PENGUIN CLASSICS

THE THEORY OF MORAL SENTIMENTS

ADAM SMITH (1723–1790) was born at Kirkcaldy, on the east coast of Scotland, in 1723, and received his early education at the local burgh school. He subsequently attended Glasgow University (1737–1740), where he studied under Francis Hutcheson, and Balliol College, Oxford (1740–1746). Two years after his return to Scotland, Smith moved to Edinburgh, where he delivered lectures on rhetoric, which did much to establish his early reputation. In 1751 Smith was appointed Professor of Logic at Glasgow, but was translated to Hutcheson's old chair of Moral Philosophy in 1752. He held this appointment until 1764, during which tenure he published, in 1759, *The Theory of Moral Sentiments*. In 1764 Smith resigned his professorship to become tutor to the young Duke of Buccleuch, at the invitation of Charles Townshend. This office took him to France, where he traveled extensively, meeting many of the leading thinkers of the day, including Voltaire, Quesnai, Turgot, and Helvetius, and where he began writing *The Wealth of Nations*. The book was published in 1776, the same year the Declaration of Independence was adopted. In 1778 Smith became a resident of Edinburgh, on his appointment as Commissioner of Customs, and remained there until his death in 1790. He was elected Lord Rector of Glasgow University in 1787, in succession to his friend Edmund Burke. Smith's life was relatively uneventful and his disposition absent-minded and retiring. Yet he wrote with vigor and did not lack personal courage, a fact attested by his defense of the character of the alleged atheist David Hume, after the latter's death.

AMARTYA SEN is Lamont University Professor at Harvard University. He won the Nobel Prize in Economics in 1998 and was Master of Trinity College, Cambridge, from 1998 until 2004. His books include *Development as Freedom*, *Identity and Violence*, and *The Idea of Justice*.

RYAN PATRICK HANLEY is the author of *Adam Smith and the Character of Virtue*. An assistant professor of political science at Marquette University, he has been the recipient of fellowships from the Mellon Foundation and the National Endowment for the Humanities.

ADAM SMITH

The Theory of Moral Sentiments

Introduction by
AMARTYA SEN

Edited with Notes by
RYAN PATRICK HANLEY

PENGUIN BOOKS

PENGUIN BOOKS
Published by the Penguin Group
Penguin Group (USA) Inc., 375 Hudson Street, New York, New York 10014, U.S.A.
Penguin Group (Canada), 90 Eglinton Avenue East, Suite 700, Toronto,
Ontario, Canada M4P 2Y3 (a division of Pearson Penguin Canada Inc.)
Penguin Books Ltd, 80 Strand, London WC2R 0RL, England
Penguin Ireland, 25 St Stephen's Green, Dublin 2, Ireland (a division of Penguin Books Ltd)
Penguin Group (Australia), 250 Camberwell Road, Camberwell,
Victoria 3124, Australia (a division of Pearson Australia Group Pty Ltd)
Penguin Books India Pvt Ltd, 11 Community Centre, Panchsheel Park, New Delhi – 110 017, India
Penguin Group (NZ), 67 Apollo Drive, Rosedale, North Shore 0632,
New Zealand (a division of Pearson New Zealand Ltd)
Penguin Books (South Africa) (Pty) Ltd, 24 Sturdee Avenue,
Rosebank, Johannesburg 2196, South Africa

Penguin Books Ltd, Registered Offices:
80 Strand, London WC2R 0RL, England

First published in Great Britain by A. Millar, London and A. Kincaid & J. Bell, Edinburgh 1759
This edition with an introduction by Amartya Sen and notes by Ryan Patrick Hanley
published in Penguin Books 2009

1   3   5   7   9   10   8   6   4   2

Introduction copyright © Amartya Sen, 2009
Notes copyright © Ryan Patrick Hanley, 2009
All rights reserved

LIBRARY OF CONGRESS CATALOGING IN PUBLICATION DATA
Smith, Adam, 1723–1790.
The theory of moral sentiments / Adam Smith ; introduction by Amartya Sen ;
edited with notes by Ryan Patrick Hanley.
p. cm.—(Penguin classics)
"The version published here is that of the sixth edition, which appeared in 1790"—P.
Includes bibliographical references (p.   ) and index.
ISBN 978-0-14-310592-3
1. Ethics—Early works to 1800.   I. Hanley, Ryan Patrick, 1974—   II. Title.
BJ1005.S6 2006
170—dc22   2009033354

Printed in the United States of America
Set in Sabon

Contents

Introduction by AMARTYA SEN   vii
Suggestions for Further Reading   xxvii
A Note on the Text   xxxi

THE THEORY OF MORAL SENTIMENTS

Advertisement   3

Contents   5

PART I. Of the propriety of action   11

PART II. Of merit and demerit; or, of the objects
of reward and punishment   79

PART III. Of the foundation of our judgments
concerning our own sentiments and conduct, and
of the sense of duty   131

PART IV. Of the effect of utility upon the sentiment
of approbation   207

PART V. Of the influence of custom and fashion
upon the sentiments of moral approbation and
disapprobation   225

PART VI. Of the character of virtue   247

PART VII. Of systems of moral philosophy   313

Considerations concerning the first formation
of languages   405

Biographical Notes   433
Textual Notes   453
Index   488

Introduction

The Theory of Moral Sentiments, Adam Smith's first book, was published in early 1759. Smith, then a young professor at the University of Glasgow, had some understandable anxiety about the public reception of the book, which was based on his quite radical lectures. On April 12, 1759, Smith heard from his friend David Hume in London about how the book was doing. If Smith was, Hume told him, prepared for "the worst," then he must now be given "the melancholy News" that unfortunately "the Public seem disposed to applaud [your book] extremely." "It was looked for by the foolish People with some Impatience; and the Mob of Literati are beginning already to be very loud in its Praises." This light-hearted intimation of the early success of Smith's first book would be followed by serious critical acclaim, bringing immediate success to one of the truly outstanding books in the intellectual history of the world.

This introduction is concerned specifically with the continued relevance of that remarkable monograph, which was published a quarter of a millennium ago. Even though Smith's investigations and analyses have had a profound impact on the world, especially the economic world, there is still much to learn from them. As it happens, after its immediate success, *Moral Sentiments* went into something of an eclipse from the beginning of the nineteenth century, and Smith was increasingly seen almost exclusively as the author of his second book that transformed the subject of economics, *An Inquiry into the Nature and Causes of the Wealth of Nations*, published in 1776. The neglect of *Moral Sentiments*, which has lasted through the nineteenth and the twentieth centuries, has had two rather unfortunate effects.

First, even though Smith was, in many ways, the pioneering

analyst of the need for impartiality and universality in ethics (the *Moral Sentiments* preceded the better-known and much more influential contributions of Immanuel Kant, who refers to Smith generously), he has been fairly comprehensively ignored in contemporary ethics and philosophy.

Second, since the ideas presented in *The Wealth of Nations* have been interpreted largely without reference to the framework of thought already developed in the *Moral Sentiments* (on which Smith substantially draws in *The Wealth of Nations*), the typical understanding of *The Wealth of Nations* has been constrained, to the detriment of economics as a subject. The neglect applies, among other issues, to the appreciation of the demands of rationality, the need for recognizing the plurality of human motivations, the connections between ethics and economics, and the co-dependent—rather than free-standing—role of institutions in general and free markets in particular in the functioning of the economy.

THE *MORAL SENTIMENTS* AND *THE WEALTH OF NATIONS*

Not only are Smith's two books related, but his ideas in them also had something of a common origin. Smith had been appointed to the professorship of logic at the University of Glasgow in 1751, but he moved to the chair of moral philosophy the following year and held that position until 1764. His lectures on the subject not only contained the material on which the *Moral Sentiments* would draw, but as one of his students—John Millar, who later became professor of law at Glasgow—noted, the last part of his four-part lecture series also "contained the substance of the work he afterwards published under the title of *An Inquiry into the Nature and Causes of the Wealth of Nations*."

Given the pervasive interdependence of these two books, it is amazing that many Smith commentators have been inclined to see a huge dichotomy between the two. Indeed, there is quite a voluminous literature on what has been called the "Adam Smith problem,"[1] the common element of which is the fanciful belief that there is an inconsistency between Smith's arguments presented in the *Moral Sentiments*, which "attributed conduct to sympathy," and in *The Wealth of Nations*, which allegedly saw behavior as "being based on selfishness." A recurrently asked question has been: Why did Smith abandon his earlier approach when he came to write *The Wealth of Nations*?

In fact, Smith never abandoned what he presented in the *Moral Sentiments*. Rather, he continued to advance that perspective, with many additional illustrations, even as he was engaged in presenting *The Wealth of Nations*.[2] The first version of the *Moral Sentiments*, published in 1759, was revised in the second edition in 1761, in the third in 1767, and in the fourth in 1774. Then, five years after the publication of *The Wealth of Nations*, came the fifth edition of *Moral Sentiments*, followed by a final—and much extended—edition, the sixth, in 1790, shortly before Smith's death the same year. It is interesting to note that Smith's first book, the *Moral Sentiments*, was also his last, in the form of the much-expanded sixth edition, with *The Wealth of Nations* coming in between.[3] Indeed in the "Advertisement" to the final edition of *Moral Sentiments*, Smith recollected the promise he had made in the earlier editions "to give an account of the general principles of law and government, and of the different revolutions they have undergone in the different ages and periods of society." He went on to say that in *The Wealth of Nations*, "I have partly executed this promise."

In each book Smith talks about a variety of human motivations, including both sympathy and self-love, and also many other concerns that drive human beings.[4] If self-love is of special relevance in seeking some particular explanation—for example, why people seek trade—then other motivations have important roles in explaining other types of choices—for example, work discipline and a commitment to obeying good rules and to treating others with respect and honour. The role of self-love in explaining particular economic phenomena does nothing to reduce the relevance of different motivations in the understanding of other economic regularities.

SYMPATHY AND SELF-LOVE

There is a strong tradition in the economic literature that has tended to assume—indeed, assert—that Smith believed "self-interest dominates the majority of men," to quote the distinguished economist George Stigler, who took this belief, which he championed, to be "on Smithian lines." A great many economists were—and some still are—evidently quite enchanted by something that has come to be called "rational choice theory," in which rationality is identified with intelligently pursuing self-interest. Further, following that fashion in modern economics, a whole generation of rational choice political analysts and of experts in so-called "law and economics" have been cheerfully practicing the same narrow art. And they have been citing Smith in alleged support of their cramped and simplistic theory of human rationality.

The conviction that Smith believed in the dominating presence—and also the rationality—of human selfishness has even found its way into English literature via a limerick by Stephen Leacock, who was both a professional economist and a talented literary writer:

> Adam, Adam, Adam Smith
> Listen what I charge you with!
> Didn't you say
> In a class one day
> That selfishness was bound to pay?
> Of all doctrines that was the Pith.
> Wasn't it, wasn't it, wasn't it, Smith?

In contrast, the *Moral Sentiments* actually begins with the following observation:

> How selfish soever man may be supposed, there are evidently some principles in his nature, which interest him in the fortune of others, and render their happiness necessary to him, though he derives nothing from it, except the pleasure of seeing it. . . . That we often derive sorrow from the sorrow of others, is of a matter of fact too obvious to require any instances to prove it; for this sentiment, like all the other original passions of human nature, is by no means confined to the virtuous and humane, though they perhaps may feel it with the most exquisite sensibility. The greatest ruffian, the most hardened violator of the laws of society, is not altogether without it.

While some men are born small and some achieve smallness, it is clear enough that Smith has had much smallness thrust upon him.

Smith famously discussed that to explain the motivation for economic exchange in the market, we do not have to invoke any objective other than the pursuit of self-interest. In his most famous and widely quoted passage from *The Wealth of Nations*, he wrote: "It is not from the benevolence of the butcher, the brewer, or the baker that we expect our dinner, but from their regard to their own interest. We address ourselves, not to their humanity but to their self-love."[5] Unfortunately, in the tradition of interpreting Smith as the guru of selfishness or self-love (as he often called it—not with great admiration), the reading of his writings does not seem to go much beyond those few lines, even though that discussion is addressed only to one very specific issue, namely *exchange* (rather than distribution or production) and, in particular, the *motivation* underlying exchange (rather than what makes normal exchanges sustainable, such as trust and confidence between the two parties). In the rest of Smith's writings there are extensive discussions of the role of other motivations that influence human action and behavior.

ECONOMICS AND THE LIMITATIONS OF THE PROFIT MOTIVE

Beyond self-love, Smith discussed how the functioning of the economic systems in general and of the markets in particular can be helped enormously by other motives. There are two distinct propositions here. The first is one of epistemology, concerning the fact that human beings are not guided only by self-gain or even prudence. The second is one of practical reason, involving the claim that there are good ethical and practical grounds for encouraging motives other than self interest—whether in the crude form of self-love or in the refined form of prudence. Indeed, Smith argues that while "prudence" was "of all the virtues that which is most helpful to the individual," "humanity, justice, generosity, and public spirit, are the qualities most useful to others."[6] These are two distinct points, and unfortunately a big part of modern economics gets both of them wrong in interpreting Smith.

The nature of the present economic crisis illustrates very clearly the need for departures from unmitigated and unrestrained self-seeking in order to have a decent society. Even John McCain, the 2008 U.S. Republican presidential candidate, complained constantly in his campaign speeches of "the greed of Wall Street." Smith had a diagnosis for this: he called promoters of excessive risk in search of profits "prodigals and projectors"—which, by the way, is quite a good description of many of the entrepreneurs of credit swaps insurances and subprime mortgages over the recent past. The term "projector" is used by Smith not in the neutral sense of "one who forms a project," but in the pejorative sense, apparently common from 1616 (so I gather from *The Shorter Oxford English Dictionary*), meaning, among other things, "a promoter of bubble companies; a speculator; a cheat." Indeed Jonathan Swift's unflattering portrait of "projectors" in *Gulliver's Travels*, published in 1726 (fifty years before *The Wealth of Nations*), corresponds closely to what Smith seems to have had in mind. Relying entirely on an unregulated market economy can result in a dire predicament in which, as Smith writes, "a great part of the capital of the country" is "kept out of the hands which were most likely to make a profitable and advantageous use of it, and thrown into those which were most likely to waste and destroy it."[7]

Smith's criticism of an unregulated market economy did not go unchallenged. It is a matter of some historical interest that Jeremy Bentham took Smith to task in a long letter he wrote to him in March 1787, arguing that Smith should leave the market alone.[8] He argued, for those whom Smith saw as "projectors"—with various projects of making quick money—were also the innovators and pioneers of change and progress. Smith was good-humored about the critique.[9] But he knew the distinction between projectors and innovators well enough, and there is little evidence, despite Bentham's expectations, that Smith wanted to revise what he had said on the need for regulation.

To understand the nature of a country's financial stability in a way that is, as it happens, immediately relevant to the current economic crisis, it is extremely important to pay attention to Smith's argument that "When the people of any particular country have such confidence in the fortune, probity, and prudence of a particular banker, as to believe that he is always ready to pay upon demand such of his promissory notes as are likely to be at any time presented to him; those notes come to have the same currency as gold and silver money, from the con-fidence that such money can at any time be had for them."¹⁰ Such confidence need not always pre-exist or survive, Smith argued; a cli-mate of mutual trust has to be cultivated and fostered. Even though the champions of the baker-brewer-butcher reading of Smith, enshrined in many economics books, may be at a complete loss about how to understand the present economic crisis (since people still have excellent reason to *seek* more trade even now, in the middle of the crisis—only far less *opportunity*), the devastating consequences of mistrust and the collapse of mutual confidence would not have puzzled Smith.

MARKETS AND THE NEED FOR OTHER INSTITUTIONS

The spirited attempt to see Smith as an advocate of pure capital-ism, with complete reliance on the market mechanism guided by pure profit motive, is altogether misconceived. Smith never used the term "capitalism" (I have certainly not found an instance). More importantly, he was not aiming to be the great champion of the profit-based market mechanism, nor was he arguing against the importance of economic institutions other than the markets. Smith was convinced of the necessity of a well-functioning market economy, but not of its sufficiency. He argued powerfully against many false diagnoses of terrible "commissions" of the market economy, and yet nowhere did he deny that the market economy yields important "omissions." He rejected *market-excluding* inter-ventions but not *market-including* interventions aimed at doing those important things that the market may leave undone.

Smith saw the task of political economy as the pursuit of "two distinct objects": "first, to provide a plentiful revenue or subsis-tence for the people, or more properly to enable them to provide such a revenue or subsistence for themselves; and secondly, to sup-ply the state or commonwealth with a revenue sufficient for the public services."¹¹ He defended such public services as free educa-tion and poverty relief while demanding greater freedom for the indigent who receives support than the rather punitive Poor Laws of his day permitted. Beyond his attention to the components and responsibilities of a well-functioning market system (such as the role of accountability and trust), he was deeply concerned about the inequality and poverty that might remain in an otherwise successful market economy. Even in dealing with regulations that restrain the markets, Smith additionally acknowledged the importance of interventions on behalf of the poor and the underdogs of society. At one stage he gives a formula of disarming simplicity: "When the regulation, therefore, is in favour of the workmen, it is always just and equitable; but it is sometimes otherwise when in favour of the masters."[12] Smith was both a proponent of a plural institutional structure and a champion of social values that transcend the profit motive in principle as well as in actual reach.

ETHICS, VIRTUE, AND CONSEQUENCES

I turn now from the relevance of *Moral Sentiments* to Smith's economic analysis to its salience to ethics and political philosophy. Smith had an abiding interest in how things actually work out, and in recommending actions and rules to be chosen he paid particular attention to the kind of world they would yield.[13] But he also noted the importance of the character of the actions themselves and the motivation behind undertaking them—not just what happens at the very end—in identifying what can be seen as virtuous.[14]

In fact, a broad ethical evaluation of the kind Smith outlined can take note of the virtues both of what actually happened and of the actions taken to produce such outcomes, going well beyond the simple-minded "consequentialist" framework made popular by theories of practical reason such as utilitarian ethics (which insists on attaching direct significance only to utilities that ultimately result). We can take note of the actions undertaken and of the ethical quality of the decision-making that led to those actions, since they are indeed part of what "really happened," without confining our scrutiny only to what occurred at the "culmination."[15] Smith's simultaneous interest in virtues and obligations and in what actually happens in the world are comprehensively integrated.

Smith makes an important distinction, in his conception of virtue, between praise and "praiseworthiness," and focuses on the latter as the legitimate basis for action.[16] It is of course the case that a praiseworthy action would also tend to generate actual praise, and this may well be pleasing to the person praised. What Smith argues for, however, is to concentrate not on what would bring praise—despite the happiness it may bring to the person involved—but on whether the action is praiseworthy.

In discussing "the different accounts which have been given of the nature of virtue," Smith distinguishes among the ways of seeing virtue: first, in terms of "propriety"; second, as fulfilling one's "private interest and happiness"; and third, as aiming "at the happiness of others."[17] These distinct views, he argues, can be integrated, and he discusses how reasoning can link them together, allowing a kind of balance that virtue and praiseworthiness would demand:

> As our most solid judgments, therefore, with regard to right and wrong, are regulated by maxims and ideas derived from an induction of reason, virtue may very properly be said to consist in a conformity to reason, and so far this faculty may be considered as the source and principle of approbation and disapprobation.[18]

POLITICAL PHILOSOPHY AND JUSTICE

I turn now from moral to political philosophy, though the two are closely related, particularly so in Smith's analysis. I will concentrate first on the kind of theory of justice that we can find in the *Moral Sentiments*, and examine it in light of mainstream theories of justice as they have emerged in recent centuries.[19]

There are two basic, and divergent, lines of reasoning about justice among leading philosophers associated with the radical thought of the Enlightenment. There is, first, the "contractarian" approach, led by the work of Thomas Hobbes in the seventeenth century, and followed in different ways by such outstanding thinkers as John Locke, Jean-Jacques Rousseau, and Immanuel Kant. In its rudimentary version, this approach concentrates on identifying "just" institutional arrangements for a society, which would yield a corresponding—hypothetical—contract. The demands of justice are, then, seen in terms of those institutional requirements, with the expectation that people would behave appropriately to make those institutions entirely effective.

The approach has two distinct features. First, it concentrates its attention on what it identifies as perfect justice, rather than on relative comparisons of justice and injustice; it tries to identify social characteristics that cannot be transcended in terms of justice, and is aimed at identifying the nature of "the just"—rather than at finding some criteria that would allow us to decide whether an alternative is "less unjust" than another. Second, in searching for perfection, transcendental institutionalism concentrates primarily on getting the institutions right, and it is only indirectly concerned with the societies that would ultimately emerge. The nature of the society that would emerge from any given set of institutions must, of course, depend on many non-institutional factors, such as actual behaviors of people and their social interactions. The traverse from institutions to social outcomes is handled by this approach with the assumption that people's behavior would be exactly what would be needed for the proper functioning of the chosen institutions.

In contrast to the social contract approach, a number of other Enlightenment theorists took a variety of comparative approaches that were concerned primarily with removing identifiable injustices in the world—such as slavery, or bureaucracy-induced poverty, or cruel and counterproductive penal codes, or rampant exploitation of labor, or the subjugation of women. The focus is on what actually happens to the lives of people, and the judgments are comparative—for example, how the world would improve if slavery were abolished. The approach of comparative realizations, as we may call it, was pursued, in different ways, not only by Smith—who was its most powerful proponent—but also by the Marquis de Condorcet (the founder of the mathematical discipline of social choice theory who was greatly influenced by Smith), Jeremy Bentham, Mary Wollstonecraft, Karl Marx, and John Stuart Mill, among others, all of whom were admirers of Smith and were clearly influenced by him, to varying extents.

As it happens, it is the first tradition—that of transcendental institutionalism—on which today's mainstream political philosophy largely draws in its exploration of the theory of justice. The most powerful and momentous exposition of this approach to justice can be found in the work of the leading political philosopher of our time, John Rawls.[20] Indeed, Rawls's "principles of justice" in *A Theory of Justice* are defined entirely for selecting perfectly just institutions. This entire tradition is very non-Smithian. Smith's focus is on actual realizations (not just on institutions and arrangements), and on comparisons rather than on transcendence. The primary concentration in the Smithian approach is on questions such as "how would justice be advanced?" rather than on, as in Rawlsian theory, "what would be perfectly just institutions?"

IMPARTIALITY AND THE IMPARTIAL SPECTATOR

An important contrast between the Smithian approach and the approach based on social contracts lies in the form in which impartiality, needed for fairness and justice, is invoked. Smith's thought experiment on impartiality invokes the device of the "impartial spectator" who can come as readily from outside of a community as from within it. This differs substantially from the admissible points of view that a "social contract" approach concentrates on, to wit, the views of the people within a polity in which the contract is being made. In Rawls's discussion of what he calls a "reflective equilibrium," distant perspectives can be invoked, but in his structured theory of "justice as fairness," the relevant points of view are confined entirely to those of the people in the society in which the so-called original position is being contemplated. In this sense, the impartiality that Rawls and the social contract approach explores is "closed"—i.e., it is confined to the members of the contracting parties (or their "representatives"). In contrast, Smith's impartial spectator takes us toward an open impartiality.

To be sure, both Smith and Kant had much to say about the importance of impartiality. Even though Smith's exposition of this idea is less remembered among contemporary moral and political philosophers, there are substantial points of similarity between the Kantian and Smithian approaches. In fact, Smith's analysis of "the impartial spectator" has some claim to being the pioneering idea in the enterprise of interpreting impartiality and formulating the demands of fairness that so engaged the world of the European enlightenment. Smith's ideas were influential not only among enlightenment thinkers such as Condorcet; Kant, too, was familiar with *The Theory of Moral Sentiments*, as we know from his correspondence with Markus Herz in 1771 (even though, alas, Herz referred to the proud Scotsman as "the Englishman Smith"),[21] which preceded by a considerable number of years Kant's own classic works *Groundwork* (1785) and *Critique of Practical Reason* (1788), and it seems quite likely that Kant was influenced by Smith.

But it is the differences between Smith on one side and Kant—and Rawls—on the other that are particularly important for the present discussion. To Smith, the internal discussion among the participants in the Rawlsian original position would appear to be inadequately scrutinized, since we have to look beyond the points of view of others in the same society, engaged in making the social contract. As Smith argued:

> We can never survey our own sentiments and motives, we can never form any judgment concerning them, unless we remove ourselves, as it were, from our own natural station, and endeavour to view them as at a certain distance from us. But we can do this in no other way than by endeavouring to view them with the eyes of other people, or as other people are likely to view them.[22]

Compared to Smith's approach, the procedural device of closed impartiality in Rawlsian "justice as fairness" can be seen as being limited in its reach. Why is this a problem? There are, in fact, two principal grounds for requiring that the encounter of public reasoning about justice go beyond boundaries of a state or region: (1) the relevance of other people's *interests*—far away from as well as close to a given society—for the sake of preventing unfairness to those who are not party to the social contract for that society; and (2) the pertinence of other people's *perspectives* to broaden our own investigation of relevant principles, for the sake of avoiding underscrutinized parochialism of values and presumptions in the local community.

INTERDEPENDENT INTERESTS AND THE IMPARTIAL SPECTATOR

By its very nature a social contract has to be confined to the members of a sovereign state—it is a contract among the citizens of that state. This makes it hard to extend the idea to the global world, as some have tried to do. Indeed, it is precisely because of the contractarian mode of reasoning that many philosophers have been tempted to argue that the idea of global justice is an absurdity at the present time, without a global sovereign state. Smith's device of the impartial spectator gets around this limitation not by posing the problem in terms of a negotiated contract for members of a sovereign state but by invoking impartial arbitrators—from far and near—whose assessments have to be considered in order to get toward impartial reasoning. Dealing with the global mess makes the Smithian engagement altogether necessary. In some ways the world is grappling with the Smithian route, and while the gradual shift from national thinking to the G-8 and now to the G-20 is a move in the right direction, we have to go much further, for Smithian reasons.

In many examples in each of his books, Smith did, in fact, make good use of the reach of global reasoning. For example, the misdeeds of early British rule in India, including the disastrous famine of 1770, engaged him greatly in *The Wealth of Nations*. When he concluded that the East India Company not only "oppresses and domineers in the East Indies" but was also "altogether unfit to govern its territorial possessions," he was drawing not on any oddly devised social contract (it would have been very hard to fit such a judgment into the contractarian framework) but on the kind of reach that the impartial spectator allows, without confining judgments of justice to the limits of a sovereign state.

Similar issues remain extremely alive today. How America tackles its economy influences not only Americans but also those in the rest of the world. AIDS and other epidemics have moved from country to country, and from continent to continent, and the medicines developed and produced in some parts of the world are important for the lives and freedoms of people far away. Also, what can be said about the environmental challenges we currently face has to be based on global reasoning about the sharing of obligations and burdens, rather than on a strictly contractarian line of analysis confined within the limits of a sovereign state.

THE IMPARTIAL SPECTATOR AND THE AVOIDANCE OF PAROCHIALISM

Another argument for an "open" approach, in Smithian lines, is that it works to avoid the trap of parochialism. If the discussion of the demands of justice is confined to a particular locality—a country or even a region larger than that—there is a possible danger of ignoring or neglecting many challenging counterarguments that might not come up in local political debates, or be accommodated in the discourse confined to the local culture, but that are eminently worth considering, from an impartial perspective.

This is still an active issue in contemporary legal debates—for example, among the judges of the U.S. Supreme Court regarding the admissibility of invoking arguments and judgments in courts in other countries in seeking an appropriate understanding of the demands of justice in the United States.[23] Smith's insistence that "the eyes of the rest of mankind" must be invoked to understand whether "a punishment appears equitable" remains deeply relevant here.

Smith was particularly keen on avoiding the grip of parochialism in jurisprudence and moral and political reasoning. In a chapter in *Moral Sentiments* revealingly entitled "Of the Influence of Custom and Fashion upon the Sentiments of Moral Approbation and Disapprobation," he gives various examples of how discussions confined within a given society can be incarcerated within a seriously narrow understanding.

> . . . the murder of new-born infants was a practice allowed of in almost all the states of Greece, even among the polite and civilized Athenians. . . . Uninterrupted custom had by this time so thoroughly authorized the practice, that not only the loose maxims of the world tolerated this barbarous prerogative, but even the doctrine of philosophers, which ought to have been more just and accurate, was led away by the established custom, and upon this, as upon many other occasions, instead of censuring, supported the horrible abuse, by far-fetched considerations of public utility. Aristotle talks of it as of what the magistrate ought upon many occasions to encourage. The humane Plato is of the same opinion, and, with all that love of mankind which seems to animate all his writings, nowhere marks this practice with disapprobation.[24]

Smith's insistence that we must view our sentiments, *inter alia*, at "a certain distance from us" thus extends, beyond the imperative to scrutinize the influence of vested interests, to the need to question the captivating hold of entrenched traditions and customs.

In scrutinizing established rules today, including the permissibility of practices as different as the stoning of adulterous women under the Taliban and the widespread use of capital punishment (with or without the public jubilation with which it is sometimes accompanied)—for example, in China, Saudi Arabia, Iran, and the United States (to name the four countries that led the world in the frequency of capital punishment in 2008)—the perspectives of other people from far as well as near have a relevance for reasons that Smith presented definitively in the *Moral Sentiments*.

INCLINATIONS, INCLUSION, AND EQUALITY

I end with some remarks on Smith's personal sentiments. This introduction has been concerned almost entirely with Smith's reasoning, rather than with his inclinations and predispositions. This has some rationale: I believe Smith was right in thinking (as I quoted him earlier) that "our most solid judgments . . . with regard to right and wrong, are regulated by maxims and ideas derived from an induction of reason." And yet Smith also argued, again quite persuasively, that our "first perceptions" of right and wrong "cannot be the object of reason, but of immediate sense and feeling."[25] Even though our first perceptions may change in response to critical examination (as Smith also noted), these perceptions can still give us interesting clues about our inclinations and emotional predispositions.

One of the striking features of Smith's personality is his inclination to be as inclusive as possible—not only locally but also globally. He does acknowledge that we may have special obligations to our neighbors, but the reach of our concern must ultimately transcend that confinement. I have already discussed the strikingly global feature of Smith's moral and political inclusiveness. To that I want to add the understanding that Smith's ethical inclusiveness is matched by a strong epistemic inclination to see people everywhere as being essentially similar. There is something quite remarkable in the ease with which Smith rides over barriers of class, gender, race, and nationality to see human beings with a presumed equality of potential, and without any innate difference in intrinsic talents and abilities.

Smith's empirical presumption of equality of potential of different human beings is stated most explicitly in *The Wealth of Nations*:

The difference of natural talents in different men is, in reality, much less than we are aware of; and the very different genius which appears to distinguish men of different professions, when grown up to maturity, is not upon many occasions so much the cause as the effect of the division of labour. The difference between the most dissimilar characters, between a philosopher and a common street porter, for example, seems to arise not so much from nature as from habit, custom, and education. When they came into the world, and for the first six or eight years of their existence, they were perhaps very much alike, and neither their parents nor playfellows could perceive any remarkable difference.[26]

It is easy to see that there is some real tension here between Smith's firmly articulated empirical view and the scientific evidence for genetic differences between individuals within the same race or nationality or class. It is not so important whether the quoted statement is correct. What is really important to appreciate is that Smith's epistemic generalization reflects not only what he very much wanted to believe, but also what he thought would be the right assumption to make—that differences between groups largely reflect differences of education and opportunities rather than differences of natural talents—when dealing with groups of people without any pre-identified genetic differentiation among them.[27]

It is not only that the working class has much less access to education—and good education in particular—than people of rank and fortune, but also that the work of the working class gives them far less occasion to cultivate their minds than the work of the privileged.

The employments of people of some rank and fortune, besides, are seldom such as harass them from morning to night. They generally have a good deal of leisure, during which they may perfect themselves in every branch either of useful or ornamental knowledge of which they may have laid the foundation, or for which they may have acquired some taste in the earlier part of life.

It is otherwise with the common people. They have little time to spare for education. Their parents can scarce afford to maintain them even in infancy. As soon as they are able to work they must apply to some trade by which they can earn their subsistence. That trade, too, is generally so simple and uniform as to give little exercise to the understanding, while, at the same time, their labour is both so constant and so severe, that it leaves them little leisure and less inclination to apply to, or even to think of, anything else.[28]

While it is important to understand Smith's inclination—indeed, longing—to believe in the equal potential of all human beings, what is crucial to his policy prescriptions is his emphasis on the class-related neglect of human talents through the lack of education and the unimaginative nature of the work that many members of the working classes are forced to do by economic circumstances. Class divisions, Smith argued, reflect this inequality of opportunity, rather than indicating differences of inborn talents and abilities.

The presumption of similarity of intrinsic talents is accepted by Smith not only within nations but also across the boundaries of states and cultures, as is clear from what he says in both the *Moral Sentiments* and *The Wealth of Nations*. The assumption of racial or regional inferiority of some people, which had quite a hold on the minds of many of his contemporaries, is completely absent in Smith's writings. And Smith does not address these points only abstractly. For example, he discusses why he thinks Chinese and Indian producers are really not in any different league of productive ability from Europeans, even though their institutions may handicap them. He is inclined to see the relative backwardness of African economic progress in terms of the continent's geographical disadvantages, having nothing like the "gulfs of Arabia, Persia, India, Bengal, and Siam, in Asia" that provide opportunities for trade to other people. Smith is also incensed by the presumption of superior racial endowments of the white man, and at one stage even bursts into unconcealed wrath: "There is not a negro from the coast of Africa who does not, in this respect, possess a degree of magnanimity which the soul of his sordid master is too often scarce capable of conceiving."[29]

Or consider Smith's odd exuberance about the nutritional benefits of the potato:

> The chairmen, porters, and coalheavers in London, and those unfortunate women who live by prostitution, the strongest men and the most beautiful women perhaps in the British dominions, are said to be the greater part of them from the lowest rank of people in Ireland, who are generally fed with this root [potato]. No food can afford a more decisive proof of its nourishing quality, or of its being peculiarly suitable to the health of the human constitution.[30]

His extraordinary excursion into nutritional wisdom serves the indirect purpose of standing up for the Irish against ridicule by the English (including the ridicule of Ireland's dependence on the potato),[31] which goes back even to Edmund Spenser's *Faerie Queene* in the sixteenth century.

The global reach of Smith's moral and political reasoning is, of course, quite a distinctive feature of his thought, but it is strongly supplemented by his belief that all humans are born with similar potential and—most importantly for policymaking—that the inequalities in the world reflect socially generated, rather than natural, disparities.

There is a vision here that has a remarkably current ring. The continuing global relevance of Smith's ideas is quite astonishing, and it is a tribute to the power of Smith's mind that this global vision is so forcefully presented by someone who, a quarter of a millennium ago, lived most of his life in considerable seclusion in a tiny coastal Scottish town.[32] Smith's analyses and explorations are of critical importance for any society in the world in which issues of morals, politics, and economics receive attention, and *The Theory of Moral Sentiments* is a global manifesto of profound significance to the interdependent world in which we live. This is indeed a book of amazing reach and contemporary relevance.[*]

AMARTYA SEN

NOTES

1. On this see D. D. Raphael and A. L. Macfie's introduction to the Clarendon Press edition of *The Theory of Moral Sentiments* (Oxford: Clarendon Press, 1976), pp. 20-25.
2. See Emma Rothschild, *Economic Sentiments: Adam Smith, Condorcet and the Enlightenment* (Cambridge, MA: Harvard University Press, 2001).
3. There is also a third book, *Lectures on Jurisprudence*, which he did not write in the form of a book, but which was posthumously put together on the basis of the lecture notes of his students.
4. See Rothschild, *Economic Sentiments* (2001). See also my *On Ethics and Economics* (Oxford: Blackwell, 1987), and Patricia

---

[*] I am most grateful to Kirsty Walker for helping me with the textual research for this introduction.

H. Werhane, *Adam Smith and His Legacy for Modern Capitalism* (New York: Oxford University Press, 1991).

5. Adam Smith, *An Inquiry into the Nature and Causes of the Wealth of Nations* (London: Penguin Classics, 1999), 1.1.2, p. 119.

6. Smith, *The Theory of Moral Sentiments*, I. iv. 2.6–9; in this edition, pp. 220–1.

7. Smith, *The Wealth of Nations*, I.II.4.14-5, p. 457.

8. Bentham included this letter in the second of the two prefaces he wrote for the second edition of his combative defense of the market economy against regulations that restrain usury, *Defence of Usury.*

9. In fact, Smith is supposed to have remarked to his friend William Adam that Bentham's book was "the work of a very superior man," and though he had given Smith some "hard knocks," "it was done in so handsome a way that he could not complain" (see John Rae's *Life of Adam Smith*, 1895 pp. 423–4) Bentham was cheered by the report of this oral conversation and went on to write to Smith on this basis: "I, have been flattered with the intelligence that, upon the whole, your sentiments with respect to the points of difference are at present the same as mine." Bentham's interpretation of Smith's good-humored reaction as substantive agreement with him would seem to be a considerable overstretch.

10. *The Wealth of Nations*, I.II.ii.2,28, p. 389.

11. *The Wealth of Nations*, I.IV. Introduction, p. 246.

12. *The Wealth of Nations*, I.i.10.ii, p. 246.

13. Smith notes: "Upon some occasions . . . those passions are restrained, not so much by a sense of their impropriety, as by prudential considerations of the bad consequences which might follow from their indulgence" (*Moral Sentiments*, VI.concl.3; p. 309).

14. An important analysis of Smith's ethics of virtue can be found in Ryan Patrick Hanley, *Adam Smith and the Character of Virtue* (Cambridge: Cambridge University Press, 2009). See also Roger Crisp and Michael Slote, eds., *Virtue Ethics* (Oxford: Clarendon Press, 1997).

15. The importance of scrutinizing "comprehensive outcomes" (including the processes involved), as opposed to only "culmination outcomes," is discussed in my "Consequential Evaluation and Practical Reason," *Journal of Philosophy*, 97 (2000), and *The Idea of Justice* (London: Allen Lane, Penguin Books, and Cambridge, Harvard University Press, 2009), especially chapter 10.

16. On the distinction involved see Ryan Patrick Hanley, *Adam Smith and the Character of Virtue* (Cambridge: Cambridge University Press, 2009). On related subjects see also Christopher Berry, "Adam Smith and the Virtues of Commerce," in John W. Clapham and William A. Galston, eds., *Nomos XXXIV: Virtue* (New York: New York

University Press, 1992); M. J. Calkins and P. H. Werhane, "Adam Smith, Aristotle, and the Virtues of Commerce," *Journal of Value Inquiry*, 32 (1998).

17. *Moral Sentiments*, VII.ii.Introduction.1-4; in this edition, p. 317.

18. *Moral Sentiments*, VII.iii.2.6; in this edition, p. 376.

19. Smith notes that the word "justice" has "several different meanings," though "there must be some natural affinity among these various significations." We follow here the most general use of the idea of justice that can be found in Smith's writings. This interpretational issue is discussed in my *The Idea of Justice* (2009).

20. John Rawls, *A Theory of Justice* (Cambridge, MA: Harvard University Press, 1971); see also his *Political Liberalism* (New York: Columbia University Press, 1993).

21. See Raphael and Macfie, "Introduction," in *The Theory of Moral Sentiments* (Clarendon Press, 1976), p. 31.

22. *Moral Sentiments*, III.1.2; in this edition p. 133.

23. An analysis of the contrasting views on this subject between Justice Scalia and Chief Justice Roberts, on one side, and Justice Ginsburg, on the other, is discussed in my *Idea of Justice* (2009), chapter 18.

24. *Moral Sentiments*, V.2.15; in this edition pp. 245–46.

25. *Moral Sentiments*, VII.iii.2.7; in this edition, pp. 376-7.

26. *The Wealth of Nations*, I.ii.4, p. 120.

27. The presumption of equal potentiality of all human beings supplements Smith's ethical belief on the priority of the interests of the poor in public policy: "No society can surely be flourishing and happy, of which the far greater part of the members are poor and miserable" (*The Wealth of Nations*, I.viii, p. 181.)

28. *The Wealth of Nations*, V.i.f.50-4, p. 371.

29. For references to Smith's remarks cited here, and to many other remarks on similar lines, see Emma Rothschild and Amartya Sen, "Adam Smith's Economics," in Knud Haakonssen ed., *The Cambridge Companion to Adam Smith* (Cambridge: Cambridge University Press, 2006).

30. *The Wealth of Nations*, I.ii.11.i, p. 265.

31. Even during the Irish famines of the 1840s (half a century after Smith's death), grossly mishandled by London, Charles Edward Trevelyan, the Head of the Treasury, would include among his reflections on the famine: "There is scarcely a woman of the peasant class in the West of Ireland whose culinary art exceeds the boiling of a potato."

32. Smith's knowledge of other towns was mainly confined to Glasgow, Edinburgh, and London (other than Oxford, which he largely hated, not least for its high-brow parochialism), and his foreign travels were confined to one visit to France and Switzerland in 1764–66.

Suggestions for Further Reading

Adam Smith once told his students that to be "an ancient" was to "have commentators." By that standard, few are more ancient than Smith. The scholarship on him is immense; what follows is merely a brief guide to some of the most helpful introductory and most essential scholarly works.

Smith's quiet life, coupled with his deathbed insistence that all his papers be destroyed, has rendered him a challenging subject for biographers. The authoritative biography is Ian S. Ross, *The Life of Adam Smith* (Oxford, 1995). A brief and lively account can be found in James Buchan, *The Authentic Adam Smith* (Norton, 2006). And still valuable is a short essay by Walter Bagehot, "Adam Smith as a Person," included in *The Collected Works of Walter Bagehot*.

Smith's intellectual context has been examined in several excellent studies; among the best introductions are Nicholas Phillipson's essay "The Scottish Enlightenment," in *The Enlightenment in National Context* (Cambridge, 1981); and *The Cambridge Companion to the Scottish Enlightenment*, edited by Alexander Broadie (Cambridge, 2003). Essential works on the moral and political thought of the Scottish Enlightenment include Istvan Hont and Michael Ignatieff, eds., *Wealth and Virtue: The Shaping of Political Economy in the Scottish Enlightenment* (Cambridge, 1983); and Christopher Berry, *Social Theory of the Scottish Enlightenment* (Edinburgh, 1997).

Among the best introductions to Smith's thought is Jerry Z. Muller, *Adam Smith in His Time and Ours* (Princeton, 1995). Comprehensive overviews can also be found in D. D. Raphael, *Adam Smith* (Oxford, 1985); and Andrew S. Skinner, *A System of Social Science* (Oxford, 1979). Readers can also look forward to two forthcoming works that promise to be of considerable interest: Phillipson's *Adam*

Smith: An Intellectual Biography (Penguin), and Eric Schliesser's study of Smith for the *Routledge Philosophers* series.

Over the course of the past century, *The Theory of Moral Sentiments* has largely lived in the shadow of *The Wealth of Nations*. Interest in Smith's moral philosophy yet owes much to the discovery of *Das Adam Smith Problem* by German scholars in the late nineteenth century. Among early important works in English is Joseph Cropsey's *Polity and Economy* (M. Nijhoff, 1957), which established Smith as a central figure in modern political philosophy, a question reconsidered in one of the most important recent works, Charles Griswold's *Adam Smith and the Virtues of Enlightenment* (Cambridge, 1999). In addition to Griswold's, other essential comprehensive studies of Smith's moral philosophy focusing on his conceptions of sympathy and spectatorship include A. L. Macfie, *The Individual in Society* (Allen and Unwin, 1967); T. D. Campbell, *Adam Smith's Science of Morals* (Allen and Unwin, 1971); and Raphael, *The Impartial Spectator* (Oxford, 2007). Smith's theory of moral judgment is examined in Samuel Fleischacker, *A Third Concept of Liberty* (Princeton, 1999); his theory of the emergence of norms through sympathy and exchange is examined in James Otteson, *Adam Smith's Marketplace of Life* (Cambridge, 2002). The context of Smith's moral and political thought is considered in Donald Winch, *Adam Smith's Politics* (Cambridge, 1978); and Leonidas Montes, *Adam Smith in Context* (Palgrave Macmillan, 2004).

Treatments of specific aspects of Smith's moral philosophy also abound. The link between his rhetoric and his ethics is examined in Vivienne Brown, *Adam Smith's Discourse* (Routledge, 1994); and Stephen J. McKenna, *Adam Smith: The Rhetoric of Propriety* (SUNY Press, 2006); the connection between his natural jurisprudence and his ethics is examined in Knud Haakonssen, *The Science of a Legislator* (Cambridge, 1981). Craig Smith examines the place of spontaneous order in *Adam Smith's Political Philosophy* (Routledge, 2005). The role of teleology in Smith is examined in James E. Alvey, *Adam Smith: Optimist or Pessimist?* (Ashgate, 2003). Smith's relationship to Rousseau is treated in Ignatieff, *The Needs of Strangers* (Picador, 1984); Pierre Force, *Self-Interest Before Adam Smith* (Cambridge, 2003); and Dennis Rasmussen, *The Problems and Promise of Commercial Society*

(Penn State, 2008). Smith's debts to the ancients are the focus of Gloria Vivenza, *Adam Smith and the Classics* (Oxford, 2001). Smith's theory of virtue is examined in Ryan Patrick Hanley, *Adam Smith and the Character of Virtue* (Cambridge, 2009), and his theory of cosmopolitanism is examined in Fonna Forman-Barzilai, *Adam Smith and the Circles of Sympathy* (Cambridge, forthcoming).

The literature on Smith's economic thought is massive, but several studies are of particular interest to readers of *The Theory of Moral Sentiments*. Important connections between Smith's ethics and his economic ideas are examined in Fleischacker, *On Adam Smith's* Wealth of Nations (Princeton, 2004); Jerry Evensky, *Adam Smith's Moral Philosophy* (Cambridge, 2005); Emma Rothschild, *Economic Sentiments* (Harvard, 2001); Winch, *Riches and Poverty* (Cambridge, 1996) and Richard F. Teichgraeber, *"Free Trade" and Moral Philosophy* (Duke, 1986). Studies of the moral implications of Smith's economic ideas include Patricia Werhane, *Adam Smith and His Legacy for Modern Capitalism* (Oxford, 1991) and Spencer J. Pack, *Capitalism as a Moral System* (Elgar, 1991).

Helpful collections of essays include Skinner and Wilson, eds., *Essays on Adam Smith* (Oxford, 1975); Montes and Schliesser, eds., *New Voices on Adam Smith* (Routledge, 2006); and Haakonssen, ed., *The Cambridge Companion to Adam Smith* (Cambridge, 2006). Many key essays have also been republished in John C. Wood, ed., *Adam Smith: Critical Assessments*, 7 vols. (Routledge, 1983); and Haakonssen, ed., *Adam Smith* (Ashgate, 1998). *The Adam Smith Review* of the International Adam Smith Society provides a forum for new scholarship.

RYAN PATRICK HANLEY

A Note on the Text

The Theory of Moral Sentiments was first published in 1759. It was subsequently revised with great care and republished in five additional editions in Smith's lifetime. The version published here is that of the sixth edition, which appeared in 1790, months before Smith's death.

The standard scholarly edition of Smith's works is the Glasgow Edition, published in hardcover by Oxford University Press and in paperback by the Liberty Fund. The Glasgow Edition includes Smith's *Wealth of Nations*, as well as student transcriptions of his lectures on jurisprudence and rhetoric, his philosophical essays, and his correspondence. Its edition of *TMS*, prepared by D. D. Raphael and A. L. Macfie, is especially valuable for having established a critical edition of the text and for its inclusion of a comprehensive textual apparatus detailing variations across editions. In an effort to present the most accurate text possible, the construction of the present edition included a thorough comparison of its text to the Glasgow Edition and to the 1790 original. In most instances of disagreement, the present edition incorporates the decisions of the Glasgow editors for the compelling reasons set forth in their notes.

The textual apparatus to the present edition includes a set of biographical notes and a set of textual notes. Historical information can be found in the biographical notes. The textual notes are of four types: definitions of words; citations of authors directly referenced or indirectly appropriated by Smith; references to key prior interventions in selected philosophical debates in which Smith is a participant; and references to parallel passages elsewhere in his corpus. Some notes also indicate the key changes that Smith made to the sixth edition; these do not, however, aspire to replicate the labors of the Glasgow Edition's editors, and readers interested in tracking these changes are encouraged to consult their thorough documentation of such. In preparing my own notes I have relied chiefly on

sources with which Smith was demonstrably familiar on the evidence
supplied by the catalogues of his library compiled by James Bonar
and Hiroshi Mizuta, and by references elsewhere in his corpus;
hence my recurrence to Johnson's *Dictionary of the English Language*, Hume's *History of England*, and the *Encyclopédie* of Diderot
and d'Alembert, among other sources ancient and modern that seem
to have been prominent in Smith's mind during the long period in
which he composed and revised his work. In all instances notes are
meant to be explicatory rather than interpretative.

All readers of Smith owe a tremendous debt to the excellent annotations of several previous editions. In addition to those of Raphael
and Macfie, these include those to be found in the editions of Knud
Haakonssen (Cambridge, 2002), of Walther Eckstein (Leipzig, 1926;
reissued Felix Meiner, 2004), and of Michaël Biziou, Claude Gautier, and Jean-François Pradeau (Presses Universitaires de France,
1999). Their notes have proven to be the inevitable and indispensible
foundation for many of my own, and I wish particularly to record
my great appreciation for and reliance on the careful work of Eckstein as well as Raphael and Macfie in documenting Smith's changes
across editions, for Haakonssen's and the French editors' references
to parallel passages in Smith's corpus and especially his jurisprudence lectures, and for the French editors' comprehensive efforts at
documenting Smith's eighteenth-century philosophical context. To
spare readers from having to witness the pedantic quarrels of editor
with editor, I have not registered my own agreements and disagreements with their annotations in individual notes, but these agreements, as well as those several instances where I have added to or felt
compelled to depart from their judgments, will be evident to any
who compare my annotations to theirs. I'm also pleased to record
here my debts to Igor Borba, Patty Rodda, Ethan Bercot, and Alan
Kellner for their invaluable assistance, and to Leon Montes, Eric
Schliesser, and Doug Den Uyl for their many helpful comments.

Preparing this edition has taught me a great deal, and only further increased my admiration for and interest in Smith. Readers
of this work are always very welcome to contact me if I can be of
any assistance in contributing to their own study of his work:
ryan.hanley@marquette.edu.

RYAN PATRICK HANLEY

The Theory of
Moral Sentiments

THE
THEORY
OF
MORAL SENTIMENTS.

By ADAM SMITH,
Professor of Moral Philosophy in the
University of Glasgow.

LONDON:
Printed for A. Millar, in the Strand;
And A. Kincaid and J. Bell, in Edinburgh.
M DCC LIX.

Facsimile title page of the first edition
of *The Theory of Moral Sentiments*

Since the first publication of THE THEORY OF MORAL SENTIMENTS, which was so long ago as the beginning of the year 1759, several corrections, and a good many illustrations of the doctrines contained in it, have occurred to me. But the various occupations in which the different accidents of my life necessarily involved me, have till now prevented me from revising this work with the care and attention which I always intended.[1] The reader will find the principal alterations which I have made in this New Edition, in the last Chapter of the third Section of Part First; and in the four first Chapters of Part Third. Part Sixth, as it stands in this New Edition, is altogether new. In Part Seventh, I have brought together the greater part of the different passages concerning the Stoical Philosophy, which, in the former Editions, had been scattered about in different parts of the work. I have likewise endeavoured to explain more fully, and examine more distinctly, some of the doctrines of that famous sect. In the fourth and last Section of the same Part, I have thrown together a few additional observations concerning the duty and principle of veracity. There are, besides, in other parts of the work, a few other alterations and corrections of no great moment.

In the last paragraph of the first Edition of the present work, I said, that I should in another discourse endeavour to give an account of the general principles of law and government, and of the different revolutions which they had undergone in the different ages and periods of society; not only in what concerns justice, but in what concerns police, revenue, and arms, and whatever else is the object of law. In the *Enquiry concerning the Nature and Causes of the Wealth of Nations*, I have partly executed this promise; at least so far as concerns police, revenue, and arms. What remains, the theory of jurisprudence, which I have long projected, I have hitherto been hindered from executing, by the same occupations which had till now prevented me from revising the present work.[2] Though my very advanced age leaves me, I acknowledge, very little expectation of ever being able to execute this great work to my own satisfaction; yet, as I have not altogether abandoned the design, and as I wish still to continue under the obligation of doing what I can, I have allowed the paragraph to remain as it was published more than thirty years ago, when I entertained no doubt of being able to execute every thing which it announced.[3]

Contents

PART I.

OF THE PROPRIETY OF ACTION   11

SECTION I.

OF THE SENSE OF PROPRIETY   13
CHAP. I.   Of Sympathy   13
CHAP. II. Of the Pleasure of mutual Sympathy   18
CHAP. III. Of the manner in which we judge of the propriety
           or impropriety of the Affections of other Men, by
           their concord or dissonance with our own   21
CHAP. IV. The same subject continued   25
CHAP. V.   Of the amiable and respectable virtues   30

SECTION II.

OF THE DEGREES OF THE DIFFERENT PASSIONS WHICH ARE CONSIS-
TENT WITH PROPRIETY   34
Introduction   34
CHAP. I.   Of the Passions which take their origin
           from the body   35
CHAP. II. Of those Passions which take their origin from a
           particular turn or habit of the imagination   39
CHAP. III. Of the unsocial Passions   42
CHAP. IV. Of the social Passions   48
CHAP. V.   Of the selfish Passions   50

SECTION III.

OF THE EFFECTS OF PROSPERITY AND ADVERSITY UPON THE
JUDGMENT OF MANKIND WITH REGARD TO THE PROPRIETY OF
ACTION; AND WHY IT IS MORE EASY TO OBTAIN THEIR APPROBATION
IN THE ONE STATE THAN IN THE OTHER   55

CHAP. I.   That though our sympathy with Sorrow is generally a
           more lively sensation than our sympathy with Joy, it
           commonly falls much more short of the violence of
           what is naturally felt by the person principally
           concerned   55

CHAP. II. Of the origin of Ambition, and of the distinction of
           Ranks   62

CHAP. III. Of the corruption of our Moral Sentiments, which is
           occasioned by this disposition to admire the rich and
           the great, and to despise or neglect persons of poor
           and mean condition   73

PART II.

OF MERIT AND DEMERIT; OR, OF THE OBJECTS OF REWARD AND
PUNISHMENT   79

SECTION I.

OF THE SENSE OF MERIT AND DEMERIT   81
Introduction   81

CHAP. I.   That whatever appears to be the proper object of grati-
           tude appears to deserve reward; and that, in the same
           manner, whatever appears to be the proper object of
           resentment, appears to deserve punishment   82

CHAP. II. Of the proper objects of gratitude and resentment 84

CHAP. III. That where there is no approbation of the conduct
           of the person who confers the benefit, there is little
           sympathy with the gratitude of him who receives
           it; and that, on the contrary, where there is no
           disapprobation of the motives of the person who
           does the mischief, there is no sort of sympathy
           with the resentment of him who suffers it   86

CHAP. IV. Recapitulation of the foregoing Chapters   88

CHAP. V.   The analysis of the sense of Merit and Demerit 90

SECTION II.

OF JUSTICE AND BENEFICENCE   95
CHAP. I.   Comparison of those two virtues   95
CHAP. II. Of the sense of Justice, of Remorse, and of the
             consciousness of Merit   100
CHAP. III. Of the utility of this constitution of Nature   103

SECTION III.

OF THE INFLUENCE OF FORTUNE UPON THE SENTIMENTS OF
  MANKIND, WITH REGARD TO THE MERIT OR DEMERIT OF ACTIONS   111
Introduction   111
CHAP. I.   Of the causes of this Influence of Fortune   112
CHAP. II. Of the extent of this Influence of Fortune   116
CHAP. III. Of the final cause of this Irregularity of Sentiments   125

PART III.

OF THE FOUNDATION OF OUR JUDGMENTS CONCERNING OUR OWN
  SENTIMENTS AND CONDUCT, AND OF THE SENSE OF DUTY   131
CHAP. I.   Of the Principle of Self-approbation and of Self-
             disapprobation   133
CHAP. II. Of the love of Praise, and of that of Praise-worthiness;
             and of the dread of Blame, and of that of Blame-
             worthiness   136
CHAP. III. Of the Influence and Authority of Conscience   156
CHAP. IV. Of the Nature of Self-deceit, and of the Origin and Use
             of general Rules   180
CHAP. V.   Of the influence and authority of the general Rules
             of Morality, and that they are justly regarded as the
             Laws of the Deity   186
CHAP. VI. In what cases the Sense of Duty ought to be the sole
             Principle of our conduct; and in what cases it ought
             to concur with other motives   197

PART IV.

OF THE EFFECT OF UTILITY UPON THE SENTIMENT
  OF APPROBATION   207

CHAP. I.   Of the beauty which the appearance of Utility
           bestows upon all the productions of Art, and of
           the extensive influence of this species of Beauty   209
CHAP. II. Of the beauty which the Appearance of Utility bestows
           upon the characters and actions of men; and how
           far the perception of this beauty may be regarded
           as one of the original principles of Approbation   218

PART V.

OF THE INFLUENCE OF CUSTOM AND FASHION UPON THE
  SENTIMENTS OF MORAL APPROBATION AND DISAPPROBATION   225
CHAP. I.   Of the Influence of Custom and Fashion upon our
           notions of Beauty and Deformity   227
CHAP. II. Of the Influence of Custom and Fashion upon Moral
           Sentiments   234

PART VI.

OF THE CHARACTER OF VIRTUE   247
Introduction   249

SECTION I.

OF THE CHARACTER OF THE INDIVIDUAL, SO FAR AS IT AFFECTS
  HIS OWN HAPPINESS; OR OF PRUDENCE   250

SECTION II.

OF THE CHARACTER OF THE INDIVIDUAL, SO FAR AS IT CAN AFFECT
  THE HAPPINESS OF OTHER PEOPLE 257
Introduction   257
CHAP. I.   Of the Order in which Individuals are recommended by
           Nature to our Care and Attention   258
CHAP. II. Of the Order in which Societies are by Nature recom-
           mended to our Beneficence   268
CHAP. III. Of universal Benevolence   276

SECTION III.

OF SELF-COMMAND   280
CONCLUSION OF THE SIXTH PART   308

PART VII.

OF SYSTEMS OF MORAL PHILOSOPHY   313

SECTION I.

OF THE QUESTIONS WHICH OUGHT TO BE EXAMINED IN A THEORY
   OF MORAL SENTIMENTS   315

SECTION II.

OF THE DIFFERENT ACCOUNTS WHICH HAVE BEEN GIVEN OF THE
   NATURE OF VIRTUE   317
Introduction   317
CHAP. I.   Of those Systems which make Virtue consist in
        Propriety   318
CHAP. II. Of those Systems which make Virtue consist in
        Prudence   346
CHAP. III. Of those Systems which make Virtue consist in
        Benevolence   353
CHAP. IV. Of licentious Systems   360

SECTION III.

OF THE DIFFERENT SYSTEMS WHICH HAVE BEEN FORMED CONCERN-
   ING THE PRINCIPLE OF APPROBATION   370
Introduction   370
CHAP. I.   Of those Systems which deduce the Principle of
        Approbation from Self-love   371
CHAP. II. Of those Systems which make Reason the Principle
        of Approbation   374
CHAP. III. Of those Systems which make Sentiment the Principle
        of Approbation   378

SECTION IV.

OF THE MANNER IN WHICH DIFFERENT AUTHORS HAVE TREATED
OF THE PRACTICAL RULES OF MORALITY   386

CONSIDERATIONS CONCERNING THE FIRST FORMATION OF
LANGUAGES, AND THE DIFFERENT GENIUS OF ORIGINAL AND
COMPOUNDED LANGUAGES.   405

PART I.

OF THE PROPRIETY
OF ACTION.

CONSISTING OF THREE SECTIONS.

SECTION I.

OF THE SENSE OF PROPRIETY.

CHAPTER I.

Of Sympathy.

How selfish soever man may be supposed, there are evidently some principles in his nature, which interest him in the fortune of others, and render their happiness necessary to him, though he derives nothing from it except the pleasure of seeing it. Of this kind is pity or compassion, the emotion which we feel for the misery of others, when we either see it, or are made to conceive it in a very lively manner. That we often derive sorrow from the sorrow of others, is a matter of fact too obvious to require any instances to prove it; for this sentiment, like all the other original passions of human nature, is by no means confined to the virtuous and humane, though they perhaps may feel it with the most exquisite sensibility. The greatest ruffian, the most hardened violator of the laws of society, is not altogether without it.[1]

As we have no immediate experience of what other men feel, we can form no idea of the manner in which they are affected, but by conceiving what we ourselves should feel in the like situation. Though our brother is upon the rack,[2] as long as we ourselves are at our ease, our senses will never inform us of what he suffers. They never did, and never can, carry us beyond our own person, and it is by the imagination only that we can form any conception of what are his sensations. Neither can that faculty help us to this any other way, than by representing to us what would be our own, if we were in his case. It is the impressions of our own senses only, not those of his, which our imaginations copy.[3] By the imagination we place ourselves in his situation, we conceive ourselves enduring all the same torments, we enter as it were into his body, and become in some measure the same person with him, and thence form some idea of his sensations, and even feel something which, though weaker in degree, is not altogether unlike them. His agonies, when they are thus brought home to ourselves, when we have thus adopted and made them our own, begin at last to affect us, and we then tremble and shudder at the thought of what he feels. For as to be in pain or distress of any kind excites the most excessive sorrow, so to conceive or to imagine that we are in it, excites some degree of the same emotion, in proportion to the vivacity or dulness of the conception.

That this is the source of our fellow-feeling for the misery of others, that it is by changing places in fancy with the sufferer, that we come either to conceive or to be affected by what he feels, may be demonstrated by many obvious observations, if it should not be thought sufficiently evident of itself. When we see a stroke aimed and just ready to fall upon the leg or arm of another person, we naturally shrink and draw back our own leg or our own arm; and when it does fall, we feel it in some measure, and are hurt by it as well as the sufferer. The mob, when they are gazing at a dancer on the slack rope, naturally writhe and twist and balance their own bodies, as they see him do, and as they feel that they themselves must do if in his situation. Persons of delicate fibres and a weak constitution of body complain, that in looking on the sores and ulcers which are exposed by beggars in the streets, they are apt to feel an itching or uneasy sensation in the correspondent part of their own bodies. The horror which they conceive at the misery of those wretches affects that particular part in themselves more than any other; because that horror arises from conceiving what they themselves would suffer, if they really were the wretches whom they are looking upon, and if that particular part in themselves was actually affected in the same miserable manner. The very force of this conception is sufficient, in their feeble frames, to produce that itching or uneasy sensation complained of. Men of the most robust make, observe that in looking upon sore eyes they often feel a very sensible soreness in their own, which proceeds from the same reason; that organ being in the strongest man more delicate, than any other part of the body is in the weakest.

Neither is it those circumstances only, which create pain or sorrow, that call forth our fellow-feeling. Whatever is the passion which arises from any object in the person principally concerned, an analogous emotion springs up, at the thought of his situation, in the breast of every attentive spectator.[4] Our joy for the deliverance of those heroes of tragedy or romance who interest us, is as sincere as our grief for their distress, and our fellow-feeling with their misery is not more real than that with their happiness. We enter into their gratitude towards those faithful friends who did not desert them in their difficulties; and we heartily go along with their resentment against those perfidious[5] traitors who injured, abandoned, or deceived them. In every passion of which the mind of man is susceptible, the emotions of the bystander always correspond to what, by bringing the case home to himself, he imagines should be the sentiments of the sufferer.

Pity and compassion are words appropriated to signify our fellow-feeling with the sorrow of others. Sympathy, though its meaning was, perhaps, originally the same, may now, however, without much impropriety, be made use of to denote our fellow-feeling with any passion whatever.[6]

Upon some occasions sympathy may seem to arise merely from the view of a certain emotion in another person. The passions, upon some occasions, may seem to be transfused from one man to another, instantaneously, and antecedent to any knowledge of what excited them in the person principally concerned. Grief and joy, for example, strongly expressed in the look and gestures of any one, at once affect the spectator with some degree of a like painful or agreeable emotion. A smiling face is, to every body that sees it, a cheerful object; as a sorrowful countenance, on the other hand, is a melancholy one.

This, however, does not hold universally, or with regard to every passion. There are some passions of which the expressions excite no sort of sympathy, but, before we are acquainted with what gave occasion to them, serve rather to disgust and provoke us against them. The furious behaviour of an angry man is more likely to exasperate us against himself than against his enemies. As we are unacquainted with his provocation, we cannot bring his case home to ourselves, nor conceive any thing like the passions which it excites. But we plainly see what is the situation of those with whom he is angry, and to what violence they may be exposed from so enraged an adversary. We readily, therefore, sympathize with their fear or resentment, and are immediately disposed to take part against the man from whom they appear to be in so much danger.

If the very appearances of grief and joy inspire us with some degree of the like emotions, it is because they suggest to us the general idea of some good or bad fortune that has befallen the person in whom we observe them: and in these passions this is sufficient to have some little influence upon us. The effects of grief and joy terminate in the person who feels those emotions, of which the expressions do not, like those of resentment, suggest to us the idea of any other person for whom we are concerned, and whose interests are opposite to his. The general idea of good or bad fortune, therefore, creates some concern for the person who has met with it, but the general idea of provocation excites no sympathy with the anger of the man who has received it. Nature, it seems, teaches us to be more averse to enter into this passion, and, till informed of its cause, to be disposed rather to take part against it.

Even our sympathy with the grief or joy of another, before we are informed of the cause of either, is always extremely imperfect. General lamentations, which express nothing but the anguish of the sufferer, create rather a curiosity to inquire into his situation, along with some disposition to sympathize with him, than any actual sympathy that is very sensible. The first question which we ask is, What has befallen you? Till this be answered, though we are uneasy both from the vague idea of his misfortune, and still more from torturing ourselves with conjectures about what it may be, yet our fellow-feeling is not very considerable.

Sympathy, therefore, does not arise so much from the view of the passion, as from that of the situation which excites it. We sometimes feel for another, a passion of which he himself seems to be altogether incapable; because, when we put ourselves in his case, that passion arises in our breast from the imagination, though it does not in his from the reality. We blush for the impudence and rudeness of another, though he himself appears to have no sense of the impropriety of his own behaviour; because we cannot help feeling with what confusion we ourselves should be covered, had we behaved in so absurd a manner.

Of all the calamities to which the condition of mortality exposes mankind, the loss of reason appears, to those who have the least spark of humanity, by far the most dreadful, and they behold that last stage of human wretchedness with deeper commiseration than any other. But the poor wretch, who is in it, laughs and sings, perhaps, and is altogether insensible of his own misery. The anguish which humanity feels, therefore, at the sight of such an object, cannot be the reflection of any sentiment of the sufferer. The compassion of the spectator must arise altogether from the consideration of what he himself would feel if he was reduced to the same unhappy situation, and, what perhaps is impossible, was at the same time able to regard it with his present reason and judgment.

What are the pangs of a mother, when she hears the moanings of her infant that, during the agony of disease cannot express what it feels? In her idea of what it suffers, she joins, to its real helplessness, her own consciousness of that helplessness, and her own terrors for the unknown consequences of its disorder; and out of all these, forms, for her own sorrow, the most complete image of misery and distress. The infant, however, feels only the uneasiness of the present instant, which can never be great. With regard to the future, it is perfectly secure, and in its thoughtlessness and want of foresight, possesses an antidote against fear and anxiety, the great tormentors of the human breast, from which reason and philosophy will, in vain, attempt to defend it, when it grows up to a man.

We sympathize even with the dead, and overlooking what is of real importance in their situation, that awful futurity which awaits them, we are chiefly affected by those circumstances which strike our senses, but can have no influence upon their happiness. It is miserable, we think, to be deprived of the light of the sun; to be shut out from life and conversation; to be laid in the cold grave, a prey to corruption and the reptiles of the earth; to be no more thought of in this world, but to be obliterated, in a little time, from the affections, and almost from the memory, of their dearest friends and relations. Surely, we imagine, we can never feel too much for those who have suffered so dreadful a calamity. The tribute of our fellow-feeling seems doubly due to them now, when they are in danger of being forgot by every body; and, by the vain honours which we pay to their memory, we endeavour, for our own misery, artificially to keep alive our melancholy remembrance of their misfortune. That our sympathy can afford them no consolation seems to be an addition to their calamity; and to think that all we can do is unavailing, and that, what alleviates all other distress, the regret, the love, and the lamentations of their friends, can yield no comfort to them, serves only to exasperate our sense of their misery. The happiness of the dead, however, most assuredly, is affected by none of these circumstances; nor is it the thought of these things which can ever disturb the profound security of their repose. The idea of that dreary and endless melancholy, which the fancy naturally ascribes to their condition, arises altogether from our joining to the change which has been produced upon them, our own consciousness of that change, from our putting ourselves in their situation, and from our lodging, if I may be allowed to say so, our own living souls in their inanimated bodies, and thence conceiving what would be our emotions in this case. It is from this very illusion of the imagination, that the foresight of our own dissolution is so terrible to us, and that the idea of those circumstances, which undoubtedly can give us no pain when we are dead, makes us miserable while we are alive.[7] And from thence arises one of the most important principles in human nature, the dread of death, the great poison to the happiness, but the great restraint upon the injustice of mankind, which, while it afflicts and mortifies the individual, guards and protects the society.

CHAPTER II.

Of the Pleasure of mutual Sympathy.

But whatever may be the cause of sympathy, or however it may be excited, nothing pleases us more than to observe in other men a fellow-feeling with all the emotions of our own breast; nor are we ever so much shocked as by the appearance of the contrary. Those who are fond of deducing all our sentiments from certain refinements of self-love, think themselves at no loss to account, according to their own principles, both for this pleasure and this pain.[8] Man, say they, conscious of his own weakness, and of the need which he has for the assistance of others, rejoices whenever he observes that they adopt his own passions, because he is then assured of that assistance; and grieves whenever he observes the contrary, because he is then assured of their opposition. But both the pleasure and the pain are always felt so instantaneously, and often upon such frivolous occasions, that it seems evident that neither of them can be derived from any such self-interested consideration. A man is mortified when, after having endeavoured to divert the company, he looks round and sees that nobody laughs at his jests but himself. On the contrary, the mirth of the company is highly agreeable to him, and he regards this correspondence of their sentiments with his own as the greatest applause.

Neither does his pleasure seem to arise altogether from the additional vivacity which his mirth may receive from sympathy with theirs, nor his pain from the disappointment he meets with when he misses this pleasure; though both the one and the other, no doubt, do in some measure. When we have read a book or poem so often that we can no longer find any amusement in reading it by ourselves, we can still take pleasure in reading it to a companion. To him it has all the graces of novelty; we enter into the surprise and admiration which it naturally excites in him, but which it is no longer capable of exciting in us; we consider all the ideas which it presents rather in the light in which they appear to him, than in that in which they appear to ourselves, and we are amused by sympathy with his amusement which thus enlivens our own. On the contrary, we should be vexed if he did not seem to be entertained with it, and we could no longer take any pleasure in reading it to him. It is the same case here. The mirth of the company, no doubt, enlivens our own mirth, and their silence, no doubt, disappoints us. But though this may contribute both to the pleasure which we derive from the one, and to the pain which we feel from the other, it is by no means the sole cause of either; and this correspondence of the sentiments of others with our own appears to be a cause of pleasure, and the want of it a cause of pain, which cannot be accounted for in this manner. The sympathy, which my friends express with my joy, might, indeed, give me pleasure by enlivening that joy: but that which they express with my grief could give me none, if it served only to enliven that grief. Sympathy, however, enlivens joy and alleviates grief. It enlivens joy by presenting another source of satisfaction; and it alleviates grief by insinuating into the heart almost the only agreeable sensation which it is at that time capable of receiving.

It is to be observed accordingly, that we are still more anxious to communicate to our friends our disagreeable than our agreeable passions, that we derive still more satisfaction from their sympathy with the former than from that with the latter, and that we are still more shocked by the want of it.

How are the unfortunate relieved when they have found out a person to whom they can communicate the cause of their sorrow? Upon his sympathy they seem to disburthen themselves of a part of their distress: he is not improperly said to share it with them. He not only feels a sorrow of the same kind with that which they feel, but as if he had derived a part of it to himself, what he feels seems to alleviate the weight of what they feel. Yet by relating their misfortunes they in some measure renew their grief. They awaken in their memory the remembrance of those circumstances which occasioned their affliction. Their tears accordingly flow faster than before, and they are apt to abandon themselves to all the weakness of sorrow. They take pleasure, however, in all this, and, it is evident, are sensibly relieved by it; because the sweetness of his sympathy more than compensates the bitterness of that sorrow, which, in order to excite this sympathy, they had thus enlivened and renewed. The cruelest insult, on the contrary, which can be offered to the unfortunate, is to appear to make light of their calamities. To seem not to be affected with the joy of our companions is but want of politeness; but not to wear a serious countenance when they tell us their afflictions, is real and gross inhumanity.

Love is an agreeable; resentment, a disagreeable passion; and accordingly we are not half so anxious that our friends should adopt our friendships, as that they should enter into our resentments. We can forgive them though they seem to be little affected with the favours which we may have received, but lose all patience if they seem indifferent about the injuries which may have been done to us: nor are we half so angry with them for not entering into our gratitude, as for not sympathizing with our resentment. They can easily avoid being friends to our friends, but can hardly avoid being enemies to those with whom we are at variance. We seldom resent their being at enmity with the first, though upon that account we may sometimes affect to make an awkward quarrel with them; but we quarrel with them in good earnest if they live in friendship with the last. The agreeable passions of love and joy can satisfy and support the heart without any auxiliary pleasure. The bitter and painful emotions of grief and resentment more strongly require the healing consolation of sympathy.

As the person who is principally interested in any event is pleased with our sympathy, and hurt by the want of it, so we, too, seem to be pleased when we are able to sympathize with him, and to be hurt when we are unable to do so. We run not only to congratulate the successful, but to condole with the afflicted; and the pleasure which we find in the conversation of one whom in all the passions of his heart we can entirely sympathize with, seems to do more than compensate the painfulness of that sorrow with which the view of his situation affects us. On the contrary, it is always disagreeable to feel that we cannot sympathize with him, and instead of being pleased with this exemption from sympathetic pain, it hurts us to find that we cannot share his uneasiness. If we hear a person loudly lamenting his misfortunes, which, however, upon bringing the case home to ourselves, we feel, can produce no such violent effect upon us, we are shocked at his grief; and, because we cannot enter into it, call it pusillanimity and weakness. It gives us the spleen,[9] on the other hand, to see another too happy or too much elevated, as we call it, with any little piece of good fortune. We are disobliged even with his joy; and, because we cannot go along with it, call it levity and folly. We are even put out of humour if our companion laughs louder or longer at a joke than we think it deserves; that is, than we feel that we ourselves could laugh at it.

CHAPTER III.

Of the manner in which we judge of the propriety or impropriety of the Affections of other Men, by their concord or dissonance with our own.

When the original passions of the person principally concerned are in perfect concord with the sympathetic emotions of the spectator, they necessarily appear to this last just and proper, and suitable to their objects; and, on the contrary, when, upon bringing the case home to himself, he finds that they do not coincide with what he feels, they necessarily appear to him unjust and improper, and unsuitable to the causes which excite them. To approve of the passions of another, therefore, as suitable to their objects, is the same thing as to observe that we entirely sympathize with them; and not to approve of them as such, is the same thing as to observe that we do not entirely sympathize with them. The man who resents the injuries that have been done to me, and observes that I resent them precisely as he does, necessarily approves of my resentment. The man whose sympathy keeps time to my grief, cannot but admit the reasonableness of my sorrow. He who admires the same poem, or the same picture, and admires them exactly as I do, must surely allow the justness of my admiration. He who laughs at the same joke, and laughs along with me, cannot well deny the propriety of my laughter. On the contrary, the person who, upon these different occasions, either feels no such emotion as that which I feel, or feels none that bears any proportion to mine, cannot avoid disapproving my sentiments on account of their dissonance with his own. If my animosity goes beyond what the indignation of my friend can correspond to; if my grief exceeds what his most tender compassion can go along with; if my admiration is either too high or too low to tally with his own; if I laugh loud and heartily when he only smiles, or, on the contrary, only smile when he laughs loud and heartily; in all these cases, as soon as he comes from considering the object, to observe how I am affected by it, according as there is more or less disproportion between his sentiments and mine, I must incur a greater or less degree of his disapprobation: and upon all occasions his own sentiments are the standards and measures by which he judges of mine.

To approve of another man's opinions is to adopt those opinions, and to adopt them is to approve of them. If the same arguments which convince you convince me likewise, I necessarily approve of your conviction; and if they do not, I necessarily disapprove of it: neither can I possibly conceive that I should do the one without the other. To approve or disapprove, therefore, of the opinions of others is acknowledged, by every body, to mean no more than to observe their agreement or disagreement with our own. But this is equally the case with regard to our approbation or disapprobation of the sentiments or passions of others.

There are, indeed, some cases in which we seem to approve without any sympathy or correspondence of sentiments, and in which, consequently, the sentiment of approbation would seem to be different from the perception of this coincidence. A little attention, however, will convince us that even in these cases our approbation is ultimately founded upon a sympathy or correspondence of this kind. I shall give an instance in things of a very frivolous nature, because in them the judgments of mankind are less apt to be perverted by wrong systems. We may often approve of a jest, and think the laughter of the company quite just and proper, though we ourselves do not laugh, because, perhaps, we are in a grave humour, or happen to have our attention engaged with other objects. We have learned, however, from experience, what sort of pleasantry is upon most occasions capable of making us laugh, and we observe that this is one of that kind. We approve, therefore, of the laughter of the company, and feel that it is natural and suitable to its object; because, though in our present mood we cannot easily enter into it, we are sensible that upon most occasions we should very heartily join in it.

The same thing often happens with regard to all the other passions. A stranger passes by us in the street with all the marks of the deepest affliction; and we are immediately told that he has just received the news of the death of his father. It is impossible that, in this case, we should not approve of his grief. Yet it may often happen, without any defect of humanity on our part, that, so far from entering into the violence of his sorrow, we should scarce conceive the first movements of concern upon his account. Both he and his father, perhaps, are entirely unknown to us, or we happen to be employed about other things, and do not take time to picture out in our imagination the different circumstances of distress which must occur to him. We have learned, however, from experience, that such a misfortune naturally excites such a degree of sorrow, and we know that if we took time to consider his situation, fully and in all its parts, we should, without doubt, most sincerely sympathize with him. It is upon the consciousness of this conditional sympathy, that our approbation of his sorrow is founded, even in those cases in which that sympathy does not actually take place; and the general rules derived from our preceding experience of what our sentiments would commonly correspond with, correct, upon this, as upon many other occasions, the impropriety of our present emotions.

The sentiment or affection of the heart from which any action proceeds, and upon which its whole virtue or vice must ultimately depend, may be considered under two different aspects, or in two different relations; first, in relation to the cause which excites it, or the motive which gives occasion to it; and secondly, in relation to the end which it proposes, or the effect which it tends to produce.

In the suitableness or unsuitableness, in the proportion or disproportion which the affection seems to bear to the cause or object which excites it, consists the propriety or impropriety, the decency or ungracefulness, of the consequent action.

In the beneficial or hurtful nature of the effects which the affection aims at, or tends to produce, consists the merit or demerit of the action, the qualities by which it is entitled to reward, or is deserving of punishment.

Philosophers have, of late years, considered chiefly the tendency of affections, and have given little attention to the relation which they stand in to the cause which excites them.[10] In common life, however, when we judge of any person's conduct, and of the sentiments which directed it, we constantly consider them under both these aspects. When we blame in another man the excesses of love, of grief, of resentment, we not only consider the ruinous effects which they tend to produce, but the little occasion which was given for them. The merit of his favourite, we say, is not so great, his misfortune is not so dreadful, his provocation is not so extraordinary, as to justify so violent a passion. We should have indulged, we say; perhaps, have approved of the violence of his emotion, had the cause been in any respect proportioned to it.

When we judge in this manner of any affection, as proportioned or disproportioned to the cause which excites it, it is scarce possible that we should make use of any other rule or canon but the correspondent affection in ourselves. If, upon bringing the case home to our own breast, we find that the sentiments which it gives occasion to, coincide and tally with our own, we necessarily approve of them as proportioned and suitable to their objects; if otherwise, we necessarily disapprove of them, as extravagant and out of proportion.

Every faculty in one man is the measure by which he judges of the like faculty in another. I judge of your sight by my sight, of your ear by my ear, of your reason by my reason, of your resentment by my resentment, of your love by my love. I neither have, nor can have, any other way of judging about them.

CHAPTER IV.

The same subject continued.

We may judge of the propriety or impropriety of the sentiments of another person by their correspondence or disagreement with our own, upon two different occasions; either, first, when the objects which excite them are considered without any peculiar relation, either to ourselves or to the person whose sentiments we judge of; or, secondly, when they are considered as peculiarly affecting one or other of us.

1. With regard to those objects which are considered without any peculiar relation either to ourselves or to the person whose sentiments we judge of; wherever his sentiments entirely correspond with our own, we ascribe to him the qualities of taste and good judgment. The beauty of a plain, the greatness of a mountain, the ornaments of a building, the expression of a picture, the composition of a discourse, the conduct of a third person, the proportions of different quantities and numbers, the various appearances which the great machine of the universe is perpetually exhibiting, with the secret wheels and springs which produce them; all the general subjects of science and taste, are what we and our companion regard as having no peculiar relation to either of us. We both look at them from the same point of view, and we have no occasion for sympathy, or for that imaginary change of situations from which it arises, in order to produce, with regard to these, the most perfect harmony of sentiments and affections. If, notwithstanding, we are often differently affected, it arises either from the different degrees of attention, which our different habits of life allow us to give easily to the several parts of those complex objects, or from the different degrees of natural acuteness in the faculty of the mind to which they are addressed.

When the sentiments of our companion coincide with our own in things of this kind, which are obvious and easy, and in which, perhaps, we never found a single person who differed from us, though we, no doubt, must approve of them, yet he seems to deserve no praise or admiration on account of them. But when they not only coincide with our own, but lead and direct our own; when in forming them he appears to have attended to many things which we had overlooked, and to have adjusted them to all the various circumstances of their objects; we not only approve of them, but wonder and are surprised at their uncommon and unexpected acuteness and comprehensiveness, and he appears to deserve a very high degree of admiration and applause. For approbation heightened by wonder and surprise, constitutes the sentiment which is properly called admiration, and of which applause is the natural expression.[11] The decision of the man who judges that exquisite beauty is preferable to the grossest deformity, or that twice two are equal to four, must certainly be approved of by all the world, but will not, surely, be much admired. It is the acute and delicate discernment of the man of taste, who distinguishes the minute, and scarce perceptible differences of beauty and deformity; it is the comprehensive accuracy of the experienced mathematician, who unravels, with ease, the most intricate and perplexed proportions; it is the great leader in science and taste, the man who directs and conducts our own sentiments, the extent and superior justness of whose talents astonish us with wonder and surprise, who excites our admiration, and seems to deserve our applause: and upon this foundation is grounded the greater part of the praise which is bestowed upon what are called the intellectual virtues.

The utility of those qualities, it may be thought, is what first recommends them to us; and, no doubt, the consideration of this, when we come to attend to it, gives them a new value.[12] Originally, however, we approve of another man's judgment, not as something useful, but as right, as accurate, as agreeable to truth and reality: and it is evident we attribute those qualities to it for no other reason but because we find that it agrees with our own. Taste, in the same manner, is originally approved of, not as useful, but as just, as delicate, and as precisely suited to its object. The idea of the utility of all qualities of this kind, is plainly an after thought, and not what first recommends them to our approbation.

2. With regard to those objects, which affect in a particular manner either ourselves or the person whose sentiments we judge of, it is at once more difficult to preserve this harmony and correspondence, and at the same time, vastly more important. My companion does not naturally look upon the misfortune that has befallen me, or the injury that has been done me, from the same point of view in which I consider them. They affect me much more nearly. We do not view them from the same station, as we do a picture, or a poem, or a system of philosophy, and are, therefore, apt to be very differently affected by them. But I can much more easily overlook the want of this correspondence of sentiments with regard to such indifferent objects as concern neither me nor my companion, than with regard to what interests me so much as the misfortune that has befallen me, or the injury that has been done me. Though you despise that picture, or that poem, or even that system of philosophy, which I admire, there is little danger of our quarrelling upon that account. Neither of us can reasonably be much interested about them. They ought all of them to be matters of great indifference to us both; so that, though our opinions may be opposite, our affections may still be very nearly the same. But it is quite otherwise with regard to those objects by which either you or I are particularly affected. Though your judgments in matters of speculation, though your sentiments in matters of taste, are quite opposite to mine, I can easily overlook this opposition; and if I have any degree of temper, I may still find some entertainment in your conversation, even upon those very subjects. But if you have either no fellow-feeling for the misfortunes I have met with, or none that bears any proportion to the grief which distracts me; or if you have either no indignation at the injuries I have suffered, or none that bears any proportion to the resentment which transports me, we can no longer converse upon these subjects. We become intolerable to one another. I can neither support your company, nor you mine. You are confounded at my violence and passion, and I am enraged at your cold insensibility and want of feeling.

In all such cases, that there may be some correspondence of sentiments between the spectator and the person principally concerned, the spectator must, first of all, endeavour, as much as he can, to put himself in the situation of the other, and to bring home to himself every little circumstance of distress which can possibly occur to the sufferer. He must adopt the whole case of his companion with all its minutest incidents; and strive to render as perfect as possible, that imaginary change of situation upon which his sympathy is founded.

After all this, however, the emotions of the spectator will still be very apt to fall short of the violence of what is felt by the sufferer. Mankind, though naturally sympathetic, never conceive, for what has befallen another, that degree of passion which naturally animates the person principally concerned. That imaginary change of situation, upon which their sympathy is founded, is but momentary. The thought of their own safety, the thought that they themselves are not really the sufferers, continually intrudes itself upon them; and though it does not hinder them from conceiving a passion somewhat analogous to what is felt by the sufferer, hinders them from conceiving any thing that approaches to the same degree of violence. The person principally concerned is sensible of this, and at the same time passionately desires a more complete sympathy. He longs for that relief which nothing can afford him but the entire concord of the affections of the spectators with his own. To see the emotions of their hearts, in every respect, beat time to his own, in the violent and disagreeable passions, constitutes his sole consolation. But he can only hope to obtain this by lowering his passion to that pitch, in which the spectators are capable of going along with him. He must flatten, if I may be allowed to say so, the sharpness of its natural tone, in order to reduce it to harmony and concord with the emotions of those who are about him. What they feel, will, indeed, always be, in some respects, different from what he feels, and compassion can never be exactly the same with original sorrow; because the secret consciousness that the change of situations, from which the sympathetic sentiment arises, is but imaginary, not only lowers it in degree, but, in some measure, varies it in kind, and gives it a quite different modification. These two sentiments, however, may, it is evident, have such a correspondence with one another, as is sufficient for the harmony of society. Though they will never be unisons, they may be concords, and this is all that is wanted or required.

In order to produce this concord, as nature teaches the spectators to assume the circumstances of the person principally concerned, so she teaches this last in some measure to assume those of the spectators. As they are continually placing themselves in his situation, and thence conceiving emotions similar to what he feels; so he is as constantly placing himself in theirs, and thence conceiving some degree of that coolness about his own fortune, with which he is sensible that they will view it. As they are constantly considering what they themselves would feel, if they actually were the sufferers, so he is as constantly led to imagine in what manner he would be affected if he was only one of the spectators of his own situation. As their sympathy makes them look at it, in some measure, with his eyes, so his sympathy makes him look at it, in some measure, with theirs, especially when in their presence, and acting under their observation: and as the reflected passion, which he thus conceives, is much weaker than the original one, it necessarily abates the violence of what he felt before he came into their presence, before he began to recollect in what manner they would be affected by it, and to view his situation in this candid and impartial light.

The mind, therefore, is rarely so disturbed, but that the company of a friend will restore it to some degree of tranquillity and sedateness. The breast is, in some measure, calmed and composed the moment we come into his presence. We are immediately put in mind of the light in which he will view our situation, and we begin to view it ourselves in the same light; for the effect of sympathy is instantaneous. We expect less sympathy from a common acquaintance than from a friend: we cannot open to the former all those little circumstances which we can unfold to the latter: we assume, therefore, more tranquillity before him, and endeavour to fix our thoughts upon those general outlines of our situation which he is willing to consider. We expect still less sympathy from an assembly of strangers, and we assume, therefore, still more tranquillity before them, and always endeavour to bring down our passion to that pitch, which the particular company we are in may be expected to go along with. Nor is this only an assumed appearance: for if we are at all masters of ourselves, the presence of a mere acquaintance will really compose us, still more than that of a friend; and that of an assembly of strangers still more than that of an acquaintance.

Society and conversation, therefore, are the most powerful remedies for restoring the mind to its tranquillity, if, at any time, it has unfortunately lost it; as well as the best preservatives of that equal and happy temper, which is so necessary to self-satisfaction and enjoyment. Men of retirement and speculation, who are apt to sit brooding at home over either grief or resentment, though they may often have more humanity, more generosity, and a nicer sense of honour, yet seldom possess that equality of temper which is so common among men of the world.

CHAPTER V.

Of the amiable and respectable virtues.

Upon these two different efforts, upon that of the spectator to enter into the sentiments of the person principally concerned, and upon that of the person principally concerned, to bring down his emotions to what the spectator can go along with, are founded two different sets of virtues. The soft, the gentle, the amiable virtues, the virtues of candid condescension and indulgent humanity, are founded upon the one: the great, the awful and respectable, the virtues of self-denial, of self-government, of that command of the passions which subjects all the movements of our nature to what our own dignity and honour, and the propriety of our own conduct require, take their origin from the other.[13]

How amiable does he appear to be, whose sympathetic heart seems to re-echo all the sentiments of those with whom he converses, who grieves for their calamities, who resents their injuries, and who rejoices at their good fortune! When we bring home to ourselves the situation of his companions, we enter into their gratitude, and feel what consolation they must derive from the tender sympathy of so affectionate a friend. And for a contrary reason, how disagreeable does he appear to be, whose hard and obdurate heart feels for himself only, but is altogether insensible to the happiness or misery of others! We enter, in this case too, into the pain which his presence must give to every mortal with whom he converses, to those especially with whom we are most apt to sympathize, the unfortunate and the injured.

On the other hand, what noble propriety and grace do we feel in the conduct of those who, in their own case, exert that recollection and self-command which constitute the dignity of every passion, and which bring it down to what others can enter into! We are disgusted with that clamorous grief, which, without any delicacy, calls upon our compassion with sighs and tears and importunate lamentations. But we reverence that reserved, that silent and majestic sorrow, which discovers itself only in the swelling of the eyes, in the quivering of the lips and cheeks, and in the distant, but affecting, coldness of the whole behaviour. It imposes the like silence upon us. We regard it with respectful attention, and watch with anxious concern over our whole behaviour, lest by any impropriety we should disturb that concerted tranquillity, which it requires so great an effort to support.

The insolence and brutality of anger, in the same manner when we indulge its fury without check or restraint, is, of all objects, the most detestable. But we admire that noble and generous resentment which governs its pursuit of the greatest injuries, not by the rage which they are apt to excite in the breast of the sufferer, but by the indignation which they naturally call forth in that of the impartial spectator; which allows no word, no gesture, to escape it beyond what this more equitable sentiment would dictate; which never, even in thought, attempts any greater vengeance, nor desires to inflict any greater punishment, than what every indifferent person would rejoice to see executed.

And hence it is, that to feel much for others and little for ourselves, that to restrain our selfish, and to indulge our benevolent affections, constitutes the perfection of human nature; and can alone produce among mankind that harmony of sentiments and passions in which consists their whole grace and propriety. As to love our neighbour as we love ourselves is the great law of Christianity,[14] so it is the great precept of nature to love ourselves only as we love our neighbour, or what comes to the same thing, as our neighbour is capable of loving us.

As taste and good judgment, when they are considered as qualities which deserve praise and admiration, are supposed to imply a delicacy of sentiment and an acuteness of understanding not commonly to be met with; so the virtues of sensibility and self-command are not apprehended to consist in the ordinary, but in the uncommon degrees of those qualities. The amiable virtue of humanity requires, surely, a sensibility, much beyond what is possessed by the rude vulgar of mankind. The great and exalted virtue of magnanimity undoubtedly demands much more than that degree of self-command, which the weakest of mortals is capable of exerting. As in the common degree of the intellectual qualities, there is no abilities; so in the common degree of the moral, there is no virtue. Virtue is excellence, something uncommonly great and beautiful, which rises far above what is vulgar and ordinary. The amiable virtues consist in that degree of sensibility which surprises by its exquisite and unexpected delicacy and tenderness. The awful and respectable, in that degree of self-command which astonishes by its amazing superiority over the most ungovernable passions of human nature.

There is, in this respect, a considerable difference between virtue and mere propriety; between those qualities and actions which deserve to be admired and celebrated, and those which simply deserve to be approved of.[15] Upon many occasions, to act with the most perfect propriety, requires no more than that common and ordinary degree of sensibility or self-command which the most worthless of mankind are possesst of, and sometimes even that degree is not necessary. Thus, to give a very low instance, to eat when we are hungry, is certainly, upon ordinary occasions, perfectly right and proper, and cannot miss being approved of as such by every body. Nothing, however, could be more absurd than to say it was virtuous.

On the contrary, there may frequently be a considerable degree of virtue in those actions which fall short of the most perfect propriety; because they may still approach nearer to perfection than could well be expected upon occasions in which it was so extremely difficult to attain it: and this is very often the case upon those occasions which require the greatest exertions of self-command. There are some situations which bear so hard upon human nature, that the greatest degree of self-government, which can belong to so imperfect a creature as man, is not able to stifle, altogether, the voice of human weakness, or reduce the violence of the passions to that pitch of moderation, in which the impartial spectator can entirely enter into them. Though in those cases, therefore, the behaviour of the sufferer fall short of the most perfect propriety, it may still deserve some applause, and even in a certain sense, may be denominated virtuous. It may still manifest an effort of generosity and magnanimity of which the greater part of men are incapable; and though it fails of absolute perfection, it may be a much nearer approximation towards perfection, than what, upon such trying occasions, is commonly either to be found or to be expected.

In cases of this kind, when we are determining the degree of blame or applause which seems due to any action, we very frequently make use of two different standards.[16] The first is the idea of complete propriety and perfection, which, in those difficult situations, no human conduct ever did, or ever can come up to; and in comparison with which the actions of all men must for ever appear blameable and imperfect. The second is the idea of that degree of proximity or distance from this complete perfection, which the actions of the greater part of men commonly arrive at. Whatever goes beyond this degree, how far soever it may be removed from absolute perfection, seems to deserve applause; and whatever falls short of it, to deserve blame.

It is in the same manner that we judge of the productions of all the arts which address themselves to the imagination. When a critic examines the work of any of the great masters in poetry or painting, he may sometimes examine it by an idea of perfection, in his own mind, which neither that nor any other human work will ever come up to; and as long as he compares it with this standard, he can see nothing in it but faults and imperfections. But when he comes to consider the rank which it ought to hold among other works of the same kind, he necessarily compares it with a very different standard, the common degree of excellence which is usually attained in this particular art; and when he judges of it by this new measure, it may often appear to deserve the highest applause, upon account of its approaching much nearer to perfection than the greater part of those works which can be brought into competition with it.

SECTION II.

OF THE DEGREES OF THE DIFFERENT PASSIONS WHICH ARE CONSISTENT WITH PROPRIETY.

INTRODUCTION.

The propriety of every passion excited by objects peculiarly related to ourselves, the pitch which the spectator can go along with, must lie, it is evident, in a certain mediocrity. If the passion is too high, or if it is too low, he cannot enter into it. Grief and resentment for private misfortunes and injuries may easily, for example, be too high, and in the greater part of mankind they are so. They may likewise, though this more rarely happens, be too low. We denominate the excess, weakness and fury: and we call the defect stupidity, insensibility, and want of spirit. We can enter into neither of them, but are astonished and confounded to see them.

This mediocrity, however, in which the point of propriety consists, is different in different passions. It is high in some, and low in others. There are some passions which it is indecent to express very strongly, even upon those occasions, in which it is acknowledged that we cannot avoid feeling them in the highest degree. And there are others of which the strongest expressions are upon many occasions extremely graceful, even though the passions themselves do not, perhaps, arise so necessarily. The first are those passions with which, for certain reasons, there is little or no sympathy: the second are those with which, for other reasons, there is the greatest. And if we consider all the different passions of human nature, we shall find that they are regarded as decent, or indecent, just in proportion as mankind are more or less disposed to sympathize with them.

CHAPTER I.

Of the Passions which take their origin from the body.

1. It is indecent to express any strong degree of those passions which arise from a certain situation or disposition of the body; because the company, not being in the same disposition, cannot be expected to sympathize with them. Violent hunger, for example, though upon many occasions not only natural, but unavoidable, is always indecent, and to eat voraciously is universally regarded as a piece of ill manners. There is, however, some degree of sympathy, even with hunger. It is agreeable to see our companions eat with a good appetite, and all expressions of loathing are offensive. The disposition of body which is habitual to a man in health, makes his stomach easily keep time, if I may be allowed so coarse an expression, with the one, and not with the other. We can sympathize with the distress which excessive hunger occasions when we read the description of it in the journal of a siege, or of a sea-voyage. We imagine ourselves in the situation of the sufferers, and thence readily conceive the grief, the fear, and consternation, which must necessarily distract them. We feel, ourselves, some degree of those passions, and therefore sympathize with them: but as we do not grow hungry by reading the description, we cannot properly, even in this case, be said to sympathize with their hunger.

It is the same case with the passion by which Nature unites the two sexes. Though naturally the most furious of all the passions, all strong expressions of it are upon every occasion indecent, even between persons in whom its most complete indulgence is acknowledged by all laws, both human and divine, to be perfectly innocent. There seems, however, to be some degree of sympathy even with this passion. To talk to a woman as we would to a man is improper: it is expected that their company should inspire us with more gaiety, more pleasantry, and more attention; and an entire insensibility to the fair sex, renders a man contemptible in some measure even to the men.

Such is our aversion for all the appetites which take their origin from the body: all strong expressions of them are loathsome and disagreeable. According to some ancient philosophers, these are the passions which we share in common with the brutes, and which having no connexion with the characteristical qualities of human nature, are upon that account beneath its dignity.[1] But there are many other passions which we share in common with the brutes, such as resentment, natural affection, even gratitude, which do not, upon that account, appear to be so brutal. The true cause of the peculiar disgust which we conceive for the appetites of the body when we see them in other men, is that we cannot enter into them. To the person himself who feels them, as soon as they are gratified, the object that excited them ceases to be agreeable: even its presence often becomes offensive to him; he looks round to no purpose for the charm which transported him the moment before, and he can now as little enter into his own passion as another person. When we have dined, we order the covers to be removed; and we should treat in the same manner the objects of the most ardent and passionate desires, if they were the objects of no other passions but those which take their origin from the body.

In the command of those appetites of the body consists that virtue which is properly called temperance. To restrain them within those bounds, which regard to health and fortune prescribes, is the part of prudence. But to confine them within those limits, which grace, which propriety, which delicacy, and modesty, require, is the office of temperance.

2. It is for the same reason that to cry out with bodily pain, how intolerable soever, appears always unmanly and unbecoming. There is, however, a good deal of sympathy even with bodily pain. If, as has already been observed,[2] I see a stroke aimed, and just ready to fall upon the leg, or arm, of another person, I naturally shrink and draw back my own leg, or my own arm: and when it does fall, I feel it in some measure, and am hurt by it as well as the sufferer. My hurt, however, is, no doubt, excessively slight, and, upon that account, if he makes any violent out-cry, as I cannot go along with him, I never fail to despise him. And this is the case of all the passions which take their origin from the body: they excite either no sympathy at all, or such a degree of it, as is altogether disproportioned to the violence of what is felt by the sufferer.

It is quite otherwise with those passions which take their origin from the imagination. The frame of my body can be but little affected by the alterations which are brought about upon that of my companion: but my imagination is more ductile, and more readily assumes, if I may say so, the shape and configuration of the imaginations of those with whom I am familiar. A disappointment in love, or ambition, will, upon this account, call forth more sympathy than the greatest bodily evil. Those passions arise altogether from the imagination. The person who has lost his whole fortune, if he is in health, feels nothing in his body. What he suffers is from the imagination only, which represents to him the loss of his dignity, neglect from his friends, contempt from his enemies, dependence, want, and misery, coming fast upon him; and we sympathize with him more strongly upon this account, because our imaginations can more readily mould themselves upon his imagination, than our bodies can mould themselves upon his body.

The loss of a leg may generally be regarded as a more real calamity than the loss of a mistress. It would be a ridiculous tragedy, however, of which the catastrophe was to turn upon a loss of that kind. A misfortune of the other kind, how frivolous soever it may appear to be, has given occasion to many a fine one.

Nothing is so soon forgot as pain. The moment it is gone the whole agony of it is over, and the thought of it can no longer give us any sort of disturbance. We ourselves cannot then enter into the anxiety and anguish which we had before conceived. An unguarded word from a friend will occasion a more durable uneasiness. The agony which this creates is by no means over with the word. What at first disturbs us is not the object of the senses, but the idea of the imagination. As it is an idea, therefore, which occasions our uneasiness, till time and other accidents have in some measure effaced it from our memory, the imagination continues to fret and rankle within, from the thought of it.

Pain never calls forth any very lively sympathy unless it is accompanied with danger. We sympathize with the fear, though not with the agony of the sufferer. Fear, however, is a passion derived altogether from the imagination, which represents, with an uncertainty and fluctuation that increases our anxiety, not what we really feel, but what we may hereafter possibly suffer. The gout or the toothache, though exquisitely painful, excite very little sympathy; more dangerous diseases, though accompanied with very little pain, excite the highest.

Some people faint and grow sick at the sight of a chirurgical operation, and that bodily pain which is occasioned by tearing the flesh, seems, in them, to excite the most excessive sympathy. We conceive in a much more lively and distinct manner the pain which proceeds from an external cause, than we do that which arises from an internal disorder. I can scarce form an idea of the agonies of my neighbour when he is tortured with the gout, or the stone; but I have the clearest conception of what he must suffer from an incision, a wound, or a fracture. The chief cause, however, why such objects produce such violent effects upon us, is their novelty. One who has been witness to a dozen dissections, and as many amputations, sees, ever after, all operations of this kind with great indifference, and often with perfect insensibility. Though we have read or seen represented more than five hundred tragedies, we shall seldom feel so entire an abatement of our sensibility to the objects which they represent to us.

In some of the Greek tragedies there is an attempt to excite compassion, by the representation of the agonies of bodily pain. Philoctetes cries out and faints from the extremity of his sufferings. Hippolytus and Hercules are both introduced as expiring under the severest tortures, which, it seems, even the fortitude of Hercules was incapable of supporting. In all these cases, however, it is not the pain which interests us, but some other circumstance. It is not the sore foot, but the solitude, of Philoctetes which affects us, and diffuses over that charming tragedy, that romantic wildness, which is so agreeable to the imagination. The agonies of Hercules and Hippolytus are interesting only because we foresee that death is to be the consequence.[3] If those heroes were to recover, we should think the representation of their sufferings perfectly ridiculous. What a tragedy would that be of which the distress consisted in a colic! Yet no pain is more exquisite. These attempts to excite compassion by the representation of bodily pain, may be regarded as among the greatest breaches of decorum of which the Greek theatre has set the example.

The little sympathy which we feel with bodily pain is the foundation of the propriety of constancy and patience in enduring it. The man, who under the severest tortures allows no weakness to escape him, vents no groan, gives way to no passion which we do not entirely enter into, commands our highest admiration. His firmness enables him to keep time with our indifference and insensibility. We admire and entirely go along with the magnanimous effort which he makes for this purpose. We approve of his behaviour, and from our experience of the common weakness of human nature, we are surprised, and wonder how he should be able to act so as to deserve approbation. Approbation, mixed and animated by wonder and surprise, constitutes the sentiment which is properly called admiration, of which, applause is the natural expression, as has already been observed.[4]

CHAPTER II.

Of those Passions which take their origin from a particular turn or habit of the Imagination.

Even of the passions derived from the imagination, those which take their origin from a peculiar turn or habit it has acquired, though they may be acknowledged to be perfectly natural, are, however, but little sympathized with. The imaginations of mankind, not having acquired that particular turn, cannot enter into them; and such passions, though they may be allowed to be almost unavoidable in some part of life, are always, in some measure, ridiculous. This is the case with that strong attachment which naturally grows up between two persons of different sexes, who have long fixed their thoughts upon one another. Our imagination not having run in the same channel with that of the lover, we cannot enter into the eagerness of his emotions. If our friend has been injured, we readily sympathize with his resentment, and grow angry with the very person with whom he is angry. If he has received a benefit, we readily enter into his gratitude, and have a very high sense of the merit of his benefactor. But if he is in love, though we may think his passion just as reasonable as any of the kind, yet we never think ourselves bound to conceive a passion of the same kind, and for the same person for whom he has conceived it. The passion appears to every body, but the man who feels it, entirely disproportioned to the value of the object; and love, though it is pardoned in a certain age because we know it is natural, is always laughed at, because we cannot enter into it. All serious and strong expressions of it appear ridiculous to a third person; and though a lover may be good company to his mistress, he is so to nobody else. He himself is sensible of this; and as long as he continues in his sober senses, endeavours to treat his own passion with raillery[5] and ridicule. It is the only style in which we care to hear of it; because it is the only style in which we ourselves are disposed to talk of it. We grow weary of the grave, pedantic, and long-sentenced love of Cowley and Petrarca, who never have done with exaggerating the violence of their attachments; but the gaiety of Ovid, and the gallantry of Horace, are always agreeable.

But though we feel no proper sympathy with an attachment of this kind, though we never approach even in imagination towards conceiving a passion for that particular person, yet as we either have conceived, or may be disposed to conceive, passions of the same kind, we readily enter into those high hopes of happiness which are proposed from its gratification, as well as into that exquisite distress which is feared from its disappointment. It interests us not as a passion, but as a situation that gives occasion to other passions which interest us; to hope, to fear, and to distress of every kind: in the same manner as in a description of a sea voyage, it is not the hunger which interests us, but the distress which that hunger occasions. Though we do not properly enter into the attachment of the lover, we readily go along with those expectations of romantic happiness which he derives from it. We feel how natural it is for the mind, in a certain situation, relaxed with indolence, and fatigued with the violence of desire, to long for serenity and quiet, to hope to find them in the gratification of that passion which distracts it, and to frame to itself the idea of that life of pastoral tranquillity and retirement which the elegant, the tender, and the passionate Tibullus takes so much pleasure in describing,[6] a life like what the poets describe in the Fortunate Islands,[7] a life of friendship, liberty, and repose; free from labour, and from care, and from all the turbulent passions which attend them. Even scenes of this kind interest us most, when they are painted rather as what is hoped, than as what is enjoyed. The grossness of that passion, which mixes with, and is, perhaps, the foundation of love, disappears when its gratification is far off and at a distance; but renders the whole offensive, when described as what is immediately possessed. The happy passion, upon this account, interests us much less than the fearful and the melancholy. We tremble for whatever can disappoint such natural and agreeable hopes: and thus enter into all the anxiety, and concern, and distress of the lover.

Hence it is, that, in some modern tragedies and romances, this passion appears so wonderfully interesting. It is not so much the love of Castalio and Monimia which attaches us in the Orphan, as the distress which that love occasions.[8] The author who should introduce two lovers, in a scene of perfect security, expressing their mutual fondness for one another, would excite laughter, and not sympathy. If a scene of this kind is ever admitted into a tragedy, it is always, in some measure, improper, and is endured, not from any sympathy with the passion that is expressed in it, but from concern for the dangers and difficulties with which the audience foresee that its gratification is likely to be attended.

The reserve which the laws of society impose upon the fair sex, with regard to this weakness, renders it more peculiarly distressful in them, and, upon that very account, more deeply interesting. We are charmed with the love of Phædra, as it is expressed in the French tragedy of that name, notwithstanding all the extravagance and guilt which attend it.[9] That very extravagance and guilt may be said, in some measure, to recommend it to us. Her fear, her shame, her remorse, her horror, her despair, become thereby more natural and interesting. All the secondary passions, if I may be allowed to call them so, which arise from the situation of love, become necessarily more furious and violent; and it is with these secondary passions only that we can properly be said to sympathize.

Of all the passions, however, which are so extravagantly disproportioned to the value of their objects, love is the only one that appears, even to the weakest minds, to have any thing in it that is either graceful or agreeable. In itself, first of all, though it may be ridiculous, it is not naturally odious; and though its consequences are often fatal and dreadful, its intentions are seldom mischievous. And then, though there is little propriety in the passion itself, there is a good deal in some of those which always accompany it. There is in love a strong mixture of humanity, generosity, kindness, friendship, esteem; passions with which, of all others, for reasons which shall be explained immediately, we have the greatest propensity to sympathize, even notwithstanding we are sensible that they are, in some measure, excessive. The sympathy which we feel with them, renders the passion which they accompany less disagreeable, and supports it in our imagination, notwithstanding all the vices which commonly go along with it; though in the one sex it necessarily leads to the last ruin and infamy; and though in the other, where it is apprehended to be least fatal, it is almost always attended with an incapacity for labour, a neglect of duty, a contempt of fame, and even of common reputation. Notwithstanding all this, the degree of sensibility and generosity with which it is supposed to be accompanied, renders it to many the object of vanity; and they are fond of appearing capable of feeling what would do them no honour if they had really felt it.

It is for a reason of the same kind, that a certain reserve is necessary when we talk of our own friends, our own studies, our own professions. All these are objects which we cannot expect should interest our companions in the same degree in which they interest us. And it is for want of this reserve, that the one half of mankind make bad company to the other. A philosopher is company to a philosopher only; the member of a club, to his own little knot of companions.

Chapter III.

Of the unsocial Passions.

There is another set of passions, which, though derived from the imagination, yet before we can enter into them, or regard them as graceful or becoming, must always be brought down to a pitch much lower than that to which undisciplined nature would raise them. These are, hatred and resentment, with all their different modifications. With regard to all such passions, our sympathy is divided between the person who feels them, and the person who is the object of them. The interests of these two are directly opposite. What our sympathy with the person who feels them would prompt us to wish for, our fellow-feeling with the other would lead us to fear. As they are both men, we are concerned for both, and our fear for what the one may suffer, damps our resentment for what the other has suffered. Our sympathy, therefore, with the man who has received the provocation, necessarily falls short of the passion which naturally animates him, not only upon account of those general causes which render all sympathetic passions inferior to the original ones, but upon account of that particular cause which is peculiar to itself, our opposite sympathy with another person. Before resentment, therefore, can become graceful and agreeable, it must be more humbled and brought down below that pitch to which it would naturally rise, than almost any other passion.

Mankind, at the same time, have a very strong sense of the injuries that are done to another. The villain, in a tragedy or romance, is as much the object of our indignation, as the hero is that of our sympathy and affection. We detest Iago as much as we esteem Othello; and delight as much in the punishment of the one, as we are grieved at the distress of the other. But though mankind have so strong a fellow-feeling with the injuries that are done to their brethren, they do not always resent them the more that the sufferer appears to resent them. Upon most occasions, the greater his patience, his mildness, his humanity, provided it does not appear that he wants spirit, or that fear was the motive of his forbearance, the higher their resentment against the person who injured him. The amiableness of the character exasperates their sense of the atrocity of the injury.

Those passions, however, are regarded as necessary parts of the character of human nature. A person becomes contemptible who tamely sits still, and submits to insults, without attempting either to repel or to revenge them. We cannot enter into his indifference and insensibility: we call his behaviour mean-spiritedness, and are as really provoked by it as by the insolence of his adversary. Even the mob are enraged to see any man submit patiently to affronts and ill usage. They desire to see this insolence resented, and resented by the person who suffers from it. They cry to him with fury, to defend, or to revenge himself. If his indignation rouses at last, they heartily applaud, and sympathize with it. It enlivens their own indignation against his enemy, whom they rejoice to see him attack in his turn, and are as really gratified by his revenge, provided it is not immoderate, as if the injury had been done to themselves.

But though the utility of those passions to the individual, by rendering it dangerous to insult or injure him, be acknowledged; and though their utility to the public, as the guardians of justice, and of the equality of its administration, be not less considerable, as shall be shown hereafter;[10] yet there is still something disagreeable in the passions themselves, which makes the appearance of them in other men the natural object of our aversion. The expression of anger towards any body present, if it exceeds a bare intimation that we are sensible of his ill usage, is regarded not only as an insult to that particular person, but as a rudeness to the whole company. Respect for them ought to have restrained us from giving way to so boisterous and offensive an emotion. It is the remote effects of these passions which are agreeable; the immediate effects are mischief to the person against whom they are directed. But it is the immediate, and not the remote effects of objects which render them agreeable or disagreeable to the imagination. A prison is certainly more useful to the public than a palace; and the person who founds the one is generally directed by a much juster spirit of patriotism, than he who builds the other. But the immediate effects of a prison, the confinement of the wretches shut up in it, are disagreeable; and the imagination either does not take time to trace out the remote ones, or sees them at too great a distance to be much affected by them. A prison, therefore, will always be a disagreeable object; and the fitter it is for the purpose for which it was intended, it will be the more so. A palace, on the contrary, will always be agreeable; yet its remote effects may often be inconvenient to the public. It may serve to promote luxury, and set the example of the dissolution of manners. Its immediate effects, however, the conveniency, the pleasure, and the gaiety of the people who live in it, being all agreeable, and suggesting to the imagination a thousand agreeable ideas, that faculty generally rests upon them, and seldom goes further in tracing its more distant consequences. Trophies of the instruments of music or of agriculture, imitated in painting or in stucco, make a common and an agreeable ornament of our halls and dining-rooms. A trophy of the same kind, composed of the instruments of surgery, of dissecting and amputation knives, of saws for cutting the bones, of trepanning instruments, &c. would be absurd and shocking. Instruments of surgery, however, are always more finely polished, and generally more nicely adapted to the purposes for which they are intended, than instruments of agriculture. The remote effects of them too, the health of the patient, is agreeable; yet as the immediate effect of them is pain and suffering, the sight of them always displeases us. Instruments of war are agreeable, though their immediate effect may seem to be in the same manner pain and suffering. But then it is the pain and suffering of our enemies, with whom we have no sympathy. With regard to us, they are immediately connected with the agreeable ideas of courage, victory, and honour. They are themselves, therefore, supposed to make one of the noblest parts of dress, and the imitation of them one of the finest ornaments of architecture. It is the same case with the qualities of the mind. The ancient stoics were of opinion, that as the world was governed by the all-ruling providence of a wise, powerful, and good God, every single event ought to be regarded, as making a necessary part of the plan of the universe, and as tending to promote the general order and happiness of the whole: that the vices and follies of mankind, therefore, made as necessary a part of this plan as their wisdom or their virtue; and by that eternal art which educes good from ill, were made to tend equally to the prosperity and perfection of the great system of nature.[11] No speculation of this kind, however, how deeply soever it might be rooted in the mind, could diminish our natural abhorrence for vice, whose immediate effects are so destructive, and whose remote ones are too distant to be traced by the imagination.

It is the same case with those passions we have been just now considering. Their immediate effects are so disagreeable, that even when they are most justly provoked, there is still something about them which disgusts us. These, therefore, are the only passions of which the expressions, as I formerly observed, do not dispose and prepare us to sympathize with them, before we are informed of the cause which excites them. The plaintive voice of misery, when heard at a distance, will not allow us to be indifferent about the person from whom it comes. As soon as it strikes our ear, it interests us in his fortune, and, if continued, forces us almost involuntarily to fly to his assistance. The sight of a smiling countenance, in the same manner, elevates even the pensive into that gay and airy mood, which disposes him to sympathize with, and share, the joy which it expresses; and he feels his heart, which with thought and care was before that shrunk and depressed, instantly expanded and elated. But it is quite otherwise with the expressions of hatred and resentment. The hoarse, boisterous, and discordant voice of anger, when heard at a distance, inspires us either with fear or aversion. We do not fly towards it, as to one who cries out with pain and agony. Women, and men of weak nerves, tremble and are overcome with fear, though sensible that themselves are not the objects of the anger. They conceive fear, however, by putting themselves in the situation of the person who is so. Even those of stouter hearts are disturbed; not indeed enough to make them afraid, but enough to make them angry; for anger is the passion which they would feel in the situation of the other person. It is the same case with hatred. Mere expressions of spite inspire it against nobody, but the man who uses them. Both these passions are by nature the objects of our aversion. Their disagreeable and boisterous appearance never excites, never prepares, and often disturbs our sympathy. Grief does not more powerfully engage and attract us to the person in whom we observe it, than these, while we are ignorant of their cause, disgust and detach us from him. It was, it seems, the intention of Nature, that those rougher and more unamiable emotions, which drive men from one another, should be less easily and more rarely communicated.

When music imitates the modulations of grief or joy, it either actually inspires us with those passions, or at least puts us in the mood which disposes us to conceive them. But when it imitates the notes of anger, it inspires us with fear. Joy, grief, love, admiration, devotion, are all of them passions which are naturally musical.[12] Their natural tones are all soft, clear, and melodious; and they naturally express themselves in periods which are distinguished by regular pauses, and which upon that account are easily adapted to the regular returns of the correspondent airs of a tune. The voice of anger, on the contrary, and of all the passions which are akin to it, is harsh and discordant. Its periods too are all irregular, sometimes very long, and sometimes very short, and distinguished by no regular pauses. It is with difficulty, therefore, that music can imitate any of those passions; and the music which does imitate them is not the most agreeable. A whole entertainment may consist, without any impropriety, of the imitation of the social and agreeable passions. It would be a strange entertainment which consisted altogether of the imitations of hatred and resentment.

If those passions are disagreeable to the spectator, they are not less so to the person who feels them. Hatred and anger are the greatest poison to the happiness of a good mind. There is, in the very feeling of those passions, something harsh, jarring, and convulsive, something that tears and distracts the breast, and is altogether destructive of that composure and tranquillity of mind which is so necessary to happiness, and which is best promoted by the contrary passions of gratitude and love. It is not the value of what they lose by the perfidy[13] and ingratitude of those they live with, which the generous and humane are most apt to regret. Whatever they may have lost, they can generally be very happy without it. What most disturbs them is the idea of perfidy and ingratitude exercised towards themselves; and the discordant and disagreeable passions which this excites, constitute, in their own opinion, the chief part of the injury which they suffer.

How many things are requisite to render the gratification of resentment completely agreeable, and to make the spectator thoroughly sympathize with our revenge? The provocation must first of all be such that we should become contemptible, and be exposed to perpetual insults, if we did not, in some measure, resent it. Smaller offences are always better neglected; nor is there any thing more despicable than that froward and captious humour which takes fire upon every slight occasion of quarrel. We should resent more from a sense of the propriety of resentment, from a sense that mankind expect and require it of us, than because we feel in ourselves the furies of that disagreeable passion. There is no passion, of which the human mind is capable, concerning whose justness we ought to be so doubtful, concerning whose indulgence we ought so carefully to consult our natural sense of propriety, or so diligently to consider what will be the sentiments of the cool and impartial spectator. Magnanimity, or a regard to maintain our own rank and dignity in society, is the only motive which can ennoble the expressions of this disagreeable passion. This motive must characterize our whole stile and deportment. These must be plain, open, and direct; determined without positiveness, and elevated without insolence; not only free from petulance and low scurrility, but generous, candid, and full of all proper regards, even for the person who has offended us. It must appear, in short, from our whole manner, without our labouring affectedly to express it, that passion has not extinguished our humanity; and that if we yield to the dictates of revenge, it is with reluctance, from necessity, and in consequence of great and repeated provocations. When resentment is guarded and qualified in this manner, it may be admitted to be even generous and noble.

CHAPTER IV.

Of the social Passions.

As it is a divided sympathy which renders the whole set of passions just now mentioned, upon most occasions, so ungraceful and disagreeable; so there is another set opposite to these, which a redoubled sympathy renders almost always peculiarly agreeable and becoming. Generosity, humanity, kindness, compassion, mutual friendship and esteem, all the social and benevolent affections, when expressed in the countenance or behaviour, even towards those who are not peculiarly connected with ourselves, please the indifferent spectator upon almost every occasion. His sympathy with the person who feels those passions, exactly coincides with his concern for the person who is the object of them. The interest, which, as a man, he is obliged to take in the happiness of this last, enlivens his fellow-feeling with the sentiments of the other, whose emotions are employed about the same object. We have always, therefore, the strongest disposition to sympathize with the benevolent affections. They appear in every respect agreeable to us. We enter into the satisfaction both of the person who feels them, and of the person who is the object of them. For as to be the object of hatred and indignation gives more pain than all the evil which a brave man can fear from his enemies; so there is a satisfaction in the consciousness of being beloved, which, to a person of delicacy and sensibility, is of more importance to happiness, than all the advantage which he can expect to derive from it. What character is so detestable as that of one who takes pleasure to sow dissension among friends, and to turn their most tender love into mortal hatred? Yet wherein does the atrocity of this so much abhorred injury consist? Is it in depriving them of the frivolous good offices, which, had their friendship continued, they might have expected from one another? It is in depriving them of that friendship itself, in robbing them of each other's affections, from which both derived so much satisfaction; it is in disturbing the harmony of their hearts, and putting an end to that happy commerce which had before subsisted between them. These affections, that harmony, this commerce, are felt, not only by the tender and the delicate, but by the rudest vulgar of mankind, to be of more importance to happiness than all the little services which could be expected to flow from them.

The sentiment of love is, in itself, agreeable to the person who feels it. It soothes and composes the breast, seems to favour the vital motions, and to promote the healthful state of the human constitution; and it is rendered still more delightful by the consciousness of the gratitude and satisfaction which it must excite in him who is the object of it. Their mutual regard renders them happy in one another, and sympathy, with this mutual regard, makes them agreeable to every other person. With what pleasure do we look upon a family, through the whole of which reign mutual love and esteem, where the parents and children are companions for one another, without any other difference than what is made by respectful affection on the one side, and kind indulgence on the other; where freedom and fondness, mutual raillery and mutual kindness, show that no opposition of interest divides the brothers, nor any rivalship of favour sets the sisters at variance, and where every thing presents us with the idea of peace, cheerfulness, harmony, and contentment? On the contrary, how uneasy are we made when we go into a house in which jarring contention sets one half of those who dwell in it against the other; where amidst affected smoothness and complaisance, suspicious looks and sudden starts of passion betray the mutual jealousies which burn within them, and which are every moment ready to burst out through all the restraints which the presence of the company imposes?

Those amiable passions, even when they are acknowledged to be excessive, are never regarded with aversion. There is something agreeable even in the weakness of friendship and humanity. The too tender mother, the too indulgent father, the too generous and affectionate friend, may sometimes, perhaps, on account of the softness of their natures, be looked upon with a species of pity, in which, however, there is a mixture of love, but can never be regarded with hatred and aversion, nor even with contempt, unless by the most brutal and worthless of mankind. It is always with concern, with sympathy and kindness, that we blame them for the extravagance of their attachment. There is a helplessness in the character of extreme humanity which more than any thing interests our pity. There is nothing in itself which renders it either ungraceful or disagreeable. We only regret that it is unfit for the world, because the world is unworthy of it, and because it must expose the person who is endowed with it as a prey to the perfidy and ingratitude of insinuating falsehood, and to a thousand pains and uneasinesses, which, of all men, he the least deserves to feel, and which generally too he is, of all men, the least capable of supporting. It is quite otherwise with hatred and resentment. Too violent a propensity to those detestable passions, renders a person the object of universal dread and abhorrence, who, like a wild beast, ought, we think, to be hunted out of all civil society.

CHAPTER V.

Of the selfish Passions.

Besides those two opposite sets of passions, the social and unsocial, there is another which holds a sort of middle place between them; is never either so graceful as is sometimes the one set, nor is ever so odious as is sometimes the other. Grief and joy, when conceived upon account of our own private good or bad fortune, constitute this third set of passions. Even when excessive, they are never so disagreeable as excessive resentment, because no opposite sympathy can ever interest us against them: and when most suitable to their objects, they are never so agreeable as impartial humanity and just benevolence; because no double sympathy can ever interest us for them. There is, however, this difference between grief and joy, that we are generally most disposed to sympathize with small joys and great sorrows. The man who, by some sudden revolution of fortune, is lifted up all at once into a condition of life, greatly above what he had formerly lived in, may be assured that the congratulations of his best friends are not all of them perfectly sincere. An upstart, though of the greatest merit, is generally disagreeable, and a sentiment of envy commonly prevents us from heartily sympathizing with his joy. If he has any judgment, he is sensible of this, and instead of appearing to be elated with his good fortune, he endeavours, as much as he can, to smother his joy, and keep down that elevation of mind with which his new circumstances naturally inspire him. He affects the same plainness of dress, and the same modesty of behaviour, which became him in his former station. He redoubles his attention to his old friends, and endeavours more than ever to be humble, assiduous, and complaisant. And this is the behaviour which in his situation we most approve of; because we expect, it seems, that he should have more sympathy with our envy and aversion to his happiness, than we have with his happiness. It is seldom that with all this he succeeds. We suspect the sincerity of his humility, and he grows weary of this constraint. In a little time, therefore, he generally leaves all his old friends behind him, some of the meanest of them excepted, who may, perhaps, condescend to become his dependents: nor does he always acquire any new ones; the pride of his new connections is as much affronted at finding him their equal, as that of his old ones had been by his becoming their superior: and it requires the most obstinate and persevering modesty to atone for this mortification to either. He generally grows weary too soon, and is provoked, by the sullen and suspicious pride of the one, and by the saucy contempt of the other, to treat the first with neglect, and the second with petulance, till at last he grows habitually insolent, and forfeits the esteem of all. If the chief part of human happiness arises from the consciousness of being beloved, as I believe it does, those sudden changes of fortune seldom contribute much to happiness. He is happiest who advances more gradually to greatness, whom the public destines to every step of his preferment long before he arrives at it, in whom, upon that account, when it comes, it can excite no extravagant joy, and with regard to whom it cannot reasonably create either any jealousy in those he overtakes, or any envy in those he leaves behind.

Mankind, however, more readily sympathize with those smaller joys which flow from less important causes. It is decent to be humble amidst great prosperity; but we can scarce express too much satisfaction in all the little occurrences of common life, in the company with which we spent the evening last night, in the entertainment that was set before us, in what was said and what was done, in all the little incidents of the present conversation, and in all those frivolous nothings which fill up the void of human life. Nothing is more graceful than habitual cheerfulness, which is always founded upon a peculiar relish for all the little pleasures which common occurrences afford. We readily sympathize with it: it inspires us with the same joy, and makes every trifle turn up to us in the same agreeable aspect in which it presents itself to the person endowed with this happy disposition. Hence it is that youth, the season of gaiety, so easily engages our affections. That propensity to joy which seems even to animate the bloom, and to sparkle from the eyes of youth and beauty, though in a person of the same sex, exalts, even the aged, to a more joyous mood than ordinary. They forget, for a time, their infirmities, and abandon themselves to those agreeable ideas and emotions to which they have long been strangers, but which, when the presence of so much happiness recalls them to their breast, take their place there, like old acquaintance, from whom they are sorry to have ever been parted, and whom they embrace more heartily upon account of this long separation.

It is quite otherwise with grief. Small vexations excite no sympathy, but deep affliction calls forth the greatest. The man who is made uneasy by every little disagreeable incident, who is hurt if either the cook or the butler have failed in the least article of their duty, who feels every defect in the highest ceremonial of politeness, whether it be shown to himself or to any other person, who takes it amiss that his intimate friend did not bid him good-morrow when they met in the forenoon, and that his brother hummed a tune all the time he himself was telling a story; who is put out of humour by the badness of the weather when in the country, by the badness of the roads when upon a journey, and by the want of company, and dulness of all public diversions when in town; such a person, I say, though he should have some reason, will seldom meet with much sympathy. Joy is a pleasant emotion, and we gladly abandon ourselves to it upon the slightest occasion. We readily, therefore, sympathize with it in others, whenever we are not prejudiced by envy. But grief is painful, and the mind, even when it is our own misfortune, naturally resists and recoils from it. We would endeavour either not to conceive it at all, or to shake it off as soon as we have conceived it. Our aversion to grief will not, indeed, always hinder us from conceiving it in our own case upon very trifling occasions, but it constantly prevents us from sympathizing with it in others when excited by the like frivolous causes: for our sympathetic passions are always less irresistible than our original ones. There is, besides, a malice in mankind, which not only prevents all sympathy with little uneasinesses, but renders them in some measure diverting. Hence the delight which we all take in raillery, and in the small vexation which we observe in our companion, when he is pushed, and urged, and teased upon all sides. Men of the most ordinary good breeding dissemble the pain which any little incident may give them; and those who are more thoroughly formed to society, turn, of their own accord, all such incidents into raillery, as they know their companions will do for them. The habit which a man, who lives in the world, has acquired of considering how every thing that concerns himself will appear to others, makes those frivolous calamities turn up in the same ridiculous light to him, in which he knows they will certainly be considered by them.

Our sympathy, on the contrary, with deep distress, is very strong and very sincere. It is unnecessary to give an instance. We weep even at the feigned representation of a tragedy. If you labour, therefore, under any signal calamity, if by some extraordinary misfortune you are fallen into poverty, into diseases, into disgrace and disappointment; even though your own fault may have been, in part, the occasion, yet you may generally depend upon the sincerest sympathy of all your friends, and, as far as interest and honour will permit, upon their kindest assistance too. But if your misfortune is not of this dreadful kind, if you have only been a little baulked in your ambition, if you have only been jilted by your mistress, or are only hen-pecked by your wife, lay your account with the raillery of all your acquaintance.

SECTION III.

OF THE EFFECTS OF PROSPERITY AND ADVER-
SITY UPON THE JUDGMENT OF MANKIND WITH
REGARD TO THE PROPRIETY OF ACTION; AND WHY
IT IS MORE EASY TO OBTAIN THEIR APPROBATION
IN THE ONE STATE THAN IN THE OTHER.

CHAPTER I.

*That though our sympathy with Sorrow is generally a more
lively sensation than our sympathy with Joy, it commonly falls
much more short of the violence of what is naturally felt by
the person principally concerned.*

Our sympathy with sorrow, though not more real, has been more
taken notice of than our sympathy with joy. The word sympathy, in
its most proper and primitive signification, denotes our fellow-feeling
with the sufferings, not that with the enjoyments, of others. A late
ingenious and subtile philosopher thought it necessary to prove, by
arguments, that we had a real sympathy with joy, and that congratulation was a principle of human nature.[1] Nobody, I believe, ever
thought it necessary to prove that compassion was such.

First of all, our sympathy with sorrow is, in some sense, more
universal than that with joy. Though sorrow is excessive, we may
still have some fellow-feeling with it. What we feel does not, indeed,
in this case, amount to that complete sympathy, to that perfect
harmony and correspondence of sentiments which constitutes
approbation. We do not weep, and exclaim, and lament, with the
sufferer. We are sensible, on the contrary, of his weakness and of
the extravagance of his passion, and yet often feel a very sensible
concern upon his account. But if we do not entirely enter into, and
go along with, the joy of another, we have no sort of regard or

fellow-feeling for it. The man who skips and dances about with that intemperate and senseless joy which we cannot accompany him in, is the object of our contempt and indignation.

Pain besides, whether of mind or body, is a more pungent sensation than pleasure, and our sympathy with pain, though it falls greatly short of what is naturally felt by the sufferer, is generally a more lively and distinct perception than our sympathy with pleasure, though this last often approaches more nearly, as I shall show immediately, to the natural vivacity of the original passion.

Over and above all this, we often struggle to keep down our sympathy with the sorrow of others. Whenever we are not under the observation of the sufferer, we endeavour, for our own sake, to suppress it as much as we can, and we are not always successful. The opposition which we make to it, and the reluctance with which we yield to it, necessarily oblige us to take more particular notice of it. But we never have occasion to make this opposition to our sympathy with joy. If there is any envy in the case, we never feel the least propensity towards it; and if there is none, we give way to it without any reluctance. On the contrary, as we are always ashamed of our own envy, we often pretend, and sometimes really wish to sympathize with the joy of others, when by that disagreeable sentiment we are disqualified from doing so. We are glad, we say, on account of our neighbour's good fortune, when in our hearts, perhaps, we are really sorry. We often feel a sympathy with sorrow when we would wish to be rid of it; and we often miss that with joy when we would be glad to have it. The obvious observation, therefore, which it naturally falls in our way to make, is, that our propensity to sympathize with sorrow must be very strong, and our inclination to sympathize with joy very weak.

Notwithstanding this prejudice, however, I will venture to affirm, that, when there is no envy in the case, our propensity to sympathize with joy is much stronger than our propensity to sympathize with sorrow; and that our fellow-feeling for the agreeable emotion approaches much more nearly to the vivacity of what is naturally felt by the persons principally concerned, than that which we conceive for the painful one.

We have some indulgence for that excessive grief which we

cannot entirely go along with. We know what a prodigious effort is requisite before the sufferer can bring down his emotions to complete harmony and concord with those of the spectator. Though he fails, therefore, we easily pardon him. But we have no such indulgence for the intemperance of joy; because we are not conscious that any such vast effort is requisite to bring it down to what we can entirely enter into. The man who, under the greatest calamities, can command his sorrow, seems worthy of the highest admiration; but he who, in the fulness of prosperity, can in the same manner master his joy, seems hardly to deserve any praise. We are sensible that there is a much wider interval in the one case than in the other, between what is naturally felt by the person principally concerned, and what the spectator can entirely go along with.

What can be added to the happiness of the man who is in health, who is out of debt, and has a clear conscience? To one in this situation all accessions of fortune may properly be said to be superfluous; and if he is much elevated upon account of them, it must be the effect of the most frivolous levity. This situation, however, may very well be called the natural and ordinary state of mankind. Notwithstanding the present misery and depravity of the world, so justly lamented, this really is the state of the greater part of men. The greater part of men, therefore, cannot find any great difficulty in elevating themselves to all the joy which any accession to this situation can well excite in their companion.

But though little can be added to this state, much may be taken from it. Though between this condition and the highest pitch of human prosperity, the interval is but a trifle; between it and the lowest depth of misery the distance is immense and prodigious. Adversity, on this account, necessarily depresses the mind of the sufferer much more below its natural state, than prosperity can elevate him above it. The spectator, therefore, must find it much more difficult to sympathize entirely, and keep perfect time, with his sorrow, than thoroughly to enter into his joy, and must depart much further from his own natural and ordinary temper of mind in the one case than in the other. It is on this account, that though our sympathy with sorrow is often a more pungent sensation than our sympathy with joy, it always falls much more short of the violence of what is naturally felt by the person principally concerned.

It is agreeable to sympathize with joy; and wherever envy does not oppose it, our heart abandons itself with satisfaction to the highest transports of that delightful sentiment. But it is painful to go along with grief, and we always enter into it with reluctance.* When we attend to the representation of a tragedy, we struggle against that sympathetic sorrow which the entertainment inspires as long as we can, and we give way to it at last only when we can no longer avoid it: we even then endeavour to cover our concern from the company. If we shed any tears, we carefully conceal them, and are afraid, lest the spectators, not entering into this excessive tenderness, should regard it as effeminacy and weakness. The wretch whose misfortunes call upon our compassion feels with what reluctance we are likely to enter into his sorrow, and therefore proposes his grief to us with fear and hesitation: he even smothers the half of it, and is ashamed, upon account of this hard heartedness of mankind, to give vent to the fulness of his affliction. It is otherwise with the man who riots in joy and success. Wherever envy does not interest us against him, he expects our completest sympathy. He does not fear, therefore, to announce himself with shouts of exultation, in full confidence that we are heartily disposed to go along with him.

Why should we be more ashamed to weep than to laugh before company? We may often have as real occasion to do the one as to do the other: but we always feel that the spectators are more likely to go along with us in the agreeable, than in the painful emotion. It is always miserable to complain, even when we are oppressed by the most dreadful calamities. But the triumph of victory is not always ungraceful. Prudence, indeed, would often advise us to bear our prosperity with more moderation; because

---

* It has been objected to me that as I found the sentiment of approbation, which is always agreeable, upon sympathy, it is inconsistent with my system to admit any disagreeable sympathy. I answer, that in the sentiment of approbation there are two things to be taken notice of; first, the sympathetic passion of the spectator; and, secondly, the emotion which arises from his observing the perfect coincidence between this sympathetic passion in himself, and the original passion in the person principally concerned. This last emotion, in which the sentiment of approbation properly consists, is always agreeable and delightful. The other may either be agreeable or disagreeable, according to the nature of the original passion, whose features it must always, in some measure, retain.[2]

prudence would teach us to avoid that envy which this very triumph is, more than any thing, apt to excite.

How hearty are the acclamations of the mob, who never bear any envy to their superiors, at a triumph or a public entry? And how sedate and moderate is commonly their grief at an execution? Our sorrow at a funeral generally amounts to no more than an affected gravity; but our mirth at a christening or a marriage, is always from the heart, and without any affectation. Upon these, and all such joyous occasions, our satisfaction, though not so durable is often as lively as that of the persons principally concerned. Whenever we cordially congratulate our friends, which, however, to the disgrace of human nature, we do but seldom, their joy literally becomes our joy: we are, for the moment, as happy as they are: our heart swells and overflows with real pleasure: joy and complacency sparkle from our eyes, and animate every feature of our countenance, and every gesture of our body.

But, on the contrary, when we condole with our friends in their afflictions, how little do we feel, in comparison of what they feel? We sit down by them, we look at them, and while they relate to us the circumstances of their misfortune, we listen to them with gravity and attention. But while their narration is every moment interrupted by those natural bursts of passion which often seem almost to choak them in the midst of it; how far are the languid emotions of our hearts from keeping time to the transports of theirs? We may be sensible, at the same time, that their passion is natural, and no greater than what we ourselves might feel upon the like occasion. We may even inwardly reproach ourselves with our own want of sensibility, and perhaps, on that account, work ourselves up into an artificial sympathy, which, however, when it is raised, is always the slightest and most transitory imaginable; and generally, as soon as we have left the room, vanishes, and is gone for ever. Nature, it seems, when she loaded us with our own sorrows, thought that they were enough, and therefore did not command us to take any further share in those of others, than what was necessary to prompt us to relieve them.

It is on account of this dull sensibility to the afflictions of others, that magnanimity amidst great distress appears always so divinely graceful. His behaviour is genteel and agreeable who can maintain his cheerfulness amidst a number of frivolous disasters.

But he appears to be more than mortal who can support in the same manner the most dreadful calamities. We feel what an immense effort is requisite to silence those violent emotions which naturally agitate and distract those in his situation. We are amazed to find that he can command himself so entirely. His firmness, at the same time, perfectly coincides with our insensibility. He makes no demand upon us for that more exquisite degree of sensibility which we find, and which we are mortified to find, that we do not possess. There is the most perfect correspondence between his sentiments and ours, and on that account the most perfect propriety in his behaviour. It is a propriety too, which, from our experience of the usual weakness of human nature, we could not reasonably have expected he should be able to maintain. We wonder with surprise and astonishment at that strength of mind which is capable of so noble and generous an effort. The sentiment of complete sympathy and approbation, mixed and animated with wonder and surprise, constitutes what is properly called admiration, as has already been more than once taken notice of. Cato, surrounded on all sides by his enemies, unable to resist them, disdaining to submit to them, and reduced, by the proud maxims of that age, to the necessity of destroying himself; yet never shrinking from his misfortunes, never supplicating with the lamentable voice of wretchedness, those miserable sympathetic tears which we are always so unwilling to give; but on the contrary, arming himself with manly fortitude, and the moment before he executes his fatal resolution, giving, with his usual tranquillity, all necessary orders for the safety of his friends; appears to Seneca, that great preacher of insensibility, a spectacle which even the gods themselves might behold with pleasure and admiration.[3]

Whenever we meet, in common life, with any examples of such heroic magnanimity, we are always extremely affected. We are more apt to weep and shed tears for such as, in this manner, seem to feel nothing for themselves, than for those who give way to all the weakness of sorrow: and in this particular case, the sympathetic grief of the spectator appears to go beyond the original passion in the person principally concerned. The friends of Socrates all wept when he drank the last potion, while he himself expressed the gayest and most cheerful tranquillity.[4] Upon all such occasions the spectator makes no effort, and has no occasion to make any, in order to conquer his sympathetic sorrow. He is under no fear that it will transport him to any thing that is extravagant and improper; he is rather pleased with the sensibility of his own heart, and gives way to it with complaisance and self-approbation. He gladly indulges, therefore, the most melancholy views which can naturally occur to him, concerning the calamity of his friend, for whom, perhaps, he never felt so exquisitely before, the tender and tearful passion of love. But it is quite otherwise with the person principally concerned. He is obliged, as much as possible, to turn away his eyes from whatever is either naturally terrible or disagreeable in his situation. Too serious an attention to those circumstances, he fears, might make so violent an impression upon him, that he could no longer keep within the bounds of moderation, or render himself the object of the complete sympathy and approbation of the spectators. He fixes his thoughts, therefore, upon those only which are agreeable, the applause and admiration which he is about to deserve by the heroic magnanimity of his behaviour. To feel that he is capable of so noble and generous an effort, to feel that in this dreadful situation he can still act as he would desire to act, animates and transports him with joy, and enables him to support that triumphant gaiety which seems to exult in the victory he thus gains over his misfortunes.

On the contrary, he always appears, in some measure, mean and despicable, who is sunk in sorrow and dejection upon account of any calamity of his own. We cannot bring ourselves to feel for him what he feels for himself, and what, perhaps, we should feel for ourselves if in his situation: we, therefore, despise him; unjustly, perhaps, if any sentiment could be regarded as unjust, to which we are by nature irresistibly determined. The weakness of sorrow never appears in any respect agreeable, except when it arises from what we feel for others more than from what we feel for ourselves. A son, upon the death of an indulgent and respectable father, may give way to it without much blame. His sorrow is chiefly founded upon a sort of sympathy with his departed parent; and we readily enter into this humane emotion. But if he should indulge the same weakness upon account of any misfortune which affected himself only, he would no longer meet with any such indulgence. If he should be reduced to beggary and ruin, if he should be exposed to the most dreadful dangers, if he should even be led out to a public execution, and there shed one single tear upon the scaffold, he would disgrace himself for ever in the opinion of all the gallant and generous part of mankind. Their compassion for him, however, would be very strong, and very sincere; but as it would still fall short of this excessive weakness, they would have no pardon for the man who could thus expose himself in the eyes of the world. His behaviour would affect them with shame rather than with sorrow; and the dishonour which he had thus brought upon himself would appear to them the most lamentable circumstance in his misfortune. How did it disgrace the memory of the intrepid Duke of Biron, who had so often braved death in the field, that he wept upon the scaffold, when he beheld the state to which he was fallen, and remembered the favour and the glory from which his own rashness had so unfortunately thrown him![5]

Chapter II.

Of the origin of Ambition, and of the distinction of Ranks.

It is because mankind are disposed to sympathize more entirely with our joy than with our sorrow, that we make parade of our riches, and conceal our poverty. Nothing is so mortifying as to be obliged to expose our distress to the view of the public, and to feel, that though our situation is open to the eyes of all mankind, no mortal conceives for us the half of what we suffer. Nay, it is chiefly from this regard to the sentiments of mankind, that we pursue riches and avoid poverty. For to what purpose is all the toil and bustle of this world? what is the end of avarice and ambition, of the pursuit of wealth, of power, and preheminence? Is it to supply the necessities of nature? The wages of the meanest labourer can supply them. We see that they afford him food and clothing, the comfort of a house, and of a family. If we examine his economy with rigour, we should find that he spends a great part of them upon conveniencies, which may be regarded as superfluities, and that, upon extraordinary occasions, he can give something even to vanity and distinction. What then is the cause of our aversion to his situation, and why should those who have been educated in the higher ranks of life, regard it as worse than death, to be reduced to live, even without labour, upon the same simple fare with him, to dwell under the same lowly roof, and to be clothed in the same humble attire? Do they imagine that their stomach is better, or their sleep sounder, in a palace than in a cottage? The contrary has been so often observed, and, indeed, is so very obvious, though it had never been observed, that there is nobody ignorant of it. From whence, then, arises that emulation which runs through all the different ranks of men, and what are the advantages which we propose by that great purpose of human life which we call bettering our condition?[6] To be observed, to be attended to, to be taken notice of with sympathy, complacency, and approbation, are all the advantages which we can propose to derive from it. It is the vanity, not the ease, or the pleasure, which interests us. But vanity is always founded upon the belief of our being the object of attention and approbation.[7] The rich man glories in his riches, because he feels that they naturally draw upon him the attention of the world, and that mankind are disposed to go along with him in all those agreeable emotions with which the advantages of his situation so readily inspire him. At the thought of this, his heart seems to swell and dilate itself within him, and he is fonder of his wealth, upon this account, than for all the other advantages it procures him. The poor man, on the contrary, is ashamed of his poverty. He feels that it either places him out of the sight of mankind, or, that if they take any notice of him, they have, however, scarce any fellow-feeling with the misery and distress which he suffers. He is mortified upon both accounts; for though to be overlooked, and to be disapproved of, are things entirely different, yet as obscurity covers us from the day-light of honour and approbation, to feel that we are taken no notice of, necessarily damps the most agreeable hope, and disappoints the most ardent desire, of human nature. The poor man goes out and comes in unheeded, and when in the midst of a crowd is in the same obscurity as if shut up in his own hovel. Those humble cares and painful attentions which occupy those in his situation, afford no amusement to the dissipated and the gay. They turn away their eyes from him, or if the extremity of his distress forces them to look at him, it is only to spurn so disagreeable an object from among them. The fortunate and the proud wonder at the insolence of human wretchedness, that it should dare to present itself before them, and with the loathsome aspect of its misery presume to disturb the serenity of their happiness. The man of rank and distinction, on the contrary, is observed by all the world. Every body is eager to look at him, and to conceive, at least by sympathy, that joy and exultation with which his circumstances naturally inspire him. His actions are the objects of the public care. Scarce a word, scarce a gesture, can fall from him that is altogether neglected. In a great assembly he is the person upon whom all direct their eyes; it is upon him that their passions seem all to wait with expectation, in order to receive that movement and direction which he shall impress upon them; and if his behaviour is not altogether absurd, he has, every moment, an opportunity of interesting mankind, and of rendering himself the object of the observation and fellow-feeling of every body about him. It is this, which, notwithstanding the restraint it imposes, notwithstanding the loss of liberty with which it is attended, renders greatness the object of envy, and compensates, in the opinion of mankind, all that toil, all that anxiety, all those mortifications which must be undergone in the pursuit of it; and what is of yet more consequence, all that leisure, all that ease, all that careless security, which are forfeited for ever by the acquisition.

When we consider the condition of the great, in those delusive colours in which the imagination is apt to paint it, it seems to be almost the abstract idea of a perfect and happy state. It is the very state which, in all our waking dreams and idle reveries, we had sketched out to ourselves as the final object of all our desires. We feel, therefore, a peculiar sympathy with the satisfaction of those who are in it. We favour all their inclinations, and forward all their wishes. What pity, we think, that any thing should spoil and corrupt so agreeable a situation! We could even wish them immortal; and it seems hard to us, that death should at last put an end to such perfect enjoyment. It is cruel, we think, in Nature to compel them from their exalted stations to that humble, but hospitable, home, which she has provided for all her children. Great King, live for ever! is the compliment, which, after the manner of eastern adulation, we should readily make them, if experience did not teach us its absurdity. Every calamity that befals them, every injury that is done them, excites in the breast of the spectator ten times more compassion and resentment than he would have felt, had the same things happened to other men. It is the misfortunes of Kings only which afford the proper subjects for tragedy. They resemble, in this respect, the misfortunes of lovers. Those two situations are the chief which interest us upon the theatre; because, in spite of all that reason and experience can tell us to the contrary, the prejudices of the imagination attach to these two states a happiness superior to any other. To disturb, or to put an end to, such perfect enjoyment, seems to be the most atrocious of all injuries. The traitor who conspires against the life of his monarch, is thought a greater monster than any other murderer. All the innocent blood that was shed in the civil wars, provoked less indignation than the death of Charles I.[8] A stranger to human nature, who saw the indifference of men about the misery of their inferiors, and the regret and indignation which they feel for the misfortunes and sufferings of those above them, would be apt to imagine, that pain must be more agonizing, and the convulsions of death more terrible to persons of higher rank, than to those of meaner stations.

Upon this disposition of mankind, to go along with all the passions of the rich and the powerful, is founded the distinction of ranks, and the order of society. Our obsequiousness to our superiors more frequently arises from our admiration for the advantages of their situation, than from any private expectations of benefit from their good-will.[9] Their benefits can extend but to a few; but their fortunes interest almost every body. We are eager to assist them in completing a system of happiness that approaches so near to perfection; and we desire to serve them for their own sake, without any other recompense but the vanity or the honour of obliging them. Neither is our deference to their inclinations founded chiefly, or altogether, upon a regard to the utility of such submission, and to the order of society, which is best supported by it. Even when the order of society seems to require that we should oppose them, we can hardly bring ourselves to do it. That kings are the servants of the people, to be obeyed, resisted, deposed, or punished, as the public conveniency may require, is the doctrine of reason and philosophy; but it is not the doctrine of Nature. Nature would teach us to submit to them for their own sake, to tremble and bow down before their exalted station, to regard their smile as a reward sufficient to compensate any services, and to dread their displeasure, though no other evil were to follow from it, as the severest of all mortifications. To treat them in any respect as men, to reason and dispute with them upon ordinary occasions, requires such resolution, that there are few men whose magnanimity can support them in it, unless they are likewise assisted by familiarity and acquaintance. The strongest motives, the most furious passions, fear, hatred, and resentment, are scarce sufficient to balance this natural disposition to respect them: and their conduct must, either justly or unjustly, have excited the highest degree of all those passions, before the bulk of the people can be brought to oppose them with violence, or to desire to see them either punished or deposed. Even when the people have been brought this length, they are apt to relent every moment, and easily relapse into their habitual state of deference to those on whom they have been accustomed to look up as their natural superiors. They cannot stand the mortification of their monarch. Compassion soon takes the place of resentment, they forget all past provocations, their old principles of loyalty revive, and they run to re-establish the ruined authority of their old masters, with the same violence with which they had opposed it. The death of Charles I. brought about the Restoration of the royal family. Compassion for James II. when he was seized by the populace in making his escape on ship-board, had almost prevented the Revolution, and made it go on more heavily than before.[10]

Do the great seem insensible of the easy price at which they may acquire the public admiration; or do they seem to imagine that to them, as to other men, it must be the purchase either of sweat or of blood? By what important accomplishments is the young nobleman instructed to support the dignity of his rank, and to render himself worthy of that superiority over his fellow-citizens, to which the virtue of his ancestors had raised them? Is it by knowledge, by industry, by patience, by self-denial, or by virtue of any kind? As all his words, as all his motions are attended to, he learns an habitual regard to every circumstance of ordinary behaviour, and studies to perform all those small duties with the most exact propriety. As he is conscious how much he is observed, and how much mankind are disposed to favour all his inclinations, he acts, upon the most indifferent occasions, with that freedom and elevation which the thought of this naturally inspires. His air, his manner, his deportment, all mark that elegant and graceful sense of his own superiority, which those who are born to inferior stations can hardly ever arrive at. These are the arts by which he proposes to make mankind more easily submit to his authority, and to govern their inclinations according to his own pleasure: and in this he is seldom disappointed. These arts, supported by rank and preheminence, are, upon ordinary occasions, sufficient to govern the world. Lewis XIV, during the greater part of his reign, was regarded, not only in France, but over all Europe, as the most perfect model of a great prince. But what were the talents and virtues by which he acquired this great reputation? Was it by the scrupulous and inflexible justice of all his undertakings, by the immense dangers and difficulties with which they were attended, or by the unwearied and unrelenting application with which he pursued them? Was it by his extensive knowledge, by his exquisite judgment, or by his heroic valour? It was by none of these qualities. But he was, first of all, the most powerful prince in Europe, and consequently held the highest rank among kings; and then, says his historian, "he surpassed all his courtiers in the gracefulness of his shape, and the majestic beauty of his features. The sound of his voice, noble and affecting, gained those hearts which his presence intimidated. He had a step and a deportment which could suit only him and his rank, and which would have been ridiculous in any other person. The embarrassment which he occasioned to those who spoke to him, flattered that secret satisfaction with which he felt his own superiority. The old officer, who was confounded and faultered in asking him a favour, and not being able to conclude his discourse, said to him: Sir, your majesty, I hope, will believe that I do not tremble thus before your enemies: had no difficulty to obtain what he demanded."[11] These frivolous accomplishments, supported by his rank, and, no doubt too, by a degree of other talents and virtues, which seems, however, not to have been much above mediocrity, established this prince in the esteem of his own age, and have drawn, even from posterity, a good deal of respect for his memory. Compared with these, in his own times, and in his own presence, no other virtue, it seems, appeared to have any merit. Knowledge, industry, valour, and beneficence, trembled, were abashed, and lost all dignity before them.

But it is not by accomplishments of this kind, that the man of inferior rank must hope to distinguish himself. Politeness is so much the virtue of the great, that it will do little honour to any body but themselves. The coxcomb,[12] who imitates their manner, and affects to be eminent by the superior propriety of his ordinary behaviour, is rewarded with a double share of contempt for his folly and presumption. Why should the man, whom nobody thinks it worth while to look at, be very anxious about the manner in which he holds up his head, or disposes of his arms while he walks through a room? He is occupied surely with a very superfluous attention, and with an attention too that marks a sense of his own importance, which no other mortal can go along with. The most perfect modesty and plainness, joined to as much negligence as is consistent with the respect due to the company, ought to be the chief characteristics of the behaviour of a private man. If ever he hopes to distinguish himself, it must be by more important virtues. He must acquire dependants to balance the dependants of the great, and he has no other fund to pay them from, but the labour of his body, and the activity of his mind. He must cultivate these therefore: he must acquire superior knowledge in his profession, and superior industry in the exercise of it. He must be patient in labour, resolute in danger, and firm in distress. These talents he must bring into public view, by the difficulty, importance, and, at the same time, good judgment of his undertakings, and by the severe and unrelenting application with which he pursues them. Probity and prudence, generosity and frankness, must characterize his behaviour upon all ordinary occasions; and he must, at the same time, be forward to engage in all those situations, in which it requires the greatest talents and virtues to act with propriety, but in which the greatest applause is to be acquired by those who can acquit themselves with honour. With what impatience does the man of spirit and ambition, who is depressed by his situation, look round for some great opportunity to distinguish himself? No circumstances, which can afford this, appear to him undesirable. He even looks forward with satisfaction to the prospect of foreign war, or civil dissension; and, with secret transport and delight, sees through all the confusion and bloodshed which attend them, the probability of those wished-for occasions presenting themselves, in which he may draw upon himself the attention and admiration of mankind. The man of rank and distinction, on the contrary, whose whole glory consists in the propriety of his ordinary behaviour, who is contented with the humble renown which this can afford him, and has no talents to acquire any other, is unwilling to embarrass himself with what can be attended either with difficulty or distress. To figure at a ball is his great triumph, and to succeed in an intrigue of gallantry, his highest exploit. He has an aversion to all public confusions, not from the love of mankind, for the great never look upon their inferiors as their fellow creatures; nor yet from want of courage, for in that he is seldom defective; but from a consciousness that he possesses none of the virtues which are required in such situations, and that the public attention will certainly be drawn away from him by others. He may be willing to expose himself to some little danger, and to make a campaign when it happens to be the fashion. But he shudders with horror at the thought of any situation which demands the continual and long exertion of patience, industry, fortitude, and application of thought. These virtues are hardly ever to be met with in men who are born to those high stations. In all governments accordingly, even in monarchies, the highest offices are generally possessed, and the whole detail of the administration conducted, by men who were educated in the middle and inferior ranks of life, who have been carried forward by their own industry and abilities, though loaded with the jealousy, and opposed by the resentment, of all those who were born their superiors, and to whom the great, after having regarded them, first with contempt, and afterwards with envy, are at last contented to truckle with the same abject meanness with which they desire that the rest of mankind should behave to themselves.

It is the loss of this easy empire over the affections of mankind which renders the fall from greatness so insupportable. When the family of the king of Macedon was led in triumph by Paulus Æmilius, their misfortunes, it is said, made them divide with their

conqueror the attention of the Roman people.[13] The sight of the
royal children, whose tender age rendered them insensible of their
situation, struck the spectators, amidst the public rejoicings and
prosperity, with the tenderest sorrow and compassion. The king
appeared next in the procession; and seemed like one confounded
and astonished, and bereft of all sentiment, by the greatness of
his calamities. His friends and ministers followed after him. As
they moved along, they often cast their eyes upon their fallen sovereign, and always burst into tears at the sight; their whole behaviour demonstrating that they thought not of their own misfortunes,
but were occupied entirely by the superior greatness of his. The
generous Romans, on the contrary, beheld him with disdain and
indignation, and regarded as unworthy of all compassion the
man who could be so mean-spirited as to bear to live under such
calamities. Yet what did those calamities amount to? According
to the greater part of historians, he was to spend the remainder of
his days, under the protection of a powerful and humane people,
in a state which in itself should seem worthy of envy, a state of
plenty, ease, leisure, and security, from which it was impossible
for him, even by his own folly to fall. But he was no longer to be
surrounded by that admiring mob of fools, flatterers, and dependants, who had formerly been accustomed to attend upon all his
motions. He was no longer to be gazed upon by multitudes, nor
to have it in his power to render himself the object of their respect,
their gratitude, their love, their admiration. The passions of nations
were no longer to mould themselves upon his inclinations. This
was that insupportable calamity which bereaved the king of all
sentiment; which made his friends forget their own misfortunes;
and which the Roman magnanimity could scarce conceive how
any man could be so mean-spirited as to bear to survive.

"Love," says my Lord Rochefoucault, "is commonly succeeded
by ambition; but ambition is hardly ever succeeded by love."[14]
That passion, when once it has got entire possession of the breast,
will admit neither a rival nor a successor. To those who have been
accustomed to the possession, or even to the hope of public
admiration, all other pleasures sicken and decay. Of all the dis-
carded statesmen who for their own ease have studied to get the
better of ambition, and to despise those honours which they
could no longer arrive at, how few have been able to succeed?

The greater part have spent their time in the most listless and insipid indolence, chagrined at the thoughts of their own insignificancy, incapable of being interested in the occupations of private life, without enjoyment, except when they talked of their former greatness, and without satisfaction, except when they were employed in some vain project to recover it. Are you in earnest resolved never to barter your liberty for the lordly servitude of a court, but to live free, fearless, and independent? There seems to be one way to continue in that virtuous resolution; and perhaps but one. Never enter the place from whence so few have been able to return; never come within the circle of ambition; nor ever bring your self into comparison with those masters of the earth who have already engrossed the attention of half mankind before you.

Of such mighty importance does it appear to be, in the imaginations of men, to stand in that situation which sets them most in the view of general sympathy and attention. And thus, place, that great object which divides the wives of aldermen, is the end of half the labours of human life; and is the cause of all the tumult and bustle, all the rapine and injustice, which avarice and ambition have introduced into this world. People of sense, it is said, indeed despise place; that is, they despise sitting at the head of the table, and are indifferent who it is that is pointed out to the company by that frivolous circumstance, which the smallest advantage is capable of overbalancing. But rank, distinction, pre-eminence, no man despises, unless he is either raised very much above, or sunk very much below, the ordinary standard of human nature; unless he is either so confirmed in wisdom and real philosophy, as to be satisfied that, while the propriety of his conduct renders him the just object of approbation, it is of little consequence though he be neither attended to, nor approved of; or so habituated to the idea of his own meanness, so sunk in slothful and sottish indifference, as entirely to have forgot the desire, and almost the very wish, for superiority.[15]

As to become the natural object of the joyous congratulations and sympathetic attentions of mankind is, in this manner, the circumstance which gives to prosperity all its dazzling splendour; so nothing darkens so much the gloom of adversity as to feel that our misfortunes are the objects, not of the fellow-feeling but of the contempt and aversion of our brethren. It is upon this account that the most dreadful calamities are not always those which it is most difficult to support. It is often more mortifying to appear in public under small disasters, than under great misfortunes. The first excite no sympathy; but the second, though they may excite none that approaches to the anguish of the sufferer, call forth, however, a very lively compassion. The sentiments of the spectators are, in this last case, less wide of those of the sufferer, and their imperfect fellow-feeling lends him some assistance in supporting his misery. Before a gay assembly, a gentleman would be more mortified to appear covered with filth and rags than with blood and wounds. This last situation would interest their pity; the other would provoke their laughter. The judge who orders a criminal to be set in the pillory, dishonours him more than if he had condemned him to the scaffold. The great prince, who, some years ago, caned a general officer at the head of his army, disgraced him irrecoverably.[16] The punishment would have been much less had he shot him through the body. By the laws of honour, to strike with a cane dishonours, to strike with a sword does not, for an obvious reason. Those slighter punishments, when inflicted on a gentleman, to whom dishonour is the greatest of all evils, come to be regarded among a humane and generous people, as the most dreadful of any. With regard to persons of that rank, therefore, they are universally laid aside, and the law, while it takes their life upon many occasions, respects their honour upon almost all. To scourge a person of quality, or to set him in the pillory, upon account of any crime whatever, is a brutality of which no European government, except that of Russia, is capable.

A brave man is not rendered contemptible by being brought to the scaffold; he is, by being set in the pillory. His behaviour in the one situation may gain him universal esteem and admiration. No behaviour in the other can render him agreeable. The sympathy of the spectators supports him in the one case, and saves him from that shame, that consciousness that his misery is felt by himself only, which is of all sentiments the most insupportable. There is no sympathy in the other; or, if there is any, it is not with his pain, which is a trifle, but with his consciousness of the want of sympathy with which this pain is attended. It is with his shame, not with his sorrow. Those who pity him, blush and hang down their heads for him. He droops in the same manner, and feels himself irrecoverably degraded by the punishment, though not by the crime. The man, on the contrary, who dies with resolution, as he is naturally regarded with the erect aspect of esteem and approbation, so he wears himself the same undaunted countenance; and, if the crime does not deprive him of the respect of others, the punishment never will. He has no suspicion that his situation is the object of contempt or derision to any body, and he can, with propriety, assume the air, not only of perfect serenity, but of triumph and exultation.

"Great dangers," says the Cardinal de Retz, "have their charms, because there is some glory to be got, even when we miscarry. But moderate dangers have nothing but what is horrible, because the loss of reputation always attends the want of success."[17] His maxim has the same foundation with what we have been just now observing with regard to punishments.

Human virtue is superior to pain, to poverty, to danger, and to death; nor does it even require its utmost efforts to despise them. But to have its misery exposed to insult and derision, to be led in triumph, to be set up for the hand of scorn to point at, is a situation in which its constancy is much more apt to fail. Compared with the contempt of mankind, all other external evils are easily supported.

CHAPTER III.

Of the corruption of our Moral Sentiments, which is occasioned by this disposition to admire the rich and the great, and to despise or neglect persons of poor and mean condition.[18]

This disposition to admire, and almost to worship, the rich and the powerful, and to despise, or, at least, to neglect persons of poor and mean condition, though necessary both to establish and to maintain the distinction of ranks and the order of society, is, at the same time, the great and most universal cause of the corruption of our moral sentiments. That wealth and greatness are often regarded with the respect and admiration which are due only to wisdom and virtue; and that the contempt, of which vice and folly are the only proper objects, is often most unjustly bestowed upon poverty and weakness, has been the complaint of moralists in all ages.[19]

We desire both to be respectable and to be respected. We dread both to be contemptible and to be contemned. But, upon coming into the world, we soon find that wisdom and virtue are by no means the sole objects of respect; nor vice and folly, of contempt. We frequently see the respectful attentions of the world more strongly directed towards the rich and the great, than towards the wise and the virtuous. We see frequently the vices and follies of the powerful much less despised than the poverty and weakness of the innocent. To deserve, to acquire, and to enjoy the respect and admiration of mankind, are the great objects of ambition and emulation. Two different roads are presented to us, equally leading to the attainment of this so much desired object; the one, by the study of wisdom and the practice of virtue; the other, by the acquisition of wealth and greatness. Two different characters are presented to our emulation; the one, of proud ambition and ostentatious avidity; the other, of humble modesty and equitable justice. Two different models, two different pictures, are held out to us, according to which we may fashion our own character and behaviour; the one more gaudy and glittering in its colouring; the other more correct and more exquisitely beautiful in its outline: the one forcing itself upon the notice of every wandering eye; the other, attracting the attention of scarce any body but the most studious and careful observer. They are the wise and the virtuous chiefly, a select, though, I am afraid, but a small party, who are the real and steady admirers of wisdom and virtue. The great mob of mankind are the admirers and worshippers, and, what may seem more extraordinary, most frequently the disinterested admirers and worshippers, of wealth and greatness.

The respect which we feel for wisdom and virtue is, no doubt, different from that which we conceive for wealth and greatness; and it requires no very nice discernment to distinguish the difference. But, notwithstanding this difference, those sentiments bear a very considerable resemblance to one another. In some particular features they are, no doubt, different, but, in the general air of the countenance, they seem to be so very nearly the same, that inattentive observers are very apt to mistake the one for the other.

In equal degrees of merit there is scarce any man who does not respect more the rich and the great, than the poor and the humble. With most men the presumption and vanity of the former are much more admired, than the real and solid merit of the latter. It is scarce agreeable to good morals, or even to good language, perhaps, to say, that mere wealth and greatness, abstracted from merit and virtue, deserve our respect. We must acknowledge, however, that they almost constantly obtain it; and that they may, therefore, be considered as, in some respects, the natural objects of it. Those exalted stations may, no doubt, be completely degraded by vice and folly. But the vice and folly must be very great, before they can operate this complete degradation. The profligacy of a man of fashion is looked upon with much less contempt and aversion, than that of a man of meaner condition. In the latter, a single transgression of the rules of temperance and propriety, is commonly more resented, than the constant and avowed contempt of them ever is in the former.

In the middling and inferior stations of life, the road to virtue and that to fortune, to such fortune, at least, as men in such stations can reasonably expect to acquire, are, happily, in most cases, very nearly the same. In all the middling and inferior professions, real and solid professional abilities, joined to prudent, just, firm, and temperate conduct, can very seldom fail of success. Abilities will even sometimes prevail where the conduct is by no means correct. Either habitual imprudence, however, or injustice, or weakness, or profligacy, will always cloud, and sometimes depress altogether, the most splendid professional abilities. Men in the inferior and middling stations of life, besides, can never be great enough to be above the law, which must generally overawe them into some sort of respect for, at least, the more important rules of justice. The success of such people, too, almost always depends upon the favour and good opinion of their neighbours and equals; and without a tolerably regular conduct these can very seldom be obtained. The good old proverb, therefore, That honesty is the best policy, holds, in such situations, almost always perfectly true. In such situations, therefore, we may generally expect a considerable degree of virtue; and, fortunately for the good morals of society, these are the situations of by far the greater part of mankind.

In the superior stations of life the case is unhappily not always the same. In the courts of princes, in the drawing-rooms of the great, where success and preferment depend, not upon the esteem of intelligent and well-informed equals, but upon the fanciful and foolish favour of ignorant, presumptuous, and proud superiors; flattery and falsehood too often prevail over merit and abilities. In such societies the abilities to please, are more regarded than the abilities to serve. In quiet and peaceable times, when the storm is at a distance, the prince, or great man, wishes only to be amused, and is even apt to fancy that he has scarce any occasion for the service of any body, or that those who amuse him are sufficiently able to serve him. The external graces, the frivolous accomplishments, of that impertinent and foolish thing called a man of fashion, are commonly more admired than the solid and masculine virtues of a warrior, a statesman, a philosopher, or a legislator. All the great and awful virtues, all the virtues which can fit, either for the council, the senate, or the field, are, by the insolent and insignificant flatterers, who commonly figure the most in such corrupted societies, held in the utmost contempt and derision. When the duke of Sully was called upon by Lewis the Thirteenth to give his advice in some great emergency, he observed the favourites and courtiers whispering to one another, and smiling at his unfashionable appearance. "Whenever your majesty's father," said the old warrior and statesman, "did me the honour to consult me, he ordered the buffoons of the court to retire into the antechamber."[20]

It is from our disposition to admire, and consequently to imitate, the rich and the great, that they are enabled to set, or to lead what is called the fashion. Their dress is the fashionable dress; the language of their conversation, the fashionable style; their air and deportment, the fashionable behaviour. Even their vices and follies are fashionable; and the greater part of men are proud to imitate and resemble them in the very qualities which dishonour and degrade them. Vain men often give themselves airs of a fashionable profligacy, which, in their hearts, they do not approve of, and of which, perhaps, they are really not guilty. They desire to be praised for what they themselves do not think praise-worthy, and

are ashamed of unfashionable virtues which they sometimes practise in secret, and for which they have secretly some degree of real
veneration. There are hypocrites of wealth and greatness, as well
as of religion and virtue; and a vain man is as apt to pretend to be
what he is not, in the one way, as a cunning man is in the other.
He assumes the equipage and splendid way of living of his superiors, without considering that whatever may be praise-worthy in
any of these, derives its whole merit and propriety from its suitableness to that situation and fortune which both require and can
easily support the expence. Many a poor man places his glory in
being thought rich, without considering that the duties (if one may
call such follies by so very venerable a name) which that reputation imposes upon him, must soon reduce him to beggary, and
render his situation still more unlike that of those whom he
admires and imitates, than it had been originally.

To attain to this envied situation, the candidates for fortune
too frequently abandon the paths of virtue; for unhappily, the
road which leads to the one, and that which leads to the other,
lie sometimes in very opposite directions. But the ambitious
man flatters himself that, in the splendid situation to which he
advances, he will have so many means of commanding the respect
and admiration of mankind, and will be enabled to act with such
superior propriety and grace, that the lustre of his future conduct
will entirely cover, or efface, the foulness of the steps by which he
arrived at that elevation. In many governments the candidates for
the highest stations are above the law; and, if they can attain the
object of their ambition, they have no fear of being called to
account for the means by which they acquired it. They often
endeavour, therefore, not only by fraud and falsehood, the ordinary and vulgar arts of intrigue and cabal; but sometimes by the
perpetration of the most enormous crimes, by murder and assassination, by rebellion and civil war, to supplant and destroy those
who oppose or stand in the way of their greatness. They more
frequently miscarry than succeed; and commonly gain nothing
but the disgraceful punishment which is due to their crimes. But,
though they should be so lucky as to attain that wished-for greatness, they are always most miserably disappointed in the happiness which they expect to enjoy in it. It is not ease or pleasure,
but always honour, of one kind or another, though frequently an

honour very ill understood, that the ambitious man really pursues. But the honour of his exalted station appears, both in his
own eyes and in those of other people, polluted and defiled by the
baseness of the means through which he rose to it. Though by the
profusion of every liberal expence; though by excessive indulgence in every profligate pleasure, the wretched, but usual, re-
source of ruined characters; though by the hurry of public business,
or by the prouder and more dazzling tumult of war, he may
endeavour to efface, both from his own memory and from that of
other people, the remembrance of what he has done; that remembrance never fails to pursue him. He invokes in vain the dark and
dismal powers of forgetfulness and oblivion. He remembers himself what he has done, and that remembrance tells him that other
people must likewise remember it. Amidst all the gaudy pomp of
the most ostentatious greatness; amidst the venal and vile adulation of the great and of the learned; amidst the more innocent,
though more foolish, acclamations of the common people; amidst
all the pride of conquest and the triumph of successful war, he is
still secretly pursued by the avenging furies of shame and remorse;
and, while glory seems to surround him on all sides, he himself,
in his own imagination, sees black and foul infamy fast pursuing
him, and every moment ready to overtake him from behind. Even
the great Caesar, though he had the magnanimity to dismiss his
guards, could not dismiss his suspicions. The remembrance of
Pharsalia still haunted and pursued him. When, at the request of
the senate, he had the generosity to pardon Marcellus, he told
that assembly, that he was not unaware of the designs which were
carrying on against his life; but that, as he had lived long enough
both for nature and for glory, he was contented to die, and therefore despised all conspiracies.[21] He had, perhaps, lived long
enough for nature. But the man who felt himself the object of
such deadly resentment, from those whose favour he wished to
gain, and whom he still wished to consider as his friends, had
certainly lived too long for real glory; or for all the happiness
which he could ever hope to enjoy in the love and esteem of his
equals.

PART II.

OF MERIT AND DEMERIT;

OR,

OF THE OBJECTS OF REWARD AND PUNISHMENT.

CONSISTING OF THREE SECTIONS.

SECTION I.

INTRODUCTION.

There is another set of qualities ascribed to the actions and conduct of mankind, distinct from their propriety or impropriety, their decency or ungracefulness, and which are the objects of a distinct species of approbation and disapprobation. These are Merit and Demerit, the qualities of deserving reward, and of deserving punishment.

It has already been observed,[1] that the sentiment or affection of the heart, from which any action proceeds, and upon which its whole virtue or vice depends, may be considered under two different aspects, or in two different relations: first, in relation to the cause or object which excites it; and, secondly, in relation to the end which it proposes, or to the effect which it tends to produce: that upon the suitableness or unsuitableness, upon the proportion or disproportion, which the affection seems to bear to the cause or object which excites it, depends the propriety or impropriety, the decency or ungracefulness of the consequent action; and that upon the beneficial or hurtful effects which the affection proposes or tends to produce, depends the merit or demerit, the good or ill desert of the action to which it gives occasion. Wherein consists our sense of the propriety or impropriety of actions, has been explained in the former part of this discourse. We come now to consider, wherein consists that of their good or ill desert.

Chapter I.

That whatever appears to be the proper object of gratitude, appears to deserve reward; and that, in the same manner, whatever appears to be the proper object of resentment, appears to deserve punishment.

To us, therefore, that action must appear to deserve reward, which appears to be the proper and approved object of that sentiment, which most immediately and directly prompts us to reward, or to do good to another. And in the same manner, that action must appear to deserve punishment, which appears to be the proper and approved object of that sentiment which most immediately and directly prompts us to punish, or to inflict evil upon another.

The sentiment which most immediately and directly prompts us to reward, is gratitude; that which most immediately and directly prompts us to punish, is resentment.

To us, therefore, that action must appear to deserve reward, which appears to be the proper and approved object of gratitude; as, on the other hand, that action must appear to deserve punishment, which appears to be the proper and approved object of resentment.

To reward, is to recompense, to remunerate, to return good for good received. To punish, too, is to recompense, to remunerate, though in a different manner; it is to return evil for evil that has been done.

There are some other passions, besides gratitude and resentment, which interest us in the happiness or misery of others; but there are none which so directly excite us to be the instruments of either. The love and esteem which grow upon acquaintance and habitual approbation, necessarily lead us to be pleased with the good fortune of the man who is the object of such agreeable emotions, and consequently, to be willing to lend a hand to promote it. Our love, however, is fully satisfied, though his good fortune should be brought about without our assistance. All that this passion desires is to see him happy, without regarding who was the author of his prosperity. But gratitude is not to be satisfied in this manner. If the person to whom we owe many obligations, is made happy without our assistance, though it pleases our love, it does not content our gratitude. Till we have recompensed him, till we ourselves have been instrumental in promoting his happiness, we feel ourselves still loaded with that debt which his past services have laid upon us.

The hatred and dislike, in the same manner, which grow upon habitual disapprobation, would often lead us to take a malicious pleasure in the misfortune of the man whose conduct and character excite so painful a passion. But though dislike and hatred harden us against all sympathy, and sometimes dispose us even to rejoice at the distress of another, yet, if there is no resentment in the case, if neither we nor our friends have received any great personal provocation, these passions would not naturally lead us to wish to be instrumental in bringing it about. Though we could fear no punishment in consequence of our having had some hand in it, we would rather that it should happen by other means. To one under the dominion of violent hatred it would be agreeable, perhaps, to hear, that the person whom he abhorred and detested was killed by some accident. But if he had the least spark of justice, which, though this passion is not very favourable to virtue, he might still have, it would hurt him excessively to have been himself, even without design, the occasion of this misfortune. Much more would the very thought of voluntarily contributing to it shock him beyond all measure. He would reject with horror even the imagination of so execrable a design; and if he could imagine himself capable of such an enormity, he would begin to regard himself in the same odious light in which he had considered the person who was the object of his dislike. But it is quite otherwise with resentment: if the person who had done us some great injury, who had murdered our father or our brother, for example, should soon afterwards die of a fever, or even be brought to the scaffold upon account of some other crime, though it might sooth our hatred, it would not fully gratify our resentment. Resentment would prompt us to desire, not only that he should be punished, but that he should be punished by our means, and upon account of that particular injury which he had done to us. Resentment cannot be fully gratified, unless the offender is not only made to grieve in his turn, but to grieve for that particular wrong which we have suffered from him. He must be made to repent and be sorry for this very action, that others, through fear of the like punishment, may be terrified from being guilty of the like offence. The natural gratification of this passion tends, of its own accord, to produce all the political ends of punishment; the correction of the criminal, and the example to the public.

Gratitude and resentment, therefore, are the sentiments which most immediately and directly prompt to reward and to punish. To us, therefore, he must appear to deserve reward, who appears to be the proper and approved object of gratitude; and he to deserve punishment, who appears to be that of resentment.

CHAPTER II.

Of the proper objects of gratitude and resentment.

To be the proper and approved object either of gratitude or resentment, can mean nothing but to be the object of that gratitude, and of that resentment, which naturally seems proper, and is approved of.

But these, as well as all the other passions of human nature, seem proper and are approved of, when the heart of every impartial spectator entirely sympathizes with them, when every indifferent by-stander entirely enters into, and goes along with them.

He, therefore, appears to deserve reward, who, to some person or persons, is the natural object of a gratitude which every human heart is disposed to beat time to, and thereby applaud: and he, on the other hand, appears to deserve punishment, who in the same manner is to some person or persons the natural object of a resentment which the breast of every reasonable man is ready to adopt and sympathize with. To us, surely, that action must appear to deserve reward, which every body who knows of it would wish to reward, and therefore delights to see rewarded: and that action must as surely appear to deserve punishment, which every body who hears of it is angry with, and upon that account rejoices to see punished.

1. As we sympathize with the joy of our companions when in prosperity, so we join with them in the complacency and satisfaction with which they naturally regard whatever is the cause of their good fortune. We enter into the love and affection which they conceive for it, and begin to love it too. We should be sorry

for their sakes if it was destroyed, or even if it was placed at too great a distance from them, and out of the reach of their care and protection, though they should lose nothing by its absence except the pleasure of seeing it. If it is man who has thus been the fortunate instrument of the happiness of his brethren, this is still more peculiarly the case. When we see one man assisted, protected, relieved, by another, our sympathy with the joy of the person who receives the benefit serves only to animate our fellow-feeling with his gratitude towards him who bestows it. When we look upon the person who is the cause of his pleasure with the eyes with which we imagine he must look upon him, his benefactor seems to stand before us in the most engaging and amiable light. We readily therefore sympathize with the grateful affection which he conceives for a person to whom he has been so much obliged; and consequently applaud the returns which he is disposed to make for the good offices conferred upon him. As we entirely enter into the affection from which these returns proceed, they necessarily seem every way proper and suitable to their object.[2]

2. In the same manner, as we sympathize with the sorrow of our fellow-creature whenever we see his distress, so we likewise enter into his abhorrence and aversion for whatever has given occasion to it. Our heart, as it adopts and beats time to his grief, so is it likewise animated with that spirit by which he endeavours to drive away or destroy the cause of it. The indolent and passive fellow-feeling, by which we accompany him in his sufferings, readily gives way to that more vigorous and active sentiment by which we go along with him in the effort he makes, either to repel them, or to gratify his aversion to what has given occasion to them. This is still more peculiarly the case, when it is man who has caused them. When we see one man oppressed or injured by another, the sympathy which we feel with the distress of the sufferer seems to serve only to animate our fellow-feeling with his resentment against the offender. We are rejoiced to see him attack his adversary in his turn, and are eager and ready to assist him whenever he exerts himself for defence, or even for vengeance, within a certain degree. If the injured should perish in the quarrel, we not only sympathize with the real resentment of his friends and relations, but with the imaginary resentment which in fancy we lend to the dead, who is no longer capable of feeling that or any other human sentiment.

But as we put ourselves in his situation, as we enter, as it were, into his body, and in our imaginations, in some measure, animate anew the deformed and mangled carcass of the slain, when we bring home in this manner his case to our own bosoms, we feel upon this, as upon many other occasions, an emotion which the person principally concerned is incapable of feeling, and which yet we feel by an illusive sympathy with him. The sympathetic tears which we shed for that immense and irretrievable loss, which in our fancy he appears to have sustained, seem to be but a small part of the duty which we owe him. The injury which he has suffered demands, we think, a principal part of our attention. We feel that resentment which we imagine he ought to feel, and which he would feel, if in his cold and lifeless body there remained any consciousness of what passes upon earth. His blood, we think, calls aloud for vengeance. The very ashes of the dead seem to be disturbed at the thought that his injuries are to pass unrevenged. The horrors which are supposed to haunt the bed of the murderer, the ghosts which, superstition imagines, rise from their graves to demand vengeance upon those who brought them to an untimely end, all take their origin from this natural sympathy with the imaginary resentment of the slain. And with regard, at least, to this most dreadful of all crimes, Nature, antecedent to all reflections upon the utility of punishment, has in this manner stamped upon the human heart, in the strongest and most indelible characters, an immediate and instinctive approbation of the sacred and necessary law of retaliation.

CHAPTER III.

That where there is no approbation of the conduct of the person who confers the benefit, there is little sympathy with the gratitude of him who receives it: and that, on the contrary, where there is no disapprobation of the motives of the person who does the mischief, there is no sort of sympathy with the resentment of him who suffers it.

It is to be observed, however, that, how beneficial soever on the one hand, or how hurtful soever on the other, the actions or intentions of the person who acts may have been to the person who is, if I may say so, acted upon, yet if in the one case there appears to have been no propriety in the motives of the agent, if we cannot enter into the affections which influenced his conduct, we have little sympathy with the gratitude of the person who receives the benefit: or if, in the other case, there appears to have been no impropriety in the motives of the agent, if, on the contrary, the affections which influenced his conduct are such as we must necessarily enter into, we can have no sort of sympathy with the resentment of the person who suffers. Little gratitude seems due in the one case, and all sort of resentment seems unjust in the other. The one action seems to merit little reward, the other to deserve no punishment.

1. First, I say, That wherever we cannot sympathize with the affections of the agent, wherever there seems to be no propriety in the motives which influenced his conduct, we are less disposed to enter into the gratitude of the person who received the benefit of his actions. A very small return seems due to that foolish and profuse generosity which confers the greatest benefits from the most trivial motives, and gives an estate to a man merely because his name and sirname happen to be the same with those of the giver. Such services do not seem to demand any proportionable recompense. Our contempt for the folly of the agent hinders us from thoroughly entering into the gratitude of the person to whom the good office has been done. His benefactor seems unworthy of it. As when we place ourselves in the situation of the person obliged, we feel that we could conceive no great reverence for such a benefactor, we easily absolve him from a great deal of that submissive veneration and esteem which we should think due to a more respectable character; and provided he always treats his weak friend with kindness and humanity, we are willing to excuse him from many attentions and regards which we should demand to a worthier patron. Those Princes, who have heaped, with the greatest profusion, wealth, power, and honours, upon their favourites, have seldom excited that degree of attachment to their persons which has often been experienced by those who were more frugal of their favours. The well-natured, but injudicious prodigality of James the First of Great Britain seems to have attached nobody to his person; and that Prince, notwithstanding his social and harmless disposition, appears to have lived and died without a friend.[3] The whole gentry and nobility

of England exposed their lives and fortunes in the cause of his more frugal and distinguishing son, notwithstanding the coldness and distant severity of his ordinary deportment.

2. Secondly, I say, That wherever the conduct of the agent appears to have been entirely directed by motives and affections which we thoroughly enter into and approve of, we can have no sort of sympathy with the resentment of the sufferer, how great soever the mischief which may have been done to him. When two people quarrel, if we take part with, and entirely adopt the resentment of one of them, it is impossible that we should enter into that of the other. Our sympathy with the person whose motives we go along with, and whom therefore, we look upon as in the right, cannot but harden us against all fellow-feeling with the other, whom we necessarily regard as in the wrong. Whatever this last, therefore, may have suffered, while it is no more than what we ourselves should have wished him to suffer, while it is no more than what our own sympathetic indignation would have prompted us to inflict upon him, it cannot either displease or provoke us. When an inhuman murderer is brought to the scaffold, though we have some compassion for his misery, we can have no sort of fellow-feeling with his resentment, if he should be so absurd as to express any against either his prosecutor or his judge. The natural tendency of their just indignation against so vile a criminal is indeed the most fatal and ruinous to him. But it is impossible that we should be displeased with the tendency of a sentiment, which, when we bring the case home to ourselves, we feel that we cannot avoid adopting.

CHAPTER IV.

Recapitulation of the foregoing chapters.

1. We do not, therefore, thoroughly and heartily sympathize with the gratitude of one man towards another, merely because this other has been the cause of his good fortune, unless he has been the cause of it from motives which we entirely go along with. Our heart must adopt the principles of the agent, and go along with all the affections which influenced his conduct, before it can entirely

sympathize with, and beat time to, the gratitude of the person who has been benefited by his actions. If in the conduct of the benefactor there appears to have been no propriety, how beneficial soever its effects, it does not seem to demand, or necessarily to require, any proportionable recompense.

But when to the beneficent tendency of the action is joined the propriety of the affection from which it proceeds, when we entirely sympathize and go along with the motives of the agent, the love which we conceive for him upon his own account, enhances and enlivens our fellow-feeling with the gratitude of those who owe their prosperity to his good conduct. His actions seem then to demand, and, if I may say so, to call aloud for a proportionable recompense. We then entirely enter into that gratitude which prompts to bestow it. The benefactor seems then to be the proper object of reward, when we thus entirely sympathize with, and approve of, that sentiment which prompts to reward him. When we approve of, and go along with, the affection from which the action proceeds, we must necessarily approve of the action, and regard the person towards whom it is directed, as its proper and suitable object.

2. In the same manner, we cannot at all sympathize with the resentment of one man against another, merely because this other has been the cause of his misfortune, unless he has been the cause of it from motives which we cannot enter into. Before we can adopt the resentment of the sufferer, we must disapprove of the motives of the agent, and feel that our heart renounces all sympathy with the affections which influenced his conduct. If there appears to have been no impropriety in these, how fatal soever the tendency of the action which proceeds from them to those against whom it is directed, it does not seem to deserve any punishment, or to be the proper object of any resentment.

But when to the hurtfulness of the action is joined the impropriety of the affection from whence it proceeds, when our heart rejects with abhorrence all fellow-feeling with the motives of the agent, we then heartily and entirely sympathize with the resentment of the sufferer. Such actions seem then to deserve, and, if I may say so, to call aloud for, a proportionable punishment; and we entirely enter into, and thereby approve of, that resentment which prompts to inflict it. The offender necessarily seems then to be the proper object of punishment, when we thus entirely sympathize with, and thereby approve of, that sentiment which prompts to punish. In this case too, when we approve, and go along with, the affection from which the action proceeds, we must necessarily approve of the action, and regard the person against whom it is directed, as its proper and suitable object.

CHAPTER V.

The analysis of the sense of Merit and Demerit.

1. As our sense, therefore, of the propriety of conduct arises from what I shall call a direct sympathy with the affections and motives of the person who acts, so our sense of its merit arises from what I shall call an indirect sympathy with the gratitude of the person who is, if I may say so, acted upon.

As we cannot indeed enter thoroughly into the gratitude of the person who receives the benefit, unless we beforehand approve of the motives of the benefactor, so, upon this account, the sense of merit seems to be a compounded sentiment, and to be made up of two distinct emotions; a direct sympathy with the sentiments of the agent, and an indirect sympathy with the gratitude of those who receive the benefit of his actions.

We may, upon many different occasions, plainly distinguish those two different emotions combining and uniting together in our sense of the good desert of a particular character or action. When we read in history concerning actions of proper and benefi-cent greatness of mind, how eagerly do we enter into such designs? How much are we animated by that high-spirited generosity which directs them? How keen are we for their success? How grieved at their disappointment? In imagination we become the very person whose actions are represented to us: we transport ourselves in fancy to the scenes of those distant and forgotten adventures, and imagine ourselves acting the part of a Scipio or a Camillus, a Timoleon or an Aristides.[4] So far our sentiments are founded upon the direct sympathy with the person who acts. Nor is the indirect sympathy with those who receive the benefit of such actions less sensibly felt. Whenever we place ourselves in the situation of these last, with what warm and affectionate fellow-feeling do we enter into their gratitude towards those who served them so essentially? We embrace, as it were, their benefactor along with them. Our heart readily sympathizes with the highest transports of their grateful affection. No honours, no rewards, we think, can be too great for them to bestow upon him. When they make this proper return for his services, we heartily applaud and go along with them; but are shocked beyond all measure, if by their conduct they appear to have little sense of the obligations conferred upon them. Our whole sense, in short, of the merit and good desert of such actions, of the propriety and fitness of recompensing them, and making the person who performed them rejoice in his turn, arises from the sympathetic emotions of gratitude and love, with which, when we bring home to our own breast the situation of those principally concerned, we feel ourselves naturally transported towards the man who could act with such proper and noble beneficence.

2. In the same manner as our sense of the impropriety of conduct arises from a want of sympathy, or from a direct antipathy to the affections and motives of the agent, so our sense of its demerit arises from what I shall here too call an indirect sympathy with the resentment of the sufferer.

As we cannot indeed enter into the resentment of the sufferer, unless our heart beforehand disapproves the motives of the agent, and renounces all fellow-feeling with them; so upon this account the sense of demerit, as well as that of merit, seems to be a compounded sentiment, and to be made up of two distinct emotions; a direct antipathy to the sentiments of the agent, and an indirect sympathy with the resentment of the sufferer.

We may here too, upon many different occasions, plainly distinguish those two different emotions combining and uniting together in our sense of the ill-desert of a particular character or action. When we read in history concerning the perfidy and cruelty of a Borgia or a Nero, our heart rises up against the detestable sentiments which influenced their conduct, and renounces with horror and abomination all fellow-feeling with such execrable motives.[5] So far our sentiments are founded upon the direct antipathy to the affections of the agent: and the indirect sympathy with the resentment of the sufferers is still more sensibly felt. When we bring home to ourselves the situation of the persons whom those scourges of mankind insulted, murdered, or betrayed, what indignation do we not feel against such insolent and inhuman oppressors of the earth? Our sympathy with the unavoidable distress of the innocent sufferers is not more real nor more lively, than our fellow-feeling with their just and natural resentment. The former sentiment only heightens the latter, and the idea of their distress serves only to inflame and blow up our animosity against those who occasioned it. When we think of the anguish of the sufferers, we take part with them more earnestly against their oppressors; we enter with more eagerness into all their schemes of vengeance, and feel ourselves every moment wreaking, in imagination, upon such violators of the laws of society, that punishment which our sympathetic indignation tells us is due to their crimes. Our sense of the horror and dreadful atrocity of such conduct, the delight which we take in hearing that it was properly punished, the indignation which we feel when it escapes this due retaliation, our whole sense and feeling, in short, of its ill desert, of the propriety and fitness of inflicting evil upon the person who is guilty of it, and of making him grieve in his turn, arises from the sympathetic indignation which naturally boils up in the breast of the spectator, whenever he thoroughly brings home to himself the case of the sufferer.*

* To ascribe in this manner our natural sense of the ill desert of human actions to a sympathy with the resentment of the sufferer, may seem, to the greater part of people, to be a degradation of that sentiment. Resentment is commonly regarded as so odious a passion, that they will be apt to think it impossible that so laudable a principle, as the sense of the ill desert of vice, should in any respect be founded upon it. They will be more willing, perhaps, to admit that our sense of the merit of good actions is founded upon a sympathy with the gratitude of the persons who receive the benefit of them; because gratitude, as well as all the other benevolent passions, is regarded as an amiable principle, which can take nothing from the worth of whatever is founded upon it. Gratitude and resentment, however, are in every respect, it is evident, counterparts to one another; and if our sense of merit arises from a sympathy with the one, our sense of demerit can scarce miss to proceed from a fellow-feeling with the other.

Let it be considered too that resentment, though, in the degrees in which we too often see it, the most odious, perhaps, of all the passions, is not disapproved of when properly humbled and entirely brought down to the level of the sympathetic indignation of the spectator. When we, who are the bystanders, feel that our own animosity entirely corresponds with that of the sufferer, when the resentment of this last does not in any respect go beyond our own, when no word, no gesture, escapes him that denotes an emotion more violent than what we can keep time to, and when he never aims at inflicting any punishment beyond what we should rejoice to see inflicted, or what we ourselves would upon this account even desire to be the instruments of inflicting, it is impossible that we should not entirely approve of his sentiments. Our own emotion in this case must, in our eyes, undoubtedly justify his. And as experience teaches us how much the greater part of mankind are incapable of this moderation, and how great an effort must be made in order to bring down the rude and undisciplined impulse of resentment to this suitable temper, we cannot avoid conceiving a considerable degree of esteem and admiration for one who appears capable of exerting so much self-command over one of the most ungovernable passions of his nature. When indeed the animosity of the sufferer exceeds, as it almost always does, what we can go along with, as we cannot enter into it, we necessarily disapprove of it. We even disapprove of it more than we should of an equal excess of almost any other passion derived from the imagination. And this too violent resentment, instead of carrying us along with it, becomes itself the object of our resentment and indignation. We enter into the opposite resentment of the person who is the object of this unjust emotion, and who is in danger of suffering from it. Revenge, therefore, the excess of resentment, appears to be the most detestable of all the passions, and is the object of the horror and indignation of every body. And as in the way in which this passion commonly discovers itself among mankind, it is excessive a hundred times for once that it is moderate, we are very apt to consider it as altogether odious and detestable, because in its most ordinary appearances it is so. Nature, however, even in the present depraved state of mankind, does not seem to have dealt so unkindly with us, as to have endowed us with any principle which is wholly and in every respect evil, or which, in no degree and in no direction, can be the proper object of praise and approbation. Upon some occasions we are sensible that this passion, which is generally too strong, may likewise be too weak. We sometimes complain that a particular person shows too little spirit, and has too little sense of the injuries that have been done to him; and we are as ready to despise him for the defect, as to hate him for the excess of this passion.

The inspired writers would not surely have talked so frequently or so strongly of the wrath and anger of God, if they had regarded every degree of those passions as vicious and evil, even in so weak and imperfect a creature as man.

Let it be considered too, that the present inquiry is not concerning a matter of right, if I may say so, but concerning a matter of fact. We are not at present examining upon what principles a perfect being would approve of the punishment of bad actions; but upon what principles so weak and imperfect a creature as man actually and in fact approves of it. The principles which I have just now mentioned, it is evident, have a very great effect upon his sentiments; and it seems wisely ordered that it should be so. The very existence of society requires that unmerited and unprovoked malice should be restrained by proper punishments; and consequently, that to inflict those punishments should be regarded as a proper and laudable action. Though man, therefore, be naturally endowed with a desire of the welfare and preservation of society, yet the Author of nature has not entrusted it to his reason to find out that a certain application of punishments is the proper means of attaining this end; but has endowed him with an immediate and instinctive approbation of that very application which is most proper to attain it. The economy of nature is in this respect exactly of a piece with what it is upon many other occasions. With regard to all those ends which, upon account of their peculiar importance, may be regarded, if such an expression is allowable, as the favourite ends of nature, she has constantly in this manner not only endowed mankind with an appetite for the end which she proposes, but likewise with an appetite for the means by which alone this end can be brought about, for their own sakes, and independent of their tendency to produce it. Thus self-preservation, and the propagation of the species, are the great ends which Nature seems to have proposed in the formation of all animals. Mankind are endowed with a desire of those ends, and an aversion to the contrary; with a love of life, and a dread of dissolution; with a desire of the continuance and perpetuity of the species, and with an aversion to the thoughts of its intire extinction. But though we are in this manner endowed with a very strong desire of those ends, it has not been entrusted to the slow and uncertain determinations of our reason, to find out the proper means of bringing them about. Nature has directed us to the greater part of these by original and immediate instincts. Hunger, thirst, the passion which unites the two sexes, the love of pleasure, and the dread of pain, prompt us to apply those means for their own sakes, and without any consideration of their tendency to those beneficent ends which the great Director of nature intended to produce by them.

Before I conclude this note, I must take notice of a difference between the approbation of propriety and that of merit or beneficence. Before we approve of the sentiments of any person as proper and suitable to their objects, we must not only be affected in the same manner as he is, but we must perceive this harmony and correspondence of sentiments between him and ourselves. Thus, though upon hearing of a misfortune that had befallen my friend, I should conceive precisely that degree of concern which he gives way to; yet till I am informed of the manner in which he behaves, till I perceive the harmony between his emotions and mine, I cannot be said to approve of the sentiments which influence his behaviour. The approbation of propriety therefore requires, not only that we should entirely sympathize with the person who acts, but that we should perceive this perfect concord between his sentiments and our own. On the contrary, when I hear of a benefit that has been bestowed upon another person, let him who has received it be affected in what manner he pleases, if, by bringing his case home to myself, I feel gratitude arise in my own breast, I necessarily approve of the conduct of his benefactor, and regard it as meritorious, and the proper object of reward. Whether the person who has received the benefit conceives gratitude or not, cannot, it is evident, in any degree alter our sentiments with regard to the merit of him who has bestowed it. No actual correspondence of sentiments, therefore, is here required. It is sufficient that if he was grateful, they would correspond; and our sense of merit is often founded upon one of those illusive sympathies, by which, when we bring home to ourselves the case of another, we are often affected in a manner in which the person principally concerned is incapable of being affected. There is a similar difference between our disapprobation of demerit, and that of impropriety.

SECTION II.

OF JUSTICE AND BENEFICENCE.

CHAPTER I.

Comparison of those two Virtues.

Actions of a beneficent tendency, which proceed from proper motives, seem alone to require reward; because such alone are the approved objects of gratitude, or excite the sympathetic gratitude of the spectator.

Actions of a hurtful tendency, which proceed from improper motives, seem alone to deserve punishment; because such alone are the approved objects of resentment, or excite the sympathetic resentment of the spectator.[1]

Beneficence is always free, it cannot be extorted by force, the mere want of it exposes to no punishment; because the mere want of beneficence tends to do no real positive evil. It may disappoint of the good which might reasonably have been expected, and upon that account it may justly excite dislike and disapprobation: it cannot, however, provoke any resentment which mankind will go along with. The man who does not recompense his benefactor, when he has it in his power, and when his benefactor needs his assistance, is, no doubt, guilty of the blackest ingratitude. The heart of every impartial spectator rejects all fellow-feeling with the selfishness of his motives, and he is the proper object of the highest disapprobation. But still he does no positive hurt to any body. He only does not do that good which in propriety he ought to have done. He is the object of hatred, a passion which is naturally excited by impropriety of sentiment and behaviour; not of resentment, a passion which is never properly called forth but by actions which tend to do real and positive hurt to some particular persons. His want of gratitude, therefore, cannot be punished.

To oblige him by force to perform what in gratitude he ought to perform, and what every impartial spectator would approve of him for performing, would, if possible, be still more improper than his neglecting to perform it. His benefactor would dishonour himself if he attempted by violence to constrain him to gratitude, and it would be impertinent for any third person, who was not the superior of either, to intermeddle. But of all the duties of beneficence, those which gratitude recommends to us approach nearest to what is called a perfect and complete obligation. What friendship, what generosity, what charity, would prompt us to do with universal approbation, is still more free, and can still less be extorted by force than the duties of gratitude. We talk of the debt of gratitude, not of charity, or generosity, nor even of friendship, when friendship is mere esteem, and has not been enhanced and complicated with gratitude for good offices.

Resentment seems to have been given us by nature for defence, and for defence only. It is the safeguard of justice and the security of innocence. It prompts us to beat off the mischief which is attempted to be done to us, and to retaliate that which is already done; that the offender may be made to repent of his injustice, and that others, through fear of the like punishment, may be terrified from being guilty of the like offence. It must be reserved therefore for these purposes, nor can the spectator ever go along with it when it is exerted for any other. But the mere want of the beneficent virtues, though it may disappoint us of the good which might reasonably be expected, neither does, nor attempts to do, any mischief from which we can have occasion to defend ourselves.

There is, however, another virtue, of which the observance is not left to the freedom of our own wills, which may be extorted by force, and of which the violation exposes to resentment, and consequently to punishment. This virtue is justice: the violation of justice is injury: it does real and positive hurt to some particular persons, from motives which are naturally disapproved of. It is, therefore, the proper object of resentment, and of punishment, which is the natural consequence of resentment. As mankind go along with, and approve of the violence employed to avenge the hurt which is done by injustice, so they much more go along with, and approve of, that which is employed to prevent and beat off the injury, and to restrain the offender from hurting his neigh-bours. The person himself who meditates an injustice is sensible of this, and feels that force may, with the utmost propriety, be made use of, both by the person whom he is about to injure, and by others, either to obstruct the execution of his crime, or to pun-ish him when he has executed it. And upon this is founded that remarkable distinction between justice and all the other social virtues, which has of late been particularly insisted upon by an author of very great and original genius, that we feel ourselves to be under a stricter obligation to act according to justice, than agreeably to friendship, charity, or generosity; that the practice of these last-mentioned virtues seems to be left in some measure to our own choice, but that, somehow or other, we feel ourselves to be in a peculiar manner tied, bound, and obliged to the observa-tion of justice.[2] We feel, that is to say, that force may, with the utmost propriety, and with the approbation of all mankind, be made use of to constrain us to observe the rules of the one, but not to follow the precepts of the other.

We must always, however, carefully distinguish what is only blameable, or the proper object of disapprobation, from what force may be employed either to punish or to prevent. That seems blameable which falls short of that ordinary degree of proper beneficence which experience teaches us to expect of every body; and, on the contrary, that seems praise-worthy which goes beyond it. The ordinary degree itself seems neither blameable nor praise-worthy. A father, a son, a brother, who behaves to the correspon-dent relation neither better nor worse than the greater part of men commonly do, seems properly to deserve neither praise nor blame. He who surprises us by extraordinary and unexpected, though still proper and suitable kindness, or on the contrary by extraordinary and unexpected, as well as unsuitable unkind-ness, seems praise-worthy in the one case, and blameable in the other.

Even the most ordinary degree of kindness or beneficence, however, cannot, among equals, be extorted by force. Among equals each individual is naturally, and antecedent to the institu-tion of civil government, regarded as having a right both to defend himself from injuries, and to exact a certain degree of pun-ishment for those which have been done to him. Every generous spectator not only approves of his conduct when he does this, but enters so far into his sentiments as often to be willing to assist him. When one man attacks, or robs, or attempts to murder another, all the neighbours take the alarm, and think that they do right when they run, either to revenge the person who has been injured, or to defend him who is in danger of being so. But when a father fails in the ordinary degree of parental affection towards a son; when a son seems to want that filial reverence which might be expected to his father; when brothers are without the usual degree of brotherly affection; when a man shuts his breast against compassion, and refuses to relieve the misery of his fellow-creatures, when he can with the greatest ease; in all these cases, though every body blames the conduct, nobody imagines that those who might have reason, perhaps, to expect more kindness, have any right to extort it by force. The sufferer can only complain, and the spectator can intermeddle no other way than by advice and persuasion. Upon all such occasions, for equals to use force against one another, would be thought the highest degree of insolence and presumption.

A superior may, indeed, sometimes, with universal approbation, oblige those under his jurisdiction to behave, in this respect, with a certain degree of propriety to one another. The laws of all civilized nations oblige parents to maintain their children, and children to maintain their parents, and impose upon men many other duties of beneficence. The civil magistrate is entrusted with the power not only of preserving the public peace by restraining injustice, but of promoting the prosperity of the commonwealth, by establishing good discipline, and by discouraging every sort of vice and impropriety; he may prescribe rules, therefore, which not only prohibit mutual injuries among fellow-citizens, but command mutual good offices to a certain degree. When the sovereign commands what is merely indifferent, and what, antecedent to his orders, might have been omitted without any blame, it becomes not only blameable but punishable to disobey him. When he commands, therefore, what, antecedent to any such order, could not have been omitted without the greatest blame, it surely becomes much more punishable to be wanting in obedience. Of all the duties of a law-giver, however, this, perhaps, is that which it requires the greatest delicacy and reserve to execute with propriety and judgment. To neglect it altogether exposes the commonwealth to many gross disorders and shocking enormities, and to push it too far is destructive of all liberty, security, and justice.[3]

Though the mere want of beneficence seems to merit no punishment from equals, the greater exertions of that virtue appear to deserve the highest reward. By being productive of the greatest good, they are the natural and approved objects of the liveliest gratitude. Though the breach of justice, on the contrary, exposes to punishment, the observance of the rules of that virtue seems scarce to deserve any reward. There is, no doubt, a propriety in the practice of justice, and it merits, upon that account, all the approbation which is due to propriety. But as it does no real positive good, it is entitled to very little gratitude. Mere justice is, upon most occasions, but a negative virtue, and only hinders us from hurting our neighbour. The man who barely abstains from violating either the person, or the estate, or the reputation of his neighbours, has surely very little positive merit. He fulfils, however, all the rules of what is peculiarly called justice, and does every thing which his equals can with propriety force him to do, or which they can punish him for not doing. We may often fulfil all the rules of justice by sitting still and doing nothing.

As every man doth, so shall it be done to him, and retaliation seems to be the great law which is dictated to us by Nature.[4] Beneficence and generosity we think due to the generous and beneficent. Those whose hearts never open to the feelings of humanity, should, we think, be shut out in the same manner, from the affections of all their fellow-creatures, and be allowed to live in the midst of society, as in a great desert where there is nobody to care for them, or to inquire after them. The violator of the laws of justice ought to be made to feel himself that evil which he has done to another; and since no regard to the sufferings of his brethren is capable of restraining him, he ought to be overawed by the fear of his own. The man who is barely innocent, who only observes the laws of justice with regard to others, and merely abstains from hurting his neighbours, can merit only that his neighbours in their turn should respect his innocence, and that the same laws should be religiously observed with regard to him.

Chapter II.

*Of the sense of Justice, of Remorse, and of the conscious-
ness of Merit.*

There can be no proper motive for hurting our neighbour, there
can be no incitement to do evil to another, which mankind will
go along with, except just indignation for evil which that other
has done to us. To disturb his happiness merely because it stands
in the way of our own, to take from him what is of real use to
him merely because it may be of equal or of more use to us, or to
indulge, in this manner, at the expence of other people, the natural
preference which every man has for his own happiness above that
of other people, is what no impartial spectator can go along with.
Every man is, no doubt, by nature, first and principally recommended to his own care; and as he is fitter to take care of himself
than of any other person, it is fit and right that it should be so.[5]
Every man, therefore, is much more deeply interested in whatever
immediately concerns himself, than in what concerns any other
man: and to hear, perhaps, of the death of another person, with
whom we have no particular connexion, will give us less concern,
will spoil our stomach, or break our rest much less than a very
insignificant disaster which has befallen ourselves. But though the
ruin of our neighbour may affect us much less than a very small
misfortune of our own, we must not ruin him to prevent that
small misfortune, nor even to prevent our own ruin. We must,
here, as in all other cases, view ourselves not so much according
to that light in which we may naturally appear to ourselves, as
according to that in which we naturally appear to others. Though
every man may, according to the proverb, be the whole world to
himself, to the rest of mankind he is a most insignificant part of
it. Though his own happiness may be of more importance to him
than that of all the world besides, to every other person it is of no
more consequence than that of any other man. Though it may be
true, therefore, that every individual, in his own breast, naturally
prefers himself to all mankind, yet he dares not look mankind in
the face, and avow that he acts according to this principle. He
feels that in this preference they can never go along with him, and
that how natural soever it may be to him, it must always appear

excessive and extravagant to them. When he views himself in the light in which he is conscious that others will view him, he sees that to them he is but one of the multitude in no respect better than any other in it.[6] If he would act so as that the impartial spectator may enter into the principles of his conduct, which is what of all things he has the greatest desire to do, he must, upon this, as upon all other occasions, humble the arrogance of his self-love, and bring it down to something which other men can go along with. They will indulge it so far as to allow him to be more anxious about, and to pursue with more earnest assiduity, his own happiness than that of any other person. Thus far, whenever they place themselves in his situation, they will readily go along with him. In the race for wealth, and honours, and preferments, he may run as hard as he can, and strain every nerve and every muscle, in order to outstrip all his competitors. But if he should justle, or throw down any of them, the indulgence of the spectators is entirely at an end.[7] It is a violation of fair play, which they cannot admit of. This man is to them, in every respect, as good as he: they do not enter into that self-love by which he prefers himself so much to this other, and can not go along with the motive from which he hurt him. They readily, therefore, sympathize with the natural resentment of the injured, and the offender becomes the object of their hatred and indignation. He is sensible that he becomes so, and feels that those sentiments are ready to burst out from all sides against him.

As the greater and more irreparable the evil that is done, the resentment of the sufferer runs naturally the higher; so does likewise the sympathetic indignation of the spectator, as well as the sense of guilt in the agent. Death is the greatest evil which one man can inflict upon another, and excites the highest degree of resentment in those who are immediately connected with the slain. Murder, therefore, is the most atrocious of all crimes which affect individuals only, in the sight both of mankind, and of the person who has committed it. To be deprived of that which we are possessed of, is a greater evil than to be disappointed of what we have only the expectation. Breach of property, therefore, theft and robbery, which take from us what we are possessed of, are greater crimes than breach of contract, which only disappoints us of what we expected. The most sacred laws of justice, therefore, those whose violation seems to call loudest for vengeance and punishment, are the laws which guard the life and person of our neighbour; the next are those which guard his property and possessions; and last of all come those which guard what are called his personal rights, or what is due to him from the promises of others.

The violator of the more sacred laws of justice can never reflect on the sentiments which mankind must entertain with regard to him, without feeling all the agonies of shame, and horror, and consternation. When his passion is gratified, and he begins coolly to reflect on his past conduct, he can enter into none of the motives which influenced it. They appear now as detestable to him as they did always to other people. By sympathizing with the hatred and abhorrence which other men must entertain for him, he becomes in some measure the object of his own hatred and abhorrence. The situation of the person, who suffered by his injustice, now calls upon his pity. He is grieved at the thought of it; regrets the unhappy effects of his own conduct, and feels at the same time that they have rendered him the proper object of the resentment and indignation of mankind, and of what is the natural consequence of resentment, vengeance and punishment. The thought of this perpetually haunts him, and fills him with terror and amazement. He dares no longer look society in the face, but imagines himself as it were rejected, and thrown out from the affections of all mankind. He cannot hope for the consolation of sympathy in this his greatest and most dreadful distress. The remembrance of his crimes has shut out all fellow-feeling with him from the hearts of his fellow-creatures. The sentiments which they entertain with regard to him, are the very thing which he is most afraid of. Every thing seems hostile, and he would be glad to fly to some inhospitable desert, where he might never more behold the face of a human creature, nor read in the countenance of mankind the condemnation of his crimes. But solitude is still more dreadful than society. His own thoughts can present him with nothing but what is black, unfortunate, and disastrous, the melancholy forebodings of incomprehensible misery and ruin. The horror of solitude drives him back into society, and he comes again into the presence of mankind, astonished to appear before them, loaded with shame and distracted with fear, in order to supplicate some little protection from the countenance of those very judges, who he knows have already all unanimously condemned him. Such is the nature of that sentiment, which is properly called remorse; of all the sentiments which can enter the human breast the most dreadful.[8] It is made up of shame from the sense of the impropriety of past conduct; of grief for the effects of it; of pity for those who suffer by it; and of the dread and terror of punishment from the consciousness of the justly-provoked resentment of all rational creatures.

The opposite behaviour naturally inspires the opposite sentiment. The man who, not from frivolous fancy, but from proper motives, has performed a generous action, when he looks forward to those whom he has served, feels himself to be the natural object of their love and gratitude, and, by sympathy with them, of the esteem and approbation of all mankind. And when he looks backward to the motive from which he acted, and surveys it in the light in which the indifferent spectator will survey it, he still continues to enter into it, and applauds himself by sympathy with the approbation of this supposed impartial judge. In both these points of view his own conduct appears to him every way agreeable. His mind, at the thought of it, is filled with cheerfulness, serenity, and composure. He is in friendship and harmony with all mankind, and looks upon his fellow-creatures with confidence and benevolent satisfaction, secure that he has rendered himself worthy of their most favourable regards. In the combination of all these sentiments consists the consciousness of merit, or of deserved reward.

CHAPTER III.

Of the utility of this constitution of Nature.

It is thus that man, who can subsist only in society, was fitted by nature to that situation for which he was made.[9] All the members of human society stand in need of each others assistance, and are likewise exposed to mutual injuries. Where the necessary assistance is reciprocally afforded from love, from gratitude, from friendship, and esteem, the society flourishes and is happy. All the different members of it are bound together by the agreeable bands of love and affection, and are, as it were, drawn to one common centre of mutual good offices.

But though the necessary assistance should not be afforded from such generous and disinterested motives, though among the different members of the society there should be no mutual love and affection, the society, though less happy and agreeable, will not necessarily be dissolved. Society may subsist among different men, as among different merchants, from a sense of its utility, without any mutual love or affection; and though no man in it should owe any obligation, or be bound in gratitude to any other, it may still be upheld by a mercenary exchange of good offices according to an agreed valuation.

Society, however, cannot subsist among those who are at all times ready to hurt and injure one another. The moment that injury begins, the moment that mutual resentment and animosity take place, all the bands of it are broke asunder, and the different members of which it consisted are, as it were, dissipated and scattered abroad by the violence and opposition of their discordant affections. If there is any society among robbers and murderers, they must at least, according to the trite observation, abstain from robbing and murdering one another.[10] Beneficence, therefore, is less essential to the existence of society than justice. Society may subsist, though not in the most comfortable state, without beneficence; but the prevalence of injustice must utterly destroy it.

Though Nature, therefore, exhorts mankind to acts of beneficence, by the pleasing consciousness of deserved reward, she has not thought it necessary to guard and enforce the practice of it by the terrors of merited punishment in case it should be neglected. It is the ornament which embellishes, not the foundation which supports the building, and which it was, therefore, sufficient to recommend, but by no means necessary to impose. Justice, on the contrary, is the main pillar that upholds the whole edifice. If it is removed, the great, the immense fabric of human society, that fabric which to raise and support seems in this world, if I may say so, to have been the peculiar and darling care of Nature, must in a moment crumble into atoms. In order to enforce the observation of justice, therefore, Nature has implanted in the human breast that consciousness of ill desert, those terrors of merited punishment which attend upon its violation, as the great safeguards of the association of mankind, to protect the weak, to curb the violent, and to chastise the guilty. Men, though naturally sympathetic, feel so little for another, with whom they have no particular connexion, in comparison of what they feel for themselves; the misery of one, who is merely their fellow-creature, is of so little importance to them in comparison even of a small conveniency of their own; they have it so much in their power to hurt him, and may have so many temptations to do so, that if this principle did not stand up within them in his defence, and overawe them into a respect for his innocence, they would, like wild beasts, be at all times ready to fly upon him; and a man would enter an assembly of men as he enters a den of lions.

In every part of the universe we observe means adjusted with the nicest artifice to the ends which they are intended to produce; and in the mechanism of a plant, or animal body, admire how every thing is contrived for advancing the two great purposes of nature, the support of the individual, and the propagation of the species. But in these, and in all such objects, we still distinguish the efficient from the final cause of their several motions and organizations. The digestion of the food, the circulation of the blood, and the secretion of the several juices which are drawn from it, are operations all of them necessary for the great purposes of animal life. Yet we never endeavour to account for them from those purposes as from their efficient causes, nor imagine that the blood circulates, or that the food digests of its own accord, and with a view or intention to the purposes of circulation or digestion. The wheels of the watch are all admirably adjusted to the end for which it was made, the pointing of the hour. All their various motions conspire in the nicest manner to produce this effect. If they were endowed with a desire and intention to produce it, they could not do it better. Yet we never ascribe any such desire or intention to them, but to the watch-maker, and we know that they are put into motion by a spring, which intends the effect it produces as little as they do. But though, in accounting for the operations of bodies, we never fail to distinguish in this manner the efficient from the final cause, in accounting for those of the mind we are very apt to confound these two different things with one another.[11] When by natural principles we are led to advance those ends, which a refined and enlightened reason would recommend to us, we are very apt to impute to that reason, as to their efficient cause, the sentiments and actions by which we advance those ends, and to imagine that to be the wisdom of man, which in reality is the wisdom of God. Upon a superficial view, this cause seems sufficient to produce the effects which are ascribed to it; and the system of human nature seems to be more simple and agreeable when all its different operations are in this manner deduced from a single principle.

As society cannot subsist unless the laws of justice are tolerably observed, as no social intercourse can take place among men who do not generally abstain from injuring one another; the consideration of this necessity, it has been thought, was the ground upon which we approved of the enforcement of the laws of justice by the punishment of those who violated them. Man, it has been said, has a natural love for society, and desires that the union of mankind should be preserved for its own sake, and though he himself was to derive no benefit from it. The orderly and flourishing state of society is agreeable to him, and he takes delight in contemplating it. Its disorder and confusion, on the contrary, is the object of his aversion, and he is chagrined at whatever tends to produce it. He is sensible, too, that his own interest is connected with the prosperity of society, and that the happiness, perhaps the preservation of his existence, depends upon its preservation. Upon every account, therefore, he has an abhorrence at whatever can tend to destroy society, and is willing to make use of every means, which can hinder so hated and so dreadful an event. Injustice necessarily tends to destroy it. Every appearance of injustice, therefore, alarms him, and he runs, if I may say so, to stop the progress of what, if allowed to go on, would quickly put an end to every thing that is dear to him. If he cannot restrain it by gentle and fair means, he must beat it down by force and violence, and at any rate must put a stop to its further progress. Hence it is, they say, that he often approves of the enforcement of the laws of justice even by the capital punishment of those who violate them. The disturber of the public peace is hereby removed out of the world, and others are terrified by his fate from imitating his example.[12]

Such is the account commonly given of our approbation of the punishment of injustice. And so far this account is undoubtedly true, that we frequently have occasion to confirm our natural sense of the propriety and fitness of punishment, by reflecting how necessary it is for preserving the order of society. When the guilty is about to suffer that just retaliation, which the natural indignation of mankind tells them is due to his crimes; when the insolence of his injustice is broken and humbled by the terror of his approaching punishment; when he ceases to be an object of fear, with the generous and humane he begins to be an object of pity. The thought of what he is about to suffer extinguishes their resentment for the sufferings of others to which he has given occasion. They are disposed to pardon and forgive him, and to save him from that punishment, which in all their cool hours they had considered as the retribution due to such crimes. Here, therefore, they have occasion to call to their assistance the consideration of the general interest of society. They counterbalance the impulse of this weak and partial humanity by the dictates of a humanity that is more generous and comprehensive. They reflect that mercy to the guilty is cruelty to the innocent, and oppose to the emotions of compassion which they feel for a particular person, a more enlarged compassion which they feel for mankind.

Sometimes too we have occasion to defend the propriety of observing the general rules of justice by the consideration of their necessity to the support of society. We frequently hear the young and the licentious ridiculing the most sacred rules of morality, and professing, sometimes from the corruption, but more frequently from the vanity of their hearts, the most abominable maxims of conduct. Our indignation rouses, and we are eager to refute and expose such detestable principles. But though it is their intrinsic hatefulness and detestableness, which originally inflames us against them, we are unwilling to assign this as the sole reason why we condemn them, or to pretend that it is merely because we ourselves hate and detest them. The reason, we think, would not appear to be conclusive. Yet why should it not; if we hate and detest them because they are the natural and proper objects of hatred and detestation? But when we are asked why we should not act in such or such a manner, the very question seems to suppose that, to those who ask it, this manner of acting does not appear to be for its own sake the natural and proper object of those sentiments. We must show them, therefore, that it ought to be so for the sake of something else. Upon this account we generally cast about for other arguments, and the consideration which first occurs to us, is the disorder and confusion of society which would result from the universal prevalence of such practices. We seldom fail, therefore, to insist upon this topic.

But though it commonly requires no great discernment to see the destructive tendency of all licentious practices to the welfare of society, it is seldom this consideration which first animates us against them. All men, even the most stupid and unthinking, abhor fraud, perfidy, and injustice, and delight to see them punished. But few men have reflected upon the necessity of justice to the existence of society, how obvious soever that necessity may appear to be.

That it is not a regard to the preservation of society, which originally interests us in the punishment of crimes committed against individuals, may be demonstrated by many obvious considerations. The concern which we take in the fortune and happiness of individuals does not, in common cases, arise from that which we take in the fortune and happiness of society. We are no more concerned for the destruction or loss of a single man, because this man is a member or part of society, and because we should be concerned for the destruction of society, than we are concerned for the loss of a single guinea, because this guinea is a part of a thousand guineas, and because we should be concerned for the loss of the whole sum. In neither case does our regard for the individuals arise from our regard for the multitude: but in both cases our regard for the multitude is compounded and made up of the particular regards which we feel for the different individuals of which it is composed. As when a small sum is unjustly taken from us, we do not so much prosecute the injury from a regard to the preservation of our whole fortune, as from a regard to that particular sum which we have lost; so when a single man is injured, or destroyed, we demand the punishment of the wrong that has been done to him, not so much from a concern for the general interest of society, as from a concern for that very individual who has been injured. It is to be observed, however, that this concern does not necessarily include in it any degree of those exquisite sentiments which are commonly called love, esteem, and affection, and by which we distinguish our particular friends and acquaintance. The concern which is requisite for this, is no more than the general fellow-feeling which we have with every man merely because he is our fellow-creature. We enter into the resentment even of an odious person, when he is injured by those to whom he has given no provocation. Our disapprobation of his ordinary character and conduct does not in this case altogether prevent our fellow-feeling with his natural indignation; though with those who are not either extremely candid, or who have not been accustomed to correct and regulate their natural sentiments by general rules, it is very apt to damp it.

Upon some occasions, indeed, we both punish and approve of punishment, merely from a view to the general interest of society, which, we imagine, cannot otherwise be secured. Of this kind are all the punishments inflicted for breaches of what is called either civil police, or military discipline. Such crimes do not immediately or directly hurt any particular person; but their remote consequences, it is supposed, do produce, or might produce, either a considerable inconveniency, or a great disorder in the society. A centinel, for example, who falls asleep upon his watch, suffers death by the laws of war, because such carelessness might endanger the whole army.[13] This severity may, upon many occasions, appear necessary, and, for that reason, just and proper. When the preservation of an individual is inconsistent with the safety of a multitude, nothing can be more just than that the many should be preferred to the one. Yet this punishment, how necessary soever, always appears to be excessively severe. The natural atrocity of the crime seems to be so little, and the punishment so great, that it is with great difficulty that our heart can reconcile itself to it. Though such carelessness appears very blameable, yet the thought of this crime does not naturally excite any such resentment, as would prompt us to take such dreadful revenge. A man of humanity must recollect himself, must make an effort, and exert his whole firmness and resolution, before he can bring himself either to inflict it, or to go along with it when it is inflicted by others. It is not, however, in this manner, that he looks upon the just punishment of an ungrateful murderer or parricide. His heart, in this case, applauds with ardour, and even with transport, the just retaliation which seems due to such detestable crimes, and which, if, by any accident, they should happen to escape, he would be highly enraged and disappointed. The very different sentiments with which the spectator views those different punishments, is a proof that his approbation of the one is far from being founded upon the same principles with that of the other. He looks upon the centinel as an unfortunate victim, who, indeed, must, and ought to be, devoted to the safety of numbers, but whom still, in his heart, he would be glad to save; and he is only sorry, that the interest of the many should oppose it. But if the murderer should escape from punishment, it would excite his highest indignation, and he would call upon God to avenge, in another world, that crime which the injustice of mankind had neglected to chastise upon earth.

For it well deserves to be taken notice of, that we are so far from imagining that injustice ought to be punished in this life, merely on account of the order of society, which cannot otherwise be maintained, that Nature teaches us to hope, and religion, we suppose, authorizes us to expect, that it will be punished even in a life to come. Our sense of its ill desert pursues it, if I may say so, even beyond the grave, though the example of its punishment there cannot serve to deter the rest of mankind, who see it not, who know it not, from being guilty of the like practices here. The justice of God, however, we think, still requires, that he should hereafter avenge the injuries of the widow and the fatherless, who are here so often insulted with impunity. In every religion, and in every superstition that the world has ever beheld, accordingly, there has been a Tartarus as well as an Elysium; a place provided for the punishment of the wicked, as well as one for the reward of the just.[14]

SECTION III.

OF THE INFLUENCE OF FORTUNE UPON THE
SENTIMENTS OF MANKIND, WITH REGARD TO
THE MERIT OR DEMERIT OF ACTIONS.

INTRODUCTION.

Whatever praise or blame can be due to any action, must belong either, first, to the intention or affection of the heart, from which it proceeds; or, secondly, to the external action or movement of the body, which this affection gives occasion to; or, lastly, to the good or bad consequences, which actually, and in fact, proceed from it. These three different things constitute the whole nature and circumstances of the action, and must be the foundation of whatever quality can belong to it.

That the two last of these three circumstances cannot be the foundation of any praise or blame, is abundantly evident; nor has the contrary ever been asserted by any body. The external action or movement of the body is often the same in the most innocent and in the most blameable actions. He who shoots a bird, and he who shoots a man, both of them perform the same external movement: each of them draws the trigger of a gun. The consequences which actually, and in fact, happen to proceed from any action, are, if possible, still more indifferent either to praise or blame, than even the external movement of the body. As they depend, not upon the agent, but upon fortune, they cannot be the proper foundation for any sentiment, of which his character and conduct are the objects.

The only consequences for which he can be answerable, or by which he can deserve either approbation or disapprobation of any kind, are those which were some way or other intended, or those which, at least, show some agreeable or disagreeable quality in the intention of the heart, from which he acted. To the intention or affection of the heart, therefore, to the propriety or impropriety, to the beneficence or hurtfulness of the design, all praise or blame, all approbation or disapprobation, of any kind, which can justly be bestowed upon any action, must ultimately belong.

When this maxim is thus proposed, in abstract and general terms, there is nobody who does not agree to it. Its self-evident justice is acknowledged by all the world, and there is not a dissenting voice among all mankind. Every body allows, that how different soever the accidental the unintended and unforeseen consequences of different actions, yet, if the intentions or affections from which they arose were, on the one hand, equally proper and equally beneficent, or, on the other, equally improper and equally malevolent, the merit or demerit of the actions is still the same, and the agent is equally the suitable object either of gratitude or of resentment.

But how well soever we may seem to be persuaded of the truth of this equitable maxim, when we consider it after this manner, in abstract, yet when we come to particular cases, the actual consequences which happen to proceed from any action, have a very great effect upon our sentiments concerning its merit or demerit, and almost always either enhance or diminish our sense of both. Scarce, in any one instance, perhaps, will our sentiments be found, after examination, to be entirely regulated by this rule, which we all acknowledge ought entirely to regulate them.

This irregularity of sentiment, which every body feels, which scarce any body is sufficiently aware of, and which nobody is willing to acknowledge, I proceed now to explain; and I shall consider, first, the cause which gives occasion to it, or the mechanism by which nature produces it; secondly, the extent of its influence; and, last of all, the end which it answers, or the purpose which the Author of nature seems to have intended by it.

CHAPTER I.

Of the causes of this Influence of Fortune.

The causes of pain and pleasure, whatever they are, or however they operate, seem to be the objects, which, in all animals, immediately excite those two passions of gratitude and resentment. They are excited by inanimated, as well as by animated objects. We are angry, for a moment, even at the stone that hurts us. A child beats it, a dog barks at it, a choleric man is apt to curse it. The least reflection, indeed, corrects this sentiment, and we soon become sensible, that what has no feeling is a very improper object of revenge. When the mischief, however, is very great, the object which caused it becomes disagreeable to us ever after, and we take pleasure to burn or destroy it. We should treat, in this manner, the instrument which had accidentally been the cause of the death of a friend, and we should often think ourselves guilty of a sort of inhumanity, if we neglected to vent this absurd sort of vengeance upon it.

We conceive, in the same manner, a sort of gratitude for those inanimated objects, which have been the causes of great, or frequent pleasure to us. The sailor, who, as soon as he got ashore, should mend his fire with the plank upon which he had just escaped from a shipwreck, would seem to be guilty of an unnatural action. We should expect that he would rather preserve it with care and affection, as a monument that was, in some measure, dear to him. A man grows fond of a snuff-box, of a pen-knife, of a staff which he has long made use of, and conceives something like a real love and affection for them. If he breaks or loses them, he is vexed out of all proportion to the value of the damage. The house which we have long lived in, the tree, whose verdure and shade we have long enjoyed, are both looked upon with a sort of respect that seems due to such benefactors. The decay of the one, or the ruin of the other, affects us with a kind of melancholy, though we should sustain no loss by it. The Dryads and the Lares of the ancients, a sort of genii of trees and houses, were probably first suggested by this sort of affection, which the authors of those superstitions felt for such objects, and which seemed unreasonable, if there was nothing animated about them.[1]

But, before any thing can be the proper object of gratitude or resentment, it must not only be the cause of pleasure or pain, it must likewise be capable of feeling them. Without this other quality, those passions cannot vent themselves with any sort of satisfaction upon it. As they are excited by the causes of pleasure and pain, so their gratification consists in retaliating those sensations upon what gave occasion to them; which it is to no purpose to attempt upon what has no sensibility. Animals, therefore, are less improper objects of gratitude and resentment than inanimated objects. The dog that bites, the ox that gores, are both of them punished. If they have been the causes of the death of any person, neither the public, nor the relations of the slain, can be satisfied, unless they are put to death in their turn: nor is this merely for the security of the living, but, in some measure, to revenge the injury of the dead. Those animals, on the contrary, that have been remarkably serviceable to their masters, become the objects of a very lively gratitude. We are shocked at the brutality of that officer, mentioned in the Turkish Spy, who stabbed the horse that had carried him across an arm of the sea, lest that animal should afterwards distinguish some other person by a similar adventure.[2]

But, though animals are not only the causes of pleasure and pain, but are also capable of feeling those sensations, they are still far from being complete and perfect objects, either of gratitude or resentment; and those passions still feel, that there is something wanting to their entire gratification. What gratitude chiefly desires, is not only to make the benefactor feel pleasure in his turn, but to make him conscious that he meets with this reward on account of his past conduct, to make him pleased with that conduct, and to satisfy him that the person upon whom he bestowed his good offices was not unworthy of them. What most of all charms us in our benefactor, is the concord between his sentiments and our own, with regard to what interests us so nearly as the worth of our own character, and the esteem that is due to us. We are delighted to find a person who values us as we value ourselves, and distinguishes us from the rest of mankind, with an attention not unlike that with which we distinguish ourselves. To maintain in him these agreeable and flattering sentiments, is one of the chief ends proposed by the returns we are disposed to make to him. A generous mind often disdains the interested thought of extorting new favours from its benefactor, by what may be called the importunities of its gratitude. But to preserve and to increase his esteem, is an interest which the greatest mind does not think unworthy of its attention. And this is the foundation of what I formerly observed, that when we cannot enter into the motives of our benefactor, when his conduct and character appear unworthy of our approbation, let his services have been ever so great, our gratitude is always sensibly diminished. We are less flattered by the distinction; and to preserve the esteem of so weak, or so worthless a patron, seems to be an object which does not deserve to be pursued for its own sake.

The object, on the contrary, which resentment is chiefly intent upon, is not so much to make our enemy feel pain in his turn, as to make him conscious that he feels it upon account of his past conduct, to make him repent of that conduct, and to make him sensible, that the person whom he injured did not deserve to be treated in that manner. What chiefly enrages us against the man who injures or insults us, is the little account which he seems to make of us, the unreasonable preference which he gives to himself above us, and that absurd self-love, by which he seems to imagine, that other people may be sacrificed at any time, to his conveniency or his humour. The glaring impropriety of this conduct, the gross insolence and injustice which it seems to involve in it, often shock and exasperate us more than all the mischief which we have suffered. To bring him back to a more just sense of what is due to other people, to make him sensible of what he owes us, and of the wrong that he has done to us, is frequently the principal end proposed in our revenge, which is always imperfect when it cannot accomplish this. When our enemy appears to have done us no injury, when we are sensible that he acted quite properly, that, in his situation, we should have done the same thing, and that we deserved from him all the mischief we met with; in that case, if we have the least spark either of candour or justice, we can entertain no sort of resentment.

Before any thing, therefore, can be the complete and proper object, either of gratitude or resentment, it must possess three different qualifications. First, it must be the cause of pleasure in the one case, and of pain in the other. Secondly, it must be capable of feeling those sensations. And, thirdly, it must not only have produced those sensations, but it must have produced them from design, and from a design that is approved of in the one case, and disapproved of in the other. It is by the first qualification, that any object is capable of exciting those passions: it is by the second, that it is in any respect capable of gratifying them: the third qualification is not only necessary for their complete satisfaction, but as it gives a pleasure or pain that is both exquisite and peculiar, it is likewise an additional exciting cause of those passions.

As what gives pleasure or pain, therefore, either in one way or another, is the sole exciting cause of gratitude and resentment; though the intentions of any person should be ever so proper and beneficent on the one hand, or ever so improper and malevolent on the other; yet, if he has failed in producing either the good or the evil which he intended, as one of the exciting causes is wanting in both cases, less gratitude seems due to him in the one, and less resentment in the other. And, on the contrary, though in the intentions of any person, there was either no laudable degree of benevolence on the one hand, or no blameable degree of malice on the other; yet, if his actions should produce either great good or great evil, as one of the exciting causes takes place upon both these occasions, some gratitude is apt to arise towards him in the one, and some resentment in the other. A shadow of merit seems to fall upon him in the first, a shadow of demerit in the second. And, as the consequences of actions are altogether under the empire of Fortune, hence arises her influence upon the sentiments of mankind with regard to merit and demerit.

CHAPTER II.

Of the extent of this Influence of Fortune.

The effect of this influence of fortune, is, first, to diminish our sense of the merit or demerit of those actions which arose from the most laudable or blameable intentions, when they fail of producing their proposed effects: and, secondly, to increase our sense of the merit or demerit of actions, beyond what is due to the motives or affections from which they proceed, when they accidentally give occasion either to extraordinary pleasure or pain.

1. First, I say, though the intentions of any person should be ever so proper and beneficent, on the one hand, or ever so improper and malevolent, on the other, yet, if they fail in producing their effects, his merit seems imperfect in the one case, and his demerit incomplete in the other. Nor is this irregularity of sentiment felt only by those who are immediately affected by the consequences of any action. It is felt, in some measure, even by the impartial

spectator. The man who solicits an office for another, without obtaining it, is regarded as his friend, and seems to deserve his love and affection. But the man who not only solicits, but procures it, is more peculiarly considered as his patron and benefactor, and is entitled to his respect and gratitude. The person obliged, we are apt to think, may, with some justice, imagine himself on a level with the first: but we cannot enter into his sentiments, if he does not feel himself inferior to the second. It is common indeed to say, that we are equally obliged to the man who has endeavoured to serve us, as to him who actually did so. It is the speech which we constantly make upon every unsuccessful attempt of this kind; but which, like all other fine speeches, must be understood with a grain of allowance. The sentiments which a man of generosity entertains for the friend who fails, may often indeed be nearly the same with those which he conceives for him who succeeds: and the more generous he is, the more nearly will those sentiments approach to an exact level. With the truly generous, to be beloved, to be esteemed by those whom they themselves think worthy of esteem, gives more pleasure, and thereby excites more gratitude, than all the advantages which they can ever expect from those sentiments. When they lose those advantages therefore, they seem to lose but a trifle, which is scarce worth regarding. They still however lose something. Their pleasure therefore, and consequently their gratitude, is not perfectly complete: and accordingly if, between the friend who fails and the friend who succeeds, all other circumstances are equal, there will, even in the noblest and the best mind, be some little difference of affection in favour of him who succeeds. Nay, so unjust are mankind in this respect, that though the intended benefit should be procured, yet if it is not procured by the means of a particular benefactor, they are apt to think that less gratitude is due to the man, who with the best intentions in the world could do no more than help it a little forward. As their gratitude is in this case divided among the different persons who contributed to their pleasure, a smaller share of it seems due to any one. Such a person, we hear men commonly say, intended no doubt to serve us; and we really believe exerted himself to the utmost of his abilities for that purpose. We are not, however, obliged to him for this benefit; since, had it not been for the concurrence of others, all that he could have done would never have brought it about. This consideration, they imagine, should, even in the eyes of the impartial spectator, diminish the debt which they owe to him. The person himself who has unsuccessfully endeavoured to confer a benefit, has by no means the same dependency upon the gratitude of the man whom he meant to oblige, nor the same sense of his own merit towards him, which he would have had in the case of success.

Even the merit of talents and abilities which some accident has hindered from producing their effects, seems in some measure imperfect, even to those who are fully convinced of their capacity to produce them. The general who has been hindered by the envy of ministers from gaining some great advantage over the enemies of his country, regrets the loss of the opportunity for ever after. Nor is it only upon account of the public that he regrets it. He laments that he was hindered from performing an action which would have added a new lustre to his character in his own eyes, as well as in those of every other person. It satisfies neither himself nor others to reflect that the plan or design was all that depended on him, that no greater capacity was required to execute it than what was necessary to concert it: that he was allowed to be every way capable of executing it, and that had he been permitted to go on, success was infallible. He still did not execute it; and though he might deserve all the approbation which is due to a magnanimous and great design, he still wanted the actual merit of having performed a great action. To take the management of any affair of public concern from the man who has almost brought it to a conclusion, is regarded as the most invidious injustice. As he had done so much, he should, we think, have been allowed to acquire the complete merit of putting an end to it. It was objected to Pompey, that he came in upon the victories of Lucullus, and gathered those laurels which were due to the fortune and valour of another. The glory of Lucullus, it seems, was less complete even in the opinion of his own friends, when he was not permitted to finish that conquest which his conduct and courage had put in the power of almost any man to finish. It mortifies an architect when his plans are either not executed at all, or when they are so far altered as to spoil the effect of the building. The plan, however, is all that depends upon the architect. The whole of his genius is, to good judges, as completely discovered in that as in the actual execution. But a plan does not, even to the most intelligent, give the same pleasure as a noble and magnificent building. They may discover as much both of taste and genius in the one as in the other. But their effects are still vastly different, and the amusement derived from the first, never approaches to the wonder and admiration which are sometimes excited by the second. We may believe of many men, that their talents are superior to those of Cæsar and Alexander; and that in the same situations they would perform still greater actions. In the meantime, however, we do not behold them with that astonishment and admiration with which those two heroes have been regarded in all ages and nations. The calm judgments of the mind may approve of them more, but they want the splendour of great actions to dazzle and transport it. The superiority of virtues and talents has not, even upon those who acknowledge that superiority, the same effect with the superiority of atchievements.

As the merit of an unsuccessful attempt to do good seems thus, in the eyes of ungrateful mankind, to be diminished by the miscarriage, so does likewise the demerit of an unsuccessful attempt to do evil. The design to commit a crime, how clearly soever it may be proved, is scarce ever punished with the same severity as the actual commission of it. The case of treason is perhaps the only exception. That crime immediately affecting the being of the government itself, the government is naturally more jealous of it than of any other. In the punishment of treason, the sovereign resents the injuries which are immediately done to himself: in the punishment of other crimes, he resents those which are done to other men. It is his own resentment which he indulges in the one case: it is that of his subjects which by sympathy he enters into in the other. In the first case, therefore, as he judges in his own cause, he is very apt to be more violent and sanguinary in his punishments than the impartial spectator can approve of. His resentment too rises here upon smaller occasions, and does not always, as in other cases, wait for the perpetration of the crime, or even for the attempt to commit it. A treasonable concert, though nothing has been done, or even attempted in consequence of it, nay, a treasonable conversation, is in many countries punished in the same manner as the actual commission of treason.[3]

With regard to all other crimes, the mere design, upon which no attempt has followed, is seldom punished at all, and is never punished severely. A criminal design, and a criminal action, it may be said indeed, do not necessarily suppose the same degree of depravity, and ought not therefore to be subjected to the same punishment. We are capable, it may be said, of resolving, and even of taking measures to execute, many things which, when it comes to the point, we feel ourselves altogether incapable of executing. But this reason can have no place when the design has been carried the length of the last attempt. The man, however, who fires a pistol at his enemy but misses him, is punished with death by the laws of scarce any country. By the old law of Scotland, though he should wound him, yet, unless death ensues within a certain time, the assassin is not liable to the last punishment.[4] The resentment of mankind, however, runs so high against this crime, their terror for the man who shows himself capable of committing it, is so great, that the mere attempt to commit it ought in all countries to be capital. The attempt to commit smaller crimes is almost always punished very lightly, and sometimes is not punished at all. The thief, whose hand has been caught in his neighbour's pocket before he had taken any thing out of it, is punished with ignominy only. If he had got time to take away a handkerchief, he would have been put to death. The house-breaker, who has been found setting a ladder to his neighbour's window, but had not got into it, is not exposed to the capital punishment. The attempt to ravish is not punished as a rape. The attempt to seduce a married woman is not punished at all, though seduction is punished severely. Our resentment against the person who only attempted to do a mischief, is seldom so strong as to bear us out in inflicting the same punishment upon him, which we should have thought due if he had actually done it. In the one case, the joy of our deliverance alleviates our sense of the atrocity of his conduct; in the other, the grief of our misfortune increases it. His real demerit, however, is undoubtedly the same in both cases, since his intentions were equally criminal; and there is in this respect, therefore, an irregularity in the sentiments of all men, and a consequent relaxation of discipline in the laws of, I believe, all nations, of the most civilized, as well as of the most barbarous. The humanity of a civilized people disposes them either to dispense with, or to mitigate punishments wherever their natural indignation is not goaded on by the consequences of the crime. Barbarians, on the other hand, when no actual consequence has happened from any action, are not apt to be very delicate or inquisitive about the motives.

The person himself who either from passion, or from the influence of bad company, has resolved, and perhaps taken measures to perpetrate some crime, but who has fortunately been prevented by an accident which put it out of his power, is sure, if he has any remains of conscience, to regard this event all his life after as a great and signal deliverance. He can never think of it without returning thanks to Heaven for having been thus graciously pleased to save him from the guilt in which he was just ready to plunge himself, and to hinder him from rendering all the rest of his life a scene of horror, remorse, and repentance. But though his hands are innocent, he is conscious that his heart is equally guilty as if he had actually executed what he was so fully resolved upon. It gives great ease to his conscience, however, to consider that the crime was not executed, though he knows that the failure arose from no virtue in him. He still considers himself as less deserving of punishment and resentment; and this good fortune either diminishes, or takes away altogether, all sense of guilt. To remember how much he was resolved upon it, has no other effect than to make him regard his escape as the greater and more miraculous: for he still fancies that he has escaped, and he looks back upon the danger to which his peace of mind was exposed, with that terror, with which one who is in safety may sometimes remember the hazard he was in of falling over a precipice, and shudder with horror at the thought.

2. The second effect of this influence of fortune, is to increase our sense of the merit or demerit of actions beyond what is due to the motives or affection from which they proceed, when they happen to give occasion to extraordinary pleasure or pain. The agreeable or disagreeable effects of the action often throw a shadow of merit or demerit upon the agent, though in his intention there was nothing that deserved either praise or blame, or at least that deserved them in the degree in which we are apt to bestow them. Thus, even the messenger of bad news is disagreeable to us, and, on the contrary, we feel a sort of gratitude for the

man who brings us good tidings. For a moment we look upon them both as the authors, the one of our good, the other of our bad fortune, and regard them in some measure as if they had really brought about the events which they only give an account of. The first author of our joy is naturally the object of a transitory gratitude: we embrace him with warmth and affection, and should be glad, during the instant of our prosperity, to reward him as for some signal service. By the custom of all courts, the officer, who brings the news of a victory, is entitled to considerable preferments, and the general always chuses one of his principal favourites to go upon so agreeable an errand. The first author of our sorrow is, on the contrary, just as naturally the object of a transitory resentment. We can scarce avoid looking upon him with chagrin and uneasiness; and the rude and brutal are apt to vent upon him that spleen which his intelligence gives occasion to. Tigranes, king of Armenia, struck off the head of the man who brought him the first account of the approach of a formidable enemy.[5] To punish in this manner the author of bad tidings, seems barbarous and inhuman: yet, to reward the messenger of good news, is not disagreeable to us; we think it suitable to the bounty of kings. But why do we make this difference, since, if there is no fault in the one, neither is there any merit in the other? It is because any sort of reason seems sufficient to authorize the exertion of the social and benevolent affections; but it requires the most solid and substantial to make us enter into that of the unsocial and malevolent.

But though in general we are averse to enter into the unsocial and malevolent affections, though we lay it down for a rule that we ought never to approve of their gratification, unless so far as the malicious and unjust intention of the person, against whom they are directed, renders him their proper object; yet, upon some occasions, we relax of this severity. When the negligence of one man has occasioned some unintended damage to another, we generally enter so far into the resentment of the sufferer, as to approve of his inflicting a punishment upon the offender much beyond what the offence would have appeared to deserve, had no such unlucky consequence followed from it.

There is a degree of negligence, which would appear to deserve some chastisement though it should occasion no damage to any body. Thus, if a person should throw a large stone over a wall into a public street without giving warning to those who might be passing by, and without regarding where it was likely to fall, he would undoubtedly deserve some chastisement. A very accurate police[6] would punish so absurd an action, even though it had done no mischief. The person who has been guilty of it, shows an insolent contempt of the happiness and safety of others. There is real injustice in his conduct. He wantonly exposes his neighbour to what no man in his senses would chuse to expose himself, and evidently wants that sense of what is due to his fellow-creatures which is the basis of justice and of society. Gross negligence therefore is, in the law, said to be almost equal to malicious design.*[7] When any unlucky consequences happen from such carelessness, the person who has been guilty of it is often punished as if he had really intended those consequences; and his conduct, which was only thoughtless and insolent, and what deserved some chastisement, is considered as atrocious, and as liable to the severest punishment. Thus if, by the imprudent action above mentioned, he should accidentally kill a man, he is, by the laws of many countries, particularly by the old law of Scotland, liable to the last punishment.[8] And though this is no doubt excessively severe, it is not altogether inconsistent with our natural sentiments. Our just indignation against the folly and inhumanity of his conduct is exasperated by our sympathy with the unfortunate sufferer. Nothing, however, would appear more shocking to our natural sense of equity, than to bring a man to the scaffold merely for having thrown a stone carelessly into the street without hurting any body. The folly and inhumanity of his conduct, however, would in this case be the same; but still our sentiments would be very different. The consideration of this difference may satisfy us how much the indignation, even of the spectator, is apt to be animated by the actual consequences of the action. In cases of this kind there will, if I am not mistaken, be found a great degree of severity in the laws of almost all nations; as I have already observed that in those of an opposite kind there was a very general relaxation of discipline.

There is another degree of negligence which does not involve in

---

* Lata culpa prope dolum est.

it any sort of injustice. The person who is guilty of it treats his neighbour as he treats himself, means no harm to any body, and is far from entertaining any insolent contempt for the safety and happiness of others. He is not, however, so careful and circumspect in his conduct as he ought to be, and deserves upon this account some degree of blame and censure, but no sort of punishment. Yet if by a negligence* of this kind he should occasion some damage to another person, he is by the laws of, I believe, all countries, obliged to compensate it. And though this is no doubt a real punishment, and what no mortal would have thought of inflicting upon him, had it not been for the unlucky accident which his conduct gave occasion to; yet this decision of the law is approved of by the natural sentiments of all mankind. Nothing, we think, can be more just than that one man should not suffer by the carelessness of another; and that the damage occasioned by blamable negligence, should be made up by the person who was guilty of it.

There is another species of negligence,† which consists merely in a want of the most anxious timidity and circumspection, with regard to all the possible consequences of our actions. The want of this painful attention, when no bad consequences follow from it, is so far from being regarded as blamable, that the contrary quality is rather considered as such. That timid circumspection which is afraid of every thing, is never regarded as a virtue, but as a quality which more than any other incapacitates for action and business. Yet when, from a want of this excessive care, a person happens to occasion some damage to another, he is often by the law obliged to compensate it. Thus, by the Aquilian law, the man, who not being able to manage a horse that had accidentally taken fright, should happen to ride down his neighbour's slave, is obliged to compensate the damage.[9] When an accident of this kind happens, we are apt to think that he ought not to have rode such a horse, and to regard his attempting it as an unpardonable levity; though without this accident we should not only have made no such reflection, but should have regarded his refusing it as the effect of timid weakness, and of an anxiety about merely possible events, which it is to no purpose to be aware of. The per-

* Culpa levis.   † Culpa levissima.

son himself, who by an accident even of this kind has involuntarily hurt another, seems to have some sense of his own ill desert, with regard to him. He naturally runs up to the sufferer to express his concern for what has happened, and to make every acknowledgment in his power. If he has any sensibility, he necessarily desires to compensate the damage, and to do every thing he can to appease that animal resentment, which he is sensible will be apt to arise in the breast of the sufferer. To make no apology, to offer no atonement, is regarded as the highest brutality. Yet why should he make an apology more than any other person? Why should he, since he was equally innocent with any other bystander, be thus singled out from among all mankind, to make up for the bad fortune of another? This task would surely never be imposed upon him, did not even the impartial spectator feel some indulgence for what may be regarded as the unjust resentment of that other.

Chapter III.

Of the final cause of this Irregularity of Sentiments.

Such is the effect of the good or bad consequences of actions upon the sentiments both of the person who performs them, and of others; and thus, Fortune, which governs the world, has some influence where we should be least willing to allow her any, and directs in some measure the sentiments of mankind, with regard to the character and conduct both of themselves and others. That the world judges by the event, and not by the design, has been in all ages the complaint, and is the great discouragement of virtue. Every body agrees to the general maxim, that as the event does not depend on the agent, it ought to have no influence upon our sentiments, with regard to the merit or propriety of his conduct. But when we come to particulars, we find that our sentiments are scarce in any one instance exactly conformable to what this equitable maxim would direct. The happy or unprosperous event of any action, is not only apt to give us a good or bad opinion of the prudence with which it was conducted, but almost always too animates our gratitude or resentment, our sense of the merit or demerit of the design.

Nature, however, when she implanted the seeds of this irregularity in the human breast, seems, as upon all other occasions, to have intended the happiness and perfection of the species. If the hurtfulness of the design, if the malevolence of the affection, were alone the causes which excited our resentment, we should feel all the furies of that passion against any person in whose breast we suspected or believed such designs or affections were harboured, though they had never broke out into any action. Sentiments, thoughts, intentions, would become the objects of punishment; and if the indignation of mankind run as high against them as against actions; if the baseness of the thought which had given birth to no action, seemed in the eyes of the world as much to call aloud for vengeance as the baseness of the action, every court of judicature would become a real inquisition. There would be no safety for the most innocent and circumspect conduct. Bad wishes, bad views, bad designs, might still be suspected; and while these excited the same indignation with bad conduct, while bad intentions were as much resented as bad actions, they would equally expose the person to punishment and resentment. Actions, therefore, which either produce actual evil, or attempt to produce it, and thereby put us in the immediate fear of it, are by the Author of nature rendered the only proper and approved objects of human punishment and resentment. Sentiments, designs, affections, though it is from these that according to cool reason human actions derive their whole merit or demerit, are placed by the great Judge of hearts beyond the limits of every human jurisdiction, and are reserved for the cognizance of his own unerring tribunal. That necessary rule of justice, therefore, that men in this life are liable to punishment for their actions only, not for their designs and intentions, is founded upon this salutary and useful irregularity in human sentiments concerning merit or demerit, which at first sight appears so absurd and unaccountable. But every part of nature, when attentively surveyed, equally demonstrates the providential care of its Author, and we may admire the wisdom and goodness of God even in the weakness and folly of man.

Nor is that irregularity of sentiments altogether without its utility, by which the merit of an unsuccessful attempt to serve, and much more that of mere good inclinations and kind wishes, appears to be imperfect. Man was made for action, and to promote by the exertion of his faculties such changes in the external circumstances both of himself and others, as may seem most favourable to the happiness of all.[10] He must not be satisfied with indolent benevolence, nor fancy himself the friend of mankind, because in his heart he wishes well to the prosperity of the world. That he may call forth the whole vigour of his soul, and strain every nerve, in order to produce those ends which it is the purpose of his being to advance, Nature has taught him, that neither himself nor mankind can be fully satisfied with his conduct, nor bestow upon it the full measure of applause, unless he has actually produced them. He is made to know, that the praise of good intentions, without the merit of good offices, will be but of little avail to excite either the loudest acclamations of the world, or even the highest degree of self-applause. The man who has performed no single action of importance, but whose whole conversation and deportment express the justest, the noblest, and most generous sentiments, can be entitled to demand no very high reward, even though his inutility should be owing to nothing but the want of an opportunity to serve. We can still refuse it him without blame. We can still ask him, What have you done? What actual service can you produce, to entitle you to so great a recompense? We esteem you, and love you; but we owe you nothing. To reward indeed that latent virtue which has been useless only for want of an opportunity to serve, to bestow upon it those honours and preferments, which, though in some measure it may be said to deserve them, it could not with propriety have insisted upon, is the effect of the most divine benevolence. To punish, on the contrary, for the affections of the heart only, where no crime has been committed, is the most insolent and barbarous tyranny. The benevolent affections seem to deserve most praise, when they do not wait till it becomes almost a crime for them not to exert themselves. The malevolent, on the contrary, can scarce be too tardy, too slow, or deliberate.

It is even of considerable importance, that the evil which is done without design should be regarded as a misfortune to the doer as well as to the sufferer. Man is thereby taught to reverence the

happiness of his brethren, to tremble lest he should, even unknow-
ingly, do any thing that can hurt them, and to dread that animal
resentment which, he feels, is ready to burst out against him, if he
should, without design, be the unhappy instrument of their
calamity.[11] As, in the ancient heathen religion, that holy ground
which had been consecrated to some god, was not to be trod
upon but upon solemn and necessary occasions, and the man
who had even ignorantly violated it, became piacular from that
moment, and, until proper atonement should be made, incurred
the vengeance of that powerful and invisible being to whom it
had been set apart; so, by the wisdom of Nature, the happiness of
every innocent man is, in the same manner, rendered holy, consecrated, and hedged round against the approach of every other
man; not to be wantonly trod upon, not even to be, in any respect,
ignorantly and involuntarily violated, without requiring some
expiation, some atonement in proportion to the greatness of such
undesigned violation. A man of humanity, who accidentally, and
without the smallest degree of blamable negligence, has been
the cause of the death of another man, feels himself piacular,
though not guilty. During his whole life he considers this accident as one of the greatest misfortunes that could have befallen
him. If the family of the slain is poor, and he himself in tolerable
circumstances, he immediately takes them under his protection,
and, without any other merit, thinks them entitled to every degree
of favour and kindness. If they are in better circumstances, he
endeavours by every submission, by every expression of sorrow,
by rendering them every good office which he can devise or they
accept of, to atone for what has happened, and to propitiate, as
much as possible, their, perhaps natural, though no doubt most
unjust resentment, for the great, though involuntary, offence
which he has given them.

The distress which an innocent person feels, who, by some
accident, has been led to do something which, if it had been done
with knowledge and design, would have justly exposed him to
the deepest reproach, has given occasion to some of the finest and
most interesting scenes both of the ancient and of the modern
drama. It is this fallacious sense of guilt, if I may call it so, which
constitutes the whole distress of Œdipus and Jocasta upon the
Greek, of Monimia and Isabella upon the English, theatre.[12] They

are all of them in the highest degree piacular, though not one of them is in the smallest degree guilty.

Notwithstanding, however, all these seeming irregularities of sentiment, if man should unfortunately either give occasion to those evils which he did not intend, or fail in producing that good which he intended, Nature has not left his innocence altogether without consolation, nor his virtue altogether without reward. He then calls to his assistance that just and equitable maxim, That those events which did not depend upon our conduct, ought not to diminish the esteem that is due to us. He summons up his whole magnanimity and firmness of soul, and strives to regard himself, not in the light in which he at present appears, but in that in which he ought to appear, in which he would have appeared had his generous designs been crowned with success, and in which he would still appear, notwithstanding their mis-carriage, if the sentiments of mankind were either altogether can-did and equitable, or even perfectly consistent with themselves. The more candid and humane part of mankind entirely go along with the effort which he thus makes to support himself in his own opinion. They exert their whole generosity and greatness of mind, to correct in themselves this irregularity of human nature, and endeavour to regard his unfortunate magnanimity in the same light in which, had it been successful, they would, without any such generous exertion, have naturally been disposed to con-sider it.

PART III.

OF THE FOUNDATION OF OUR JUDGMENTS

CONCERNING OUR

OWN SENTIMENTS AND CONDUCT, AND OF THE SENSE OF DUTY.

Chapter I.

Of the Principle of Self-approbation and of Self-disapprobation.

In the two foregoing parts of this discourse, I have chiefly considered the origin and foundation of our judgments concerning the sentiments and conduct of others. I come now to consider more particularly the origin of those concerning our own.

The principle by which we naturally either approve or disapprove of our own conduct, seems to be altogether the same with that by which we exercise the like judgments concerning the conduct of other people. We either approve or disapprove of the conduct of another man according as we feel that, when we bring his case home to ourselves, we either can or cannot entirely sympathize with the sentiments and motives which directed it. And, in the same manner, we either approve or disapprove of our own conduct, according as we feel that, when we place ourselves in the situation of another man, and view it, as it were, with his eyes and from his station, we either can or cannot entirely enter into and sympathize with the sentiments and motives which influenced it. We can never survey our own sentiments and motives, we can never form any judgment concerning them, unless we remove ourselves, as it were, from our own natural station, and endeavour to view them as at a certain distance from us. But we can do this in no other way than by endeavouring to view them with the eyes of other people, or as other people are likely to view them. Whatever judgment we can form concerning them, accordingly, must always bear some secret reference, either to what are, or to what, upon a certain condition, would be, or to what, we imagine, ought to be the judgment of others. We endeavour to examine our own conduct as we imagine any other fair and impartial spectator would examine it. If, upon placing ourselves in his situation, we thoroughly enter into all the passions and motives which influenced it, we approve of it, by sympathy with the approbation of this supposed equitable judge. If otherwise, we enter into his disapprobation, and condemn it.

Were it possible that a human creature could grow up to manhood in some solitary place, without any communication with his own species, he could no more think of his own character, of the propriety or demerit of his own sentiments and conduct, of the beauty or deformity of his own mind, than of the beauty or deformity of his own face. All these are objects which he cannot easily see, which naturally he does not look at, and with regard to which he is provided with no mirror which can present them to his view. Bring him into society, and he is immediately provided with the mirror which he wanted before.[1] It is placed in the countenance and behaviour of those he lives with, which always mark when they enter into, and when they disapprove of his sentiments; and it is here that he first views the propriety and impropriety of his own passions, the beauty and deformity of his own mind. To a man who from his birth was a stranger to society, the objects of his passions, the external bodies which either pleased or hurt him, would occupy his whole attention. The passions themselves, the desires or aversions, the joys or sorrows, which those objects excited, though of all things the most immediately present to him, could scarce ever be the objects of his thoughts. The idea of them could never interest him so much as to call upon his attentive consideration. The consideration of his joy could in him excite no new joy, nor that of his sorrow any new sorrow, though the consideration of the causes of those passions might often excite both. Bring him into society, and all his own passions will immediately become the causes of new passions. He will observe that mankind approve of some of them, and are disgusted by others. He will be elevated in the one case, and cast down in the other; his desires and aversions, his joys and sorrows, will now often become the causes of new desires and new aversions, new joys and new sorrows: they will now, therefore, interest him deeply, and often call upon his most attentive consideration.

Our first ideas of personal beauty and deformity, are drawn from the shape and appearance of others, not from our own. We soon become sensible, however, that others exercise the same criticism upon us. We are pleased when they approve of our figure, and are disobliged when they seem to be disgusted. We become anxious to know how far our appearance deserves either their blame or approbation. We examine our persons limb by limb, and by placing ourselves before a looking-glass, or by some such expedient, endeavour, as much as possible, to view ourselves at the distance and with the eyes of other people. If, after this examination, we are satisfied with our own appearance, we can more easily support the most disadvantageous judgments of others. If, on the contrary, we are sensible that we are the natural objects of distaste, every appearance of their disapprobation mortifies us beyond all measure. A man who is tolerably handsome, will allow you to laugh at any little irregularity in his person; but all such jokes are commonly unsupportable to one who is really deformed. It is evident, however, that we are anxious about our own beauty and deformity, only upon account of its effect upon others. If we had no connexion with society, we should be altogether indifferent about either.

In the same manner our first moral criticisms are exercised upon the characters and conduct of other people; and we are all very forward to observe how each of these affects us. But we soon learn, that other people are equally frank with regard to our own. We become anxious to know how far we deserve their censure or applause, and whether to them we must necessarily appear those agreeable or disagreeable creatures which they represent us. We begin, upon this account, to examine our own passions and conduct, and to consider how these must appear to them, by considering how they would appear to us if in their situation. We suppose ourselves the spectators of our own behaviour, and endeavour to imagine what effect it would, in this light, produce upon us. This is the only looking-glass by which we can, in some measure, with the eyes of other people, scrutinize the propriety of our own conduct. If in this view it pleases us, we are tolerably satisfied. We can be more indifferent about the applause, and, in some measure, despise the censure of the world; secure that, however misunderstood or misrepresented, we are the natural and proper objects of approbation. On the contrary, if we are doubtful about it, we are often, upon that very account, more anxious to gain their approbation, and, provided we have not already, as they say, shaken hands with infamy, we are altogether distracted at the thoughts of their censure, which then strikes us with double severity.

When I endeavour to examine my own conduct, when I endeavour to pass sentence upon it, and either to approve or condemn it, it is evident that, in all such cases, I divide myself, as it were, into two persons; and that I, the examiner and judge, represent a different character from that other I, the person whose conduct is examined into and judged of. The first is the spectator, whose sentiments with regard to my own conduct I endeavour to enter into, by placing myself in his situation, and by considering how it would appear to me, when seen from that particular point of view. The second is the agent, the person whom I properly call myself, and of whose conduct, under the character of a spectator, I was endeavouring to form some opinion. The first is the judge; the second the person judged of. But that the judge should, in every respect, be the same with the person judged of, is as impossible, as that the cause should, in every respect, be the same with the effect.

To be amiable and to be meritorious; that is, to deserve love and to deserve reward, are the great characters of virtue; and to be odious and punishable, of vice. But all these characters have an immediate reference to the sentiments of others. Virtue is not said to be amiable, or to be meritorious, because it is the object of its own love, or of its own gratitude; but because it excites those sentiments in other men. The consciousness that it is the object of such favourable regards, is the source of that inward tranquillity and self-satisfaction with which it is naturally attended, as the suspicion of the contrary gives occasion to the torments of vice. What so great happiness as to be beloved, and to know that we deserve to be beloved? What so great misery as to be hated, and to know that we deserve to be hated?

CHAPTER II.

Of the love of Praise, and of that of Praise-worthiness; and of the dread of Blame, and of that of Blame-worthiness.[1]

Man naturally desires, not only to be loved, but to be lovely; or to be that thing which is the natural and proper object of love. He naturally dreads, not only to be hated, but to be hateful; or to be that thing which is the natural and proper object of hatred. He desires, not only praise, but praise-worthiness; or to be that thing which, though it should be praised by nobody, is, however, the natural and proper object of praise. He dreads, not only blame, but blame-worthiness; or to be that thing which, though it should be blamed by nobody, is, however, the natural and proper object of blame.

The love of praise-worthiness is by no means derived altogether from the love of praise. Those two principles, though they resemble one another, though they are connected, and often blended with one another, are yet, in many respects, distinct and independent of one another.

The love and admiration which we naturally conceive for those whose character and conduct we approve of, necessarily dispose us to desire to become ourselves the objects of the like agreeable sentiments, and to be as amiable and as admirable as those whom we love and admire the most. Emulation,[2] the anxious desire that we ourselves should excel, is originally founded in our admiration of the excellence of others. Neither can we be satisfied with being merely admired for what other people are admired. We must at least believe ourselves to be admirable for what they are admirable. But, in order to attain this satisfaction, we must become the impartial spectators of our own character and conduct. We must endeavour to view them with the eyes of other people, or as other people are likely to view them. When seen in this light, if they appear to us as we wish, we are happy and contented. But it greatly confirms this happiness and contentment when we find that other people, viewing them with those very eyes with which we, in imagination only, were endeavouring to view them, see them precisely in the same light in which we ourselves had seen them. Their approbation necessarily confirms our own self-approbation. Their praise necessarily strengthens our own sense of our own praise-worthiness. In this case, so far is the love of praise-worthiness from being derived altogether from that of praise; that the love of praise seems, at least in a great measure; to be derived from that of praise-worthiness.

The most sincere praise can give little pleasure when it cannot be considered as some sort of proof of praise-worthiness. It is by no means sufficient that, from ignorance or mistake, esteem and admiration should, in some way or other, be bestowed upon us. If we are conscious that we do not deserve to be so favourably thought of, and that if the truth were known, we should be regarded with very different sentiments, our satisfaction is far from being complete. The man who applauds us either for actions which we did not perform, or for motives which had no sort of influence upon our conduct, applauds not us, but another person. We can derive no sort of satisfaction from his praises. To us they should be more mortifying than any censure, and should perpetually call to our minds, the most humbling of all reflections, the reflection of what we ought to be, but what we are not. A woman who paints,[3] could derive, one should imagine, but little vanity from the compliments that are paid to her complexion. These, we should expect, ought rather to put her in mind of the sentiments which her real complexion would excite, and mortify her the more by the contrast. To be pleased with such groundless applause is a proof of the most superficial levity and weakness. It is what is properly called vanity, and is the foundation of the most ridiculous and contemptible vices, the vices of affectation and common lying; follies which, if experience did not teach us how common they are, one should imagine the least spark of common sense would save us from. The foolish liar, who endeavours to excite the admiration of the company by the relation of adventures which never had any existence; the important coxcomb, who gives himself airs of rank and distinction which he well knows he has no just pretensions to; are both of them, no doubt, pleased with the applause which they fancy they meet with. But their vanity arises from so gross an illusion of the imagination, that it is difficult to conceive how any rational creature should be imposed upon by it. When they place themselves in the situation of those whom they fancy they have deceived, they are struck with the highest admiration for their own persons. They look upon themselves, not in that light in which, they know, they ought to appear to their companions, but in that in which they believe their companions actually look upon them. Their superficial weakness and trivial folly hinder them from ever turning their eyes inwards, or from seeing themselves in that despicable point of view in which their own consciences must tell them that they would appear to every body, if the real truth should ever come to be known.

As ignorant and groundless praise can give no solid joy, no satisfaction that will bear any serious examination, so, on the contrary, it often gives real comfort to reflect, that though no praise should actually be bestowed upon us, our conduct, however, has been such as to deserve it, and has been in every respect suitable to those measures and rules by which praise and approbation are naturally and commonly bestowed. We are pleased, not only with praise, but with having done what is praise-worthy. We are pleased to think that we have rendered ourselves the natural objects of approbation, though no approbation should ever actually be bestowed upon us: and we are mortified to reflect that we have justly merited the blame of those we live with, though that sentiment should never actually be exerted against us. The man who is conscious to himself that he has exactly observed those measures of conduct which experience informs him are generally agreeable, reflects with satisfaction on the propriety of his own behaviour. When he views it in the light in which the impartial spectator would view it, he thoroughly enters into all the motives which influenced it. He looks back upon every part of it with pleasure and approbation, and though mankind should never be acquainted with what he has done, he regards himself, not so much according to the light in which they actually regard him, as according to that in which they would regard him if they were better informed. He anticipates the applause and admiration which in this case would be bestowed upon him, and he applauds and admires himself by sympathy with sentiments, which do not indeed actually take place, but which the ignorance of the public alone hinders from taking place, which he knows are the natural and ordinary effects of such conduct, which his imagination strongly connects with it, and which he has acquired a habit of conceiving as something that naturally and in propriety ought to follow from it. Men have voluntarily thrown away life to acquire after death a renown which they could no longer enjoy. Their imagination, in the meantime, anticipated that fame which was in future times to be bestowed upon them. Those applauses which they were never to hear rung in their ears; the thoughts of that admiration, whose effects they were never to feel, played about their hearts, banished from their breasts the strongest of all natural fears, and transported them to perform actions which seem almost beyond the reach of human nature. But in point of reality there is surely no great difference between that approbation which is not to be bestowed till we can no longer enjoy it, and that which, indeed, is never to be bestowed, but which would be bestowed, if the world was ever made to understand properly the real circumstances of our behaviour. If the one often produces such violent effects, we cannot wonder that the other should always be highly regarded.

Nature, when she formed man for society, endowed him with an original desire to please, and an original aversion to offend his brethren.[4] She taught him to feel pleasure in their favourable, and pain in their unfavourable regard. She rendered their approbation most flattering and most agreeable to him for its own sake; and their disapprobation most mortifying and most offensive.

But this desire of the approbation, and this aversion to the disapprobation of his brethren, would not alone have rendered him fit for that society for which he was made. Nature, accordingly, has endowed him, not only with a desire of being approved of, but with a desire of being what ought to be approved of; or of being what he himself approves of in other men. The first desire could only have made him wish to appear to be fit for society. The second was necessary in order to render him anxious to be really fit. The first could only have prompted him to the affectation of virtue, and to the concealment of vice. The second was necessary in order to inspire him with the real love of virtue, and with the real abhorrence of vice.[5] In every well-formed mind this second desire seems to be the strongest of the two. It is only the weakest and most superficial of mankind who can be much delighted with that praise which they themselves know to be altogether unmerited. A weak man may sometimes be pleased with it, but a wise man rejects it upon all occasions. But, though a wise man feels little pleasure from praise where he knows there is no praise-worthiness, he often feels the highest in doing what he knows to be praise-worthy, though he knows equally well that no praise is ever to be bestowed upon it. To obtain the approbation of mankind, where no approbation is due, can never be an object of any importance to him. To obtain that approbation where it is really due, may sometimes be an object of no great importance to him. But to be that thing which deserves approbation, must always be an object of the highest.

To desire, or even to accept of praise, where no praise is due, can be the effect only of the most contemptible vanity. To desire it where it is really due, is to desire no more than that a most essential act of justice should be done to us. The love of just fame, of true glory, even for its own sake, and independent of any advantage which he can derive from it, is not unworthy even of a wise man. He sometimes, however, neglects, and even despises it; and he is never more apt to do so than when he has the most perfect assurance of the perfect propriety of every part of his own conduct. His self-approbation, in this case, stands in need of no confirmation from the approbation of other men. It is alone sufficient, and he is contented with it. This self-approbation, if not the only, is at least the principal object, about which he can or ought to be anxious. The love of it, is the love of virtue.

As the love and admiration which we naturally conceive for some characters, dispose us to wish to become ourselves the proper objects of such agreeable sentiments; so the hatred and contempt which we as naturally conceive for others, dispose us, perhaps still more strongly, to dread the very thought of resembling them in any respect. Neither is it, in this case, too, so much the thought of being hated and despised that we are afraid of, as that of being hateful and despicable. We dread the thought of doing any thing which can render us the just and proper objects of the hatred and contempt of our fellow-creatures; even though we had the most perfect security that those sentiments were never actually to be exerted against us. The man who has broke through all those measures of conduct, which can alone render him agreeable to mankind, though he should have the most perfect assurance that what he had done was for ever to be concealed from every human eye, it is all to no purpose. When he looks back upon it, and views it in the light in which the impartial spectator would view it, he finds that he can enter into none of the motives which influenced it. He is abashed and confounded at the thoughts of it, and necessarily feels a very high degree of that shame which he would be exposed to, if his actions should ever come to be generally known. His imagination, in this case too, anticipates the contempt and derision from which nothing saves him but the ignorance of those he lives with. He still feels that he is the natural object of these sentiments, and still trembles at the thought of what he would suffer, if they were ever actually exerted against him. But if what he had been guilty of was not merely one of those improprieties which are the objects of simple disapprobation, but one of those enormous crimes which excite detestation and resentment, he could never think of it, as long as he had any sensibility left, without feeling all the agony of horror and remorse; and though he could be assured that no man was ever to know it, and could even bring himself to believe that there was no God to revenge it, he would still feel enough of both these sentiments to embitter the whole of his life: he would still regard himself as the natural object of the hatred and indignation of all his fellow-creatures; and, if his heart was not grown callous by the habit of crimes, he could not think without terror and astonishment even of the manner in which mankind would look upon him, of what would be the expression of their countenance and of their eyes, if the dreadful truth should ever come to be known. These natural pangs of an affrighted conscience are the daemons, the avenging furies, which, in this life, haunt the guilty, which allow them neither quiet nor repose, which often drive them to despair and distraction, from which no assurance of secrecy can protect them, from which no principles of irreligion can entirely deliver them, and from which nothing can free them but the vilest and most abject of all states, a complete insensibility to honour and infamy, to vice and virtue. Men of the most detestable characters, who, in the execution of the most dreadful crimes, had taken their measures so coolly as to avoid even the suspicion of guilt, have sometimes been driven, by the horror of their situation, to discover, of their own accord, what no human sagacity could ever have investigated. By acknowledging their guilt, by submitting themselves to the resentment of their offended fellow-citizens, and, by thus satiating that vengeance of which they were sensible that they had become the proper objects, they hoped, by their death to reconcile themselves, at least in their own imagination, to the natural sentiments of mankind; to be able to consider themselves as less worthy of hatred and resentment; to atone, in some measure, for their crimes, and, by thus becoming the objects, rather of compassion than of horror, if possible, to die in peace and with the forgiveness of all their fellow-creatures.

Compared to what they felt before the discovery, even the thought of this, it seems, was happiness.

In such cases, the horror of blame-worthiness seems, even in persons who cannot be suspected of any extraordinary delicacy or sensibility of character, completely to conquer the dread of blame. In order to allay that horror, in order to pacify, in some degree, the remorse of their own consciences, they voluntarily submitted themselves both to the reproach and to the punishment which they knew were due to their crimes, but which, at the same time, they might easily have avoided.

They are the most frivolous and superficial of mankind only who can be much delighted with that praise which they themselves know to be altogether unmerited. Unmerited reproach, however, is frequently capable of mortifying very severely even men of more than ordinary constancy. Men of the most ordinary constancy, indeed, easily learn to despise those foolish tales which are so frequently circulated in society, and which, from their own absurdity and falsehood, never fail to die away in the course of a few weeks, or of a few days. But an innocent man, though of more than ordinary constancy, is often, not only shocked, but most severely mortified by the serious, though false, imputation of a crime; especially when that imputation happens unfortunately to be supported by some circumstances which give it an air of probability. He is humbled to find that any body should think so meanly of his character as to suppose him capable of being guilty of it. Though perfectly conscious of his own innocence, the very imputation seems often, even in his own imagination, to throw a shadow of disgrace and dishonour upon his character. His just indignation, too, at so very gross an injury, which, however, it may frequently be improper, and sometimes even impossible to revenge, is itself a very painful sensation. There is no greater tormentor of the human breast than violent resentment which cannot be gratified. An innocent man, brought to the scaffold by the false imputation of an infamous or odious crime, suffers the most cruel misfortune which it is possible for innocence to suffer. The agony of his mind may, in this case, frequently be greater than that of those who suffer for the like crimes, of which they have been actually guilty. Profligate criminals, such as common thieves

and highwaymen, have frequently little sense of the baseness of
their own conduct, and consequently no remorse. Without trou-
bling themselves about the justice or injustice of the punishment,
they have always been accustomed to look upon the gibbet[6] as a
lot very likely to fall to them. When it does fall to them, therefore,
they consider themselves only as not quite so lucky as some of
their companions, and submit to their fortune, without any other
uneasiness than what may arise from the fear of death; a fear
which, even by such worthless wretches, we frequently see, can be
so easily, and so very completely conquered. The innocent man,
on the contrary, over and above the uneasiness which this fear
may occasion, is tormented by his own indignation at the injustice
which has been done to him. He is struck with horror at the
thoughts of the infamy which the punishment may shed upon his
memory, and foresees, with the most exquisite anguish, that he is
hereafter to be remembered by his dearest friends and relations,
not with regret and affection, but with shame, and even with horror for his supposed disgraceful conduct: and the shades of death
appear to close round him with a darker and more melancholy
gloom than naturally belongs to them. Such fatal accidents, for
the tranquillity of mankind, it is to be hoped, happen very rarely
in any country; but they happen sometimes in all countries, even
in those where justice is in general very well administered. The
unfortunate Calas, a man of much more than ordinary constancy
(broke upon the wheel and burnt at Tholouse for the supposed
murder of his own son, of which he was perfectly innocent),
seemed, with his last breath, to deprecate, not so much the cruelty
of the punishment, as the disgrace which the imputation might
bring upon his memory. After he had been broke, and was just
going to be thrown into the fire, the monk, who attended the execution, exhorted him to confess the crime for which he had been
condemned. My Father, said Calas, can you yourself bring yourself to believe that I am guilty?[7]

To persons in such unfortunate circumstances, that humble
philosophy which confines its views to this life, can afford, perhaps, but little consolation. Every thing that could render either
life or death respectable is taken from them. They are condemned
to death and to everlasting infamy. Religion can alone afford
them any effectual comfort. She alone can tell them, that it is of

little importance what man may think of their conduct, while the all-seeing Judge of the world approves of it. She alone can present to them the view of another world; a world of more candour, humanity, and justice, than the present; where their innocence is in due time to be declared, and their virtue to be finally rewarded: and the same great principle which can alone strike terror into triumphant vice, affords the only effectual consolation to disgraced and insulted innocence.

In smaller offences, as well as in greater crimes, it frequently happens that a person of sensibility is much more hurt by the unjust imputation, than the real criminal is by the actual guilt. A woman of gallantry laughs even at the well-founded surmises which are circulated concerning her conduct. The worst-founded surmise of the same kind is a mortal stab to an innocent virgin. The person who is deliberately guilty of a disgraceful action, we may lay it down, I believe, as a general rule, can seldom have much sense of the disgrace; and the person who is habitually guilty of it, can scarce ever have any.

When every man, even of middling understanding, so readily despises unmerited applause, how it comes to pass that unmerited reproach should often be capable of mortifying so severely men of the soundest and best judgment, may, perhaps, deserve some consideration.

Pain, I have already had occasion to observe,[8] is, in almost all cases, a more pungent sensation than the opposite and correspondent pleasure. The one, almost always, depresses us much more below the ordinary, or what may be called the natural state of our happiness, than the other ever raises us above it. A man of sensibility is apt to be more humiliated by just censure than he is ever elavated by just applause. Unmerited applause a wise man rejects with contempt upon all occasions; but he often feels very severely the injustice of unmerited censure. By suffering himself to be applauded for what he has not performed, by assuming a merit which does not belong to him, he feels that he is guilty of a mean falsehood, and deserves, not the admiration, but the contempt of those very persons who, by mistake, had been led to admire him. It may, perhaps, give him some well-founded pleasure to find that he has been, by many people, thought capable of performing what he did not perform. But, though he may be obliged to his friends for their good opinion, he would think himself guilty of the greatest baseness if he did not immediately undeceive them. It gives him little pleasure to look upon himself in the light in which other people actually look upon him, when he is conscious that, if they knew the truth, they would look upon him in a very different light. A weak man, however, is often much delighted with viewing himself in this false and delusive light. He assumes the merit of every laudable action that is ascribed to him, and pretends to that of many which nobody ever thought of ascribing to him. He pretends to have done what he never did, to have written what another wrote, to have invented what another discovered; and is led into all the miserable vices of plagiarism and common lying. But though no man of middling good sense can derive much pleasure from the imputation of a laudable action which he never performed, yet a wise man may suffer great pain from the serious imputation of a crime which he never committed. Nature, in this case, has rendered the pain, not only more pungent than the opposite and correspondent pleasure, but she has rendered it so in a much greater than the ordinary degree. A denial rids a man at once of the foolish and ridiculous pleasure; but it will not always rid him of the pain. When he refuses the merit which is ascribed to him, nobody doubts his veracity. It may be doubted when he denies the crime which he is accused of. He is at once enraged at the falsehood of the imputation, and mortified to find that any credit should be given to it. He feels that his character is not sufficient to protect him. He feels that his brethren, far from looking upon him in that light in which he anxiously desires to be viewed by them, think him capable of being guilty of what he is accused of. He knows perfectly that he has not been guilty. He knows perfectly what he has done; but, perhaps, scarce any man can know perfectly what he himself is capable of doing. What the peculiar constitution of his own mind may or may not admit of, is, perhaps, more or less a matter of doubt to every man. The trust and good opinion of his friends and neighbours, tends more than any thing to relieve him from this most disagreeable doubt; their distrust and unfavourable opinion to increase it. He may think himself very confident that their unfavourable judgment is wrong: but this confidence can seldom be so great as to hinder that judgment from making some impression upon him; and the greater his sensibility, the greater his delicacy, the greater his worth in short, this impression is likely to be the greater.

The agreement or disagreement both of the sentiments and judgments of other people with our own, is, in all cases, it must be observed, of more or less importance to us, exactly in proportion as we ourselves are more or less uncertain about the propriety of our own sentiments, about the accuracy of our own judgments.

A man of sensibility may sometimes feel great uneasiness lest he should have yielded too much even to what may be called an honourable passion; to his just indignation, perhaps, at the injury which may have been done either to himself or to his friend. He is anxiously afraid lest, meaning only to act with spirit, and to do justice, he may, from the too great vehemence of his emotion, have done a real injury to some other person; who, though not innocent, may not have been altogether so guilty as he at first apprehended. The opinion of other people becomes, in this case, of the utmost importance to him. Their approbation is the most healing balsam; their disapprobation, the bitterest and most tormenting poison that can be poured into his uneasy mind. When he is perfectly satisfied with every part of his own conduct, the judgment of other people is often of less importance to him.

There are some very noble and beautiful arts, in which the degree of excellence can be determined only by a certain nicety of taste, of which the decisions, however, appear always, in some measure, uncertain. There are others, in which the success admits, either of clear demonstration, or very satisfactory proof. Among the candidates for excellence in those different arts, the anxiety about the public opinion is always much greater in the former than in the latter.

The beauty of poetry is a matter of such nicety, that a young beginner can scarce ever be certain that he has attained it. Nothing delights him so much, therefore, as the favourable judgments of his friends and of the public; and nothing mortifies him so severely as the contrary. The one establishes, the other shakes, the good opinion which he is anxious to entertain concerning his own performances. Experience and success may in time give him a little more confidence in his own judgment. He is at all times, however, liable to be most severely mortified by the unfavourable judgments of the public. Racine was so disgusted by the indifferent success of his Phædra, the finest tragedy, perhaps, that is extant in any language, that, though in the vigour of his life, and at the height of his abilities, he resolved to write no more for the stage. That great poet used frequently to tell his son, that the most paltry and impertinent criticism had always given him more pain, than the highest and justest eulogy had ever given him pleasure.[9] The extreme sensibility of Voltaire to the slightest censure of the same kind is well known to every body.[10] The Dunciad of Mr. Pope is an everlasting monument of how much the most correct, as well as the most elegant and harmonious of all the English poets, had been hurt by the criticisms of the lowest and most contemptible authors.[11] Gray (who joins to the sublimity of Milton the elegance and harmony of Pope, and to whom nothing is wanting to render him, perhaps, the first poet in the English language, but to have written a little more) is said to have been so much hurt, by a foolish and impertinent parody of two of his finest odes, that he never afterwards attempted any considerable work.[12] Those men of letters who value themselves upon what is called fine writing in prose, approach somewhat to the sensibility of poets.

Mathematicians, on the contrary, who may have the most perfect assurance, both of the truth and of the importance of their discoveries, are frequently very indifferent about the reception which they may meet with from the public. The two greatest mathematicians that I ever have had the honour to be known to, and, I believe, the two greatest that have lived in my time, Dr. Robert Simpson of Glasgow, and Dr. Matthew Stewart of Edinburgh, never seemed to feel even the slightest uneasiness from the neglect with which the ignorance of the public received some of their most valuable works. The great work of Sir Isaac Newton, his *Mathematical Principles of Natural Philosophy*, I have been told, was for several years neglected by the public. The tranquillity of that great man, it is probable, never suffered, upon that account, the interruption of a single quarter of an hour.[13] Natural philosophers, in their independency upon the public opinion, approach nearly to mathematicians, and, in their judgments concerning the merit of their own discoveries and observations, enjoy some degree of the same security and tranquillity.

The morals of those different classes of men of letters are, perhaps, sometimes somewhat affected by this very great difference in their situation with regard to the public.

Mathematicians and natural philosophers, from their independency upon the public opinion, have little temptation to form themselves into factions and cabals, either for the support of their own reputation, or for the depression of that of their rivals. They are almost always men of the most amiable simplicity of manners, who live in good harmony with one another, are the friends of one another's reputation, enter into no intrigue in order to secure the public applause, but are pleased when their works are approved of, without being either much vexed or very angry when they are neglected.

It is not always the same case with poets, or with those who value themselves upon what is called fine writing. They are very apt to divide themselves into a sort of literary factions; each cabal being often avowedly, and almost always secretly, the mortal enemy of the reputation of every other, and employing all the mean arts of intrigue and solicitation to preoccupy the public opinion in favour of the works of its own members, and against those of its enemies and rivals. In France, Despreaux and Racine did not think it below them to set themselves at the head of a literary cabal, in order to depress the reputation, first of Quinault and Perreault, and afterwards of Fontenelle and La Motte, and even to treat the good La Fontaine with a species of most disrespectful kindness.[14] In England, the amiable Mr. Addison did not think it unworthy of his gentle and modest character to set himself at the head of a little cabal of the same kind, in order to keep down the rising reputation of Mr. Pope.[15] Mr. Fontenelle, in writing the lives and characters of the members of the academy of sciences, a society of mathematicians and natural philosophers, has frequent opportunities of celebrating the amiable simplicity of their manners; a quality which, he observes, was so universal among them as to be characteristical, rather of that whole class of men of letters, than of any individual.[16] Mr. D'Alembert, in writing the lives and characters of the members of the French academy, a society of poets and fine writers, or of those who are supposed to be such, seems not to have had such frequent opportunities of making any remark of this kind, and nowhere pretends to represent this amiable quality as characteristical of that class of men of letters whom he celebrates.

Our uncertainty concerning our own merit, and our anxiety to think favourably of it, should together naturally enough make us desirous to know the opinion of other people concerning it; to be more than ordinarily elevated when that opinion is favourable, and to be more than ordinarily mortified when it is otherwise: but they should not make us desirous either of obtaining the favourable, or of avoiding the unfavourable opinion, by intrigue and cabal. When a man has bribed all the judges, the most unanimous decision of the court, though it may gain him his law-suit, cannot give him any assurance that he was in the right: and had he carried on his law-suit merely to satisfy himself that he was in the right, he never would have bribed the judges. But though he wished to find himself in the right, he wished likewise to gain his law-suit; and therefore he bribed the judges. If praise were of no consequence to us, but as a proof of our own praise-worthiness, we never should endeavour to obtain it by unfair means. But, though to wise men it is, at least in doubtful cases, of principal consequence upon this account; it is likewise of some consequence upon its own account: and therefore (we cannot, indeed, upon such occasions, call them wise men, but) men very much above the common level have sometimes attempted both to obtain praise, and to avoid blame, by very unfair means.

Praise and blame express what actually are; praise-worthiness and blame-worthiness, what naturally ought to be the sentiments of other people with regard to our character and conduct. The love of praise is the desire of obtaining the favourable sentiments of our brethren. The love of praise-worthiness is the desire of rendering ourselves the proper objects of those sentiments. So far those two principles resemble and are akin to one another. The like affinity and resemblance take place between the dread of blame and that of blame-worthiness.

The man who desires to do, or who actually does, a praise-worthy action, may likewise desire the praise which is due to it, and sometimes, perhaps, more than is due to it. The two principles are in this case blended together. How far his conduct may have been influenced by the one, and how far by the other, may frequently be unknown even to himself. It must almost always be so to other people. They who are disposed to lessen the merit of his conduct, impute it chiefly or altogether to the mere love of praise, or to what they call mere vanity. They who are disposed to think more favourably of it, impute it chiefly or altogether to the love of praise-worthiness; to the love of what is really honourable and noble in human conduct; to the desire, not merely of obtaining, but of deserving the approbation and applause of his brethren. The imagination of the spectator throws upon it either the one colour or the other, according either to his habits of thinking, or to the favour or dislike which he may bear to the person whose conduct he is considering.

Some splenetic philosophers, in judging of human nature, have done as peevish individuals are apt to do in judging of the conduct of one another, and have imputed to the love of praise, or to what they call vanity, every action which ought to be ascribed to that of praise-worthiness. I shall hereafter have occasion to give an account of some of their systems,[17] and shall not at present stop to examine them.

Very few men can be satisfied with their own private consciousness that they have attained those qualities, or performed those actions, which they admire and think praise-worthy in other people; unless it is, at the same time, generally acknowledged that they possess the one, or have performed the other; or, in other words, unless they have actually obtained that praise which they think due both to the one and to the other. In this respect, however, men differ considerably from one another. Some seem indifferent about the praise, when, in their own minds, they are perfectly satisfied that they have attained the praise-worthiness. Others appear much less anxious about the praise-worthiness than about the praise.

No man can be completely, or even tolerably satisfied, with having avoided every thing blame-worthy in his conduct; unless he has likewise avoided the blame or the reproach. A wise man may frequently neglect praise, even when he has best deserved it; but, in all matters of serious consequence, he will most carefully endeavour so to regulate his conduct as to avoid, not only

blame-worthiness, but, as much as possible, every probable imputation of blame. He will never, indeed, avoid blame by doing any
thing which he judges blame-worthy; by omitting any part of his
duty, or by neglecting any opportunity of doing any thing which
he judges to be really and greatly praise-worthy. But, with these
modifications, he will most anxiously and carefully avoid it. To
show much anxiety about praise, even for praise-worthy actions,
is seldom a mark of great wisdom, but generally of some degree
of weakness. But, in being anxious to avoid the shadow of blame
or reproach, there may be no weakness, but frequently the most
praise-worthy prudence.

"Many people," says Cicero, "despise glory, who are yet most
severely mortified by unjust reproach; and that most inconsistently."[18] This inconsistency, however, seems to be founded in the
unalterable principles of human nature.

The all-wise Author of Nature has, in this manner, taught man
to respect the sentiments and judgments of his brethren; to be
more or less pleased when they approve of his conduct, and to
be more or less hurt when they disapprove of it. He has made
man, if I may say so, the immediate judge of mankind; and has,
in this respect, as in many others, created him after his own
image, and appointed him his vicegerent upon earth, to superintend the behaviour of his brethren.[19] They are taught by nature,
to acknowledge that power and jurisdiction which has thus been
conferred upon him, to be more or less humbled and mortified
when they have incurred his censure, and to be more or less elated
when they have obtained his applause.

But though man has, in this manner, been rendered the immediate judge of mankind, he has been rendered so only in the first
instance; and an appeal lies from his sentence to a much higher
tribunal, to the tribunal of their own consciences, to that of the
supposed impartial and well-informed spectator, to that of the
man within the breast, the great judge and arbiter of their conduct. The jurisdictions of those two tribunals are founded upon
principles which, though in some respects resembling and akin,
are, however, in reality different and distinct. The jurisdiction of
the man without, is founded altogether in the desire of actual
praise, and in the aversion to actual blame. The jurisdiction
of the man within, is founded altogether in the desire of praise-

worthiness, and in the aversion to blame-worthiness; in the desire of possessing those qualities, and performing those actions, which we love and admire in other people; and in the dread of possessing those qualities, and performing those actions, which we hate and despise in other people. If the man without should applaud us, either for actions which we have not performed, or for motives which had no influence upon us; the man within can immediately humble that pride and elevation of mind which such groundless acclamations might otherwise occasion, by telling us, that as we know that we do not deserve them, we render ourselves despicable by accepting them. If, on the contrary, the man without should reproach us, either for actions which we never performed, or for motives which had no influence upon those which we may have performed; the man within may immediately correct this false judgment, and assure us, that we are by no means the proper objects of that censure which has so unjustly been bestowed upon us. But in this and in some other cases, the man within seems sometimes, as it were, astonished and confounded by the vehemence and clamour of the man without. The violence and loudness, with which blame is sometimes poured out upon us, seems to stupify and benumb our natural sense of praise-worthiness and blame-worthiness; and the judgments of the man within, though not, perhaps, absolutely altered or perverted, are, however, so much shaken in the steadiness and firmness of their decision, that their natural effect, in securing the tranquillity of the mind, is frequently in a great measure destroyed. We scarce dare to absolve ourselves, when all our brethren appear loudly to condemn us. The supposed impartial spectator of our conduct seems to give his opinion in our favour with fear and hesitation; when that of all the real spectators, when that of all those with whose eyes and from whose station he endeavours to consider it, is unanimously and violently against us. In such cases, this demigod within the breast appears, like the demigods of the poets, though partly of immortal, yet partly too of mortal extraction. When his judgments are steadily and firmly directed by the sense of praise-worthiness and blame-worthiness, he seems to act suitably to his divine extraction: But when he suffers himself to be astonished and confounded by the judgments of ignorant and weak man, he discovers his connexion with mortality, and appears to act suitably, rather to the human, than to the divine, part of his origin.

In such cases, the only effectual consolation of humbled and afflicted man lies in an appeal to a still higher tribunal, to that of the all-seeing Judge of the world, whose eye can never be deceived, and whose judgments can never be perverted. A firm confidence in the unerring rectitude of this great tribunal, before which his innocence is in due time to be declared, and his virtue to be finally rewarded, can alone support him under the weakness and despondency of his own mind, under the perturbation and astonishment of the man within the breast, whom nature has set up as, in this life, the great guardian, not only of his innocence, but of his tranquillity. Our happiness in this life is thus, upon many occasions, dependent upon the humble hope and expectation of a life to come: a hope and expectation deeply rooted in human nature; which can alone support its lofty ideas of its own dignity; can alone illumine the dreary prospect of its continually approaching mortality, and maintain its cheerfulness under all the heaviest calamities to which, from the disorders of this life, it may sometimes be exposed. That there is a world to come, where exact justice will be done to every man, where every man will be ranked with those who, in the moral and intellectual qualities, are really his equals; where the owner of those humble talents and virtues which, from being depressed by fortune, had, in this life, no opportunity of displaying themselves; which were unknown, not only to the public, but which he himself could scarce be sure that he possessed, and for which even the man within the breast could scarce venture to afford him any distinct and clear testimony; where that modest, silent, and unknown merit, will be placed upon a level, and sometimes above those who, in this world, had enjoyed the highest reputation, and who, from the advantage of their situation, had been enabled to perform the most splendid and dazzling actions; is a doctrine, in every respect so venerable, so comfortable to the weakness, so flattering to the grandeur of human nature, that the virtuous man who has the misfortune to doubt of it, cannot possibly avoid wishing most earnestly and anxiously to believe it. It could never have been exposed to the derision of the scoffer, had not the distribution of rewards and punishments, which some of its most zealous assertors have

taught us was to be made in that world to come, been too frequently in direct opposition to all our moral sentiments.

That the assiduous courtier is often more favoured than the
faithful and active servant; that attendance and adulation are
often shorter and surer roads to preferment than merit or service;
and that a campaign at Versailles or St. James's[20] is often worth
two either in Germany or Flanders, is a complaint which we have
all heard from many a venerable, but discontented, old officer. But
what is considered as the greatest reproach even to the weakness
of earthly sovereigns, has been ascribed, as an act of justice, to
divine perfection; and the duties of devotion, the public and private worship of the Deity, have been represented, even by men of
virtue and abilities, as the sole virtues which can either entitle to
reward or exempt from punishment in the life to come. They
were the virtues, perhaps, most suitable to their station, and
in which they themselves chiefly excelled; and we are all naturally disposed to overrate the excellencies of our own characters.
In the discourse which the eloquent and philosophical Massillon
pronounced, on giving his benediction to the standards of
the regiment of Catinat, there is the following address to the offi-
cers: "What is most deplorable in your situation, Gentlemen, is,
that in a life hard and painful, in which the services and the
duties sometimes go beyond the rigour and severity of the most
austere cloisters; you suffer always in vain for the life to come,
and frequently even for this life. Alas! the solitary monk in his
cell, obliged to mortify the flesh and to subject it to the spirit, is
supported by the hope of an assured recompence, and by the
secret unction of that grace which softens the yoke of the Lord.
But you, on the bed of death, can you dare to represent to Him
your fatigues and the daily hardships of your employment? can
you dare to solicit Him for any recompence? and in all the exertions that you have made, in all the violences that you have done
to yourselves, what is there that He ought to place to His own
account? The best days of your life, however, have been sacrificed to your profession, and ten years service has more worn out
your body, than would, perhaps, have done a whole life of repentance and mortification. Alas! my brother, one single day of those
sufferings, consecrated to the Lord, would, perhaps, have obtained
you an eternal happiness. One single action, painful to nature,

and offered up to Him, would, perhaps, have secured to you the inheritance of the Saints. And you have done all this, and in vain, for this world."[21]

To compare, in this manner, the futile mortifications of a monastery, to the ennobling hardships and hazards of war; to suppose that one day, or one hour, employed in the former should, in the eye of the great Judge of the world, have more merit than a whole life spent honourably in the latter, is surely contrary to all our moral sentiments; to all the principles by which nature has taught us to regulate our contempt or admiration. It is this spirit, however, which, while it has reserved the celestial regions for monks and friars, or for those whose conduct and conversation resembled those of monks and friars, has condemned to the infernal all the heroes, all the statesmen and lawgivers, all the poets and philosophers of former ages; all those who have invented, improved, or excelled in the arts which contribute to the subsistence, to the conveniency, or to the ornament of human life; all the great protectors, instructors, and benefactors of mankind; all those to whom our natural sense of praise-worthiness forces us to ascribe the highest merit and most exalted virtue. Can we wonder that so strange an application of this most respectable doctrine should sometimes have exposed it to contempt and derision; with those at least who had themselves, perhaps, no great taste or turn for the devout and contemplative virtues?*

CHAPTER III.

Of the Influence and Authority of Conscience.

But though the approbation of his own conscience can scarce, upon some extraordinary occasions, content the weakness of man; though the testimony of the supposed impartial spectator, of the great inmate of the breast, cannot always alone support him;

* See Voltaire.

Vous y grillez sage et docte Platon,
Divin Homere, eloquent Ciceron, &c.[22]

yet the influence and authority of this principle is, upon all occasions, very great; and it is only by consulting this judge within, that we can ever see what relates to ourselves in its proper shape and dimensions; or that we can ever make any proper comparison between our own interests and those of other people.

As to the eye of the body, objects appear great or small, not so much according to their real dimensions, as according to the nearness or distance of their situation; so do they likewise to what may be called the natural eye of the mind: and we remedy the defects of both these organs pretty much in the same manner. In my present situation an immense landscape of lawns, and woods, and distant mountains, seems to do no more than cover the little window which I write by, and to be out of all proportion less than the chamber in which I am sitting. I can form a just comparison between those great objects and the little objects around me, in no other way, than by transporting myself, at least in fancy, to a different station, from whence I can survey both at nearly equal distances, and thereby form some judgment of their real proportions. Habit and experience have taught me to do this so easily and so readily, that I am scarce sensible that I do it; and a man must be, in some measure, acquainted with the philosophy of vision, before he can be thoroughly convinced, how little those distant objects would appear to the eye, if the imagination, from a knowledge of their real magnitudes, did not swell and dilate them.[1]

In the same manner, to the selfish and original passions of human nature, the loss or gain of a very small interest of our own, appears to be of vastly more importance, excites a much more passionate joy or sorrow, a much more ardent desire or aversion, than the greatest concern of another with whom we have no particular connexion. His interests, as long as they are surveyed from this station, can never be put into the balance with our own, can never restrain us from doing whatever may tend to promote our own, how ruinous soever to him. Before we can make any proper comparison of those opposite interests, we must change our position. We must view them, neither from our own place nor yet from his, neither with our own eyes nor yet with his, but from the place and with the eyes of a third person, who has no particular connexion with either, and who judges with impartiality between us. Here, too, habit and experience have

taught us to do this so easily and so readily, that we are scarce
sensible that we do it; and it requires, in this case too, some
degree of reflection, and even of philosophy, to convince us, how
little interest we should take in the greatest concerns of our neighbour, how little we should be affected by whatever relates to him,
if the sense of propriety and justice did not correct the otherwise
natural inequality of our sentiments.

Let us suppose that the great empire of China, with all its myr-
iads of inhabitants, was suddenly swallowed up by an earthquake, and let us consider how a man of humanity in Europe,
who had no sort of connexion with that part of the world, would
be affected upon receiving intelligence of this dreadful calamity.[2]
He would, I imagine, first of all, express very strongly his sorrow
for the misfortune of that unhappy people, he would make many
melancholy reflections upon the precariousness of human life,
and the vanity of all the labours of man, which could thus be
annihilated in a moment. He would too, perhaps, if he was a
man of speculation, enter into many reasonings concerning the
effects which this disaster might produce upon the commerce of
Europe, and the trade and business of the world in general. And
when all this fine philosophy was over, when all these humane
sentiments had been once fairly expressed, he would pursue his
business or his pleasure, take his repose or his diversion, with the
same ease and tranquillity, as if no such accident had happened.
The most frivolous disaster which could befal himself would
occasion a more real disturbance. If he was to lose his little finger
to-morrow, he would not sleep to-night; but, provided he never
saw them, he will snore with the most profound security over the
ruin of a hundred millions of his brethren, and the destruction of
that immense multitude seems plainly an object less interesting to
him, than this paltry misfortune of his own.[3] To prevent, therefore, this paltry misfortune to himself, would a man of humanity
be willing to sacrifice the lives of a hundred millions of his brethren, provided he had never seen them? Human nature startles
with horror at the thought, and the world, in its greatest depravity and corruption, never produced such a villain as could be capable of entertaining it. But what makes this difference? When
our passive feelings are almost always so sordid and so selfish,
how comes it that our active principles should often be so gener-

ous and so noble? When we are always so much more deeply
affected by whatever concerns ourselves, than by whatever concerns other men; what is it which prompts the generous, upon all
occasions, and the mean upon many, to sacrifice their own interests to the greater interests of others? It is not the soft power of
humanity, it is not that feeble spark of benevolence which Nature
has lighted up in the human heart, that is thus capable of coun-
teracting the strongest impluses of self-love. It is a stronger power,
a more forcible motive, which exerts itself upon such occasions.
It is reason, principle, conscience, the inhabitant of the breast,
the man within, the great judge and arbiter of our conduct. It is
he who, whenever we are about to act so as to affect the happiness of others, calls to us, with a voice capable of astonishing the
most presumptuous of our passions, that we are but one of the
multitude, in no respect better than any other in it; and that when
we prefer ourselves so shamefully and so blindly to others, we
become the proper objects of resentment, abhorrence, and exe-
cration. It is from him only that we learn the real littleness of
ourselves, and of whatever relates to ourselves, and the natural
misrepresentations of self-love can be corrected only by the eye of
this impartial spectator. It is he who shows us the propriety of
generosity and the deformity of injustice; the propriety of resign-
ing the greatest interests of our own, for the yet greater interests
of others, and the deformity of doing the smallest injury to
another, in order to obtain the greatest benefit to ourselves. It is
not the love of our neighbour, it is not the love of mankind, which
upon many occasions prompts us to the practice of those divine
virtues. It is a stronger love, a more powerful affection, which
generally takes place upon such occasions; the love of what is
honourable and noble, of the grandeur, and dignity, and superiority of our own characters.[4]

When the happiness or misery of others depends in any respect
upon our conduct, we dare not, as self-love might suggest to us,
prefer the interest of one to that of many. The man within immediately calls to us, that we value ourselves too much and other people
too little, and that, by doing so, we render ourselves the proper
object of the contempt and indignation of our brethren.[5] Neither is
this sentiment confined to men of extraordinary magnanimity and
virtue. It is deeply impressed upon every tolerably good soldier,

who feels that he would become the scorn of his companions, if he could be supposed capable of shrinking from danger, or of hesitating, either to expose or to throw away his life, when the good of the service required it.

One individual must never prefer himself so much even to any other individual, as to hurt or injure that other, in order to benefit himself, though the benefit to the one should be much greater than the hurt or injury to the other. The poor man must neither defraud nor steal from the rich, though the acquisition might be much more beneficial to the one than the loss could be hurtful to the other. The man within immediately calls to him, in this case too, that he is no better than his neighbour, and that by this unjust preference he renders himself the proper object of the contempt and indignation of mankind; as well as of the punishment which that contempt and indignation must naturally dispose them to inflict, for having thus violated one of those sacred rules, upon the tolerable observation of which depend the whole security and peace of human society. There is no commonly honest man who does not more dread the inward disgrace of such an action, the indelible stain which it would for ever stamp upon his own mind, than the greatest external calamity which, without any fault of his own, could possibly befal him; and who does not inwardly feel the truth of that great stoical maxim, that for one man to deprive another unjustly of any thing, or unjustly to promote his own advantage by the loss or disadvantage of another, is more contrary to nature, than death, than poverty, than pain, than all the misfortunes which can affect him, either in his body, or in his external circumstances.[6]

When the happiness or misery of others, indeed, in no respect depends upon our conduct, when our interests are altogether separated and detached from theirs, so that there is neither connexion nor competition between them, we do not always think it so necessary to restrain, either our natural, and perhaps, improper anxiety about our own affairs, or our natural, and perhaps, equally improper indifference about those of other men. The most vulgar education teaches us to act, upon all important occasions, with some sort of impartiality between ourselves and others, and even the ordinary commerce of the world is capable of adjusting our active principles to some degree of propriety. But it is the most artificial and refined education only, it has been said, which can correct the inequalities of our passive feelings; and we must for this purpose, it has been pretended, have recourse to the severest, as well as to the profoundest philosophy.

Two different sets of philosophers have attempted to teach us this hardest of all the lessons of morality. One set have laboured to increase our sensibility to the interests of others; another, to diminish that to our own. The first would have us feel for others as we naturally feel for ourselves. The second would have us feel for ourselves as we naturally feel for others. Both, perhaps, have carried their doctrines a good deal beyond the just standard of nature and propriety.

The first are those whining and melancholy moralists, who are perpetually reproaching us with our happiness, while so many of our brethren are in misery,* who regard as impious the natural joy of prosperity, which does not think of the many wretches that are at every instant labouring under all sorts of calamities, in the langour of poverty, in the agony of disease, in the horrors of death, under the insults and oppression of their enemies. Commiseration for those miseries which we never saw, which we never heard of, but which we may be assured are at all times infesting such numbers of our fellow-creatures, ought, they think, to damp the pleasures of the fortunate, and to render a certain melancholy dejection habitual to all men. But first of all, this extreme sympathy with misfortunes which we know nothing about, seems altogether absurd and unreasonable. Take the whole earth at an average, for one man who suffers pain or misery, you will find twenty in prosperity and joy, or at least in tolerable circumstances. No reason, surely, can be assigned why we should rather weep with the one than rejoice with the twenty. This artificial commiseration, besides, is not only absurd, but seems altogether unattainable; and those who affect this character have commonly nothing but a certain affected and sentimental sadness, which, without reaching the heart, serves only to render the countenance and conversation impertinently dismal and disagreeable. And last of all, this

* See Thomson's *Seasons*, Winter:

"Ah! little think the gay licentious proud," &c.
See also Pascal.[7]

disposition of mind, though it could be attained, would be perfectly useless, and could serve no other purpose than to render miserable the person who possessed it. Whatever interest we take in the fortune of those with whom we have no acquaintance or connexion, and who are placed altogether out of the sphere of our activity, can produce only anxiety to ourselves, without any manner of advantage to them. To what purpose should we trouble ourselves about the world in the moon? All men, even those at the greatest distance, are no doubt entitled to our good wishes, and our good wishes we naturally give them. But if, notwithstanding, they should be unfortunate, to give ourselves any anxiety upon that account, seems to be no part of our duty. That we should be but little interested, therefore, in the fortune of those whom we can neither serve nor hurt, and who are in every respect so very remote from us, seems wisely ordered by Nature; and if it were possible to alter in this respect the original constitution of our frame, we could yet gain nothing by the change.

It is never objected to us that we have too little fellow-feeling with the joy of success. Wherever envy does not prevent it, the favour which we bear to prosperity is rather apt to be too great; and the same moralists who blame us for want of sufficient sympathy with the miserable, reproach us for the levity with which we are too apt to admire and almost to worship the fortunate, the powerful, and the rich.

Among the moralists who endeavour to correct the natural inequality of our passive feelings by diminishing our sensibility to what peculiarly concerns ourselves, we may count all the ancient sects of philosophers, but particularly the ancient Stoics. Man, according to the Stoics, ought to regard himself, not as something separated and detached, but as a citizen of the world, a member of the vast commonwealth of nature.[8] To the interest of this great community, he ought at all times to be willing that his own little interest should be sacrificed. Whatever concerns himself, ought to affect him no more than whatever concerns any other equally important part of this immense system. We should view ourselves, not in the light in which our own selfish passions are apt to place us, but in the light in which any other citizen of the world would view us. What befalls ourselves we should regard as what befalls our neighbour, or, what comes to the same thing, as our neighbour regards what befalls us. "When our neighbour," says Epictetus, "loses his wife, or his son, there is nobody who is not sensible that this is a human calamity, a natural event altogether according to the ordinary course of things; but, when the same thing happens to ourselves, then we cry out, as if we had suffered the most dreadful misfortune. We ought, however, to remember how we were affected when this accident happened to another, and such as we were in his case, such ought we to be in our own."[9]

Those private misfortunes, for which our feelings are apt to go beyond the bounds of propriety, are of two different kinds.[10] They are either such as affect us only indirectly, by affecting, in the first place, some other persons who are particularly dear to us; such as our parents, our children, our brothers and sisters, our intimate friends; or they are such as affect ourselves immediately and directly, either in our body, in our fortune, or in our reputation; such as pain, sickness, approaching death, poverty, disgrace, &c.

In misfortunes of the first kind, our emotions may, no doubt, go very much beyond what exact propriety will admit of; but they may likewise fall short of it, and they frequently do so. The man who should feel no more for the death or distress of his own father, or son, than for those of any other man's father or son, would appear neither a good son nor a good father. Such unnatural indifference, far from exciting our applause, would incur our highest disapprobation. Of those domestic affections, however, some are most apt to offend by their excess, and others by their defect. Nature, for the wisest purposes, has rendered, in most men, perhaps in all men, parental tenderness a much stronger affection than filial piety. The continuance and propagation of the species depend altogether upon the former, and not upon the latter. In ordinary cases, the existence and preservation of the child depend altogether upon the care of the parents. Those of the parents seldom depend upon that of the child. Nature, therefore, has rendered the former affection so strong, that it generally requires not to be excited, but to be moderated; and moralists seldom endeavour to teach us how to indulge, but generally how to restrain our fondness, our excessive attachment, the unjust preference which we are disposed to give to our own children above those of other

people. They exhort us, on the contrary, to an affectionate attention to our parents, and to make a proper return to them, in their
old age, for the kindness which they had shown to us in our infancy
and youth. In the Decalogue we are commanded to honour our
fathers and mothers.[11] No mention is made of the love of our children. Nature had sufficiently prepared us for the performance of
this latter duty. Men are seldom accused of affecting to be fonder
of their children than they really are. They have sometimes been
suspected of displaying their piety to their parents with too much
ostentation. The ostentatious sorrow of widows has, for a like
reason, been suspected of insincerity. We should respect, could we
believe it sincere, even the excess of such kind affections; and
though we might not perfectly approve, we should not severely
condemn it. That it appears praise-worthy, at least in the eyes of
those who affect it, the very affectation is a proof.

Even the excess of those kind affections which are most apt to
offend by their excess, though it may appear blameable, never
appears odious. We blame the excessive fondness and anxiety of
a parent, as something which may, in the end, prove hurtful to
the child, and which, in the meantime, is excessively inconvenient
to the parent; but we easily pardon it, and never regard it with
hatred and detestation. But the defect of this usually excessive
affection appears always peculiarly odious. The man who appears
to feel nothing for his own children, but who treats them upon all
occasions with unmerited severity and harshness, seems of all
brutes the most detestable. The sense of propriety, so far from
requiring us to eradicate altogether that extraordinary sensibility, which we naturally feel for the misfortunes of our nearest
connections, is always much more offended by the defect, than it
ever is by the excess of that sensibility. The stoical apathy is, in
such cases, never agreeable, and all the metaphysical sophisms by
which it is supported can seldom serve any other purpose than to
blow up the hard insensibility of a coxcomb to ten times its native
impertinence. The poets and romance writers, who best paint the
refinements and delicacies of love and friendship, and of all other
private and domestic affections, Racine and Voltaire; Richardson, Maurivaux, and Riccoboni; are, in such cases, much better
instructors than Zeno, Chrysippus, or Epictetus.[12]

That moderated sensibility to the misfortunes of others, which does not disqualify us for the performance of any duty; the melancholy and affectionate remembrance of our departed friends; *the pang,* as Gray says, *to secret sorrow dear*; are by no means undelicious sensations.[13] Though they outwardly wear the features of pain and grief, they are all inwardly stamped with the ennobling characters of virtue and self-approbation.

It is otherwise in the misfortunes which affect ourselves immediately and directly, either in our body, in our fortune, or in our reputation. The sense of propriety is much more apt to be offended by the excess, than by the defect of our sensibility, and there are but very few cases in which we can approach too near to the stoical apathy and indifference.

That we have very little fellow-feeling with any of the passions which take their origin from the body, has already been observed.[14] That pain which is occasioned by an evident cause; such as, the cutting or tearing of the flesh; is, perhaps, the affection of the body with which the spectator feels the most lively sympathy. The approaching death of his neighbour, too, seldom fails to affect him a good deal. In both cases, however, he feels so very little in comparison of what the person principally concerned feels, that the latter can scarce ever offend the former by appearing to suffer with too much ease.

The mere want of fortune, mere poverty, excites little compassion. Its complaints are too apt to be the objects rather of contempt than of fellow-feeling.[15] We despise a beggar; and, though his importunities may extort an alms from us, he is scarce ever the object of any serious commiseration. The fall from riches to poverty, as it commonly occasions the most real distress to the sufferer, so it seldom fails to excite the most sincere commiseration in the spectator. Though, in the present state of society, this misfortune can seldom happen without some misconduct, and some very considerable misconduct too, in the sufferer; yet he is almost always so much pitied that he is scarce ever allowed to fall into the lowest state of poverty; but by the means of his friends, frequently by the indulgence of those very creditors who have much reason to complain of his imprudence, is almost always supported in some degree of decent, though humble, mediocrity. To persons under such misfortunes, we could, perhaps, easily pardon some degree of weakness; but, at the same time, they who carry the firmest countenance, who accommodate themselves with the greatest ease to their new situation, who seem to feel no humiliation from the change, but to rest their rank in the society, not upon their fortune, but upon their character and conduct, are always the most approved of, and never fail to command our highest and most affectionate admiration.

As, of all the external misfortunes which can affect an innocent man immediately and directly, the undeserved loss of reputation is certainly the greatest; so a considerable degree of sensibility to whatever can bring on so great a calamity, does not always appear ungraceful or disagreeable. We often esteem a young man the more, when he resents, though with some degree of violence, any unjust reproach that may have been thrown upon his character or his honour. The affliction of an innocent young lady, on account of the groundless surmises which may have been circulated concerning her conduct, appears often perfectly amiable. Persons of an advanced age, whom long experience of the folly and injustice of the world, has taught to pay little regard, either to its censure or to its applause, neglect and despise obloquy, and do not even deign to honour its futile authors with any serious resentment. This indifference, which is founded altogether on a firm confidence in their own well-tried and well-established characters, would be disagreeable in young people, who neither can nor ought to have any such confidence. It might in them be supposed to forebode, in their advancing years, a most improper insensibility to real honour and infamy.

In all other private misfortunes which affect ourselves immediately and directly, we can very seldom offend by appearing to be too little affected. We frequently remember our sensibility to the misfortunes of others with pleasure and satisfaction. We can seldom remember that to our own, without some degree of shame and humiliation.

If we examine the different shades and gradations of weakness and self-command, as we meet with them in common life, we shall very easily satisfy ourselves that this control of our passive feelings must be acquired, not from the abstruse syllogisms of a quibbling dialectic, but from that great discipline which Nature has established for the acquisition of this and of every other virtue; a regard to the sentiments of the real or supposed spectator of our conduct.

A very young child has no self-command; but, whatever are its emotions, whether fear, or grief, or anger, it endeavours always, by the violence of its outcries, to alarm, as much as it can, the attention of its nurse, or of its parents. While it remains under the custody of such partial protectors, its anger is the first and, perhaps, the only passion which it is taught to moderate. By noise and threatening they are, for their own ease, often obliged to frighten it into good temper; and the passion which incites it to attack, is restrained by that which teaches it to attend to its own safety. When it is old enough to go to school, or to mix with its equals, it soon finds that they have no such indulgent partiality. It naturally wishes to gain their favour, and to avoid their hatred or contempt. Regard even to its own safety teaches it to do so; and it soon finds that it can do so in no other way than by moderating, not only its anger, but all its other passions, to the degree which its play-fellows and companions are likely to be pleased with. It thus enters into the great school of self-command, it studies to be more and more master of itself, and begins to exercise over its own feelings a discipline which the practice of the longest life is very seldom sufficient to bring to complete perfection.

In all private misfortunes, in pain, in sickness, in sorrow, the weakest man, when his friend, and still more when a stranger visits him, is immediately impressed with the view in which they are likely to look upon his situation. Their view calls off his attention from his own view; and his breast is, in some measure, becalmed the moment they come into his presence. This effect is produced instantaneously and, as it were, mechanically; but, with a weak man, it is not of long continuance. His own view of his situation immediately recurs upon him. He abandons himself, as before, to sighs and tears and lamentations; and endeavours, like a child that has not yet gone to school, to produce some sort of harmony between his own grief and the compassion of the spectator, not by moderating the former, but by importunately calling upon the latter.

With a man of a little more firmness, the effect is somewhat more permanent. He endeavours, as much as he can, to fix his attention upon the view which the company are likely to take of his situation. He feels, at the same time, the esteem and approbation which they naturally conceive for him when he thus preserves his tranquillity; and, though under the pressure of some recent and great calamity, appears to feel for himself no more than what they really feel for him. He approves and applauds himself by sympathy with their approbation, and the pleasure which he derives from this sentiment supports and enables him more easily to continue this generous effort. In most cases he avoids mentioning his own misfortune; and his company, if they are tolerably well bred, are careful to say nothing which can put him in mind of it. He endeavours to entertain them, in his usual way, upon indifferent subjects, or, if he feels himself strong enough to venture to mention his misfortune, he endeavours to talk of it as, he thinks, they are capable of talking of it, and even to feel it no further than they are capable of feeling it. If he has not, however, been well inured to the hard discipline of self-command, he soon grows weary of this restraint. A long visit fatigues him; and, towards the end of it, he is constantly in danger of doing, what he never fails to do the moment it is over, of abandoning himself to all the weakness of excessive sorrow. Modern good manners, which are extremely indulgent to human weakness, forbid, for some time, the visits of strangers to persons under great family distress, and permit those only of the nearest relations and most intimate friends. The presence of the latter, it is thought, will impose less restraint than that of the former; and the sufferers can more easily accommodate themselves to the feelings of those, from whom they have reason to expect a more indulgent sympathy. Secret enemies, who fancy that they are not known to be such, are frequently fond of making those charitable visits as early as the most intimate friends. The weakest man in the world, in this case, endeavours to support his manly countenance, and, from indignation and contempt of their malice, to behave with as much gaiety and ease as he can.

The man of real constancy and firmness, the wise and just man who has been thoroughly bred in the great school of self-command, in the bustle and business of the world, exposed, perhaps, to the violence and injustice of faction, and to the hardships and hazards of war, maintains this control of his passive feelings upon all occasions; and whether in solitude or in society, wears nearly the same countenance, and is affected very nearly in the same manner. In success and in disappointment, in prosperity and in adversity, before friends and before enemies, he has often been under the necessity of supporting this manhood. He has never dared to forget for one moment the judgment which the impartial spectator would pass upon his sentiments and conduct. He has never dared to suffer the man within the breast to be absent one moment from his attention. With the eyes of this great inmate he has always been accustomed to regard whatever relates to himself. This habit has become perfectly familiar to him. He has been in the constant practice, and, indeed, under the constant necessity, of modelling, or of endeavouring to model, not only his outward conduct and behaviour, but, as much as he can, even his inward sentiments and feelings, according to those of this awful and respectable judge. He does not merely affect the sentiments of the impartial spectator. He really adopts them. He almost identifies himself with, he almost becomes himself that impartial spectator, and scarce even feels but as that great arbiter of his conduct directs him to feel.

The degree of the self-approbation with which every man, upon such occasions, surveys his own conduct, is higher or lower, exactly in proportion to the degree of self-command which is necessary in order to obtain that self-approbation. Where little self-command is necessary, little self-approbation is due. The man who has only scratched his finger, cannot much applaud himself, though he should immediately appear to have forgot this paltry misfortune. The man who has lost his leg by a cannon shot, and who, the moment after, speaks and acts with his usual coolness and tranquillity, as he exerts a much higher degree of self-command, so he naturally feels a much higher degree of self-approbation. With most men, upon such an accident, their own natural view of their own misfortune would force itself upon them with such a vivacity and strength of colouring, as would entirely efface all thought of every other view. They would feel nothing, they could attend to nothing, but their own pain and their own fear; and not only the judgment of the ideal man within the breast, but that of the real spectators who might happen to be present, would be entirely overlooked and disregarded.

The reward which Nature bestows upon good behaviour under

misfortune, is thus exactly proportioned to the degree of that good behaviour. The only compensation she could possibly make for the bitterness of pain and distress is thus too, in equal degrees of good behaviour, exactly proportioned to the degree of that pain and distress. In proportion to the degree of the self-command which is necessary in order to conquer our natural sensibility, the pleasure and pride of the conquest are so much the greater; and this pleasure and pride are so great that no man can be altogether unhappy who completely enjoys them. Misery and wretchedness can never enter the breast in which dwells complete self-satisfaction; and though it may be too much, perhaps, to say, with the Stoics, that, under such an accident as that above mentioned, the happiness of a wise man is in every respect equal to what it could have been under any other circumstances; yet it must be acknowledged, at least, that this complete enjoyment of his own self-applause, though it may not altogether extinguish, must certainly very much alleviate his sense of his own sufferings.

In such paroxysms[16] of distress, if I may be allowed to call them so, the wisest and firmest man, in order to preserve his equanimity, is obliged, I imagine, to make a considerable, and even a painful exertion. His own natural feeling of his own distress, his own natural view of his own situation, presses hard upon him, and he cannot, without a very great effort, fix his attention upon that of the impartial spectator. Both views present themselves to him at the same time. His sense of honour, his regard to his own dignity, directs him to fix his whole attention upon the one view. His natural, his untaught and undisciplined feelings, are continually calling it off to the other. He does not, in this case, perfectly identify himself with the ideal man within the breast, he does not become himself the impartial spectator of his own conduct. The different views of both characters exist in his mind separate and distinct from one another, and each directing him to a behaviour different from that to which the other directs him. When he follows that view which honour and dignity point out to him, Nature does not, indeed, leave him without a recompense. He enjoys his own complete self-approbation, and the applause of every candid and impartial spectator. By her unalterable laws, however, he still suffers; and the recompense which she bestows, though very considerable, is not sufficient completely to compensate the sufferings which those laws inflict. Neither is it fit that it should. If it did completely compensate them, he could, from self-interest, have no motive for avoiding an accident which must necessarily diminish his utility both to himself and to society; and Nature, from her parental care of both, meant that he should anxiously avoid all such accidents. He suffers, therefore, and though, in the agony of the paroxysm, he maintains, not only the manhood of his countenance, but the sedateness and sobriety of his judgment, it requires his utmost and most fatiguing exertions to do so.

By the constitution of human nature, however, agony can never be permanent; and, if he survives the paroxysm, he soon comes, without any effort, to enjoy his ordinary tranquillity. A man with a wooden leg suffers, no doubt, and foresees that he must continue to suffer during the remainder of his life, a very considerable inconveniency. He soon comes to view it, however, exactly as every impartial spectator views it; as an inconveniency under which he can enjoy all the ordinary pleasures both of solitude and of society. He soon identifies himself with the ideal man within the breast, he soon becomes himself the impartial spectator of his own situation. He no longer weeps, he no longer laments, he no longer grieves over it, as a weak man may sometimes do in the beginning. The view of the impartial spectator becomes so perfectly habitual to him, that, without any effort, without any exertion, he never thinks of surveying his misfortune in any other view.

The never-failing certainty with which all men, sooner or later, accommodate themselves to whatever becomes their permanent situation, may, perhaps, induce us to think that the Stoics were, at least, thus far very nearly in the right; that, between one permanent situation and another, there was, with regard to real happiness, no essential difference: or that, if there were any difference, it was no more than just sufficient to render some of them the objects of simple choice or preference; but not of any earnest or anxious desire: and others, of simple rejection, as being fit to be set aside or avoided; but not of any earnest or anxious aversion.[17] Happiness consists in tranquillity and enjoyment. Without tranquillity there can be no enjoyment; and where there is perfect tranquillity there is scarce anything which is not capable of amusing. But in every permanent situation, where there is no expectation of change, the mind of every man, in a longer or shorter time, returns to its natural and usual state of tranquillity. In prosperity, after a certain time, it falls back to that state; in adversity, after a certain time, it rises up to it. In the confinement and solitude of the Bastile, after a certain time, the fashionable and frivolous Count de Lauzun recovered tranquillity enough to be capable of amusing himself with feeding a spider.[18] A mind better furnished would, perhaps, have both sooner recovered its tranquillity, and sooner found, in its own thoughts, a much better amusement.

The great source of both the misery and disorders of human life, seems to arise from over-rating the difference between one permanent situation and another. Avarice over-rates the difference between poverty and riches: ambition, that between a private and a public station: vain-glory, that between obscurity and extensive reputation. The person under the influence of any of those extravagant passions, is not only miserable in his actual situation, but is often disposed to disturb the peace of society, in order to arrive at that which he so foolishly admires. The slightest observation, however, might satisfy him, that, in all the ordinary situations of human life, a well-disposed mind may be equally calm, equally cheerful, and equally contented. Some of those situations may, no doubt, deserve to be preferred to others: but none of them can deserve to be pursued with that passionate ardour which drives us to violate the rules either of prudence or of justice; or to corrupt the future tranquillity of our minds, either by shame from the remembrance of our own folly, or by remorse from the horror of our own injustice. Wherever prudence does not direct, wherever justice does not permit, the attempt to change our situation, the man who does attempt it, plays at the most unequal of all games of hazard, and stakes every thing against scarce any thing. What the favourite of the king of Epirus said to his master, may be applied to men in all the ordinary situations of human life. When the King had recounted to him, in their proper order, all the conquests which he proposed to make, and had come to the last of them; And what does your Majesty propose to do then? said the Favourite.—I propose then, said the King, to enjoy myself with my friends, and endeavour to be good company over a bottle.—And what hinders your Majesty from doing so now?

replied the Favourite.[19] In the most glittering and exalted situation that our idle fancy can hold out to us, the pleasures from which we propose to derive our real happiness, are almost always the same with those which, in our actual, though humble station, we have at all times at hand, and in our power. Except the frivolous pleasures of vanity and superiority, we may find, in the most humble station, where there is only personal liberty, every other which the most exalted can afford; and the pleasures of vanity and superiority are seldom consistent with perfect tranquillity, the principle and foundation of all real and satisfactory enjoyment. Neither is it always certain that, in the splendid situation which we aim at, those real and satisfactory pleasures can be enjoyed with the same security as in the humble one which we are so very eager to abandon. Examine the records of history, recollect what has happened within the circle of your own experience, consider with attention what has been the conduct of almost all the greatly unfortunate, either in private or public life, whom you may have either read of, or heard of, or remember, and you will find that the misfortunes of by far the greater part of them have arisen from their not knowing when they were well, when it was proper for them to sit still and to be contented. The inscription upon the tomb-stone of the man who had endeavoured to mend a tolerable constitution by taking physic; "*I was well, I wished to be better; here I am*"; may generally be applied with great justness to the distress of disappointed avarice and ambition.[20]

It may be thought a singular, but I believe it to be a just observation, that, in the misfortunes which admit of some remedy, the greater part of men do not either so readily or so universally recover their natural and usual tranquillity, as in those which plainly admit of none. In misfortunes of the latter kind, it is chiefly in what may be called the paroxysm, or in the first attack, that we can discover any sensible difference between the sentiments and behaviour of the wise and those of the weak man. In the end, Time, the great and universal comforter, gradually composes the weak man to the same degree of tranquillity which a regard to his own dignity and manhood teaches the wise man to assume in the beginning. The case of the man with the wooden leg is an obvious example of this. In the irreparable misfortunes occasioned by the death of children, or of friends and relations, even a wise man may for some time indulge himself in some degree of moderated sorrow. An affectionate, but weak woman, is often, upon such occasions, almost perfectly distracted. Time, however, in a longer or shorter period, never fails to compose the weakest woman to the same degree of tranquillity as the strongest man. In all the irreparable calamities which affect himself immediately and directly, a wise man endeavours, from the beginning, to anticipate and to enjoy before-hand, that tranquillity which he foresees the course of a few months, or a few years, will certainly restore to him in the end.

In the misfortunes for which the nature of things admits, or seems to admit, of a remedy, but in which the means of applying that remedy are not within the reach of the sufferer, his vain and fruitless attempts to restore himself to his former situation, his continual anxiety for their success, his repeated disappointments upon their miscarriage, are what chiefly hinder him from resuming his natural tranquillity, and frequently render miserable, during the whole of his life, a man to whom a greater misfortune, but which plainly admitted of no remedy, would not have given a fortnight's disturbance. In the fall from royal favour to disgrace, from power to insignificancy, from riches to poverty, from liberty to confinement, from strong health to some lingering, chronical, and perhaps incurable disease, the man who struggles the least, who most easily and readily acquiesces in the fortune which has fallen to him, very soon recovers his usual and natural tranquillity, and surveys the most disagreeable circumstances of his actual situation in the same light, or, perhaps, in a much less unfavourable light, than that in which the most indifferent spectator is disposed to survey them. Faction, intrigue, and cabal, disturb the quiet of the unfortunate statesman. Extravagant projects, visions of gold mines, interrupt the repose of the ruined bankrupt. The prisoner, who is continually plotting to escape from his confinement, cannot enjoy that careless security which even a prison can afford him. The medicines of the physician are often the greatest torment of the incurable patient. The monk who, in order to comfort Joanna of Castile, upon the death of her husband Philip, told her of a King, who, fourteen years after his decease, had been restored to life again, by the prayers of his afflicted queen, was not likely, by his legendary tale, to restore sedateness to the distempered mind of that unhappy Princess. She endeavoured to repeat the same experiment in hopes of the same success; resisted for a long time the burial of her husband, soon after raised his body from the grave, attended it almost constantly herself, and watched, with all the impatient anxiety of frantic expectation, the happy moment when her wishes were to be gratified by the revival of her beloved Philip.*

Our sensibility to the feelings of others, so far from being inconsistent with the manhood of self-command, is the very principle upon which that manhood is founded. The very same principle or instinct which, in the misfortune of our neighbour, prompts us to compassionate his sorrow; in our own misfortune, prompts us to restrain the abject and miserable lamentations of our own sorrow. The same principle or instinct which, in his prosperity and success, prompts us to congratulate his joy; in our own prosperity and success, prompts us to restrain the levity and intemperance of our own joy. In both cases, the propriety of our own sentiments and feelings seems to be exactly in proportion to the vivacity and force with which we enter into and conceive his sentiments and feelings.

The man of the most perfect virtue, the man whom we naturally love and revere the most, is he who joins, to the most perfect command of his own original and selfish feelings, the most exquisite sensibility both to the original and sympathetic feelings of others. The man who, to all the soft, the amiable, and the gentle virtues, joins all the great, the awful, and the respectable, must surely be the natural and proper object of our highest love and admiration.

The person best fitted by nature for acquiring the former of those two sets of virtues, is likewise necessarily best fitted for acquiring the latter. The man who feels the most for the joys and sorrows of others, is best fitted for acquiring the most complete control of his own joys and sorrows. The man of the most exquisite humanity, is naturally the most capable of acquiring the highest degree of self-command. He may not, however, always have acquired it; and it very frequently happens that he has not. He may have lived too much in ease and tranquillity. He may have never been exposed to the violence of faction, or to the hardships

* See Robertson's *Charles V.*, vol. ii. pp. 14 and 15, first edition.[21]

and hazards of war. He may have never experienced the insolence of his superiors, the jealous and malignant envy of his equals, or the pilfering injustice of his inferiors. When, in an advanced age, some accidental change of fortune exposes him to all these, they all make too great an impression upon him. He has the disposition which fits him for acquiring the most perfect self-command; but he has never had the opportunity of acquiring it. Exercise and practice have been wanting; and without these no habit can ever be tolerably established. Hardships, dangers, injuries, misfortunes, are the only masters under whom we can learn the exercise of this virtue. But these are all masters to whom nobody willingly puts himself to school.

The situations in which the gentle virtue of humanity can be most happily cultivated, are by no means the same with those which are best fitted for forming the austere virtue of self-command. The man who is himself at ease can best attend to the distress of others. The man who is himself exposed to hardships is most immediately called upon to attend to, and to control his own feelings. In the mild sunshine of undisturbed tranquillity, in the calm retirement of undissipated and philosophical leisure, the soft virtue of humanity flourishes the most, and is capable of the highest improvement. But, in such situations, the greatest and noblest exertions of self-command have little exercise. Under the boisterous and stormy sky of war and faction, of public tumult and confusion, the sturdy severity of self-command prospers the most, and can be the most successfully cultivated. But, in such situations, the strongest suggestions of humanity must frequently be stifled or neglected; and every such neglect necessarily tends to weaken the principle of humanity. As it may frequently be the duty of a soldier not to take, so it may sometimes be his duty not to give quarter; and the humanity of the man who has been several times under the necessity of submitting to this disagreeable duty, can scarce fail to suffer a considerable diminution. For his own ease, he is too apt to learn to make light of the misfortunes which he is so often under the necessity of occasioning; and the situations which call forth the noblest exertions of self-command, by imposing the necessity of violating sometimes the property, and sometimes the life of our neighbour, always tend to diminish, and too often to extinguish altogether, that sacred regard to both, which is the foundation of justice and humanity. It is upon this account, that we so frequently find in the world men of great humanity who have little self-command, but who are indolent and irresolute, and easily disheart-ened, either by difficulty or danger, from the most honourable pursuits; and, on the contrary, men of the most perfect self-command, whom no difficulty can discourage, no danger appal, and who are at all times ready for the most daring and desperate enterprizes, but who, at the same time, seem to be hardened against all sense either of justice or humanity.

In solitude, we are apt to feel too strongly whatever relates to ourselves: we are apt to overrate the good offices we may have done, and the injuries we may have suffered: we are apt to be too much elated by our own good, and too much dejected by our own bad fortune. The conversation of a friend brings us to a bet-ter, that of a stranger to a still better temper. The man within the breast, the abstract and ideal spectator of our sentiments and conduct, requires often to be awakened and put in mind of his duty, by the presence of the real spectator: and it is always from that spectator, from whom we can expect the least sympathy and indulgence, that we are likely to learn the most complete lesson of self-command.

Are you in adversity? Do not mourn in the darkness of solitude, do not regulate your sorrow according to the indulgent sympathy of your intimate friends; return, as soon as possible, to the day-light of the world and of society. Live with strangers, with those who know nothing, or care nothing about your misfortune; do not even shun the company of enemies; but give yourself the pleasure of mortifying their malignant joy, by making them feel how little you are affected by your calamity, and how much you are above it.

Are you in prosperity? Do not confine the enjoyment of your good fortune to your own house, to the company of your own friends, perhaps of your flatterers, of those who build upon your fortune the hopes of mending their own; frequent those who are independent of you, who can value you only for your character and conduct, and not for your fortune. Neither seek nor shun, neither intrude yourself into nor run away from the society of those who were once your superiors, and who may be hurt at finding you their equal, or, perhaps, even their superior. The impertinence of their pride may, perhaps, render their company too disagreeable: but if it should not, be assured that it is the best company you can possibly keep; and if, by the simplicity of your unassuming demeanour, you can gain their favour and kindness, you may rest satisfied that you are modest enough, and that your head has been in no respect turned by your good fortune.

The propriety of our moral sentiments is never so apt to be corrupted, as when the indulgent and partial spectator is at hand, while the indifferent and impartial one is at a great distance.

Of the conduct of one independent nation towards another, neutral nations are the only indifferent and impartial spectators. But they are placed at so great a distance that they are almost quite out of sight. When two nations are at variance, the citizen of each pays little regard to the sentiments which foreign nations may entertain concerning his conduct. His whole ambition is to obtain the approbation of his own fellow-citizens; and as they are all animated by the same hostile passions which animate himself, he can never please them so much as by enraging and offending their enemies. The partial spectator is at hand: the impartial one at a great distance. In war and negotiation, therefore, the laws of justice are very seldom observed. Truth and fair dealing are almost totally disregarded. Treaties are violated; and the violation, if some advantage is gained by it, sheds scarce any dishonour upon the violator. The ambassador who dupes the minister of a foreign nation, is admired and applauded. The just man who disdains either to take or to give any advantage, but who would think it less dishonourable to give than to take one; the man who, in all private transactions, would be the most beloved and the most esteemed; in those public transactions is regarded as a fool and an idiot, who does not understand his business; and he incurs always the contempt, and sometimes even the detestation of his fellow-citizens. In war, not only what are called the laws of nations, are frequently violated, without bringing (among his own fellow-citizens, whose judgments he only regards) any considerable dishonour upon the violator; but those laws themselves are, the greater part of them, laid down with very little regard to the plainest and most obvious rules of justice. That the innocent, though they may have some connexion or dependency upon the guilty (which, perhaps, they themselves cannot help), should not, upon that account, suffer or be punished for the guilty, is one of the plainest and most obvious rules of justice. In the most unjust war, however, it is commonly the sovereign or the rulers only who are guilty. The subjects are almost always perfectly innocent. Whenever it suits the conveniency of a public enemy, however, the goods of the peaceable citizens are seized both at land and at sea; their lands are laid waste, their houses are burnt, and they themselves, if they presume to make any resistance, are murdered or led into captivity; and all this in the most perfect conformity to what are called the laws of nations.[22]

The animosity of hostile factions, whether civil or ecclesiastical, is often still more furious than that of hostile nations; and their conduct towards one another is often still more atrocious. What may be called the laws of faction have often been laid down by grave authors with still less regard to the rules of justice than what are called the laws of nations. The most ferocious patriot never stated it as a serious question, Whether faith ought to be kept with public enemies? Whether faith ought to be kept with rebels? Whether faith ought to be kept with heretics? are questions which have been often furiously agitated by celebrated doctors both civil and ecclesiastical. It is needless to observe, I presume, that both rebels and heretics are those unlucky persons, who, when things have come to a certain degree of violence, have the misfortune to be of the weaker party. In a nation distracted by faction, there are, no doubt, always a few, though commonly but a very few, who preserve their judgment untainted by the general contagion. They seldom amount to more than, here and there, a solitary individual, without any influence, excluded, by his own candour, from the confidence of either party, and who, though he may be one of the wisest, is necessarily, upon that very account, one of the most insignificant men in the society. All such people are held in contempt and derision, frequently in detestation, by the furious zealots of both parties. A true party-man hates and despises candour; and, in reality, there is no vice which could so effectually disqualify him for the trade of a party-man as that single virtue. The real, revered, and impartial spectator, therefore, is, upon no occasion, at a greater distance than amidst the violence and rage of contending parties. To them, it may be said, that such a spectator scarce exists anywhere in the universe. Even to the great Judge of the universe, they impute all their own prejudices, and often view that Divine Being as animated by all their own vindictive and implacable passions. Of all the corrupters of moral sentiments, therefore, faction and fanaticism have always been by far the greatest.[23]

Concerning the subject of self-command, I shall only observe further, that our admiration for the man who, under the heaviest and most unexpected misfortunes, continues to behave with fortitude and firmness, always supposes that his sensibility to those misfortunes is very great, and such as it requires a very great effort to conquer or command. The man who was altogether insensible to bodily pain, could deserve no applause from enduring the torture with the most perfect patience and equanimity. The man who had been created without the natural fear of death, could claim no merit from preserving his coolness and presence of mind in the midst of the most dreadful dangers. It is one of the extravagancies of Seneca, that the Stoical wise man was, in this respect, superior even to a God; that the security of the God was altogether the benefit of nature, which had exempted him from suffering; but that the security of the wise man was his own benefit, and derived altogether from himself and from his own exertions.[24]

The sensibility of some men, however, to some of the objects which immediately affect themselves, is sometimes so strong as to render all self-command impossible. No sense of honour can control the fears of the man who is weak enough to faint, or to fall into convulsions, upon the approach of danger. Whether such weakness of nerves, as it has been called, may not, by gradual exercise and proper discipline, admit of some cure, may, perhaps, be doubtful. It seems certain that it ought never to be trusted or employed.

CHAPTER IV.

Of the Nature of Self-deceit, and of the Origin and Use of general Rules.

In order to pervert the rectitude of our own judgments concerning the propriety of our own conduct, it is not always necessary that the real and impartial spectator should be at a great distance.

When he is at hand, when he is present, the violence and injustice of our own selfish passions are sometimes sufficient to induce the man within the breast to make a report very different from what the real circumstances of the case are capable of authorising.

There are two different occasions upon which we examine our own conduct, and endeavour to view it in the light in which the impartial spectator would view it: first, when we are about to act; and secondly, after we have acted. Our views are apt to be very partial in both cases; but they are apt to be most partial when it is of most importance that they should be otherwise.

When we are about to act, the eagerness of passion will seldom allow us to consider what we are doing, with the candour of an indifferent person. The violent emotions which at that time agitate us, discolour our views of things, even when we are endeavouring to place ourselves in the situation of another, and to regard the objects that interest us in the light in which they will naturally appear to him. The fury of our own passions constantly calls us back to our own place, where every thing appears magnified and misrepresented by self-love. Of the manner in which those objects would appear to another, of the view which he would take of them, we can obtain, if I may say so, but instantaneous glimpses, which vanish in a moment, and which, even while they last, are not altogether just. We cannot even for that moment divest ourselves entirely of the heat and keenness with which our peculiar situation inspires us, nor consider what we are about to do with the complete impartiality of an equitable judge. The passions, upon this account, as father Malebranche says, all justify themselves, and seem reasonable and proportioned to their objects, as long as we continue to feel them.[1]

When the action is over, indeed, and the passions which prompted it have subsided, we can enter more coolly into the sentiments of the indifferent spectator. What before interested us is now become almost as indifferent to us as it always was to him, and we can now examine our own conduct with his candour and impartiality. The man of to-day is no longer agitated by the same passions which distracted the man of yesterday: and when the paroxysm of emotion, in the same manner as when the paroxysm of distress, is fairly over, we can identify ourselves, as it were, with the ideal man within the breast, and, in our own character, view, as in the one case, our own situation, so in the other, our own conduct, with the severe eyes of the most impartial spectator. But our judgments now are often of little importance in comparison of what they were before; and can frequently produce nothing but vain regret and unavailing repentance; without always securing us from the like errors in time to come. It is seldom, however, that they are quite candid even in this case. The opinion which we entertain of our own character depends entirely on our judgment concerning our past conduct. It is so disagreeable to think ill of ourselves, that we often purposely turn away our view from those circumstances which might render that judgment unfavourable. He is a bold surgeon, they say, whose hand does not tremble when he performs an operation upon his own person; and he is often equally bold who does not hesitate to pull off the mysterious veil of self-delusion, which covers from his view the deformities of his own conduct. Rather than see our own behaviour under so disagreeable an aspect, we too often, foolishly and weakly, endeavour to exasperate anew those unjust passions which had formerly misled us; we endeavour by artifice to awaken our old hatreds, and irritate afresh our almost forgotten resentments: we even exert ourselves for this miserable purpose, and thus persevere in injustice, merely because we once were unjust, and because we are ashamed and afraid to see that we were so.

So partial are the views of mankind with regard to the propriety of their own conduct, both at the time of action and after it; and so difficult is it for them to view it in the light in which any indifferent spectator would consider it. But if it was by a peculiar faculty, such as the moral sense is supposed to be, that they judged of their own conduct, if they were endued with a particular power of perception, which distinguished the beauty or deformity of passions and affections; as their own passions would be more immediately exposed to the view of this faculty, it would judge with more accuracy concerning them, than concerning those of other men, of which it had only a more distant prospect.[2]

This self-deceit, this fatal weakness of mankind, is the source of half the disorders of human life. If we saw ourselves in the light in which others see us, or in which they would see us if they knew all, a reformation would generally be unavoidable. We could not otherwise endure the sight.

Nature, however, has not left this weakness, which is of so much importance, altogether without a remedy; nor has she abandoned us entirely to the delusions of self-love. Our continual observations upon the conduct of others, insensibly lead us to form to ourselves certain general rules concerning what is fit and proper either to be done or to be avoided. Some of their actions shock all our natural sentiments. We hear every body about us express the like detestation against them. This still further confirms, and even exasperates our natural sense of their deformity. It satisfies us that we view them in the proper light, when we see other people view them in the same light. We resolve never to be guilty of the like, nor ever, upon any account, to render ourselves in this manner the objects of universal disapprobation. We thus naturally lay down to ourselves a general rule, that all such actions are to be avoided, as tending to render us odious, contemptible, or punishable, the objects of all those sentiments for which we have the greatest dread and aversion. Other actions, on the contrary, call forth our approbation, and we hear every body around us express the same favourable opinion concerning them. Every body is eager to honour and reward them. They excite all those sentiments for which we have by nature the strongest desire; the love, the gratitude, the admiration of mankind. We become ambitious of performing the like; and thus naturally lay down to ourselves a rule of another kind, that every opportunity of acting in this manner is carefully to be sought after.

It is thus that the general rules of morality are formed. They are ultimately founded upon experience of what, in particular instances, our moral faculties, our natural sense of merit and propriety, approve, or disapprove of. We do not originally approve or condemn particular actions; because, upon examination, they appear to be agreeable or inconsistent with a certain general rule. The general rule, on the contrary, is formed, by finding from experience, that all actions of a certain kind, or circumstanced in a certain manner, are approved or disapproved of. To the man who first saw an inhuman murder, committed from avarice, envy, or unjust resentment, and upon one too that loved and trusted the murderer, who beheld the last agonies of the dying person, who heard him, with his expiring breath, complain more of the perfidy and ingratitude of his false friend, than of the violence which had

been done to him, there could be no occasion, in order to conceive how horrible such an action was, that he should reflect, that
one of the most sacred rules of conduct was what prohibited the
taking away the life of an innocent person, that this was a plain
violation of that rule, and consequently a very blamable action.
His detestation of this crime, it is evident, would arise instantaneously and antecedent to his having formed to himself any such
general rule. The general rule, on the contrary, which he might
afterwards form, would be founded upon the detestation which
he felt necessarily arise in his own breast, at the thought of this,
and every other particular action of the same kind.

When we read in history or romance, the account of actions
either of generosity or of baseness, the admiration which we conceive for the one, and the contempt which we feel for the other,
neither of them arise from reflecting that there are certain general
rules which declare all actions of the one kind admirable, and all
actions of the other contemptible. Those general rules, on the contrary, are all formed from the experience we have had of the effects
which actions of all different kinds naturally produce upon us.

An amiable action, a respectable action, an horrid action, are all
of them actions which naturally excite for the person who performs
them, the love, the respect, or the horror of the spectator. The general rules which determine what actions are, and what are not, the
objects of each of those sentiments, can be formed no other way
than by observing what actions actually and in fact excite them.

When these general rules, indeed, have been formed, when
they are universally acknowledged and established, by the con-
curring sentiments of mankind, we frequently appeal to them as
to the standards of judgment, in debating concerning the degree
of praise or blame that is due to certain actions of a complicated
and dubious nature. They are upon these occasions commonly
cited as the ultimate foundations of what is just and unjust in
human conduct; and this circumstance seems to have misled several very eminent authors, to draw up their systems in such a
manner, as if they had supposed that the original judgments of
mankind with regard to right and wrong, were formed like the
decisions of a court of judicatory, by considering first the general
rule, and then, secondly, whether the particular action under
consideration fell properly within its comprehension.

Those general rules of conduct, when they have been fixed in our mind by habitual reflection, are of great use in correcting the misrepresentations of self-love concerning what is fit and proper to be done in our particular situation. The man of furious resentment, if he was to listen to the dictates of that passion, would perhaps regard the death of his enemy, as but a small compensation for the wrong, he imagines, he has received; which, however, may be no more than a very slight provocation. But his observations upon the conduct of others, have taught him how horrible all such sanguinary revenges appear. Unless his education has been very singular, he has laid it down to himself as an inviolable rule, to abstain from them upon all occasions. This rule preserves its authority with him, and renders him incapable of being guilty of such a violence. Yet the fury of his own temper may be such, that had this been the first time in which he considered such an action, he would undoubtedly have determined it to be quite just and proper, and what every impartial spectator would approve of. But that reverence for the rule which past experience has impressed upon him, checks the impetuosity of his passion, and helps him to correct the too partial views which self-love might otherwise suggest, of what was proper to be done in his situation. If he should allow himself to be so far transported by passion as to violate this rule, yet, even in this case, he cannot throw off altogether the awe and respect with which he has been accustomed to regard it. At the very time of acting, at the moment in which passion mounts the highest, he hesitates and trembles at the thought of what he is about to do: he is secretly conscious to himself that he is breaking through those measures of conduct which, in all his cool hours, he had resolved never to infringe, which he had never seen infringed by others without the highest disapprobation, and of which the infringement, his own mind forebodes, must soon render him the object of the same disagreeable sentiments. Before he can take the last fatal resolution, he is tormented with all the agonies of doubt and uncertainty; he is terrified at the thought of violating so sacred a rule, and at the same time is urged and goaded on by the fury of his desires to violate it. He changes his purpose every moment; sometimes he resolves to adhere to his principle, and not indulge a passion which may corrupt the remaining part of his life with the horrors of shame and repentance; and a momentary calm takes possession of his breast, from the prospect of that security and tranquillity which he will enjoy when he thus determines not to expose himself to the hazard of a contrary conduct. But immediately the passion rouses anew, and with fresh fury drives him on to commit what he had the instant before resolved to abstain from. Wearied and distracted with those continual irresolutions, he at length, from a sort of despair, makes the last fatal and irrecoverable step; but with that terror and amazement with which one flying from an enemy, throws himself over a precipice, where he is sure of meeting with more certain destruction than from any thing that pursues him from behind. Such are his sentiments even at the time of acting; though he is then, no doubt, less sensible of the impropriety of his own conduct than afterwards, when his passion being gratified and palled, he begins to view what he has done in the light in which others are apt to view it; and actually feels, what he had only foreseen very imperfectly before, the stings of remorse and repentance begin to agitate and torment him.

CHAPTER V.

Of the influence and authority of the general Rules of Morality, and that they are justly regarded as the Laws of the Deity.

The regard to those general rules of conduct, is what is properly called a sense of duty, a principle of the greatest consequence in human life, and the only principle by which the bulk of mankind are capable of directing their actions. Many men behave very decently, and through the whole of their lives avoid any considerable degree of blame, who yet, perhaps, never felt the sentiment upon the propriety of which we found our approbation of their conduct, but acted merely from a regard to what they saw were the established rules of behaviour. The man who has received great benefits from another person, may, by the natural coldness of his temper, feel but a very small degree of the sentiment of gratitude. If he has been virtuously educated, however, he will often have been made to observe how odious those actions appear which denote a want of this sentiment, and how amiable the contrary. Though his heart therefore is not warmed with any grateful affection, he will strive to act as if it was, and will endeavour to pay all those regards and attentions to his patron which the liveliest gratitude could suggest. He will visit him regularly; he will behave to him respectfully; he will never talk of him but with expressions of the highest esteem, and of the many obligations which he owes to him. And what is more, he will carefully embrace every opportunity of making a proper return for past services. He may do all this too without any hypocrisy or blamable dissimulation, without any selfish intention of obtaining new favours, and without any design of imposing either upon his benefactor or the public. The motive of his actions may be no other than a reverence for the established rule of duty, a serious and earnest desire of acting, in every respect, according to the law of gratitude. A wife, in the same manner, may sometimes not feel that tender regard for her husband which is suitable to the relation that subsists between them. If she has been virtuously educated, however, she will endeavour to act as if she felt it, to be careful, officious, faithful, and sincere, and to be deficient in none of those attentions which the sentiment of conjugal affection could have prompted her to perform. Such a friend, and such a wife, are neither of them, undoubtedly, the very best of their kinds; and though both of them may have the most serious and earnest desire to fulfil every part of their duty, yet they will fail in many nice and delicate regards, they will miss many opportunities of obliging, which they could never have overlooked if they had possessed the sentiment that is proper to their situation. Though not the very first of their kinds, however, they are perhaps the second; and if the regard to the general rules of conduct has been very strongly impressed upon them, neither of them will fail in any very essential part of their duty. None but those of the happiest mould are capable of suiting, with exact justness, their sentiments and behaviour to the smallest difference of situation, and of acting upon all occasions with the most delicate and accurate propriety. The coarse clay of which the bulk of mankind are formed, cannot be wrought up to such perfection. There is scarce any man, however, who by discipline, education, and example, may not be so impressed with a regard to general rules, as to act upon almost every occasion with tolerable decency, and through the whole of his life to avoid any considerable degree of blame.

Without this sacred regard to general rules, there is no man whose conduct can be much depended upon. It is this which constitutes the most essential difference between a man of principle and honour and a worthless fellow. The one adheres, on all occasions, steadily and resolutely to his maxims, and preserves through the whole of his life one even tenour of conduct. The other, acts variously and accidentally, as humour, inclination, or interest chance to be uppermost. Nay, such are the inequalities of humour to which all men are subject, that without this principle, the man who, in all his cool hours, had the most delicate sensibility to the propriety of conduct, might often be led to act absurdly upon the most frivolous occasions, and when it was scarce possible to assign any serious motive for his behaving in this manner. Your friend makes you a visit when you happen to be in a humour which makes it disagreeable to receive him: in your present mood his civility is very apt to appear an impertinent intrusion; and if you were to give way to the views of things which at this time occur, though civil in your temper, you would behave to him with coldness and contempt. What renders you incapable of such a rudeness, is nothing but a regard to the general rules of civility and hospitality, which prohibit it. That habitual reverence which your former experience has taught you for these, enables you to act, upon all such occasions, with nearly equal propriety, and hinders those inequalities of temper, to which all men are subject, from influencing your conduct in any very sensible degree. But if without regard to these general rules, even the duties of politeness, which are so easily observed, and which one can scarce have any serious motive to violate, would yet be so frequently violated, what would become of the duties of justice, of truth, of chastity, of fidelity, which it is often so difficult to observe, and which there may be so many strong motives to violate? But upon the tolerable observance of these duties, depends the very existence of human society, which would crumble into nothing if mankind were not generally impressed with a reverence for those important rules of conduct.

This reverence is still further enhanced by an opinion which is first impressed by nature, and afterwards confirmed by reasoning and philosophy, that those important rules of morality are the commands and laws of the Deity, who will finally reward the obedient, and punish the transgressors of their duty.

This opinion or apprehension, I say, seems first to be impressed by nature. Men are naturally led to ascribe to those mysterious beings, whatever they are, which happen, in any country, to be the objects of religious fear, all their own sentiments and passions. They have no other, they can conceive no other to ascribe to them. Those unknown intelligences which they imagine but see not, must necessarily be formed with some sort of resemblance to those intelligences of which they have experience. During the ignorance and darkness of pagan superstition, mankind seem to have formed the ideas of their divinities with so little delicacy, that they ascribed to them, indiscriminately, all the passions of human nature, those not excepted which do the least honour to our species, such as lust, hunger, avarice, envy, revenge. They could not fail, therefore, to ascribe to those beings, for the excellence of whose nature they still conceived the highest admiration, those sentiments and qualities which are the great ornaments of humanity, and which seem to raise it to a resemblance of divine perfection, the love of virtue and beneficence, and the abhorrence of vice and injustice. The man who was injured, called upon Jupiter to be witness of the wrong that was done to him, and could not doubt, but that divine being would behold it with the same indignation which would animate the meanest of mankind, who looked on when injustice was committed. The man who did the injury, felt himself to be the proper object of the detestation and resentment of mankind; and his natural fears led him to impute the same sentiments to those awful beings, whose presence he could not avoid, and whose power he could not resist. These natural hopes and fears, and suspicions, were propagated by sympathy, and confirmed by education; and the gods were universally represented and believed to be the rewarders of humanity and mercy, and the avengers of perfidy and injustice. And thus religion, even in its rudest form, gave a sanction to the rules of morality, long before the age of artificial reasoning and philosophy. That the terrors of religion should thus enforce the natural sense of duty, was of too much importance to the happiness of mankind, for nature to leave it dependent upon the slowness and uncertainty of philosophical researches.

These researches, however, when they came to take place, confirmed those original anticipations of nature. Upon whatever we suppose that our moral faculties are founded, whether upon a certain modification of reason, upon an original instinct, called a moral sense, or upon some other principle of our nature, it cannot be doubted, that they were given us for the direction of our conduct in this life. They carry along with them the most evident badges of this authority, which denote that they were set up within us to be the supreme arbiters of all our actions, to superintend all our senses, passions, and appetites, and to judge how far each of them was either to be indulged or restrained. Our moral faculties are by no means, as some have pretended, upon a level in this respect with the other faculties and appetites of our nature, endowed with no more right to restrain these last, than these last are to restrain them. No other faculty or principle of action judges of any other. Love does not judge of resentment, nor resentment of love. Those two passions may be opposite to one another, but cannot, with any propriety, be said to approve or disapprove of one another. But it is the peculiar office of those faculties now under our consideration to judge, to bestow censure or applause upon all the other principles of our nature. They may be considered as a sort of senses of which those principles are the objects. Every sense is supreme over its own objects. There is no appeal from the eye with regard to the beauty of colours, nor from the ear with regard to the harmony of sounds, nor from the taste with regard to the agreeableness of flavours. Each of those senses judges in the last resort of its own objects. Whatever gratifies the taste is sweet, whatever pleases the eye is beautiful, whatever soothes the ear is harmonious. The very essence of each of those qualities consists in its being fitted to please the sense to which it is addressed. It belongs to our moral faculties, in the same manner to determine when the ear ought to be soothed, when the eye ought to be indulged, when the taste ought to be gratified, when and how far every other principle of our nature ought either to be indulged or restrained. What is agreeable to our moral faculties, is fit, and right, and proper to be done; the contrary wrong, unfit, and improper. The sentiments which they approve of, are graceful and becoming: the contrary, ungraceful and unbecoming. The very words, right, wrong, fit, improper, graceful, unbecoming, mean only what pleases or displeases those faculties.

Since these, therefore, were plainly intended to be the governing principles of human nature, the rules which they prescribe are to be regarded as the commands and laws of the Deity, promulgated by those vicegerents[1] which he has thus set up within us. All general rules are commonly denominated laws: thus the general rules which bodies observe in the communication of motion, are called the laws of motion. But those general rules which our moral faculties observe in approving or condemning whatever sentiment or action is subjected to their examination, may much more justly be denominated such. They have a much greater resemblance to what are properly called laws, those general rules which the sovereign lays down to direct the conduct of his subjects. Like them they are rules to direct the free actions of men: they are prescribed most surely by a lawful superior, and are attended too with the sanction of rewards and punishments. Those vicegerents of God within us, never fail to punish the violation of them, by the torments of inward shame, and self-condemnation; and on the contrary, always reward obedience with tranquillity of mind, with contentment, and self-satisfaction.

There are innumerable other considerations which serve to confirm the same conclusion. The happiness of mankind, as well as of all other rational creatures, seems to have been the original purpose intended by the Author of nature, when he brought them into existence. No other end seems worthy of that supreme wisdom and divine benignity which we necessarily ascribe to him; and this opinion, which we are led to by the abstract consideration of his infinite perfections, is still more confirmed by the examination of the works of nature, which seem all intended to promote happiness, and to guard against misery. But by acting according to the dictates of our moral faculties, we necessarily pursue the most effectual means for promoting the happiness of mankind, and may therefore be said, in some sense, to co-operate with the Deity, and to advance as far as in our power the plan of Providence. By acting otherwise, on the contrary, we seem to obstruct, in some measure, the scheme which the Author of nature has established for the happiness and perfection of the world, and to declare ourselves, if I may say so, in some measure the enemies of God. Hence we are naturally encouraged to hope for his extraordinary favour and reward in the one case, and to dread his vengeance and punishment in the other.

There are besides many other reasons, and many other natural principles, which all tend to confirm and inculcate the same salutary doctrine. If we consider the general rules by which external prosperity and adversity are commonly distributed in this life, we shall find, that notwithstanding the disorder in which all things appear to be in this world, yet even here every virtue naturally meets with its proper reward, with the recompense which is most fit to encourage and promote it; and this too so surely, that it requires a very extraordinary concurrence of circumstances entirely to disappoint it. What is the reward most proper for encouraging industry, prudence, and circumspection? Success in every sort of business. And is it possible that in the whole of life these virtues should fail of attaining it? Wealth and external honours are their proper recompense, and the recompense which they can seldom fail of acquiring. What reward is most proper for promoting the practice of truth, justice, and humanity? The confidence, the esteem, and love of those we live with. Humanity does not desire to be great, but to be beloved. It is not in being rich that truth and justice would rejoice, but in being trusted and believed, recompenses which those virtues must almost always acquire. By some very extraordinary and unlucky circumstance, a good man may come to be suspected of a crime of which he was altogether incapable, and upon that account be most unjustly exposed for the remaining part of his life to the horror and aversion of mankind. By an accident of this kind he may be said to lose his all, notwithstanding his integrity and justice; in the same manner as a cautious man, notwithstanding his utmost circumspection, may be ruined by an earthquake or an inundation. Accidents of the first kind, however, are perhaps still more rare, and still more contrary to the common course of things than those of the second; and it still remains true, that the practice of truth, justice, and humanity is a certain and almost infallible method of acquiring what those virtues chiefly aim at, the confidence and love of those we live with.

A person may be very easily misrepresented with regard to a particular action; but it is scarce possible that he should be so with regard to the general tenor of his conduct. An innocent man may be believed to have done wrong: this, however, will rarely happen. On the contrary, the established opinion of the innocence of his manners, will often lead us to absolve him where he has really been in the fault, notwithstanding very strong presumptions. A knave, in the same manner, may escape censure, or even meet with applause, for a particular knavery, in which his conduct is not understood.[2] But no man was ever habitually such, without being almost universally known to be so, and without being even frequently suspected of guilt, when he was in reality perfectly innocent. And so far as vice and virtue can be either punished or rewarded by the sentiments and opinions of mankind, they both, according to the common course of things, meet even here with something more than exact and impartial justice.

But though the general rules by which prosperity and adversity are commonly distributed, when considered in this cool and philosophical light, appear to be perfectly suited to the situation of mankind in this life, yet they are by no means suited to some of our natural sentiments. Our natural love and admiration for some virtues is such, that we should wish to bestow on them all sorts of honours and rewards, even those which we must acknowledge to be the proper recompenses of other qualities, with which those virtues are not always accompanied. Our detestation, on the contrary, for some vices is such, that we should desire to heap upon them every sort of disgrace and disaster, those not excepted which are the natural consequences of very different qualities. Magnanimity, generosity, and justice, command so high a degree of admiration, that we desire to see them crowned with wealth, and power, and honours of every kind, the natural consequences of prudence, industry, and application; qualities with which those virtues are not inseparably connected. Fraud, falsehood, brutality, and violence, on the other hand, excite in every human breast such scorn and abhorrence, that our indignation rouses to see them possess those advantages which they may in some sense be said to have merited, by the diligence and industry with which they are sometimes attended. The industrious knave cultivates the soil; the indolent good man leaves it uncultivated. Who ought to reap the harvest? Who starve, and who live in plenty? The natural course of things decides it in favour of the knave: the natural sentiments of mankind in favour of the man of virtue. Man judges, that the good qualities of the one are greatly over-recompensed by those advantages which they tend to procure him, and that the omissions of the other are by far too severely punished by the distress which they naturally bring upon him; and human laws, the consequences of human sentiments, forfeit the life and the estate of the industrious and cautious traitor, and reward, by extraordinary recompenses, the fidelity and public spirit of the improvident and careless good citizen. Thus man is by Nature directed to correct, in some measure, that distribution of things which she herself would otherwise have made. The rules which for this purpose she prompts him to follow, are different from those which she herself observes. She bestows upon every virtue, and upon every vice, that precise reward or punishment which is best fitted to encourage the one, or to restrain the other. She is directed by this sole consideration, and pays little regard to the different degrees of merit and demerit, which they may seem to possess in the sentiments and passions of man. Man, on the contrary, pays regard to this only, and would endeavour to render the state of every virtue precisely proportioned to that degree of love and esteem, and of every vice to that degree of contempt and abhorrence, which he himself conceives for it. The rules which she follows are fit for her, those which he follows for him: but both are calculated to promote the same great end, the order of the world, and the perfection and happiness of human nature.

But though man is thus employed to alter that distribution of things which natural events would make, if left to themselves; though, like the gods of the poets, he is perpetually interposing, by extraordinary means, in favour of virtue, and in opposition to vice, and, like them, endeavours to turn away the arrow that is aimed at the head of the righteous, but to accelerate the sword of destruction that is lifted up against the wicked; yet he is by no means able to render the fortune of either quite suitable to his own sentiments and wishes. The natural course of things cannot be entirely controlled by the impotent endeavours of man: the current is too rapid and too strong for him to stop it; and though the rules which direct it appear to have been established for the wisest and best purposes, they sometimes produce effects which shock all his natural sentiments. That a great combination of men should prevail over a small one; that those who engage in an enterprise with forethought and all necessary preparation, should prevail over such as oppose them without any; and that every end should be acquired by those means only which Nature has established for acquiring it, seems to be a rule not only necessary and unavoidable in itself, but even useful and proper for rousing the industry and attention of mankind. Yet, when, in consequence of this rule, violence and artifice prevail over sincerity and justice, what indignation does it not excite in the breast of every human spectator? What sorrow and compassion for the sufferings of the innocent, and what furious resentment against the success of the oppressor? We are equally grieved and enraged at the wrong that is done, but often find it altogether out of our power to redress it. When we thus despair of finding any force upon earth which can check the triumph of injustice, we naturally appeal to heaven, and hope, that the great Author of our nature will himself execute hereafter, what all the principles which he has given us for the direction of our conduct, prompt us to attempt even here; that he will complete the plan which he himself has thus taught us to begin; and will, in a life to come, render to every one according to the works which he has performed in this world. And thus we are led to the belief of a future state, not only by the weaknesses, by the hopes and fears of human nature, but by the noblest and best principles which belong to it, by the love of virtue, and by the abhorrence of vice and injustice.

"Does it suit the greatness of God," says the eloquent and philosophical bishop of Clermont, with that passionate and exaggerating force of imagination, which seems sometimes to exceed the bounds of decorum; "does it suit the greatness of God, to leave the world which he has created in so universal a disorder? To see the wicked prevail almost always over the just; the innocent dethroned by the usurper; the father become the victim of the ambition of an unnatural son; the husband expiring under the stroke of a barbarous and faithless wife? From the height of his greatness ought God to behold those melancholy events as a fantastical amusement, without taking any share in them? Because he is great, should he be weak, or unjust, or barbarous? Because men are little, ought they to be allowed either to be dissolute without punishment, or virtuous with out reward? O God! if this is the character of your Supreme Being; if it is you whom we adore under such dreadful ideas; I can no longer acknowledge you for my father, for my protector, for the comforter of my sorrow, the support of my weakness, the rewarder of my fidelity. You would then be no more than an indolent and fantastical tyrant, who sacrifices mankind to his insolent vanity, and who has brought them out of nothing, only to make them serve for the sport of his leisure and of his caprice."[3]

When the general rules which determine the merit and demerit of actions, come thus to be regarded as the laws of an All-powerful Being, who watches over our conduct, and who, in a life to come, will reward the observance, and punish the breach of them; they necessarily acquire a new sacredness from this consideration. That our regard to the will of the Deity ought to be the supreme rule of our conduct, can be doubted of by nobody who believes his existence. The very thought of disobedience appears to involve in it the most shocking impropriety. How vain, how absurd would it be for man, either to oppose or to neglect the commands that were laid upon him by Infinite Wisdom, and Infinite Power! How unnatural, how impiously ungrateful not to reverence the precepts that were prescribed to him by the infinite goodness of his Creator, even though no punishment was to follow their violation. The sense of propriety too is here well supported by the strongest motives of self-interest. The idea that, however we may escape the observation of man, or be placed above the reach of human punishment, yet we are always acting under the eye, and exposed to the punishment of God, the great avenger of injustice, is a motive capable of restraining the most headstrong passions, with those at least who, by constant reflection, have rendered it familiar to them.

It is in this manner that religion enforces the natural sense of duty: and hence it is, that mankind are generally disposed to place great confidence in the probity of those who seem deeply impressed with religious sentiments. Such persons, they imagine, act under an additional tie, besides those which regulate the conduct of other men. The regard to the propriety of action, as well as to reputation, the regard to the applause of his own breast, as well as to that of others, are motives which they suppose have the same influence over the religious man, as over the man of the world. But the former lies under another restraint, and never acts deliberately but as in the presence of that Great Superior who is finally to recompense him according to his deeds. A greater trust is reposed, upon this account, in the regularity and exactness of his conduct. And wherever the natural principles of religion are not corrupted by the factious and party zeal of some worthless cabal; wherever the first duty which it requires, is to fulfil all the obligations of morality; wherever men are not taught to regard frivolous observances, as more immediate duties of religion, than acts of justice and beneficence; and to imagine, that by sacrifices, and ceremonies, and vain supplications, they can bargain with the Deity for fraud, and perfidy, and violence, the world undoubt-edly judges right in this respect, and justly places a double confi-dence in the rectitude of the religious man's behaviour.

CHAPTER VI.

In what cases the Sense of Duty ought to be the sole principle of our conduct; and in what cases it ought to concur with other motives.

Religion affords such strong motives to the practice of virtue, and guards us by such powerful restraints from the temptations of vice, that many have been led to suppose, that religious principles were the sole laudable motives of action. We ought neither, they said, to reward from gratitude, nor punish from resentment; we ought neither to protect the helplessness of our children, nor afford sup-port to the infirmities of our parents, from natural affection. All affections for particular objects, ought to be extinguished in our breast, and one great affection take the place of all others, the love of the Deity, the desire of rendering ourselves agreeable to him, and of directing our conduct, in every respect, according to his will. We ought not to be grateful from gratitude, we ought not to be charitable from humanity, we ought not to be public-spirited from the love of our country, nor generous and just from the love of mankind. The sole principle and motive of our conduct in the performance of all those different duties, ought to be a sense that God has commanded us to perform them. I shall not at present take time to examine this opinion particularly; I shall only observe, that we should not have expected to have found it entertained by any sect, who professed themselves of a religion in which, as it is the first precept to love the Lord our God with all our heart, with all our soul, and with all our strength, so it is the second to love our neighbour as we love ourselves;[1] and we love ourselves surely for our own sakes, and not merely because we are commanded to do so. That the sense of duty should be the sole principle of our conduct, is no where the precept of Christianity; but that it should be the ruling and the governing one, as philosophy, and as, indeed, common sense directs. It may be a question, however, in what cases our actions ought to arise chiefly or entirely from a sense of duty, or from a regard to general rules; and in what cases some other sentiment or affection ought to concur, and have a principal influence.

The decision of this question, which cannot, perhaps, be given with any very great accuracy, will depend upon two different circumstances; first, upon the natural agreeableness or deformity of the sentiment or affection which would prompt us to any action independent of all regard to general rules; and, secondly, upon the precision and exactness, or the looseness and inaccuracy, of the general rules themselves.

I. First, I say, it will depend upon the natural agreeableness or deformity of the affection itself, how far our actions ought to arise from it, or entirely proceed from a regard to the general rule.

All those graceful and admired actions, to which the benevolent affections would prompt us, ought to proceed as much from the passions themselves, as from any regard to the general rules of conduct. A benefactor thinks himself but ill requited, if the person upon whom he has bestowed his good offices, repays them merely from a cold sense of duty, and without any affection to his person. A husband is dissatisfied with the most obedient wife, when he imagines her conduct is animated by no other principle besides her regard to what the relation she stands in requires. Though a son should fail in none of the offices of filial duty, yet if he wants that affectionate reverence which it so well becomes him to feel, the parent may justly complain of his indifference. Nor could a son be quite satisfied with a parent who, though he performed all the duties of his situation, had nothing of that fatherly fondness which might have been expected from him. With regard to all such benevolent and social affections, it is agreeable to see the sense of duty employed rather to restrain than to enliven them, rather to hinder us from doing too much, than to prompt us to do what we ought. It gives us pleasure to see a father obliged to check his own fondness, a friend obliged to set bounds to his natural generosity, a person who has received a benefit, obliged to restrain the too sanguine gratitude of his own temper.

The contrary maxim takes place with regard to the malevolent and unsocial passions. We ought to reward from the gratitude and generosity of our own hearts, without any reluctance, and without being obliged to reflect how great the propriety of rewarding: but we ought always to punish with reluctance, and more from a sense of the propriety of punishing, than from any savage disposition to revenge. Nothing is more graceful than the behaviour of the man who appears to resent the greatest injuries, more from a sense that they deserve, and are the proper objects of resentment, than from feeling himself the furies of that disagreeable passion; who, like a judge, considers only the general rule, which determines what vengeance is due for each particular offence; who, in executing that rule, feels less for what himself has suffered, than for what the offender is about to suffer; who, though in wrath, remembers mercy, and is disposed to interpret the rule in the most gentle and favourable manner, and to allow all the alleviations which the most candid humanity could, consistently with good sense, admit of.

As the selfish passions according to what has formerly been observed, hold, in other respects, a sort of middle place, between the social and unsocial affections, so do they likewise in this. The pursuit of the objects of private interest, in all common, little, and ordinary cases, ought to flow rather from a regard to the general rules which prescribe such conduct, than from any passion for the objects themselves; but upon more important and extraordinary occasions, we should be awkward, insipid, and ungraceful, if the objects themselves did not appear to animate us with a considerable degree of passion. To be anxious, or to be laying a plot either to gain or to save a single shilling, would degrade the most vulgar tradesman in the opinion of all his neighbours. Let his circumstances be ever so mean, no attention to any such small matters, for the sake of the things themselves, must appear in his conduct. His situation may require the most severe economy and the most exact assiduity: but each particular exertion of that economy and assiduity must proceed, not so much from a regard for that particular saving or gain, as for the general rule which to him prescribes, with the utmost rigour, such a tenor of conduct. His parsimony to-day must not arise from a desire of the particular three-pence which he will save by it, nor his attendance in his shop from a passion for the particular tenpence which he will acquire by it: both the one and the other ought to proceed solely from a regard to the general rule, which prescribes, with the most unrelenting severity, this plan of conduct to all persons in his way of life. In this consists the difference between the character of a miser and that of a person of exact economy and assiduity. The one is anxious about small matters for their own sake; the other attends to them only in consequence of the scheme of life which he has laid down to himself.

It is quite otherwise with regard to the more extraordinary and important objects of self-interest. A person appears mean-spirited, who does not pursue these with some degree of earnestness for their own sake. We should despise a prince who was not anxious about conquering or defending a province. We should have little respect for a private gentleman who did not exert himself to gain an estate, or even a considerable office, when he could acquire them without either meanness or injustice. A member of parliament who shows no keenness about his own election, is abandoned by his friends, as altogether unworthy of their attachment. Even a tradesman is thought a poor-spirited fellow among his neighbours, who does not bestir himself to get what they call an extraordinary job, or some uncommon advantage. This spirit and keenness constitutes the difference between the man of enterprise and the man of dull regularity. Those great objects of self-interest, of which the loss or acquisition quite changes the rank of the person, are the objects of the passion properly called ambition; a passion, which when it keeps within the bounds of prudence and justice, is always admired in the world, and has even sometimes a certain irregular greatness, which dazzles the imagination, when it passes the limits of both these virtues, and is not only unjust but extravagant. Hence the general admiration for heroes and conquerors, and even for statesmen, whose projects have been very daring and extensive, though altogether devoid of justice; such as those of the Cardinals of Richlieu and of Retz. The objects of avarice and ambition differ only in their greatness. A miser is as furious about a halfpenny, as a man of ambition about the conquest of a kingdom.

II. Secondly, I say, it will depend partly upon the precision and exactness, or the looseness and inaccuracy of the general rules themselves, how far our conduct ought to proceed entirely from a regard to them.

The general rules of almost all the virtues, the general rules which determine what are the offices of prudence, of charity, of generosity, of gratitude, of friendship, are in many respects loose and inaccurate, admit of many exceptions, and require so many modifications, that it is scarce possible to regulate our conduct entirely by a regard to them. The common proverbial maxims of prudence, being founded in universal experience, are perhaps the best general rules which can be given about it. To affect, however, a very strict and literal adherence to them would evidently be the most absurd and ridiculous pedantry. Of all the virtues I have just now mentioned, gratitude is that, perhaps, of which the rules are the most precise, and admit of the fewest exceptions. That as soon as we can we should make a return of equal, and, if possible, of superior value to the services we have received, would seem to be a pretty plain rule, and one which admitted of scarce any exceptions. Upon the most superficial examination, however, this rule will appear to be in the highest degree loose and inaccurate, and to admit of ten thousand exceptions. If your benefactor attended you in your sickness, ought you to attend him in his? or can you fulfil the obligation of gratitude, by making a return of a different kind? If you ought to attend him, how long ought you to attend him? The same time which he attended you, or longer, and how much longer? If your friend lent you money in your distress, ought you to lend him money in his? How much ought you to lend him? When ought you to lend him? Now, or to-morrow, or next month? And for how long a time? It is evident, that no general rule can be laid down, by which a precise answer can, in all cases, be given to any of these questions. The difference between his character and yours, between his circumstances and yours, may be such, that you may be perfectly grateful, and justly refuse to lend him a halfpenny: and, on the contrary, you may be willing to lend, or even to give him ten times the sum which he lent you, and yet justly be accused of the blackest ingratitude, and of not having fulfilled the hundredth part of the obligation you lie under. As the duties of gratitude, however, are perhaps the most sacred of all those which the beneficent virtues prescribe to us, so the general rules which determine them are, as I said before, the most accurate. Those which ascertain the actions required by friendship, humanity, hospitality, generosity, are still more vague and indeterminate.

There is, however, one virtue of which the general rules determine with the greatest exactness every external action which it requires. This virtue is justice. The rules of justice are accurate in the highest degree, and admit of no exceptions or modifications, but such as may be ascertained as accurately as the rules themselves, and which generally, indeed, flow from the very same principles with them. If I owe a man ten pounds, justice requires that I should precisely pay him ten pounds, either at the time agreed upon, or when he demands it. What I ought to perform, how much I ought to perform, when and where I ought to perform it, the whole nature and circumstances of the action prescribed, are all of them precisely fixt and determined. Though it may be awkward and pedantic, therefore, to affect too strict an adherence to the common rules of prudence or generosity, there is no pedantry in sticking fast by the rules of justice. On the contrary, the most sacred regard is due to them; and the actions which this virtue requires are never so properly performed, as when the chief motive for performing them is a reverential and religious regard to those general rules which require them. In the practice of the other virtues, our conduct should rather be directed by a certain idea of propriety, by a certain taste for a particular tenor of conduct, than by any regard to a precise maxim or rule; and we should consider the end and foundation of the rule, more than the rule itself. But it is otherwise with regard to justice: the man who in that refines the least, and adheres with the most obstinate stedfastness to the general rules themselves, is the most commendable, and the most to be depended upon. Though the end of the rules of justice be, to hinder us from hurting our neighbour, it may frequently be a crime to violate them, though we could pretend, with some pretext of reason, that this particular violation could do no hurt. A man often becomes a villain the moment he begins, even in his own heart, to chicane in this manner. The moment he thinks of departing from the most staunch and positive adherence to what those inviolable precepts prescribe to him, he is no longer to be trusted, and no man can say what degree of guilt he may not arrive at. The thief imagines he does no evil, when he steals from the rich, what he supposes they may easily want, and what possibly they may never even know has been stolen from them. The adulterer imagines he does no evil, when he corrupts the wife of his friend, provided he covers his intrigue from the suspicion of the husband, and does not disturb the peace of the family. When once we begin to give way to such refinements, there is no enormity so gross of which we may not be capable.

The rules of justice may be compared to the rules of grammar; the rules of the other virtues, to the rules which critics lay down for the attainment of what is sublime and elegant in composition. The one, are precise, accurate, and indispensable. The other, are loose, vague, and indeterminate, and present us rather with a general idea of the perfection we ought to aim at, than afford us any certain and infallible directions for acquiring it.[2] A man may learn to write grammatically by rule, with the most absolute infallibility; and so, perhaps, he may be taught to act justly. But there are no rules whose observance will infallibly lead us to the attainment of elegance or sublimity in writing; though there are some which may help us, in some measure, to correct and ascertain the vague ideas which we might otherwise have entertained of those perfections. And there are no rules by the knowledge of which we can infallibly be taught to act upon all occasions with prudence, with just magnanimity, or proper beneficence: though there are some which may enable us to correct and ascertain, in several respects, the imperfect ideas which we might otherwise have entertained of those virtues.

It may sometimes happen, that with the most serious and earnest desire of acting so as to deserve approbation, we may mistake the proper rules of conduct, and thus be misled by that very principle which ought to direct us. It is in vain to expect, that in this case mankind should entirely approve of our behaviour. They cannot enter into that absurd idea of duty which influenced us, nor go along with any of the actions which follow from it. There is still, however, something respectable in the character and behaviour of one who is thus betrayed into vice, by a wrong sense of duty, or by what is called an erroneous conscience. How fatally soever he may be misled by it, he is still, with the generous and humane, more the object of commiseration than of hatred or resentment. They lament the weakness of human nature, which exposes us to such unhappy delusions, even while we are most sincerely labouring after perfection, and endeavouring to act according to the best principle which can possibly direct us. False notions of religion are almost the only causes which can occasion any very gross perversion of our natural sentiments in this way; and that principle which gives the greatest authority to the rules of duty, is alone capable of distorting our ideas of them in any considerable degree.[3] In all other cases common sense is sufficient to direct us, if not to the most exquisite propriety of conduct, yet to something which is not very far from it; and provided we are in earnest desirous to do well, our behaviour will always, upon the whole, be praise-worthy. That to obey the will of the Deity, is the first rule of duty, all men are agreed. But concerning the particular commandments which that will may impose upon us, they differ widely from one another. In this, therefore, the greatest mutual forbearance and toleration is due; and though the defence of society requires that crimes should be punished, from whatever motives they proceed, yet a good man will always punish them with reluctance, when they evidently proceed from false notions of religious duty. He will never feel against those who commit them that indignation which he feels against other criminals, but will rather regret, and sometimes even admire their unfortunate firmness and magnanimity, at the very time that he punishes their crime. In the tragedy of Mahomet, one of the finest of Mr. Voltaire's, it is well represented, what ought to be our sentiments for crimes which proceed from such motives. In that

tragedy, two young people of different sexes, of the most innocent and virtuous dispositions, and without any other weakness
except what endears them the more to us, a mutual fondness for
one another, are instigated by the strongest motives of a false
religion, to commit a horrid murder, that shocks all the principles
of human nature. A venerable old man, who had expressed the
most tender affection for them both, for whom, notwithstanding
he was the avowed enemy of their religion, they had both conceived the highest reverence and esteem, and who was in reality
their father, though they did not know him to be such, is pointed
out to them as a sacrifice which God had expressly required at
their hands, and they are commanded to kill him. While they are
about executing this crime, they are tortured with all the agonies
which can arise from the struggle between the idea of the indis-
pensableness of religious duty on the one side, and compassion,
gratitude, reverence for the age, and love for the humanity and
virtue of the person whom they are going to destroy, on the other.
The representation of this exhibits one of the most interesting,
and perhaps the most instructive spectacle that was ever introduced upon any theatre.[4] The sense of duty, however, at last prevails over all the amiable weaknesses of human nature. They
execute the crime imposed upon them; but immediately discover
their error, and the fraud which had deceived them, and are distracted with horror, remorse, and resentment. Such as are our
sentiments for the unhappy Seid and Palmira, such ought we to
feel for every person who is in this manner misled by religion,
when we are sure that it is really religion which misleads him,
and not the pretence of it, which is made a cover to some of the
worst of human passions.

As a person may act wrong by following a wrong sense of duty,
so nature may sometimes prevail, and lead him to act right in
opposition to it. We cannot in this case be displeased to see that
motive prevail, which we think ought to prevail, though the person himself is so weak as to think otherwise. As his conduct,
however, is the effect of weakness, not principle, we are far from
bestowing upon it any thing that approaches to complete approbation. A bigotted Roman Catholic, who, during the massacre of
St. Bartholomew, had been so overcome by compassion, as to save
some unhappy Protestants, whom he thought it his duty to destroy,

would not seem to be entitled to that high applause which we should have bestowed upon him, had he exerted the same generosity with complete self-approbation.[5] We might be pleased with the humanity of his temper, but we should still regard him with a sort of pity which is altogether inconsistent with the admiration that is due to perfect virtue. It is the same case with all the other passions. We do not dislike to see them exert themselves properly, even when a false notion of duty would direct the person to restrain them. A very devout Quaker, who upon being struck upon one cheek, instead of turning up the other, should so far forget his literal interpretation of our Saviour's precept, as to bestow some good discipline upon the brute that insulted him, would not be disagreeable to us. We should laugh and be diverted with his spirit, and rather like him the better for it. But we should by no means regard him with that respect and esteem which would seem due to one who, upon a like occasion, had acted properly from a just sense of what was proper to be done. No action can properly be called virtuous, which is not accompanied with the sentiment of self-approbation.

PART IV.

OF THE EFFECT OF UTILITY UPON THE SENTIMENT OF APPROBATION.

CONSISTING OF ONE SECTION.

CHAPTER I.

Of the beauty which the appearance of Utility bestows upon all the productions of art, and of the extensive influence of this species of Beauty.

That utility is one of the principal sources of beauty has been observed by every body, who has considered with any attention what constitutes the nature of beauty. The conveniency of a house gives pleasure to the spectator as well as its regularity, and he is as much hurt when he observes the contrary defect, as when he sees the correspondent windows of different forms, or the door not placed exactly in the middle of the building. That the fitness of any system or machine to produce the end for which it was intended, bestows a certain propriety and beauty upon the whole, and renders the very thought and contemplation of it agreeable, is so very obvious that nobody has overlooked it.[1]

The cause too, why utility pleases, has of late been assigned by an ingenious and agreeable philosopher, who joins the greatest depth of thought to the greatest elegance of expression, and possesses the singular and happy talent of treating the abstrusest subjects not only with the most perfect perspicuity, but with the most lively eloquence.[2] The utility of any object, according to him, pleases the master by perpetually suggesting to him the pleasure or conveniency which it is fitted to promote. Every time he looks at it, he is put in mind of this pleasure; and the object in this manner becomes a source of perpetual satisfaction and enjoyment. The spectator enters by sympathy into the sentiments of the master, and necessarily views the object under the same agreeable aspect. When we visit the palaces of the great, we cannot help conceiving the satisfaction we should enjoy if we ourselves were the masters, and were possessed of so much artful and ingenuously contrived accommodation. A similar account is given why the appearance of inconveniency should render any object disagreeable both to the owner and to the spectator.

But that this fitness, this happy contrivance of any production of art, should often be more valued, than the very end for which it was intended; and that the exact adjustment of the means for attaining any conveniency or pleasure, should frequently be more regarded, than that very conveniency or pleasure, in the attainment of which their whole merit would seem to consist, has not, so far as I know, been yet taken notice of by any body. That this however is very frequently the case, may be observed in a thousand instances, both in the most frivolous and in the most important concerns of human life.

When a person comes into his chamber, and finds the chairs all standing in the middle of the room, he is angry with his servant, and rather than see them continue in that disorder, perhaps takes the trouble himself to set them all in their places with their backs to the wall. The whole propriety of this new situation arises from its superior conveniency in leaving the floor free and disengaged. To attain this conveniency he voluntarily puts himself to more trouble than all he could have suffered from the want of it; since nothing was more easy, than to have set himself down upon one of them, which is probably what he does when his labour is over. What he wanted therefore, it seems, was not so much this conveniency, as that arrangement of things which promotes it. Yet it is this conveniency which ultimately recommends that arrangement, and bestows upon it the whole of its propriety and beauty.

A watch, in the same manner, that falls behind above two minutes in a day, is despised by one curious in watches. He sells it perhaps for a couple of guineas, and purchases another at fifty, which will not lose above a minute in a fortnight. The sole use of watches however, is to tell us what o'clock it is, and to hinder us from breaking any engagement, or suffering any other inconveniency by our ignorance in that particular point. But the person so nice with regard to this machine, will not always be found either more scrupulously punctual than other men, or more anxiously concerned upon any other account, to know precisely what time of day it is. What interests him is not so much the attainment of this piece of knowledge, as the perfection of the machine which serves to attain it.

How many people ruin themselves by laying out money on trinkets of frivolous utility? What pleases these lovers of toys is not so much the utility, as the aptness of the machines which are fitted to promote it. All their pockets are stuffed with little conveniencies. They contrive new pockets, unknown in the clothes of other people, in order to carry a greater number. They walk

about loaded with a multitude of baubles,[3] in weight and sometimes in value not inferior to an ordinary Jew's-box, some of
which may sometimes be of some little use, but all of which might
at all times be very well spared, and of which the whole utility is
certainly not worth the fatigue of bearing the burden.

Nor is it only with regard to such frivolous objects that our
conduct is influenced by this principle; it is often the secret motive
of the most serious and important pursuits of both private and
public life.

The poor man's son, whom heaven in its anger has visited with
ambition, when he begins to look around him, admires the condition of the rich. He finds the cottage of his father too small for his
accommodation, and fancies he should be lodged more at his ease
in a palace. He is displeased with being obliged to walk a-foot, or
to endure the fatigue of riding on horseback. He sees his superiors
carried about in machines, and imagines that in one of these he
could travel with less inconveniency. He feels himself naturally
indolent, and willing to serve himself with his own hands as little
as possible; and judges, that a numerous retinue of servants would
save him from a great deal of trouble. He thinks if he had attained
all these, he would sit still contentedly, and be quiet, enjoying
himself in the thought of the happiness and tranquillity of his situation. He is enchanted with the distant idea of this felicity.
It appears in his fancy like the life of some superior rank of beings,
and, in order to arrive at it, he devotes himself for ever to the pursuit of wealth and greatness. To obtain the conveniencies which
these afford, he submits in the first year, nay in the first month of
his application, to more fatigue of body and more uneasiness
of mind than he could have suffered through the whole of his
life from the want of them. He studies to distinguish himself
in some laborious profession. With the most unrelenting industry
he labours night and day to acquire talents superior to all his
competitors. He endeavours next to bring those talents into
public view, and with equal assiduity solicits every opportunity of
employment. For this purpose he makes his court to all mankind;
he serves those whom he hates, and is obsequious to those whom
he despises.[4] Through the whole of his life he pursues the idea of
a certain artificial and elegant repose which he may never arrive
at, for which he sacrifices a real tranquillity that is at all times in

his power, and which, if in the extremity of old age he should at last attain to it, he will find to be in no respect preferable to that humble security and contentment which he had abandoned for it. It is then, in the last dregs of life, his body wasted with toil and diseases, his mind galled and ruffled by the memory of a thousand injuries and disappointments which he imagines he has met with from the injustice of his enemies, or from the perfidy and ingratitude of his friends, that he begins at last to find that wealth and greatness are mere trinkets of frivolous utility, no more adapted for procuring ease of body or tranquillity of mind than the tweezer-cases of the lover of toys; and like them too, more troublesome to the person who carries them about with him than all the advantages they can afford him are commodious. There is no other real difference between them, except that the conveniencies of the one are somewhat more observable than those of the other. The palaces, the gardens, the equipage, the retinue of the great, are objects of which the obvious conveniency strikes every body. They do not require that their masters should point out to us wherein consists their utility. Of our own accord we readily enter into it, and by sympathy enjoy and thereby applaud the satisfaction which they are fitted to afford him. But the curiosity of a tooth-pick, of an ear-picker, of a machine for cutting the nails, or of any other trinket of the same kind, is not so obvious. Their conveniency may perhaps be equally great, but it is not so striking, and we do not so readily enter into the satisfaction of the man who possesses them. They are therefore less reasonable subjects of vanity than the magnificence of wealth and greatness; and in this consists the sole advantage of these last. They more effectually gratify that love of distinction so natural to man. To one who was to live alone in a desolate island it might be a matter of doubt, perhaps, whether a palace, or a collection of such small conveniencies as are commonly contained in a tweezer-case, would contribute most to his happiness and enjoyment. If he is to live in society, indeed, there can be no comparison, because in this, as in all other cases, we constantly pay more regard to the sentiments of the spectator, than to those of the person principally concerned, and consider rather how his situation will appear to other people, than how it will appear to himself. If we examine, however, why the spectator distinguishes with such admiration the condition of the rich and the great, we shall find that it is not so much upon account of the superior ease or pleasure which they are supposed to enjoy, as of the numberless artificial and elegant contrivances for promoting this ease or pleasure. He does not even imagine that they are really happier than other people: but he imagines that they possess more means of happiness. And it is the ingenious and artful adjustment of those means to the end for which they were intended, that is the principal source of his admiration. But in the languor of disease and the weariness of old age, the pleasures of the vain and empty distinctions of greatness disappear. To one, in this situation, they are no longer capable of recommending those toilsome pursuits in which they had formerly engaged him. In his heart he curses ambition, and vainly regrets the ease and the indolence of youth, pleasures which are fled for ever, and which he has foolishly sacrificed for what, when he has got it, can afford him no real satisfaction. In this miserable aspect does greatness appear to every man when reduced either by spleen or disease to observe with attention his own situation, and to consider what it is that is really wanting to his happiness. Power and riches appear then to be, what they are, enormous and operose[5] machines contrived to produce a few trifling conveniencies to the body, consisting of springs the most nice and delicate, which must be kept in order with the most anxious attention, and which in spite of all our care are ready every moment to burst into pieces, and to crush in their ruins their unfortunate possessor. They are immense fabrics, which it requires the labour of a life to raise, which threaten every moment to overwhelm the person that dwells in them, and which while they stand, though they may save him from some smaller inconveniencies, can protect him from none of the severer inclemencies of the season. They keep off the summer shower, not the winter storm, but leave him always as much, and sometimes more exposed than before, to anxiety, to fear, and to sorrow; to diseases, to danger, and to death.

But though this splenetic philosophy, which in time of sickness or low spirits is familiar to every man, thus entirely depreciates those great objects of human desire, when in better health and in better humour, we never fail to regard them under a more agreeable aspect. Our imagination, which in pain and sorrow seems to be confined and cooped up within our own persons, in times of ease and prosperity expands itself to every thing around us. We are then charmed with the beauty of that accommodation which reigns in the palaces and economy of the great; and admire how every thing is adapted to promote their ease, to prevent their wants, to gratify their wishes, and to amuse and entertain their most frivolous desires. If we consider the real satisfaction which all these things are capable of affording, by itself and separated from the beauty of that arrangement which is fitted to promote it, it will always appear in the highest degree contemptible and trifling. But we rarely view it in this abstract and philosophical light. We naturally confound it in our imagination with the order, the regular and harmonious movement of the system, the machine or economy by means of which it is produced. The pleasures of wealth and greatness, when considered in this complex view, strike the imagination as something grand and beautiful and noble, of which the attainment is well worth all the toil and anxiety which we are so apt to bestow upon it.

And it is well that nature imposes upon us in this manner.[6] It is this deception which rouses and keeps in continual motion the industry of mankind. It is this which first prompted them to cultivate the ground, to build houses, to found cities and commonwealths, and to invent and improve all the sciences and arts, which ennoble and embellish human life; which have entirely changed the whole face of the globe, have turned the rude forests of nature into agreeable and fertile plains, and made the trackless and barren ocean a new fund of subsistence, and the great high road of communication to the different nations of the earth. The earth by these labours of mankind has been obliged to redouble her natural fertility, and to maintain a greater multitude of inhabitants. It is to no purpose, that the proud and unfeeling landlord views his extensive fields, and without a thought for the wants of his brethren, in imagination consumes himself the whole harvest that grows upon them. The homely and vulgar proverb, that the eye is larger than the belly, never was more fully verified than with regard to him. The capacity of his stomach bears no proportion to the immensity of his desires, and will receive no more than that of the meanest peasant. The rest he is obliged to distribute among those, who prepare, in the nicest manner, that little which he himself makes use of, among those who fit up the palace in which this little is to be consumed, among those who provide and keep in order all the different baubles and trinkets, which are employed in the economy of greatness; all of whom thus derive from his luxury and caprice, that share of the necessaries of life, which they would in vain have expected from his humanity or his justice. The produce of the soil maintains at all times nearly that number of inhabitants which it is capable of maintaining. The rich only select from the heap what is most precious and agreeable. They consume little more than the poor, and in spite of their natural selfishness and rapacity, though they mean only their own conveniency, though the sole end which they propose from the labours of all the thousands whom they employ, be the gratification of their own vain and insatiable desires, they divide with the poor the produce of all their improvements.[7] They are led by an invisible hand to make nearly the same distribution of the necessaries of life, which would have been made, had the earth been divided into equal portions among all its inhabitants, and thus without intending it, without knowing it, advance the interest of the society, and afford means to the multiplication of the species.[8] When Providence divided the earth among a few lordly masters, it neither forgot nor abandoned those who seemed to have been left out in the partition. These last too enjoy their share of all that it produces. In what constitutes the real happiness of human life, they are in no respect inferior to those who would seem so much above them. In ease of body and peace of mind, all the different ranks of life are nearly upon a level, and the beggar, who suns himself by the side of the highway, possesses that security which kings are fighting for.

The same principle, the same love of system, the same regard to the beauty of order, of art and contrivance, frequently serves to recommend those institutions which tend to promote the public welfare. When a patriot exerts himself for the improvement of any part of the public police, his conduct does not always arise from pure sympathy with the happiness of those who are to reap the benefit of it. It is not commonly from a fellow-feeling with carriers and waggoners that a public-spirited man encourages the mending of high roads. When the legislature establishes premiums and other encouragements to advance the linen or woollen manufactures, its conduct seldom proceeds from pure sympathy with the wearer of cheap or fine cloth, and much less from that with the manufacturer or merchant. The perfection of police, the extension of trade and manufactures, are noble and magnificent objects. The contemplation of them pleases us, and we are interested in whatever can tend to advance them. They make part of the great system of government, and the wheels of the political machine seem to move with more harmony and ease by means of them. We take pleasure in beholding the perfection of so beautiful and grand a system, and we are uneasy till we remove any obstruction that can in the least disturb or encumber the regularity of its motions. All constitutions of government, however, are valued only in proportion as they tend to promote the happiness of those who live under them. This is their sole use and end. From a certain spirit of system, however, from a certain love of art and contrivance, we sometimes seem to value the means more than the end, and to be eager to promote the happiness of our fellow-creatures, rather from a view to perfect and improve a certain beautiful and orderly system, than from any immediate sense or feeling of what they either suffer or enjoy. There have been men of the greatest public spirit, who have shown themselves in other respects not very sensible to the feelings of humanity. And on the contrary, there have been men of the greatest humanity, who seem to have been entirely devoid of public spirit. Every man may find in the circle of his acquaintance instances both of the one kind and the other. Who had ever less humanity, or more public spirit, than the celebrated legislator of Muscovy? The social and well-natured James the First of Great Britain seems, on the contrary, to have had scarce any passion, either for the glory or the interest of his country. Would you awaken the industry of the man who seems almost dead to ambition, it will often be to no purpose to describe to him the happiness of the rich and the great; to tell him that they are generally sheltered from the sun and the rain, that they are seldom hungry, that they are seldom cold, and that they are rarely exposed to weariness, or to want of any kind. The most eloquent exhortation of this kind will have little effect upon him. If you would hope to succeed, you must describe to him the conveniency and arrangement of the different apartments in their palaces; you must explain to him the propriety of their equipages, and point out to him the number, the order, and the different offices of all their attendants. If any thing is capable of making impression upon him, this will. Yet all these things tend only to keep off the sun and the rain, to save them from hunger and cold, from want and weariness. In the same manner, if you would implant public virtue in the breast of him who seems heedless of the interest of his country, it will often be to no purpose to tell him, what superior advantages the subjects of a well-governed state enjoy; that they are better lodged, that they are better clothed, that they are better fed. These considerations will commonly make no great impression. You will be more likely to persuade, if you describe the great system of public police which procures these advantages, if you explain the connexions and dependencies of its several parts, their mutual subordination to one another, and their general subserviency to the happiness of the society; if you show how this system might be introduced into his own country, what it is that hinders it from taking place there at present, how those obstructions might be removed, and all the several wheels of the machine of government be made to move with more harmony and smoothness, without grating upon one another, or mutually retarding one another's motions. It is scarce possible that a man should listen to a discourse of this kind, and not feel himself animated to some degree of public spirit. He will, at least for the moment, feel some desire to remove those obstructions, and to put into motion so beautiful and so orderly a machine. Nothing tends so much to promote public spirit as the study of politics, of the several systems of civil government, their advantages and disadvantages, of the constitution of our own country, its situation, and interest with regard to foreign nations, its commerce, its defence, the disadvantages it labours under, the dangers to which it may be exposed, how to remove the one, and how to guard against the other. Upon this account political disquisitions, if just, and reasonable, and practicable, are of all the works of speculation the most useful. Even the weakest and the worst of them are not altogether without their utility. They serve at least to animate the public passions of men, and rouse them to seek out the means of promoting the happiness of the society.

CHAPTER II.

Of the beauty which the appearance of Utility bestows upon the characters and actions of men; and how far the perception of this beauty may be regarded as one of the original principles of approbation.

The characters of men, as well as the contrivances of art, or the institutions of civil government, may be fitted either to promote or to disturb the happiness both of the individual and of the society. The prudent, the equitable, the active, resolute, and sober character promises prosperity and satisfaction, both to the person himself and to every one connected with him. The rash, the insolent, the slothful, effeminate, and voluptuous, on the contrary, forebodes ruin to the individual, and misfortune to all who have any thing to do with him. The first turn of mind has at least all the beauty which can belong to the most perfect machine that was ever invented for promoting the most agreeable purpose: and the second, all the deformity of the most awkward and clumsy contrivance. What institution of government could tend so much to promote the happiness of mankind as the general prevalence of wisdom and virtue? All government is but an imperfect remedy for the deficiency of these. Whatever beauty, therefore, can belong to civil government upon account of its utility, must in a far superior degree belong to these. On the contrary, what civil policy can be so ruinous and destructive as the vices of men? The fatal effects of bad government arise from nothing, but that it does not sufficiently guard against the mischiefs which human wickedness gives occasion to.

This beauty and deformity which characters appear to derive from their usefulness or inconveniency, are apt to strike, in a peculiar manner, those who consider, in an abstract and philosophical light, the actions and conduct of mankind. When a philosopher goes to examine why humanity is approved of, or cruelty condemned, he does not always form to himself, in a very clear and distinct manner, the conception of any one particular action either of cruelty or of humanity, but is commonly contented with the vague and indeterminate idea which the general names of those qualities suggest to him. But it is in particular instances only that the propriety or impropriety, the merit or demerit of actions is very obvious and discernible. It is only when particular examples are given that we perceive distinctly either the concord or disagreement between our own affections and those of the agent, or feel a social gratitude arise towards him in the one case, or a sympathetic resentment in the other. When we consider virtue and vice in an abstract and general manner, the qualities by which they excite these several sentiments seem in a great measure to disappear, and the sentiments themselves become less obvious and discernible. On the contrary, the happy effects of the one and the fatal consequences of the other seem then to rise up to the view, and as it were to stand out and distinguish themselves from all the other qualities of either.

The same ingenious and agreeable author who first explained why utility pleases, has been so struck with this view of things, as to resolve our whole approbation of virtue into a perception of this species of beauty which results from the appearance of utility. No qualities of the mind, he observes, are approved of as virtuous, but such as are useful or agreeable either to the person himself or to others; and no qualities are disapproved of as vicious but such as have a contrary tendency.[1] And Nature, indeed, seems to have so happily adjusted our sentiments of approbation and disapprobation, to the conveniency both of the individual and of the society, that after the strictest examination it will be found, I believe, that this is universally the case. But still I affirm, that it is not the view of this utility or hurtfulness which is either the first or principal source of our approbation and disapprobation. These sentiments are no doubt enhanced and enlivened by the perception of the beauty or deformity which results from this utility or hurt-fulness. But still, I say, they are originally and essentially different from this perception.

For first of all, it seems impossible that the approbation of virtue should be a sentiment of the same kind with that by which we approve of a convenient and well-contrived building; or that we should have no other reason for praising a man than that for which we commend a chest of drawers.[2]

And secondly, it will be found, upon examination, that the usefulness of any disposition of mind is seldom the first ground of our approbation; and that the sentiment of approbation always involves in it a sense of propriety quite distinct from the perception of utility. We may observe this with regard to all the qualities which are approved of as virtuous, both those which, according to this system, are originally valued as useful to ourselves, as well as those which are esteemed on account of their usefulness to others.

The qualities most useful to ourselves are, first of all, superior reason and understanding, by which we are capable of discerning the remote consequences of all our actions, and of foreseeing the advantage or detriment which is likely to result from them: and secondly, self-command, by which we are enabled to abstain from present pleasure or to endure present pain, in order to obtain a greater pleasure or to avoid a greater pain in some future time. In the union of those two qualities consists the virtue of prudence, of all the virtues that which is most useful to the individual.

With regard to the first of those qualities, it has been observed on a former occasion,[3] that superior reason and understanding are originally approved of as just and right and accurate, and not merely as useful or advantageous. It is in the abstruser sciences, particularly in the higher parts of mathematics, that the greatest and most admired exertions of human reason have been displayed. But the utility of those sciences, either to the individual or to the public, is not very obvious, and to prove it, requires a discussion which is not always very easily comprehended. It was not, therefore, their utility which first recommended them to the public admiration. This quality was but little insisted upon, till it became necessary to make some reply to the reproaches of those, who, having themselves no taste for such sublime discoveries, endeavoured to depreciate them as useless.[4]

That self-command, in the same manner, by which we restrain our present appetites, in order to gratify them more fully upon another occasion, is approved of, as much under the aspect of propriety, as under that of utility. When we act in this manner, the sentiments which influence our conduct seem exactly to coincide with those of the spectator. The spectator does not feel the solicitations of our present appetites. To him the pleasure which we are to enjoy a week hence, or a year hence, is just as interesting as that which we are to enjoy this moment. When for the sake of the present, therefore, we sacrifice the future, our conduct appears to him absurd and extravagant in the highest degree, and he cannot enter into the principles which influence it. On the contrary, when we abstain from present pleasure, in order to secure greater pleasure to come, when we act as if the remote object interested us as much as that which immediately presses upon the senses, as our affections exactly correspond with his own, he cannot fail to approve of our behaviour: and as he knows from experience, how few are capable of this self-command, he looks upon our conduct with a considerable degree of wonder and admiration. Hence arises that eminent esteem with which all men naturally regard a steady perseverance in the practice of frugality, industry, and application, though directed to no other purpose than the acquisition of fortune. The resolute firmness of the person who acts in this manner, and in order to obtain a great though remote advantage, not only gives up all present pleasures, but endures the greatest labour both of mind and body, necessarily commands our approbation. That view of his interest and happiness which appears to regulate his conduct, exactly tallies with the idea which we naturally form of it. There is the most perfect correspondence between his sentiments and our own, and at the same time, from our experience of the common weakness of human nature, it is a correspondence which we could not reasonably have expected. We not only approve, therefore, but in some measure admire his conduct, and think it worthy of a considerable degree of applause. It is the consciousness of this merited approbation and esteem which is alone capable of supporting the agent in this tenour of conduct.[5] The pleasure which we are to enjoy ten years hence interests us so little in comparison with that which we may enjoy to-day, the passion which the first excites, is naturally so weak in comparison with that violent emotion which the second is apt to give occasion to, that the one could never be any balance to the other, unless it was supported by the sense of propriety, by the consciousness that we merited the esteem and approbation of every body, by acting in the one way, and that we became the proper objects of their contempt and derision by behaving in the other.

Humanity, justice, generosity, and public spirit, are the qualities most useful to others. Wherein consists the propriety of humanity and justice has been explained upon a former occasion,[6] where it was shown how much our esteem and approbation of those qualities depended upon the concord between the affections of the agent and those of the spectators.

The propriety of generosity and public spirit is founded upon the same principle with that of justice. Generosity is different from humanity. Those two qualities, which at first sight seem so nearly allied, do not always belong to the same person. Humanity is the virtue of a woman, generosity of a man.[7] The fair-sex, who have commonly much more tenderness than ours, have seldom so much generosity. That women rarely make considerable donations, is an observation of the civil law.* Humanity consists merely in the exquisite fellow-feeling which the spectator entertains with the sentiments of the persons principally concerned, so as to grieve for their sufferings, to resent their injuries, and to rejoice at their good fortune. The most humane actions require no self-denial, no self-command, no great exertion of the sense of propriety. They consist only in doing what this exquisite sympathy would of its own accord prompt us to do. But it is otherwise with generosity. We never are generous except when in some respect we prefer some other person to ourselves, and sacrifice some great and important interest of our own to an equal interest of a friend or of a superior. The man who gives up his pretensions to an office that was the great object of his ambition, because he imagines that the services of another are better entitled to it; the man who exposes his life to defend that of his friend, which he judges to be of more importance; neither of them act from humanity, or because they feel more exquisitely what concerns that other person than what concerns themselves. They both consider those opposite interests, not in the light in which they naturally appear to themselves, but in that in which they appear to others. To every bystander, the success or preservation of this other person may justly be more interesting than their own; but it cannot be so to themselves. When to the interest of this other person, therefore, they sacrifice their own, they accommodate themselves to the sentiments of the spectator, and by an effort of magnanimity act according to those views of things which, they feel, must naturally occur to any third person. The soldier who throws away his life in order to defend that of his officer, would perhaps be but little affected by the death of that officer, if it should happen without any fault of his own; and a very small disaster which had befallen himself might excite a much more lively sorrow. But when

* Raro mulieres donare solent.[8]

he endeavours to act so as to deserve applause, and to make the impartial spectator enter into the principles of his conduct, he feels, that to every body but himself, his own life is a trifle compared with that of his officer, and that when he sacrifices the one to the other, he acts quite properly and agreeably to what would be the natural apprehensions of every impartial bystander.

It is the same case with the greater exertions of public spirit. When a young officer exposes his life to acquire some inconsiderable addition to the dominions of his sovereign, it is not because the acquisition of the new territory is, to himself, an object more desirable than the preservation of his own life. To him his own life is of infinitely more value than the conquest of a whole kingdom for the state which he serves. But when he compares those two objects with one another, he does not view them in the light in which they naturally appear to himself, but in that in which they appear to the nation he fights for. To them the success of the war is of the highest importance; the life of a private person of scarce any consequence. When he puts himself in their situation, he immediately feels that he cannot be too prodigal of his blood, if, by shedding it, he can promote so valuable a purpose. In thus thwarting, from a sense of duty and propriety, the strongest of all natural propensities, consists the heroism of his conduct. There is many an honest Englishman, who, in his private station, would be more seriously disturbed by the loss of a guinea than by the national loss of Minorca, who yet, had it been in his power to defend that fortress, would have sacrificed his life a thousand times rather than, through his fault, have let it fall into the hands of the enemy.[9] When the first Brutus led forth his own sons to a capital punishment, because they had conspired against the rising liberty of Rome,[10] he sacrificed what, if he had consulted his own breast only, would appear to be the stronger to the weaker affection. Brutus ought naturally to have felt much more for the death of his own sons, than for all that probably Rome could have suffered from the want of so great an example. But he viewed them, not with the eyes of a father, but with those of a Roman citizen. He entered so thoroughly into the sentiments of this last character, that he paid no regard to that tie, by which he himself was connected with them; and to a Roman citizen, the sons even of Brutus seemed contemptible when put into the balance with the smallest interest of Rome. In these and in all other cases of this kind, our admiration is not so much founded upon the utility, as upon the unexpected, and on that account the great, the noble, and exalted propriety of such actions. This utility, when we come to view it, bestows upon them, undoubtedly, a new beauty, and upon that account still further recommends them to our approbation. This beauty, however, is chiefly perceived by men of reflection and speculation, and is by no means the quality which first recommends such actions to the natural sentiments of the bulk of mankind.

It is to be observed, that so far as the sentiment of approbation arises from the perception of this beauty of utility, it has no reference of any kind to the sentiments of others. If it was possible, therefore, that a person should grow up to manhood without any communication with society, his own actions might, notwithstanding, be agreeable or disagreeable to him on account of their tendency to his happiness or disadvantage. He might perceive a beauty of this kind in prudence, temperance, and good conduct, and a deformity in the opposite behaviour: he might view his own temper and character with that sort of satisfaction with which we consider a well-contrived machine, in the one case; or with that sort of distaste and dissatisfaction with which we regard a very awkward and clumsy contrivance, in the other. As these perceptions, however, are merely a matter of taste, and have all the feebleness and delicacy of that species of perceptions, upon the justness of which what is properly called taste is founded, they probably would not be much attended to by one in this solitary and miserable condition. Even though they should occur to him, they would by no means have the same effect upon him, antecedent to his connexion with society, which they would have in consequence of that connexion. He would not be cast down with inward shame at the thought of this deformity; nor would he be elevated with secret triumph of mind from the consciousness of the contrary beauty. He would not exult from the notion of deserving reward in the one case, nor tremble from the suspicion of meriting punishment in the other. All such sentiments suppose the idea of some other being, who is the natural judge of the person that feels them; and it is only by sympathy with the decisions of this arbiter of his conduct, that he can conceive, either the triumph of self-applause, or the shame of self-condemnation.

PART V.

OF THE

INFLUENCE OF CUSTOM AND FASHION

UPON THE

SENTIMENTS OF MORAL APPROBATION AND DISAPPROBATION.

CONSISTING OF ONE SECTION.

CHAPTER I.

Of the Influence of Custom and Fashion upon our notions of Beauty and Deformity.

There are other principles besides those already enumerated, which have a considerable influence upon the moral sentiments of mankind, and are the chief causes of the many irregular and discordant opinions which prevail in different ages and nations concerning what is blameable or praise-worthy. These principles are custom and fashion, principles which extend their dominion over our judgments concerning beauty of every kind.

When two objects have frequently been seen together, the imagination acquires a habit of passing easily from the one to the other. If the first appear, we lay our account that the second is to follow. Of their own accord they put us in mind of one another, and the attention glides easily along them. Though, independent of custom, there should be no real beauty in their union, yet when custom has thus connected them together, we feel an impropriety in their separation. The one we think is awkward when it appears without its usual companion. We miss something which we expected to find, and the habitual arrangement of our ideas is disturbed by the disappointment. A suit of clothes, for example, seems to want something if they are without the most insignificant ornament which usually accompanies them, and we find a meanness or awkwardness in the absence even of a haunch button. When there is any natural propriety in the union, custom increases our sense of it, and makes a different arrangement appear still more disagreeable than it would otherwise seem to be. Those who have been accustomed to see things in a good taste, are more disgusted by whatever is clumsy or awkward. Where the conjunction is improper, custom either diminishes, or takes away altogether, our sense of the impropriety. Those who have been accustomed to slovenly disorder lose all sense of neatness or elegance. The modes of furniture or dress which seem ridiculous to strangers, give no offence to the people who are used to them.

Fashion is different from custom, or rather is a particular species of it. That is not the fashion which every body wears, but which those wear who are of a high rank, or character. The graceful, the easy, and commanding manners of the great, joined to the usual richness and magnificence of their dress, give a grace to the very form which they happen to bestow upon it. As long as they continue to use this form, it is connected in our imaginations with the idea of something that is genteel and magnificent, and though in itself it should be indifferent, it seems, on account of this relation, to have something about it that is genteel and magnificent too. As soon as they drop it, it loses all the grace, which it had appeared to possess before, and being now used only by the inferior ranks of people, seems to have something of their meanness and awkwardness.

Dress and furniture are allowed by all the world to be entirely under the dominion of custom and fashion. The influence of those principles, however, is by no means confined to so narrow a sphere, but extends itself to whatever is in any respect the object of taste, to music, to poetry, to architecture. The modes of dress and furniture are continually changing, and that fashion appearing ridiculous to-day which was admired five years ago, we are experimentally convinced that it owed its vogue chiefly or entirely to custom and fashion. Clothes and furniture are not made of very durable materials. A well-fancied coat is done in a twelve-month, and cannot continue longer to propagate, as the fashion, that form according to which it was made. The modes of furniture change less rapidly than those of dress; because furniture is commonly more durable. In five or six years, however, it generally undergoes an entire revolution, and every man in his own time sees the fashion in this respect change many different ways. The productions of the other arts are much more lasting, and, when happily imagined, may continue to propagate the fashion of their make for a much longer time. A well-contrived building may endure many centuries: a beautiful air may be delivered down by a sort of tradition, through many successive generations: a well-written poem may last as long as the world; and all of them continue for ages together, to give the vogue to that particular style, to that particular taste or manner, according to which each of them was composed. Few men have an opportunity of seeing in their own times the fashion in any of these arts change very considerably. Few men have so much experience and acquaintance with the different modes which have obtained in remote ages and nations, as to be thoroughly reconciled to them, or to judge with impartiality between them, and what takes place in their own age and country. Few men therefore are willing to allow, that custom or fashion have much influence upon their judgments concerning what is beautiful, or otherwise, in the productions of any of those arts; but imagine, that all the rules, which they think ought to be observed in each of them, are founded upon reason and nature, not upon habit or prejudice. A very little attention, however, may convince them of the contrary, and satisfy them, that the influence of custom and fashion over dress and furniture, is not more absolute than over architecture, poetry, and music.

Can any reason, for example, be assigned why the Doric capital should be appropriated to a pillar, whose height is equal to eight diameters; the Ionic volute to one of nine; and the Corinthian foliage to one of ten? The propriety of each of those appropriations can be founded upon nothing but habit and custom. The eye having been used to see a particular proportion connected with a particular ornament, would be offended if they were not joined together. Each of the five orders has its peculiar ornaments, which cannot be changed for any other, without giving offence to all those who know anything of the rules of architecture. According to some architects, indeed, such is the exquisite judgment with which the ancients have assigned to each order its proper ornaments, that no others can be found which are equally suitable. It seems, however, a little difficult to be conceived that these forms, though, no doubt, extremely agreeable, should be the only forms which can suit those proportions, or that there should not be five hundred others which, antecedent to established custom, would have fitted them equally well. When custom, however, has established particular rules of building, provided they are not absolutely unreasonable, it is absurd to think of altering them for others which are only equally good, or even for others which, in point of elegance and beauty, have naturally some little advantage over them.[1] A man would be ridiculous who should appear in public with a suit of clothes quite different from those which are commonly worn, though the new dress should in itself be ever so graceful or convenient. And there seems to be an absurdity of the same kind in ornamenting a house after a quite different manner from that which custom and fashion have prescribed; though the new ornaments should in themselves be somewhat superior to the common ones.

According to the ancient rhetoricians, a certain measure of verse was by nature appropriated to each particular species of writing, as being naturally expressive of that character, sentiment, or passion, which ought to predominate in it.[2] One verse, they said, was fit for grave and another for gay works, which could not, they thought, be interchanged without the greatest impropriety. The experience of modern times, however, seems to contradict this principle, though in itself it would appear to be extremely probable. What is the burlesque verse in English, is the heroic verse in French. The tragedies of Racine and the Henriad of Voltaire, are nearly in the same verse with,

"Let me have your advice in a weighty affair."

The burlesque verse in French, on the contrary, is pretty much the same with the heroic verse of ten syllables in English. Custom has made the one nation associate the ideas of gravity, sublimity, and seriousness, to that measure which the other has connected with whatever is gay, flippant, and ludicrous. Nothing would appear more absurd in English than a tragedy written in the Alexandrine verses of the French; or in French, than a work of the same kind in verses of ten syllables.

An eminent artist will bring about a considerable change in the established modes of each of those arts, and introduce a new fashion of writing, music, or architecture. As the dress of an agreeable man of high rank recommends itself, and how peculiar and fantastical soever, comes soon to be admired and imitated; so the excellencies of an eminent master recommend his peculiarities, and his manner becomes the fashionable style in the art which he practises. The taste of the Italians in music and architecture has, within these fifty years, undergone a considerable change, from imitating the peculiarities of some eminent masters in each of those arts. Seneca is accused by Quintilian of having corrupted the taste of the Romans, and of having introduced a frivolous prettiness in the room of majestic reason and masculine eloquence.[3] Sallust and Tacitus have by others been charged with the same accusation, though in a different manner. They gave reputation, it is pretended, to a style, which though in the highest degree concise, elegant, expressive, and even poetical, wanted, however, ease, simplicity, and nature, and was evidently the production of the most laboured and studied affectation. How many great qualities must that writer possess, who can thus render his very faults agreeable? After the praise of refining the taste of a nation, the highest eulogy, perhaps, which can be bestowed upon any author, is to say, that he corrupted it. In our own language, Mr. Pope and Dr. Swift have each of them introduced a manner different from what was practised, before into all works that are written in rhyme, the one in long verses, the other in short. The quaintness of Butler has given place to the plainness of Swift. The rambling freedom of Dryden, and the correct but often tedious and prosaic languor of Addison, are no longer the objects of imitation, but all long verses are now written after the manner of the nervous precision of Mr. Pope.

Neither is it only over the productions of the arts, that custom and fashion exert their dominion. They influence our judgments, in the same manner, with regard to the beauty of natural objects. What various and opposite forms are deemed beautiful in different species of things? The proportions which are admired in one animal, are altogether different from those which are esteemed in another. Every class of things has its own peculiar conformation, which is approved of, and has a beauty of its own, distinct from that of every other species. It is upon this account that a learned Jesuit, father Buffier, has determined that the beauty of every object consists in that form and colour, which is most usual among things of that particular sort to which it belongs.[4] Thus, in the human form, the beauty of each feature lies in a certain middle, equally removed from a variety of other forms that are ugly. A beautiful nose, for example, is one that is neither very long, nor very short, neither very straight, nor very crooked, but a sort of middle among all these extremes, and less different from any one of them than all of them, are from one another. It is the form which Nature seems to have aimed at in them all, which, however, she deviates from in a great variety of ways, and very seldom hits exactly; but to which all those deviations still bear a very strong resemblance. When a number of drawings are made after one pattern, though they may all miss it in some respects, yet they will all resemble it more than they resemble one another; the general character of the pattern will run through them all; the most singular and odd will be those which are most wide of it; and though very few will copy it exactly, yet the most accurate delineations will bear a greater resemblance to the most careless, than the careless ones will bear to one another. In the same manner, in each species of creatures, what is most beautiful bears the strongest characters of the general fabric of the species, and has the strongest resemblance to the greater part of the individuals with which it is classed. Monsters, on the contrary, or what is perfectly deformed, are always most singular and odd, and have the least resemblance to the generality of that species to which they belong. And thus the beauty of each species, though in one sense the rarest of all things, because few individuals hit this middle form exactly, yet in another is the most common, because all the deviations from it resemble it more than they resemble one another. The most customary form, therefore, is in each species of things, according to him, the most beautiful. And hence it is that a certain practice and experience in contemplating each species of objects is requisite, before we can judge of its beauty, or know wherein the middle and most usual form consists. The nicest judgment concerning the beauty of the human species, will not help us to judge of that of flowers, or horses, or any other species of things. It is for the same reason that in different climates, and where different customs and ways of living take place, as the generality of any species receives a different conformation from those circumstances, so different ideas of its beauty prevail. The beauty of a Moorish is not exactly the same with that of an English horse. What different ideas are formed in different nations concerning the beauty of the human shape and countenance? A fair complexion is a shocking deformity upon the coast of Guinea. Thick lips and a flat nose are a beauty. In some nations long ears that hang down upon the shoulders are the objects of universal admiration.[5] In China if a lady's foot is so large as to be fit to walk upon, she is regarded as a monster of ugliness. Some of the savage nations in North-America tie four boards round the heads of their children, and thus squeeze them, while the bones are tender and gristly, into a form that is almost perfectly square. Europeans are astonished at the absurd barbarity of this practice, to which some missionaries have imputed the singular stupidity of those nations among whom it prevails. But when they condemn those savages, they do not reflect that the ladies in Europe had, till within these very few years, been endeavouring, for near a century past, to squeeze the beautiful roundness of their natural shape into a square form of the same kind. And that, notwithstanding the many distortions and diseases which this practice was known to occasion, custom had rendered it agreeable among some of the most civilized nations which, perhaps, the world ever beheld.

Such is the system of this learned and ingenious Father, concerning the nature of beauty; of which the whole charm, according to him, would thus seem to arise from its falling in with the habits which custom had impressed upon the imagination, with regard to things of each particular kind. I cannot, however, be induced to believe that our sense even of external beauty is founded altogether on custom. The utility of any form, its fitness for the useful purposes for which it was intended, evidently recommends it, and renders it agreeable to us, independent of custom. Certain colours are more agreeable than others, and give more delight to the eye the first time it ever beholds them. A smooth surface is more agreeable than a rough one. Variety is more pleasing than a tedious undiversified uniformity. Connected variety, in which each new appearance seems to be introduced by what went before it, and in which all the adjoining parts seem to have some natural relation to one another, is more agreeable than a disjointed and disorderly assemblage of unconnected objects. But though I cannot admit that custom is the sole principle of beauty, yet I can so far allow the truth of this ingenious system as to grant, that there is scarce any one external form so beautiful as to please, if quite contrary to custom, and unlike whatever we have been used to in that particular species of things: or so deformed as not to be agreeable, if custom uniformly supports it, and habituates us to see it in every single individual of the kind.

CHAPTER II.

Of the Influence of Custom and Fashion upon Moral Sentiments.

Since our sentiments concerning beauty of every kind, are so much influenced by custom and fashion, it cannot be expected, that those, concerning the beauty of conduct, should be entirely exempted from the dominion of those principles. Their influence here, however, seems to be much less than it is every where else. There is, perhaps, no form of external objects, how absurd and fantastical soever, to which custom will not reconcile us, or which fashion will not render even agreeable. But the characters and conduct of a Nero, or a Claudius, are what no custom will ever reconcile us to, what no fashion will ever render agreeable; but the one will always be the object of dread and hatred; the other of scorn and derision.[1] The principles of the imagination, upon which our sense of beauty depends, are of a very nice and delicate nature, and may easily be altered by habit and education: but the sentiments of moral approbation and disapprobation, are founded on the strongest and most vigorous passions of human nature; and though they may be somewhat warpt, cannot be entirely perverted.

But though the influence of custom and fashion upon moral sentiments is not altogether so great, it is however perfectly similar to what it is everywhere else. When custom and fashion coincide with the natural principles of right and wrong, they heighten the delicacy of our sentiments, and increase our abhorrence for everything which approaches to evil. Those who have been educated in what is really good company, not in what is commonly called such, who have been accustomed to see nothing in the persons whom they esteemed and lived with, but justice, modesty, humanity, and good order; are more shocked with whatever seems to be inconsistent with the rules which those virtues prescribe. Those, on the contrary, who have had the misfortune to be brought up amidst violence, licentiousness, falsehood, and injustice; lose, though not all sense of the impropriety of such conduct, yet all sense of its dreadful enormity, or of the vengeance and punishment due to it. They have been familiarized with it from their infancy, custom has rendered it habitual to them, and they are very apt to regard it as, what is called, the way of the world, something which either may, or must be practised, to hinder us from being the dupes of our own integrity.

Fashion too will sometimes give reputation to a certain degree of disorder, and, on the contrary, discountenance qualities which deserve esteem. In the reign of Charles II. a degree of licentiousness was deemed the characteristic of a liberal education. It was connected, according to the notions of those times, with generosity, sincerity, magnanimity, loyalty, and proved that the person who acted in this manner, was a gentleman, and not a puritan. Severity of manners and regularity of conduct, on the other hand, were altogether unfashionable, and were connected, in the imagination of that age, with cant, cunning, hypocrisy, and low manners. To superficial minds, the vices of the great seem at all times agreeable. They connect them, not only with the splendour of fortune, but with many superior virtues, which they ascribe to their superiors; with the spirit of freedom and independency, with frankness, generosity, humanity, and politeness. The virtues of the inferior ranks of people, on the contrary, their parsimonious frugality, their painful industry, and rigid adherence to rules, seem to them mean and disagreeable. They connect them, both with the meanness of the station to which those qualities commonly belong, and with many great vices, which, they suppose, usually accompany them; such as an abject, cowardly, ill-natured, lying, pilfering disposition.

The objects with which men in the different professions and states of life are conversant, being very different, and habituating them to very different passions, naturally form in them very different characters and manners. We expect in each rank and profession, a degree of those manners, which, experience has taught us, belonged to it. But as in each species of things, we are particularly pleased with the middle conformation, which, in every part and feature, agrees most exactly with the general standard which nature seems to have established for things of that kind; so in each rank, or, if I may say so, in each species of men, we are particularly pleased, if they have neither too much, nor too little of the character which usually accompanies their particular condition and situation. A man, we say, should look like his trade and profession; yet the pedantry of every profession is disagreeable.

The different periods of life have, for the same reason, different manners assigned to them. We expect in old age, that gravity and sedateness which its infirmities, its long experience, and its worn-out sensibility seem to render both natural and respectable; and we lay our account to find in youth that sensibility, that gaiety and sprightly vivacity which experience teaches us to expect from the lively impressions that all interesting objects are apt to make upon the tender and unpractised senses of that early period of life. Each of those two ages, however, may easily have too much of the peculiarities which belong to it. The flirting levity of youth, and the immoveable insensibility of old age, are equally disagreeable. The young, according to the common saying, are most agreeable when in their behaviour there is something of the manners of the old, and the old, when they retain something of the gaiety of the young. Either of them, however, may easily have too much of the manners of the other. The extreme coldness, and dull formality, which are pardoned in old age, make youth ridiculous. The levity, the carelessness, and the vanity, which are indulged in youth, render old age contemptible.

The peculiar character and manners which we are led by custom to appropriate to each rank and profession, have sometimes perhaps, a propriety independent of custom; and are what we should approve of for their own sakes, if we took into consideration all the different circumstances which naturally affect those in each different state of life. The propriety of a person's behaviour, depends not upon its suitableness to any one circumstance of his situation, but to all the circumstances, which, when we bring his case home to ourselves, we feel, should naturally call upon his attention. If he appears to be so much occupied by any one of them, as entirely to neglect the rest, we disapprove of his conduct, as something which we cannot entirely go along with, because not properly adjusted to all the circumstances of his situation: yet, perhaps, the emotion he expresses for the object which principally interests him, does not exceed what we should entirely sympathize with, and approve of, in one whose attention was not required by any other thing. A parent in private life might, upon the loss of an only son, express without blame a degree of grief and tenderness, which would be unpardonable in a general at the head of an army, when glory, and the public safety, demanded so great a part of his attention. As different objects ought, upon common occasions, to occupy the attention of men of different professions, so different passions ought naturally to become habitual to them; and when we bring home to ourselves their situation in this particular respect, we must be sensible, that every occurrence should naturally affect them more or less, according as the emotion which it excites, coincides or disagrees with the fixt habit and temper of their minds. We cannot expect the same sensibility to the gay pleasures and amusements of life in a clergyman, which we lay our account with in an officer. The man whose peculiar occupation it is to keep the world in mind of that awful futurity which awaits them, who is to announce what may be the fatal consequences of every deviation from the rules of duty, and who is himself to set the example of the most exact conformity, seems to be the messenger of tidings, which cannot, in propriety, be delivered either with levity or indifference. His mind is supposed to be continually occupied with what is too grand and solemn, to leave any room for the impressions of those frivolous objects, which fill up the attention of the dissipated and the gay. We readily feel therefore, that, independent of custom, there is a propriety in the manners which custom has allotted to this profession; and that nothing can be more suitable to the character of a clergyman, than that grave, that austere and abstracted severity, which we are habituated to expect in his behaviour. These reflections are so very obvious, that there is scarce any man so inconsiderate, as not, at some time, to have made them, and to have accounted to himself in this manner for his approbation of the usual character of this order.

The foundation of the customary character of some other professions is not so obvious, and our approbation of it is founded entirely in habit, without being either confirmed, or enlivened by any reflections of this kind. We are led by custom, for example, to annex the character of gaiety, levity, and sprightly freedom, as well as of some degree of dissipation, to the military profession. Yet, if we were to consider what mood or tone of temper would be most suitable to this situation, we should be apt to determine, perhaps, that the most serious and thoughtful turn of mind would best become those whose lives are continually exposed to uncommon danger, and who should therefore be more

constantly occupied with the thoughts of death and its consequences than other men. It is this very circumstance, however,
which is not improbably the occasion why the contrary turn of
mind prevails so much among men of this profession. It requires
so great an effort to conquer the fear of death, when we survey it
with steadiness and attention, that those who are constantly
exposed to it, find it easier to turn away their thoughts from it
altogether, to wrap themselves up in careless security and indifference, and to plunge themselves, for this purpose, into every
sort of amusement and dissipation. A camp is not the element of
a thoughtful or a melancholy man: persons of that cast, indeed,
are often abundantly determined, and are capable, by a great
effort, of going on with inflexible resolution to the most unavoidable death. But to be exposed to continual, though less imminent
danger, to be obliged to exert, for a long time, a degree of this
effort, exhausts and depresses the mind, and renders it incapable
of all happiness and enjoyment. The gay and careless, who have
occasion to make no effort at all, who fairly resolve never to look
before them, but to lose in continual pleasures and amusements
all anxiety about their situation, more easily support such circumstances. Whenever, by any peculiar circumstances, an officer
has no reason to lay his account with being exposed to any
uncommon danger, he is very apt to lose the gaiety and dissipated
thoughtlessness of his character. The captain of a city-guard is
commonly as sober, careful, and penurious an animal as the rest
of his fellow-citizens. A long peace is, for the same reason, very
apt to diminish the difference between the civil and the military
character. The ordinary situation, however, of men of this profession, renders gaiety, and a degree of dissipation, so much their
usual character; and custom has, in our imagination, so strongly
connected this character with this state of life, that we are very
apt to despise any man, whose peculiar humour or situation, renders him incapable of acquiring it. We laugh at the grave and
careful faces of a city-guard, which so little resemble those of
their profession. They themselves seem often to be ashamed of
the regularity of their own manners, and, not to be out of the
fashion of their trade, are fond of affecting that levity, which is
by no means natural to them. Whatever is the deportment which
we have been accustomed to see in a respectable order of men, it

comes to be so associated in our imagination with that order, that whenever we see the one, we lay our account that we are to meet with the other, and when disappointed, miss something which we expected to find. We are embarrassed, and put to a stand, and know not how to address ourselves to a character, which plainly affects to be of a different species from those with which we should have been disposed to class it.

The different situations of different ages and countries are apt, in the same manner, to give different characters to the generality of those who live in them, and their sentiments concerning the particular degree of each quality, that is either blamable or praise-worthy, vary, according to that degree which is usual in their own country, and in their own times.[2] That degree of politeness, which would be highly esteemed, perhaps, would be thought effeminate adulation, in Russia, would be regarded as rudeness and barbarism at the court of France. That degree of order and frugality, which, in a Polish nobleman, would be considered as excessive parsimony, would be regarded as extravagance in a citizen of Amsterdam. Every age and country look upon that degree of each quality, which is commonly to be met with in those who are esteemed among themselves, as the golden mean of that particular talent or virtue. And as this varies, according as their different circumstances render different qualities more or less habitual to them, their sentiments concerning the exact propriety of character and behaviour vary accordingly.

Among civilized nations, the virtues which are founded upon humanity, are more cultivated than those which are founded upon self-denial and the command of the passions.[3] Among rude and barbarous nations, it is quite otherwise, the virtues of self-denial are more cultivated than those of humanity. The general security and happiness which prevail in ages of civility and politeness, afford little exercise to the contempt of danger, to patience in enduring labour, hunger, and pain. Poverty may easily be avoided, and the contempt of it therefore almost ceases to be a virtue. The abstinence from pleasure becomes less necessary, and the mind is more at liberty to unbend itself, and to indulge its natural inclinations in all those particular respects.

Among savages and barbarians it is quite otherwise. Every savage undergoes a sort of Spartan discipline, and by the necessity

of his situation is inured to every sort of hardship.[4] He is in continual danger: he is often exposed to the greatest extremities of
hunger, and frequently dies of pure want. His circumstances not
only habituate him to every sort of distress, but teach him to give
way to none of the passions which that distress is apt to excite.
He can expect from his countrymen no sympathy or indulgence
for such weakness. Before we can feel much for others, we must
in some measure be at ease ourselves. If our own misery pinches
us very severely, we have no leisure to attend to that of our neighbour: and all savages are too much occupied with their own
wants and necessities, to give much attention to those of another
person. A savage, therefore, whatever be the nature of his distress, expects no sympathy from those about him, and disdains,
upon that account, to expose himself, by allowing the least weakness to escape him. His passions, how furious and violent soever,
are never permitted to disturb the serenity of his countenance or
the composure of his conduct and behaviour. The savages in
North America, we are told, assume upon all occasions the greatest indifference, and would think themselves degraded if they
should ever appear in any respect to be overcome, either by love,
or grief, or resentment. Their magnanimity and self-command, in
this respect, are almost beyond the conception of Europeans. In a
country in which all men are upon a level, with regard to rank
and fortune, it might be expected that the mutual inclinations of
the two parties should be the only thing considered in marriages,
and should be indulged without any sort of control. This, however, is the country in which all marriages, without exception,
are made up by the parents, and in which a young man would
think himself disgraced for ever, if he showed the least preference
of one woman above another, or did not express the most complete indifference, both about the time when, and the person to
whom he was to be married.[5] The weakness of love, which is so
much indulged in ages of humanity and politeness, is regarded
among savages as the most unpardonable effeminacy. Even after
the marriage, the two parties seem to be ashamed of a connexion
which is founded upon so sordid a necessity. They do not live
together. They see one another by stealth only. They both continue
to dwell in the houses of their respective fathers, and the open
cohabitation of the two sexes, which is permitted without blame

in all other countries, is here considered as the most indecent and unmanly sensuality. Nor is it only over this agreeable passion that they exert this absolute self-command. They often bear, in the sight of all their countrymen, with injuries, reproach, and the grossest insults, with the appearance of the greatest insensibility, and without expressing the smallest resentment. When a savage is made prisoner of war, and receives, as is usual, the sentence of death from his conquerors, he hears it without expressing any emotion, and afterwards submits to the most dreadful torments, without ever bemoaning himself, or discovering any other passion but contempt of his enemies.[6] While he is hung by the shoulders over a slow fire, he derides his tormentors, and tells them with how much more ingenuity he himself had tormented such of their countrymen as had fallen into his hands. After he has been scorched and burnt, and lacerated in all the most tender and sensible parts of his body for several hours together, he is often allowed, in order to prolong his misery, a short respite, and is taken down from the stake: he employs this interval in talking upon all indifferent subjects, inquires after the news of the country, and seems indifferent about nothing but his own situation. The spectators express the same insensibility; the sight of so horrible an object seems to make no impression upon them; they scarce look at the prisoner, except when they lend a hand to torment him. At other times they smoke tobacco, and amuse themselves with any common object, as if no such matter was going on. Every savage is said to prepare himself from his earliest youth for this dreadful end. He composes, for this purpose, what they call the song of death, a song which he is to sing when he has fallen into the hands of his enemies, and is expiring under the tortures which they inflict upon him. It consists of insults upon his tormentors, and expresses the highest contempt of death and pain. He sings this song upon all extraordinary occasions, when he goes out to war, when he meets his enemies in the field, or whenever he has a mind to show that he has familiarized his imagination to the most dreadful misfortunes, and that no human event can daunt his resolution, or alter his purpose. The same contempt of death and torture prevails among all other savage nations. There is not a negro from the coast of Africa who does not, in this respect, possess a degree of magnanimity which the

soul of his sordid master is too often scarce capable of conceiving. Fortune never exerted more cruelly her empire over mankind,
than when she subjected those nations of heroes to the refuse of
the jails of Europe, to wretches who possess the virtues neither of
the countries which they come from, nor of those which they go
to, and whose levity, brutality, and baseness, so justly expose
them to the contempt of the vanquished.

This heroic and unconquerable firmness, which the custom
and education of his country demand of every savage, is not
required of those who are brought up to live in civilized societies.
If these last complain when they are in pain, if they grieve when
they are in distress, if they allow themselves either to be overcome by love, or to be discomposed by anger, they are easily pardoned. Such weaknesses are not apprehended to affect the
essential parts of their character. As long as they do not allow
themselves to be transported to do any thing contrary to justice
or humanity, they lose but little reputation, though the serenity
of their countenance, or the composure of their discourse and
behaviour, should be somewhat ruffled and disturbed. A humane
and polished people, who have more sensibility to the passions of
others, can more readily enter into an animated and passionate
behaviour, and can more easily pardon some little excess. The
person principally concerned is sensible of this; and being assured
of the equity of his judges, indulges himself in stronger expressions of passion, and is less afraid of exposing himself to their
contempt by the violence of his emotions. We can venture to
express more emotion in the presence of a friend than in that of a
stranger, because we expect more indulgence from the one than
from the other. And in the same manner the rules of decorum
among civilized nations, admit of a more animated behaviour,
than is approved of among barbarians. The first converse together
with the openness of friends; the second with the reserve of
strangers. The emotion and vivacity with which the French and
the Italians, the two most polished nations upon the continent,
express themselves on occasions that are at all interesting, surprise at first those strangers who happen to be travelling among
them, and who, having been educated among a people of duller
sensibility, cannot enter into this passionate behaviour, of which
they have never seen any example in their own country. A young

French nobleman will weep in the presence of the whole court, upon being refused a regiment. An Italian, says the abbot Dû Bos, expresses more emotion on being condemned in a fine of twenty shillings, than an Englishman on receiving the sentence of death.[7] Cicero, in the times of the highest Roman politeness, could, without degrading himself, weep with all the bitterness of sorrow in the sight of the whole senate and the whole people; as it is evident he must have done in the end of almost every oration. The orators of the earlier and ruder ages of Rome could not probably, consistent with the manners of the times, have expressed themselves with so much emotion. It would have been regarded, I suppose, as a violation of nature and propriety in the Scipios, in the Leliuses, and in the elder Cato, to have exposed so much tenderness to the view of the public. Those ancient warriors could express themselves with order, gravity, and good judgment; but are said to have been strangers to that sublime and passionate eloquence which was first introduced into Rome, not many years before the birth of Cicero, by the two Gracchi, by Crassus, and by Sulpitius.[8] This animated eloquence, which has been long practised, with or without success, both in France and Italy, is but just beginning to be introduced into England. So wide is the difference between the degrees of self-command which are required in civilized and in barbarous nations, and by such different standards do they judge of the propriety of behaviour.

This difference gives occasion to many others that are not less essential. A polished people being accustomed to give way, in some measure, to the movements of nature, become frank, open, and sincere. Barbarians, on the contrary, being obliged to smother and conceal the appearance of every passion, necessarily acquire the habits of falsehood and dissimulation. It is observed by all those who have been conversant with savage nations, whether in Asia, Africa, or America, that they are all equally impenetrable, and that, when they have a mind to conceal the truth, no examination is capable of drawing it from them. They cannot be trepanned by the most artful questions. The torture itself is incapable of making them confess any thing which they have no mind to tell. The passions of a savage too, though they never express themselves by any outward emotion, but lie concealed in the breast of the sufferer, are, notwithstanding, all mounted to the highest pitch of fury. Though he seldom shows any symptoms of anger, yet his vengeance, when he comes to give way to it, is always sanguinary and dreadful. The least affront drives him to despair. His countenance and discourse indeed are still sober and composed, and express nothing but the most perfect tranquillity of mind: but his actions are often the most furious and violent. Among the North-Americans it is not uncommon for persons of the tenderest age and more fearful sex to drown themselves upon receiving only a slight reprimand from their mothers, and this too without expressing any passion, or saying any thing, except *you shall no longer have a daughter.*[9] In civilized nations the passions of men are not commonly so furious or so desperate. They are often clamorous and noisy, but are seldom very hurtful; and seem frequently to aim at no other satisfaction, but that of convincing the spectator, that they are in the right to be so much moved, and of procuring his sympathy and approbation.

All these effects of custom and fashion, however, upon the moral sentiments of mankind, are inconsiderable, in comparison of those which they give occasion to in some other cases; and it is not concerning the general style of character and behaviour, that those principles produce the greatest perversion of judgment, but concerning the propriety or impropriety of particular usages.

The different manners which custom teaches us to approve of in the different professions and states of life, do not concern things of the greatest importance. We expect truth and justice from an old man as well as from a young, from a clergyman as well as from an officer; and it is in matters of small moment only that we look for the distinguishing marks of their respective characters. With regard to these too, there is often some unobserved circumstance which, if it was attended to, would show us, that, independent of custom, there was a propriety in the character which custom had taught us to allot to each profession. We cannot complain, therefore, in this case, that the perversion of natural sentiment is very great. Though the manners of different nations require different degrees of the same quality, in the character which they think worthy of esteem, yet the worst that can be said to happen even here, is that the duties of one virtue are sometimes extended so as to encroach a little upon the precincts of some other. The rustic hospitality that is in fashion among the

Poles encroaches, perhaps, a little upon economy and good order; and the frugality that is esteemed in Holland, upon generosity and good-fellowship. The hardiness demanded of savages diminishes their humanity; and, perhaps, the delicate sensibility required in civilized nations sometimes destroys the masculine firmness of the character. In general, the style of manners which takes place in any nation, may commonly upon the whole be said to be that which is most suitable to its situation. Hardiness is the character most suitable to the circumstances of a savage; sensibility to those of one who lives in a very civilized society. Even here, therefore, we cannot complain that the moral sentiments of men are very grossly perverted.

It is not therefore in the general style of conduct or behaviour that custom authorises the widest departure from what is the natural propriety of action. With regard to particular usages, its influence is often much more destructive of good morals, and it is capable of establishing, as lawful and blameless, particular actions, which shock the plainest principles of right and wrong.

Can there be greater barbarity, for example, than to hurt an infant? Its helplessness, its innocence, its amiableness, call forth the compassion, even of an enemy, and not to spare that tender age is regarded as the most furious effort of an enraged and cruel conqueror. What then should we imagine must be the heart of a parent who could injure that weakness which even a furious enemy is afraid to violate? Yet the exposition, that is, the murder of new-born infants, was a practice allowed of in almost all the states of Greece, even among the polite and civilized Athenians; and whenever the circumstances of the parent rendered it inconvenient to bring up the child, to abandon it to hunger, or to wild beasts, was regarded without blame or censure. This practice had probably begun in times of the most savage barbarity. The imaginations of men had been first made familiar with it in that earliest period of society, and the uniform continuance of the custom had hindered them afterwards from perceiving its enormity. We find, at this day, that this practice prevails among all savage nations;[10] and in that rudest and lowest state of society it is undoubtedly more pardonable than in any other. The extreme indigence of a savage is often such that he himself is frequently exposed to the greatest extremity of hunger, he often dies of pure want, and it is frequently impossible for him to support both himself and his child. We cannot wonder, therefore, that in this case he should abandon it. One who, in flying from an enemy, whom it was impossible to resist, should throw down his infant, because it retarded his flight, would surely be excusable; since, by attempting to save it, he could only hope for the consolation of dying with it. That in this state of society, therefore, a parent should be allowed to judge whether he can bring up his child, ought not to surprise us so greatly. In the latter ages of Greece, however, the same thing was permitted from views of remote interest or conveniency, which could by no means excuse it. Uninterrupted custom had by this time so thoroughly authorised the practice, that not only the loose maxims of the world tolerated this barbarous prerogative, but even the doctrine of philosophers, which ought to have been more just and accurate, was led away by the established custom, and upon this, as upon many other occasions, instead of censuring, supported the horrible abuse, by far-fetched considerations of public utility. Aristotle talks of it as of what the magistrate ought upon many occasions to encourage. The humane Plato is of the same opinion, and, with all that love of mankind which seems to animate all his writings, no where marks this practice with disapprobation.[11] When custom can give sanction to so dreadful a violation of humanity, we may well imagine that there is scarce any particular practice so gross which it cannot authorise. Such a thing, we hear men every day saying, is commonly done, and they seem to think this a sufficient apology for what, in itself, is the most unjust and unreasonable conduct.

There is an obvious reason why custom should never pervert our sentiments with regard to the general style and character of conduct and behaviour, in the same degree as with regard to the propriety or unlawfulness of particular usages. There never can be any such custom. No society could subsist a moment, in which the usual strain of men's conduct and behaviour was of a piece with the horrible practice I have just now mentioned.

PART VI.

OF THE CHARACTER
OF VIRTUE.

CONSISTING OF THREE SECTIONS.[1]

INTRODUCTION.

When we consider the character of any individual, we naturally view it under two different aspects; first, as it may affect his own happiness; and secondly, as it may affect that of other people.

SECTION I.

OF THE CHARACTER OF THE INDIVIDUAL, SO
FAR AS IT AFFECTS HIS OWN HAPPINESS; OR OF
PRUDENCE.

The preservation and healthful state of the body seem to be the
objects which Nature first recommends to the care of every individual. The appetites of hunger and thirst, the agreeable or disagreeable sensations of pleasure and pain, of heat and cold, &c.
may be considered as lessons delivered by the voice of Nature
herself, directing him what he ought to chuse, and what he ought
to avoid, for this purpose. The first lessons which he is taught by
those to whom his childhood is entrusted, tend, the greater part of
them, to the *same* purpose. Their principal object is to teach him
how to keep out of harm's way.

As he grows up, he soon learns that some care and foresight
are necessary for providing the means of gratifying those natural
appetites, of procuring pleasure and avoiding pain, of procuring
the agreeable and avoiding the disagreeable temperature of heat
and cold. In the proper direction of this care and foresight consists the art of preserving and increasing what is called his external fortune.

Though it is in order to supply the necessities and conveniencies
of the body, that the advantages of external fortune are originally
recommended to us, yet we cannot live long in the world without
perceiving that the respect of our equals, our credit and rank
in the society we live in, depend very much upon the degree in
which we possess, or are supposed to possess, those advantages.
The desire of becoming the proper objects of this respect, of
deserving and obtaining this credit and rank among our equals,
is, perhaps, the strongest of all our desires, and our anxiety to
obtain the advantages of fortune is accordingly much more
excited and irritated by this desire, than by that of supplying all

the necessities and conveniencies of the body, which are always very easily supplied.

Our rank and credit among our equals, too, depend very much upon, what, perhaps, a virtuous man would wish them to depend entirely, our character and conduct, or upon the confidence, esteem, and good-will, which these naturally excite in the people we live with.

The care of the health, of the fortune, of the rank and reputation of the individual, the objects upon which his comfort and happiness in this life are supposed principally to depend, is considered as the proper business of that virtue which is commonly called Prudence.

We suffer more, it has already been observed,[2] when we fall from a better to a worse situation, than we ever enjoy when we rise from a worse to a better. Security, therefore, is the first and the principal object of prudence. It is averse to expose our health, our fortune, our rank, or reputation, to any sort of hazard. It is rather cautious than enterprising, and more anxious to preserve the advantages which we already possess, than forward to prompt us to the acquisition of still greater advantages. The methods of improving our fortune, which it principally recommends to us, are those which expose to no loss or hazard; real knowledge and skill in our trade or profession, assiduity and industry in the exercise of it, frugality, and even some degree of parsimony, in all our expences.

The prudent man always studies seriously and earnestly to understand whatever he professes to understand, and not merely to persuade other people that he understands it; and though his talents may not always be very brilliant, they are always perfectly genuine. He neither endeavours to impose upon you by the cunning devices of an artful impostor, nor by the arrogant airs of an assuming pedant, nor by the confident assertions of a superficial and impudent pretender. He is not ostentatious even of the abilities which he really possesses. His conversation is simple and modest, and he is averse to all the quackish arts by which other people so frequently thrust themselves into public notice and reputation. For reputation in his profession he is naturally disposed to rely a good deal upon the solidity of his knowledge and abilities; and he does not always think of cultivating the favour of

those little clubs and cabals, who, in the superior arts and sciences, so often erect themselves into the supreme judges of merit;
and who make it their business to celebrate the talents and virtues of one another, and to decry whatever can come into competition with them. If he ever connects himself with any society of
this kind, it is merely in self-defence, not with a view to impose
upon the public, but to hinder the public from being imposed
upon, to his disadvantage, by the clamours, the whispers, or the
intrigues, either of that particular society, or of some other of the
same kind.

The prudent man is always sincere, and feels horror at the very
thought of exposing himself to the disgrace which attends upon
the detection of falsehood. But though always sincere, he is not
always frank and open; and though he never tells any thing but
the truth, he does not always think himself bound, when not
properly called upon, to tell the whole truth. As he is cautious in
his actions, so he is reserved in his speech; and never rashly or
unnecessarily obtrudes his opinion concerning either things or
persons.

The prudent man, though not always distinguished by the most
exquisite sensibility, is always very capable of friendship. But his
friendship is not that ardent and passionate, but too often transitory affection, which appears so delicious to the generosity of
youth and inexperience. It is a sedate, but steady and faithful
attachment to a few well-tried and well-chosen companions; in
the choice of whom he is not guided by the giddy admiration of
shining accomplishments, but by the sober esteem of modesty,
discretion, and good conduct. But though capable of friendship,
he is not always much disposed to general sociality. He rarely fre-
quents, and more rarely figures in those convivial societies which
are distinguished for the jollity and gaiety of their conversation.
Their way of life might too often interfere with the regularity of
his temperance, might interrupt the steadiness of his industry, or
break in upon the strictness of his frugality.

But though his conversation may not always be very sprightly
or diverting, it is always perfectly inoffensive. He hates the thought
of being guilty of any petulance or rudeness. He never assumes
impertinently over any body, and, upon all common occasions, is
willing to place himself rather below than above his equals. Both

in his conduct and conversation, he is an exact observer of decency, and respects with an almost religious scrupulosity, all the established decorums and ceremonials of society. And, in this respect, he sets a much better example than has frequently been done by men of much more splendid talents and virtues; who, in all ages, from that of Socrates and Aristippus, down to that of Dr. Swift and Voltaire, and from that of Philip and Alexander the Great, down to that of the great Czar Peter of Moscovy, have too often distinguished themselves by the most improper and even insolent contempt of all the ordinary decorums of life and conversation, and who have thereby set the most pernicious example to those who wish to resemble them, and who too often content themselves with imitating their follies, without even attempting to attain their perfections.

In the steadiness of his industry and frugality, in his steadily sacrificing the ease and enjoyment of the present moment for the probable expectation of the still greater ease and enjoyment of a more distant but more lasting period of time, the prudent man is always both supported and rewarded by the entire approbation of the impartial spectator, and of the representative of the impartial spectator, the man within the breast. The impartial spectator does not feel himself worn out by the present labour of those whose conduct he surveys; nor does he feel himself solicited by the importunate calls of their present appetites. To him their present, and what is likely to be their future situation, are very nearly the same: he sees them nearly at the same distance, and is affected by them very nearly in the same manner. He knows, however, that to the persons principally concerned, they are very far from being the same, and that they naturally affect *them* in a very different manner. He cannot therefore but approve, and even applaud, that proper exertion of self-command, which enables them to act as if their present and their future situation affected them nearly in the same manner in which they affect him.

The man who lives within his income is naturally contented with his situation, which, by continual, though small accumulations, is growing better and better every day. He is enabled gradually to relax, both in the rigour of his parsimony and in the severity of his application; and he feels with double satisfaction this gradual increase of ease and enjoyment, from having felt before the hardship which attended the want of them. He has no anxiety to change so comfortable a situation, and does not go in quest of new enterprises and adventures, which might endanger, but could not well increase, the secure tranquillity which he actually enjoys. If he enters into any new projects or enterprises, they are likely to be well concerted and well prepared. He can never be hurried or drove into them by any necessity, but has always time and leisure to deliberate soberly and coolly concerning what are likely to be their consequences.

The prudent man is not willing to subject himself to any responsibility which his duty does not impose upon him. He is not a bustler in business where he has no concern; is not a meddler in other people's affairs; is not a professed counsellor or adviser, who obtrudes his advice where nobody is asking it. He confines himself, as much as his duty will permit, to his own affairs, and has no taste for that foolish importance which many people wish to derive from appearing to have some influence in the management of those of other people. He is averse to enter into any party disputes, hates faction, and is not always very forward to listen to the voice even of noble and great ambition. When distinctly called upon, he will not decline the service of his country, but he will not cabal in order to force himself into it, and would be much better pleased that the public business were well managed by some other person, than that he himself should have the trouble, and incur the responsibility, of managing it. In the bottom of his heart he would prefer the undisturbed enjoyment of secure tranquillity, not only to all the vain splendour of successful ambition, but to the real and solid glory of performing the greatest and most magnanimous actions.

Prudence, in short, when directed merely to the care of the health, of the fortune, and of the rank and reputation of the individual, though it is regarded as a most respectable, and even, in some degree, as an amiable and agreeable quality, yet it never is considered as one, either of the most endearing, or of the most ennobling of the virtues. It commands a certain cold esteem, but seems not entitled to any very ardent love or admiration.

Wise and judicious conduct, when directed to greater and nobler purposes than the care of the health, the fortune, the rank and reputation of the individual, is frequently and very properly called prudence. We talk of the prudence of the great general, of the great statesman, of the great legislator. Prudence is, in all these cases, combined with many greater and more splendid virtues, with valour, with extensive and strong benevolence, with a sacred regard to the rules of justice, and all these supported by a proper degree of self-command. This superior prudence, when carried to the highest degree of perfection, necessarily supposes the art, the talent, and the habit or disposition of acting with the most perfect propriety in every possible circumstance and situation. It necessarily supposes the utmost perfection of all the intellectual and of all the moral virtues. It is the best head joined to the best heart. It is the most perfect wisdom combined with the most perfect virtue. It constitutes very nearly the character of the Academical or Peripatetic sage, as the inferior prudence does that of the Epicurean.[3]

Mere imprudence, or the mere want of the capacity to take care of one's self, is, with the generous and humane, the object of compassion; with those of less delicate sentiments, of neglect, or, at worst, of contempt, but never of hatred or indignation. When combined with other vices, however, it aggravates in the highest degree the infamy and disgrace which would otherwise attend them. The artful knave, whose dexterity and address exempt him, though not from strong suspicions, yet from punishment or distinct detection, is too often received in the world with an indulgence which he by no means deserves. The awkward and foolish one, who, for want of this dexterity and address, is convicted and brought to punishment, is the object of universal hatred, contempt, and derision. In countries where great crimes frequently pass unpunished, the most atrocious actions become almost familiar, and cease to impress the people with that horror which is universally felt in countries where an exact administration of justice takes place. The injustice is the same in both countries; but the imprudence is often very different. In the latter, great crimes are evidently great follies. In the former, they are not always considered as such. In Italy, during the greater part of the sixteenth century, assassinations, murders, and even murders under trust, seem to have been almost familiar among the superior ranks of people. Cæsar Borgia invited four of the little princes in his neighbourhood, who all possessed little sovereignties, and commanded little armies of their own, to a friendly conference at Senigaglia, where, as soon as they arrived, he put them all to death. This infamous action, though certainly not approved of even in that age of crimes, seems to have contributed very little to the discredit, and not in the least to the ruin of the perpetrator. That ruin happened a few years after from causes altogether disconnected with this crime. Machiavel, not indeed a man of the nicest morality even for his own times, was resident, as minister from the republic of Florence, at the court of Cæsar Borgia when this crime was committed. He gives a very particular account of it, and in that pure, elegant, and simple language which distinguishes all his writings. He talks of it very coolly; is pleased with the address with which Cæsar Borgia conducted it; has much contempt for the dupery and weakness of the sufferers; but no compassion for their miserable and untimely death, and no sort of indignation at the cruelty and falsehood of their murderer.[4] The violence and injustice of great conquerors are often regarded with foolish wonder and admiration; those of petty thieves, robbers, and murderers, with contempt, hatred, and even horror upon all occasions. The former, though they are a hundred times more mischievous and destructive, yet when successful, they often pass for deeds of the most heroic magnanimity. The latter are always viewed with hatred and aversion, as the follies, as well as the crimes, of the lowest and most worthless of mankind. The injustice of the former is certainly, at least, as great as that of the latter; but the folly and imprudence are not near so great. A wicked and worthless man of parts often goes through the world with much more credit than he deserves. A wicked and worthless fool appears always, of all mortals, the most hateful, as well as the most contemptible. As prudence combined with other virtues, constitutes the noblest; so imprudence combined with other vices, constitutes the vilest of all characters.

SECTION II.

OF THE CHARACTER OF THE INDIVIDUAL, SO FAR AS IT CAN AFFECT THE HAPPINESS OF OTHER PEOPLE.

INTRODUCTION.

The character of every individual, so far as it can affect the happiness of other people, must do so by its disposition either to hurt or to benefit them.

Proper resentment for injustice attempted, or actually committed, is the only motive which, in the eyes of the impartial spectator, can justify our hurting or disturbing in any respect the happiness of our neighbour. To do so from any other motive is itself a violation of the laws of justice, which force ought to be employed either to restrain or to punish. The wisdom of every state or commonwealth endeavours, as well as it can, to employ the force of the society to restrain those who are subject to its authority, from hurting or disturbing the happiness of one another. The rules which it establishes for this purpose, constitute the civil and criminal law of each particular state or country. The principles upon which those rules either are, or ought to be founded, are the subject of a particular science, of all sciences by far the most important, but hitherto, perhaps, the least cultivated, that of natural jurisprudence; concerning which it belongs not to our present subject to enter into any detail. A sacred and religious regard not to hurt or disturb in any respect the happiness of our neighbour, even in those cases where no law can properly protect him, constitutes the character of the perfectly innocent and just man; a character which, when carried to a certain delicacy of attention, is always highly respectable and even venerable for its own sake, and can scarce ever fail to be accompanied with many other virtues, with great feeling for other people, with great humanity and great benevolence. It is a character sufficiently understood, and requires no further explanation. In the present section I shall only endeavour to explain the foundation of that order which nature seems to have traced out for the distribution of our good offices, or for the direction and employment of our very limited powers of beneficence: first, towards individuals; and secondly, towards societies.

The same unerring wisdom, it will be found, which regulates every other part of her conduct, directs, in this respect too, the order of her recommendations; which are always stronger or weaker in proportion as our beneficence is more or less necessary, or can be more or less useful.

CHAPTER I.

Of the Order in which Individuals are recommended by Nature to our care and attention.[1]

Every man, as the Stoics used to say, is first and principally recommended to his own care; and every man is certainly, in every respect, fitter and abler to take care of himself than of any other person. Every man feels his own pleasures and his own pains more sensibly than those of other people. The former are the original sensations; the latter the reflected or sympathetic images of those sensations. The former may be said to be the substance; the latter the shadow.

After himself, the members of his own family, those who usually live in the same house with him, his parents, his children, his brothers and sisters, are naturally the objects of his warmest affections. They are naturally and usually the persons upon whose happiness or misery his conduct must have the greatest influence. He is more habituated to sympathize with them. He knows better how every thing is likely to affect them, and his sympathy with them is more precise and determinate, than it can be with the greater part of other people. It approaches nearer, in short, to what he feels for himself.

This sympathy too, and the affections which are founded on

it, are by nature more strongly directed towards his children than towards his parents, and his tenderness for the former seems generally a more active principle, than his reverence and gratitude towards the latter. In the natural state of things, it has already been observed,[2] the existence of the child, for some time after it comes into the world, depends altogether upon the care of the parent; that of the parent does not naturally depend upon the care of the child. In the eye of nature, it would seem, a child is a more important object than an old man; and excites a much more lively, as well as a much more universal sympathy. It ought to do so. Every thing may be expected, or at least hoped, from the child. In ordinary cases, very little can be either expected or hoped from the old man. The weakness of childhood interests the affections of the most brutal and hard-hearted. It is only to the virtuous and humane, that the infirmities of old age are not the objects of contempt and aversion. In ordinary cases, an old man dies without being much regretted by any body. Scarce a child can die without rending asunder the heart of somebody.

The earliest friendships, the friendships which are naturally contracted when the heart is most susceptible of that feeling, are those among brothers and sisters. Their good agreement, while they remain in the same family, is necessary for its tranquillity and happiness. They are capable of giving more pleasure or pain to one another, than to the greater part of other people. Their situation renders their mutual sympathy of the utmost importance to their common happiness; and, by the wisdom of nature, the same situation, by obliging them to accommodate to one another, renders that sympathy more habitual, and thereby more lively, more distinct, and more determinate.

The children of brothers and sisters are naturally connected by the friendship which, after separating into different families, continues to take place between their parents. Their good agreement improves the enjoyment of that friendship; their discord would disturb it. As they seldom live in the same family, however, though of more importance to one another, than to the greater part of other people, they are of much less than brothers and sisters. As their mutual sympathy is less necessary, so it is less habitual, and therefore proportionably weaker.

The children of cousins, being still less connected, are of still less importance to one another; and the affection gradually diminishes as the relation grows more and more remote.

What is called affection, is in reality nothing but habitual sympathy. Our concern in the happiness or misery of those who are the objects of what we call our affections; our desire to promote the one, and to prevent the other; are either the actual feeling of that habitual sympathy, or the necessary consequences of that feeling. Relations being usually placed in situations which naturally create this habitual sympathy, it is expected that a suitable degree of affection should take place among them. We generally find that it actually does take place; we therefore naturally expect that it should; and we are, upon that account, more shocked when, upon any occasion, we find that it does not. The general rule is established, that persons related to one another in a certain degree ought always to be affected towards one another in a certain manner, and that there is always the highest impropriety, and sometimes even a sort of impiety, in their being affected in a different manner. A parent without parental tenderness, a child devoid of all filial reverence, appear monsters, the objects, not of hatred only, but of horror.

Though in a particular instance, the circumstances which usually produce those natural affections, as they are called, may, by some accident, not have taken place, yet respect for the general rule will frequently, in some measure, supply their place, and produce something which, though not altogether the same, may bear, however, a very considerable resemblance to those affections. A father is apt to be less attached to a child, who, by some accident, has been separated from him in its infancy, and who does not return to him till it is grown up to manhood. The father is apt to feel less paternal tenderness for the child; the child, less filial reverence for the father. Brothers and sisters, when they have been educated in distant countries, are apt to feel a similar diminution of affection. With the dutiful and the virtuous, however, respect for the general rule will frequently produce something which, though by no means the same, yet may very much resemble those natural affections. Even during the separation, the father and the child, the brothers or the sisters, are by no means indifferent to one another. They all consider one another as persons to and from whom certain affections are due, and they live in the hopes of being some time or another in a situation to enjoy that friendship which ought naturally to have taken place among persons so nearly connected. Till they meet, the absent son, the absent brother, are frequently the favourite son, the favourite brother. They have never offended, or, if they have, it is so long ago, that the offence is forgotten, as some childish trick not worth the remembering. Every account they have heard of one another, if conveyed by people of any tolerable good nature, has been, in the highest degree, flattering and favourable. The absent son, the absent brother, is not like other ordinary sons and brothers; but an all-perfect son, an all-perfect brother; and the most romantic hopes are entertained of the happiness to be enjoyed in the friendship and conversation of such persons. When they meet, it is often with so strong a disposition to conceive that habitual sympathy which constitutes the family affection, that they are very apt to fancy they have actually conceived it, and to behave to one another as if they had. Time and experience, however, I am afraid, too frequently undeceive them. Upon a more familiar acquaintance, they frequently discover in one another habits, humours, and inclinations, different from what they expected, to which, from want of habitual sympathy, from want of the real principle and foundation of what is properly called family-affection, they cannot now easily accommodate themselves. They have never lived in the situation which almost necessarily forces that easy accommodation, and though they may now be sincerely desirous to assume it, they have really become incapable of doing so. Their familiar conversation and intercourse soon become less pleasing to them, and, upon that account, less frequent. They may continue to live with one another in the mutual exchange of all essential good offices, and with every other external appearance of decent regard. But that cordial satisfaction, that delicious sympathy, that confidential openness and ease, which naturally take place in the conversation of those who have lived long and familiarly with one another, it seldom happens that they can completely enjoy.

It is only, however, with the dutiful and the virtuous, that the general rule has even this slender authority. With the dissipated, the profligate, and the vain, it is entirely disregarded. They are so far from respecting it, that they seldom talk of it but with the most indecent derision; and an early and long separation of this kind never fails to estrange them most completely from one another. With such persons, respect for the general rule can at best produce only a cold and affected civility (a very slender semblance of real regard); and even this, the slightest offence, the smallest opposition of interest, commonly puts an end to altogether.

The education of boys at distant great schools, of young men at distant colleges, of young ladies in distant nunneries and boarding-schools, seems, in the higher ranks of life, to have hurt most essentially the domestic morals, and consequently the domestic happiness, both of France and England.[3] Do you wish to educate your children to be dutiful to their parents, to be kind and affectionate to their brothers and sisters? put them under the necessity of being dutiful children, of being kind and affectionate brothers and sisters: educate them in your own house. From their parents' house they may, with propriety and advantage, go out every day to attend public schools: but let their dwelling be always at home. Respect for you must always impose a very useful restraint upon their conduct; and respect for them may frequently impose no useless restraint upon your own. Surely no acquirement, which can possibly be derived from what is called a public education, can make any sort of compensation for what is almost certainly and necessarily lost by it. Domestic education is the institution of nature; public education, the contrivance of man. It is surely unnecessary to say, which is likely to be the wisest.

In some tragedies and romances, we meet with many beautiful and interesting scenes, founded upon, what is called, the force of blood, or upon the wonderful affection which near relations are supposed to conceive for one another, even before they know that they have any such connection. This force of blood, however, I am afraid, exists no-where but in tragedies and romances. Even in tragedies and romances, it is never supposed to take place between any relations, but those who are naturally bred up in the same house; between parents and children, between brothers and sisters. To imagine any such mysterious affection between cousins, or even between aunts or uncles, and nephews or nieces, would be too ridiculous.

In pastoral countries, and in all countries where the authority of law is not alone sufficient to give perfect security to every member of the state, all the different branches of the same family commonly chuse to live in the neighbourhood of one another. Their association is frequently necessary for their common defence. They are all, from the highest to the lowest, of more or less importance to one another. Their concord strengthens their necessary association; their discord always weakens, and might destroy it. They have more intercourse with one another, than with the members of any other tribe. The remotest members of the same tribe claim some connexion with one another; and, where all other circumstances are equal, expect to be treated with more distinguished attention than is due to those who have no such pretensions. It is not many years ago that, in the Highlands of Scotland, the Chieftain used to consider the poorest man of his clan, as his cousin and relation. The same extensive regard to kindred is said to take place among the Tartars, the Arabs, the Turkomans, and, I believe, among all other nations who are nearly in the same state of society in which the Scots Highlanders were about the beginning of the present century.

In commercial countries, where the authority of law is always perfectly sufficient to protect the meanest man in the state, the descendants of the same family, having no such motive for keeping together, naturally separate and disperse, as interest or inclination may direct. They soon cease to be of importance to one another; and, in a few generations, not only lose all care about one another, but all remembrance of their common origin, and of the connection which took place among their ancestors. Regard for remote relations becomes, in every country, less and less, according as this state of civilization has been longer and more completely established. It has been longer and more completely established in England than in Scotland; and remote relations are, accordingly, more considered in the latter country than in the former, though, in this respect, the difference between the two countries is growing less and less every day. Great lords, indeed, are, in every country, proud of remembering and acknowledging their connection with one another, however remote. The remembrance of such illustrious relations flatters not a little the family pride of them all; and it is neither from affection, nor from any thing which resembles affection, but from the most frivolous and childish of all vanities, that this remembrance is so carefully kept up. Should some more humble, though, perhaps, much nearer kinsman, presume to put such great men in mind of his relation to their family, they seldom fail to tell him that they are bad genealogists, and miserably ill-informed concerning their own family history. It is not in that order, I am afraid, that we are to expect any extraordinary extension of, what is called, natural affection.

I consider what is called natural affection as more the effect of the moral than of the supposed physical connection between the parent and the child. A jealous husband, indeed, notwithstanding the moral connection, notwithstanding the child's having been educated in his own house, often regards, with hatred and aversion, that unhappy child which he supposes to be the offspring of his wife's infidelity. It is the lasting monument of a most disagreeable adventure; of his own dishonour, and of the disgrace of his family.

Among well-disposed people, the necessity or conveniency of mutual accommodation, very frequently produces a friendship not unlike that which takes place among those who are born to live in the same family. Colleagues in office, partners in trade, call one another brothers; and frequently feel towards one another as if they really were so. Their good agreement is an advantage to all; and, if they are tolerably reasonable people, they are naturally disposed to agree. We expect that they should do so; and their disagreement is a sort of a small scandal. The Romans expressed this sort of attachment by the word *necessitudo*, which, from the etymology, seems to denote that it was imposed by the necessity of the situation.[4]

Even the trifling circumstance of living in the same neighbourhood, has some effect of the same kind. We respect the face of a man whom we see every day, provided he has never offended us. Neighbours can be very convenient, and they can be very troublesome, to one another. If they are good sort of people, they are naturally disposed to agree. We expect their good agreement; and to be a bad neighbour is a very bad character. There are certain small good offices, accordingly, which are universally allowed to be due to a neighbour in preference to any other person who has no such connection.

This natural disposition to accommodate and to assimilate, as much as we can, our own sentiments, principles, and feelings, to those which we see fixed and rooted in the persons whom we are obliged to live and converse a great deal with, is the cause of the contagious effects of both good and bad company. The man who associates chiefly with the wise and the virtuous, though he may not himself become either wise or virtuous, cannot help conceiving a certain respect at least for wisdom and virtue; and the man who associates chiefly with the profligate and the dissolute, though he may not himself become profligate and dissolute, must soon lose, at least, all his original abhorrence of profligacy and dissolution of manners. The similarity of family characters, which we so frequently see transmitted through several successive generations, may, perhaps, be partly owing to this disposition, to assimilate ourselves to those whom we are obliged to live and converse a great deal with. The family character, however, like the family countenance, seems to be owing, not altogether to the moral, but partly too to the physical connection. The family countenance is certainly altogether owing to the latter.

But of all attachments to an individual, that which is founded altogether upon esteem and approbation of his good conduct and behaviour, confirmed by much experience and long acquaintance, is, by far, the most respectable. Such friendships, arising not from a constrained sympathy, not from a sympathy which has been assumed and rendered habitual for the sake of conveniency and accommodation; but from a natural sympathy, from an involuntary feeling that the persons to whom we attach ourselves are the natural and proper objects of esteem and approbation; can exist only among men of virtue. Men of virtue only can feel that entire confidence in the conduct and behaviour of one another, which can, at all times, assure them that they can never either offend or be offended by one another. Vice is always capricious: virtue only is regular and orderly. The attachment which is founded upon the love of virtue, as it is certainly, of all attachments, the most virtuous; so it is likewise the happiest, as well as the most permanent and secure. Such friendships need not be confined to a single person, but may safely embrace all the wise and virtuous, with whom we have been long and intimately acquainted, and upon whose wisdom and virtue we can, upon that account, entirely depend. They who would confine friendship to two persons, seem to confound the wise security of friendship with the jealousy and folly of love. The hasty, fond, and foolish intimacies of young people, founded, commonly, upon some slight similarity of character, altogether unconnected with good conduct, upon a taste, perhaps, for the same studies, the same amusements, the same diversions, or upon their agreement in some singular principle or opinion, not commonly adopted; those intimacies which a freak begins, and which a freak puts an end to, how agreeable soever they may appear while they last, can by no means deserve the sacred and venerable name of friendship.[5]

Of all the persons, however, whom nature points out for our peculiar beneficence, there are none to whom it seems more properly directed than to those whose beneficence we have ourselves already experienced. Nature, which formed men for that mutal kindness, so necessary for their happiness, renders every man the peculiar object of kindness, to the persons to whom he himself has been kind. Though their gratitude should not always correspond to his beneficence, yet the sense of his merit, the sympathetic gratitude of the impartial spectator, will always correspond to it. The general indignation of other people, against the baseness of their ingratitude, will even, sometimes, increase the general sense of his merit. No benevolent man ever lost altogether the fruits of his benevolence. If he does not always gather them from the persons from whom he ought to have gathered them, he seldom fails to gather them, and with a tenfold increase, from other people. Kindness is the parent of kindness; and if to be beloved by our brethren be the great object of our ambition, the surest way of obtaining it is, by our conduct to show that we really love them.

After the persons who are recommended to our beneficence, either by their connection with ourselves, by their personal qualities, or by their past services, come those who are pointed out, not indeed to, what is called, our friendship, but to our benevolent attention and good offices; those who are distinguished by their extraordinary situation; the greatly fortunate and the greatly unfortunate, the rich and the powerful, the poor and the wretched. The distinction of ranks, the peace and order of society, are, in a great measure, founded upon the respect which we naturally conceive for the former. The relief and consolation of human misery depend altogether upon our compassion for the latter. The peace and order of society, is of more importance than even the relief of the miserable. Our respect for the great, accordingly, is most apt to offend by its excess; our fellow-feeling for the miserable, by its defect. Moralists exhort us to charity and compassion. They warn us against the fascination of greatness. This fascination, indeed, is so powerful, that the rich and the great are too often preferred to the wise and the virtuous. Nature has wisely judged that the distinction of ranks, the peace and order of society, would rest more securely upon the plain and palpable difference of birth and fortune, than upon the invisible and often uncertain difference of wisdom and virtue. The undistinguishing eyes of the great mob of mankind can well enough perceive the former: it is with difficulty that the nice discernment of the wise and the virtuous can sometimes distinguish the latter. In the order of all those recommendations, the benevolent wisdom of nature is equally evident.

It may, perhaps, be unnecessary to observe, that the combination of two, or more, of those exciting causes of kindness, increases the kindness. The favour and partiality which, when there is no envy in the case, we naturally bear to greatness, are much increased when it is joined with wisdom and virtue. If, notwithstanding that wisdom and virtue, the great man should fall into those misfortunes, those dangers and distresses, to which the most exalted stations are often the most exposed, we are much more deeply interested in his fortune than we should be in that of a person equally virtuous, but in a more humble situation. The most interesting subjects of tragedies and romances are the misfortunes of virtuous and magnanimous kings and princes. If, by the wisdom and manhood of their exertions, they should extricate themselves from those misfortunes, and recover completely their former superiority and security, we cannot help viewing them with the most enthusiastic and even extravagant admiration. The grief which we felt for their distress, the joy which we feel for their prosperity, seem to combine together in enhancing that partial admiration which we naturally conceive both for the station and the character.

When those different beneficent affections happen to draw different ways, to determine by any precise rules in what cases we ought to comply with the one, and in what with the other, is, perhaps, altogether impossible. In what cases friendship ought to yield to gratitude, or gratitude to friendship; in what cases the strongest of all natural affections ought to yield to a regard for the safety of those superiors upon whose safety often depends that of the whole society; and in what cases natural affection may, without impropriety, prevail over that regard; must be left altogether to the decision of the man within the breast, the supposed impartial spectator, the great judge and arbiter of our conduct. If we place ourselves completely in his situation, if we really view ourselves with his eyes, and as he views us, and listen with diligent and reverential attention to what he suggests to us, his voice will never deceive us. We shall stand in need of no casuistic rules to direct our conduct. These it is often impossible to accommodate to all the different shades and gradations of circumstance, character, and situation, to differences and distinctions which, though not imperceptible, are, by their nicety and delicacy, often altogether undefinable.[6] In that beautiful tragedy of Voltaire, the Orphan of China,[7] while we admire the magnanimity of Zamti, who is willing to sacrifice the life of his own child, in order to preserve that of the only feeble remnant of his ancient sovereigns and masters; we not only pardon, but love the maternal tenderness of Idame, who, at the risk of discovering the important secret of her husband, reclaims her infant from the cruel hands of the Tartars, into which it had been delivered.

Chapter II.

Of the order in which Societies are by nature recommended to our Beneficence.

The same principles that direct the order in which individuals are recommended to our beneficence, direct that likewise in which societies are recommended to it. Those to which it is, or may be of most importance, are first and principally recommended to it.

The state or sovereignty in which we have been born and educated, and under the protection of which we continue to live, is, in ordinary cases, the greatest society upon whose happiness or misery our good or bad conduct can have much influence. It is accordingly, by nature, most strongly recommended to us. Not only we ourselves, but all the objects of our kindest affections, our children, our parents, our relations, our friends, our benefactors, all those whom we naturally love and revere the most, are commonly comprehended within it; and their prosperity and safety depend in some measure upon its prosperity and safety. It is by nature, therefore, endeared to us, not only by all our selfish, but by all our private benevolent affections. Upon account of our own connexion with it, its prosperity and glory seem to reflect some sort of honour upon ourselves. When we compare it with other societies of the same kind, we are proud of its superiority, and mortified in some degree, if it appears in any respect below them. All the illustrious characters which it has produced in former times (for against those of our own times envy may sometimes prejudice us a little), its warriors, its statesmen, its poets, its philosophers, and men of letters of all kinds; we are disposed to view with the most partial admiration, and to rank them (sometimes most unjustly) above those of all other nations. The patriot who lays down his life for the safety, or even for the vain-glory of this society, appears to act with the most exact propriety. He appears to view himself in the light in which the impartial spectator naturally and necessarily views him, as but one of the multitude, in the eye of that equitable judge, of no more consequence than any other in it, but bound at all times to sacrifice and devote himself to the safety, to the service, and even to the glory of the greater number. But though this sacrifice appears to be perfectly just and proper, we know how difficult it is to make it, and how few people are capable of making it. His conduct, therefore, excites not only our entire approbation, but our highest wonder and admiration, and seems to merit all the applause which can be due to the most heroic virtue. The traitor, on the contrary, who, in some peculiar situation, fancies he can promote his own little interest by betraying to the public enemy that of his native country; who, regardless of the judgment of the man within the breast, prefers himself, in this respect so shamefully and so basely, to all those with whom he has any connexion; appears to be of all villains the most detestable.

The love of our own nation often disposes us to view, with the most malignant jealousy and envy, the prosperity and aggrandisement of any other neighbouring nation. Independent and neighbouring nations, having no common superior to decide their disputes, all live in continual dread and suspicion of one another. Each sovereign, expecting little justice from his neighbours, is disposed to treat them with as little as he expects from them. The regard for the laws of nations, or for those rules which independent states profess or pretend to think themselves bound to observe in their dealings with one another, is often very little more than mere pretence and profession. From the smallest interest, upon the slightest provocation, we see those rules every day, either evaded or directly violated without shame or remorse. Each nation foresees, or imagines it foresees, its own subjugation in the increasing power and aggrandisement of any of its neighbours; and the mean principle of national prejudice is often founded upon the noble one of the love of our own country. The sentence with which the elder Cato is said to have concluded every speech which he made in the senate, whatever might be the subject, "*It is my opinion likewise that Carthage ought to be destroyed*," was the natural expression of the savage patriotism of a strong but coarse mind, enraged almost to madness against a foreign nation from which his own had suffered so much. The more humane sentence with which Scipio Nasica is said to have concluded all his speeches, "*It is my opinion likewise that Carthage ought not to be destroyed*," was the liberal expression of a more enlarged and enlightened mind, who felt no aversion to the prosperity even of an old enemy, when reduced to a state which could no longer be formidable to Rome.[8] France and England may each of them have some reason to dread the increase of the naval and military power of the other; but for either of them to envy the internal happiness and prosperity of the other, the cultivation of its lands, the advancement of its manufactures, the increase of its commerce, the security and number of its ports and harbours, its proficiency in all the liberal arts and sciences, is surely beneath the dignity of two such great nations. These are all real improvements of the world we live in. Mankind are benefited, human nature is ennobled by them. In such improvements each nation ought, not only to endeavour itself to excel, but from the love of mankind, to promote, instead of obstructing the excellence of its neighbours. These are all proper objects of national emulation, not of national prejudice or envy.[9]

The love of our own country seems not to be derived from the love of mankind. The former sentiment is altogether independent of the latter, and seems sometimes even to dispose us to act inconsistently with it. France may contain, perhaps, near three times the number of inhabitants which Great Britain contains. In the great society of mankind, therefore, the prosperity of France should appear to be an object of much greater importance than that of Great Britain. The British subject, however, who, upon that account, should prefer upon all occasions the prosperity of the former to that of the latter country, would not be thought a good citizen of Great Britain. We do not love our country merely as a part of the great society of mankind: we love it for its own sake, and independently of any such consideration. That wisdom which contrived the system of human affections, as well as that of every other part of nature, seems to have judged that the interest of the great society of mankind would be best promoted by directing the principal attention of each individual to that particular portion of it, which was most within the sphere both of his abilities and of his understanding.

National prejudices and hatreds seldom extend beyond neighbouring nations. We very weakly and foolishly, perhaps, call the French our natural enemies; and they perhaps, as weakly and foolishly, consider us in the same manner. Neither they nor we bear any sort of envy to the prosperity of China or Japan. It very rarely happens, however, that our good-will towards such distant countries can be exerted with much effect.

The most extensive public benevolence which can commonly be exerted with any considerable effect, is that of the statesmen, who project and form alliances among neighbouring or not very distant nations, for the preservation either of, what is called, the balance of power, or of the general peace and tranquillity of the states within the circle of their negotiations. The statesmen, however, who plan and execute such treaties, have seldom any thing in view but the interest of their respective countries. Sometimes, indeed, their views are more extensive. The Count d'Avaux, the plenipotentiary of France, at the treaty of Munster, would have been willing to sacrifice his life (according to the Cardinal de Retz, a man not over-credulous in the virtue of other people) in order to have restored, by that treaty, the general tranquillity of

Europe.[10] King William seems to have had a real zeal for the liberty and independency of the greater part of the sovereign states of Europe; which, perhaps, might be a good deal stimulated by his particular aversion to France, the state from which, during his time, that liberty and independency were principally in danger. Some share of the same spirit seems to have descended to the first ministry of Queen Anne.

Every independent state is divided into many different orders and societies, each of which has its own particular powers, privileges, and immunities. Every individual is naturally more attached to his own particular order or society, than to any other. His own interest, his own vanity, the interest and vanity of many of his friends and companions, are commonly a good deal connected with it. He is ambitious to extend its privileges and immunities. He is zealous to defend them against the encroachments of every other order or society.

Upon the manner in which any state is divided into the different orders and societies which compose it, and upon the particular distribution which has been made of their respective powers, privileges, and immunities, depends, what is called, the constitution of that particular state.

Upon the ability of each particular order or society to maintain its own powers, privileges, and immunities, against the encroachments of every other, depends the stability of that particular constitution. That particular constitution is necessarily more or less altered, whenever any of its subordinate parts is either raised above or depressed below whatever had been its former rank and condition.

All those different orders and societies are dependent upon the state to which they owe their security and protection. That they are all subordinate to that state, and established only in subserviency to its prosperity and preservation, is a truth acknowledged by the most partial member of every one of them. It may often, however, be hard to convince him that the prosperity and preservation of the state require any diminution of the powers, privileges, and immunities of his own particular order or society. This partiality, though it may sometimes be unjust, may not, upon that account be useless. It checks the spirit of innovation. It tends to preserve whatever is the established balance among the different orders and societies into which the state is divided; and while it sometimes appears to obstruct some alterations of government which may be fashionable and popular at the time, it contributes in reality to the stability and permanency of the whole system.

The love of our country seems, in ordinary cases, to involve in it two different principles; first, a certain respect and reverence for that constitution or form of government which is actually established; and secondly, an earnest desire to render the condition of our fellow-citizens as safe, respectable, and happy as we can. He is not a citizen who is not disposed to respect the laws and to obey the civil magistrate; and he is certainly not a good citizen who does not wish to promote, by every means in his power, the welfare of the whole society of his fellow-citizens.

In peaceable and quiet times, those two principles generally coincide and lead to the same conduct. The support of the established government seems evidently the best expedient for maintaining the safe, respectable, and happy situation of our fellow-citizens; when we see that this government actually maintains them in that situation. But in times of public discontent, faction, and disorder, those two different principles may draw different ways, and even a wise man may be disposed to think some alteration necessary in that constitution or form of government, which, in its actual condition, appears plainly unable to maintain the public tranquillity. In such cases, however, it often requires, perhaps, the highest effort of political wisdom to determine when a real patriot ought to support and endeavour to re-establish the authority of the old system, and when he ought to give way to the more daring, but often dangerous spirit of innovation.

Foreign war and civil faction are the two situations which afford the most splendid opportunities for the display of public spirit. The hero who serves his country successfully in foreign war gratifies the wishes of the whole nation, and is, upon that account, the object of universal gratitude and admiration. In times of civil discord, the leaders of the contending parties, though they may be admired by one half of their fellow-citizens, are commonly execrated by the other. Their characters and the merit of their respective services appear commonly more doubtful. The glory which is acquired by foreign war is, upon this account, almost always more pure and more splendid than that which can be acquired in civil faction.

The leader of the successful party, however, if he has authority enough to prevail upon his own friends to act with proper temper and moderation (which he frequently has not), may sometimes render to his country a service much more essential and important than the greatest victories and the most extensive conquests. He may re-establish and improve the constitution, and from the very doubtful and ambiguous character of the leader of a party, he may assume the greatest and noblest of all characters, that of the reformer and legislator of a great state; and, by the wisdom of his institutions, secure the internal tranquillity and happiness of his fellow-citizens for many succeeding generations.

Amidst the turbulence and disorder of faction, a certain spirit of system is apt to mix itself with that public spirit which is founded upon the love of humanity, upon a real fellow-feeling with the inconveniencies and distresses to which some of our fellow-citizens may be exposed. This spirit of system commonly takes the direction of that more gentle public spirit; always animates it, and often inflames it even to the madness of fanaticism. The leaders of the discontented party seldom fail to hold out some plausible plan of reformation which, they pretend, will not only remove the inconveniencies and relieve the distresses immediately complained of, but will prevent, in all time coming, any return of the like inconveniencies and distresses. They often propose, upon this account, to new-model the constitution, and to alter, in some of its most essential parts, that system of government under which the subjects of a great empire have enjoyed, perhaps, peace, security, and even glory, during the course of several centuries together. The great body of the party are commonly intoxicated with the imaginary beauty of this ideal system, of which they have no experience, but which has been represented to them in all the most dazzling colours in which the eloquence of their leaders could paint it. Those leaders themselves, though they originally may have meant nothing but their own aggrandisement, become many of them in time the dupes of their own sophistry, and are as eager for this great reformation as the weakest and foolishest of their followers. Even though the leaders should have preserved their own heads, as indeed they commonly do, free from this fanaticism, yet they dare not always disappoint the expectation of their followers; but are often obliged, though contrary to their principle and their conscience, to act as if they were under the common delusion. The violence of the party, refusing all palliatives, all temperaments, all reasonable accommodations, by requiring too much frequently obtains nothing; and those inconveniencies and distresses which, with a little moderation, might in a great measure have been removed and relieved, are left altogether without the hope of a remedy.

The man whose public spirit is prompted altogether by humanity and benevolence, will respect the established powers and privileges even of individuals, and still more those of the great orders and societies, into which the state is divided. Though he should consider some of them as in some measure abusive, he will content himself with moderating, what he often cannot annihilate without great violence. When he cannot conquer the rooted prejudices of the people by reason and persuasion, he will not attempt to subdue them by force; but will religiously observe what, by Cicero, is justly called the divine maxim of Plato, never to use violence to his country no more than to his parents.[11] He will accommodate, as well as he can, his public arrangements to the confirmed habits and prejudices of the people; and will remedy as well as he can, the inconveniencies which may flow from the want of those regulations which the people are averse to submit to. When he cannot establish the right, he will not disdain to ameliorate the wrong; but like Solon, when he cannot establish the best system of laws, he will endeavour to establish the best that the people can bear.

The man of system, on the contrary, is apt to be very wise in his own conceit; and is often so enamoured with the supposed beauty of his own ideal plan of government, that he cannot suffer the smallest deviation from any part of it. He goes on to establish it completely and in all its parts, without any regard either to the great interests or to the strong prejudices which may oppose it. He seems to imagine that he can arrange the different members of a great society with as much ease as the hand arranges the different pieces upon a chess-board. He does not consider that the pieces upon the chess-board have no other principle of motion besides that which the hand impresses upon them; but that, in the great chess-board of human society, every single piece has a principle of motion of its own, altogether different from that which the legislature might chuse to impress upon it. If those two principles

coincide and act in the same direction, the game of human society will go on easily and harmoniously, and is very likely to be
happy and successful. If they are opposite or different, the game
will go on miserably, and the society must be at all times in the
highest degree of disorder.

Some general, and even systematical, idea of the perfection of
policy and law, may no doubt be necessary for directing the views
of the statesman. But to insist upon establishing, and upon establishing all at once, and in spite of all opposition, every thing which
that idea may seem to require, must often be the highest degree of
arrogance. It is to erect his own judgment into the supreme standard of right and wrong. It is to fancy himself the only wise and
worthy man in the commonwealth, and that his fellow-citizens
should accommodate themselves to him and not he to them.[12] It is
upon this account, that of all political speculators, sovereign princes
are by far the most dangerous. This arrogance is perfectly familiar to them. They entertain no doubt of the immense superiority
of their own judgment. When such imperial and royal reformers,
therefore, condescend to contemplate the constitution of the country which is committed to their government, they seldom see any
thing so wrong in it as the obstructions which it may sometimes
oppose to the execution of their own will. They hold in contempt
the divine maxim of Plato, and consider the state as made for
themselves, not themselves for the state. The great object of their
reformation, therefore, is to remove those obstructions; to reduce
the authority of the nobility; to take away the privileges of cities
and provinces, and to render both the greatest individuals and the
greatest orders of the state, as incapable of opposing their commands as the weakest and most insignificant.

CHAPTER III.

Of universal Benevolence.

Though our effectual good offices can very seldom be extended to
any wider society than that of our own country; our good-will is
circumscribed by no boundary, but may embrace the immensity of

the universe. We cannot form the idea of any innocent and sensible being, whose happiness we should not desire, or to whose misery, when distinctly brought home to the imagination, we should not have some degree of aversion. The idea of a mischievous, though sensible, being, indeed, naturally provokes our hatred: but the ill-will which, in this case, we bear to it, is really the effect of our universal benevolence. It is the effect of the sympathy which we feel with the misery and resentment of those other innocent and sensible beings, whose happiness is disturbed by its malice.

This universal benevolence, how noble and generous soever, can be the source of no solid happiness to any man who is not thoroughly convinced that all the inhabitants of the universe, the meanest as well as the greatest, are under the immediate care and protection of that great, benevolent, and all-wise Being, who directs all the movements of nature; and who is determined, by his own unalterable perfections, to maintain in it at all times the greatest possible quantity of happiness.[13] To this universal benevolence, on the contrary, the very suspicion of a fatherless world, must be the most melancholy of all reflections; from the thought that all the unknown regions of infinite and incomprehensible space may be filled with nothing but endless misery and wretchedness. All the splendour of the highest prosperity can never enlighten the gloom with which so dreadful an idea must necessarily over-shadow the imagination; nor, in a wise and virtuous man, can all the sorrow of the most afflicting adversity ever dry up the joy which necessarily springs from the habitual and thorough conviction of the truth of the contrary system.

The wise and virtuous man is at all times willing that his own private interest should be sacrificed to the public interest of his own particular order or society. He is at all times willing, too, that the interest of this order or society should be sacrificed to the greater interest of the state or sovereignty, of which it is only a subordinate part. He should, therefore, be equally willing that all those inferior interests should be sacrificed to the greater interest of the universe, to the interest of that great society of all sensible and intelligent beings, of which God himself is the immediate administrator and director. If he is deeply impressed with the habitual and thorough conviction that this benevolent and all-wise Being can admit into the system of his government, no partial evil which is not necessary for the universal good, he must consider all the misfortunes which may befal himself, his friends, his society, or his country, as necessary for the prosperity of the universe, and, therefore as what he ought, not only to submit to with resignation, but as what he himself, if he had known all the connexions and dependencies of things, ought sincerely and devoutly to have wished for.

Nor does this magnanimous resignation to the will of the great Director of the universe, seem in any respect beyond the reach of human nature. Good soldiers, who both love and trust their general, frequently march with more gaiety and alacrity to the forlorn station, from which they never expect to return, than they would to one where there was neither difficulty nor danger. In marching to the latter, they could feel no other sentiment than that of the dulness of ordinary duty: in marching to the former, they feel that they are making the noblest exertion which it is possible for man to make. They know that their general would not have ordered them upon this station, had it not been necessary for the safety of the army, for the success of the war. They cheerfully sacrifice their own little systems to the prosperity of a greater system. They take an affectionate leave of their comrades, to whom they wish all happiness and success; and march out, not only with submissive obedience, but often with shouts of the most joyful exultation, to that fatal, but splendid and honourable station to which they are appointed. No conductor of an army can deserve more unlimited trust, more ardent and zealous affection, than the great Conductor of the universe. In the greatest public as well as private disasters, a wise man ought to consider that he himself, his friends and countrymen, have only been ordered upon the forlorn station of the universe; that had it not been necessary for the good of the whole, they would not have been so ordered; and that it is their duty, not only with humble resignation to submit to this allotment, but to endeavour to embrace it with alacrity and joy. A wise man should surely be capable of doing what a good soldier holds himself at all times in readiness to do.

The idea of that divine Being, whose benevolence and wisdom have, from all eternity, contrived and conducted the immense machine of the universe, so as at all times to produce the greatest possible quantity of happiness, is certainly of all the objects of human contemplation by far the most sublime. Every other thought necessarily appears mean in the comparison. The man whom we believe to be principally occupied in this sublime contemplation, seldom fails to be the object of our highest veneration; and though his life should be altogether contemplative, we often regard him with a sort of religious respect much superior to that with which we look upon the most active and useful servant of the commonwealth. The Meditations of Marcus Antoninus, which turn principally upon this subject, have contributed more, perhaps, to the general admiration of his character, than all the different transactions of his just, merciful, and beneficent reign.[14]

The administration of the great system of the universe, however, the care of the universal happiness of all rational and sensible beings, is the business of God and not of man. To man is allotted a much humbler department, but one much more suitable to the weakness of his powers, and to the narrowness of his comprehension; the care of his own happiness, of that of his family, his friends, his country: that he is occupied in contemplating the more sublime, can never be an excuse for his neglecting the more humble department; and he must not expose himself to the charge which Avidius Cassius is said to have brought, perhaps unjustly, against Marcus Antoninus; that while he employed himself in philosophical speculations, and contemplated the prosperity of the universe, he neglected that of the Roman empire.[15] The most sublime speculation of the contemplative philosopher can scarce compensate the neglect of the smallest active duty.

SECTION III.

OF SELF-COMMAND.

The man who acts according to the rules of perfect prudence, of strict justice, and of proper benevolence, may be said to be perfectly virtuous. But the most perfect knowledge of those rules will not alone enable him to act in this manner: his own passions are very apt to mislead him; sometimes to drive him and sometimes to seduce him to violate all the rules which he himself, in all his sober and cool hours, approves of. The most perfect knowledge, if it is not supported by the most perfect self-command, will not always enable him to do his duty.

Some of the best of the ancient moralists seem to have considered those passions as divided into two different classes: first, into those which it requires a considerable exertion of self-command to restrain even for a single moment; and secondly, into those which it is easy to restrain for a single moment, or even for a short period of time; but which, by their continual and almost incessant solicitations, are, in the course of a life, very apt to mislead into great deviations.¹

Fear and anger, together with some other passions which are mixed or connected with them, constitute the first class. The love of ease, of pleasure, of applause, and of many other selfish gratifications, constitute the second. Extravagant fear and furious anger, it is often difficult to restrain even for a single moment. The love of ease, of pleasure, of applause, and other selfish gratifications, it is always easy to restrain for a single moment, or even for a short period of time; but, by their continual solicitations, they often mislead us into many weaknesses which we have afterwards much reason to be ashamed of. The former set of passions may often be said to drive, the latter, to seduce us from our duty. The command of the former was, by the ancient moralists above alluded to,

denominated fortitude, manhood, and strength of mind; that of
the latter, temperance, decency, modesty, and moderation.

The command of each of those two sets of passions, independent of the beauty which it derives from its utility; from its
enabling us upon all occasions to act according to the dictates of
prudence, of justice, and of proper benevolence; has a beauty of
its own, and seems to deserve for its own sake a certain degree
of esteem and admiration. In the one case, the strength and greatness of the exertion excites some degree of that esteem and admiration. In the other, the uniformity, the equality and unremitting
steadiness of that exertion.

The man who, in danger, in torture, upon the approach of
death, preserves his tranquillity unaltered, and suffers no word,
no gesture to escape him which does not perfectly accord with
the feelings of the most indifferent spectator, necessarily commands
a very high degree of admiration. If he suffers in the cause of liberty and justice, for the sake of humanity and the love of his
country, the most tender compassion for his sufferings, the strongest
indignation against the injustice of his persecutors, the warmest
sympathetic gratitude for his beneficent intentions, the highest
sense of his merit, all join and mix themselves with the admiration of his magnanimity, and often inflame that sentiment into
the most enthusiastic and rapturous veneration. The heroes of
ancient and modern history, who are remembered with the most
peculiar favour and affection, are, many of them, those who, in
the cause of truth, liberty, and justice, have perished upon the
scaffold, and who behaved there with that ease and dignity which
became them. Had the enemies of Socrates suffered him to die
quietly in his bed, the glory even of that great philosopher might
possibly never have acquired that dazzling splendour in which it
has been beheld in all succeeding ages.[2] In the English history,
when we look over the illustrious heads which have been engraven
by Vertue and Howbraken, there is scarce any body, I imagine,
who does not feel that the axe, the emblem of having been
beheaded, which is engraved under some of the most illustrious
of them; under those of the Sir Thomas Mores, of the Rhaleighs,
the Russels, the Sydneys, &c. sheds a real dignity and interesting-
ness over the characters to which it is affixed, much superior

to what they can derive from all the futile ornaments of heraldry, with which they are sometimes accompanied.[3]

Nor does this magnanimity give lustre only to the characters of innocent and virtuous men. It draws some degree of favourable regard even upon those of the greatest criminals; and when a robber or highwayman is brought to the scaffold, and behaves there with decency and firmness, though we perfectly approve of his punishment, we often cannot help regretting that a man who possessed such great and noble powers should have been capable of such mean enormities.

War is the great school both for acquiring and exercising this species of magnanimity. Death, as we say, is the king of terrors; and the man who has conquered the fear of death is not likely to lose his presence of mind at the approach of any other natural evil. In war, men become familiar with death and are thereby necessarily cured of that superstitious horror with which it is viewed by the weak and unexperienced. They consider it merely as the loss of life, and as no further the object of aversion than as life may happen to be that of desire. They learn from experience, too, that many seemingly great dangers are not so great as they appear; and that, with courage, activity, and presence of mind, there is often a good probability of extricating themselves with honour from situations where at first they could see no hope. The dread of death is thus greatly diminished; and the confidence or hope of escaping it, augmented. They learn to expose themselves to danger with less reluctance. They are less anxious to get out of it, and less apt to lose their presence of mind while they are in it. It is this habitual contempt of danger and death which ennobles the profession of a soldier, and bestows upon it, in the natural apprehensions of mankind, a rank and dignity superior to that of any other profession. The skilful and successful exercise of this profession, in the service of their country, seems to have constituted the most distinguishing feature in the character of the favourite heroes of all ages.

Great warlike exploit, though undertaken contrary to every principle of justice, and carried on without any regard to humanity, sometimes interests us, and commands even some degree of a certain sort of esteem for the very worthless characters which conduct it. We are interested even in the exploits of the Buccaneers;[4]

and read with some sort of esteem and admiration, the history of the most worthless men, who, in pursuit of the most criminal purposes, endured greater hardships, surmounted greater difficulties, and encountered greater dangers, than, perhaps, any which the ordinary course of history gives an account of.

The command of anger appears upon many occasions not less generous and noble than that of fear. The proper expression of just indignation composes many of the most splendid and admired passages both of ancient and modern eloquence. The Philippics of Demosthenes, the Catilinarians of Cicero, derive their whole beauty from the noble propriety with which this passion is expressed.[5] But this just indignation is nothing but anger restrained and properly attempered to what the impartial spectator can enter into. The blustering and noisy passion which goes beyond this, is always odious and offensive, and interests us, not for the angry man, but for the man with whom he is angry. The nobleness of pardoning appears, upon many occasions, superior even to the most perfect propriety of resenting. When either proper acknowledgments have been made by the offending party; or, even without any such acknowledgments, when the public interest requires that the most mortal enemies should unite for the discharge of some important duty, the man who can cast away all animosity, and act with confidence and cordiality towards the person who had most grievously offended him, seems justly to merit our highest admiration.

The command of anger, however, does not always appear in such splendid colours. Fear is contrary to anger, and is often the motive which restrains it; and in such cases the meanness of the motive takes away all the nobleness of the restraint. Anger prompts to attack, and the indulgence of it seems sometimes to show a sort of courage and superiority to fear. The indulgence of anger is sometimes an object of vanity. That of fear never is. Vain and weak men, among their inferiors, or those who dare not resist them, often affect to be ostentatiously passionate, and fancy that they show what is called, spirit in being so. A bully tells many stories of his own insolence, which are not true, and imagines that he thereby renders himself, if not more amiable and respectable, at least more formidable to his audience. Modern manners, which, by favouring the practice of duelling, may be said, in some cases, to encourage private revenge, contribute, perhaps, a good deal to render, in modern times, the restraint of anger by fear still more contemptible than it might otherwise appear to be. There is always something dignified in the command of fear, whatever may be the motive upon which it is founded. It is not so with the command of anger. Unless it is founded altogether in the sense of decency, of dignity, and propriety, it never is perfectly agreeable.

To act according to the dictates of prudence, of justice, and proper beneficence, seems to have no great merit where there is no temptation to do otherwise. But to act with cool deliberation in the midst of the greatest dangers and difficulties; to observe religiously the sacred rules of justice in spite both of the greatest interests which might tempt, and the greatest injuries which might provoke us to violate them; never to suffer the benevolence of our temper to be damped or discouraged by the malignity and ingratitude of the individuals towards whom it may have been exercised; is the character of the most exalted wisdom and virtue. Self-command is not only itself a great virtue, but from it all the other virtues seem to derive their principal lustre.

The command of fear, the command of anger, are always great and noble powers. When they are directed by justice and benevolence, they are not only great virtues, but increase the splendour of those other virtues. They may, however, sometimes be directed by very different motives; and in this case, though still great and respectable, they may be excessively dangerous. The most intrepid valour may be employed in the cause of the greatest injustice. Amidst great provocations, apparent tranquillity and good-humour may sometimes conceal the most determined and cruel resolution to revenge. The strength of mind requisite for such dissimulation, though always and necessarily contaminated by the baseness of falsehood, has, however, been often much admired by many people of no contemptible judgment. The dissimulation of Catharine of Medicis is often celebrated by the profound historian Davila; that of Lord Digby, afterwards Earl of Bristol, by the grave and conscientious Lord Clarendon; that of the first Ashley Earl of Shaftesbury, by the judicious Mr. Locke.[6] Even Cicero seems to consider this deceitful character, not indeed as of the highest dignity, but as not unsuitable to a certain flexibility of manners, which, he thinks, may, notwithstanding, be, upon the whole, both agreeable and respectable. He exemplifies it by the characters of Homer's Ulysses, of the Athenian Themistocles, of the Spartan Lysander, and of the Roman Marcus Crassus.[7] This character of dark and deep dissimulation occurs most commonly in times of great public disorder; amidst the violence of faction and civil war. When law has become in a great measure impotent, when the most perfect innocence cannot alone insure safety, regard to self-defence obliges the greater part of men to have recourse to dexterity, to address, and to apparent accommodation to whatever happens to be, at the moment, the prevailing party. This false character, too, is frequently accompanied with the coolest and most determined courage. The proper exercise of it imposes that courage, as death is commonly the certain consequence of detection. It may be employed indifferently, either to exasperate or to allay those furious animosities of adverse factions which impose the necessity of assuming it; and though it may sometimes be useful, it is at least equally liable to be excessively pernicious.

The command of the less violent and turbulent passions seems much less liable to be abused to any pernicious purpose. Temperance, decency, modesty, and moderation, are always amiable, and can seldom be directed to any bad end. It is from the unremitting steadiness of those gentler exertions of self-command, that the amiable virtue of chastity, that the respectable virtues of industry and frugality, derive all that sober lustre which attends them. The conduct of all those who are contented to walk in the humble paths of private and peaceable life, derives from the same principle the greater part of the beauty and grace which belong to it; a beauty and grace, which, though much less dazzling, is not always less pleasing than those which accompany the more splendid actions of the hero, the statesman, or the legislator.

After what has already been said, in several different parts of this discourse, concerning the nature of self-command, I judge it unnecessary to enter into any further detail concerning those virtues. I shall only observe at present, that the point of propriety, the degree of any passion which the impartial spectator approves of, is differently situated in different passions. In some passions the excess is less disagreeable than the defect; and in such passions the point of propriety seems to stand high, or nearer to the excess than to the defect. In other passions, the defect is less disagreeable than the excess; and in such passions the point of propriety seems to stand low, or nearer to the defect than to the excess. The former are the passions which the spectator is most, the latter, those which he is least disposed to sympathize with. The former, too, are the passions of which the immediate feeling or sensation is agreeable to the person principally concerned; the latter, those of which it is disagreeable. It may be laid down as a general rule, that the passions which the spectator is most disposed to sympathize with, and in which, upon that account, the point of propriety may be said to stand high, are those of which the immediate feeling or sensation is more or less agreeable to the person principally concerned: and that, on the contrary, the passions which the spectator is least disposed to sympathize with, and in which, upon that account, the point of propriety may be said to stand low, are those of which the immediate feeling or sensation is more or less disagreeable, or even painful, to the person principally concerned. This general rule, so far as I have been able to observe, admits not of a single exception. A few examples will at once, both sufficiently explain it and demonstrate the truth of it.

The disposition to the affections which tend to unite men in society, to humanity, kindness, natural affection, friendship, esteem, may sometimes be excessive. Even the excess of this disposition, however, renders a man interesting to every body. Though we blame it, we still regard it with compassion, and even with kindness, and never with dislike. We are more sorry for it than angry at it. To the person himself, the indulgence even of such excessive affections is, upon many occasions, not only agreeable, but delicious. Upon some occasions, indeed, especially when directed, as is too often the case, towards unworthy objects, it exposes him to much real and heart-felt distress. Even upon such occasions, however, a well-disposed mind regards him with the most exquisite pity, and feels the highest indignation against those who affect to despise him for his weakness and imprudence. The defect of this disposition, on the contrary, what is called hardness of heart, while it renders a man insensible to the feelings and distresses of other people, renders other people equally insensible to his; and, by excluding him from the friendship of all the world, excludes him from the best and most comfortable of all social enjoyments.

The disposition to the affections which drive men from one another, and which tend, as it were, to break the bands of human society; the disposition to anger, hatred, envy, malice, revenge; is, on the contrary, much more apt to offend by its excess than by its defect. The excess renders a man wretched and miserable in his own mind, and the object of hatred, and sometimes even of horror, to other people. The defect is very seldom complained of. It may, however, be defective. The want of proper indignation is a most essential defect in the manly character, and, upon many occasions, renders a man incapable of protecting either himself or his friends from insult and injustice. Even that principle, in the excess and improper direction of which consists the odious and detestable passion of envy, may be defective. Envy is that passion which views with malignant dislike the superiority of those who are really entitled to all the superiority they possess. The man, however, who, in matters of consequence, tamely suffers other people, who are entitled to no such superiority, to rise above him or get before him, is justly condemned as mean-spirited. This weakness is commonly founded in indolence, sometimes in good-nature, in an aversion to opposition, to bustle and solicitation, and sometimes, too, in a sort of ill-judged magnanimity, which fancies that it can always continue to despise the advantage which it then despises, and, therefore, so easily gives up. Such weakness, however, is commonly followed by much regret and repentance; and what had some appearance of magnanimity in the beginning frequently gives place to a most malignant envy in the end, and to a hatred of that superiority, which those who have once attained it, may often become really entitled to, by the very circumstance of having attained it. In order to live comfortably in the world, it is, upon all occasions, as necessary to defend our dignity and rank, as it is to defend our life or our fortune.

Our sensibility to personal danger and distress, like that to personal provocation, is much more apt to offend by its excess than by its defect. No character is more contemptible than that of a coward; no character is more admired than that of the man who faces death with intrepidity, and maintains his tranquillity and presence of mind amidst the most dreadful dangers. We esteem the man who supports pain and even torture with man-hood and firmness; and we can have little regard for him who sinks under them, and abandons himself to useless outcries and womanish lamentations. A fretful temper, which feels, with too much sensibility, every little cross accident, renders a man miserable in himself and offensive to other people. A calm one, which does not allow its tranquillity to be disturbed, either by the small injuries, or by the little disasters incident to the usual course of human affairs; but which, amidst the natural and moral evils infesting the world, lays its account and is contented to suffer a little from both, is a blessing to the man himself, and gives ease and security to all his companions.

Our sensibility, however, both to our own injuries and to our own misfortunes, though generally too strong, may likewise be too weak. The man who feels little for his own misfortunes must always feel less for those of other people, and be less disposed to relieve them. The man who has little resentment for the injuries which are done to himself, must always have less for those which are done to other people, and be less disposed either to protect or to avenge them. A stupid insensibility to the events of human life necessarily extinguishes all that keen and earnest attention to the propriety of our own conduct, which constitutes the real essence of virtue. We can feel little anxiety about the propriety of our own actions, when we are indifferent about the events which may result from them. The man who feels the full distress of the calamity which has befallen him, who feels the whole baseness of the injustice which has been done to him, but who feels still more strongly what the dignity of his own character requires; who does not abandon himself to the guidance of the undisciplined passions which his situation might naturally inspire; but who governs his whole behaviour and conduct according to those restrained and corrected emotions which the great inmate, the great demi-god within the breast prescribes and approves of; is alone the real man of virtue, the only real and proper object of love, respect, and admiration. Insensibility and that noble firmness, that exalted self-command, which is founded in the sense of dignity and propriety, are so far from being altogether the same, that in proportion as the former takes place, the merit of the latter is, in many cases, entirely taken away.

But though the total want of sensibility to personal injury, to personal danger and distress, would, in such situations, take away the whole merit of self-command, that sensibility, however, may very easily be too exquisite, and it frequently is so. When the sense of propriety, when the authority of the judge within the breast, can control this extreme sensibility, that authority must no doubt appear very noble and very great. But the exertion of it may be too fatiguing; it may have too much to do. The individual, by a great effort, may behave perfectly well. But the contest between the two principles, the warfare within the breast, may be too violent to be at all consistent with internal tranquillity and happiness. The wise man whom Nature has endowed with this too exquisite sensibility, and whose too lively feelings have not been sufficiently blunted and hardened by early education and proper exercise, will avoid, as much as duty and propriety will permit, the situations for which he is not perfectly fitted. The man whose feeble and delicate constitution renders him too sensible to pain, to hardship, and to every sort of bodily distress, should not wantonly embrace the profession of a soldier. The man of too much sensibility to injury, should not rashly engage in the contests of faction. Though the sense of propriety should be strong enough to command all those sensibilities, the composure of the mind must always be disturbed in the struggle. In this disorder the judgment cannot always maintain its ordinary acuteness and precision; and though he may always mean to act properly, he may often act rashly and imprudently, and in a manner which he himself will, in the succeeding part of his life, be for ever ashamed of. A certain intrepidity, a certain firmness of nerves and hardiness of constitution, whether natural or acquired, are undoubtedly the best preparatives for all the great exertions of self-command.

Though war and faction are certainly the best schools for forming every man to this hardiness and firmness of temper, though they are the best remedies for curing him of the opposite weaknesses, yet, if the day of trial should happen to come before he has completely learned his lesson, before the remedy has had time to produce its proper effect, the consequences might not be agreeable.

Our sensibility to the pleasures, to the amusements and enjoyments of human life, may offend, in the same manner, either by its excess or by its defect. Of the two, however, the excess seems less disagreeable than the defect. Both to the spectator and to the person principally concerned, a strong propensity to joy is certainly more pleasing than a dull insensibility to the objects of amusement and diversion. We are charmed with the gaiety of youth, and even with the playfulness of childhood: but we soon grow weary of the flat and tasteless gravity which too frequently accompanies old age. When this propensity, indeed, is not restrained by the sense of propriety, when it is unsuitable to the time or to the place, to the age or to the situation of the person, when, to indulge it, he neglects either his interest or his duty; it is justly blamed as excessive, and as hurtful both to the individual and to the society. In the greater part of such cases, however, what is chiefly to be found fault with is, not so much the strength of the propensity to joy as the weakness of the sense of propriety and duty. A young man who has no relish for the diversions and amusements that are natural and suitable to his age, who talks of nothing but his book or his business, is disliked as formal and pedantic; and we give him no credit for his abstinence even from improper indulgences, to which he seems to have so little inclination.

The principle of self-estimation may be too high, and it may likewise be too low. It is so very agreeable to think highly, and so very disagreeable to think meanly of ourselves, that, to the person himself, it cannot well be doubted, but that some degree of excess must be much less disagreeable than any degree of defect. But to the impartial spectator, it may perhaps be thought, things must appear quite differently, and that to him, the defect must always be less disagreeable than the excess. And in our companions, no doubt, we much more frequently complain of the latter than of the former. When they assume upon us, or set themselves before us, their self-estimation mortifies our own. Our own pride and vanity prompt us to accuse them of pride and vanity, and we cease to be the impartial spectators of their conduct. When the same companions, however, suffer any other man to assume over them a superiority which does not belong to him, we not only blame them, but often despise them as mean-spirited. When, on the contrary, among other people, they push themselves a little more forward, and scramble to an elevation disproportioned, as we think, to their merit, though we may not perfectly approve of their conduct, we are often, upon the whole, diverted with it; and, where there is no envy in the case, we are almost always much less displeased with them, than we should have been, had they suffered themselves to sink below their proper station.

In estimating our own merit, in judging of our own character and conduct, there are two different standards to which we naturally compare them. The one is the idea of exact propriety and perfection, so far as we are each of us capable of comprehending that idea. The other is that degree of approximation to this idea which is commonly attained in the world, and which the greater part of our friends and companions, of our rivals and competitors, may have actually arrived at. We very seldom (I am disposed to think, we never) attempt to judge of ourselves without giving more or less attention to both these different standards. But the attention of different men, and even of the same man at different times, is often very unequally divided between them; and is sometimes principally directed towards the one, and sometimes towards the other.

So far as our attention is directed towards the first standard, the wisest and best of us all, can, in his own character and conduct, see nothing but weakness and imperfection; can discover no ground for arrogance and presumption, but a great deal for humility, regret, and repentance. So far as our attention is directed towards the second, we may be affected either in the one way or in the other, and feel ourselves, either really above, or really below, the standard to which we compare ourselves.

The wise and virtuous man directs his principal attention to the first standard; the idea of exact propriety and perfection. There exists in the mind of every man, an idea of this kind, gradually formed from his observations upon the character and conduct both of himself and of other people. It is the slow, gradual, and progressive work of the great demigod within the breast, the great judge and arbiter of conduct. This idea is in every man more or less accurately drawn, its colouring is more or less just, its outlines are more or less exactly designed, according to the delicacy and acuteness of that sensibility, with which those observations were made, and according to the care and attention employed in making them. In the wise and virtuous man they have been made with the most acute and delicate sensibility, and the utmost care and attention have been employed in making them. Every day some feature is improved; every day some blemish is corrected. He has studied this idea more than other people, he comprehends it more distinctly, he has formed a much more correct image of it, and is much more deeply enamoured of its exquisite and divine beauty. He endeavours as well as he can, to assimilate his own character to this archetype of perfection. But he imitates the work of a divine artist, which can never be equalled. He feels the imperfect success of all his best endeavours, and sees, with grief and affliction, in how many different features the mortal copy falls short of the immortal original. He remembers, with concern and humiliation, how often, from want of attention, from want of judgment, from want of temper, he has, both in words and actions, both in conduct and conversation, violated the exact rules of perfect propriety; and has so far departed from that model, according to which he wished to fashion his own character and conduct. When he directs his attention towards the second standard, indeed, that degree of excellence which his friends and acquaintances have commonly arrived at, he may be sensible of his own superiority. But, as his principal attention is always directed towards the first standard, he is necessarily much more humbled by the one comparison, than he ever can be elevated by the other. He is never so elated as to look down with insolence even upon those who are really below him. He feels so well his own imperfection, he knows so well the difficulty with which he attained his own distant approximation to rectitude, that he cannot regard with contempt the still greater imperfection of other people. Far from insulting over their inferiority, he views it with the most indulgent commiseration, and, by his advice as well as example, is at all times willing to promote their further advancement. If, in any particular qualification, they happen to be superior to him (for who is so perfect as not to have many superiors in many different qualifications?), far from envying their superiority, he, who knows how difficult it is to excel, esteems and honours their excellence, and never fails to bestow upon it the full measure of applause which it deserves. His whole mind, in short, is deeply impressed, his whole behaviour and deportment are distinctly stamped with the character of real modesty; with that of a very moderate estimation of his own merit, and, at the same time, of a full sense of the merit of other people.

In all the liberal and ingenious arts, in painting, in poetry, in music, in eloquence, in philosophy, the great artist feels always the real imperfection of his own best works, and is more sensible than any man how much they fall short of that ideal perfection of which he has formed some conception, which he imitates as well as he can, but which he despairs of ever equalling. It is the inferior artist only, who is ever perfectly satisfied with his own performances. He has little conception of this ideal perfection, about which he has little employed his thoughts; and it is chiefly to the works of other artists, of, perhaps, a still lower order, that he deigns to compare his own works. Boileau, the great French poet (in some of his works, perhaps not inferior to the greatest poet of the same kind, either ancient or modern), used to say, that no great man was ever completely satisfied with his own works. His acquaintance Santeuil (a writer of Latin verses, and who, on account of that school boy accomplishment, had the weakness to fancy himself a poet), assured him, that he himself was always completely satisfied with *his* own. Boileau replied, with, perhaps, an arch ambiguity, That he certainly was the only great man that ever was so.[8] Boileau, in judging of his own works, compared them with the standard of ideal perfection which, in his own particular branch of the poetic art, he had, I presume, meditated as deeply, and conceived as distinctly, as it is possible for man to conceive it. Santeuil, in judging of *his* own works, compared them, I suppose, chiefly to those of the other Latin poets of his own time, to the greater part of whom he was certainly very far from being inferior. But to support and finish off, if I may say so, the conduct and conversation of a whole life to some resemblance of this ideal perfection, is surely much more difficult than to work up to an equal resemblance any of the productions of any of the ingenious arts. The artist sits down to his work undisturbed, at leisure, in the full possession and recollection of all his skill, experience, and knowledge. The wise man must support the propriety of his own conduct in health and in sickness, in success and in disappointment, in the hour of fatigue and drowsy indolence, as well as in that of the most awakened attention. The most sudden and unexpected assaults of difficulty and distress must never surprise him. The injustice of other people must never provoke him to injustice. The violence of faction must never confound him. All the hardships and hazards of war must never either dishearten or appal him.

Of the persons who, in estimating their own merit, in judging of their own character and conduct, direct by far the greater part of their attention to the second standard, to that ordinary degree of excellence which is commonly attained by other people, there are some who really and justly feel themselves very much above it, and who, by every intelligent and impartial spectator, are acknowledged to be so. The attention of such persons, however, being always principally directed, not to the standard of ideal, but to that of ordinary perfection, they have little sense of their own weaknesses and imperfections; they have little modesty; are often assuming, arrogant, and presumptuous; great admirers of themselves, and great contemners of other people. Though their characters are in general much less correct, and their merit much inferior to that of the man of real and modest virtue; yet their excessive presumption, founded upon their own excessive self-admiration, dazzles the multitude, and often imposes even upon those who are much superior to the multitude. The frequent, and often wonderful, success of the most ignorant quacks and impostors, both civil and religious, sufficiently demonstrate how easily the multitude are imposed upon by the most extravagant and groundless pretensions. But when those pretensions are supported by a very high degree of real and solid merit, when they are displayed with all the splendour which ostentation can bestow upon them, when they are supported by high rank and great power, when they have often been successfully exerted, and are, upon that account, attended by the loud acclamations of the multitude; even the man of sober judgment often abandons himself to the general admiration. The very noise of those foolish acclamations often contributes to confound his understanding, and while he sees those great men only at a certain distance, he is often disposed to worship them with a sincere admiration, superior even to that with which they appear to worship themselves. When there is no envy in the case, we all take pleasure in admiring, and are, upon that account, naturally disposed, in our own fancies, to render complete and perfect in every respect the characters which, in many respects, are so very worthy of admiration. The excessive self-admiration of those great men is well understood, perhaps, and even seen through, with some degree of derision, by those wise men who are much in their familiarity, and who secretly smile at those lofty pretensions, which, by people at a distance, are often regarded with reverence, and almost with adoration. Such, however, have been, in all ages, the greater part of those men who have procured to themselves the most noisy fame, the most extensive reputation; a fame and reputation, too, which have often descended to the remotest posterity.

Great success in the world, great authority over the sentiments and opinions of mankind, have very seldom been acquired without some degree of this excessive self-admiration. The most splendid characters, the men who have performed the most illustrious actions, who have brought about the greatest revolutions, both in the situations and opinions of mankind; the most successful warriors, the greatest statesmen and legislators, the eloquent founders and leaders of the most numerous and most successful sects and parties; have many of them been, not more distinguished for their very great merit, than for a degree of presumption and self-admiration altogether disproportioned even to that very great merit. This presumption was, perhaps, necessary, not only to prompt them to undertakings which a more sober mind would never have thought of, but to command the submission and obedience of their followers to support them in such undertakings. When crowned with success, accordingly, this presumption has often betrayed them into a vanity that approached almost to insanity and folly. Alexander the Great appears, not only to have wished that other people should think him a God, but to have been at least very well disposed to fancy himself such. Upon his death-bed, the most ungodlike of all situations, he requested of his friends that, to the respectable list of Deities, into which himself had long before been inserted, his old mother Olympia might likewise have the honour of being added.[9] Amidst the respectful admiration of his followers and disciples, amidst the universal applause of the public, after the oracle, which probably had followed the voice of that applause, had pronounced him the wisest of men, the great wisdom of Socrates, though it did not suffer him to fancy himself a God, yet was not great enough to hinder him from fancying that he had secret and frequent intimations from some invisible and divine Being.[10] The sound head of Caesar was not so perfectly sound as to hinder him from being much pleased with his divine genealogy from the goddess Venus; and, before the temple of this pretended great-grandmother, to receive, without rising from his seat, the Roman Senate, when that illustrious body came to present him with some decrees conferring upon him the most extravagant honours.[11] This insolence, joined to some other acts of an almost childish vanity, little to be expected from an understanding at once so very acute and comprehensive, seems, by exasperating the public jealousy, to have emboldened his assassins, and to have hastened the execution of their conspiracy. The religion and manners of modern times give our great men little encouragement to fancy themselves either Gods or even Prophets. Success, however, joined to great popular favour, has often so far turned the heads of the greatest of them, as to make them ascribe to themselves both an importance and an ability much beyond what they really possessed; and, by this presumption, to precipitate themselves into many rash and sometimes ruinous adventures. It is a characteristic almost peculiar to the great Duke of Marlborough, that ten years of such uninterrupted and such splendid success as scarce any other general could boast of, never betrayed him into a single rash action, scarce into a single rash word or expression. The same temperate coolness and self-command cannot, I think, be ascribed to any other great warrior of later times; not to Prince Eugene, not to the late King of Prussia, not to the great Prince of Conde, not even to Gustavus Adolphus. Turrenne seems to have approached the nearest to it; but several different transactions of his life sufficiently demonstrate that it was in him by no means so perfect as in the great Duke of Marlborough.

In the humble projects of private life, as well as in the ambitious and proud pursuits of high stations, great abilities and successful enterprise, in the beginning, have frequently encouraged to undertakings which necessarily led to bankruptcy and ruin in the end.

The esteem and admiration which every impartial spectator conceives for the real merit of those spirited, magnanimous, and high-minded persons, as it is a just and well-founded sentiment, so it is a steady and permanent one, and altogether independent of their good or bad fortune. It is otherwise with that admiration which he is apt to conceive for their excessive self-estimation and presumption. While they are successful, indeed, he is often perfectly conquered and overborne by them. Success covers from his eyes, not only the great imprudence, but frequently the great injustice of their enterprises; and, far from blaming this defective part of their character, he often views it with the most enthusiastic admiration. When they are unfortunate, however, things change their colours and their names. What was before heroic magnanimity, resumes its proper appellation of extravagant rashness and folly; and the blackness of that avidity and injustice, which was before hid under the splendour of prosperity, comes full into view, and blots the whole lustre of their enterprise. Had Caesar, instead of gaining, lost the battle of Pharsalia, his character would, at this hour, have ranked a little above that of Catiline, and the weakest man would have viewed his enterprise against the laws of his country in blacker colours, than, perhaps even Cato, with all the animosity of a party-man, ever viewed it at the time.[12] His real merit, the justness of his taste, the simplicity and elegance of his writings, the propriety of his eloquence, his skill in war, his resources in distress, his cool and sedate judgment in danger, his faithful attachment to his friends, his unexampled generosity to his enemies, would all have been acknowledged; as the real merit of Catiline, who had many great qualities, is acknowledged at this day. But the insolence and injustice of his all-grasping ambition would have darkened and extinguished the glory of all that real merit. Fortune has in this, as well as in some other respects already mentioned, great influence over the moral sentiments of mankind, and, according as she is either favourable or adverse, can render the same character the object, either of general love and admiration, or of universal hatred and contempt. This great disorder in our moral sentiments is by no means, however, without its utility; and we may on this, as well as on many other occasions, admire the wisdom of God even in the weakness and folly of man. Our admiration of success is founded upon the same principle with our respect for wealth and greatness, and is equally necessary for establishing the distinction of ranks and the order of society. By this admiration of success we are taught to submit more easily to those superiors, whom the course of human affairs may assign to us; to regard with reverence, and sometimes even with a sort of respectful affection, that fortunate violence which we are no longer capable of resisting; not only the violence of such splendid characters as those of a Caesar or an

Alexander, but often that of the most brutal and savage barbarians, of an Attila, a Gengis, or a Tamerlane. To all such mighty conquerors the great mob of mankind are naturally disposed to look up with a wondering, though, no doubt, with a very weak and foolish admiration. By this admiration, however, they are taught to acquiesce with less reluctance under that government which an irresistible force imposes upon them, and from which no reluctance could deliver them.

Though in prosperity, however, the man of excessive self-estimation may sometimes appear to have some advantage over the man of correct and modest virtue; though the applause of the multitude, and of those who see them both only at a distance, is often much louder in favour of the one than it ever is in favour of the other; yet, all things fairly computed, the real balance of advantage is, perhaps in all cases, greatly in favour of the latter and against the former. The man who neither ascribes to himself, nor wishes that other people should ascribe to him, any other merit besides that which really belongs to him, fears no humiliation, dreads no detection; but rests contented and secure upon the genuine truth and solidity of his own character. His admirers may neither be very numerous nor very loud in their applauses; but the wisest man who sees him the nearest and who knows him the best, admires him the most. To a real wise man the judicious and well-weighed approbation of a single wise man, gives more heartfelt satisfaction than all the noisy applauses of ten thousand ignorant though enthusiastic admirers. He may say with Parmenides, who, upon reading a philosophical discourse before a public assembly at Athens, and observing that, except Plato, the whole company had left him, continued, notwithstanding, to read on, and said that Plato alone was audience sufficient for him.[13]

It is otherwise with the man of excessive self-estimation. The wise men who see him the nearest, admire him the least. Amidst the intoxication of prosperity, their sober and just esteem falls so far short of the extravagance of his own self-admiration, that he regards it as mere malignity and envy. He suspects his best friends. Their company becomes offensive to him. He drives them from his presence: and often rewards their services, not only with ingratitude, but with cruelty and injustice. He abandons his confidence to flatterers and traitors, who pretend to idolize his vanity and presumption; and that character which in the beginning, though in some respects defective, was, upon the whole, both amiable and respectable, becomes contemptible and odious in the end. Amidst the intoxication of prosperity, Alexander killed Clytus, for having preferred the exploits of his father Philip to his own; put Calisthenes to death in torture, for having refused to adore him in the Persian manner; and murdered the great friend of his father, the venerable Parmenio, after having, upon the most groundless suspicions, sent first to the torture and afterwards to the scaffold the only remaining son of that old man, the rest having all before died in his own service. This was that Parmenio of whom Philip used to say, that the Athenians were very fortunate who could find ten generals every year, while he himself, in the whole course of his life, could never find one but Parmenio. It was upon the vigilance and attention of this Parmenio that he reposed at all times with confidence and security, and, in his hours of mirth and jollity, used to say, Let us drink, my friends, we may do it with safety, for Parmenio never drinks.[14] It was this same Parmenio, with whose presence and counsel, it had been said, Alexander had gained all his victories; and without whose presence and counsel, he had never gained a single victory. The humble, admiring, and flattering friends, whom Alexander left in power and authority behind him, divided his empire among themselves, and after having thus robbed his family and kindred of their inheritance, put, one after another, every single surviving individual of them, whether male or female, to death.

We frequently, not only pardon, but thoroughly enter into and sympathize with the excessive self-estimation of those splendid characters in which we observe a great and distinguished superiority above the common level of mankind. We call them spirited, magnanimous, and high-minded; words which all involve in their meaning a considerable degree of praise and admiration. But we cannot enter into and sympathize with the excessive self-estimation of those characters in which we can discern no such distinguished superiority. We are disgusted and revolted by it; and it is with some difficulty that we can either pardon or suffer it. We call it pride or vanity; two words, of which the latter always, and the former for the most part, involve in their meaning a considerable degree of blame.

Those two vices, however, though resembling, in some respects, as being both modifications of excessive self-estimation, are yet, in many respects, very different from one another.

The proud man is sincere, and, in the bottom of his heart, is convinced of his own superiority; though it may sometimes be difficult to guess upon what that conviction is founded. He wishes you to view him in no other light than that in which, when he places himself in your situation, he really views himself. He demands no more of you than, what he thinks, justice. If you appear not to respect him as he respects himself, he is more offended than mortified, and feels the same indignant resentment as if he had suffered a real injury. He does not even then, however, deign to explain the grounds of his own pretensions. He disdains to court your esteem. He affects even to despise it, and endeavours to maintain his assumed station, not so much by making you sensible of his superiority, as of your own meanness. He seems to wish, not so much to excite your esteem for *himself,* as to mortify *that* for *yourself.*

The vain man is not sincere, and, in the bottom of his heart, is very seldom convinced of that superiority which he wishes you to ascribe to him. He wishes you to view him in much more splendid colours than those in which, when he places himself in your situation, and supposes you to know all that he knows, he can really view himself. When you appear to view him, therefore, in different colours, perhaps in his proper colours, he is much more mortified than offended. The grounds of his claim to that character which he wishes you to ascribe to him, he takes every opportunity of displaying, both by the most ostentatious and unnecessary exhibition of the good qualities and accomplishments which he possesses in some tolerable degree, and sometimes even by false pretensions to those which he either possesses in no degree, or in so very slender a degree that he may well enough be said to possess them in no degree. Far from despising your esteem, he courts it with the most anxious assiduity. Far from wishing to mortify your self-estimation, he is happy to cherish it, in hopes that in return you will cherish his own. He flatters in order to be flattered. He studies to please, and endeavours to bribe you into a good opinion of him by politeness and complaisance, and sometimes even by real and essential good offices, though often displayed, perhaps, with unnecessary ostentation.

The vain man sees the respect which is paid to rank and fortune, and wishes to usurp this respect, as well as that for talents
and virtues. His dress, his equipage, his way of living, accordingly, all announce both a higher rank and a greater fortune than
really belong to him; and in order to support this foolish imposition for a few years in the beginning of his life, he often reduces
himself to poverty and distress long before the end of it. As long
as he can continue his expence, however, his vanity is delighted
with viewing himself, not in the light in which you would view
him if you knew all that he knows; but in that in which, he imagines, he has, by his own address, induced you actually to view him.
Of all the illusions of vanity this is, perhaps, the most common.
Obscure strangers who visit foreign countries, or who, from a
remote province, come to visit, for a short time, the capital of their
own country, most frequently attempt to practise it. The folly of
the attempt, though always very great and most unworthy of a
man of sense, may not be altogether so great upon such as upon
most other occasions. If their stay is short, they may escape any
disgraceful detection; and, after indulging their vanity for a few
months or a few years, they may return to their own homes, and
repair, by future parsimony, the waste of their past profusion.

The proud man can very seldom be accused of this folly. His
sense of his own dignity renders him careful to preserve his independency, and, when his fortune happens not to be large, though
he wishes to be decent, he studies to be frugal and attentive in all
his expences. The ostentatious expence of the vain man is highly
offensive to him. It outshines, perhaps, his own. It provokes his
indignation as an insolent assumption of a rank which is by no
means due; and he never talks of it without loading it with the
harshest and severest reproaches.

The proud man does not always feel himself at his ease in the
company of his equals, and still less in that of his superiors. He
cannot lay down his lofty pretensions, and the countenance and
conversation of such company overawe him so much that he dare
not display them. He has recourse to humbler company, for which
he has little respect, which he would not willingly chuse; and
which is by no means agreeable to him; that of his inferiors, his
flatterers, and dependants. He seldom visits his superiors, or, if he
does, it is rather to show that he is entitled to live in such company,

than for any real satisfaction that he enjoys in it. It is, as Lord Clarendon says of the Earl of Arundel, that he sometimes went to court, because he could there only find a greater man than himself; but that he went very seldom, because he found there a greater man than himself.[15]

It is quite otherwise with the vain man. He courts the company of his superiors as much as the proud man shuns it. Their splendour, he seems to think, reflects a splendour upon those who are much about them. He haunts the courts of kings and the levees[16] of ministers, and gives himself the air of being a candidate for fortune and preferment, when in reality he possesses the much more precious happiness, if he knew how to enjoy it, of not being one. He is fond of being admitted to the tables of the great, and still more fond of magnifying to other people the familiarity with which he is honoured there. He associates himself, as much as he can, with fashionable people, with those who are supposed to direct the public opinion, with the witty, with the learned, with the popular; and he shuns the company of his best friends whenever the very uncertain current of public favour happens to run in any respect against them. With the people to whom he wishes to recommend himself, he is not always very delicate about the means which he employs for that purpose; unnecessary ostentation, groundless pretensions, constant assentation, frequently flattery, though for the most part a pleasant and a sprightly flattery, and very seldom the gross and fulsome flattery of a parasite. The proud man, on the contrary, never flatters, and is frequently scarce civil to any body.

Notwithstanding all its groundless pretensions, however, vanity is almost always a sprightly and a gay, and very often a good-natured passion. Pride is always a grave, a sullen, and a severe one. Even the falsehoods of the vain man are all innocent falsehoods, meant to raise himself, not to lower other people. To do the proud man justice, he very seldom stoops to the baseness of falsehood. When he does, however, his falsehoods are by no means so innocent. They are all mischievous, and meant to lower other people. He is full of indignation at the unjust superiority, as he thinks it, which is given to them. He views them with malignity and envy, and, in talking of them, often endeavours, as much as he can, to extenuate and lessen whatever are the grounds upon which their superiority is supposed to be founded. Whatever tales are circulated to their disadvantage, though he seldom forges them himself, yet he often takes pleasure in believing them, is by no means unwilling to repeat them, and even sometimes with some degree of exaggeration. The worst falsehoods of vanity are all what we call white lies: those of pride, whenever it condescends to falsehood, are all of the opposite complexion.

Our dislike to pride and vanity generally disposes us to rank the persons whom we accuse of those vices rather below than above the common level. In this judgment, however, I think, we are most frequently in the wrong, and that both the proud and the vain man are often (perhaps for the most part) a good deal above it; though not near so much as either the one really thinks himself, or as the other wishes you to think him. If we compare them with their own pretensions, they may appear the just objects of contempt. But when we compare them with what the greater part of their rivals and competitors really are, they may appear quite otherwise, and very much above the common level. Where there is this real superiority, pride is frequently attended with many respectable virtues; with truth, with integrity, with a high sense of honour, with cordial and steady friendship, with the most inflexible firmness and resolution. Vanity, with many amiable ones; with humanity, with politeness, with a desire to oblige in all little matters, and sometimes with a real generosity in great ones; a generosity, however, which it often wishes to display in the most splendid colours that it can. By their rivals and enemies, the French, in the last century, were accused of vanity; the Spaniards, of pride; and foreign nations were disposed to consider the one as the more amiable; the other, as the more respectable people.

The words *vain* and *vanity* are never taken in a good sense. We sometimes say of a man, when we are talking of him in good-humour, that he is the better for his vanity, or that his vanity is more diverting than offensive; but we still consider it as a foible and a ridicule in his character.

The words *proud* and *pride*, on the contrary, are sometimes taken in a good sense. We frequently say of a man, that he is too proud, or that he has too much noble pride, ever to suffer himself to do a mean thing. Pride is, in this case, confounded with magnanimity. Aristotle, a philosopher who certainly knew the world, in drawing the character of the magnanimous man, paints him with many features which, in the two last centuries, were commonly ascribed to the Spanish character: that he was deliberate in all his resolutions; slow, and even tardy, in all his actions; that his voice was grave, his speech deliberate, his step and motion slow; that he appeared indolent and even slothful, not at all disposed to bustle about little matters, but to act with the most determined and vigorous resolution upon all great and illustrious occasions; that he was not a lover of danger, or forward to expose himself to little dangers, but to great dangers; and that, when he exposed himself to danger, he was altogether regardless of his life.[17]

The proud man is commonly too well contented with himself to think that his character requires any amendment. The man who feels himself all-perfect, naturally enough despises all further improvement. His self-sufficiency and absurd conceit of his own superiority, commonly attend him from his youth to his most advanced age; and he dies, as Hamlet says, with all his sins upon his head, unanointed, unanealed.[18]

It is frequently quite otherwise with the vain man. The desire of the esteem and admiration of other people, when for qualities and talents which are the natural and proper objects of esteem and admiration, is the real love of true glory; a passion which, if not the very best passion of human nature, is certainly one of the best. Vanity is very frequently no more than an attempt prematurely to usurp that glory before it is due. Though your son, under five-and-twenty years of age, should be but a coxcomb; do not, upon that account, despair of his becoming, before he is forty, a very wise and worthy man, and a real proficient in all those talents and virtues to which, at present, he may only be an ostentatious and empty pretender. The great secret of education is to direct vanity to proper objects.[19] Never suffer him to value himself upon trivial accomplishments. But do not always discourage his pretensions to those that are of real importance. He would not pretend to them if he did not earnestly desire to possess them. Encourage this desire; afford him every means to facilitate the acquisition; and do not take too much offence, although he should sometimes assume the air of having attained it a little before the time.

Such, I say, are the distinguishing characteristics of pride and vanity, when each of them acts according to its proper character. But the proud man is often vain; and the vain man is often proud. Nothing can be more natural than that the man, who thinks much more highly of himself than he deserves, should wish that other people should think still more highly of him: or that the man, who wishes that other people should think more highly of him than he thinks of himself, should, at the same time, think much more highly of himself than he deserves. Those two vices being frequently blended in the same character, the characteristics of both are necessarily confounded; and we sometimes find the superficial and impertinent ostentation of vanity joined to the most malignant and derisive insolence of pride. We are sometimes, upon that account, at a loss how to rank a particular character, or whether to place it among the proud or among the vain.

Men of merit considerably above the common level, sometimes under-rate as well as over-rate themselves. Such characters, though not very dignified, are often, in private society, far from being disagreeable. His companions all feel themselves much at their ease in the society of a man so perfectly modest and unassuming. If those companions, however, have not both more discernment and more generosity than ordinary, though they may have some kindness for him, they have seldom much respect; and the warmth of their kindness is very seldom sufficient to compensate the coldness of their respect. Men of no more than ordinary discernment never rate any person higher than he appears to rate himself. He seems doubtful himself, they say, whether he is perfectly fit for such a situation or such an office; and immediately give the preference to some impudent blockhead who entertains no doubt about his own qualifications. Though they should have discernment, yet, if they want generosity, they never fail to take advantage of his simplicity, and to assume over him an impertinent superiority which they are by no means entitled to. His good nature may enable him to bear this for some time; but he grows weary at last, and frequently when it is too late, and when that rank, which he ought to have assumed, is lost irrecoverably, and usurped, in consequence of his own backwardness, by some of his more forward, though much less meritorious companions. A man of this character must have been very fortunate in the early choice of his companions, if, in going through the world, he meets always with fair justice, even from those whom, from his own past kindness, he might have some reason to consider as his best friends; and a youth, too unassuming and too unambitious, is frequently followed by an insignificant, complaining, and discontented old age.

Those unfortunate persons whom nature has formed a good deal below the common level, seem sometimes to rate themselves still more below it than they really are. This humility appears sometimes to sink them into idiotism. Whoever has taken the trouble to examine idiots with attention, will find that, in many of them, the faculties of the understanding are by no means weaker than in several other people, who, though acknowledged to be dull and stupid, are not, by any body, accounted idiots. Many idiots, with no more than ordinary education, have been taught to read, write, and account tolerably well. Many persons, never accounted idiots, notwithstanding the most careful education, and notwithstanding that, in their advanced age, they have had spirit enough to attempt to learn what their early education had not taught them, have never been able to acquire, in any tolerable degree, any one of those three accomplishments. By an instinct of pride, however, they set themselves upon a level with their equals in age and situation; and, with courage and firmness, maintain their proper station among their companions. By an opposite instinct, the idiot feels himself below every company into which you can introduce him. Ill-usage, to which he is extremely liable, is capable of throwing him into the most violent fits of rage and fury. But no good usage, no kindness or indulgence, can ever raise him to converse with you as your equal. If you can bring him to converse with you at all, however, you will frequently find his answers sufficiently pertinent, and even sensible. But they are always stamped with a distinct consciousness of his own great inferiority. He seems to shrink and, as it were to retire from your look and conversation; and to feel, when he places himself in your situation, that, notwithstanding your apparent condescension, you cannot help considering him as immensely below you. Some idiots, perhaps the greater part, seem to be so, chiefly or altogether, from a certain numbness or torpidity in the faculties of the understanding. But there are others, in whom those faculties do not appear more torpid or benumbed than in many other people who are not accounted idiots. But that instinct of pride, necessary to support them upon an equality with their brethren, seems totally wanting in the former and not in the latter.

That degree of self-estimation, therefore, which contributes most to the happiness and contentment of the person himself, seems likewise most agreeable to the impartial spectator. The man who esteems himself as he ought, and no more than he ought, seldom fails to obtain from other people all the esteem that he himself thinks due. He desires no more than is due to him, and he rests upon it with complete satisfaction.

The proud and the vain man, on the contrary, are constantly dissatisfied. The one is tormented with indignation at the unjust superiority, as he thinks it, of other people. The other is in continual dread of the shame which, he foresees, would attend upon the detection of his groundless pretensions. Even the extravagant pretensions of the man of real magnanimity, though, when supported by splendid abilities and virtues, and, above all, by good fortune, they impose upon the multitude, whose applauses he little regards, do not impose upon those wise men whose approbation he can only value, and whose esteem he is most anxious to acquire. He feels that they see through, and suspects that they despise his excessive presumption; and he often suffers the cruel misfortune of becoming, first the jealous and secret, and at last the open, furious, and vindictive enemy of those very persons, whose friendship it would have given him the greatest happiness to enjoy with unsuspicious security.

Though our dislike to the proud and the vain often disposes us to rank them rather below than above their proper station, yet, unless we are provoked by some particular and personal impertinence, we very seldom venture to use them ill. In common cases, we endeavour, for our own ease, rather to acquiesce, and, as well as we can, to accommodate ourselves to their folly. But, to the man who under-rates himself, unless we have both more discernment and more generosity than belong to the greater part of men, we seldom fail to do, at least, all the injustice which he does to himself, and frequently a great deal more. He is not only more unhappy in his own feelings than either the proud or the vain, but he is much more liable to every sort of ill-usage from other people.

In almost all cases, it is better to be a little too proud, than, in any respect, too humble; and, in the sentiment of self-estimation, some degree of excess seems, both to the person himself and to the impartial spectator, to be less disagreeable than any degree of defect.

In this, therefore, as well as in every other emotion, passion, and habit, the degree that is most agreeable to the impartial spectator is likewise most agreeable to the person himself; and according as either the excess or the defect is least offensive to the former, so, either the one or the other is in proportion least disagreeable to the latter.

CONCLUSION OF THE SIXTH PART.

Concern for our own happiness recommends to us the virtue of prudence: concern for that of other people, the virtues of justice and beneficence; of which, the one restrains us from hurting, the other prompts us to promote that happiness. Independent of any regard either to what are, or to what ought to be, or to what upon a certain condition would be, the sentiments of other people, the first of those three virtues is originally recommended to us by our selfish, the other two by our benevolent affections. Regard to the sentiments of other people, however, comes afterwards both to enforce and to direct the practice of all those virtues; and no man during, either the whole course of his life, or that of any considerable part of it, ever trod steadily and uniformly in the paths of prudence, of justice, or of proper beneficence, whose conduct was not principally directed by a regard to the sentiments of the supposed impartial spectator, of the great inmate of the breast, the great judge and arbiter of conduct. If in the course of the day we have swerved in any respect from the rules which he prescribes to us; if we have either exceeded or relaxed in our frugality; if we have either exceeded or relaxed in our industry; if, through passion or inadvertency, we have hurt in any respect the interest or happiness of our neighbour; if we have neglected a plain and proper opportunity of promoting that interest and happiness; it is this inmate who, in the evening, calls us to an account for all those omissions and violations, and his reproaches often make us blush inwardly both for our folly and inattention to our own happiness, and for our still greater indifference and inattention, perhaps, to that of other people.

But though the virtues of prudence, justice, and beneficence, may, upon different occasions, be recommended to us almost equally by two different principles; those of self-command are, upon most occasions, principally and almost entirely recommended to us by one; by the sense of propriety, by regard to the sentiments of the supposed impartial spectator. Without the restraint which this principle imposes, every passion would, upon most occasions, rush headlong, if I may say so, to its own gratification. Anger would follow the suggestions of its own fury; fear those of its own violent agitations. Regard to no time or place would induce vanity to refrain from the loudest and most impertinent ostentation; or voluptuousness from the most open, indecent, and scandalous indulgence. Respect for what are, or for what ought to be, or for what upon a certain condition would be, the sentiments of other people, is the sole principle which, upon most occasions, overawes all those mutinous and turbulent passions into that tone and temper which the impartial spectator can enter into and sympathize with.

Upon some occasions, indeed, those passions are restrained, not so much by a sense of their impropriety, as by prudential considerations of the bad consequences which might follow from their indulgence. In such cases, the passions, though restrained, are not always subdued, but often remain lurking in the breast with all their original fury. The man whose anger is restrained by fear, does not always lay aside his anger, but only reserves its gratification for a more safe opportunity. But the man who, in relating to some other person the injury which has been done to him, feels at once the fury of his passion cooled and becalmed by sympathy with the more moderate sentiments of his companion, who at once adopts those more moderate sentiments, and comes to view that injury, not in the black and atrocious colours in which he had originally beheld it, but in the much milder and fairer light in which his companion naturally views it; not only restrains, but in some measure subdues his anger. The passion becomes really less than it was before, and less capable of exciting him to the violent and bloody revenge which at first, perhaps, he might have thought of inflicting.

Those passions which are restrained by the sense of propriety, are all in some degree moderated and subdued by it. But those which are restrained only by prudential considerations of any kind, are, on the contrary, frequently inflamed by the restraint, and sometimes (long after the provocation given, and when nobody is thinking about it) burst out absurdly and unexpectedly, and with tenfold fury and violence.

Anger, however, as well as every other passion, may, upon many occasions, be very properly restrained by prudential considerations. Some exertion of manhood and self-command is even necessary for this sort of restraint; and the impartial spectator may sometimes view it with that sort of cold esteem due to that species of conduct which he considers as a mere matter of vulgar prudence; but never with that affectionate admiration with which he surveys the same passions, when, by the sense of propriety, they are moderated and subdued to what he himself can readily enter into. In the former species of restraint, he may frequently discern some degree of propriety, and, if you will, even of virtue; but it is a propriety and virtue of a much inferior order to those which he always feels with transport and admiration in the latter.

The virtues of prudence, justice, and beneficence, have no tendency to produce any but the most agreeable effects. Regard to those effects, as it originally recommends them to the actor, so does it afterwards to the impartial spectator. In our approbation of the character of the prudent man, we feel, with peculiar complacency, the security which he must enjoy while he walks under the safeguard of that sedate and deliberate virtue. In our approbation of the character of the just man, we feel, with equal complacency, the security which all those connected with him, whether in neighbourhood, society, or business, must derive from his scrupulous anxiety never either to hurt or offend. In our approbation of the character of the beneficent man, we enter into the gratitude of all those who are within the sphere of his good offices, and conceive with them the highest sense of his merit. In our approbation of all those virtues, our sense of their agreeable effects, of their utility, either to the person who exercises them, or to some other persons, joins with our sense of their propriety, and constitutes always a considerable, frequently the greater part of that approbation.

But in our approbation of the virtues of self-command, complacency with their effects sometimes constitutes no part, and frequently but a small part, of that approbation. Those effects may sometimes be agreeable, and sometimes disagreeable; and though our approbation is no doubt stronger in the former case, it is by no means altogether destroyed in the latter. The most heroic valour may be employed indifferently in the cause either of justice or of injustice; and though it is no doubt much more loved and admired in the former case, it still appears a great and respectable quality even in the latter. In that, and in all the other virtues of self-command, the splendid and dazzling quality seems always to be the greatness and steadiness of the exertion, and the strong sense of propriety which is necessary in order to make and to maintain that exertion. The effects are too often but too little regarded.

PART VII.

OF SYSTEMS OF MORAL PHILOSOPHY.

CONSISTING OF FOUR SECTIONS.

SECTION I.

OF THE QUESTIONS WHICH OUGHT TO BE EXAM-
INED IN A THEORY OF MORAL SENTIMENTS.

If we examine the most celebrated and remarkable of the different theories which have been given concerning the nature and
origin of our moral sentiments, we shall find that almost all of
them coincide with some part or other of that which I have been
endeavouring to give an account of; and that if every thing which
has already been said be fully considered, we shall be at no loss
to explain what was the view or aspect of nature which led each
particular author to form his particular system. From some one
or other of those principles which I have been endeavouring to
unfold, every system of morality that ever had any reputation in
the world has, perhaps, ultimately been derived. As they are all of
them, in this respect, founded upon natural principles, they are
all of them in some measure in the right. But as many of them
are derived from a partial and imperfect view of nature, there are
many of them too in some respects in the wrong.

In treating of the principles of morals there are two questions
to be considered. First, wherein does virtue consist? Or what is
the tone of temper, and tenour of conduct, which constitutes the
excellent and praise-worthy character, the character which is the
natural object of esteem, honour, and approbation? And, secondly, by what power or faculty in the mind is it, that this character, whatever it be, is recommended to us? Or in other words,
how and by what means does it come to pass, that the mind prefers one tenour of conduct to another, denominates the one right
and the other wrong; considers the one as the object of approbation, honour, and reward, and the other of blame, censure, and
punishment?

We examine the first question when we consider whether virtue
consists in benevolence, as Dr. Hutcheson imagines; or in acting

suitably to the different relations we stand in, as Dr. Clarke supposes; or in the wise and prudent pursuit of our own real and solid happiness, as has been the opinion of others.[1]

We examine the second question, when we consider, whether the virtuous character, whatever it consists in, be recommended to us by self-love, which makes us perceive that this character, both in ourselves and others, tends most to promote our own private interest; or by reason, which points out to us the difference between one character and another, in the same manner as it does that between truth and falsehood; or by a peculiar power of perception, called a moral sense, which this virtuous character gratifies and pleases, as the contrary disgusts and displeases it; or last of all, by some other principle in human nature, such as a modification of sympathy, or the like.[2]

I shall begin with considering the systems which have been formed concerning the first of these questions, and shall proceed afterwards to examine those concerning the second.

SECTION II.

OF THE DIFFERENT ACCOUNTS WHICH HAVE BEEN GIVEN OF THE NATURE OF VIRTUE.

INTRODUCTION.

The different accounts which have been given of the nature of virtue, or of the temper of mind which constitutes the excellent and praise-worthy character, may be reduced to three different classes. According to some, the virtuous temper of mind does not consist in any one species of affections, but in the proper government and direction of all our affections, which may be either virtuous or vicious according to the objects which they pursue, and the degree of vehemence with which they pursue them. According to these authors, therefore, virtue consists in propriety.

According to others, virtue consists in the judicious pursuit of our own private interest and happiness, or in the proper government and direction of those selfish affections which aim solely at this end. In the opinion of these authors, therefore, virtue consists in prudence.

Another set of authors make virtue consist in those affections only which aim at the happiness of others, not in those which aim at our own. According to them, therefore, disinterested benevolence is the only motive which can stamp upon any action the character of virtue.

The character of virtue, it is evident, must either be ascribed indifferently to all our affections, when under proper government and direction; or it must be confined to some one class or division of them.[1] The great division of our affections is into the selfish and the benevolent. If the character of virtue, therefore, cannot be ascribed indifferently to all our affections, when under proper government and direction, it must be confined either to those which aim directly at our own private happiness, or to those which aim directly at that of others. If virtue, therefore, does not consist in propriety, it must consist either in prudence or in benevolence. Besides these three, it is scarce possible to imagine that any other account can be given of the nature of virtue. I shall endeavour to show hereafter how all the other accounts, which are seemingly different from any of these, coincide at bottom with some one or other of them.

CHAPTER I.

Of those Systems which make Virtue consist in Propriety.

According to Plato, to Aristotle, and to Zeno, virtue consists in the propriety of conduct, or in the suitableness of the affection from which we act to the object which excites it.

I. In the system of Plato* the soul is considered as something like a little state or republic, composed of three different faculties or orders.²

The first is the judging faculty, the faculty which determines not only what are the proper means for attaining any end, but also what ends are fit to be pursued, and what degree of relative value we ought to put upon each. This faculty Plato called, as it is very properly called, reason, and considered it as what had a right to be the governing principle of the whole.³ Under this appellation, it is evident, he comprehended not only that faculty by which we judge of truth and falsehood, but that by which we judge of the propriety or impropriety of desires and affections.

The different passions and appetites, the natural subjects of this ruling principle, but which are so apt to rebel against their master, he reduced to two different classes or orders. The first consisted of those passions, which are founded in pride and resentment, or in what the schoolmen called the irascible part of the soul; ambition, animosity, the love of honour, and the dread of shame, the desire of victory, superiority, and revenge; all those passions,

---

* See Plato de Rep. lib. iv.

in short, which are supposed either to rise from, or to denote what, by a metaphor in our language, we commonly call spirit or natural fire. The second consisted of those passions which are founded in the love of pleasure, or in what the schoolmen called the concupiscible part of the soul. It comprehended all the appetites of the body, the love of ease and security, and of all sensual gratifications.[4]

It rarely happens that we break in upon that plan of conduct, which the governing principle prescribes, and which in all our cool hours we had laid down to ourselves as what was most proper for us to pursue, but when prompted by one or other of those two different sets of passions; either by ungovernable ambition and resentment, or by the importunate solicitations of present ease and pleasure. But though these two orders of passions are so apt to mislead us, they are still considered as necessary parts of human nature: the first having been given to defend us against injuries, to assert our rank and dignity in the world, to make us aim at what is noble and honourable, and to make us distinguish those who act in the same manner; the second, to provide for the support and necessities of the body.

In the strength, acuteness, and perfection of the governing principle was placed the essential virtue of prudence, which, according to Plato, consisted in a just and clear discernment, founded upon general and scientific ideas, of the ends which were proper to be pursued, and of the means which were proper for attaining them.[5]

When the first set of passions, those of the irascible part of the soul, had that degree of strength and firmness which enabled them, under the direction of reason, to despise all dangers in the pursuit of what was honourable and noble; it constituted the virtue of fortitude and magnanimity. This order of passions, according to this system, was of a more generous and noble nature than the other. They were considered upon many occasions as the auxiliaries of reason, to check and restrain the inferior and brutal appetites. We are often angry at ourselves, it was observed, we often become the objects of our own resentment and indignation, when the love of pleasure prompts to do what we disapprove of; and the irascible part of our nature is in this manner called in to assist the rational against the concupiscible.[6]

When all those three different parts of our nature were in perfect concord with one another, when neither the irascible nor concupiscible passions ever aimed at any gratification which reason did not approve of, and when reason never commanded any thing but what these of their own accord were willing to perform: this happy composure, this perfect and complete harmony of soul, constituted that virtue which in their language is expressed by a word which we commonly translate temperance, but which might more properly be translated good temper, or sobriety and moderation of mind.[7]

Justice, the last and greatest of the four cardinal virtues, took place, according to this system, when each of those three faculties of the mind confined itself to its proper office, without attempting to encroach upon that of any other; when reason directed and passion obeyed, and when each passion performed its proper duty, and exerted itself towards its proper object, easily and without reluctance, and with that degree of force and energy, which was suitable to the value of what it pursued. In this consisted that complete virtue, that perfect propriety of conduct, which Plato, after some of the ancient Pythagoreans, denominated Justice.[8]

The word, it is to be observed, which expresses justice in the Greek language, has several different meanings; and as the correspondent word in all other languages, so far as I know, has the same, there must be some natural affinity among those various significations. In one sense we are said to do justice to our neighbour when we abstain from doing him any positive harm, and do not directly hurt him, either in his person, or in his estate, or in his reputation. This is that justice which I have treated of above,[9] the observance of which may be extorted by force, and the violation of which exposes to punishment. In another sense we are said not to do justice to our neighbour unless we conceive for him all that love, respect, and esteem, which his character, his situation, and his connexion with ourselves, render suitable and proper for us to feel, and unless we act accordingly. It is in this sense that we are said to do injustice to a man of merit who is connected with us, though we abstain from hurting him in every respect, if we do not exert ourselves to serve him and to place him in that situation in which the impartial spectator would be pleased to see him. The first sense of the word coincides with what Aristotle and the Schoolmen call commutative justice, and with what Grotius calls the *justitia expletrix*, which consists in abstaining from what is another's, and in doing voluntarily whatever we can with propriety be forced to do. The second sense of the word coincides with what some have called distributive justice,* and with the *justitia attributrix* of Grotius, which consists in proper beneficence, in the becoming use of what is our own, and in the applying it to those purposes either of charity or generosity, to which it is most suitable, in our situation, that it should be applied.[10] In this sense justice comprehends all the social virtues. There is yet another sense in which the word justice is sometimes taken, still more extensive than either of the former, though very much akin to the last; and which runs too, so far as I know, through all languages. It is in this last sense that we are said to be unjust, when we do not seem to value any particular object with that degree of esteem, or to pursue it with that degree of ardour which to the impartial spectator it may appear to deserve or to be naturally fitted for exciting. Thus we are said to do injustice to a poem or a picture, when we do not admire them enough, and we are said to do them more than justice when we admire them too much. In the same manner we are said to do injustice to ourselves when we appear not to give sufficient attention to any particular object of self-interest. In this last sense, what is called justice means the same thing with exact and perfect propriety of conduct and behaviour, and comprehends in it, not only the offices of both commutative and distributive justice, but of every other virtue, of prudence, of fortitude, of temperance. It is in this last sense that Plato evidently understands what he calls justice, and which, therefore, according to him, comprehends in it the perfection of every sort of virtue.

Such is the account given by Plato of the nature of virtue, or of that temper of mind which is the proper object of praise and approbation. It consists, according to him, in that state of mind in which every faculty confines itself within its proper sphere

---

* The distributive justice of Aristotle is somewhat different. It consists in the proper distribution of rewards from the public stock of a community. See Aristotle Ethic. Nic. l. v. c. 2.

without encroaching upon that of any other, and performs its proper office with that precise degree of strength and vigour which belongs to it.[11] His account, it is evident, coincides in every respect with what we have said above concerning the propriety of conduct.

II. Virtue, according to Aristotle,* consists in the habit of mediocrity according to right reason.[12] Every particular virtue, according to him, lies in a kind of middle between two opposite vices, of which the one offends from being too much, the other from being too little affected by a particular species of objects. Thus the virtue of fortitude or courage lies in the middle between the opposite vices of cowardice and of presumptuous rashness, of which the one offends from being too much, and the other from being too little affected by the objects of fear. Thus too the virtue of frugality lies in a middle between avarice and profusion, of which the one consists in an excess, the other in a defect of the proper attention to the objects of self-interest. Magnanimity, in the same manner, lies in a middle between the excess of arrogance and the defect of pusillanimity, of which the one consists in too extravagant, the other in too weak a sentiment of our own worth and dignity.[13] It is unnecessary to observe that this account of virtue corresponds too pretty exactly with what has been said above concerning the propriety and impropriety of conduct.

According to Aristotle,† indeed, virtue did not so much consist in those moderate and right affections, as in the habit of this moderation. In order to understand this, it is to be observed, that virtue may be considered either as the quality of an action, or as the quality of a person. Considered as the quality of an action, it consists, even according to Aristotle, in the reasonable moderation of the affection from which the action proceeds, whether this disposition be habitual to the person or not. Considered as the quality of a person, it consists in the habit of this reasonable moderation, in its having become the customary and usual disposition of the mind. Thus the action which proceeds from an occasional fit of generosity is undoubtedly a generous action, but the

---

* See Aristotle, Ethic. Nic. l. ii. c. 5, et seq. et l. iii. c. 5, et seq.

† See Aristotle, Ethic. Nic. lib. ii. ch. 1, 2, 3, and 4.

man who performs it, is not necessarily a generous person, because it may be the single action of the kind which he ever performed. The motive and disposition of heart, from which this action was performed, may have been quite just and proper: but as this happy mood seems to have been the effect rather of accidental humour than of any thing steady or permanent in the character, it can reflect no great honour on the performer. When we denominate a character generous or charitable, or virtuous in any respect, we mean to signify that the disposition expressed by each of those appellations is the usual and customary disposition of the person. But single actions of any kind, how proper and suitable soever, are of little consequence to show that this is the case.[14] If a single action was sufficient to stamp the character of any virtue upon the person who performed it, the most worthless of mankind might lay claim to all the virtues; since there is no man who has not, upon some occasions, acted with prudence, justice, temperance, and fortitude. But though single actions, how laudable soever, reflect very little praise upon the person who performs them, a single vicious action performed by one whose conduct is usually very regular, greatly diminishes and sometimes destroys altogether our opinion of his virtue. A single action of this kind sufficiently shows that his habits are not perfect, and that he is less to be depended upon, than, from the usual train of his behaviour, we might have been apt to imagine.

Aristotle too,* when he made virtue to consist in practical habits, had it probably in his view to oppose the doctrine of Plato, who seems to have been of opinion that just sentiments and reasonable judgments concerning what was fit to be done or to be avoided, were alone sufficient to constitute the most perfect virtue.[15] Virtue, according to Plato, might be considered as a species of science, and no man, he thought, could see clearly and demonstratively what was right and what was wrong, and not act accordingly. Passion might make us act contrary to doubtful and uncertain opinions, not to plain and evident judgments. Aristotle, on the contrary, was of opinion, that no conviction of the understanding was capable of getting the better of inveterate habits, and that good morals arose not from knowledge but from action.

* See Aristotle Mag. Mor. lib. i. ch. 1.

III. According to Zeno,*[16] the founder of the Stoical doctrine, every animal was by nature recommended to its own care, and was endowed with the principle of self-love, that it might endeavour to preserve, not only its existence, but all the different parts of its nature, in the best and most perfect state of which they were capable.[17]

The self-love of man embraced, if I may say so, his body and all its different members, his mind and all its different faculties and powers, and desired the preservation and maintenance of them all in their best and most perfect condition. Whatever tended to support this state of existence was, therefore, by nature pointed out to him as fit to be chosen; and whatever tended to destroy it, as fit to be rejected. Thus health, strength, agility and ease of body as well as the external conveniencies which could promote these; wealth, power, honours, the respect and esteem of those we live with; were naturally pointed out to us as things eligible, and of which the possession was preferable to the want. On the other hand, sickness, infirmity, unwieldiness, pain of body, as well as all the external inconveniencies which tend to occasion or bring on any of them; poverty, the want of authority, the contempt or hatred of those we live with; were, in the same manner, pointed out to us as things to be shunned and avoided.[18] In each of those two opposite classes of objects, there were some which appeared to be more the objects either of choice or rejection, than others in the same class. Thus, in the first class, health appeared evidently preferable to strength, and strength to agility; reputation to power, and power to riches. And thus too, in the second class, sickness was more to be avoided than unwieldiness of body, ignominy than poverty, and poverty than the loss of power. Virtue and the propriety of conduct consisted in choosing and rejecting all different objects and circumstances according as they were by nature rendered more or less the objects of choice or rejection; in selecting always from among the several objects of choice presented to us, that which was most to be chosen, when we could not obtain them all; and in selecting too, out of the several objects of rejection offered to us, that which was least to be

* See Cicero de finibus, lib. iii.; also Diogenes Laertius in Zenone, lib. vii. segment 84.

avoided, when it was not in our power to avoid them all. By choosing and rejecting with this just and accurate discernment, by thus bestowing upon every object the precise degree of attention it deserved, according to the place which it held in this natural scale of things, we maintained, according to the Stoics, that perfect rectitude of conduct which constituted the essence of virtue. This was what they called to live consistently, to live according to nature, and to obey those laws and directions which nature, or the Author of nature, had prescribed for our conduct.[19]

So far the Stoical idea of propriety and virtue is not very different from that of Aristotle and the ancient Peripatetics.[20]

Among those primary objects which nature had recommended to us as eligible, was the prosperity of our family, of our relations, of our friends, of our country, of mankind, and of the universe in general.[21] Nature, too, had taught us, that as the prosperity of two was preferable to that of one, that of many, or of all, must be infinitely more so. That we ourselves were but one, and that consequently wherever our prosperity was inconsistent with that, either of the whole, or of any considerable part of the whole, it ought, even in our own choice, to yield to what was so vastly preferable. As all the events in this world were conducted by the providence of a wise, powerful, and good God, we might be assured that whatever happened tended to the prosperity and perfection of the whole.[22] If we ourselves, therefore, were in poverty, in sickness, or in any other calamity, we ought, first of all, to use our utmost endeavours, so far as justice and our duty to others would allow, to rescue ourselves from this disagreeable circumstance. But if, after all we could do, we found this impossible, we ought to rest satisfied that the order and perfection of the universe required that we should in the mean time continue in this situation. And as the prosperity of the whole should, even to us, appear preferable to so insignificant a part as ourselves, our situation, whatever it was, ought from that moment to become the object of our liking, if we would maintain that complete propriety and rectitude of sentiment and conduct in which consisted the perfection of our nature. If, indeed, any opportunity of extricating ourselves should offer, it became our duty to embrace it. The order of the universe, it was evident, no longer required our continuance in this situation, and the great Director of the world plainly called upon us to leave it, by so clearly pointing out the road which we were to follow. It was the same case with the adversity of our relations, our friends, our country. If, without violating any more sacred obligation, it was in our power to prevent or put an end to their calamity, it undoubtedly was our duty to do so. The propriety of action, the rule which Jupiter had given us for the direction of our conduct, evidently required this of us. But if it was altogether out of our power to do either, we ought then to consider this event as the most fortunate which could possibly have happened; because we might be assured that it tended most to the prosperity and order of the whole, which was what we ourselves, if we were wise and equitable, ought most of all to desire. It was our own final interest considered as a part of that whole, of which the prosperity ought to be, not only the principal but the sole object of our desire.

"In what sense," says Epictetus, "are some things said to be according to our nature, and others contrary to it? It is in that sense in which we consider ourselves as separated and detached from all other things. For thus it may be said to be according to the nature of the foot to be always clean. But if you consider it as a foot, and not as something detached from the rest of the body, it must behove it sometimes to trample in the dirt, and sometimes to tread upon thorns, and sometimes, too, to be cut off for the sake of the whole body; and if it refuses this, it is no longer a foot. Thus, too, ought we to conceive with regard to ourselves. What are you? A man. If you consider yourself as something separated and detached, it is agreeable to your nature to live to old age, to be rich, to be in health. But if you consider yourself as a man, and as a part of a whole, upon account of that whole, it will behove you sometimes to be in sickness, sometimes to be exposed to the inconveniency of a sea-voyage, sometimes to be in want; and at last, perhaps, to die before your time. Why then do you complain? Do not you know that by doing so, as the foot ceases to be a foot, so you cease to be a man?"[23]

A wise man never complains of the destiny of Providence, nor thinks the universe in confusion when he is out of order.[24] He does not look upon himself as a whole, separated and detached from every other part of nature, to be taken care of by itself and for itself. He regards himself in the light in which he imagines the great genius of human nature, and of the world, regards him. He enters, if I may say so, into the sentiments of that divine Being, and considers himself as an atom, a particle, of an immense and infinite system, which must and ought to be disposed of, according to the conveniency of the whole. Assured of the wisdom which directs all the events of human life, whatever lot befalls him, he accepts it with joy, satisfied that, if he had known all the connections and dependencies of the different parts of the universe, it is the very lot which he himself would have wished for. If it is life, he is contented to live; and if it is death, as nature must have no further occasion for his presence here, he willingly goes where he is appointed. I accept, said a cynical philosopher, whose doctrines were in this respect the same as those of the Stoics, I accept, with equal joy and satisfaction, whatever fortune can befall me. Riches or poverty, pleasure or pain, health or sickness, all is alike: nor would I desire that the Gods should in any respect change my destination.[25] If I was to ask of them any thing beyond what their bounty has already bestowed, it should be that they would inform me beforehand what it was their pleasure should be done with me, that I might of my own accord place myself in this situation, and demonstrate the cheerfulness with which I embraced their allotment. If I am going to sail, says Epictetus, I chuse the best ship and the best pilot, and I wait for the fairest weather that my circumstances and duty will allow. Prudence and propriety, the principles which the Gods have given me for the direction of my conduct, require this of me; but they require no more: and if, notwithstanding, a storm arises, which neither the strength of the vessel nor the skill of the pilot are likely to withstand, I give myself no trouble about the consequence. All that I had to do is done already. The directors of my conduct never command me to be miserable, to be anxious, desponding, or afraid. Whether we are to be drowned, or to come to a harbour, is the business of Jupiter, not mine. I leave it entirely to his determination, nor ever break my rest with considering which way he is likely to decide it, but receive whatever comes with equal indifference and security.[26]

From this perfect confidence in that benevolent wisdom which governs the universe, and from this entire resignation to whatever order that wisdom might think proper to establish, it necessarily followed, that, to the Stoical wise man all the events of human life must be in a great measure indifferent. His happiness consisted altogether, first, in the contemplation of the happiness and perfection of the great system of the universe, of the good government of the great republic of Gods and men, of all rational and sensible beings; and, secondly, in discharging his duty, in acting properly in the affairs of this great republic whatever little part that wisdom had assigned to him. The propriety or impropriety of his endeavours might be of great consequence to him. Their success or disappointment could be of none at all; could excite no passionate joy or sorrow, no passionate desire or aversion. If he preferred some events to others, if some situations were the objects of his choice and others of his rejection, it was not because he regarded the one as in themselves in any respect better than the other, or thought that his own happiness would be more complete in what is called the fortunate than in what is regarded as the distressful situation; but because the propriety of action, the rule which the Gods had given him for the direction of his conduct, required him to chuse and reject in this manner. All his affections were absorbed and swallowed up in two great affections; in that for the discharge of his own duty, and in that for the greatest possible happiness of all rational and sensible beings. For the gratification of this latter affection, he rested with the most perfect security upon the wisdom and power of the great Superintendent of the universe. His sole anxiety was about the gratification of the former; not about the event, but about the propriety of his own endeavours. Whatever the event might be, he trusted to a superior power and wisdom for turning it to promote that great end which he himself was most desirous of promoting.[27]

This propriety of chusing and rejecting, though originally pointed out to us, and as it were recommended and introduced to our acquaintance by the things, and for the sake of the things, chosen and rejected; yet when we had once become thoroughly acquainted with it, the order, the grace, the beauty, which we discerned in this conduct, the happiness which we felt resulted from it, necessarily appeared to us of much greater value than the actual obtaining of all the different objects of choice, or the actual avoiding of all those of rejection. From the observation of this propriety arose the happiness and the glory; from the neglect of it, the misery and the disgrace of human nature.

But to a wise man, to one whose passions were brought under perfect subjection to the ruling principles of his nature, the exact observation of this propriety was equally easy upon all occasions. Was he in prosperity, he returned thanks to Jupiter for having joined him with circumstances which were easily mastered, and in which there was little temptation to do wrong. Was he in adversity, he equally returned thanks to the director of this spectacle of human life, for having opposed to him a vigorous athlete, over whom, though the contest was likely to be more violent, the victory was more glorious, and equally certain. Can there be any shame in that distress which is brought upon us without any fault of our own, and in which we behave with perfect propriety? There can, therefore, be no evil, but, on the contrary, the greatest good and advantage. A brave man exults in those dangers in which, from no rashness of his own, his fortune has involved him. They afford an opportunity of exercising that heroic intrepidity, whose exertion gives the exalted delight which flows from the consciousness of superior propriety and deserved admiration.[28] One who is master of all his exercises has no aversion to measure his strength and activity with the strongest. And, in the same manner, one who is master of all his passions, does not dread any circumstance in which the Superintendent of the universe may think proper to place him. The bounty of that divine Being has provided him with virtues which render him superior to every situation. If it is pleasure, he has temperance to refrain from it; if it is pain, he has constancy to bear it; if it is danger or death, he has magnanimity and fortitude to despise it. The events of human life can never find him unprepared, or at a loss how to maintain that propriety of sentiment and conduct which, in his own apprehension, constitutes at once his glory and his happiness.[29]

Human life the Stoics appear to have considered as a game of great skill; in which, however, there was a mixture of chance, or of what is vulgarly understood to be chance. In such games the stake is commonly a trifle, and the whole pleasure of the game arises from playing well, from playing fairly, and playing skilfully. If notwithstanding all his skill, however, the good player should, by the influence of chance, happen to lose, the loss ought to be a matter, rather of merriment, than of serious sorrow. He has made no false stroke; he has done nothing which he ought to be ashamed of; he has enjoyed completely the whole pleasure of the game. If, on the contrary, the bad player, notwithstanding all his blunders, should, in the same manner, happen to win, his success can give him but little satisfaction. He is mortified by the remembrance of all the faults which he committed. Even during the play he can enjoy no part of the pleasure which it is capable of affording. From ignorance of the rules of the game, fear and doubt and hesitation are the disagreeable sentiments that precede almost every stroke which he plays; and when he has played it, the mortification of finding it a gross blunder, commonly completes the unpleasing circle of his sensations. Human life, with all the advantages which can possibly attend it, ought, according to the Stoics, to be regarded but as a mere two-penny stake; a matter by far too insignificant to merit any anxious concern. Our only anxious concern ought to be, not about the stake, but about the proper method of playing. If we placed our happiness in winning the stake, we placed it in what depended upon causes beyond our power, and out of our direction. We necessarily exposed ourselves to perpetual fear and uneasiness, and frequently to grievous and mortifying disappointments. If we placed it in playing well, in playing fairly, in playing wisely and skilfully; in the propriety of our own conduct in short; we placed it in what, by proper discipline, education, and attention, might be altogether in our own power, and under our own direction. Our happiness was perfectly secure, and beyond the reach of fortune. The event of our actions, if it was out of our power, was equally out of our concern, and we could never feel either fear or anxiety about it; nor ever suffer any grievous, or even any serious disappointment.[30]

Human life itself, as well as every different advantage or disadvantage which can attend it, might, they said, according to different circumstances, be the proper object either of our choice or of our rejection. If, in our actual situation, there were more circumstances agreeable to nature than contrary to it; more circumstances which were the objects of choice than of rejection; life, in this case was, upon the whole, the proper object of choice, and the propriety of conduct required that we should remain in it. If, on the other hand, there were, in our actual situation, without any probable hope of amendment, more circumstances contrary to nature than agreeable to it; more circumstances which were the objects of rejection than of choice; life itself, in this case, became, to a wise man, the object of rejection, and he was not only at liberty to remove out of it, but the propriety of conduct, the rule which the Gods had given him for the direction of his conduct, required him to do so. I am ordered, says Epictetus, not to dwell at Nicopolis. I do not dwell there. I am ordered not to dwell at Athens. I do not dwell at Athens. I am ordered not to dwell in Rome. I do not dwell in Rome. I am ordered to dwell in the little and rocky island of Gyaræ. I go and dwell there. But the house smokes in Gyaræ. If the smoke is moderate, I will bear it, and stay there. If it is excessive, I will go to a house from whence no tyrant can remove me. I keep in mind always that the door is open, that I can walk out when I please, and retire to that hospitable house which is at all times open to all the world; for beyond my undermost garment, beyond my body, no man living has any power over me.[31] If your situation is upon the whole disagreeable; if your house smokes too much for you, said the Stoics, walk forth by all means. But walk forth without repining; without murmuring or complaining. Walk forth calm, contented, rejoicing, returning thanks to the Gods, who, from their infinite bounty, have opened the safe and quiet harbour of death, at all times ready to receive us from the stormy ocean of human life; who have prepared this sacred, this inviolable, this great asylum, always open, always accessible; altogether beyond the reach of human rage and injustice; and large enough to contain both all those who wish, and all those who do not wish to retire to it: an asylum which takes away from every man every pretence of complaining, or even of fancying that there can be any evil in human life, except such as he may suffer from his own folly and weakness.[32]

The Stoics, in the few fragments of their philosophy which have come down to us, sometimes talk of leaving life with a gaiety, and even with a levity, which, were we to consider those passages by themselves, might induce us to believe that they imagined we could with propriety leave it whenever we had a mind, wantonly and capriciously, upon the slightest disgust or uneasiness. "When you sup with such a person," says Epictetus, "you complain of the long stories which he tells you about his Mysian wars.

'Now my friend, says he, having told you how I took possession of an eminence at such a place, I will tell you how I was besieged in such another place.' But if you have a mind not to be troubled with his long stories, do not accept of his supper. If you accept of his supper, you have not the least pretence to complain of his long stories. It is the same case with what you call the evils of human life. Never complain of that of which it is at all times in your power to rid yourself."[33] Notwithstanding this gaiety and even levity of expression, however, the alternative of leaving life, or of remaining in it, was, according to the Stoics, a matter of the most serious and important deliberation. We ought never to leave it till we were distinctly called upon to do so by that superintending Power which had originally placed us in it. But we were to consider ourselves as called upon to do so, not merely at the appointed and unavoidable term of human life. Whenever the providence of that superintending power had rendered our condition in life upon the whole the proper object rather of rejection than of choice; the great rule which he had given us for the direction of our conduct, then required us to leave it. We might then be said to hear the awful and benevolent voice of that divine Being distinctly calling upon us to do so.

It was upon this account that, according to the Stoics, it might be the duty of a wise man to remove out of life though he was perfectly happy; while, on the contrary, it might be the duty of a weak man to remain in it, though he was necessarily miserable.[34] If, in the situation of the wise man, there were more circumstances which were the natural objects of rejection than of choice, the whole situation became the object of rejection, and the rule which the Gods had given him for the direction of his conduct, required that he should remove out of it as speedily as particular circumstances might render convenient. He was, however, perfectly happy even during the time that he might think proper to remain in it. He had placed his happiness, not in obtaining the objects of his choice, or in avoiding those of his rejection; but in always choosing and rejecting with exact propriety; not in the success, but in the fitness of his endeavours and exertions. If, in the situation of the weak man, on the contrary, there were more circumstances which were the natural objects of choice than of rejection; his whole situation became the proper object of choice, and it was his duty to remain in it. He was unhappy, however, from not knowing how to use those circumstances. Let his cards be ever so good, he did not know how to play them, and could enjoy no sort of real satisfaction, either in the progress, or in the event of the game, in whatever manner it might happen to turn out.*

The propriety, upon some occasions, of voluntary death, though it was, perhaps, more insisted upon by the Stoics, than by any other sect of ancient philosophers, was, however, a doctrine common to them all, even to the peaceable and indolent Epicureans. During the age in which flourished the founders of all the principal sects of ancient philosophy; during the Peloponnesian war and for many years after its conclusion, all the different republics of Greece were, at home, almost always distracted by the most furious factions; and abroad, involved in the most sanguinary wars, in which each sought, not merely superiority or dominion, but either completely to extirpate all its enemies, or, what was not less cruel, to reduce them into the vilest of all states, that of domestic slavery, and to sell them, man, woman, and child, like so many herds of cattle, to the highest bidder in the market. The smallness of the greater part of those states, too, rendered it, to each of them, no very improbable event, that it might itself fall into that very calamity which it had so frequently, either, perhaps, actually inflicted, or at least attempted to inflict upon some of its neighbours. In this disorderly state of things, the most perfect innocence, joined to both the highest rank and the greatest public services, could give no security to any man that, even at home and among his own relations and fellow-citizens, he was not, at some time or another, from the prevalence of some hostile and furious faction, to be condemned to the most cruel and ignominious punishment. If he was taken prisoner in war, or if the city of which he was a member was conquered, he was exposed, if possible, to still greater injuries and insults. But every man naturally, or rather necessarily, familiarizes his imagination with the distresses to which he foresees that his situation may frequently expose him. It is impossible that a sailor should not frequently think of storms and shipwrecks, and foundering at sea, and of how he himself is likely both to feel and to act upon such

* See Cicero de finibus, lib. iii. c. 13. Olivet's edition.

occasions. It was impossible, in the same manner, that a Grecian patriot or hero should not familiarize his imagination with all the different calamities to which he was sensible his situation must frequently, or rather constantly expose him. As an American savage prepares his death-song, and considers how he should act when he has fallen into the hands of his enemies, and is by them put to death in the most lingering tortures, and amidst the insults and derision of all the spectators; so a Grecian patriot or hero could not avoid frequently employing his thoughts in considering what he ought both to suffer and to do in banishment, in captivity, when reduced to slavery, when put to the torture, when brought to the scaffold. But the philosophers of all the different sects very justly represented virtue; that is, wise, just, firm, and temperate conduct; not only as the most probable, but as the certain and infallible road to happiness even in this life. This conduct, however, could not always exempt, and might even sometimes expose the person who followed it to all the calamities which were incident to that unsettled situation of public affairs. They endeavoured, therefore, to show that happiness was either altogether, or at least in a great measure, independent of fortune; the Stoics, that it was so altogether; the Academic and Peripatetic philosophers, that it was so in a great measure. Wise, prudent, and good conduct was, in the first place, the conduct most likely to ensure success in every species of undertaking; and secondly, though it should fail of success, yet the mind was not left without consolation. The virtuous man might still enjoy the complete approbation of his own breast; and might still feel that, how untoward soever things might be without, all was calm and peace and concord within. He might generally comfort himself, too, with the assurance that he possessed the love and esteem of every intelligent and impartial spectator, who could not fail both to admire his conduct, and to regret his misfortune.

Those philosophers endeavoured, at the same time, to show, that the greatest misfortunes to which human life was liable, might be supported more easily than was commonly imagined. They endeavoured to point out the comforts which a man might still enjoy when reduced to poverty, when driven into banishment, when exposed to the injustice of popular clamour, when labouring under blindness, under deafness, in the extremity of old age,

upon the approach of death. They pointed out, too, the considerations which might contribute to support his constancy under the
agonies of pain and even of torture, in sickness, in sorrow for the
loss of children, for the death of friends and relations, &c. The
few fragments which have come down to us of what the ancient
philosophers had written upon these subjects, form, perhaps, one
of the most instructive, as well as one of the most interesting
remains of antiquity. The spirit and manhood of their doctrines
make a wonderful contrast with the desponding, plaintive, and
whining tone of some modern systems.[35]

But while those ancient philosophers endeavoured in this manner to suggest every consideration which could, as Milton says,
arm the obdured breast with stubborn patience, as with triple
steel;[36] they, at the same time, laboured above all to convince
their followers that there neither was nor could be any evil in
death; and that, if their situation became at any time too hard for
their constancy to support, the remedy was at hand, the door was
open, and they might, without fear, walk out when they pleased.
If there was no world beyond the present, death, they said, could
be no evil; and if there was another world, the Gods must likewise
be in that other, and a just man could fear no evil while under
their protection. Those philosophers, in short, prepared a
death-song, if I may say so, which the Grecian patriots and heroes
might make use of upon the proper occasions; and, of all the different sects, the Stoics, I think it must be acknowledged, had prepared by far the most animated and spirited song.

Suicide, however, never seems to have been very common
among the Greeks. Excepting Cleomenes, I cannot at present recollect any very illustrious either patriot or hero of Greece, who
died by his own hand.[37] The death of Aristomenes is as much
beyond the period of true history as that of Ajax.[38] The common
story of the death of Themistocles, though within that period, bears
upon its face all the marks of a most romantic fable.[39] Of all the
Greek heroes whose lives have been written by Plutarch, Cleomenes
appears to have been the only one who perished in this manner.
Theramines, Socrates, and Phocion, who certainly did not want
courage, suffered themselves to be sent to prison, and submitted
patiently to that death to which the injustice of their fellow-citizens
had condemned them.[40] The brave Eumenes allowed himself to

be delivered up, by his own mutinous soldiers, to his enemy Antigonus, and was starved to death, without attemping any violence.[41] The gallant Philopœmen suffered himself to be taken prisoner by the Messenians, was thrown into a dungeon, and was supposed to have been privately poisoned.[42] Several of the philosophers, indeed, are said to have died in this manner; but their lives have been so very foolishly written, that very little credit is due to the greater part of the tales which are told of them.[43] Three different accounts have been given of the death of Zeno the Stoic.[44] One is, that after enjoying, for ninety-eight years, the most perfect state of health, he happened, in going out of his school, to fall; and though he suffered no other damage than that of breaking or dislocating one of his fingers, he struck the ground with his hand, and, in the words of the Niobe of Euripides, said, *I come, why doest thou call me?* and immediately went home and hanged himself. At that great age, one should think, he might have had a little more patience. Another account is, that, at the same age, and in consequence of a like accident, he starved himself to death. The third account is, that, at seventy-two years of age, he died in the natural way; by far the most probable account of the three, and supported too by the authority of a contemporary, who must have had every opportunity of being well informed; of Persæus, originally the slave, and afterwards the friend and disciple of Zeno.[45] The first account is given by Apollonius of Tyre, who flourished about the time of Augustus Cæsar, between two and three hundred years after the death of Zeno.[46] I know not who is the author of the second account. Apollonius, who was himself a Stoic, had probably thought it would do honour to the founder of a sect which talked so much about voluntary death, to die in this manner by his own hand. Men of letters, though, after their death, they are frequently more talked of than the greatest princes or statesmen of their times, are generally, during their life, so obscure and insignificant that their adventures are seldom recorded by contemporary historians. Those of after-ages, in order to satisfy the public curiosity, and having no authentic documents either to support or to contradict their narratives, seem frequently to have fashioned them according to their own fancy; and almost always with a great mixture of the marvellous. In this particular case the marvellous, though supported by no authority, seems to have prevailed over the probable, though supported by the best. Diogenes Laertius plainly gives the preference to the story of Apollonius. Lucian and Lactantius appear both to have given credit to that of the great age and of the violent death.[47]

This fashion of voluntary death appears to have been much more prevalent among the proud Romans, than it ever was among the lively, ingenious, and accommodating Greeks. Even among the Romans, the fashion seems not to have been established in the early and, what are called, the virtuous ages of the republic. The common story of the death of Regulus, though probably a fable, could never have been invented, had it been supposed that any dishonour could fall upon that hero, from patiently submitting to the tortures which the Carthaginians are said to have inflicted upon him.[48] In the later ages of the republic some dishonour, I apprehend, would have attended this submission. In the different civil wars which preceded the fall of the commonwealth, many of the eminent men of all the contending parties chose rather to perish by their own hands, than to fall into those of their enemies. The death of Cato, celebrated by Cicero, and censured by Cæsar, and become the subject of a very serious controversy between, perhaps, the two most illustrious advocates that the world had ever beheld, stamped a character of splendour upon this method of dying which it seems to have retained for several ages after.[49] The eloquence of Cicero was superior to that of Cæsar. The admiring prevailed greatly over the censuring party, and the lovers of liberty, for many ages afterwards, looked up to Cato as to the most venerable martyr of the republican party. The head of a party, the Cardinal de Retz observes, may do what he pleases; as long as he retains the confidence of his own friends, he can never do wrong; a maxim of which his Eminence had himself, upon several occasions, an opportunity of experiencing the truth.[50] Cato, it seems, joined to his other virtues that of an excellent bottle companion. His enemies accused him of drunkenness, but, says Seneca, whoever objected this vice to Cato, will find it much easier to prove that drunkenness is a virtue, than that Cato could be addicted to any vice.[51]

Under the Emperors this method of dying seems to have been, for a long time, perfectly fashionable. In the epistles of Pliny we find an account of several persons who chose to die in this manner, rather from vanity and ostentation, it would seem, than from what would appear, even to a sober and judicious Stoic, any proper or necessary reason.[52] Even the ladies, who are seldom behind in following the fashion, seem frequently to have chosen, most unnecessarily, to die in this manner; and, like the ladies in Bengal, to accompany, upon some occasions, their husbands to the tomb. The prevalence of this fashion certainly occasioned many deaths which would not otherwise have happened. All the havoc, however, which this, perhaps the highest exertion of human vanity and impertinence, could occasion, would, probably, at no time, be very great.

The principle of suicide, the principle which would teach us, upon some occasions, to consider that violent action as an object of applause and approbation, seems to be altogether a refinement of philosophy.[53] Nature, in her sound and healthful state, seems never to prompt us to suicide. There is, indeed, a species of melancholy (a disease to which human nature, among its other calamities, is unhappily subject) which seems to be accompanied with, what one may call, an irresistible appetite for self-destruction. In circumstances often of the highest external prosperity, and sometimes too, in spite even of the most serious and deeply impressed sentiments of religion, this disease has frequently been known to drive its wretched victims to this fatal extremity. The unfortunate persons who perish in this miserable manner, are the proper objects, not of censure, but of commiseration. To attempt to punish them, when they are beyond the reach of all human punishment, is not more absurd than it is unjust. That punishment can fall only on their surviving friends and relations, who are always perfectly innocent, and to whom the loss of their friend, in this disgraceful manner, must always be alone a very heavy calamity. Nature, in her sound and healthful state, prompts us to avoid distress upon all occasions; upon many occasions to defend ourselves against it, though at the hazard, or even with the certainty of perishing in that defence. But, when we have neither been able to defend ourselves from it, nor have perished in that defence, no natural principle, no regard to the approbation of the supposed impartial spectator, to the judgment of the man within the breast, seems to call upon us to escape from it by destroying ourselves. It is only the consciousness of our own weakness, of our own incapacity to support the calamity with proper manhood and firmness, which can drive us to this resolution. I do not remember to have either read or heard of any American savage, who, upon being taken prisoner by some hostile tribe, put himself to death, in order to avoid being afterwards put to death in torture, and amidst the insults and mockery of his enemies. He places his glory in supporting those torments with manhood, and in retorting those insults with tenfold contempt and derision.

This contempt of life and death, however, and, at the same time, the most entire submission to the order of Providence; the most complete contentment with every event which the current of human affairs could possibly cast up, may be considered as the two fundamental doctrines upon which rested the whole fabric of Stoical morality. The independent and spirited, but often harsh Epictetus, may be considered as the great apostle of the first of those doctrines: the mild, the humane, the benevolent Antoninus, of the second.[54]

The emancipated slave of Epaphriditus, who, in his youth, had been subjected to the insolence of a brutal master, who, in his riper years, was, by the jealousy and caprice of Domitian, banished from Rome and Athens, and obliged to dwell at Nicopolis, and who, by the same tyrant, might expect every moment to be sent to Gyaræ, or, perhaps, to be put to death; could preserve his tranquillity only by fostering in his mind the most sovereign contempt of human life.[55] He never exults so much, accordingly his eloquence is never so animated as when he represents the futility and nothingness of all its pleasures and all its pains.

The good-natured Emperor, the absolute sovereign of the whole civilized part of the world, who certainly had no peculiar reason to complain of his own allotment, delights in expressing his contentment with the ordinary course of things, and in pointing out beauties even in those parts of it where vulgar observers are not apt to see any. There is a propriety and even an engaging grace, he observes, in old age as well as in youth; and the weakness and decrepitude of the one state are as suitable to nature as the bloom and vigour of the other. Death, too, is just as proper a termination of old age, as youth is of childhood, or manhood of youth.[56] As we frequently say, he remarks upon another occasion, that the physician has ordered to such a man to ride on horseback, or to

use the cold bath, or to walk barefooted; so ought we to say, that
Nature, the great conductor and physician of the universe, has
ordered to such a man a disease, or the amputation of a limb, or
the loss of a child.[57] By the prescriptions of ordinary physicians
the patient swallows many a bitter potion; undergoes many a
painful operation. From the very uncertain hope, however, that
health may be the consequence, he gladly submits to all. The
harshest prescriptions of the great Physician of nature, the patient
may, in the same manner, hope will contribute to his own health,
to his own final prosperity and happiness: and he may be perfectly
assured that they not only contribute, but are indispensably necessary to the health, to the prosperity and happiness of the universe,
to the furtherance and advancement of the great plan of Jupiter.
Had they not been so, the universe would never have produced
them; its all-wise Architect and Conductor would never have suffered them to happen. As all, even the smallest of the co-existent
parts of the universe, are exactly fitted to one another, and all
contribute to compose one immense and connected system; so all,
even apparently the most insignificant of the successive events
which follow one another, make parts, and necessary parts, of
that great chain of causes and effects which had no beginning,
and which will have no end; and which, as they all necessarily
result from the original arrangement and contrivance of the whole;
so they are all essentially necessary, not only to its prosperity, but
to its continuance and preservation. Whoever does not cordially
embrace whatever befals him, whoever is sorry that it has befallen
him, whoever wishes that it had not befallen him, wishes, so far
as in him lies, to stop the motion of the universe, to break that
great chain of succession, by the progress of which that system
can alone be continued and preserved, and, for some little conveniency of his own, to disorder and discompose the whole machine
of the world. "O world," says he, in another place, "all things are
suitable to me which are suitable to thee. Nothing is too early or
too late to me which is seasonable for thee. All is fruit to me which
thy seasons bring forth. From thee are all things; in thee are all
things; for thee are all things. One man says, O beloved city of
Cecrops. Wilt not thou say, O beloved city of God?"[58]

From these very sublime doctrines the Stoics, or at least some
of the Stoics, attempted to deduce all their paradoxes.[59]

The Stoical wise man endeavoured to enter into the views of the great Superintendent of the universe, and to see things in the same light in which that divine Being beheld them. But, to the great Superintendent of the universe, all the different events which the course of his providence may bring forth, what to us appear the smallest and the greatest, the bursting of a bubble, as Mr. Pope says,[60] and that of a world, for example, were perfectly equal, were equally parts of that great chain which he had pre-destined from all eternity, were equally the effects of the same unerring wisdom, of the same universal and boundless benevolence. To the Stoical wise man, in the same manner, all those different events were perfectly equal. In the course of those events, indeed, a little department, in which he had himself some little management and direction, had been assigned to him. In this department he endeavoured to act as properly as he could, and to conduct himself according to those orders which, he understood, had been prescribed to him. But he took no anxious or passionate concern either in the success, or in the disappointment of his own most faithful endeavours. The highest prosperity and the total destruction of that little department, of that little system which had been in some measure committed to his charge, were perfectly indifferent to him. If those events had depended upon him, he would have chosen the one, and he would have rejected the other. But as they did not depend upon him, he trusted to a superior wisdom, and was perfectly satisfied that the event which happened, whatever it might be, was the very event which he himself, had he known all the connections and dependencies of things, would most earnestly and devoutly have wished for. Whatever he did under the influence and direction of those principles was equally perfect; and when he stretched out his finger, to give the example which they commonly made use of, he performed an action in every respect as meritorious, as worthy of praise and admiration, as when he laid down his life for the service of his country.[61] As, to the great Superintendent of the universe, the greatest and the smallest exertions of his power, the formation and dissolution of a world, the formation and dissolution of a bubble, were equally easy, were equally admirable, and equally the effects of the same divine wisdom and benevolence; so, to the Stoical wise man, what we would call the great action, required no more exertion than the little one, was equally easy, proceeded from exactly the same principles, was in no respect more meritorious, nor worthy of any higher degree of praise and admiration.

As all those who had arrived at this state of perfection, were equally happy; so all those who fell in the smallest degree short of it, how nearly soever they might approach to it, were equally miserable. As the man, they said, who was but an inch below the surface of the water, could no more breathe than he who was an hundred yards below it;[62] so the man who had not completely subdued all his private, partial, and selfish passions, who had any other earnest desire but that for the universal happiness, who had not completely emerged from that abyss of misery and disorder into which his anxiety for the gratification of those private, partial, and selfish passions had involved him, could no more breathe the free air of liberty and independency, could no more enjoy the security and happiness of the wise man, than he who was most remote from that situation. As all the actions of the wise man were perfect, and equally perfect; so all those of the man who had not arrived at this supreme wisdom were faulty, and, as some Stoics pretended, equally faulty. As one truth, they said, could not be more true, nor one falsehood more false than another; so an honourable action could not be more honourable, nor a shameful one more shameful than another. As in shooting at a mark, the man who missed it by an inch had equally missed it with him who had done so by a hundred yards; so the man who, in what to us appears the most insignificant action, had acted improperly and without a sufficient reason, was equally faulty with him who had done so in, what to us appears, the most important; the man who has killed a cock, for example, improperly and without a sufficient reason, with him who had murdered his father.

If the first of those two paradoxes should appear sufficiently violent, the second is evidently too absurd to deserve any serious consideration. It is, indeed, so very absurd that one can scarce help suspecting that it must have been in some measure misunderstood or misrepresented. At any rate, I cannot allow myself to believe that such men as Zeno or Cleanthes, men, it is said, of the most simple as well as of the most sublime eloquence, could be the authors, either of these, or of the greater part of the other Stoical paradoxes, which are in general mere impertinent quibbles, and do so little honour to their system that I shall give no further account of them. I am disposed to impute them rather to Chrysippus, the disciple and follower, indeed, of Zeno and Cleanthes, but who, from all that has been delivered down to us concerning him, seems to have been a mere dialectical pedant, without taste or elegance of any kind.[63] He may have been the first who reduced their doctrines into a scholastic or technical system of artificial definitions, divisions, and subdivisions; one of the most effectual expedients, perhaps, for extinguishing whatever degree of good sense there may be in any moral or metaphysical doctrine. Such a man may very easily be supposed to have understood too literally some animated expressions of his masters in describing the happiness of the man of perfect virtue, and the unhappiness of whoever fell short of that character.

The Stoics in general seem to have admitted that there might be a degree of proficiency in those who had not advanced to perfect virtue and happiness. They distributed those proficients into different classes, according to the degree of their advancement; and they called the imperfect virtues which they supposed them capable of exercising, not rectitudes, but proprieties, fitnesses, decent and becoming actions, for which a plausible or probable reason could be assigned, what Cicero expresses by the Latin word *officia*, and Seneca, I think more exactly, by that of *convenientia*. The doctrine of those imperfect, but attainable virtues, seems to have constituted what we may call the practical morality of the Stoics. It is the subject of Cicero's Offices; and is said to have been that of another book written by Marcus Brutus, but which is now lost.[64]

The plan and system which Nature has sketched out for our conduct, seems to be altogether different from that of the Stoical philosophy.

By Nature the events which immediately affect that little department in which we ourselves have some little management and direction, which immediately affect ourselves, our friends, our country, are the events which interest us the most, and which chiefly excite our desires and aversions, our hopes and fears, our joys and sorrows. Should those passions be, what they are very apt to be, too vehement, Nature has provided a proper remedy and correction. The real or even the imaginary presence of the impartial spectator, the authority of the man within the breast, is always at hand to overawe them into the proper tone and temper of moderation.

If, notwithstanding our most faithful exertions, all the events which can affect this little department, should turn out the most unfortunate and disastrous, Nature has by no means left us without consolation. That consolation may be drawn, not only from the complete approbation of the man within the breast, but, if possible, from a still nobler and more generous principle, from a firm reliance upon, and a reverential submission to, that benevolent wisdom which directs all the events of human life, and which, we may be assured, would never have suffered those misfortunes to happen, had they not been indispensably necessary for the good of the whole.

Nature has not prescribed to us this sublime contemplation as the great business and occupation of our lives. She only points it out to us as the consolation of our misfortunes. The Stoical philosophy prescribes it as the great business and occupation of our lives.[65] That philosophy teaches us to interest ourselves earnestly and anxiously in no events, external to the good order of our own minds, to the propriety of our own choosing and rejecting, except in those which concern a department where we neither have nor ought to have any sort of management or direction, the department of the great Superintendent of the universe. By the perfect apathy which it prescribes to us, by endeavouring, not merely to moderate, but to eradicate all our private, partial, and selfish affections, by suffering us to feel for whatever can befall ourselves, our friends, our country, not even the sympathetic and reduced passions of the impartial spectator, it endeavours to render us altogether indifferent and unconcerned in the success or miscarriage of every thing which Nature has prescribed to us as the proper business and occupation of our lives.[66]

The reasonings of philosophy, it may be said, though they may confound and perplex the understanding, can never break down the necessary connection which Nature has established between causes and their effects. The causes which naturally excite our desires and aversions, our hopes and fears, our joys and sorrows, would no doubt, notwithstanding all the reasonings of Stoicism, produce upon each individual, according to the degree of his actual sensibility, their proper and necessary effects. The judgments of the man within the breast, however, might be a good deal affected by those reasonings, and that great inmate might be taught by them to attempt to overawe all our private, partial, and selfish affections into a more or less perfect tranquillity. To direct the judgments of this inmate is the great purpose of all systems of morality. That the Stoical philosophy had very great influence upon the character and conduct of its followers, cannot be doubted; and that though it might sometimes incite them to unnecessary violence, its general tendency was to animate them to actions of the most heroic magnanimity and most extensive benevolence.

IV. Besides these ancient, there are some modern systems, according to which virtue consists in propriety; or in the suitableness of the affection from which we act, to the cause or object which excites it. The system of Dr. Clark, which places virtue in acting according to the relations of things, in regulating our conduct according to the fitness or incongruity which there may be in the application of certain actions to certain things, or to certain relations: that of Mr. Woollaston, which places it in acting according to the truth of things, according to their proper nature and essence, or in treating them as what they really are, and not as what they are not: that of my Lord Shaftesbury, which places it in maintaining a proper balance of the affections, and in allowing no passion to go beyond its proper sphere; are all of them more or less inaccurate descriptions of the same fundamental idea.[67]

None of those systems either give, or even pretend to give, any precise or distinct measure by which this fitness or propriety of affection can be ascertained or judged of. That precise and distinct measure can be found nowhere but in the sympathetic feelings of the impartial and well-informed spectator.

The description of virtue, besides, which is either given, or at least meant and intended to be given in each of those systems, for some of the modern authors are not very fortunate in their manner of expressing themselves, is no doubt quite just, so far as it goes. There is no virtue without propriety, and wherever there is propriety some degree of approbation is due. But still this description is imperfect. For though propriety is an essential

ingredient in every virtuous action, it is not always the sole ingredient. Beneficent actions have in them another quality by which
they appear not only to deserve approbation but recompense.
None of those systems account either easily or sufficiently for
that superior degree of esteem which seems due to such actions,
or for that diversity of sentiment which they naturally excite.
Neither is the description of vice more complete. For, in the same
manner, though impropriety is a necessary ingredient in every
vicious action, it is not always the sole ingredient; and there is
often the highest degree of absurdity and impropriety in very
harmless and insignificant actions. Deliberate actions, of a pernicious tendency to those we live with, have, besides their impropriety, a peculiar quality of their own by which they appear to
deserve, not only disapprobation, but punishment; and to be the
objects, not of dislike merely, but of resentment and revenge: and
none of those systems easily and sufficiently account for that
superior degree of detestation which we feel for such actions.

CHAPTER II.

Of those Systems which make Virtue consist in Prudence.

The most ancient of those systems which make virtue consist
in prudence, and of which any considerable remains have come
down to us, is that of Epicurus, who is said, however, to have
borrowed all the leading principles of his philosophy from some
of those who had gone before him, particularly from Aristippus;
though it is very probable, notwithstanding this allegation of his
enemies, that at least his manner of applying those principles was
altogether his own.[68]

According to Epicurus,*[69] bodily pleasure and pain were the
sole ultimate objects of natural desire and aversion. That they
were always the natural objects of those passions, he thought
required no proof.[70] Pleasure might, indeed, appear sometimes to
be avoided; not, however, because it was pleasure, but because,

---

* See Cicero de finibus, lib. i. Diogenes Laert. l.x.

by the enjoyment of it, we should either forfeit some greater pleasure, or expose ourselves to some pain that was more to be avoided than this pleasure was to be desired. Pain, in the same manner, might appear sometimes to be eligible; not, however, because it was pain, but because by enduring it we might either avoid a still greater pain, or acquire some pleasure of much more importance. That bodily pain and pleasure, therefore, were always the natural objects of desire and aversion, was, he thought, abundantly evident. Nor was it less so, he imagined, that they were the sole ultimate objects of those passions. Whatever else was either desired or avoided, was so, according to him, upon account of its tendency to produce one or other of those sensations. The tendency to procure pleasure rendered power and riches desirable, as the contrary tendency to produce pain made poverty and insignificancy the objects of aversion. Honour and reputation were valued, because the esteem and love of those we live with were of the greatest consequence both to procure pleasure and to defend us from pain. Ignominy and bad fame, on the contrary, were to be avoided, because the hatred, contempt, and resentment of those we lived with, destroyed all security, and necessarily exposed us to the greatest bodily evils.

All the pleasures and pains of the mind were, according to Epicurus, ultimately derived from those of the body. The mind was happy when it thought of the past pleasures of the body, and hoped for others to come: and it was miserable when it thought of the pains which the body had formerly endured, and dreaded the same or greater thereafter.

But the pleasures and pains of the mind, though ultimately derived from those of the body, were vastly greater than their originals. The body felt only the sensation of the present instant, whereas the mind felt also the past and the future, the one by remembrance, the other by anticipation, and consequently both suffered and enjoyed much more. When we are under the greatest bodily pain, he observed, we shall always find, if we attend to it, that it is not the suffering of the present instant which chiefly torments us, but either the agonizing remembrance of the past, or the yet more horrible dread of the future. The pain of each instant, considered by itself, and cut off from all that goes before and all that comes after it, is a trifle, not worth the regarding. Yet this is all which the body can ever be said to suffer. In the same manner, when we enjoy the greatest pleasure, we shall always find that the bodily sensation, the sensation of the present instant, makes but a small part of our happiness, that our enjoyment chiefly arises either from the cheerful recollection of the past, or the still more joyous anticipation of the future, and that the mind always contributes by much the largest share of the entertainment.

Since our happiness and misery, therefore, depended chiefly on the mind, if this part of our nature was well disposed, if our thoughts and opinions were as they should be, it was of little importance in what manner our body was affected. Though under great bodily pain, we might still enjoy a considerable share of happiness, if our reason and judgment maintained their superiority. We might entertain ourselves with the remembrance of past, and with the hopes of future pleasure; we might soften the rigour of our pains, by recollecting what it was which, even in this situation, we were under any necessity of suffering. That this was merely the bodily sensation, the pain of the present instant, which by itself could never be very great. That whatever agony we suffered from the dread of its continuance, was the effect of an opinion of the mind, which might be corrected by juster sentiments; by considering that, if our pains were violent, they would probably be of short duration; and that if they were of long continuance, they would probably be moderate, and admit of many intervals of ease; and that, at any rate, death was always at hand and within call to deliver us, which as, according to him, it put an end to all sensation, either of pain or pleasure, could not be regarded as an evil. When we are, said he, death is not; and when death is, we are not; death therefore can be nothing to us.[71]

If the actual sensation of positive pain was in itself so little to be feared, that of pleasure was still less to be desired. Naturally the sensation of pleasure was much less pungent than that of pain. If, therefore, this last could take so very little from the happiness of a well-disposed mind, the other could add scarce any thing to it. When the body was free from pain and the mind from fear and anxiety, the superadded sensation of bodily pleasure could be of very little importance; and though it might diversify, could not properly be said to increase the happiness of this situation.[72]

In ease of body, therefore, and in security or tranquillity of mind, consisted, according to Epicurus, the most perfect state of human nature, the most complete happiness which man was capable of enjoying. To obtain this great end of natural desire was the sole object of all the virtues, which, according to him, were not desirable upon their own account, but upon account of their tendency to bring about this situation.[73]

Prudence, for example, though, according to this philosophy, the source and principle of all the virtues, was not desirable upon its own account.[74] That careful and laborious and circumspect state of mind, ever watchful and ever attentive to the most distant consequences of every action, could not be a thing pleasant or agreeable for its own sake, but upon account of its tendency to procure the greatest goods and to keep off the greatest evils.

To abstain from pleasure too, to curb and restrain our natural passions for enjoyment, which was the office of temperance, could never be desirable for its own sake. The whole value of this virtue arose from its utility, from its enabling us to postpone the present enjoyment for the sake of a greater to come, or to avoid a greater pain that might ensue from it. Temperance, in short, was nothing but prudence with regard to pleasure.

To support labour, to endure pain, to be exposed to danger or to death, the situations which fortitude would often lead us into, were surely still less the objects of natural desire. They were chosen only to avoid greater evils. We submitted to labour, in order to avoid the greater shame and pain of poverty, and we exposed ourselves to danger and to death in defence of our liberty and property, the means and instruments of pleasure and happiness; or in defence of our country, in the safety of which our own was necessarily comprehended. Fortitude enabled us to do all this cheerfully, as the best which, in our present situation, could possibly be done, and was in reality no more than prudence, good judgment, and presence of mind in properly appreciating pain, labour, and danger, always choosing the less in order to avoid the greater.

It is the same case with justice. To abstain from what is another's was not desirable on its own account, and it could not surely be better for you, that I should possess what is my own, than that you should possess it. You ought, however, to abstain from whatever belongs to me, because by doing otherwise you will provoke the resentment and indignation of mankind. The security and tranquillity of your mind will be entirely destroyed. You will be filled with fear and consternation at the thought of that punishment which you will imagine that men are at all times ready to inflict upon you, and from which no power, no art, no concealment, will ever, in your own fancy, be sufficient to protect you. That other species of justice which consists in doing proper good offices to different persons, according to the various relations of neighbours, kinsmen, friends, benefactors, superiors, or equals, which they may stand in to us, is recommended by the same reasons. To act properly in all these different relations procures us the esteem and love of those we live with; as to do otherwise excites their contempt and hatred. By the one we naturally secure, by the other we necessarily endanger our own ease and tranquillity, the great and ultimate objects of all our desires. The whole virtue of justice, therefore, the most important of all the virtues, is no more than discreet and prudent conduct with regard to our neighbours.

Such is the doctrine of Epicurus concerning the nature of virtue. It may seem extraordinary that this philosopher, who is described as a person of the most amiable manners,[75] should never have observed, that, whatever may be the tendency of those virtues, or of the contrary vices, with regard to our bodily ease and security, the sentiments which they naturally excite in others are the objects of a much more passionate desire or aversion than all their other consequences; that to be amiable, to be respectable, to be the proper object of esteem, is by every well-disposed mind more valued than all the ease and security which love, respect, and esteem can procure us; that, on the contrary, to be odious, to be contemptible, to be the proper object of indignation, is more dreadful than all that we can suffer in our body from hatred, contempt, or indignation; and that consequently our desire of the one character, and our aversion to the other, cannot arise from any regard to the effects which either of them is likely to produce upon the body.[76]

This system is, no doubt, altogether inconsistent with that which I have been endeavouring to establish. It is not difficult, however, to discover from what phasis,[77] if I may say so, from what particular view or aspect of nature, this account of things derives its probability. By the wise contrivance of the Author of nature, virtue is upon all ordinary occasions, even with regard to this life, real wisdom, and the surest and readiest means of obtaining both safety and advantage. Our success or disappointment in our undertakings must very much depend upon the good or bad opinion which is commonly entertained of us, and upon the general disposition of those we live with, either to assist or to oppose us. But the best, the surest, the easiest, and the readiest way of obtaining the advantageous and of avoiding the unfavourable judgments of others, is undoubtedly to render ourselves the proper objects of the former and not of the latter. "Do you desire," said Socrates, "the reputation of a good musician? The only sure way of obtaining it, is to become a good musician. Would you desire in the same manner to be thought capable of serving your country either as a general or as a statesman? The best way in this case too is really to acquire the art and experience of war and government, and to become really fit to be a general or a statesman. And in the same manner if you would be reckoned sober, temperate, just, and equitable, the best way of acquiring this reputation is to become sober, temperate, just, and equitable. If you can really render yourself amiable, respectable, and the proper object of esteem, there is no fear of your not soon acquiring the love, the respect, and esteem of those you live with." [78] Since the practice of virtue, therefore, is in general so advantageous, and that of vice so contrary to our interest, the consideration of those opposite tendencies undoubtedly stamps an additional beauty and propriety upon the one, and a new deformity and impropriety upon the other. Temperance, magnanimity, justice, and beneficence, come thus to be approved of, not only under their proper characters, but under the additional character of the highest wisdom and most real prudence. And in the same manner, the contrary vices of intemperance, pusillanimity, injustice, and either malevolence or sordid selfishness, come to be disapproved of, not only under their proper characters, but under the additional character of the most short-sighted folly and weakness. Epicurus appears in every virtue to have attended to this species of propriety only. It is that which is most apt to occur to those who are endeavouring to persuade others to regularity of conduct. When men by their practice, and perhaps too by their maxims, manifestly show that the natural beauty of virtue is not like to have much effect upon them, how is it possible to move them but by representing the folly of their conduct, and how much they themselves are in the end likely to suffer by it?

By running up all the different virtues too to this one species of propriety, Epicurus indulged a propensity, which is natural to all men, but which philosophers in particular are apt to cultivate with a peculiar fondness, as the great means of displaying their ingenuity, the propensity to account for all appearances from as few principles as possible. And he, no doubt, indulged this propensity still further, when he referred all the primary objects of natural desire and aversion to the pleasures and pains of the body. The great patron of the atomical philosophy,[79] who took so much pleasure in deducing all the powers and qualities of bodies from the most obvious and familiar, the figure, motion, and arrangement of the small parts of matter, felt no doubt a similar satisfaction, when he accounted, in the same manner, for all the sentiments and passions of the mind from those which are most obvious and familiar.[80]

The system of Epicurus agreed with those of Plato, Aristotle, and Zeno, in making virtue consist in acting in the most suitable manner to obtain* the primary objects of natural desire. It differed from all of them in two other respects; first, in the account which it gave of those primary objects of natural desire; and secondly, in the account which it gave of the excellence of virtue, or of the reason why that quality ought to be esteemed.

The primary objects of natural desire consisted, according to Epicurus, in bodily pleasure and pain, and in nothing else: whereas, according to the other three philosophers, there were many other objects, such as knowledge, such as the happiness of our relations, of our friends, of our country, which were ultimately desirable for their own sakes.

Virtue too, according to Epicurus, did not deserve to be pursued for its own sake, nor was itself one of the ultimate objects of natural appetite, but was eligible only upon account of its tendency to prevent pain and to procure ease and pleasure. In the

* Prima naturæ[81]

opinion of the other three, on the contrary, it was desirable, not merely as the means of procuring the other primary objects of natural desire, but as something which was in itself more valuable than them all. Man, they thought, being born for action, his happiness must consist, not merely in the agreeableness of his passive sensations, but also in the propriety of his active exertions.[82]

CHAPTER III.

Of those Systems which make Virtue consist in Benevolence.

The system which makes virtue consist in benevolence, though I think not so ancient as all of those which I have already given an account of, is, however, of very great antiquity. It seems to have been the doctrine of the greater part of those philosophers who, about and after the age of Augustus, called themselves Eclectics, who pretended to follow chiefly the opinions of Plato and Pythagoras, and who upon that account are commonly known by the name of the later Platonists.[83]

In the divine nature, according to these authors, benevolence or love was the sole principle of action, and directed the exertion of all the other attributes. The wisdom of the Deity was employed in finding out the means for bringing about those ends which his goodness suggested, as his infinite power was exerted to execute them. Benevolence, however, was still the supreme and governing attribute, to which the others were subservient, and from which the whole excellency, or the whole morality, if I may be allowed such an expression, of the divine operations, was ultimately derived. The whole perfection and virtue of the human mind consisted in some resemblance or participation of the divine perfections, and, consequently, in being filled with the same principle of benevolence and love which influenced all the actions of the Deity. The actions of men which flowed from this motive were alone truly praise-worthy, or could claim any merit in the sight of the Deity. It was by actions of charity and love only that we could imitate, as became us, the conduct of God, that we could express our humble and devout admiration of his infinite perfections, that by fostering in our own minds the same divine principle, we could bring our own affections to a greater resemblance with his holy attributes, and thereby become more proper objects of his love and esteem; till at last we arrived at that immediate converse and communication with the Deity to which it was the great object of this philosophy to raise us.

This system, as it was much esteemed by many ancient fathers of the Christian church, so after the Reformation it was adopted by several divines of the most eminent piety and learning and of the most amiable manners; particularly, by Dr. Ralph Cudworth, by Dr. Henry More, and by Mr. John Smith of Cambridge.[84] But of all the patrons of this system, ancient or modern, the late Dr. Hutcheson was undoubtedly, beyond all comparison, the most acute, the most distinct, the most philosophical, and what is of the greatest consequence of all, the soberest and most judicious.

That virtue consists in benevolence is a notion supported by many appearances in human nature. It has been observed already,[85] that proper benevolence is the most graceful and agreeable of all the affections, that it is recommended to us by a double sympathy, that as its tendency is necessarily beneficent, it is the proper object of gratitude and reward, and that upon all these accounts it appears to our natural sentiments to possess a merit superior to any other. It has been observed too, that even the weaknesses of benevolence are not very disagreeable to us, whereas those of every other passion are always extremely disgusting. Who does not abhor excessive malice, excessive selfishness, or excessive resentment? But the most excessive indulgence even of partial friendship is not so offensive. It is the benevolent passions only which can exert themselves without any regard or attention to propriety, and yet retain something about them which is engaging. There is something pleasing even in mere instinctive good-will which goes on to do good offices without once reflecting whether by this conduct it is the proper object either of blame or approbation. It is not so with the other passions. The moment they are deserted, the moment they are unaccompanied by the sense of propriety, they cease to be agreeable.

As benevolence bestows upon those actions which proceed from it, a beauty superior to all others, so the want of it, and much more the contrary inclination, communicates a peculiar deformity to whatever evidences such a disposition. Pernicious actions are often punishable for no other reason than because they show a want of sufficient attention to the happiness of our neighbour.[86]

Besides all this, Dr. Hutcheson* observed, that whenever in any action, supposed to proceed from benevolent affections, some other motive had been discovered, our sense of the merit of this action was just so far diminished as this motive was believed to have influenced it. If an action, supposed to proceed from gratitude, should be discovered to have arisen from an expectation of some new favour, or if what was apprehended to proceed from public spirit, should be found out to have taken its origin from the hope of a pecuniary reward, such a discovery would entirely destroy all notion of merit or praise-worthiness in either of these actions. Since, therefore, the mixture of any selfish motive, like that of a baser alloy, diminished or took away altogether the merit which would otherwise have belonged to any action, it was evident, he imagined, that virtue must consist in pure and disinterested benevolence alone.[87]

When those actions, on the contrary, which are commonly supposed to proceed from a selfish motive, are discovered to have arisen from a benevolent one, it greatly enhances our sense of their merit. If we believed of any person that he endeavoured to advance his fortune from no other view but that of doing friendly offices, and of making proper returns to his benefactors, we should only love and esteem him the more. And this observation seemed still more to confirm the conclusion, that it was benevolence only which could stamp upon any action the character of virtue.

Last of all, what, he imagined, was an evident proof of the justness of this account of virtue, in all the disputes of casuists concerning the rectitude of conduct, the public good, he observed, was the standard to which they constantly referred; thereby universally acknowledging that whatever tended to promote the happiness of mankind was right and laudable and virtuous, and the contrary, wrong, blamable, and vicious. In the late debates about passive obedience and the right of resistance, the sole point in controversy among men of sense was, whether universal submission would

* See Inquiry concerning Virtue, sect. i. and ii.

probably be attended with greater evils than temporary insurrections when privileges were invaded. Whether what, upon the whole, tended most to the happiness of mankind, was not also morally good, was never once, he said, made a question.[88]

Since benevolence, therefore, was the only motive which could bestow upon any action the character of virtue, the greater the benevolence which was evidenced by any action, the greater the praise which must belong to it.

Those actions which aimed at the happiness of a great community, as they demonstrated a more enlarged benevolence than those which aimed only at that of a smaller system, so were they, likewise, proportionally the more virtuous. The most virtuous of all affections, therefore, was that which embraced as its objects the happiness of all intelligent beings. The least virtuous, on the contrary, of those to which the character of virtue could in any respect belong, was that which aimed no further than at the happiness of an individual, such as a son, a brother, a friend.[89]

In directing all our actions to promote the greatest possible good, in submitting all inferior affections to the desire of the general happiness of mankind, in regarding one's self but as one of the many,[90] whose prosperity was to be pursued no further than it was consistent with, or conducive to that of the whole, consisted the perfection of virtue.

Self-love was a principle which could never be virtuous in any degree or in any direction. It was vicious whenever it obstructed the general good. When it had no other effect than to make the individual take care of his own happiness, it was merely innocent, and though it deserved no praise, neither ought it to incur any blame. Those benevolent actions which were performed, notwithstanding some strong motive from self-interest, were the more virtuous upon that account. They demonstrated the strength and vigour of the benevolent principle.

Dr. Hutcheson* was so far from allowing self-love to be in any case a motive of virtuous actions, that even a regard to the pleasure of self-approbation, to the comfortable applause of our own consciences, according to him, diminished the merit of a benevolent

* Inquiry concerning virtue, sect. ii. art. 4; also Illustrations on the moral sense, sect. v. last paragraph.[91]

action. This was a selfish motive, he thought, which, so far as it contributed to any action, demonstrated the weakness of that pure and disinterested benevolence which could alone stamp upon the conduct of man the character of virtue. In the common judgments of mankind, however, this regard to the approbation of our own minds is so far from being considered as what can in any respect diminish the virtue of any action, that it is rather looked upon as the sole motive which deserves the appellation of virtuous.

Such is the account given of the nature of virtue in this amiable system, a system which has a peculiar tendency to nourish and support in the human heart the noblest and the most agreeable of all affections, and not only to check the injustice of self-love, but in some measure to discourage that principle altogether, by representing it as what could never reflect any honour upon those who were influenced by it.

As some of the other systems which I have already given an account of, do not sufficiently explain from whence arises the peculiar excellency of the supreme virtue of beneficence, so this system seems to have the contrary defect, of not sufficiently explaining from whence arises our approbation of the inferior virtues of prudence, vigilance, circumspection, temperance, constancy, firmness. The view and aim of our affections, the beneficent and hurtful effects which they tend to produce, are the only qualities at all attended to in this system. Their propriety and impropriety, their suitableness and unsuitableness, to the cause which excites them, are disregarded altogether.[92]

Regard to our own private happiness and interest, too, appear upon many occasions very laudable principles of action. The habits of economy, industry, discretion, attention, and application of thought, are generally supposed to be cultivated from self-interested motives, and at the same time are apprehended to be very praiseworthy qualities, which deserve the esteem and approbation of every body. The mixture of a selfish motive, it is true, seems often to sully the beauty of those actions which ought to arise from a benevolent affection. The cause of this, however, is not that self-love can never be the motive of a virtuous action, but that the benevolent principle appears in this particular case to want its due degree of strength, and to be altogether unsuitable to its object. The character, therefore, seems evidently imperfect, and upon the whole to deserve blame rather than praise. The mixture of a benevolent motive in an action to which self-love alone ought to be sufficient to prompt us, is not so apt indeed to diminish our sense of its propriety, or of the virtue of the person who performs it. We are not ready to suspect any person of being defective in selfishness. This is by no means the weak side of human nature, or the failing of which we are apt to be suspicious. If we could really believe, however, of any man, that, was it not from a regard to his family and friends, he would not take that proper care of his health, his life, or his fortune, to which self-preservation alone ought to be sufficient to prompt him, it would undoubtedly be a failing, though one of those amiable failings, which render a person rather the object of pity than of contempt or hatred. It would still, however, somewhat diminish the dignity and respectableness of his character. Carelessness and want of economy are universally disapproved of, not, however, as proceeding from a want of benevolence, but from a want of the proper attention to the objects of self-interest.

Though the standard by which casuists frequently determine what is right or wrong in human conduct, be its tendency to the welfare or disorder of society, it does not follow that a regard to the welfare of society should be the sole virtuous motive of action, but only that, in any competition, it ought to cast the balance against all other motives.

Benevolence may, perhaps, be the sole principle of action in the Deity, and there are several, not improbable, arguments which tend to persuade us that it is so. It is not easy to conceive what other motive an independent and all-perfect Being, who stands in need of nothing external, and whose happiness is complete in himself, can act from. But whatever may be the case with the Deity, so imperfect a creature as man, the support of whose existence requires so many things external to him, must often act from many other motives. The condition of human nature were peculiarly hard, if those affections, which, by the very nature of our being, ought frequently to influence our conduct, could upon no occasion appear virtuous, or deserve esteem and commendation from any body.

Those three systems, that which places virtue in propriety, that which places it in prudence, and that which makes it consist in benevolence, are the principal accounts which have been given of the nature of virtue. To one or other of them, all the other descriptions of virtue, how different soever they may appear, are easily reducible.

That system which places virtue in obedience to the will of the Deity, may be counted either among those which make it consist in prudence, or among those which make it consist in propriety. When it is asked, why we ought to obey the will of the Deity, this question, which would be impious and absurd in the highest degree, if asked from any doubt that we ought to obey him, can admit but of two different answers. It must either be said that we ought to obey the will of the Deity because he is a Being of infinite power, who will reward us eternally if we do so, and punish us eternally if we do otherwise: or it must be said, that independent of any regard to our own happiness, or to rewards and punishments of any kind, there is a congruity and fitness that a creature should obey its creator, that a limited and imperfect being should submit to one of infinite and incomprehensible perfections. Besides one or other of these two, it is impossible to conceive that any other answer can be given to this question. If the first answer be the proper one, virtue consists in prudence, or in the proper pursuit of our own final interest and happiness; since it is upon this account that we are obliged to obey the will of the Deity. If the second answer be the proper one, virtue must consist in propriety, since the ground of our obligation to obedience is the suitableness or congruity of the sentiments of humility and submission to the superiority of the object which excites them.

That system which places virtue in utility, coincides too with that which makes it consist in propriety. According to this system, all those qualities of the mind which are agreeable or advantageous, either to the person himself or to others, are approved of as virtuous, and the contrary disapproved of as vicious. But the agreeableness or utility of any affection depends upon the degree which it is allowed to subsist in. Every affection is useful when it is confined to a certain degree of moderation; and every affection is disadvantageous when it exceeds the proper bounds. According to this system therefore, virtue consists not in any one affection, but in the proper degree of all the affections.[93] The only difference between it and that which I have been endeavouring to

establish, is, that it makes utility, and not sympathy, or the correspondent affection of the spectator, the natural and original
measure of this proper degree.

CHAPTER IV.

Of licentious Systems.

All those systems, which I have hitherto given an account of, suppose that there is a real and essential distinction between vice and
virtue, whatever these qualities may consist in. There is a real and
essential difference between the propriety and impropriety of any
affection, between benevolence and any other principle of action,
between real prudence and short-sighted folly or precipitate rashness. In the main too all of them contribute to encourage the
praise-worthy, and to discourage the blamable disposition.

It may be true, perhaps, of some of them, that they tend, in some
measure, to break the balance of the affections, and to give the
mind a particular bias to some principles of action, beyond the proportion that is due to them. The ancient systems, which place virtue in propriety, seem chiefly to recommend the great, the Lawful,
and the respectable virtues, the virtues of self-government and
self-command; fortitude, magnanimity, independency upon fortune, the contempt of all outward accidents, of pain, poverty, exile,
and death. It is in these great exertions that the noblest propriety
of conduct is displayed. The soft, the amiable, the gentle virtues,
all the virtues of indulgent humanity are, in comparison, but little
insisted upon, and seem, on the contrary, by the Stoics in particular, to have been often regarded as mere weaknesses which it
behoved a wise man not to harbour in his breast.

The benevolent system, on the other hand, while it fosters and
encourages all those milder virtues in the highest degree, seems
entirely to neglect the more lawful and respectable qualities of
the mind. It even denies them the appellation of virtues. It calls
them moral abilities, and treats them as qualities which do not
deserve the same sort of esteem and approbation, that is due to
what is properly denominated virtue. All those principles of

action which aim only at our own interest, it treats, if that be possible, still worse. So far from having any merit of their own, they diminish, it pretends, the merit of benevolence, when they co-operate with it: and prudence, it is asserted, when employed only in promoting private interest, can never even be imagined a virtue.

That system, again, which makes virtue consist in prudence only, while it gives the highest encouragement to the habits of caution, vigilance, sobriety, and judicious moderation, seems to degrade equally both the amiable and respectable virtues, and to strip the former of all their beauty, and the latter of all their grandeur.

But notwithstanding these defects, the general tendency of each of those three systems is to encourage the best and most laudable habits of the human mind: and it were well for society, if, either mankind in general, or even those few who pretend to live according to any philosophical rule, were to regulate their conduct by the precepts of any one of them. We may learn from each of them something that is both valuable and peculiar. If it was possible, by precept and exhortation, to inspire the mind with fortitude and magnanimity, the ancient systems of propriety would seem sufficient to do this. Or if it was possible, by the same means, to soften it into humanity, and to awaken the affections of kindness and general love towards those we live with, some of the pictures with which the benevolent system presents us, might seem capable of producing this effect. We may learn from the system of Epicurus, though undoubtedly the most imperfect of all the three, how much the practice of both the amiable and respectable virtues is conducive to our own interest, to our own ease and safety and quiet even in this life. As Epicurus placed happiness in the attainment of ease and security, he exerted himself in a particular manner to show that virtue was, not merely the best and the surest, but the only means of acquiring those invaluable possessions.[94] The good effects of virtue, upon our inward tranquillity and peace of mind, are what other philosophers have chiefly celebrated. Epicurus, without neglecting this topic, has chiefly insisted upon the influence of that amiable quality on our outward prosperity and safety. It was upon this account that his writings were so much studied in the ancient world by men of all different philosophical parties. It is from him that Cicero, the great enemy of the Epicurean system, borrows his most agreeable proofs that virtue alone is sufficient to secure happiness. Seneca, though a Stoic, the sect most opposite to that of Epicurus, yet quotes this philosopher more frequently than any other.

There is, however, another system which seems to take away altogether the distinction between vice and virtue, and of which the tendency is, upon that account, wholly pernicious: I mean the system of Dr. Mandeville.[95] Though the notions of this author are in almost every respect erroneous, there are, however, some appearances in human nature, which, when viewed in a certain manner, seem at first sight to favour them. These, described and exaggerated by the lively and humorous, though coarse and rustic eloquence of Dr. Mandeville, have thrown upon his doctrines an air of truth and probability which is very apt to impose upon the unskilful.[96]

Dr. Mandeville considers whatever is done from a sense of propriety, from a regard to what is commendable and praise-worthy, as being done from a love of praise and commendation, or as he calls it from vanity. Man, he observes, is naturally much more interested in his own happiness than in that of others, and it is impossible that in his heart he can ever really prefer their prosperity to his own. Whenever he appears to do so, we may be assured that he imposes upon us, and that he is then acting from the same selfish motives as at all other times.[97] Among his other selfish passions, vanity is one of the strongest, and he is always easily flattered and greatly delighted with the applauses of those about him. When he appears to sacrifice his own interest to that of his companions, he knows that his conduct will be highly agreeable to their self-love, and that they will not fail to express their satisfaction by bestowing upon him the most extravagant praises. The pleasure which he expects from this, over-balances, in his opinion, the interest which he abandons in order to procure it. His conduct, therefore, upon this occasion, is in reality just as selfish, and arises from just as mean a motive, as upon any other. He is flattered, however, and he flatters himself, with the belief that it is entirely disinterested; since, unless this was supposed, it would not seem to merit any commendation either in his own eyes or in those of others. All public spirit, therefore, all preference of public to private interest, is, according to him, a mere cheat and imposition upon mankind; and that human virtue which is so much boasted of, and which is the occasion of so much emulation among men, is the mere offspring of flattery begot upon pride.[98]

Whether the most generous and public spirited actions may not, in some sense, be regarded as proceeding from self-love, I shall not at present examine. The decision of this question is not, I apprehend, of any importance towards establishing the reality of virtue, since self-love may frequently be a virtuous motive of action. I shall only endeavour to show that the desire of doing what is honourable and noble, of rendering ourselves the proper objects of esteem and approbation, cannot with any propriety be called vanity.[99] Even the love of well grounded fame and reputation, the desire of acquiring esteem by what is really estimable, does not deserve that name. The first is the love of virtue, the noblest and the best passion of human nature. The second is the love of true glory, a passion inferior no doubt to the former, but which in dignity appears to come immediately after it. He is guilty of vanity who desires praise for qualities which are either not praise-worthy in any degree, or not in that degree in which he expects to be praised for them; who sets his character upon the frivolous ornaments of dress and equipage, or upon the equally frivolous accomplishments of ordinary behaviour. He is guilty of vanity who desires praise for what indeed very well deserves it, but what he perfectly knows does not belong to him. The empty coxcomb who gives himself airs of importance which he has no title to, the silly liar who assumes the merit of adventures which never happened, the foolish plagiary who gives himself out for the author of what he has no pretensions to, are properly accused of this passion. He too is said to be guilty of vanity who is not contented with the silent sentiments of esteem and approbation, who seems to be fonder of their noisy expressions and acclamations than of the sentiments themselves, who is never satisfied but when his own praises are ringing in his ears, and who solicits with the most anxious importunity all external marks of respect, is fond of titles, of compliments, of being visited, of being attended, of being taken notice of in public places with the appearance of deference and attention. This frivolous passion is altogether different from either of the two former, and is the passion of the lowest and the least of mankind, as they are of the noblest and the greatest.

But though these three passions, the desire of rendering ourselves the proper objects of honour and esteem; or of becoming what is honourable and estimable; the desire of acquiring honour and esteem by really deserving those sentiments; and the frivolous desire of praise at any rate, are widely different; though the two former are always approved of, while the latter never fails to be despised; there is, however, a certain remote affinity among them, which, exaggerated by the humorous and diverting eloquence of this lively author, has enabled him to impose upon his readers.[100] There is an affinity between vanity and the love of true glory, as both these passions aim at acquiring esteem and approbation. But they are different in this, that the one is a just, reasonable, and equitable passion, while the other is unjust, absurd, and ridiculous. The man who desires esteem for what is really estimable, desires nothing but what he is justly entitled to, and what cannot be refused him without some sort of injury. He, on the contrary, who desires it upon any other terms, demands what he has no just claim to. The first is easily satisfied, is not apt to be jealous or suspicious that we do not esteem him enough, and is seldom solicitous about receiving many external marks of our regard. The other, on the contrary, is never to be satisfied, is full of jealousy and suspicion that we do not esteem him so much as he desires, because he has some secret consciousness that he desires more than he deserves. The least neglect of ceremony, he considers as a mortal affront, and as an expression of the most determined contempt. He is restless and impatient, and perpetually afraid that we have lost all respect for him, and is upon this account always anxious to obtain new expressions of esteem, and cannot be kept in temper but by continual attendance and adulation.

There is an affinity too between the desire of becoming what is honourable and estimable, and the desire of honour and esteem, between the love of virtue and the love of true glory. They resemble one another not only in this respect, that both aim at really being what is honourable and noble, but even in that respect in which the love of true glory resembles what is properly called vanity, some reference to the sentiments of others. The man of the greatest magnanimity, who desires virtue for its own sake, and is most indifferent about what actually are the opinions of mankind with regard to him, is still, however, delighted with the thoughts of what they should be, with the consciousness that though he may neither be honoured nor applauded, he is still the proper object of honour and applause, and that if mankind were cool and candid and consistent with themselves, and properly informed of the motives and circumstances of his conduct, they would not fail to honour and applaud him. Though he despises the opinions which are actually entertained of him, he has the highest value for those which ought to be entertained of him. That he might think himself worthy of those honourable sentiments, and, whatever was the idea which other men might conceive of his character, that when he should put himself in their situation, and consider, not what was, but what ought to be their opinion, he should always have the highest idea of it himself, was the great and exalted motive of his conduct. As even in the love of virtue, therefore, there is still some reference, though not to what is, yet to what in reason and propriety ought to be, the opinion of others, there is even in this respect some affinity between it, and the love of true glory. There is, however, at the same time, a very great difference between them. The man who acts solely from a regard to what is right and fit to be done, from a regard to what is the proper object of esteem and approbation, though these sentiments should never be bestowed upon him, acts from the most sublime and godlike motive which human nature is even capable of conceiving. The man, on the other hand, who while he desires to merit approbation is at the same time anxious to obtain it, though he too is laudable in the main, yet his motives have a greater mixture of human infirmity. He is in danger of being mortified by the ignorance and injustice of mankind, and his happiness is exposed to the envy of his rivals and the folly of the public. The happiness of the other, on the contrary, is altogether secure and independent of fortune, and of the caprice of those he lives with. The contempt and hatred which may be thrown upon him by the ignorance of mankind, he considers as not belonging to him, and is not at all mortified by it. Mankind despise and hate him from a false notion of his character and conduct. If they knew him better, they would esteem and love him. It is not him whom, properly speaking, they hate and despise, but another person whom they mistake him to be. Our friend, whom we should meet at a masquerade in the garb of our enemy, would be more diverted than mortified, if under that disguise we should vent our indignation against him. Such are the sentiments of a man of real magnanimity, when exposed to unjust censure. It seldom happens, however, that human nature arrives at this degree of firmness. Though none but the weakest and most worthless of mankind are much delighted with false glory, yet, by a strange inconsistency, false ignominy is often capable of mortifying those who appear the most resolute and determined.

Dr. Mandeville is not satisfied with representing the frivolous motive of vanity, as the source of all those actions which are commonly accounted virtuous. He endeavours to point out the imperfection of human virtue in many other respects. In every case, he pretends, it falls short of that complete self-denial which it pretends to, and, instead of a conquest, is commonly no more than a concealed indulgence of our passions. Wherever our reserve with regard to pleasure falls short of the most ascetic abstinence, he treats it as gross luxury and sensuality. Every thing, according to him, is luxury which exceeds what is absolutely necessary for the support of human nature, so that there is vice even in the use of a clean shirt, or of a convenient habitation. The indulgence of the inclination to sex, in the most lawful union, he considers as the same sensuality with the most hurtful gratification of that passion, and derides that temperance and that chastity which can be practised at so cheap a rate.[101] The ingenious sophistry of his reasoning, is here, as upon many other occasions, covered by the ambiguity of language. There are some of our passions which have no other names except those which mark the disagreeable and offensive degree. The spectator is more apt to take notice of them in this degree than in any other. When they shock his own sentiments, when they give him some sort of antipathy and uneasiness, he is necessarily obliged to attend to them, and is from thence naturally led to give them a name. When they fall in with the natural state of his own mind, he is very apt to overlook them altogether, and either gives them no name at all, or, if he give them any, it is one which marks rather the subjection and restraint of the passion, than the degree which it still is allowed to subsist in, after it is so subjected and restrained. Thus the common names* of the love of pleasure, and of the love of sex, denote a vicious and offensive degree of those passions. The words temperance and chastity, on the other hand, seem to mark rather the restraint and subjection which they are kept under, than the degree which they are still allowed to subsist in. When he can show, therefore, that they still subsist in some degree, he imagines, he has entirely demolished the reality of the virtues of temperance and chastity, and shown them to be mere impositions upon the inattention and simplicity of mankind. Those virtues, however, do not require an entire insensibility to the objects of the passions which they mean to govern. They only aim at restraining the violence of those passions so far as not to hurt the individual, and neither disturb nor offend the society.

It is the great fallacy of Dr. Mandeville's book† to represent every passion as wholly vicious, which is so in any degree and in any direction. It is thus that he treats every thing as vanity which has any reference, either to what are, or to what ought to be the sentiments of others, and it is by means of this sophistry, that he establishes his favourite conclusion, that private vices are public benefits. If the love of magnificence, a taste for the elegant arts and improvements of human life, for whatever is agreeable in dress, furniture, or equipage, for architecture, statuary, painting, and music, is to be regarded as luxury, sensuality, and ostentation, even in those whose situation allows, without any inconveniency, the indulgence of those passions, it is certain that luxury, sensuality, and ostentation are public benefits: since without the qualities upon which he thinks proper to bestow such approbrious names, the arts of refinement could never find encouragement, and must languish for want of employment. Some popular ascetic doctrines which had been current before his time, and which placed virtue in the entire extirpation and annihilation of all our passions, were the real foundation of this licentious system.[102] It was easy for Dr. Mandeville to prove, first, that this

---

* Luxury and lust.

† Fable of the Bees.

entire conquest never actually took place among men; and secondly, that, if it was to take place universally, it would be pernicious to society, by putting an end to all industry and commerce, and in a manner to the whole business of human life. By the first of these propositions he seemed to prove that there was no real virtue, and that what pretended to be such, was a mere cheat and imposition upon mankind; and by the second, that private vices were public benefits, since without them no society could prosper or flourish.

Such is the system of Dr. Mandeville, which once made so much noise in the world, and which, though, perhaps, it never gave occasion to more vice than what would have been without it, at least taught that vice, which arose from other causes, to appear with more effrontery, and to avow the corruption of its motives with a profligate audaciousness which had never been heard of before.

But how destructive soever this system may appear, it could never have imposed upon so great a number of persons, nor have occasioned so general an alarm among those who are the friends of better principles, had it not in some respects bordered upon the truth. A system of natural philosophy may appear very plausible, and be for a long time very generally received in the world, and yet have no foundation in nature, nor any sort of resemblance to the truth. The vortices of Des Cartes were regarded by a very ingenious nation, for near a century together, as a most satisfactory account of the revolutions of the heavenly bodies. Yet it has been demonstrated, to the conviction of all mankind, that these pretended causes of those wonderful effects, not only do not actually exist, but are utterly impossible, and if they did exist, could produce no such effects as are ascribed to them.[103] But it is otherwise with systems of moral philosophy, and an author who pretends to account for the origin of our moral sentiments, cannot deceive us so grossly, nor depart so very far from all resemblance to the truth. When a traveller gives an account of some distant country, he may impose upon our credulity the most groundless and absurd fictions as the most certain matters of fact. But when a person pretends to inform us of what passes in our neighbourhood, and of the affairs of the very parish which we live in, though here too, if we are so careless as not to examine things with our own eyes, he may deceive us in many respects, yet the greatest falsehoods which he imposes upon us must bear some resemblance to the truth, and must even have a considerable mixture of truth in them. An author who treats of natural philosophy, and pretends to assign the causes of the great phaenomena of the universe, pretends to give an account of the affairs of a very distant country, concerning which he may tell us what he pleases, and as long as his narration keeps within the bounds of seeming possibility, he need not despair of gaining our belief. But when he proposes to explain the origin of our desires and affections, of our sentiments of approbation and disapprobation, he pretends to give an account, not only of the affairs of the very parish that we live in, but of our own domestic concerns. Though here too, like indolent masters who put their trust in a steward who deceives them, we are very liable to be imposed upon, yet we are incapable of passing any account which does not preserve some little regard to the truth. Some of the articles, at least, must be just, and even those which are most overcharged must have had some foundation, otherwise the fraud would be detected even by that careless inspection which we are disposed to give. The author who should assign, as the cause of any natural sentiment, some principle which neither had any connexion with it, nor resembled any other principle which had some such connexion, would appear absurd and ridiculous to the most injudicious and unexperienced reader.

SECTION III.

OF THE DIFFERENT SYSTEMS WHICH HAVE
BEEN FORMED CONCERNING THE PRINCIPLE OF
APPROBATION.

INTRODUCTION.

After the inquiry concerning the nature of virtue, the next question of importance in Moral Philosophy, is concerning the principle of approbation, concerning the power or faculty of the mind which renders certain characters agreeable or disagreeable to us, makes us prefer one tenour of conduct to another, denominate the one right and the other wrong, and consider the one as the object of approbation, honour, and reward; the other as that of blame, censure, and punishment.

Three different accounts have been given of this principle of approbation.[1] According to some, we approve and disapprove both of our own actions and of those of others, from self-love only, or from some view of their tendency to our own happiness or disadvantage: according to others, reason, the same faculty by which we distinguish between truth and falsehood, enables us to distinguish between what is fit and unfit both in actions and affections: according to others this distinction is altogether the effect of immediate sentiment and feeling, and arises from the satisfaction or disgust with which the view of certain actions or affections inspires us. Self-love, reason, and sentiment, therefore, are the three different sources which have been assigned for the principle of approbation.

Before I proceed to give an account of those different systems, I must observe, that the determination of this second question, though of the greatest importance in speculation, is of none in practice. The question concerning the nature of virtue necessarily has some influence upon our notions of right and wrong in many particular cases. That concerning the principle of approbation can possibly have no such effect. To examine from what contrivance or mechanism within, those different notions or sentiments arise, is a mere matter of philosophical curiosity.

CHAPTER I.

Of those Systems which deduce the Principle of Approbation from Self-love.

Those who account for the principle of approbation from self-love, do not all account for it in the same manner, and there is a good deal of confusion and inaccuracy in all their different systems. According to Mr. Hobbes, and many of his followers,*[2] man is driven to take refuge in society, not by any natural love which he bears to his own kind, but because without the assistance of others, he is incapable of subsisting with ease or safety. Society, upon this account, becomes necessary to him, and whatever tends to its support and welfare, he considers as having a remote tendency to his own interest; and, on the contrary, whatever is likely to disturb or destroy it, he regards as in some measure hurtful or pernicious to himself.[3] Virtue is the great support, and vice the great disturber of human society. The former, therefore, is agreeable, and the latter offensive to every man; as from the one he foresees the prosperity, and from the other the ruin and disorder of what is so necessary for the comfort and security of his existence.

That the tendency of virtue to promote, and of vice to disturb the order of society, when we consider it coolly and philosophically, reflects a very great beauty upon the one, and a very great deformity upon the other, cannot, as I have observed upon a former occasion,[4] be called in question. Human society, when we contemplate it in a certain abstract and philosophical light, appears like a great, an immense machine, whose regular and harmonious movements produce a thousand agreeable effects. As in any other beautiful and noble machine that was the production

* Puffendorff, Mandeville.

of human art, whatever tended to render its movements more smooth and easy, would derive a beauty from this effect, and, on the contrary, whatever tended to obstruct them would displease upon that account: so virtue, which is, as it were, the fine polish to the wheels of society, necessarily pleases; while vice, like the vile rust, which makes them jar and grate upon one another, is as necessarily offensive. This account, therefore, of the origin of approbation and disapprobation, so far as it derives them from a regard to the order of society, runs into that principle which gives beauty to utility, and which I have explained upon a former occasion; and it is from thence that this system derives all that appearance of probability which it possesses. When those authors describe the innumerable advantages of a cultivated and social, above a savage and solitary life; when they expatiate upon the necessity of virtue and good order for the maintenance of the one, and demonstrate how infallibly the prevalence of vice and disobedience to the laws tend to bring back the other, the reader is charmed with the novelty and grandeur of those views which they open to him: he sees plainly a new beauty in virtue, and a new deformity in vice, which he had never taken notice of before, and is commonly so delighted with the discovery, that he seldom takes time to reflect, that this political view, having never occurred to him in his life before, cannot possibly be the ground of that approbation and disapprobation with which he has always been accustomed to consider those different qualities.[5]

When those authors, on the other hand, deduce from self-love the interest which we take in the welfare of society, and the esteem which upon that account we bestow upon virtue, they do not mean, that when we in this age applaud the virtue of Cato, and detest the villany of Catiline, our sentiments are influenced by the notion of any benefit we receive from the one, or of any detriment we suffer from the other. It was not because the prosperity or subversion of society, in those remote ages and nations, was apprehended to have any influence upon our happiness or misery in the present times; that according to those philosophers, we esteemed the virtuous, and blamed the disorderly character. They never imagined that our sentiments were influenced by any benefit or damage which we supposed actually to redound to us, from either; but by that which might have redounded to us, had we lived in those distant ages and countries; or by that which might still redound to us, if in our own times we should meet with characters of the same kind. The idea, in short, which those authors were groping about, but which they were never able to unfold distinctly, was that indirect sympathy which we feel with the gratitude or resentment of those who received the benefit or suffered the damage resulting from such opposite characters: and it was this which they were indistinctly pointing at, when they said, that it was not the thought of what we had gained or suffered which prompted our applause or indignation, but the conception or imagination of what we might gain or suffer if we were to act in society with such associates.[6]

Sympathy, however, cannot, in any sense, be regarded as a selfish principle. When I sympathize with your sorrow or your indignation, it may be pretended, indeed, that my emotion is founded in self-love, because it arises from bringing your case home to myself, from putting myself in your situation, and thence conceiving what I should feel in the like circumstances. But though sympathy is very properly said to arise from an imaginary change of situations with the person principally concerned, yet this imaginary change is not supposed to happen to me in my own person and character, but in that of the person with whom I sympathize. When I condole with you for the loss of your only son, in order to enter into your grief, I do not consider what I, a person of such a character and profession, should suffer, if I had a son, and if that son was unfortunately to die: but I consider what I should suffer if I was really you, and I not only change circumstances with you, but I change persons and characters. My grief therefore, is entirely upon your account, and not in the least upon my own. It is not, therefore, in the least selfish. How can that be regarded as a selfish passion, which does not arise even from the imagination of any thing that has befallen, or that relates to myself, in my own proper person and character, but which is entirely occupied about what relates to you? A man may sympathize with a woman in child-bed; though it is impossible that he should conceive himself as suffering her pains in his own proper person and character. That whole account of human nature, however, which deduces all sentiments and affections from self-love, which has made so much noise in the world, but which, so far as I know, has never yet been fully and distinctly explained, seems to me to have arisen from some confused misapprehension of the system of sympathy.

CHAPTER II.

Of those Systems which make Reason the Principle of Approbation.

It is well known to have been the doctrine of Mr. Hobbes, that a state of nature is a state of war; and that antecedent to the institution of civil government, there could be no safe or peaceable society among men.[7] To preserve society, therefore, according to him, was to support civil government, and to destroy civil government was the same thing as to put an end to society. But the existence of civil government depends upon the obedience that is paid to the supreme magistrate. The moment he loses his authority, all government is at an end. As self-preservation, therefore, teaches men to applaud whatever tends to promote the welfare of society, and to blame whatever is likely to hurt it; so the same principle, if they would think and speak consistently, ought to teach them to applaud upon all occasions obedience to the civil magistrate, and to blame all disobedience and rebellion. The very ideas of laudable and blamable, ought to be the same with those of obedience and disobedience. The laws of the civil magistrate, therefore, ought to be regarded as the sole ultimate standards of what was just and unjust, of what was right and wrong.[8]

It was the avowed intention of Mr. Hobbes, by propagating these notions, to subject the consciences of men immediately to the civil, and not to the ecclesiastical powers, whose turbulence and ambition, he had been taught, by the example of his own times, to regard as the principal source of the disorders of society.[9] His doctrine, upon this account, was peculiarly offensive to theologians, who accordingly did not fail to vent their indignation against him with great asperity and bitterness. It was likewise offensive to all sound moralists, as it supposed that there was no natural distinction between right and wrong, that these were mutable and changeable, and depended upon the mere arbitrary will of the civil magistrate. This account of things, therefore, was attacked from all quarters, and by all sorts of weapons, by sober reason as well as by furious declamation.

In order to confute so odious a doctrine, it was necessary to prove, that antecedent to all law or positive institution, the mind was naturally endowed with a faculty, by which it distinguished in certain actions and affections, the qualities of right, laudable, and virtuous, and in others those of wrong, blamable, and vicious.

Law, it was justly observed by Dr. Cudworth,* could not be the original source of those distinctions; since upon the supposition of such a law, it must either be right to obey it, and wrong to disobey it, or indifferent whether we obeyed it, or disobeyed it.[10] That law which it was indifferent whether we obeyed or disobeyed, could not, it was evident, be the source of those distinctions; neither could that which it was right to obey and wrong to disobey, since even this still supposed the antecedent notions or ideas of right and wrong, and that obedience to the law was conformable to the idea of right, and disobedience to that of wrong.

Since the mind, therefore, had a notion of those distinctions antecedent to all law, it seemed necessarily to follow, that it derived this notion from reason, which pointed out the difference between right and wrong, in the same manner in which it did that between truth and falsehood:[11] and this conclusion, which, though true in some respects, is rather hasty in others, was more easily received at a time when the abstract science of human nature was but in its infancy, and before the distinct offices and powers of the different faculties of the human mind had been carefully examined and distinguished from one another. When this controversy with Mr. Hobbes was carried on with the greatest warmth and keenness, no other faculty had been thought of from which any such ideas could possibly be supposed to arise. It became at this time, therefore, the popular doctrine, that the essence of virtue and vice did not consist in the conformity or disagreement of human actions with the law of a superior, but in their conformity or disagreement with reason, which was thus

* Immutable Morality, l. 1.

considered as the original source and principle of approbation and disapprobation.

That virtue consists in conformity to reason, is true in some respects, and this faculty may very justly be considered as, in some sense, the source and principle of approbation and disapprobation, and of all solid judgments concerning right and wrong. It is by reason that we discover those general rules of justice by which we ought to regulate our actions: and it is by the same faculty that we form those more vague and indeterminate ideas of what is prudent, of what is decent, of what is generous or noble, which we carry constantly about with us, and according to which we endeavour, as well as we can, to model the tenor of our conduct. The general maxims of morality are formed, like all other general maxims, from experience and induction. We observe in a great variety of particular cases what pleases or displeases our moral faculties, what these approve or disapprove of, and, by induction from this experience, we establish those general rules. But induction is always regarded as one of the operations of reason. From reason, therefore, we are very properly said to derive all those general maxims and ideas. It is by these, however, that we regulate the greater part of our moral judgments, which would be extremely uncertain and precarious if they depended altogether upon what is liable to so many variations as immediate sentiment and feeling, which the different states of health and humour are capable of altering so essentially. As our most solid judgments, therefore, with regard to right and wrong, are regulated by maxims and ideas derived from an induction of reason, virtue may very properly be said to consist in a conformity to reason, and so far this faculty may be considered as the source and principle of approbation and disapprobation.

But though reason is undoubtedly the source of the general rules of morality, and of all the moral judgments which we form by means of them; it is altogether absurd and unintelligible to suppose that the first perceptions of right and wrong can be derived from reason, even in those particular cases upon the experience of which the general rules are formed. These first perceptions, as well as all other experiments upon which any general rules are founded, cannot be the object of reason, but of immediate sense and feeling. It is by finding in a vast variety of instances that one tenor of conduct constantly pleases in a certain manner, and that another as constantly displeases the mind, that we form the general rules of morality. But reason cannot render any particular object either agreeable or disagreeable to the mind for its own sake. Reason may show that this object is the means of obtaining some other which is naturally either pleasing or displeasing, and in this manner may render it either agreeable or disagreeable for the sake of something else. But nothing can be agreeable or disagreeable for its own sake, which is not rendered such by immediate sense and feeling. If virtue, therefore, in every particular instance, necessarily pleases for its own sake, and if vice as certainly displeases the mind, it cannot be reason, but immediate sense and feeling, which, in this manner, reconciles us to the one, and alienates us from the other.

Pleasure and pain are the great objects of desire and aversion: but these are distinguished not by reason, but by immediate sense and feeling. If virtue, therefore, be desirable for its own sake, and if vice be, in the same manner, the object of aversion, it cannot be reason which originally distinguishes those different qualities, but immediate sense and feeling.

As reason, however, in a certain sense, may justly be considered as the principle of approbation and disapprobation, these sentiments were, through inattention, long regarded as originally flowing from the operations of this faculty. Dr. Hutcheson had the merit of being the first who distinguished with any degree of precision in what respect all moral distinctions may be said to arise from reason, and in what respect they are founded upon immediate sense and feeling.[12] In his illustrations upon the moral sense he has explained this so fully, and, in my opinion, so unanswerably, that, if any controversy is still kept up about this subject, I can impute it to nothing, but either to inattention to what that gentleman has written, or to a superstitious attachment to certain forms of expression, a weakness not very uncommon among the learned, especially in subjects so deeply interesting as the present, in which a man of virtue is often loath to abandon, even the propriety of a single phrase which he has been accustomed to.

CHAPTER III.

Of those Systems which make Sentiment the Principle of Approbation.

Those systems which make sentiment the principle of approbation may be divided into two different classes.

I. According to some the principle of approbation is founded upon a sentiment of a peculiar nature, upon a particular power of perception exerted by the mind at the view of certain actions or affections; some of which affecting this faculty in an agreeable and others in a disagreeable manner, the former are stamped with the characters of right, laudable, and virtuous; the latter with those of wrong, blamable, and vicious. This sentiment being of a peculiar nature distinct from every other, and the effect of a particular power of perception, they give it a particular name, and call it a moral sense.[13]

II. According to others, in order to account for the principle of approbation, there is no occasion for supposing any new power of perception which had never been heard of before: Nature, they imagine, acts here, as in all other cases, with the strictest economy, and produces a multitude of effects from one and the same cause; and sympathy, a power which has always been taken notice of, and with which the mind is manifestly endowed, is, they think, sufficient to account for all the effects ascribed to this peculiar faculty.[14]

I. Dr. Hutcheson* had been at great pains to prove that the principle of approbation was not founded on self-love.[15] He had demonstrated too that it could not arise from any operation of reason. Nothing remained, he thought, but to suppose it a faculty of a peculiar kind, with which Nature had endowed the human mind, in order to produce this one particular and important effect. When self-love and reason were both excluded, it did not occur to him that there was any other known faculty of the mind which could in any respect answer this purpose.

This new power of perception he called a moral sense, and supposed it to be somewhat analogous to the external senses. As the

* Inquiry concerning Virtue.

bodies around us, by affecting these in a certain manner, appear to possess the different qualities of sound, taste, odour, colour; so the various affections of the human mind, by touching this particular faculty in a certain manner, appear to possess the different qualities of amiable and odious, of virtuous and vicious, of right and wrong.[16]

The various senses or powers of perception,* from which the human mind derives all its simple ideas, were, according to this system, of two different kinds, of which the one were called the direct or antecedent, the other, the reflex or consequent senses.[17] The direct senses were those faculties from which the mind derived the perception of such species of things as did not presuppose the antecedent perception of any other. Thus sounds and colours were objects of the direct senses. To hear a sound or to see a colour does not presuppose the antecedent perception of any other quality or object. The reflex or consequent senses, on the other hand, were those faculties from which the mind derived the perception of such species of things as presupposed the antecedent perception of some other. Thus harmony and beauty were objects of the reflex senses. In order to perceive the harmony of a sound, or the beauty of a colour, we must first perceive the sound or the colour. The moral sense was considered as a faculty of this kind. That faculty, which Mr. Locke calls reflection, and from which he derived the simple ideas of the different passions and emotions of the human mind, was, according to Dr. Hutcheson, a direct internal sense. That faculty again by which we perceived the Beauty or deformity, the virtue or vice of those different passions and emotions, was a reflex, internal sense.

Dr. Hutcheson endeavoured still further to support this doctrine, by showing that it was agreeable to the analogy of nature, and that the mind was endowed with a variety of other reflex senses exactly similar to the moral sense; such as a sense of beauty and deformity in external objects; a public sense, by which we sympathize with the happiness or misery of our fellow-creatures; a sense of shame and honour, and a sense of ridicule.[18]

But notwithstanding all the pains which this ingenious philosopher has taken to prove that the principle of approbation is

* Treatise of the Passions.

founded in a peculiar power of perception, somewhat analogous to the external senses, there are some consequences, which he acknowledges to follow from this doctrine, that will, perhaps, be regarded by many as a sufficient confutation of it. The qualities, he allows,*[19] which belong to the objects of any sense, cannot, without the greatest absurdity, be ascribed to the sense itself. Who ever thought of calling the sense of seeing black or white, the sense of hearing loud or low, or the sense of tasting sweet or bitter? And, according to him, it is equally absurd to call our moral faculties virtuous or vicious, morally good or evil. These qualities belong to the objects of those faculties, not to the faculties themselves. If any man, therefore, was so absurdly constituted as to approve of cruelty and injustice as the highest virtues, and to disapprove of equity and humanity as the most pitiful vices, such a constitution of mind might indeed be regarded as inconvenient both to the individual and to the society, and likewise as strange, surprising, and unnatural in itself; but it could not, without the greatest absurdity, be denominated vicious or morally evil.

Yet surely if we saw any man shouting with admiration and applause at a barbarous and unmerited execution, which some insolent tyrant had ordered, we should not think we were guilty of any great absurdity in denominating this behaviour vicious and morally evil in the highest degree, though it expressed nothing but depraved moral faculties, or an absurd approbation of this horrid action, as of what was noble, magnanimous, and great. Our heart, I imagine, at the sight of such a spectator, would forget for a while its sympathy with the sufferer, and feel nothing but horror and detestation, at the thought of so execrable a wretch. We should abominate him even more than the tyrant who might be goaded on by the strong passions of jealousy, fear, and resentment, and upon that account be more excusable. But the sentiments of the spectator would appear altogether without cause or motive, and therefore most perfectly and completely detestable. There is no perversion of sentiment or affection which our heart would be more averse to enter into, or which it would reject with greater hatred and indignation than one of this kind; and so far

* Illustrations upon the Moral Sense, sect. i. p. 237, et seq.; third edition.

from regarding such a constitution of mind as being merely something strange or inconvenient, and not in any respect vicious or morally evil, we should rather consider it as the very last and most dreadful stage of moral depravity.

Correct moral sentiments, on the contrary, naturally appear in some degree laudable and morally good. The man, whose censure and applause are upon all occasions suited with the greatest accuracy to the value or unworthiness of the object, seems to deserve a degree even of moral approbation. We admire the delicate precision of his moral sentiments: they lead our own judgments, and, upon account of their uncommon and surprising justness, they even excite our wonder and applause. We cannot indeed be always sure that the conduct of such a person would be in any respect correspondent to the precision and accuracy of his judgments concerning the conduct of others. Virtue requires habit and resolution of mind, as well as delicacy of sentiment; and unfortunately the former qualities are sometimes wanting, where the latter is in the greatest perfection. This disposition of mind, however, though it may sometimes be attended with imperfections, is incompatible with any thing that is grossly criminal, and is the happiest foundation upon which the superstructure of perfect virtue can be built. There are many men who mean very well, and seriously purpose to do what they think their duty, who notwithstanding are disagreeable on account of the coarseness of their moral sentiments.

It may be said, perhaps, that though the principle of approbation is not founded upon any power of perception that is in any respect analogous to the external senses, it may still be founded upon a peculiar sentiment which answers this one particular purpose and no other. Approbation and disapprobation, it may be pretended, are certain feelings or emotions which arise in the mind upon the view of different characters and actions; and as resentment might be called a sense of injuries, or gratitude a sense of benefits, so these may very properly receive the name of a sense of right and wrong, or of a moral sense.

But this account of things, though it may not be liable to the same objections with the foregoing, is exposed to others which are equally unanswerable.

First of all, whatever variations any particular emotion may undergo, it still preserves the general features which distinguish it to be an emotion of such a kind, and these general features are always more striking and remarkable than any variation which it may undergo in particular cases. Thus anger is an emotion of a particular kind: and accordingly its general features are always more distinguishable than all the variations it undergoes in particular cases. Anger against a man is, no doubt, somewhat different from anger against a woman, and that again from anger against a child. In each of those three cases, the general passion of anger receives a different modification from the particular character of its object, as may easily be observed by the attentive. But still the general features of the passion predominate in all these cases. To distinguish these, requires no nice observation: a very delicate attention, on the contrary, is necessary to discover their variations: every body takes notice of the former; scarce any body observes the latter. If approbation and disapprobation, therefore, were, like gratitude and resentment, emotions of a particular kind, distinct from every other, we should expect that in all the variations which either of them might undergo, it would still retain the general features which mark it to be an emotion of such a particular kind, clear, plain, and easily distinguishable. But in fact it happens quite otherwise. If we attend to what we really feel when upon different occasions we either approve or disapprove, we shall find that our emotion in one case is often totally different from that in another, and that no common features can possibly be discovered between them. Thus the approbation with which we view a tender, delicate, and humane sentiment, is quite different from that with which we are struck by one that appears great, daring, and magnanimous. Our approbation of both may, upon different occasions, be perfect and entire; but we are softened by the one, and we are elevated by the other, and there is no sort of resemblance between the emotions which they excite in us. But, according to that system which I have been endeavouring to establish, this must necessarily be the case. As the emotions of the person whom we approve of, are, in those two cases, quite opposite to one another, and as our approbation arises from sympathy with those opposite emotions, what we feel upon the one occasion, can have no sort of resemblance to what we feel upon the other. But this could not happen if approbation consisted in a peculiar emotion which had nothing in common with the sentiments we approved of, but which arose at the view of those sentiments, like any other passion at the view of its proper object. The same thing holds true with regard to disapprobation. Our horror for cruelty has no sort of resemblance to our contempt for mean-spiritedness. It is quite a different species of discord which we feel at the view of those two different vices, between our own minds and those of the person whose sentiments and behaviour we consider.

Secondly, I have already observed, that not only the different passions or affections of the human mind which are approved or disapproved of, appear morally good or evil, but that proper and improper approbation appear, to our natural sentiments, to be stamped with the same characters. I would ask, therefore, how it is, that, according to this system, we approve or disapprove of proper or improper approbation? To this question there is, I imagine, but one reasonable answer, which can possibly be given. It must be said, that when the approbation with which our neighbour regards the conduct of a third person coincides with our own, we approve of his approbation, and consider it as, in some measure, morally good; and that, on the contrary, when it does not coincide with our own sentiments, we disapprove of it, and consider it as, in some measure, morally evil. It must be allowed, therefore, that, at least in this one case, the coincidence or opposition of sentiments, between the observer and the person observed, constitutes moral approbation or disapprobation. And if it does so in this one case, I would ask, why not in every other? Or to what purpose imagine a new power of perception in order to account for those sentiments?

Against every account of the principle of approbation, which makes it depend upon a peculiar sentiment, distinct from every other, I would object; that it is strange that this sentiment, which Providence undoubtedly intended to be the governing principle of human nature, should hitherto have been so little taken notice of, as not to have got a name in any language. The word moral sense is of very late formation, and cannot yet be considered as making part of the English tongue. The word approbation has but within these few years been appropriated to denote peculiarly any thing of this kind. In propriety of language we approve of whatever is

entirely to our satisfaction, of the form of a building, of the contrivance of a machine, of the flavour of a dish of meat. The word
conscience does not immediately denote any moral faculty by
which we approve or disapprove.[20] Conscience supposes, indeed,
the existence of some such faculty, and properly signifies our consciousness of having acted agreeably or contrary to its directions.
When love, hatred, joy, sorrow, gratitude, resentment, with so
many other passions which are all supposed to be the subjects of
this principle, have made themselves considerable enough to get
titles to know them by, is it not surprising that the sovereign of
them all should hitherto have been so little heeded, that, a few
philosophers excepted, nobody has yet thought it worth while to
bestow a name upon it?

When we approve of any character or action, the sentiments
which we feel, are, according to the foregoing system, derived
from four sources, which are in some respects different from one
another. First, we sympathize with the motives of the agent; secondly, we enter into the gratitude of those who receive the benefit
of his actions; thirdly, we observe that his conduct has been
agreeable to the general rules by which those two sympathies
generally act; and, last of all, when we consider such actions as
making a part of a system of behaviour which tends to promote
the happiness either of the individual or of the society, they
appear to derive a beauty from this utility, not unlike that which
we ascribe to any well-contrived machine. After deducting, in
any one particular case, all that must be acknowledged to proceed from some one or other of these four principles, I should be
glad to know what remains, and I shall freely allow this overplus
to be ascribed to a moral sense, or to any other peculiar faculty,
provided any body will ascertain precisely what this overplus is.
It might be expected, perhaps, that if there was any such peculiar
principle, such as this moral sense is supposed to be, we should
feel it, in some particular cases, separated and detached from
every other, as we often feel joy, sorrow, hope, and fear, pure and
unmixed with any other emotion. This however, I imagine, cannot even be pretended. I have never heard any instance alleged in
which this principle could be said to exert itself alone and
unmixed with sympathy or antipathy, with gratitude or resentment, with the perception of the agreement or disagreement of

any action to an established rule, or last of all with that general taste for beauty and order which is excited by inanimated as well as by animated objects.

II. There is another system which attempts to account for the origin of our moral sentiments from sympathy, distinct from that which I have been endeavouring to establish. It is that which places virtue in utility, and accounts for the pleasure with which the spectator surveys the utility of any quality from sympathy with the happiness of those who are affected by it. This sympathy is different both from that by which we enter into the motives of the agent, and from that by which we go along with the gratitude of the persons who are benefited by his actions. It is the same principle with that by which we approve of a well-contrived machine. But no machine can be the object of either of those two last mentioned sympathies. I have already, in the fourth part of this discourse, given some account of this system.[21]

SECTION IV.

OF THE MANNER IN WHICH DIFFERENT AUTHORS HAVE TREATED OF THE PRACTICAL RULES OF MORALITY.

It was observed in the third part of this discourse, that the rules of justice are the only rules of morality which are precise and accurate; that those of all the other virtues are loose, vague, and indeterminate; that the first may be compared to the rules of grammar; the others to those which critics lay down for the attainment of what is sublime and elegant in composition, and which present us rather with a general idea of the perfection we ought to aim at, than afford us any certain and infallible directions for acquiring it.

As the different rules of morality admit such different degrees of accuracy, those authors who have endeavoured to collect and digest them into systems have done it in two different manners; and one set has followed through the whole that loose method to which they were naturally directed by the consideration of one species of virtues; while another has as universally endeavoured to introduce into their precepts that sort of accuracy of which only some of them are susceptible. The first wrote like critics, the second like grammarians.

I. The first, among whom we may count all the ancient moralists, have contented themselves with describing in a general manner the different vices and virtues, and with pointing out the deformity and misery of the one disposition as well as the propriety and happiness of the other, but have not affected to lay down many precise rules that are to hold good unexceptionably in all particular cases. They have only endeavoured to ascertain, as far as language is capable of ascertaining, first, wherein consists the sentiment of the heart, upon which each particular virtue is founded, what sort of internal feeling or emotion it is which constitutes the essence of friendship, of humanity, of generosity, of justice, of magnanimity, and of all the other virtues, as well as of the vices which are opposed to them: and, secondly, what is the general way of acting, the ordinary tone and tenor of conduct to which each of those sentiments would direct us, or how it is that a friendly, a generous, a brave, a just, and a humane man, would, upon ordinary occasions, chuse to act.

To characterize the sentiment of the heart, upon which each particular virtue is founded, though it requires both a delicate and an accurate pencil, is a task, however, which may be executed with some degree of exactness. It is impossible, indeed, to express all the variations which each sentiment either does or ought to undergo, according to every possible variation of circumstances. They are endless, and language wants names to mark them by. The sentiment of friendship, for example, which we feel for an old man is different from that which we feel for a young: that which we entertain for an austere man different from that which we feel for one of softer and gentler manners: and that again from what we feel for one of gay vivacity and spirit. The friendship which we conceive for a man is different from that with which a woman affects us, even where there is no mixture of any grosser passion. What author could enumerate and ascertain these and all the other infinite varieties which this sentiment is capable of undergoing? But still the general sentiment of friendship and familiar attachment which is common to them all, may be ascertained with a sufficient degree of accuracy. The picture which is drawn of it, though it will always be in many respects incomplete, may, however, have such a resemblance as to make us know the original when we meet with it, and even distinguish it from other sentiments to which it has a considerable resemblance, such as good-will, respect, esteem, admiration.

To describe, in a general manner, what is the ordinary way of acting to which each virtue would prompt us, is still more easy. It is, indeed, scarce possible to describe the internal sentiment or emotion upon which it is founded, without doing something of this kind. It is impossible by language to express, if I may say so, the invisible features of all the different modifications of passion as they show themselves within. There is no other way of marking and distinguishing them from one another, but by describing the effects which they produce without, the alterations which they occasion in the countenance, in the air and external behaviour, the resolutions they suggest, the actions they prompt to. It is thus that Cicero, in the first book of his Offices, endeavours to direct us to the practice of the four cardinal virtues, and that Aristotle in the practical parts of his Ethics,[1] points out to us the different habits by which he would have us regulate our behaviour, such as liberality, magnificence, magnanimity, and even jocularity and good humour, qualities which that indulgent philosopher has thought worthy of a place in the catalogue of the virtues, though the lightness of that approbation which we naturally bestow upon them, should not seem to entitle them to so venerable a name.

Such works present us with agreeable and lively pictures of manners. By the vivacity of their descriptions they inflame our natural love of virtue, and increase our abhorrence of vice: by the justness as well as delicacy of their observations they may often help both to correct and to ascertain our natural sentiments with regard to the propriety of conduct, and suggesting many nice and delicate attentions, form us to a more exact justness of behaviour, than what, without such instruction, we should have been apt to think of. In treating of the rules of morality, in this manner, consists the science which is properly called Ethics, a science which, though like criticism it does not admit of the most accurate precision, is, however, both highly useful and agreeable. It is of all others the most susceptible of the embellishments of eloquence, and by means of them of bestowing, if that be possible, a new importance upon the smallest rules of duty. Its precepts, when thus dressed and adorned, are capable of producing upon the flexibility of youth, the noblest and most lasting impressions, and as they fall in with the natural magnanimity of that generous age, they are able to inspire, for a time at least, the most heroic resolutions, and thus tend both to establish and confirm the best and most useful habits of which the mind of man is susceptible. Whatever precept and exhortation can do to animate us to the practice of virtue, is done by this science delivered in this manner.

II. The second set of moralists, among whom we may count all the casuists of the middle and latter ages of the christian church, as well as all those who in this and in the preceding century have treated of what is called natural jurisprudence, do not content themselves with characterizing in this general manner that tenor of conduct which they would recommend to us, but endeavour to lay down exact and precise rules for the direction of every circumstance of our behaviour.[2] As justice is the only virtue with regard to which such exact rules can properly be given; it is this virtue, that has chiefly fallen under the consideration of those two different sets of writers. They treat of it, however, in a very different manner.

Those who write upon the principles of jurisprudence, consider only what the person to whom the obligation is due, ought to think himself entitled to exact by force; what every impartial spectator would approve of him for exacting, or what a judge or arbiter, to whom he had submitted his case, and who had undertaken to do him justice, ought to oblige the other person to suffer or to perform. The casuists, on the other hand, do not so much examine what it is, that might properly be exacted by force, as what it is, that the person who owes the obligation ought to think himself bound to perform from the most sacred and scrupulous regard to the general rules of justice, and from the most conscientious dread, either of wronging his neighbour, or of violating the integrity of his own character. It is the end of jurisprudence to prescribe rules for the decisions of judges and arbiters. It is the end of casuistry to prescribe rules for the conduct of a good man. By observing all the rules of jurisprudence, supposing them ever so perfect, we should deserve nothing but to be free from external punishment. By observing those of casuistry, supposing them such as they ought to be, we should be entitled to considerable praise, by the exact and scrupulous delicacy of our behaviour.

It may frequently happen that a good man ought to think himself bound, from a sacred and conscientious regard to the general rules of justice, to perform many things which it would be the highest injustice to extort from him, or for any judge or arbiter to impose upon him by force. To give a trite example; a highwayman,[3] by the fear of death, obliges a traveller to promise him a certain sum of money. Whether such a promise, extorted in this manner by unjust force, ought to be regarded as obligatory, is a question that has been very much debated.[4]

If we consider it merely as a question of jurisprudence, the decision can admit of no doubt. It would be absurd to suppose that the highwayman can be entitled to use force to constrain the other to perform. To extort the promise was a crime which deserved the highest punishment, and to extort the performance would only be adding a new crime to the former. He can complain of no injury who has been only deceived by the person by whom he might justly have been killed. To suppose that a judge ought to enforce the obligation of such promises, or that the magistrate ought to allow them to sustain action at law, would be the most ridiculous of all absurdities. If we consider this question, therefore, as a question of jurisprudence, we can be at no loss about the decision.

But if we consider it as a question of casuistry, it will not be so easily determined. Whether a good man, from a conscientious regard to that most sacred rule of justice, which commands the observance of all serious promises, would not think himself bound to perform, is at least much more doubtful. That no regard is due to the disappointment of the wretch who brings him into this situation, that no injury is done to the robber, and consequently that nothing can be extorted by force, will admit of no sort of dispute. But whether some regard is not, in this case, due to his own dignity and honour, to the inviolable sacredness of that part of his character which makes him reverence the law of truth and abhor every thing that approaches to treachery and falsehood, may, perhaps, more reasonably be made a question. The casuists accordingly are greatly divided about it. One party, with whom we may count Cicero among the ancients, among the moderns, Puffendorf, Barbeyrac his commentator, and above all the late Dr. Hutcheson, one who in most cases was by no means a loose casuist, determine, without any hesitation, that no sort of regard is due to any such promise, and that to think otherwise is mere weakness and superstition.[5] Another party, among whom we may reckon* some of the ancient fathers of the church, as well as some very eminent modern casuists, have been of another opinion, and have judged all such promises obligatory.[6]

If we consider the matter according to the common sentiments of mankind, we shall find that some regard would be thought due

* St Augustine, La Placette.

even to a promise of this kind; but that it is impossible to determine how much, by any general rule that will apply to all cases without exception. The man who was quite frank and easy in making promises of this kind, and who violated them with as little ceremony, we should not chuse for our friend and companion. A gentleman who should promise a highwayman five pounds and not perform, would incur some blame. If the sum promised, however, was very great, it might be more doubtful, what was proper to be done. If it was such, for example, that the payment of it would entirely ruin the family of the promiser, if it was so great as to be sufficient for promoting the most useful purposes, it would appear in some measure criminal, at least extremely improper, to throw it, for the sake of a punctilio,[7] into such worthless hands. The man who should beggar himself, or who should throw away an hundred thousand pounds, though he could afford that vast sum, for the sake of observing such a parole[8] with a thief, would appear to the common sense of mankind, absurd and extravagant in the highest degree. Such profusion would seem inconsistent with his duty, with what he owed both to himself and others, and what, therefore, regard to a promise extorted in this manner, could by no means authorize. To fix, however, by any precise rule, what degree of regard ought to be paid to it, or what might be the greatest sum which could be due from it, is evidently impossible. This would vary according to the characters of the persons, according to their circumstances, according to the solemnity of the promise, and even according to the incidents of the rencounter:[9] and if the promiser had been treated with a great deal of that sort of gallantry, which is sometimes to be met with in persons of the most abandoned characters, more would seem due than upon other occasions. It may be said in general, that exact propriety requires the observance of all such promises, wherever it is not inconsistent with some other duties that are more sacred; such as regard to the public interest, to those whom gratitude, whom natural affection, or whom the laws of proper beneficence, should prompt us to provide for. But, as was formerly taken notice of, we have no precise rules to determine what external actions are due from a regard to such motives, nor, consequently, when it is that those virtues are inconsistent with the observance of such promises.

It is to be observed, however, that whenever such promises are violated, though for the most necessary reasons, it is always with some degree of dishonour to the person who made them. After they are made, we may be convinced of the impropriety of observing them. But still there is some fault in having made them. It is at least a departure from the highest and noblest maxims of magnanimity and honour. A brave man ought to die, rather than make a promise which he can neither keep without folly, nor violate without ignominy. For some degree of ignominy always attends a situation of this kind. Treachery and falsehood are vices so dangerous, so dreadful, and, at the same time, such as may so easily, and, upon many occasions, so safely be indulged, that we are more jealous of them than of almost any other. Our imagination therefore attaches the idea of shame to all violations of faith, in every circumstance and in every situation. They resemble, in this respect, the violations of chastity in the fair sex, a virtue of which, for the like reasons, we are excessively jealous; and our sentiments are not more delicate with regard to the one, than with regard to the other. Breach of chastity dishonours irretrievably. No circumstances, no solicitation can excuse it; no sorrow, no repentance atone for it. We are so nice in this respect that even a rape dishonours, and the innocence of the mind cannot, in our imagination, wash out the pollution of the body. It is the same case with the violation of faith, when it has been solemnly pledged, even to the most worthless of mankind. Fidelity is so necessary a virtue, that we apprehend it in general to be due even to those to whom nothing else is due, and whom we think it lawful to kill and destroy. It is to no purpose that the person who has been guilty of the breach of it, urges that he promised in order to save his life, and that he broke his promise because it was inconsistent with some other respectable duty to keep it. These circumstances may alleviate, but cannot entirely wipe out his dishonour. He appears to have been guilty of an action with which, in the imaginations of men, some degree of shame is inseparably connected. He has broke a promise which he had solemnly averred he would maintain; and his character, if not irretrievably stained and polluted, has at least a ridicule affixed to it, which it will be very difficult entirely to efface; and no man, I imagine, who had gone through an adventure of this kind would be fond of telling the story.

This instance may serve to show wherein consists the difference between casuistry and jurisprudence, even when both of them consider the obligations of the general rules of justice.

But though this difference be real and essential, though those two sciences propose quite different ends, the sameness of the subject has made such a similarity between them, that the greater part of authors whose professed design was to treat of jurisprudence, have determined the different questions they examine, sometimes according to the principles of that science, and sometimes according to those of casuistry, without distinguishing, and, perhaps, without being themselves aware when they did the one, and when the other.

The doctrine of the casuists, however, is by no means confined to the consideration of what a conscientious regard to the general rules of justice would demand of us. It embraces many other parts of Christian and moral duty. What seems principally to have given occasion to the cultivation of this species of science was the custom of auricular confession, introduced by the Roman Catholic superstition, in times of barbarism and ignorance. By that institution the most secret actions, and even the thoughts of every person, which could be suspected of receding in the smallest degree from the rules of Christian purity, were to be revealed to the confessor. The confessor informed his penitents whether, and in what respect they had violated their duty, and what penance it behoved them to undergo, before he could absolve them in the name of the offended Deity.

The consciousness, or even the suspicion of having done wrong, is a load upon every mind, and is accompanied with anxiety and terror in all those who are not hardened by long habits of iniquity. Men, in this, as in all other distresses, are naturally eager to disburthen themselves of the oppression which they feel upon their thoughts, by unbosoming the agony of their mind to some person whose secrecy and discretion they can confide in. The shame, which they suffer from this acknowledgment, is fully compensated by that alleviation of their uneasiness which the sympathy of their confidant seldom fails to occasion. It relieves them to find that they are not altogether unworthy of regard, and that however their past conduct may be censured, their present disposition is at least approved of, and is perhaps sufficient to compensate the other, at least to maintain them in some degree of esteem with their friend. A numerous and artful clergy had, in those times of superstition, insinuated themselves into the confidence of almost every private family. They possessed all the little learning which the times could afford, and their manners, though in many respects rude and disorderly, were polished and regular compared with those of the age they lived in. They were regarded, therefore, not only as the great directors of all religious, but of all moral duties. Their familiarity gave reputation to whoever was so happy as to possess it, and every mark of their disapprobation stamped the deepest ignominy upon all who had the misfortune to fall under it. Being considered as the great judges of right and wrong, they were naturally consulted about all scruples that occurred, and it was reputable for any person to have it known that he made those holy men the confidants of all such secrets, and took no important or delicate step in his conduct without their advice and approbation. It was not difficult for the clergy, therefore, to get it established as a general rule, that they should be entrusted with what it had already become fashionable to entrust them, and with what they generally would have been entrusted, though no such rule had been established. To qualify themselves for confessors became thus a necessary part of the study of churchmen and divines, and they were thence led to collect what are called cases of conscience, nice and delicate situations in which it is hard to determine whereabouts the propriety of conduct may lie. Such works, they imagined, might be of use both to the directors of consciences and to those who were to be directed; and hence the origin of books of casuistry.

The moral duties which fell under the consideration of the casuists were chiefly those which can, in some measure at least, be circumscribed within general rules, and of which the violation is naturally attended with some degree of remorse and some dread of suffering punishment. The design of that institution which gave occasion to their works, was to appease those terrors of conscience which attend upon the infringement of such duties. But it is not every virtue of which the defect is accompanied with any very severe compunctions of this kind, and no man applies to his confessor for absolution, because he did not perform the most generous, the most friendly, or the most magnanimous action which, in his circumstances, it was possible to perform. In failures of this kind, the rule that is violated is commonly not very determinate, and is generally of such a nature too, that though the observance of it might entitle to honour and reward, the violation seems to expose to no positive blame, censure, or punishment. The exercise of such virtues the casuists seem to have regarded as a sort of works of supererogation, which could not be very strictly exacted, and which it was therefore unnecessary for them to treat of.

The breaches of moral duty, therefore, which came before the tribunal of the confessor, and upon that account fell under the cognizance of the casuists, were chiefly of three different kinds.

First and principally, breaches of the rules of justice. The rules here are all express and positive, and the violation of them is naturally attended with the consciousness of deserving, and the dread of suffering, punishment both from God and man.

Secondly, breaches of the rules of chastity. These in all grosser instances are real breaches of the rules of justice, and no person can be guilty of them without doing the most unpardonable injury to some other. In smaller instances, when they amount only to a violation of those exact decorums which ought to be observed in the conversation of the two sexes, they cannot indeed justly be considered as violations of the rules of justice. They are generally, however, violations of a pretty plain rule, and, at least in one of the sexes, tend to bring ignominy upon the person who has been guilty of them, and, consequently to be attended in the scrupulous with some degree of shame and contrition of mind.

Thirdly, breaches of the rules of veracity. The violation of truth, it is to be observed, is not always a breach of justice, though it is so upon many occasions, and consequently cannot always expose to any external punishment. The vice of common lying, though a most miserable meanness, may frequently do hurt to nobody, and in this case no claim of vengeance or satisfaction can be due either to the persons imposed upon, or to others. But though the violation of truth is not always a breach of justice, it is always a breach of a very plain rule, and what naturally tends to cover with shame the person who has been guilty of it.

There seems to be in young children an instinctive disposition to believe whatever they are told.[10] Nature seems to have judged it necessary for their preservation that they should, for some time at least, put implicit confidence in those to whom the care of their childhood, and of the earliest and most necessary parts of their education, is intrusted. Their credulity, accordingly, is excessive, and it requires long and much experience of the falsehood of mankind to reduce them to a reasonable degree of diffidence and distrust. In grown-up people the degrees of credulity are, no doubt, very different. The wisest and most experienced are generally the least credulous. But the man scarce lives who is not more credulous than he ought to be, and who does not, upon many occasions, give credit to tales, which not only turn out to be perfectly false, but which a very moderate degree of reflection and attention might have taught him could not well be true. The natural disposition is always to believe. It is acquired wisdom and experience only that teach incredulity, and they very seldom teach it enough. The wisest and most cautious of us all frequently gives credit to stories which he himself is afterwards both ashamed and astonished that he could possibly think of believing.

The man whom we believe is necessarily, in the things concerning which we believe him, our leader and director, and we look up to him with a certain degree of esteem and respect. But as from admiring other people we come to wish to be admired ourselves; so from being led and directed by other people we learn to wish to become ourselves leaders and directors. And as we cannot always be satisfied merely with being admired, unless we can at the same time persuade ourselves that we are in some degree really worthy of admiration; so we cannot always be satisfied merely with being believed, unless we are at the same time conscious that we are really worthy of belief. As the desire of praise and that of praise-worthiness, though very much akin, are yet distinct and separate desires; so the desire of being believed and that of being worthy of belief, though very much akin too, are equally distinct and separate desires.

The desire of being believed, the desire of persuading, of leading and directing other people, seems to be one of the strongest of all our natural desires. It is, perhaps, the instinct upon which is founded the faculty of speech, the characteristical faculty of human nature. No other animal possesses this faculty, and we cannot discover in any other animal any desire to lead and direct the judgment and conduct of its fellows. Great ambition, the desire of real superiority, of leading and directing, seems to be altogether peculiar to man, and speech is the great instrument of ambition, of real superiority, of leading and directing the judgments and conduct of other people.

It is always mortifying not to be believed, and it is doubly so when we suspect that it is because we are supposed to be unworthy of belief and capable of seriously and wilfully deceiving. To tell a man that he lies, is of all affronts the most mortal. But whoever seriously and wilfully deceives is necessarily conscious to himself that he merits this affront, that he does not deserve to be believed, and that he forfeits all title to that sort of credit from which alone he can derive any sort of ease, comfort, or satisfaction, in the society of his equals. The man who had the misfortune to imagine that nobody believed a single word he said, would feel himself the outcast of human society, would dread the very thought of going into it, or of presenting himself before it, and could scarce fail, I think, to die of despair. It is probable, however, that no man ever had just reason to entertain this humiliating opinion of himself. The most notorious liar, I am disposed to believe, tells the fair truth at least twenty times for once that he seriously and deliberately lies; and, as in the most cautious the disposition to believe is apt to prevail over that to doubt and distrust; so in those who are the most regardless of truth, the natural disposition to tell it prevails upon most occasions over that to deceive, or in any respect to alter or disguise it.

We are mortified when we happen to deceive other people, though unintentionally, and from having been ourselves deceived. Though this involuntary falsehood may frequently be no mark of any want of veracity, of any want of the most perfect love of truth, it is always in some degree a mark of want of judgment, of want of memory, of improper credulity, of some degree of precipitancy and rashness. It always diminishes our authority to persuade, and always brings some degree of suspicion upon our fitness to lead and direct. The man who sometimes misleads from mistake, however, is widely different from him who is capable of wilfully deceiving. The former may safely be trusted upon many occasions; the latter very seldom upon any.

Frankness and openness conciliate confidence.[11] We trust the man who seems willing to trust us. We see clearly, we think, the road by which he means to conduct us, and we abandon ourselves with pleasure to his guidance and direction. Reserve and concealment, on the contrary, call forth diffidence. We are afraid to follow the man who is going we do not know where. The great pleasure of conversation and society, besides, arises from a certain correspondence of sentiments and opinions, from a certain harmony of minds, which like so many musical instruments coincide and keep time with one another. But this most delightful harmony cannot be obtained unless there is a free communication of sentiments and opinions. We all desire, upon this account, to feel how each other is affected, to penetrate into each other's bosoms, and to observe the sentiments and affections which really subsist there. The man who indulges us in this natural passion, who invites us into his heart, who, as it were, sets open the gates of his breast to us, seems to exercise a species of hospitality more delightful than any other. No man, who is in ordinary good temper, can fail of pleasing, if he has the courage to utter his real sentiments as he feels them, and because he feels them. It is this unreserved sincerity which renders even the prattle of a child agreeable. How weak and imperfect soever the views of the open-hearted, we take pleasure to enter into them, and endeavour, as much as we can, to bring down our own understanding to the level of their capacities, and to regard every subject in the particular light in which they appear to have considered it. This passion to discover the real sentiments of others is naturally so strong, that it often degenerates into a troublesome and impertinent curiosity to pry into those secrets of our neighbours which they have very justifiable reasons for concealing; and, upon many occasions, it requires prudence and a strong sense of propriety to govern this, as well as all the other passions of human nature, and to reduce it to that pitch which any impartial spectator can approve of. To disappoint this curiosity, however, when it is kept within proper bounds, and aims at nothing which there can be any just reason for concealing, is equally disagreeable in its turn. The man who eludes our most innocent questions, who gives no satisfaction to our most inoffensive inquiries, who plainly wraps himself up in impenetrable obscurity, seems, as it were, to build a wall about his breast. We run forward to get within it, with all the eagerness of harmless curiosity; and feel ourselves all at once pushed back with the rudest and most offensive violence.

The man of reserve and concealment, though seldom a very amiable character, is not disrespected or despised. He seems to feel coldly towards us, and we feel as coldly towards him. He is not much praised or beloved, but he is as little hated or blamed. He very seldom, however, has occasion to repent of his caution, and is generally disposed rather to value himself upon the prudence of his reserve. Though his conduct, therefore, may have been very faulty, and sometimes even hurtful, he can very seldom be disposed to lay his case before the casuists, or to fancy that he has any occasion for their acquittal or approbation.

It is not always so with the man, who, from false information, from inadvertency, from precipitancy and rashness, has involuntarily deceived. Though it should be in a matter of little consequence, in telling a piece of common news, for example, if he is a real lover of truth, he is ashamed of his own carelessness, and never fails to embrace the first opportunity of making the fullest acknowledgments. If it is in a matter of some consequence, his contrition is still greater; and if any unlucky or fatal consequence has followed from his misinformation, he can scarce ever forgive himself. Though not guilty, he feels himself to be in the highest degree, what the ancients called, piacular,[12] and is anxious and eager to make every sort of atonement in his power. Such a person might frequently be disposed to lay his case before the casuists, who have in general been very favourable to him, and though they have sometimes justly condemned him for rashness, they have universally acquitted him of the ignominy of falsehood.

But the man who had the most frequent occasion to consult them, was the man of equivocation and mental reservation, the man who seriously and deliberately meant to deceive, but who, at the same time, wished to flatter himself that he had really told the truth. With him they have dealt variously. When they approved very much of the motives of his deceit, they have sometimes acquitted him, though, to do them justice, they have in general and much more frequently condemned him.

The chief subjects of the works of the casuists, therefore, were the conscientious regard that is due to the rules of justice; how far we ought to respect the life and property of our neighbour; the duty of restitution; the laws of chastity and modesty, and wherein consisted what, in their language, are called the sins of concupiscence; the rules of veracity, and the obligation of oaths, promises, and contracts of all kinds.

It may be said in general of the works of the casuists that they attempted, to no purpose, to direct by precise rules what it belongs to feeling and sentiment only to judge of. How is it possible to ascertain by rules the exact point at which, in every case, a delicate sense of justice begins to run into a frivolous and weak scrupulosity of conscience? When it is that secrecy and reserve begin to grow into dissimulation? How far an agreeable irony may be carried, and at what precise point it begins to degenerate into a detestable lie? What is the highest pitch of freedom and ease of behaviour which can be regarded as graceful and becoming, and when it is that it first begins to run into a negligent and thoughtless licentiousness? With regard to all such matters, what would hold good in any one case would scarce do so exactly in any other, and what constitutes the propriety and happiness of behaviour varies in every case with the smallest variety of situation. Books of casuistry, therefore, are generally as useless as they are commonly tiresome. They could be of little use to one who should consult them upon occasion, even supposing their decisions to be just; because, notwithstanding the multitude of cases collected in them, yet upon account of the still greater variety of possible circumstances, it is a chance, if among all those cases there be found one exactly parallel to that under consideration. One, who is really anxious to do his duty, must be very weak, if he can imagine that he has much occasion for them; and with regard to one who is negligent of it, the style of those writings is not such as is likely to awaken him to more attention. None of them tend to animate us to what is generous and noble. None of them tend to soften us to what is gentle and humane. Many of them, on the contrary, tend rather to teach us to chicane with our own consciences, and by their vain subtilties serve to authorise innumerable evasive refinements with regard to the most essential articles of our duty. That frivolous accuracy which they attempted to introduce into subjects which do not admit of it, almost necessarily betrayed them into those dangerous errors, and at the same time rendered their works dry and disagreeable, abounding in abstruse and metaphysical distinctions, but incapable of exciting in the heart any of those emotions which it is the principal use of books of morality to excite.

The two useful parts of moral philosophy, therefore, are Ethics and Jurisprudence:[13] casuistry ought to be rejected altogether; and the ancient moralists appear to have judged much better, who, in treating of the same subjects, did not affect any such nice exactness, but contented themselves with describing, in a general manner, what is the sentiment upon which justice, modesty, and veracity are founded, and what is the ordinary way of acting to which those virtues would commonly prompt us.

Something, indeed, not unlike the doctrine of the casuists, seems to have been attempted by several philosophers. There is something of this kind in the third book of Cicero's Offices, where he endeavours like a casuist to give rules for our conduct in many nice cases, in which it is difficult to determine whereabouts the point of propriety may lie.[14] It appears too, from many passages in the same book, that several other philosophers had attempted something of the same kind before him. Neither he nor they, however, appear to have aimed at giving a complete system of this sort, but only meant to show how situations may occur, in which it is doubtful, whether the highest propriety of conduct consists in observing or in receding from what, in ordinary cases, are the rules of duty.

Every system of positive law may be regarded as a more or less imperfect attempt towards a system of natural jurisprudence, or towards an enumeration of the particular rules of justice. As the violation of justice is what men will never submit to from one another, the public magistrate is under a necessity of employing the power of the commonwealth to enforce the practice of this virtue. Without this precaution, civil society would become a scene of bloodshed and disorder, every man revenging himself at his own hand whenever he fancied he was injured. To prevent the confusion which would attend upon every man's doing justice to himself, the magistrate, in all governments that have acquired any considerable authority, undertakes to do justice to all, and promises to hear and to redress every complaint of injury. In all well-governed states too, not only judges are appointed for

determining the controversies of individuals, but rules are prescribed for regulating the decisions of those judges; and these
rules are, in general, intended to coincide with those of natural
justice. It does not, indeed, always happen that they do so in
every instance. Sometimes what is called the constitution of the
state, that is, the interest of the government; sometimes the interest of particular orders of men who tyrannize the government,
warp the positive laws of the country from what natural justice
would prescribe. In some countries, the rudeness and barbarism
of the people hinder the natural sentiments of justice from arriving
at that accuracy and precision which, in more civilized nations,
they naturally attain to. Their laws are, like their manners, gross
and rude and undistinguishing. In other countries the unfortunate constitution of their courts of judicature hinders any regular
system of jurisprudence from ever establishing itself among them,
though the improved manners of the people may be such as would
admit of the most accurate. In no country do the decisions of
positive law coincide exactly, in every case, with the rules which
the natural sense of justice would dictate. Systems of positive law,
therefore, though they deserve the greatest authority, as the
records of the sentiments of mankind in different ages and
nations, yet can never be regarded as accurate systems of the
rules of natural justice.

It might have been expected that the reasonings of lawyers,
upon the different imperfections and improvements of the laws of
different countries, should have given occasion to an inquiry into
what were the natural rules of justice independent of all positive
institution. It might have been expected that these reasonings
should have led them to aim at establishing a system of what
might properly be called natural jurisprudence, or a theory of the
general principles which ought to run through and be the foundation of the laws of all nations. But though the reasonings of
lawyers did produce something of this kind, and though no man
has treated systematically of the laws of any particular country,
without intermixing in his work many observations of this sort;
it was very late in the world before any such general system was
thought of, or before the philosophy of law was treated of by
itself, and without regard to the particular institutions of any one
nation. In none of the ancient moralists, do we find any attempt

towards a particular enumeration of the rules of justice. Cicero in his Offices, and Aristotle in his Ethics, treat of justice in the same general manner in which they treat of all the other virtues.[15] In the laws of Cicero and Plato, where we might naturally have expected some attempts towards an enumeration of those rules of natural equity, which ought to be enforced by the positive laws of every country, there is, however, nothing of this kind. Their laws are laws of police, not of justice.[16] Grotius seems to have been the first who attempted to give the world any thing like a system of those principles which ought to run through, and be the foundation of the laws of all nations; and his treatise of the laws of war and peace, with all its imperfections, is perhaps at this day the most complete work that has yet been given upon this subject.[17] I shall in another discourse endeavour to give an account of the general principles of law and government, and of the different revolutions they have undergone in the different ages and periods of society, not only in what concerns justice, but in what concerns police, revenue, and arms, and whatever else is the object of law. I shall not, therefore, at present enter into any further detail concerning the history of jurisprudence.

THE END.

CONSIDERATIONS

CONCERNING THE

FIRST FORMATION OF LANGUAGES,

AND THE

DIFFERENT GENIUS OF ORIGINAL AND COMPOUNDED LANGUAGES.

CONSIDERATIONS

CONCERNING THE

FIRST FORMATION OF LANGUAGES, &C.[1]

The assignation of particular names, to denote particular objects, that is, the institution of nouns substantive, would probably, be one of the first steps towards the formation of language.[2] Two savages, who had never been taught to speak, but had been bred up remote from the societies of men, would naturally begin to form that language by which they would endeavour to make their mutual wants intelligible to each other, by uttering certain sounds, whenever they meant to denote certain objects. Those objects only which were most familiar to them, and which they had most frequent occasion to mention, would have particular names assigned to them. The particular cave whose covering sheltered them from the weather, the particular tree whose fruit relieved their hunger, the particular fountain whose water allayed their thirst, would first be denominated by the words *cave, tree, fountain*, or by whatever other appellations they might think proper, in that primitive jargon, to mark them. Afterwards, when the more enlarged experience of these savages had led them to observe, and their necessary occasions obliged them to make mention of other caves, and other trees, and other fountains, they would naturally bestow, upon each of those new objects, the same name, by which they had been accustomed to express the similar object they were first acquainted with. The new objects had none of them any name of its own, but each of them exactly resembled another object, which had such an appellation. It was impossible that those savages could behold the new objects, without recollecting the old ones; and the name of the old ones, to which the new bore so close a resemblance. When they had occasion, therefore, to mention, or to point out to each other, any of the new objects, they would naturally utter the name of the correspondent old one, of which the idea could not fail, at that instant, to present itself to their memory in the strongest and liveliest manner. And thus, those words, which were originally the proper names of individuals, would each of them insensibly become the common name of a multitude. A child that is just learning to speak, calls every person who comes to the house its papa or its mama; and thus bestows upon the whole species those names which it had been taught to apply to two individuals. I have known a clown, who did not know the proper name of the river which ran by his own door. It was *the river*, he said, and he never heard any other name for it. His experience, it seems, had not led him to observe any other river. The general word *river*, therefore, was, it is evident, in his acceptance of it, a proper name, signifying an individual object. If this person had been carried to another river, would he not readily have called it a river? Could we suppose any person living on the banks of the Thames so ignorant, as not to know the general word *river*, but to be acquainted only with the particular word *Thames*, if he was brought to any other river, would he not readily call it *a Thames*? This, in reality, is no more than what they, who are well acquainted with the general word, are very apt to do. An Englishman, describing any great river which he may have seen in some foreign country, naturally says, that it is another Thames. The Spaniards, when they first arrived upon the coast of Mexico, and observed the wealth, populousness, and habitations of that fine country, so much superior to the savage nations which they had been visiting for some time before, cried out, that it was another Spain. Hence it was called New Spain; and this name has stuck to that unfortunate country ever since. We say, in the same manner, of a hero, that he is an Alexander; of an orator, that he is a Cicero; of a philosopher, that he is a Newton. This way of speaking, which the grammarians call an Antonomasia, and which is still extremely common, though now not at all necessary, demonstrates how much mankind are naturally disposed to give to one object the name of any other, which nearly resembles it, and thus to denominate a multitude, by what originally was intended to express an individual.

It is this application of the name of an individual to a great multitude of objects, whose resemblance naturally recalls the idea of that individual, and of the name which expresses it, that seems originally to have given occasion to the formation of those classes and assortments, which, in the schools, are called genera and species, and of which the ingenious and eloquent M. Rousseau of Geneva* finds himself so much at a loss to account for the origin.³ What constitutes a species is merely a number of objects, bearing a certain degree of resemblance to one another, and on that account denominated by a single appellation, which may be applied to express any one of them.

When the greater part of objects had thus been arranged under their proper classes and assortments, distinguished by such general names, it was impossible that the greater part of that almost infinite number of individuals, comprehended under each particular assortment or species, could have any peculiar or proper names of their own, distinct from the general name of the species. When there was occasion, therefore, to mention any particular object, it often became necessary to distinguish it from the other objects comprehended under the same general name, either, first, by its peculiar qualities; or, secondly, by the peculiar relation which it stood in to some other things. Hence the necessary origin of two other sets of words, of which the one should express quality; the other, relation.

Nouns adjective are the words which express quality considered as qualifying, or, as the schoolmen say, in concrete with, some particular subject. Thus the word *green* expresses a certain quality considered as qualifying, or as in concrete with, the particular subject to which it may be applied. Words of this kind, it is evident, may serve to distinguish particular objects from others comprehended under the same general appellation. The words *green tree*, for example, might serve to distinguish a particular tree from others that were withered or blasted.⁴

Prepositions are the words which express relation considered, in the same manner, in concrete with the co-relative object. Thus the prepositions *of, to, for, with, by, above, below*, &c. denote some relation subsisting between the objects expressed by the

* Origine de l'Inegalité. Partie Premiere, p. 376, 377. Edition d'Amsterdam des Oeuvres diverses de J. J. Rousseau.

words between which the prepositions are placed; and they denote that this relation is considered in concrete with the co-relative object. Words of this kind serve to distinguish particular objects from others of the same species, when those particular objects cannot be so properly marked out by any peculiar qualities of their own. When we say, *the green tree of the meadow*, for example, we distinguish a particular tree, not only by the quality which belongs to it, but by the relation which it stands in to another object.

As neither quality nor relation can exist in abstract, it is natural to suppose that the words which denote them considered in concrete, the way in which we always see them subsist, would be of much earlier invention than those which express them considered in abstract, the way in which we never see them subsist. The words *green* and *blue* would, in all probability, be sooner invented than the words *greenness* and *blueness*; the words *above* and *below*, than the words *superiority* and *inferiority*. To invent words of the latter kind requires a much greater effort of abstraction than to invent those of the former. It is probable, therefore, that such abstract terms would be of much later institution. Accordingly, their etymologies generally show that they are so, they being generally derived from others that are concrete.

But though the invention of nouns adjective be much more natural than that of the abstract nouns substantive derived from them, it would still, however, require a considerable degree of abstraction and generalization. Those, for example, who first invented the words *green, blue, red*, and the other names of colours, must have observed and compared together a great number of objects, must have remarked their resemblances and dissimilitudes in respect of the quality of colour, and must have arranged them, in their own minds, into different classes and assortments, according to those resemblances and dissimilitudes. An adjective is by nature a general, and in some measure, an abstract word, and necessarily presupposes the idea of a certain species or assortment of things, to all of which it is equally applicable. The word *green* could not, as we were supposing might be the case of the word *cave*, have been originally the name of an individual, and afterwards have become, by what grammarians call an Antonomasia, the name of a species. The word *green*

denoting, not the name of a substance, but the peculiar quality of
a substance, must from the very first, have been a general word,
and considered as equally applicable to any other substance possessed of the same quality. The man who first distinguished a
particular object by the epithet of *green*, must have observed
other objects that were not *green*, from which he meant to
separate it by this appellation. The institution of this name, therefore, supposes comparison. It likewise supposes some degree of
abstraction. The person who first invented this appellation must
have distinguished the quality from the object to which it
belonged, and must have conceived the object as capable of subsisting without the quality. The invention, therefore, even of the
simplest nouns adjective, must have required more metaphysics
than we are apt to be aware of. The different mental operations,
of arrangement or classing, of comparison, and of abstraction,
must all have been employed, before even the names of the different colours, the least metaphysical of all nouns adjective, could
be instituted. From all which I infer, that when languages were
beginning to be formed, nouns adjective would by no means be
the words of the earliest invention.

There is another expedient for denoting the different qualities
of different substances, which as it requires no abstraction, nor
any conceived separation of the quality from the subject, seems
more natural than the invention of nouns adjective, and which,
upon this account, could hardly fail, in the first formation of language, to be thought of before them. This expedient is to make
some variation upon the noun substantive itself, according to the
different qualities which it is endowed with. Thus, in many languages, the qualities both of sex and of the want of sex, are
expressed by different terminations in the nouns substantive, which
denote objects so qualified. In Latin, for example, *lupus, lupa;
equus, equa; juvencus, juvenca; Julius, Julia; Lucretius, Lucretia*, &c. denote the qualities of male and female in the animals
and persons to whom such appellations belong, without needing
the addition of any adjective for this purpose. On the other hand,
the words *forum, pratum, plaustrum*, denote by their peculiar
termination the total absence of sex in the different substances
which they stand for. Both sex, and the want of all sex, being
naturally considered as qualities modifying and inseparable from

the particular substances to which they belong, it was natural to express them rather by a modification in the noun substantive, than by any general and abstract word expressive of this particular species of quality. The expression bears, it is evident, in this way, a much more exact analogy to the idea or object which it denotes, than in the other. The quality appears, in nature, as a modification of the substance, and as it is thus expressed, in language, by a modification of the noun substantive, which denotes that substance, the quality and the subject are, in this case, blended together, if I may say so, in the expression, in the same manner as they appear to be in the object and in the idea. Hence the origin of the masculine, feminine, and neutral genders, in all the ancient languages. By means of these, the most important of all distinctions, that of substances into animated and inanimated, and that of animals into male and female, seem to have been sufficiently marked without the assistance of adjectives, or of any general names denoting this most extensive species of qualifications.

There are no more than these three genders in any of the languages with which I am acquainted; that is to say, the formation of nouns substantive can, by itself, and without the accompaniment of adjectives, express no other qualities but those three above mentioned, the qualities of male, of female, of neither male nor female. I should not, however, be surprised, if, in other languages with which I am unacquainted, the different formations of nouns substantive should be capable of expressing many other different qualities. The different diminutives of the Italian, and of some other languages, do, in reality, sometimes, express a great variety of different modifications in the substances denoted by those nouns which undergo such variations.

It was impossible, however, that nouns substantive could, without losing altogether their original form, undergo so great a number of variations, as would be sufficient to express that almost infinite variety of qualities, by which it might, upon different occasions, be necessary to specify and distinguish them. Though the different formation of nouns substantive, therefore, might, for some time, forestall the necessity of inventing nouns adjective, it was impossible that this necessity could be forestalled altogether. When nouns adjective came to be invented, it was natural that they should be formed with some similarity to the substantives, to which they were to serve as epithets or qualifications. Men would naturally give them the same terminations with the substantives to which they were first applied, and from that love of similarity of sound, from that delight in the returns of the same syllables, which is the foundation of analogy in all languages, they would be apt to vary the termination of the same adjective, according as they had occasion to apply it to a masculine, to a feminine, or to a neutral substantive. They would say, *magnus lupus, magna lupa, magnum pratum*, when they meant to express a great *he wolf*, a great *she wolf*, a great *meadow*.

This variation, in the termination of the noun adjective, according to the gender of the substantive, which takes place in all the ancient languages, seems to have been introduced chiefly for the sake of a certain similarity of sound, of a certain species of rhyme, which is naturally so very agreeable to the human ear. Gender, it is to be observed, cannot properly belong to a noun adjective, the signification of which is always precisely the same, to whatever species of substantives it is applied. When we say, *a great man, a great woman*, the word *great* has precisely the same meaning in both cases, and the difference of the sex in the subjects to which it may be applied, makes no sort of difference in its signification. *Magnus, magna, magnum*, in the same manner, are words which express precisely the same quality, and the change of the termination is accompanied with no sort of variation in the meaning. Sex and gender are qualities which belong to substances, but cannot belong to the qualities of substances. In general, no quality, when considered in concrete, or as qualifying some particular subject, can itself be conceived as the subject of any other quality; though when considered in abstract it may. No adjective therefore can qualify any other adjective. A *great good man*, means a man who is both *great* and *good*. Both the adjectives qualify the substantive; they do not qualify one another. On the other hand, when we say, the *great goodness* of the man, the word *goodness* denoting a quality considered in abstract, which may itself be the subject of other qualities, is upon that account capable of being qualified by the word *great*.

If the original invention of nouns adjective would be attended with so much difficulty, that of prepositions would be accompanied with yet more. Every preposition, as I have already observed, denotes some relation considered in concrete with the co-relative object. The preposition *above*, for example, denotes the relation of superiority, not in abstract, as it is expressed by the word *superiority*, but in concrete with some co-relative object. In this phrase, for example, *the tree above the cave*, the word *above* expresses a certain relation between the *tree* and the *cave*, and it expresses this relation in concrete with the co-relative object, *the cave*. A preposition always requires, in order to complete the sense, some other word to come after it; as may be observed in this particular instance. Now, I say, the original invention of such words would require a yet greater effort of abstraction and generalization than that of nouns adjective. First of all, a relation is, in itself, a more metaphysical object than a quality. Nobody can be at a loss to explain what is meant by a quality; but few people will find themselves able to express, very distinctly, what is understood by a relation. Qualities are almost always the objects of our external senses; relations never are.[5] No wonder, therefore, that the one set of objects should be so much more comprehensible than the other. Secondly, though prepositions always express the relation which they stand for, in concrete with the co-relative object, they could not have originally been formed without a considerable effort of abstraction. A preposition denotes a relation, and nothing but a relation. But before men could institute a word, which signified a relation, and nothing but a relation, they must have been able, in some measure, to consider this relation abstractedly from the related objects; since the idea of those objects does not, in any respect, enter into the signification of the preposition. The invention of such a word, therefore, must have required a considerable degree of abstraction. Thirdly, a preposition is from its nature a general word, which, from its very first institution, must have been considered as equally applicable to denote any other similar relation. The man who first invented the word *above*, must not only have distinguished, in some measure, the relation of *superiority* from the objects which were so related, but he must also have distinguished this relation from other relations, such as, from the relation of *inferiority* denoted by the word *below*, from the relation of *juxtaposition*, expressed by the word *beside*, and the like. He must have conceived this word, therefore, as expressive of a particular sort or species of relation distinct from every other, which could not be done without a considerable effort of comparison and generalization.

Whatever were the difficulties, therefore, which embarrassed the first invention of nouns adjective, the same, and many more, must have embarrassed that of prepositions. If mankind, therefore, in the first formation of languages, seem to have, for some time, evaded the necessity of nouns adjective, by varying the termination of the names of substances, according as these varied in some of their most important qualities, they would much more find themselves under the necessity of evading, by some similar contrivance, the yet more difficult invention of prepositions. The different cases in the ancient languages is a contrivance of precisely the same kind. The genitive and dative cases, in Greek and Latin, evidently supply the place of the prepositions; and by a variation in the noun substantive, which stands for the co-relative term, express the relation which subsists between what is denoted by that noun substantive, and what is expressed by some other word in the sentence. In these expressions, for example, *fructus arboris, the fruit of the tree; sacer Herculi, sacred to Hercules;* the variations made in the co-relative words, *arbor* and *Hercules,* express the same relations which are expressed in English by the prepositions *of* and *to.*

To express a relation in this manner, did not require any effort of abstraction. It was not here expressed by a peculiar word denoting relation and nothing but relation, but by a variation upon the co-relative term. It was expressed here, as it appears in nature, not as something separated and detached, but as thoroughly mixed and blended with the co-relative object.

To express relation in this manner, did not require any effort of generalization. The words *arboris* and *Herculi,* while they involve in their signification the same relation expressed by the English prepositions *of* and *to,* are not, like those prepositions, general words, which can be applied to express the same relation between whatever other objects it might be observed to subsist.

To express relation in this manner did not require any effort of comparison. The words *arboris* and *Herculi* are not general words intended to denote a particular species of relations which the inventors of those expressions meant, in consequence of some sort of comparison, to separate and distinguish from every other sort of relation. The example, indeed, of this contrivance would soon probably be followed, and whoever had occasion to express a similar relation between any other objects would be very apt to do it by making a similar variation on the name of the co-relative object. This, I say, would probably, or rather certainly happen; but it would happen without any intention or foresight in those who first set the example, and who never meant to establish any general rule. The general rule would establish itself insensibly, and by slow degrees, in consequence of that love of analogy and similarity of sound, which is the foundation of by far the greater part of the rules of grammar.[6]

To express relation, therefore, by a variation in the name of the co-relative object, requiring neither abstraction nor generalization, nor comparison of any kind, would, at first, be much more natural and easy, than to express it by those general words called prepositions, of which the first invention must have demanded some degree of all those operations.

The number of cases is different in different languages. There are five in the Greek, six in the Latin, and there are said to be ten in the Armenian language. It must have naturally happened that there should be a greater or a smaller number of cases, according as in the terminations of nouns substantive the first formers of any language happened to have established a greater or a smaller number of variations, in order to express the different relations they had occasion to take notice of, before the invention of those more general and abstract prepositions which could supply their place.

It is, perhaps, worth while to observe that those prepositions, which in modern languages hold the place of the ancient cases, are, of all others, the most general, and abstract, and metaphysical; and of consequence, would probably be the last invented. Ask any man of common acuteness, What relation is expressed by the preposition *above*? He will readily answer, that of *superiority*. By the preposition *below*? He will as quickly reply, that of *inferiority*. But ask him, what relation is expressed by the preposition *of*, and, if he has not beforehand employed his thoughts a good deal upon these subjects, you may safely allow him a week to consider of his answer. The prepositions *above* and *below* do not denote any of the relations expressed by the cases in the ancient languages. But the preposition *of,* denotes the same relation, which is in them expressed by the genitive case; and which, it is easy to observe, is of a very metaphysical nature. The preposition *of,* denotes relation in general, considered in concrete with the co-relative object. It marks that the noun substantive which goes before it, is somehow or other related to that which comes after it, but without in any respect ascertaining, as is done by the preposition *above,* what is the peculiar nature of that relation. We often apply it, therefore, to express the most opposite relations; because, the most opposite relations agree so far that each of them comprehends in it the general idea or nature of a relation. We say, *the father of the son,* and *the son of the father; the fir-trees of the forest,* and the *forest of the fir-trees.* The relation in which the father stands to the son, is, it is evident, a quite opposite relation to that in which the son stands to the father; that in which the parts stand to the whole, is quite opposite to that in which the whole stands to the parts. The word *of,* however, serves very well to denote all those relations, because in itself it denotes no particular relation, but only relation in general; and so far as any particular relation is collected from such expressions, it is inferred by the mind, not from the preposition itself, but from the nature and arrangement of the substantives, between which the preposition is placed.

What I have said concerning the preposition *of,* may in some measure be applied to the prepositions *to, for, with, by,* and to whatever other prepositions are made use of in modern languages, to supply the place of the ancient cases. They all of them express very abstract and metaphysical relations, which any man, who takes the trouble to try it, will find it extremely difficult to express by nouns substantive, in the same manner as we may express the relation denoted by the preposition *above,* by the noun substantive *superiority.* They all of them, however, express some specific relation, and are, consequently, none of them so abstract as the preposition *of,* which may be regarded as by far the most metaphysical of all prepositions. The prepositions, therefore, which are capable of supplying the place of the ancient cases, being more abstract than the other prepositions, would naturally be of more difficult invention. The relations at the same time which those prepositions express, are, of all others, those which we have most frequent occasion to mention. The prepositions *above, below, near, within, without, against,* &c. are much more rarely made use of, in modern languages, than the prepositions *of, to, for, with, from, by.* A preposition of the former kind will not occur twice in a page; we can scarce compose a single sentence without the assistance of one or two of the latter. If these latter prepositions, therefore, which supply the place of the cases, would be of such difficult invention on account of their abstractedness, some expedient, to supply their place, must have been of indispensable necessity, on account of the frequent occasion which men have to take notice of the relations which they denote. But there is no expedient so obvious, as that of varying the termination of one of the principal words.

It is, perhaps, unnecessary to observe, that there are some of the cases in the ancient languages, which, for particular reasons, cannot be represented by any prepositions. These are the nominative, accusative, and vocative cases. In those modern languages, which do not admit of any such variety in the terminations of their nouns substantive, the correspondent relations are expressed by the place of the words, and by the order and construction of the sentence.

As men have frequently occasion to make mention of multitudes as well as of single objects, it became necessary that they should have some method of expressing number. Number may be expressed either by a particular word, expressing number in general, such as the words *many, more,* &c. or by some variation upon the words which express the things numbered. It is this last expedient which mankind would probably have recourse to, in the infancy of language. Number, considered in general, without relation to any particular set of objects numbered, is one of the most abstract and metaphysical ideas, which the mind of man is capable of forming; and, consequently, is not an idea, which would readily occur to rude mortals, who were just beginning to form a language. They would naturally, therefore, distinguish when they talked of a single, and when they talked of a multitude of objects, not by any metaphysical adjectives, such as the English *a, an, many,* but by a variation upon the termination of the word which signified the objects numbered. Hence the origin of the singular and plural numbers, in all the ancient languages; and the same distinction has likewise been retained in all the modern languages, at least, in the greater part of words.

All primitive and uncompounded languages seem to have a dual, as well as a plural number. This is the case of the Greek, and I am told of the Hebrew, of the Gothic, and of many other languages. In the rude beginnings of society, *one, two,* and *more*, might possibly be all the numeral distinctions which mankind would have any occasion to take notice of. These they would find it more natural to express, by a variation upon every particular noun substantive, than by such general and abstract words as *one, two, three, four,* &c. These words, though custom has rendered them familiar to us, express, perhaps, the most subtile and refined abstractions, which the mind of man is capable of forming. Let any one consider within himself, for example, what he means by the word *three*, which signifies neither three shillings, nor three pence, nor three men, nor three horses, but three in general; and he will easily satisfy himself that a word, which denotes so very metaphysical an abstraction, could not be either a very obvious or a very early invention. I have read of some savage nations, whose language was capable of expressing no more than the three first numeral distinctions. But whether it expressed those distinctions by three general words, or by variations upon the nouns substantive, denoting the things numbered, I do not remember to have met with any thing which could determine.

As all the same relations which subsist between single, may likewise subsist between numerous objects, it is evident there would be occasion for the same number of cases in the dual and in the plural, as in the singular number. Hence the intricacy and complexness of the declensions in all the ancient languages. In the Greek there are five cases in each of the three numbers, consequently fifteen in all.

As nouns adjective, in the ancient languages, varied their terminations according to the gender of the substantive to which they were applied, so did they likewise, according to the case and the number. Every noun adjective in the Greek language, therefore, having three genders, and three numbers, and five cases in each number, may be considered as having five-and-forty different variations. The first formers of language seem to have varied the termination of the adjective, according to the case and the number of the substantive, for the same reason which made them vary it according to the gender; the love of analogy, and of a certain regularity of sound. In the signification of adjectives there is neither case nor number, and the meaning of such words is always precisely the same, notwithstanding all the variety of termination under which they appear. *Magnus vir, magni viri, magnorum virorum; a great man, of a great man, of great men;* in all these expressions the words *magnus, magni, magnorum,* as well as the word *great,* have precisely one and the same signification, though the substantives to which they are applied have not. The difference of termination in the noun adjective is accompanied with no sort of difference in the meaning. An adjective denotes the qualification of a noun substantive. But the different relations in which that noun substantive may occasionally stand, can make no sort of difference upon its qualification.

If the declensions of the ancient languages are so very complex, their conjugations are infinitely more so. And the complexness of the one is founded upon the same principle with that of the other, the difficulty of forming, in the beginnings of language, abstract and general terms.

Verbs must necessarily have been coëval with the very first attempts towards the formation of language. No affirmation can be expressed without the assistance of some verb. We never speak but in order to express our opinion that something either is or is not. But the word denoting this event, or this matter of fact, which is the subject of our affirmation, must always be a verb.

Impersonal verbs, which express in one word a complete event, which preserve in the expression that perfect simplicity and unity, which there always is in the object and in the idea, and which suppose no abstraction, or metaphysical division of the event into its several constitutent members of subject and attribute, would, in all probability, be the species of verbs first invented. The verbs *pluit, it rains; ningit, it snows; tonat, it thunders; lucet, it is day; turbatur, there is a confusion,* &c. each of them express a complete affirmation, the whole of an event, with that perfect simplicity and unity with which the mind conceives it in nature. On the contrary, the phrases, *Alexander ambulat, Alexander walks; Petrus sedet, Peter sits,* divide the event, as it were, into two parts, the person or subject, and the attribute, or matter of fact, affirmed of that subject. But in nature, the idea or conception of Alexander walking, is as perfectly and completely one simple conception, as that of Alexander not walking. The division of this event, therefore, into two parts, is altogether artificial, and is the effect of the imperfection of language, which, upon this, as upon many other occasions, supplies, by a number of words, the want of one, which could express at once the whole matter of fact that was meant to be affirmed. Every body must observe how much more simplicity there is in the natural expression, *pluit*, than in the more artificial expressions, *imber decidit, the rain falls;* or *tempestas est pluvia, the weather is rainy.* In these two last expressions, the simple event, or matter of fact, is artificially split and divided in the one, into two; in the other, into three parts. In each of them it is expressed by a sort of grammatical circumlocution, of which the significancy is founded upon a certain metaphysical analysis of the component parts of the idea expressed by the word *pluit.* The first verbs, therefore, perhaps even the first words, made use of in the beginnings of language, would in all probability be such impersonal verbs. It is observed accordingly, I am told, by the Hebrew grammarians, that the radical words of their language, from which all the others are derived, are all of them verbs, and impersonal verbs.

It is easy to conceive how, in the progress of language, those impersonal verbs should become personal. Let us suppose, for example, that the word *venit, it comes,* was originally an impersonal verb, and that it denoted, not the coming of something in general, as at present, but the coming of a particular object, such as *the Lion.* The first savage inventors of language, we shall suppose, when they observed the approach of this terrible animal, were accustomed to cry out to one another, *venit,* that is, *the lion comes;* and that this word thus expressed a complete event, without the assistance of any other. Afterwards, when, on the further progress of language, they had begun to give names to particular substances, whenever they observed the approach of any other terrible object, they would naturally join the name of that object to the word *venit,* and cry out, *venit ursus, venit lupus.* By degrees the word *venit* would thus come to signify the coming of any terrible object, and not merely the coming of the lion. It would now, therefore, express, not the coming of a particular object, but the coming of an object of a particular kind. Having become more general in its signification, it could no longer represent any particular distinct event by itself, and without the assistance of a noun substantive, which might serve to ascertain and determine its signification. It would now, therefore, have become a personal, instead of an impersonal verb. We may easily conceive how, in the further progress of society, it might still grow more general in its signification, and come to signify, as at present, the approach of any thing whatever, whether good, bad, or indifferent.

It is probably in some such manner as this, that almost all verbs have become personal, and that mankind have learned by degrees to split and divide almost every event into a great number of metaphysical parts, expressed by the different parts of speech, variously combined in the different members of every phrase and sentence.* The same sort of progress seems to have been made in the art of speaking as in the art of writing. When mankind first began to attempt to express their ideas by writing, every character represented a whole word. But the number of words being almost infinite, the memory found itself quite loaded and oppressed by the multitude of characters which it was obliged to retain. Necessity taught them, therefore, to divide words into their elements, and to invent characters which should represent, not the words themselves, but the elements of which they were composed. In consequence of this invention, every particular word came to be represented, not by one character, but by a multitude of characters; and the expression of it in writing became much more intricate and complex than before. But though particular words were thus represented by a greater number of characters, the whole language was expressed by a much smaller, and about four and twenty letters were found capable of supplying

* As the far greater part of verbs express, at present, not an event, but the attribute of an event, and, consequently, require a subject, or nominative case, to complete their signification, some grammarians, not having attended to this progress of nature, and being desirous to make their common rules quite universal, and without any exception, have insisted that all verbs required a nominative, either expressed or understood; and have, accordingly, put themselves to the torture to find some awkward nominatives to those few verbs, which still expressing a complete event, plainly admit of none. *Pluit*, for example, according to *Sanctius*, means *pluvia pluit*, in English, the *rain rains*. See Sanctii Minerva, l. iii. c. 1.[7]

the place of that immense multitude of characters, which were requisite before. In the same manner, in the beginnings of language, men seem to have attempted to express every particular event, which they had occasion to take notice of, by a particular word, which expressed at once the whole of that event. But as the number of words must, in this case, have become really infinite, in consequence of the really infinite variety of events, men found themselves partly compelled by necessity, and partly conducted by nature, to divide every event into what may be called its metaphysical elements, and to institute words, which should denote not so much the events, as the elements of which they were composed. The expression of every particular event, became in this manner more intricate and complex, but the whole system of the language became more coherent, more connected, more easily retained and comprehended.

When verbs, from being originally impersonal, had thus, by the division of the event into its metaphysical elements, become personal, it is natural to suppose that they would first be made use of in the third person singular. No verb is ever used impersonally in our language, nor, so far as I know, in any other modern tongue. But in the ancient languages, whenever any verb is used impersonally, it is always in the third person singular. The termination of those verbs, which are still always impersonal, is constantly the same with that of the third person singular of personal verbs. The consideration of these circumstances, joined to the naturalness of the thing itself, may serve to convince us that verbs first became personal in what is now called the third person singular.

But as the event, or matter of fact, which is expressed by a verb, may be affirmed either of the person who speaks, or of the person who is spoken to, as well as of some third person or object, it became necessary to fall upon some method of expressing these two peculiar relations of the event. In the English language this is commonly done, by prefixing, what are called the personal pronouns, to the general word which expresses the event affirmed. *I came, you came, he* or *it came;* in these phrases the event of having come is, in the first, affirmed of the speaker; in the second, of the person spoken to; in the third, of some other person, or object. The first formers of language, it may be imagined, might have done the same thing, and prefixing in the same manner the two first personal pronouns, to the same termination of the verb, which expressed the third person singular, might have said *ego venit, tu venit*, as well as *ille* or *illud venit*. And I make no doubt but they would have done so, if at the time when they had first occasion to express these relations of the verb, there had been any such words as either *ego* or *tu* in their language. But in this early period of the language, which we are now endeavouring to describe, it is extremely improbable that any such words would be known. Though custom has now rendered them familiar to us, they, both of them, express ideas extremely metaphysical and abstract. The word *I*, for example, is a word of a very particular species. Whatever speaks may denote itself by this personal pronoun. The word *I*, therefore, is a general word, capable of being predicated, as the logicians say, of an infinite variety of objects. It differs, however, from all other general words in this respect; that the objects of which it may be predicated, do not form any particular species of objects distinguished from all others. The word *I*, does not, like the word *man*, denote a particular class of objects, separated from all others by peculiar qualities of their own. It is far from being the name of a species, but, on the contrary, whenever it is made use of, it always denotes a precise individual, the particular person who then speaks. It may be said to be, at once, both what the logicians call, a singular, and what they call, a common term; and to join in its signification the seemingly opposite qualities of the most precise individuality, and the most extensive generalization. This word, therefore, expressing so very abstract and metaphysical an idea, would not easily or readily occur to the first formers of language. What are called the personal pronouns, it may be observed, are among the last words of which children learn to make use. A child, speaking of itself, says, *Billy walks, Billy sits*, instead of *I walk, I sit*. As in the beginnings of language, therefore, mankind seem to have evaded the invention of at least the more abstract prepositions, and to have expressed the same relations which these *now* stand for, by varying the termination of the co-relative term, so they likewise would naturally attempt to evade the necessity of inventing those more abstract pronouns by varying the termination of the verb, according as the event which it expressed was intended to be affirmed of the first, second, or third person. This seems, accordingly, to be the universal practice of all the ancient languages. In Latin, *veni, venisti, venit*, sufficiently denote, without any other addition, the different events expressed by the English phrases, *I came, you came, he* or *it came.* The verb would, for the same reason, vary its termination, according as the event was intended to be affirmed of the first, second, or third persons plural; and what is expressed by the English phrases, *we came, ye came, they came*, would be denoted by the Latin words, *venimus, venistis, venerunt.* Those primitive languages, too, which, upon account of the difficulty of inventing numeral names, had introduced a dual, as well as a plural number, into the declension of their nouns substantive, would probably, from analogy, do the same thing in the conjugations of their verbs. And thus, in all those original languages, we might expect to find, at least six, if not eight or nine variations, in the termination of every verb, according as the event which it denoted was meant to be affirmed of the first, second, or third persons singular, dual, or plural. These variations again being repeated, along with others, through all its different tenses, through all its different modes, and through all its different voices, must necessarily have rendered their conjugations still more intricate and complex than their declensions.

Language would probably have continued upon this footing in all countries, nor would ever have grown more simple in its declensions and conjugations, had it not become more complex in its composition, in consequence of the mixture of several languages with one another, occasioned by the mixture of different nations. As long as any language was spoke by those only who learned it in their infancy, the intricacy of its declensions and conjugations could occasion no great embarrassment. The far greater part of those who had occasion to speak it, had acquired it at so very early a period of their lives, so insensibly and by such slow degrees, that they were scarce ever sensible of the difficulty. But when two nations came to be mixed with one another, either by conquest or migration, the case would be very different. Each nation, in order to make itself intelligible to those with whom it was under the necessity of conversing, would be obliged to learn the language of the other. The greater part of individuals too, learning the new language, not by art, or by remounting to its rudiments and first principles, but by rote, and by what they commonly heard in conversation, would be extremely perplexed by the intricacy of its declensions and conjugations. They would endeavour, therefore, to supply their ignorance of these, by whatever shift the language could afford them. Their ignorance of the declensions they would naturally supply by the use of prepositions; and a Lombard, who was attempting to speak Latin, and wanted to express that such a person was a citizen of Rome, or a benefactor to Rome, if he happened not to be acquainted with the genitive and dative cases of the word *Roma*, would naturally express himself by prefixing the prepositions *ad* and *de* to the nominative; and, instead of *Romae*, would say, *ad Roma*, and *de Roma*. *Al Roma* and *di Roma*, accordingly, is the manner in which the present Italians, the descendants of the ancient Lombards and Romans, express this and all other similar relations. And in this manner prepositions seem to have been introduced, in the room of the ancient declensions. The same alteration has, I am informed, been produced upon the Greek language, since the taking of Constantinople by the Turks. The words are, in a great measure, the same as before; but the grammar is entirely lost, prepositions having come in the place of the old declensions. This change is undoubtedly a simplification of the language, in point of rudiments and principle. It introduces, instead of a great variety of declensions, one universal declension, which is the same in every word, of whatever gender, number, or termination.

A similar expedient enables men, in the situation above mentioned, to get rid of almost the whole intricacy of their conjugations. There is in every language a verb, known by the name of the substantive verb; in Latin, *sum;* in English, *I am*. This verb denotes not the existence of any particular event, but existence in general. It is, upon this account, the most abstract and metaphysical of all verbs; and, consequently, could by no means be a word of early invention. When it came to be invented, however, as it had all the tenses and modes of any other verb, by being joined with the passive participle, it was capable of supplying the place of the whole passive voice, and of rendering this part of their conjugations as simple and uniform, as the use of prepositions had rendered their declensions. A Lombard, who wanted to say, *I am loved*, but could not recollect the word *amor*, naturally endeavoured to supply his ignorance, by saying, *ego sum amatus*.

Io sono amato, is at this day the Italian expression, which corresponds to the English phrase above mentioned.

There is another verb, which, in the same manner, runs through all languages, and which is distinguished by the name of the possessive verb; in Latin, *habeo;* in English, *I have.* This verb, likewise, denotes an event of an extremely abstract and metaphysical nature, and, consequently, cannot be supposed to have been a word of the earliest invention. When it came to be invented, however, by being applied to the passive participle, it was capable of supplying a great part of the active voice, as the substantive verb had supplied the whole of the passive. A Lombard, who wanted to say, *I had loved*, but could not recollect the word *amaveram*, would endeavour to supply the place of it, by saying either *ego habebam amatum*, or *ego habui amatum. Io avevá amato*, or *Io ebbi amato*, are the correspondent Italian expressions at this day. And thus upon the intermixture of different nations with one another, the conjugations, by means of different auxiliary verbs, were made to approach towards the simplicity and uniformity of the declensions.

In general it may be laid down for a maxim, that the more simple any language is in its composition, the more complex it must be in its declensions and conjugations; and, on the contrary, the more simple it is in its declensions and conjugations, the more complex it must be in its composition.[8]

The Greek seems to be, in a great measure, a simple, uncompounded language, formed from the primitive jargon of those wandering savages, the ancient Hellenians and Pelasgians, from whom the Greek nation is said to have been descended. All the words in the Greek language are derived from about three hundred primitives, a plain evidence that the Greeks formed their language almost entirely among themselves, and that when they had occasion for a new word, they were not accustomed, as we are, to borrow it from some foreign language, but to form it, either by composition, or derivation from some other word or words, in their own. The declensions and conjugations, therefore, of the Greek are much more complex than those of any other European language with which I am acquainted.

The Latin is a composition of the Greek and of the ancient Tuscan languages. Its declensions and conjugations accordingly are much less complex than those of the Greek; it has dropt the dual number in both. Its verbs have no optative mood distinguished by any peculiar termination. They have but one future. They have no aorist distinct from the preterit-perfect; they have no middle voice; and even many of their tenses in the passive voice are eked out, in the same manner as in the modern languages, by the help of the substantive verb joined to the passive participle. In both the voices, the number of infinitives and participles is much smaller in the Latin than in the Greek.

The French and Italian languages are each of them compounded, the one of the Latin, and the language of the ancient Franks, the other of the same Latin, and the language of the ancient Lombards. As they are both of them, therefore, more complex in their composition than the Latin, so are they likewise more simple in their declensions and conjugations. With regard to their declensions, they have both of them lost their cases altogether; and with regard to their conjugations, they have both of them lost the whole of the passive, and some part of the active voices of their verbs. The want of the passive voice they supply entirely by the substantive verb joined to the passive participle; and they make out part of the active, in the same manner, by the help of the possessive verb and the same passive participle.

The English is compounded of the French and the ancient Saxon languages. The French was introduced into Britain by the Norman conquest, and continued, till the time of Edward III, to be the sole language of the law as well as the principal language of the court. The English, which came to be spoken afterwards, and which continues to be spoken now, is a mixture of the ancient Saxon and this Norman French. As the English language, therefore, is more complex in its composition than either the French or the Italian, so is it likewise more simple in its declensions and conjugations. Those two languages retain, at least, a part of the distinction of genders, and their adjectives vary their termination according as they are applied to a masculine or to a feminine substantive. But there is no such distinction in the English language, whose adjectives admit of no variety of termination. The French and Italian languages have, both of them, the remains of a conjugation; and all those tenses of the active voice, which cannot be expressed by the possessive verb joined to the passive participle, as well as many of those which can, are, in those languages, marked by varying the termination of the principal verb. But almost all those other tenses are in the English eked out by other auxiliary verbs, so that there is in this language scarce even the remains of a conjugation. *I love, I loved, loving*, are all the varieties of termination which the greater part of English verbs admit of. All the different modifications of meaning, which cannot be expressed by any of those three terminations, must be made out by different auxiliary verbs joined to some one or other of them. Two auxiliary verbs supply all the deficiencies of the French and Italian conjugations; it requires more than half a dozen to supply those of the English, which, besides the substantive and possessive verbs, makes use of *do, did; will, would; shall, should; can, could; may, might.*

It is in this manner that language becomes more simple in its rudiments and principles, just in proportion as it grows more complex in its composition, and the same thing has happened in it, which commonly happens with regard to mechanical engines. All machines are generally, when first invented, extremely complex in their principles, and there is often a particular principle of motion for every particular movement which it is intended they should perform. Succeeding improvers observe, that one principle may be so applied as to produce several of those movements; and thus the machine becomes gradually more and more simple, and produces its effects with fewer wheels, and fewer principles of motion. In language, in the same manner, every case of every noun, and every tense of every verb, was originally expressed by a particular distinct word, which served for this purpose and for no other. But succeeding observation discovered, that one set of words was capable of supplying the place of all that infinite number, and that four or five prepositions, and half a dozen auxiliary verbs, were capable of answering the end of all the declensions, and of all the conjugations in the ancient languages.

But this simplification of languages, though it arises, perhaps, from similar causes, has by no means similar effects with the correspondent simplification of machines. The simplification of machines renders them more and more perfect, but this simplification of the rudiments of languages renders them more and more imperfect, and less proper for many of the purposes of language: and this for the following reasons.[9]

First of all, languages are by this simplification rendered more prolix, several words having become necessary to express what could have been expressed by a single word before. Thus the words, *Dei* and *Deo*, in the Latin, sufficiently show, without any addition, what relation the object signified is understood to stand in to the objects expressed by the other words in the sentence. But to express the same relation in English, and in all other modern languages, we must make use of, at least, two words, and say, *of God, to God*. So far as the declensions are concerned, therefore, the modern languages are much more prolix than the ancient. The difference is still greater with regard to the conjugations. What a Roman expressed by the single word, *amavissem*, an Englishman is obliged to express by four different words, *I should have loved*. It is unnecessary to take any pains to show how much this prolixness must enervate the eloquence of all modern languages. How much the beauty of any expression depends upon its conciseness, is well known to those who have any experience in composition.

Secondly, this simplification of the principles of languages renders them less agreeable to the ear. The variety of termination in the Greek and Latin, occasioned by their declensions and conjugations, gives a sweetness to their language altogether unknown to ours, and a variety unknown to any other modern language. In point of sweetness, the Italian, perhaps, may surpass the Latin, and almost equal the Greek; but in point of variety, it is greatly inferior to both.

Thirdly, this simplification, not only renders the sounds of our language less agreeable to the ear, but it also restrains us from disposing such sounds as we have, in the manner that might be most agreeable. It ties down many words to a particular situation, though they might often be placed in another with much more beauty. In the Greek and Latin, though the adjective and substantive were separated from one another, the correspondence of their terminations still showed their mutual reference, and the separation did not necessarily occasion any sort of confusion. Thus in the first line of Virgil,

> Tityre tu patulæ recubans sub tegmine fagi;

we easily see that *tu* refers to *recubans*, and *patulae* to *fagi*; though the related words are separated from one another by the intervention of several others; because the terminations, showing the correspondence of their cases, determine their mutual reference. But if we were to translate this line literally into English, and say, *Tityrus, thou of spreading reclining under the shade beech*, Œdipus himself could not make sense of it; because there is here no difference of termination, to determine which substantive each adjective belongs to. It is the same case with regard to verbs. In Latin the verb may often be placed, without any inconveniency or ambiguity, in any part of the sentence. But in English its place is almost always precisely determined. It must follow the subjective and precede the objective member of the phrase in almost all cases. Thus in Latin whether you say, *Joannem verberavit Robertus*, or *Robertus verberavit Joannem*, the meaning is precisely the same, and the termination fixes John to be the sufferer in both cases. But in English *John beat Robert*, and *Robert beat John*, have by no means the same signification. The place therefore of the three principal members of the phrase is in the English, and for the same reason in the French and Italian languages, almost always precisely determined; whereas in the ancient languages a greater latitude is allowed, and the place of those members is often, in a great measure, indifferent. We must have recourse to Horace, in order to interpret some parts of Milton's literal translation;

> Who now enjoys thee credulous all gold,
> Who always vacant, always amiable
> Hopes thee; of flattering gales
> Unmindful—[10]

are verses which it is impossible to interpret by any rules of our language. There are no rules in our language, by which any man could discover, that, in the first line, *credulous* referred to *who*, and not to *thee;* or that *all gold* referred to any thing; or, that in the fourth line, *unmindful*, referred to *who*, in the second, and not to *thee* in the third; or, on the contrary, that, in the second line, *always vacant, always amiable*, referred to *thee* in the third, and not to *who* in the same line with it. In the Latin, indeed, all this is abundantly plain.

> Qui nunc te fruitur credulus aureâ,
> Qui semper vacuam, semper amabilem
> Sperat te; nescius auræ fallacis.

Because the terminations in the Latin determine the reference of each adjective to its proper substantive, which it is impossible for any thing in the English to do: How much this power of transposing the order of their words must have facilitated the composition of the ancients, both in verse and prose, can hardly be imagined. That it must greatly have facilitated their versification it is needless to observe; and in prose, whatever beauty depends upon the arrangement and construction of the several members of the period, must to them have been acquirable with much more ease, and to much greater perfection, than it can be to those whose expression is constantly confined by the prolixness, constraint, and monotony of modern languages.[11]

FINIS.

Biographical Notes

Addison, Joseph (1672–1719), English essayist and Whig politician; author of the popular tragedy *Cato* (1713) and editor of *The Spectator* (1711–1712), each of which were influential contributions to defining Enlightenment conceptions of virtue and politeness.

Ajax, Greek hero renowned for his strength; his exploits at Troy were chronicled in Homer's *Iliad*, and his reputed suicide, committed in anger at having been passed over for the honor of bearing the arms of Achilles, was dramatized by Sophocles.

Alembert, Jean Le Rond d' (1717–1783), French mathematician, philosopher, and, with Denis Diderot, editor of the monumental *Encyclopédie*; his writings include the *Preliminary Discourse* and several articles for the *Encyclopédie*, numerous scientific essays, a treatise on music, and a collection of *éloges* of his fellow members of the Académie Française.

Alexander the Great (356–323 BC), son of Philip II of Macedon, student of Aristotle, and king of the Macedonian Empire; his military genius enabled him to extend his empire as far as India, but his reign was marked by ruthless and violent persecution of those who opposed his imperial ambitions and his grandiose conception of his own divinity.

Anne (1665–1714), queen of Great Britain and Ireland from 1702 until her death; her first ministry witnessed the beginning of the string of victories earned by her principal military commander, the Duke of Marlborough, in the War of Spanish Succession.

Antigonus (ca. 382–301 BC), Macedonian general and governor of Asian provinces; after Alexander's death he was among the foremost of the ambitious successors vying for supremacy, but ultimately proved unsuccessful despite besting Eumenes.

Antoninus: See Marcus Antoninus.

Apollonius of Tyre (mid–1st c. BC), Stoic philosopher reported to have authored a lost commentary on Zeno.

Aristides (5th c. BC), Athenian commander and politician; renowned for his righteousness and often contrasted with the opportunism of Themistocles, he played a prominent military role in the Persian Wars.

Aristippus (5th c. BC), Greek philosopher from Cyrene and student of Socrates; notable for having ostensibly founded the Cyrenaic school, for having advocated a hedonism that challenged Athenian propriety, and for being the first of Socrates' students to charge his own students fees.

Aristomenes (7th c. BC), Messian warrior and subject of a patriotic hero-cult that regarded him as a symbol of resistance to the Spartans.

Aristotle (384–322 BC), Greek philosopher who studied in the Academy of Athens and founded the Peripatetic school; his extant writings cover a tremendous range from aesthetics to zoology, but he is principally discussed in *TMS* as a moral philosopher and author of *Nicomachean Ethics*.

Arrian (Lucius Flavius Arrianus; ca. AD 86–160), Greek philosopher and historian; author of a celebratory historical account of Alexander's military achievements and transcriber of the teachings of Epictetus.

Arundel, Thomas Howard, Earl of (1585–1646; also 4th Earl of Surrey and 1st Earl of Norfolk, and variously numbered as 21st or 14th or 2nd Earl of Arundel), English courtier and ambassador, chiefly remembered today as patron and collector of the arts and subject of portraits by Rubens and Van Dyck.

Attila (406–453), king of the Huns from 434 until his death; his eastern and central European empire was a chief rival of the Roman Empire, but came to be regarded as a symbol of barbarism and brutal violence.

Augustine, Saint (354–430), Bishop of Hippo and one of the principal Doctors of the Church; his principal works include his autobiographical *Confessions*, which tells the story of his conversion, and *City of God*, which exercised a lasting influence on Western conceptions of human nature, sin, and divine redemption.

Augustus Caesar (Gaius Julius Caesar Octavianus; 63 BC–AD 14), Roman emperor from 27 BC until his death.

Avaux, Claude de Mesmes, Comte d' (1595–1650), French statesman and ambassador; among his achievements was his participation in the French delegation to Münster in 1648 that negotiated and ratified the treaty that established the Peace of Westphalia, ending the Thirty Years' War.

Avidius Cassius (Gaius Avidius Cassius; ca. 130–175 AD), Roman consul, governor of Syria, and for three months acting Roman emperor in the east in the wake of a false report of the death of Marcus Aurelius.

Barbeyrac, Jean (1674–1744), French scholar of natural jurisprudence, chiefly known for his French translations of Latin works by Grotius and Pufendorf, which featured extensive and essential textual notes and commentaries.

Berkeley, George (1685–1753), Irish philosopher and clergyman, remembered today for his challenges to materialism and atheism (*Treatise Concerning the Principles of Human Knowledge*, 1710); for Smith he is a theorist of vision (*Essay Towards a New Theory of Vision*, 1709), an opponent of Mandeville (*Alciphron*, 1732), and a proponent of Irish economic reform (*The Querist*, 1735–37).

Birch, Thomas (1705–1766), historian and secretary to the Royal Society from 1752 to 1765, and recipient of a presentation copy of the first edition of TMS; among the many projects he edited was *The Heads of Illustrious Persons of Great Britain* (1743, with second volume in 1752), which featured short biographical sketches and engraved portraits by Jacobus Houbraken and George Vertue.

Biron, Charles de Gontaut, first Duc de (1562–1602), French military commander under Henri IV, executed for treason stemming from his efforts to secure favors from French enemies abroad.

Boileau-Despréaux, Nicolas (1636–1711), French author, courtier, and member of the Académie Française; known for his translation of and commentary on Longinus, his contributions on behalf of the ancients to the Quarrel of the Ancients and the Moderns, his poetic epistles, and several satires.

Borgia, Cesare (1475–1507), Italian military and political leader whose grandiose ambitions and criminal methods were memorialized by Machiavelli.

Bristol, George Digby, second Earl of (1612–1677), English statesman and principal figure in the civil wars in which he was a royalist sympathizer and later the great rival of Clarendon.

Brutus (1) (Lucius Junius Brutus; 6th c. BC), honored by tradition as founder of the Roman Republic for having cast out the Tarquin kings following the rape and suicide of Lucretia in 509 BC; as consul he presided over the indictment and execution of his two sons for their participation in the conspiracy to restore the Tarquins.

Brutus (2) (Marcus Junius Brutus; 85–42 BC), Roman politician who played a chief role in the conspiracy to murder Julius Caesar in 44 BC and variously regarded by posterity as a republican hero or ambitious regicide.

Buffier, Claude (1661–1737), French Jesuit and philosopher and author of several works on metaphysics, epistemology, and language; his chief work, *Treatise on First Truths* (1717), set forth a theory of self-knowledge founded on common sense similar to that developed by several Scottish thinkers.

Butler, Joseph (1692–1752), English philosopher and Bishop of Durham; chiefly known today for the collection of his sermons preached at Rolls Chapel (*Fifteen Sermons*, 1726) which examined the psychology of self-love and benevolence and criticized psychological egoism, and for his study of natural religion and personal identity (*Analogy of Religion*, 1736).

Butler, Samuel (1613–1680), English poet, chiefly known for his satirical *Hudibras*, published in three parts between 1662 and 1678.

Caesar (Gaius Julius Caesar; 100–44 BC), Roman commander, consul, and dictator; established supremacy in Rome through defeat of Pompey at Pharsalus, which ended the civil wars in 48 BC; assassinated four years later by conspirators jealous of his power and suspicious of his ambitions.

Calas, Jean (1698–1762), merchant of Toulouse, executed for the crime of murdering his son for converting to Catholicism; his trial proceeded without evidence (the son in fact committed suicide) leading Voltaire to become a vocal advocate of Calas's innocence.

Callisthenes (ca. 360–327 BC), Macedonian author of a celebratory account of Alexander's exploits; executed for his opposition to Alexander's importation into Macedonia of the Persian custom of *proskynesis*, the prostration of inferior before superior.

Camillus (Marcus Furius Camillus; 4th c. BC), Roman tribune and dictator celebrated for his role in preserving Rome from the invasion of the Gauls.

Catherine de Medici (1519–1589), queen of France as wife of Henry II, but exercised chief political influence as advisor to her three sons, who ruled after her husband's death in 1559 and whose reigns witnessed the height of the French Wars of Religion, including the St. Bartholomew's Day massacre of 1572.

Catiline (Lucius Sergius Catilina; 1st c. BC), Roman praetor and aspiring consul whose conspiracy was discovered and denounced by Cicero; driven from Rome, he was killed in battle in 62 BC.

Catinat, Nicholas (1637–1712), French commander under Louis XIV; elected Marshal of France for his early victories, he was defeated by Prince Eugene of Savoy in the War of Spanish Succession.

Cato (1) (Marcus Porcius Cato, Cato the Elder, or Cato the Censor; 234–149 BC), Roman consul and great-grandfather of Cato the Younger, and a prominent orator famed for his moral and political rigidity.

Cato (2) (Marcus Porcius Cato, Cato the Younger, or Cato of Utica; 95–46 BC), Roman republican hero renowned for his Stoic self-command, antipathy to corruption, and dedication to public service; he committed suicide after Caesar's victory at Thapsus so as not to be subjected to Caesar's rule.

Charles I (1600–1649), king of England, Scotland, and Ireland from 1625 until his death; his reign witnessed the English civil wars that culminated in his trial, conviction, and execution for treason, which came to be hailed as a martyrdom.

Charles II (1630–1685), son of Charles I and brother of James II, and king of England, Scotland, and Ireland from the Restoration of the monarchy in 1660 until his death.

Charlevoix, Pierre-François-Xavier de (1682–1761), French Jesuit missionary and author of *History and General Description of New France, with the Historical Journal of a Journey to North America* (1744).

Chrysippus (ca. 280–207 BC), Stoic philosopher who followed Cleanthes as third head of the Stoic school in 232; chiefly commended for his diligent codification of Stoic doctrine. .

Cicero (Marcus Tullius Cicero; 106–43 BC), Roman statesman, orator, and philosopher; his political career ended with the ascendency of Casear, which prompted him in his retirement to turn to the composition of major works of moral philosophy which exercised a significant influence on Smith and the Scottish Enlightenment, including *De legibus* (*On Laws*), *De officiis* (*On Duties*), *De finibus* (*On Ends*), and *De natura deorum* (*On the Nature of the Gods*).

Clarendon, Edward Hyde, first Earl of (1609–1674), English politician and historian who, as a moderate royalist, was a principal figure in the struggles he chronicled in his *History of the Rebellion and Civil Wars in England.*

Clarke, Samuel (1675–1729), English philosopher with principal contributions in metaphysics and natural theology; particularly influential were his two Boyle lectures of 1704 and 1705 in which he responded to the materialism and atheism of Hobbes and Spinoza: *A Demonstration of the Being and Attributes of God* and *A Discourse Concerning the Unchangeable Obligations of Natural Religion.*

Claudius (Tiberius Claudius Drusus; 10 BC–AD 54), Roman emperor from 41 until his death, upon which he was succeeded by his adoptive son, Nero.

Cleanthes (ca. 331–232 BC), Greek philosopher and successor to Zeno as second head of the Stoic school.

Cleomenes III (3rd c. BC), king of Sparta from 235 to 222; after having been driven out of the Peloponnesus by Antigonus, he traveled to Alexandria, where he committed suicide in 220 after failing to instigate a popular revolt.

Clermont, Bishop of. See Massillon.

Clytus (Cleitus; 4th c. BC), Macedonian noble and cavalry commander; once a favorite of Alexander for having saved his life in 330 in the battle against the Persians at the Granicus, he was murdered by Alexander at a drinking party in 328 for having dared to criticize Alexander's divine pretentions.

Condé, Louis II de Bourbon, Prince de (1621–1686), French commander under Louis XIV, chief figure in the aristocratic unrest of mid-century (the Fronde), and renowned as one of the great military geniuses of his age.

Cowley, Abraham (1618–1667), English poet who wrote on political, biblical, and classical themes; his chief work of love poetry was *The Mistress* (1647).

Crassus (1) (Marcus Licinius Crassus; 1st c. BC), Roman commander and statesman, remembered for his suppression of the slave revolt of Spartacus, his membership in the First Triumvirate with Casear and Pompey, and his wealth and ostensible greed.

Crassus (2) (Lucius Licinius Crassus; 140–91 BC), Roman statesman and orator, particularly celebrated by Cicero for his rhetorical abilities.

Cudworth, Ralph (1617–1688), English philosopher and one of the principal Cambridge Platonists; author of *The True Intellectual System of the Universe* (1678), which sought to reconcile Platonism and revealed religion in countering atheism, and the *Treatise Concerning Eternal and Immutable Morality* (pub. 1731), which sought to counter Epicurean and Hobbesian positivism.

Czar Peter of Muscovy: see Peter the Great.

Davila, Arrigo Caterino (1576–1631), Italian historian and author of *The History of the Civil Wars in France* (1630); he was a first-hand participant in the subjects he chronicled, having served as a soldier in France and as a page in the court of Catherine de Medici.

Demosthenes (384–322 BC), Athenian statesman and orator particularly famed for his *Philippics*, a series of speeches delivered between 351 and 341 to encourage Athenian military resistance to the Macedonian king Philip.

Descartes, René (1596–1650), French mathematician and philosopher with important contributions in metaphysics, epistemology, and ethics that shaped Enlightenment philosophical debates; Smith's engagement with Descartes is largely limited to the physical and astronomical ideas of his *Principles of Philosophy* (1644).

Diogenes Laertius (3rd c. AD), Greek historian of philosophy about whom almost nothing is known; his *Lives and Opinions of Eminent Philosophers* provides biographical and intellectual sketches that have been generally poorly regarded as philosophical commentaries but greatly valued for their quotations and transcriptions of works otherwise lost.

Domitian (Titus Flavius Domitanus, AD 51–96), Roman emperor from 81 until his death; his heavy-handed administration saw the banishment of philosophers from Rome in 89.

Dryden, John (1631–1700), English poet, playwright, critic, and translator; among his many well-known poetic works is his *Absalom and Achitophel* (1681).

Dubos, Jean-Baptiste, Abbé (1670–1742), French author of works of history and literary criticism; chiefly known for the aesthetic and psychological theories set forth in his *Critical Reflections on Poetry and Painting* (1719).

Epaphroditus (1st c. AD), former slave of Nero, secretary to Nero and Domitian, and himself master of Epictetus.

Epictetus (1st–2nd c. AD), Roman Stoic philosopher whose life and writings are principally dedicated to matters of practical morality; he wrote nothing, dedicating himself exclusively to teaching, but his lessons were transcribed by his student Arrian under the title *Discourses*.

Epicurus (341–270 BC), Greek philosopher whose hedonistic moral philosophy was built on the foundations of a materialist metaphysics derived from earlier atomistic theories.

Eugene, Prince of Savoy (1663–1736), French military commander whose chief renown came from his service to the Austrian state and the Hapsburgs in their battles against the Ottoman Empire and in the War of Spanish Succession.

Eumenes (ca. 361–316 BC), Macedonian military commander; a favorite of Alexander, he was one of the chief generals vying for supremacy in the wake of Alexander's death, but was defeated by Antigonus at Gabiene.

Euripides (5th c. BC), with Sophocles and Aeschylus, one of the three principal dramatists of the golden age of Athenian tragedy; among his nineteen extant plays are several dealing with figures and themes with which Smith engaged, including *Hippolytus*.

Fontenelle, Bernard Le Bovier, Sieur de (1657–1757), French author and key figure of the early Enlightenment; renowned for his dialogues on astronomy and Copernican cosmology (*Conversations on the Plurality of Worlds*, 1686), his defense of the moderns against the ancients, and his *éloges* of his fellow members of the French Academy of Sciences.

Frederick II (Frederick the Great; 1712–1786), king of Prussia from 1740 to his death, and renowned for his success as a military commander, his study and patronage of Enlightenment philosophers, and an approach to domestic administration that combined moderate liberal reforms with strong centralized authority (so-called enlightened absolutism).

Genghis Khan (ca. 1162–1227), Mongol emperor from 1206 to his death; at its height his empire stretched from modern China to the Middle East, and was reputed for the brutal destruction that accompanied its expansion.

Gracchi (Tiberius Sempronius Gracchus; ca. 164–133 BC) and his younger brother Gaius Sempronius Gracchus (154–121 BC) were Roman tribunes who advocated moderate legal reforms that generally benefited the plebs they represented.

Gray, Thomas (1716–1771), English poet greatly admired by Smith;

chiefly known for his *Odes* and his *Elegy Written in a Country Church-yard* (1751).

Grotius, Hugo (1583–1645), Dutch theorist of natural jurisprudence; his *De Jure Belli ac Pacis* (*Of the Rights of War and Peace*, 1625) was a preeminent and influential text of Protestant natural law, much admired by Smith, and he also wrote a number of influential theological texts in defense of revealed religion, including *Of the Truth of the Christian Religion* (1627).

Gustavus Adolphus (1594–1632), king of Sweden; a highly successful military commander during the Thirty Years' War, he pioneered several innovations in military techniques.

Hercules, Greek hero famed for the Twelve Labors that displayed his immense physical strength, and the subject of tragedies by Euripides and Sophocles.

Hippolytus, Greek tragic figure and subject of several tragedies ancient and modern that recount his refusal of his stepmother Phaedra's illicit love and the death he suffered following the intervention of Neptune, to whom his enraged father Theseus had appealed.

Hobbes, Thomas (1588–1679), English philosopher whose vast interests and influence on scientific and political thinking were communicated in a translation of Thucydides (1629), treatises on human nature and political philosophy (*De cive*, pub. 1642; *Leviathan*, pub. 1651) and an account of the English civil war (*Behemoth*, pub. 1679); the Scottish Enlightenment tended to regard him as an exponent of metaphysical materialism and ethical egoism.

Homer (ca. 8th c. BC), Greek epic poet who wrote the *Iliad*, which tells the story of the siege of Troy, and the *Odyssey*, which recounts the trials of Odysseus on his voyage home to Ithaca from the Trojan War.

Horace (65–8 BC), Roman poet and satirist, famed for his lyric *Odes*, which were particularly beloved in early modern England.

Hume, David (1711–1776), Scottish philosopher renowned for works of immediate and lasting impact across a range of fields, including metaphysics and epistemology (*A Treatise of Human Nature*, 1739–1740; *An Enquiry Concerning Human Understanding*, 1748), ethics (*An Enquiry Concerning the Principles of Morals*, 1751), aesthetics, belles lettres and political economy (*Essays*, 1753), history (*History of England*, 1754–1762), and natural theology (*Dialogues Concerning Natural Religion*, pub. 1779); whether Smith shared his skepticism is a matter of considerable debate, yet the two were lasting friends with Smith eulogizing Hume in a notorious public letter published upon his death.

Hutcheson, Francis (1694–1746), Irish-born philosopher and Presbyterian clergyman and principal figure of the early Scottish Enlightenment, he was the author of several influential texts, including *An Inquiry into the Original of Our Ideas of Beauty and Virtue* (1725), *An Essay on the Nature and Conduct of the Passions and Affections. With Illustrations on the Moral Sense* (1728), *Philosophiae Moralis Institutio Compendiaria* (trans. as *Short Introduction to Moral Philosophy*, 1747), and *A System of Moral Philosophy* (pub. 1755); as professor of moral philosophy at Glasgow, he was both Smith's teacher as well as his predecessor, and Smith was greatly influenced by his efforts to reconcile classical conceptions of virtue with Christian ethical conceptions.

Iago: See Othello.

James I (1566–1625), king of Scotland (as James VI) from 1567, and king of England and Ireland (as James I) from 1603 to his death; succeeded by his son, Charles I.

James II (1633–1701), king of England, Scotland, and Ireland from 1685 to 1689; the younger surviving son of Charles I, he ascended to the throne on the death of his brother Charles II with his reign ending when William of Orange compelled his abdication.

Joanna of Castile (Joanna the Mad; 1479–1555), queen of Castile; daughter of Ferdinand and Isabella of Spain, mother of Holy Roman Emperor Charles V, and sister of Catherine of Aragon, she is remembered principally as the dependent wife of Philip who slipped into insanity upon his death.

Jocasta: see Oedipus.

Kames, Henry Home, Lord (1696–1782), Scottish man of letters and civic administrator; his works covered a remarkably wide span, including influential contributions on ethics and natural theology (*Essays on the Principles of Morality and Natural Religion*, 1751); criticism (*Elements of Criticism*, 1762); legal history (*Historical Law-Tracts*, 1758), anthropology, and conjectural history (*Sketches of the History of Man*, 1774); and education (*Loose Hints Upon Education*, 1781); Kames was also the sponsor of Smith's lectures on rhetoric delivered in Edinburgh in 1749.

King of Epirus: See Pyrrhus.

King of Macedon: See Perseus.

Lactantius (ca. AD 240–320), religious apologist; known as the "Christian Cicero," his major work, *Divine Institutions*, sought to explain and defend Christianity before a Roman audience.

Lafitau, Joseph-François (1681–1746), French Jesuit missionary to Canada, where his skills at naturalism led him to the discovery of North American ginseng (fueling a European craze for the root previously available only from China); his careful and detailed observations of the Iroquois, *Manners of the American Savages, Compared to the Manners of the Earliest Times* (1724), proved to be an influential account of the native North Americans and an important early instance of comparative anthropology.

La Fontaine, Jean de (1621–1695), French author and moralist, noted for his *Fables* (1668, with successive volumes in 1678 and 1694), which received wide audiences in England in part thanks to Mandeville's translations; he took the side of the ancients in the quarrel of the ancients and the moderns.

La Motte, Antoine Houdar de (1672–1731), French poet, dramatist, and critic; author of a series of *Odes* and *Fables* on moral themes, and in the quarrel of the ancients and the moderns a partisan of the latter.

La Placette, Jean (1639–1718), French theologian; he fled for Copenhagen on the revocation of the Edict of Nantes, and there authored several works developing a moderated Calvinist conception of self-love, including treatises on pride (1692), on conscience (1695), and a collection of moral essays (1697).

La Rochefoucauld, François, Duc de (1613–1680), French moralist and author of *Maxims* (1665), an influential collection of aphorisms chiefly intended to demonstrate the primacy of self-love in human psychology and action, earning their author a reputation as a champion of ethical egoism.

Lauzun, Antonin-Nompar de Caumont, Duc de (1633–1723), French courtier, military officer, and diplomat under Louis XIV. He was imprisoned three times, twice for short stays in the Bastille, and once for ten years in the fortress at Pignerol.

"Leliuses" (Gaius Laelius the Elder; ca. 235–160 BC), Roman military commander and statesman; and Gaius Laelius the Younger (ca. 190–129 BC), renowned for his oratory (celebrated by Cicero in his *Brutus*), and his friendship of virtue with Scipio Aemilianus (memorialized by Cicero in his *De amicitia*).

Locke, John (1632–1704), English philosopher with chief contributions in epistemology (*An Essay Concerning Human Understanding*, 1690), political theory (*Two Treatises* and *Letter Concerning Toleration*, pub. 1689), education (*Some Thoughts Concerning Education*, 1693), and apologetics (*The Reasonableness of Christianity*, 1695); he was also physician and secretary to the first earl of Shaftesbury and tutor to the third earl.

Louis XIII (1601–1643), king of France and father of his successor, Louis XIV; his reign witnessed the beginning of the Thirty Years' War.

Louis XIV (1638–1715), king of France from 1661 to his death; his reign witnessed the centralization of power in the court, the advancement of French interests abroad through a succession of gifted military commanders and diplomats, and a remarkable flourishing of French arts and letters.

Lucian (2nd c. AD), Greek satirist greatly admired by Smith, who identifies him with Epicureanism and the Cyrenaics; a prolific writer, his *Dialogues of the Dead* and *Dialogues of the Gods* were especially popular in the eighteenth century.

Lucullus (Lucius Licinius Lucullus; ca. 118–57 BC), Roman statesman and commander; he invaded Armenia and battled Tigranes II and Mithradates VI, but was removed from command and replaced by Pompey in 66, who went on to victory and further great success in the eastern provinces.

Lysander (5th c. BC), Spartan commander who compelled Athens to surrender in 404, ending the Peloponnesian War.

Machiavelli, Niccolò (1469–1527), Florentinian philosopher and political administrator, known chiefly for his *History of Florence*, his *Discourses on Livy*, and his manual *The Prince*.

Malebranche, Nicolas (1638–1715), French philosopher and priest; his major work of epistemology, *The Search After Truth* (1674–1675), was an influential engagement with Cartesian conceptions of mind and matter from an Augustinian perspective.

Mandeville, Bernard (1670–1733), Dutch physician and essayist who emigrated to London and became notorious for his *Fable of the Bees* (1714); the subtitle of the *Fable* (*Private Vices, Publick Benefits*) has often been taken to represent the whole of his thought, leading proponents to herald him as a precursor of laissez-faire and unintended order theories and detractors to regard him as an advocate of libertinism and nihilism under the guise of moral rigorism.

Marcellus (Marcus Claudius Marcellus; 1st c. BC), Roman consul who sided with Pompey and the *optimates* against Caesar and the *populares*;

after Pharsalus he went into voluntary exile but was officially pardoned by Caesar in 46 BC.

Marcus Antoninus (Marcus Aurelius Antoninus; AD 121–180), Roman emperor from 161 until his death, and author of the *Meditations*, one of the foremost works of later Stoic moral philosophy.

Marivaux, Pierre Carlet de (1688–1763), French playwright and novelist and one of the principal representatives of sentimentalism in eighteenth-century literature; he also edited a French version of *Spectator* (1722) that took Addison's for its model.

Marlborough, John Churchill, first Duke of (1650–1722), British commander in chief of the forces allied against the French in the War of the Spanish Succession, winning particularly brilliant victories at Blenheim (1704), Ramillies (1706) and Oudenarde (1708).

Massillon, Jean-Baptiste (1663–1742), Bishop of Clermont-Ferrand and popular preacher admired by both Voltaire and Louis XIV (for whom he also delivered a funeral oration); his sermons tend to focus on questions of moral psychology rather than points of orthodoxy.

Milton, John (1608–1674), English poet and political writer whose political writings include several antimonarchical treatises defending republican freedoms; chief among his poetic works is *Paradise Lost* (1667).

More, Henry (1614–1687), English philosopher and one of the principal Cambridge Platonists who sought to counter Hobbesian and Spinozistic materialism; his theological and ethical works include his *Antidote Against Atheism* (1653) and *Enchiridion Ethicum* (*Account of Virtue*, 1667).

More, Sir Thomas (1478–1535), Lord Chancellor of England and author of influential theological and political writings, including *Utopia* (1516), a classic study in the political philosophy of the best regime; he was executed for high treason as a result of his opposition to Henry VIII's assumption of supreme ecclesiastical authority.

Nero (Nero Claudius Caesar; AD 37–68), Roman emperor from AD 54 until his death, renowned for his moral corruption and viciousness.

Newton, Sir Isaac (1642–1727), English mathematician and natural philosopher whose chief renown rests on his contributions to scientific method and to the study of gravitation and of light, as set forth in such works as his *Principia Mathematica* (1687) and his *Optics* (1704).

Oedipus, ancient king of Thebes whose tragic murder of his father and unwitting incest with his mother, Jocasta, was recounted in Sophocles' *Oedipus the King*, Euripides' *Phoenician Women*, and Seneca's *Oedipus*.

Othello, title character of Shakespeare's tragedy that chronicles his rival Iago's successful scheme to dupe Othello into the jealous murder of his love, and ends with the arrest of the guilty Iago and the suicide of Othello.

Ovid (43 BC–AD 17), Roman poet, famed for his *Metamorphoses* and love poetry collected in the *Amores* and *Ars Amatoria*.

Parmenides (early 5th c. BC), Greek pre-Socratic philosopher, and subject of a dialogue by Plato.

Parmenion (ca. 400–330 BC), chief Macedonian commander under Philip; though instrumental to Alexander's solidification of his authority after Philip's death, his resistance to Alexander's increasingly grandiose ambitions led to his and his son's executions under the pretext of treason.

Pascal, Blaise (1623–1662), French philosopher and mathematician associated with the circles at Port-Royal; his major works include the *Provincial Letters* (1656–1657), which criticize the Jesuits and defend the stricter and more rigorous Jansenist ethical view, further developed in the fragmentary set of *Pensée*s, which strikingly develop man's dependence on God and the anxiety of human existence.

Paulus Aemilius (Lucius Aemlius Paullus; ca. 229–160 BC), Roman commander and statesman; the peak of his career was his victory over Perseus at Pydna in 168 that ended the Third Macedonian War, and for which he was awarded the triumphal procession in Rome mentioned by Smith.

Perrault, Charles (1628–1703), French poet and belles-lettrist who espoused the side of the moderns in the Quarrel of the Ancients and the Moderns and engaged in a running polemical battle with Boileau in the last two decades of the seventeenth century.

Persaeus (ca. 306–243 BC), Stoic philosopher and commander, was raised and taught by Zeno.

Perseus (ca. 213–160 BC), king of Macedonia from 179 to 168 BC, was defeated by the Romans and led in the triumphal procession of Lucius Aemilius Paullus in 167 BC.

Peter the Great (1672–1725), tsar of Russia from 1682 to his death; his reign witnessed military struggle with Charles XII of Sweden, expansion of Russian influence throughout the Baltic, and the emergence of Russia into European prominence.

Petrarca, Francesco (Petrarch, 1304–1374), Italian Renaissance poet and humanist famed for his love sonnets to Laura.

Phaedra, wife of the Athenian king Theseus and stepmother of Hippolytus; the story of her illicit love for her stepson and her ensuing guilt and suicide is recounted in extant tragedies by Euripides, Seneca, and Racine.

Philip of Castile (Philip I; 1478–1506), king of Castile from 1504 to his death, son of the Habsburg Maximilian I, husband of Joanna (see above), and father of Charles V.

Philip of Macedon (Philip II; 382–336 BC), king of Macedon and father of Alexander the Great, under whose rule the Macedonian Empire reached its height and asserted its supremacy in Greece.

Philoctetes, Greek tragic figure and the subject of a surviving tragedy by Sophocles that recounts his abandonment on the island of Lemnos because of an infected snakebite while en route to Troy.

Philopoemen (ca. 253–182 BC), Greek military commander and general of the Achaean Confederacy whose hard-line policies on Sparta provoked resentment and rebellion, which ultimately culminated in his capture and poisoning.

Phocion (402–318 BC), Athenian general and student of Plato who sought to preserve Athenian interests in the face of Macedonian aggression; executed following the democratic revolution of 318.

Plato (429–347 BC), Athenian philosopher, student of Socrates, and teacher of Aristotle; immensely influential on all fields of philosophy, Plato is in *TMS* principally a moral and political philosopher and author of *Republic* and *Laws*.

Pliny (Gaius Plinius Caecilius Secundus, Pliny the Younger; ca. AD 61–112), Roman statesman, orator, and author of a collection of *Epistles* renowned for their rhetorical sophistication.

Plutarch (ca. AD 50–120), prolific author of dialogues, moral essays, and histories, principally famous for his *Parallel Lives*; Smith draws on his biographical sketches of ancient figures but elsewhere calls him "as bad a critic in philosophy as in history."

Pompey (Gnaeus Pompeius Magnus, Pompey the Great; 106–48 BC), Roman statesman and commander whose foreign military career witnessed many successes but also accusations of seeking to steal glory from Crassus for defeating Spartacus and from Lucullus for defeating Mithradates; he was an early associate of Caesar in the First Triumvirate but ultimately struggled with Caesar until being defeated by him at Pharsalus.

Pope, Alexander (1688–1744), English poet, translator of Homer, and author of the *Essay on Man* (1734–35), a principal statement of Enlightenment ideals.

Pufendorf, Samuel (1632–1694), German philosopher of natural law, and author of numerous works on European political and ecclesiastical history in addition to his influential jurisprudential works, which include *De Jure Naturae et Gentium* (*Of the Law of Nature and Nations*, 1672) and *De Officio Hominis et Civis* (*Of the Duty of Man and Citizen*, 1673).

Pyrrhus (319–272 BC), Greek commander and king of Epirus; waged ambitious struggles with Rome, Macedonia and Sparta.

Pythagoras (ca. 6th c. BC), Greek philosopher and mathematician whose cosmological theories were grounded in theories of numerical harmony; his school was traditionally assumed to have been an important influence on Plato.

Quinault, Phillipe (1635–1688), French playwright and librettist; his play *Astrate* (1664) was particularly criticized by Boileau-Despréaux.

Quintilian (Marcus Fabius Quintilianus; ca. AD 35–100), Roman orator and teacher; his *Institutio Oratoria* was an influential handbook of judgments on classical authors and the teaching and practice of rhetoric.

Racine, Jean (1639–1699), playwright, royal historiographer, and member of the Académie Française. His greatest plays include *Phèdre* (1677).

Raleigh, Sir Walter (ca. 1552–1618), English explorer of the New World; he was imprisoned by James I in 1603 for alleged conspiracy, then released to head a second, unsuccessful expedition in search of gold, but tried and executed on his return.

Regulus (Marcus Atilius Regulus; 3rd c. BC), Roman statesman and general defeated by Carthaginians in 255 BC; according to patriotic legend, he was released from captivity for purposes of negotiation but on returning to Rome insisted that no quarter be given to its enemies, following which he willingly returned to Carthage to face imprisonment, torture, and execution.

Retz, Paul de Gondi, Cardinal de (1614–1679), Archbishop of Paris and principal figure in a series of political intrigues in France and across Europe, and chronicled in his *Mémoires* (pub. 1717) with a series of character sketches and reflections on the politics of the age of Louis XIV.

Riccoboni, Marie-Jeanne (1713–1792), French novelist known for her contributions to the growth of sentimental literature; she became an admirer of Smith after their meeting in Paris in 1766.

Richardson, Samuel (1689–1761), English novelist famed for his epistolary novel *Pamela* (1740) and his *Clarissa* (1748), chief exemplars of eighteenth-century English sentimental fiction.

Richelieu, Armand Jean du Plessis, Cardinal de (1585–1642), French clergyman and politician; the author of influential works on the catechism, he was also principal minister of Louis XIII, in which capacity he sought to promote royal absolutism and weaken Protestant resistance within France, and to advance French interests abroad.

Robertson, William (1721–1793), Scottish historian, clergyman, and principal of the University of Edinburgh; with Hume and Gibbon, one of the main 18th c. British philosophical historians and the author of a *History of Scotland* (1759) and a *History of the Reign of Emperor Charles V* (1769), which included his influential "View of the Progress of Society in Europe."

Rousseau, Jean-Jacques (1712–1778), Genevan philosopher of politics, ethics, education and the arts; his corpus was well known to Smith, who particularly engaged with his key works of the period from 1755 to 1762, including the *Discourse on the Origins of Inequality* (1755), the *Letter to d'Alembert* (1758), *Emile, or On Education* (1762), and the *Social Contract* (1762).

Russell, William, Lord (1639–1683), English politician prominent in Whig circles, and executed alongside Algernon Sidney for his participation in the Rye House Plot.

Sallust (Gaius Sallustius Crispus; ca. 86–35 BC), Roman statesman and historian who withdrew from practical political life to write histories of the Catilinian conspiracy and the Jugurthan War.

Santeuil, Jean (1630–1697), French poet and author of sacred hymns and Latin verses.

Scipio Aemilianus (Publius Cornelius Scipio Aemilianus Africanus Minor; 185–129 BC), Roman general and statesman, adopted grandson of Scipio Africanus, and conqueror of Carthage.

Scipio Africanus (Publius Cornelius Scipio Africanus Major; 236–183 BC), Roman general and statesman famed as the victor over Hannibal in 202.

Scipio Nasica (Publius Cornelius Scipio Nasica Corculum; 2nd c. BC), Roman statesman and son-in-law of Scipio Africanus.

Seneca (Lucius Annaeus Seneca, Seneca the Younger; 4 BC–AD 65), Roman author and advisor to Nero; his political career was dominated by his efforts to moderate Nero's tyranny, and his prose and poetic works, which included moral treatises, shorter moral epistles, and several tragedies, were marked by an ascetic Stoicism.

Shaftesbury, Anthony Ashley Cooper, first Earl of (1621–1683), English statesman who found favor under both Cromwell and Charles II, but was forced into exile prior to the accession of James II; grandfather to the third Earl, he employed John Locke as secretary and tutor.

Shaftesbury, Anthony Ashley Cooper, third Earl of (1671–1713), English philosopher and author of the influential *Characteristicks of Men, Manners, Opinions, Times* (1711), which included his *Inquiry Concerning Virtue, or Merit*, and which collectively became a key text in eighteenth-century debates over psychological egoism and moral sense theory, classical conceptions of virtue, and deism and Christianity.

Sidney, Algernon (1623–1683), English politician and author whose practical service and writings (most notably the *Discourses Concerning Government*, pub. 1698) championed republican moral and political principles; he was executed for participation in the Rye House Plot that targeted Charles II.

Simson, Robert (1687–1768), Scottish professor of mathematics who was both Smith's professor at Glasgow and later his faculty colleague; known for his work on conic sections and his edition of Euclid's *Elements*, Hutcheson called him "the best geometer in the world."

Smith, John (1618–1652), English philosopher and one of the principal Cambridge Platonists; his chief work was his *Select Discourses* (1660), which examines epistemological questions concerning man's knowledge of God as well as ethical questions concerning the nature of love.

Socrates (ca. 469–399 BC), Athenian philosopher whose teachings were memorialized by Plato and Xenophon and who was executed for alleged religious heterodoxy and corruption of the city's youth.

Solon (ca. 630–560 BC), Athenian lawgiver and poet famed for moderation in reforming the severe law code established by Draco, including a series of progressive reforms for debt relief and a more democratic distribution of power.

Sophocles (5th c. BC), Athenian playwright who, with Euripides and Aeschylus, is one of the three principal playwrights of the golden age of Athenian tragedy.

Stewart, Matthew (1717–1785), Scottish professor of mathematics at Edinburgh, and with Smith a former student of Robert Simson.

Sully, Maximilien de Béthune, Duc de (1559–1641), French administrator who advocated a series of progressive economic reforms as minister under Henri IV; his actions are detailed in his memoirs, published in 1638.

Sulpitius (Publius Sulpicius Rufus; ca. 121–88 BC), Roman statesman and orator particularly praised by Cicero for his rhetorical abilities.

Swift, Jonathan (1667–1745), Irish satirist and moralist and Dean of St. Patrick's, Dublin; Smith engaged with Swift's literary masterpieces, including his popular novel *Gulliver's Travels* (1726), as well as his Anglo-Irish political and economic writings, including *Drapier's Letters* (1725).

Tacitus (ca. AD 56–118), Roman historian whose *Histories* and *Annals* chronicle Roman politics under the emperors from Tiberius to Domitian; his studies of political intrigue were of particular interest to early modern readers who alternately found in him republican and authoritarian sympathies.

Tamerlane (1337–1405), Turko-Mongol conqueror and founder of central Asian empire.

Themistocles (ca. 524–459 BC) Athenian politician and commander who played a principal role in the Persian Wars; ultimately ostracized from Athens for suspected intrigue with the Persians, he traveled to Asia Minor, where he is thought to have died a natural death as governor of Magnesia.

Theramenes (5th c. BC), Athenian politician and one of the Thirty Tyrants established in Athens after its defeat by Sparta in 404 BC; his moderation was despised by the hard-line oligarchists who had him put to death.

Thomson, James (1700–1748), Scottish poet who composed plays on classical themes but whose principal fame rests on *The Seasons* (1730).

Tibullus (ca. 55–19 BC), Roman poet whose works focus on romantic love and the pleasures of rural life and psychological tranquility.

Tigranes II (1st c. AD), king of Armenia and head of empire in Syria until defeat by Roman expedition commanded by Lucullus and then by Pompey in AD 66.

Timoleon (4th c. BC), Corinthian commander renowned for deposing Syracusan and Sicilian tyrants and for his victory over Carthage.

Turenne, Henri de La Tour d'Auvergne, Vicomte de (1611–1675), celebrated French commander under Louis XIV whose genius was displayed in a series of successful campaigns throughout the Thirty Years' War, the Fronde, and the Dutch War.

Ulysses (Roman name for Odysseus), king of Ithaca whose efforts to return home after the Trojan War are chronicled in Homer's *Odyssey*.

Voltaire (François-Marie Arouet, 1694–1778), French philosopher, playwright, poet, historian, and essayist who championed the liberal values of the Enlightenment in his *Philosophical Letters* (1734), his *Age of Louis XIV* (1752), and his *Treatise on Toleration* (1763); Smith was a particular admirer of Voltaire's dramatic works, and sought him out for a personal visit at his estate in Ferney outside of Geneva during his travels in France.

William III (1650–1702), Prince of Orange and King of England from 1689 until his death; on the invitation of leading English politicians he left Holland to assume the throne abdicated by James II.

Wollaston, William (1659–1724), English moral philosopher and author of a single but influential treatise on natural religion, *The Religion of Nature Delineated* (1724).

Zeno of Citium (335–263 BC), Greek philosopher who traveled to Athens and founded the Stoic school and set forth initial statements of Stoic logic, ethics, and metaphysics.

Textual Notes

ADVERTISEMENT

1. Smith's "various occupations" over his career included professor of logic and then moral philosophy at Glasgow (1751–64); tutor to the third Duke of Buccleuch (1764–66); and Commissioner of Customs for Scotland (1778–90).
2. The *Wealth of Nations* was published in 1776. Smith lectured on jurisprudence at Glasgow, and while he did not live to complete the work here mentioned, student transcriptions of his lectures have been published as part of the Glasgow Edition as the *Lectures on Jurisprudence*.
3. The "Advertisement" was new to the sixth edition of 1790; the final paragraph here mentioned was original to the first edition of 1759.

PART I, SECTION I

1. Smith introduces his work as an intervention in the debate over the relative degrees of selfishness and benevolence in human nature. The classical debate was defined by the contest of Stoicism with Epicureanism; Smith's more immediate interlocutors include those who sought to defend pity and compassion and similar other-directed sentiments against the egoism of Hobbes and Mandeville, esp. Shaftesbury, *Inquiry Concerning Virtue* 2; Hutcheson, *Essay with Illustrations* 1.3–4 and 2 Preface and *System* 1.1.5–6; Butler, *Fifteen Sermons*, esp. 1 and 5; Hume, *Enquiry Concerning Morals* App. 2; Kames, *Essays on the Principles of Morality and Natural Religion* 1.1 and 1.2.5; and Rousseau, *Discourse on Inequality*, passim.
2. rack: "an engine to torture" (Johnson).
3. Smith here draws on the terms of Hume's epistemology. For Hume's account of the copy mechanism, see *A Treatise of Human Nature* 1.1.1, 1.2.3.2–3; on the productive capacities of the imagination, see *Treatise* 1.1.3, 1.4.2.31–37. For commentary on Smith's debts to Hume's conception of the imagination, see esp. Skinner, Griswold, and Raphael.

4. The spectator is one of Smith's principal categories. Here he uses the term in the sense of an audience member at a theatrical spectacle; elsewhere he uses it to describe a range of ethical acts, from the spectatorship of the actions and character of others that provides the principal data that we use to construct ethical norms, to the idea of the "impartial spectator" whose apprehension of and judgments upon the self are the main agents of moral reform. Though Smith is the first to build a theory around spectatorship, the concept was central to several texts with which Smith engaged, including Addison's *Spectator*; Hutcheson's *Essay with Illustrations*; Hume's *Enquiry Concerning Morals*; and Rousseau's *Letter to d'Alembert*.

5. perfidious: "treacherous; false to trust; guilty of violated faith" (Johnson).

6. Sympathy is a central concept of Smith's ethics. Prior to Smith it played an important role in several ethical systems; see Hutcheson, *Short Introduction* 1.1.9; Kames, *Essays on Morality and Religion* 1.1; Burke, *Philosophical Enquiry* 1.13–15; and esp. Hume, *Treatise* 2.1.11, 2.2.5–9 and 3.3.1–3. Smith's use of the term is anticipated and clarified by Johnson, who defines it broadly as "fellow-feeling; mutual sensibility; the quality of being affected by the affection of another," but limits pity to "sympathy with misery" and compassion to "painful sympathy."

7. In speaking of the "illusions of the imagination" here and in 3.2 and 4.1, Smith may have Hume in mind; see, e.g., *Treatise* 1.3.5.4, 1.4.2.29, 1.4.7.6.

8. In 7.3.1 (p. 371), Smith names Hobbes, Pufendorf, and Mandeville as self-love theorists and refers to their various teachings on sociability and dependence.

9. spleen: "anger; spite; ill-humour" or "melancholy; hypochondriacal vapours" (Johnson).

10. For explication, see Smith's review of Hutcheson and Hume at 7.2.3 (p. 353).

11. On the intellectual sentiments of admiration, wonder, and surprise, see esp. Smith's *History of Astronomy* 1–2; for commentary, see Eric Schliesser in *British Journal for the History of Philosophy 13* (2005).

12. Smith's response to this position is further developed in 4.2 (p. 218).

13. Smith's distinction between the amiable and the awful virtues is anticipated by several others; see, e.g., Hume, *Treatise* 3.3.4.2 and *Enquiry Concerning Morals* App. 4.6; Burke, *Philosophical Enquiry* 3.10. The distinction plays a principal role in his thought

and that of other main figures of the Scottish Enlightenment insofar as the distinction between the awful and amiable virtues represented more generally a distinction between the demanding virtues revered by classical antiquity and savage societies and the more polite and gentle virtues of commercial modernity. This theme reappears in remarks on savagery (5.2), human excellence (6), and Stoicism (7.2.1); a key discussion of Smith's immediate context is Hume, *Enquiry Concerning Morals* 7.11–18.

14. Matthew 22:36–40; Mark 12:30–31; John 13:34–35; 1 Corinthians 13:13; see also 3.6 (p. 197).

15. Smith's distinction between propriety and virtue is fundamental to his thought as it both distinguishes the subjects of Part 1 from those of Part 6 and anticipates his distinction between the ordinary objects of praise, and the noble and honorable actions associated with praiseworthiness (3.2). In distinguishing mere propriety from true virtue, Smith may have in mind the distinction of *decorum* (propriety) and *honestum* (honorable and noble) fundamental to Cicero (see, e.g., *De officiis* 1.93–95), and revived in the Scottish Enlightenment in part via Hutcheson's reminder of the difference between the ordinary duties described in Cicero's *De officiis* and the supreme goods examined in his *De finibus* (*Short Introduction* Preface). Smith explicitly invokes the concept of offices on other occasions (e.g. 2.1.2, 7.2.1).

16. Smith returns to this point in his discussion of the wise and virtuous man at 6.3 (p. 280); see also Cicero, *De officiis* 3.15.

PART I, SECTION II

1. Among ancient treatments, see, e.g., Aristotle, *Politics* 1.2, 1252a25–1253a25; Epictetus, *Discourses* 1.3.3, 1.6.12–22; Marcus Aurelius, *Meditations* 3.16, 6.23; Cicero, *De officiis* 1.105–7. The comparison of animal to human nature was a prominent theme in Descartes, Locke, and Malebranche; in Smith's more immediate context, see, e.g., Hume, *Treatise* 2.1.12 and 2.2.12; Rousseau, *Discourse on Inequality* 1.

2. See 1.1.1 above.

3. In his *Philoctetes*, Sophocles recounts Philoctetes' laments at the injustice of his abandonment and his physical suffering (l. 732–821). Sophocles' *Trachinian Women* recounts Heracles' pain following his wife's inadvertent poisoning and his plea to his son to put him out of his misery (l. 749–812, 971–1278). In *Hippolytus*, Euripides portrays the suffering and death of Hippolytus after having been dragged by his horses (l. 1173–1254, 1347–1466).

4. See 1.1.4 (p. 25).

5. raillery: "slight satire; satirical merriment" (Johnson).

6. For Tibullus' praises of tranquil country life, see, e.g., 1.1, 1.5, 2.1; for his critique of the pursuit of wealth as inimical to tranquility, see, e.g., 1.1, 1.9, 1.10, 2.2. His poetry was often bound with that of his contemporary Propertius (as in the 1753 edition published in Glasgow owned by Smith); Smith's disparaging reference to Petrarch in the previous paragraph had been to Propertius in all editions prior to 1790.

7. The afterlife paradise of the ancients; see, e.g., Marcus Aurelius, *Meditations* 10.8.

8. Thomas Otway's play *The Orphan*.

9. Racine's *Phèdre* was a retelling of Euripides' *Hippolytus*, referenced by Smith throughout called "the finest tragedy, perhaps, that is extant in any language."

10. See 2.2.3 (p. 103).

11. For the Stoic conception of providentialism, see 7.2.1 below and accompanying notes.

12. Smith elaborates on the "musical passions" in his essay "The Imitative Arts" (esp. 2.13); see also his discussions of musical education in *Wealth of Nations* 5.1.f and *Rhetoric* 2.117.

13. perfidy: "treachery; want of faith; breach of faith" (Johnson).

PART I, SECTION III

1. Smith here refers to Hutcheson, who argues for the existence of a "natural disposition to congratulation with others in their joys" in *System* 1.2.3 and 1.4.10; see also *Short Introduction* 1.1.15; and *Essay with Illustrations* 1.3.4.

2. After reading the first edition, Hume wrote Smith to suggest that he clarify his account of sympathy (*Correspondence* 36). Smith wrote a draft of this note later that year in response and included it in the second and all subsequent editions of *TMS*.

3. Cato's character and suicide were important themes across the eighteenth century owing in part to their depiction in Addison's play. For Seneca's portrait, see *De providentia* 2.9–12.

4. See Plato, *Phaedo* 117a–e.

5. Contemporary accounts of the execution describe Biron's last moments as frantic and furious, emphasizing his threat to strangle the executioner rather than his tears of remorse or regret for lost greatness. Other accounts known to Smith, including that in the *Mémoires* of the Duc de Sully, do note Biron's tears (see Bk. 13, for the year 1602); of these, Smith's account is perhaps most similar to that of Helvétius in *De l'esprit* (see 3.28), published in 1758, a year before *TMS*—a work Hume recommended to Smith in 1759, but

which Smith, in a 1763 letter to Hume, claimed not to have read prior to the publication of the first edition of *TMS*.

6. Smith's locution may be inspired by La Rochefoucauld, who writes of "un désir de rendre notre condition meilleure" (*Maxims* 82), or Mandeville, who writes of our "indefatigable desire of meliorating our condition" (*Fable*, Remark V) and of man's "restless desire of mending their condition" (*Enquiry into the Origin of Honour*, Dialogue 1). The idea would play a principal role in Smith's political economy; see, e.g., *Wealth of Nations* 2.3, 3.3.

7. Smith's discussion of vanity is an intervention in a contemporary debate over the moral status of luxury and the love of esteem. The roots of that debate lie in the writings of the principal seventeenth-century French moralists (e.g., La Rochefoucauld, La Bruyère, La Fontaine, and Fénelon); important eighteenth-century interventions include, among others, those by Hume ("Of Refinement in the Arts") and Voltaire (e.g., "The Worldling"). Particularly relevant in the present context are Mandeville's theory of "self-liking" (esp. *Enquiry into the Origin of Honour*, Dialogue 1), Rousseau's conception of *amour-propre* (esp. *Discourse on Inequality* 2 and n15), and Hume's conception of "our esteem for the rich and powerful" (esp. *Treatise* 2.2.5).

8. Charles's indignation at his trial, together with the posthumous circulation of the *Eikon Basilike* (purportedly his final statement), generated a popular sympathy that grew during the Interregnum and culminated in the restoration of the monarchy and the proclamation of his martyrdom; Hume describes his trial as exciting "contagious sympathy," his execution as a scene of "grief, indignation, and astonishment," and the *Eikon* as exciting a "general compassion" (*History* 59).

9. On obsequiousness, see also 4.1 (p. 209) and the accompanying note on Rousseau.

10. James's first flight attempt ended in failure when his escape boat was captured. Returned to London under guard, he was welcomed by the crowds. Hume remarks that "the populace, moved by compassion for his unhappy fate, and actuated by their own levity, had received him with shouts and acclamations" (*History* 71).

11. Louis XIV's historian was Voltaire; the passage Smith here quotes is drawn from Voltaire, *Siècle de Louis XIV* 24.

12. coxcomb: "a fop; a superficial pretender" (Johnson).

13. Smith's account of the triumph is derived from Plutarch, *Lives*, "Aemilius Paulus," 33–34.

14. Smith quotes *Maximes* 490; see also the note below on Mandeville.

15. The first five editions of *TMS* here included a separate chapter

with the title "Of the stoical philosophy"; some material from that chapter was incorporated into the discussion of Stoicism at 7.2.1 (p. 318).

16. Smith may have in mind a notorious incident concerning the future Frederick II (Frederick the Great) and his father, Frederick Wilhelm I. In June 1730, both were present at a parade given at the camp at Mühlberg in honor of the Elector of Saxony. While there, Frederick's tyrannical father, who had long been given to humiliating his son for his effeminacy, caned him in view of the assembled regiments. Frederick was by then an officer, having received the commission of lieutenant-colonel and the command of two battalions in 1728; see David Fraser, *Frederick the Great* (2000), pp. 24, 28.

17. See Cardinal de Retz, *Mémoires* (p. 110 in the modern Pléiade edition); Smith also cites this passage in *Rhetoric* 2.42.

18. This chapter was an addition to the sixth edition of 1790. For Smith's views on corruption and the obligation to remedy it, see esp. *Jurisprudence* B 328–333.

19. Having established the economic utility of vanity and the propensity to worship the rich and powerful (see 1.3.1 and 4.1 below), Smith in this chapter examines the moral effects of such a disposition. Among the "moralists" who take up the question of the best form of life, see, e.g., Plato, *Republic* 10, 613b–621d; Aristotle, *Nicomachean Ethics* 1.5, 1095b14–1096a10; Cicero, *De officiis* 1.116–18.

20. The quotation is drawn from the "Supplement" to the *Mémoires* of the Duc de Sully (vol. 8, pp. 338–39 in the 1752 London edition that Smith owned).

21. See Cicero, *Pro Marcello* 25.

PART II, SECTION I

1. See 1.1.3 (p. 21).

2. Smith's discussions of gratitude here and esp. 3.6 are indebted to several previous discussions of gratitude; see esp. Hutcheson's claim that there is "no obligation more sacred than that of gratitude" in *Short Introduction* 2.4.6 (which cites Cicero; see *De officiis* 1.47); as well as Hutcheson, *Inquiry into Beauty and Virtue* 2.5.2.

3. Hume describes James I as "little enterprising" and "inoffensive," emphasizing that his pacifism bordered on mere "pusillanimity," and his efforts to "acquire the good will of all" through neutrality enabled him to garner "the esteem and regard of none" (*History* 49).

4. Their "actions of proper and beneficent greatness" can be read in the histories of Herodotus (8.79–81 on Aristides); Polybius (10, 14–15 on Scipio); Cornelius Nepos (who wrote lives of Timoleon and Aristides);

Livy (5.19–6.27 on Camillus; 26–30 on Scipio); Diodorus Siculus (16.65–90 on Timoleon); and Plutarch (who wrote lives of Camillus, Timoleon, and Aristides). Smith's observation is an intervention in a contemporary debate over the grounds of our admiration of virtue in distant ages; he returns to this debate in 7.3.1 below.

5. For Borgia's cruelty, see, e.g., Machiavelli, *Prince* 7 and 17; Nero's vices were condemned by Tacitus, Suetonius, Pliny, and Cassius Dio.

PART II, SECTION II

1. Smith's contrast below of the negative duties of justice with the positive duties of beneficence is anticipated in several accounts of the social virtues; see Cicero, *De officiis* 1.20; and Hume, *Enquiry Concerning Morals* 1.11.

2. Smith has in mind Kames, *Essays on Morality and Religion* 1.2.3–4. Kames's comments on duty, conscience, sympathy, consciousness of merit, and virtue as benevolence in these passages also merit comparison to Smith's comments here and elsewhere.

3. Smith's discussion here of the "duties of a law-giver" is tied to his broader conception of the "science of the legislator," a key concept of his political philosophy; see esp. 6.2.2 (p. 268) and *Wealth of Nations* 4.2, and Rousseau, "Geneva Manuscript," 1.4, 2.1–6. Smith's emphasis here and elsewhere on moderation in statesmanship is anticipated by several other thinkers; see esp. Montesquieu, *The Spirit of the Laws* 19.5–6, 19.14 and 26.23; and Hume, "Of Commerce" and "Idea of a Perfect Commonwealth."

4. See, e.g., Leviticus 24:19.

5. That our primary regard is to ourselves rather than to others (which is also Smith's point of departure in Part 6) was commonly accepted by all parties to the debate over self-love and benevolence. In antiquity it was shared by both Stoics and Epicureans among others (see Cicero, *De finibus* 5.24–30; *De officiis* 1.11); in the Enlightenment the primacy of the concern for self-preservation is reiterated by such prominent advocates of benevolence as Shaftesbury (*Inquiry Concerning Virtue* 1.2.2) and Hutcheson (*Short Introduction* 1.6.3).

6. Smith uses this location on three separate occasions in *TMS*; see his accounts of the earthquake in China in 3.3 (p. 156), and of patriotism in 6.2.2 (p. 268).

7. Smith borrows the race metaphor from Cicero (see *De officiis* 3.42), perhaps as reported by Pufendorf (see *Of the Law of Nature and Nations* 2.3.16n).

8. On the anguish of remorse, see esp. Hutcheson, *Essay with Illus-*

trations 1.5.5 and *Short Introduction* 1.2.9; and Kames, *Essays on Morality and Religion* 1.2.3 and 1.3.

9. Smith here intervenes in an ancient debate over the question of whether human beings are by nature self-sufficient or dependent on others—a prominent theme in Marcus Aurelius (see, e.g., *Meditations* 2.1, 5.16, 8.59) and Cicero (see, e.g., *De officiis* 1.22, 2.15), and revived by both Rousseau in his *Discourse on Inequality* and the thinkers reviewed in 7.2–3 in their debates over self-love and benevolence. Smith's own understanding of human interdependence is central to his political economy; see esp. *Wealth of Nations* 1.1–2.

10. See, e.g., Hume, *Enquiry Concerning Morals* 4.15.

11. Here and in 2.3.3 (p. 125) Smith invokes the doctrine of "final causes" originally associated with Aristotelian teleology, which referred to the end or purpose (*telos*) specific to a given action or organism. In the Scottish Enlightenment the debate over final causes ranged from those who incorporated final causes into their providentialist conceptions of cosmology and ethics (such as Hutcheson) to those skeptical of our capacity to apprehend such ends (such as Hume). For commentary, see Alvey.

12. Smith's account of our approbation of the punishment of injustice (mirrored in his account at *Jurisprudence* A 2.90ff) refers principally to the theories of punishment developed by those he associates with natural sociability (esp. Grotius, Pufendorf, and Hutcheson). For their views on natural sociability, see the notes to 7.3 (p. 485); for their theories of punishment (including capital punishment), see Grotius, *Rights of War and Peace* 2.20.1–9; Pufendorf, *Law of Nature and Nations* 8.3.1–12 and *Duty of Man and Citizen* 2.13; Hutcheson, *Short Introduction* 3.8.9–10 and *System* 3.9.10–15. On the general claim concerning the indispensability of justice to the preservation of society, see esp. Hobbes, *Leviathan* 15; and Hume, *Enquiry Concerning Morals* 4.

13. See Polybius 6.36–37.

14. This final sentence was an addition to the sixth edition, replacing a longer passage on the relationship of humanity to divinity. Smith's study of the wise and virtuous man in 6.3 (p. 280) also treats this theme. More broadly, Smith's argument in 2.2.3 is an intervention in the debate over the relationship of a belief in the afterlife to justice (e.g., Plato, *Republic* 10, 613b–621d; Rousseau, *The Social Contract* 4.8), revived in terms anticipating Smith by Hutcheson (e.g. *Essay With Illustrations* 1.6.4). Smith returns to this question, see esp. 3.5, 6.2.3.

PART II, SECTION III

1. The Dryads were ancient Greek tree nymphs, and the Lares ancient Roman household gods responsible for protecting households and localities.

2. The punishment of the ox is drawn from Exodus 21:28; the same example reappears at *Jurisprudence* A 2.118–19. Rules for punishing animals formed a significant component of jurisprudential treatments of negligence; see 2.3.2 (p. 116) and the sources there cited. The story of the officer and his horse is drawn from an anonymous epistolary collection, *Letters Writ by a Turkish Spy*, vol. 4, book 3, letter 10.

3. For elaboration see *Jurisprudence* A 5.61–62 and B 80.

4. See, e.g., Alexander Bayne, *Institutions of the Criminal Law of Scotland* (Edinburgh, 1730), which reports it to have been "general custom and practice of courts" to attribute to natural causes the death of any victim of attempted homicide who expires 40 days after the injury (p. 89).

5. See Plutarch, *Lives*, "Lucullus" 25.

6. police: "the regulation and government of a city or country, so far as regards the inhabitants" (Johnson).

7. Smith's distinction of three species of negligence is an intervention in an ongoing debate in natural jurisprudence over negligence and compensation; see, e.g., Grotius, *Rights of War and Peace* 2.17; Pufendorf, *Duty of Man and Citizen* 1.6.9; Hutcheson, *Short Introduction* 2.15.1–3. Smith reiterates the distinction at *Jurisprudence* A 2.78 and 2.88–89.

8. Smith reiterates the lack of distinction between murder and manslaughter in *Jurisprudence* A 2.112 and B 187.

9. The *Lex Aquilia* of the third c. BC was a Roman private law statute governing compensation for damaged or destroyed property. It was included as part of the *Corpus Iuris Civilis* (Justinian's *Institutes* 4.3.8); it emphasizes the negligence of one unable to control his horse by "weakness or lack of skill," clarifying Smith's discussion here.

10. For anticipations of Smith's claim, see, e.g., Shaftesbury, *Inquiry Concerning Virtue* 1.2.1; Hutcheson, *Short Introduction* 1.1.10, 1.2.7. Smith uses similar language in the conclusion of his comparison of Epicurus to Aristotle, Plato and Zeno (7.2.2, p. 346).

11. The discussion of guilt and atonement that occupies the remainder of this paragraph and the next was an addition to the sixth edition of 1790.

12. Smith's three examples refer to cases of unintentional transgressions of sexual norms: Oedipus's unwitting incest with his mother

(in Sophocles, *Oedipus the King*), Monimia's unwitting relationship with her brother-in-law (in Otway, *The Orphan*), and Isabelle's remarriage while her husband was still living (in Thomas Southerne, *The Fatal Marriage*).

PART III, CHAPTER I

1. Hume uses the same metaphor in *Treatise* 2.2.5.21.

PART III, CHAPTER II

1. Most of this chapter was an addition to the sixth edition. The distinction between what is merely praised and what is genuinely praiseworthy is fundamental to Smith's ethics, and has important implications for his attempts to preserve moral sentimentalism from degenerating into moral relativism. The nature and reality of this distinction between praise and virtue or praiseworthiness had also been examined by several others before Smith; see esp. Marcus Aurelius, *Meditations* 4.20, 8.1; Seneca, *De otio* 1.3; Cicero, *De officiis* 1.14–15; *De finibus* 2.49–50; Locke, *Essay Concerning Human Understanding* 2.28.10–11; Hutcheson, *Essay with Illustrations* 2.5; Hume, *Enquiry Concerning Morals* 1.10 and "Of the Dignity or Meanness of Human Nature."

2. emulation: "rivalry; desire of superiority" or "envy; desire of depressing another; contest; contention" (Johnson).

3. paint: "to lay colours on the face" (Johnson); to use makeup.

4. This paragraph and the two paragraphs that follow were added to the sixth edition; they restate the distinction between three levels of praise that Smith draws in his discussion of Mandeville in 7.2.4 (p. 362).

5. Smith's distinction between the desire to appear virtuous and the desire of being virtuous is central to his efforts to preserve his sentimentalist theory from relativism. The distinction has an important history (e.g., Plato, *Republic* 2, 360e–361d; Sallust, *Conspiracy of Catiline* 53–55); particularly important interlocutors include Mandeville (see 7.2.4, p. 362) and Rousseau, whose passage on the distinction between being and appearing was one of three passages from the *Discourse on Inequality* that Smith translated in his *Letter to the Edinburgh Review* (in *Essays on Philosophical Subjects*, pp. 252–53).

6. gibbet: "a gallows; the post on which malefactors are hanged, or on which their carcasses are exposed" (Johnson).

7. Voltaire reported the last words of Calas differently in his *History of Elisabeth Canning, and of Jean Calas* (1762) but likewise emphasized his magnanimity and protestations of innocence. Smith's account is likely less indebted to print sources than to con-

versations with Voltaire in 1765, and with those he met in Toulouse during his stay there from 1764–65.

8. See 1.3.1 (p. 55).

9. Throughout his life Racine was caught in a complex web of literary jealousy, with rival factions sponsoring competing versions of both his *Iphigénie* and *Phèdre*. Smith's story is likely drawn from the extracted version of the memoirs of Racine's life commonly prefaced to the first volume of eighteenth-century collections of Racine's works.

10. Among examples of Voltaire's vanity known to Smith would have been Voltaire's angry reaction to Kames's relatively innocuous criticism in *Elements of Criticism* 22.

11. The *Dunciad*, published in various successively expanded editions between 1728 and 1743, was a satirical assault on Whig literary and political circles.

12. Smith reiterates elsewhere his admiration for Gray (see *Rhetoric* 2.96 and the remark reported at *Rhetoric*, p. 230), who treats several characteristically Smithean themes, including the torments of ambition and envy ("Ode on a Distant Prospect of Eton-College"), fellow-feeling and "sympathetic tears" ("Ode to Adversity" and "The Progress of Poesy," 3.1), and the vanity of glory ("Elegy Written in a Country Church-yard"). Two of Gray's odes ("Progress of Poesy" and "The Bard") were parodied in 1760, but most reports emphasize that Gray remained unruffled; see, e.g., Johnson, *Lives of the Poets*, "Gray" 14–16.

13. Several eighteenth-century accounts of Newton's genius emphasize his tranquility and indifference to fame in manners that anticipate Smith; see, e.g., Hume, *History of England* 71; and esp. Fontenelle's *éloge* of Newton in the collection to which Smith refers three paragraphs down, which emphasizes that Newton had "not the least sentiment of vanity" and that his *Principia* "had not at first all the praise it merited."

14. Smith refers here to the "Quarrel of the Ancients and the Moderns" in which those here named were all principal figures. The dispute concerned the imitation of the classical style in seventeenth-century French literature and other arts, with the advocates of the superiority of the ancient literature—esp. Racine and Boileau-Despréaux—ranged against advocates of the moderns—esp. Perrault, Fontenelle, and La Motte. In his *éloge* to Boileau-Despréaux in the collection to which the end of the present paragraph alludes, d'Alembert details Boileau-Despréaux's struggles with the above-named rivals.

15. Smith refers to the support of Addison's "Buttonian" circle for a

translation of the *Iliad* prepared by one of Addison's protégés—a resentment that culminated in Pope's attack on the cowardly deference of Addison's circle in his "Epistle to Dr. Arbuthnot" (1734).

16. Fontenelle comments on the simplicity of manners in several places in his *éloges*; some are helpfully detailed in Gregory Matthew Adkins in *Journal of the History of Ideas* 61 (2000).

17. See 7.2.4 (p. 360).

18. See Cicero, *De officiis* 1.71.

19. Genesis 1:26–27; for commentary, see Otteson, chs. 1 and 6. A related idea is central to Stoicism; see, e.g., Epictetus, *Discourses* 2.8.9–23; Marcus Aurelius, *Meditations* 12.26.

20. Respectively the courts of France and Great Britain.

21. Smith here translates a passage from Massillon's *Discours prononcé à une bénédiction des drapeaux du régiment de Catinat*.

22. The quotation is from Voltaire's *La Pucelle d'Orléans*, chant 5.

PART III, CHAPTER III

1. Smith engages with the theory of vision at greater length in his "Of the External Senses"; a helpful introduction to the debate over the theories of vision is provided in Kames, *Essays on Morality and Religion* 2.3.

2. Smith may have in mind the Lisbon earthquake of 1755, which elicited a notorious exchange between Voltaire and Rousseau. Voltaire himself mentions a Chinese earthquake of 1699 that claimed the lives of 400,000, far eclipsing those of Lima and Lisbon; see his preface to his *Poem upon the Destruction of Lisbon* and his *Essai sur les moeurs* 195.

3. A similar example is used in Hume, *Treatise* 2.3.3.6.

4. The category of "the honourable and noble" here invoked plays a central role in several other passages in *TMS*; see, e.g., 3.2–3, 7.2.1, 7.2.4. The category is perhaps best regarded as Smith's rendering of the perfect moral beauty and worthiness that is suggested in Greek by *to kalon* (Aristotle, *Nicomachean Ethics* 3.7; 1115b12–13) and in Latin by *honestum* (Cicero, *De finibus* 2.44–50). In identifying this category with conscience Smith may also have in mind Hutcheson's identification of conscience with "the sense of what is right and honourable" (*Short Introduction* 1.2.7); though see also Shaftesbury, *Inquiry Concerning Virtue* 2.2.1; and the opening of Butler, *Dissertation on the Nature of Virtue*.

5. The remainder of this paragraph and the whole of the next paragraph were additions to the sixth edition of 1790.

6. While common to speak of "Stoic maxims," Smith's discussions of

such maxims is likely to have been indebted to the collection of "Maxims of the Stoics" assembled and annotated by Thomas Gataker and included in Hutcheson's translation of Marcus Aurelius's *Meditations* (see also the notes to 7.2, p. 476). Gataker's efforts to harmonize Stoic and Christian ethics on the grounds of their shared emphases on active beneficence, indifference to the things of this world, and belief in providence, influenced Hutcheson's presentation of the *Meditations* and thereby much Scottish thinking on Stoicism.

7. Smith quotes from *The Seasons, Winter*, l. 322–28, which focuses on the indifference of the wealthy and powerful to the sufferings of others. In referring to Pascal, Smith likely has in mind Pascal's *Pensées*, which treat several of the leading themes of 3.3 at length, including vanity, restlessness, and happiness.

8. For the Stoic concept of the "citizen of the world," see, e.g., Epictetus, *Discourses* 1.9.1; Marcus Aurelius, *Meditations* 6.44.

9. From Epictetus, *Enchiridion* 26.

10. The remainder of this chapter was an addition to the sixth edition of 1790.

11. Exodus 20:12. The obligations of children to parents were a prominent component of the inquiries of natural lawyers and other "moralists"; see, e.g., Pufendorf, *On the Duty of Man and Citizen* 2.3.9, 2.3.12; Hutcheson, *Short Introduction* 3.2.4; and Smith's own comments at *Jurisprudence* A 3.78–87.

12. See also Smith's more elaborate discussion of Stoicism in 7.2.1 (p. 318). Here he makes his own intervention in the Quarrel in advocating modern sentimentalism over ancient Stoicism as a source of instruction in manners. For related critiques of Stoic apathy as an extension of selfishness, see, e.g., Hutcheson, *Essay with Illustrations* 1.4.5; and Hume, "The Stoic."

13. From Gray, "Epitaph on Mrs Clerke" (1758).

14. See 1.2.1 (p. 35).

15. Smith returns to this theme in several places; see, e.g., 1.3.3 (p. 73); *Rhetoric* 1.107–110, 2.90–91; and *Jurisprudence* B 12–13.

16. paroxysm: "a fit; periodical exacerbation of a disease" (Johnson).

17. Smith elaborates on these points in 7.2.1 (p. 318).

18. The story of Lauzun's spider-training was well known in the eighteenth century; among authors known to Smith, see, e.g., Helvétius, *De l'esprit* 4.10; William Eden, *Principles of Penal Law* 6; and Kames, *Sketches of the History of Man* 2.1. Most accounts, including these, use the anecdote to illustrate malevolence, calling attention to the jailer's squashing of the spider and the grief Lauzun consequently suffered.

19. See Plutarch, *Lives*, "Pyrrhus" 14.

20. The maxim reappears in several eighteenth-century texts known to Smith; see most prominently Addison, *Spectator* 25.

21. Robertson includes the story about Joanna as evidence of "the disorder of her understanding, and her incapacity for government," and mentions neither the monk's endorsement of prayer nor the queen's efforts at such (see *Reign of Charles V*, Book 1, under marginal note "The disorder of Joanna's mind increases").

22. Smith elaborates on his theory of "the laws of nations" at greater length at *Jurisprudence* B 339–358. For the context of his critical discussion here of the relationship between ordinary morality and the laws of war as represented by the "laws of nations," see esp. Pufendorf, *Duty of Man and Citizen* 2.16 (and the several citations to Grotius there); Hutcheson, *Short Introduction* 3.9 and *System* 3.10; and Hume, *Treatise* 3.2.11.

23. See also Smith's discussions of corruption in 1.3.3, and his discussions of faction in *Wealth of Nations*, esp. 5.1.f–g.

24. See Seneca, *De providentia* 6.6.

PART III, CHAPTER IV

1. See Malebranche, *Search After Truth* 5.11; Smith also cites the passage in *Astronomy* 3.1.

2. See also 7.3.3 (p. 378).

PART III, CHAPTER V

1. vicegerent: "a lieutenant; one who is entrusted with the power of the superiour" (Johnson); see also 3.2 (p. 136).

2. See also Hume's account of the sensible knave in *Enquiry Concerning Morals* 9.22–23.

3. Smith here translates a passage from Massillon's sermon for the first Sunday of Lent in his popular collection of Lenten sermons. Its topic is the truth of a future state, which would naturally have been of interest to Smith given his own emphasis in the ways in which belief in the afterlife promotes happiness and justice.

PART III, CHAPTER VI

1. Matthew 22:36–40; Mark 12:30–31; Galatians 5:14. Smith's insistence on the centrality of love to Christian ethics, coupled with his critique of an ethics limited to divine command further develops his conception of the "natural principles of religion" introduced in 3.5 (p. 186).

2. Smith returns to the distinction between critics and grammarians at 7.4 (p. 386).

3. Smith here contributes to the distinction between "false religion" and "true religion" fundamental to the Scottish Enlightenment; see Shaftesbury, *Inquiry Concerning Virtue* 2.2.1; Hutcheson, *Short Introduction* 1.2.7; Hume, "Of Superstition and Enthusiasm."

4. Voltaire's play of 1742 (full title *Fanaticism, or Mahomet the Prophet*), chronicles the tyrannical methods of its title character to gratify his passion for Palmira, including manipulating Palmira's pious lover, Seid, into murdering Mahomet's political rival, Zopir, (also the father of Palmira and Seid, unbeknownst to all but Mahomet). The "instructive spectacle" celebrated by Smith comes in Act 4, Scene 3.

5. The St. Bartholomew's Day Massacre (August 1572) is thought to have begun when Catherine de Medici approved the assassination of several leading Huguenots; the spreading violence ultimately claimed the lives of several thousand Protestants in Paris and beyond.

PART IV, CHAPTER I

1. Among eighteenth-century British writers who speak of utility as a source of beauty, see, e.g., Berkeley, *Alciphron* 3.8–9; Hume, *Treatise* 2.1.8.2 and 3.3.1.8; and (after 1759) Kames, *Elements of Criticism* 1.3. For important countering views, see Hutcheson, *Enquiry into Beauty and Virtue* 1.1.15; and Burke, *Philosophical Enquiry* 3.6. For helpful context, see Paul Guyer in *Eighteenth Century Studies* 35 (2002).

2. Smith is thinking of Hume; for the arguments summarized here, see *Treatise* 2.2.5.14–20, 3.3.5.5 and *Enquiry Concerning Morals* 5.19–20, 6.33n. For helpful commentary on Smith's critique of Hume, see Marie Martin in *Hume Studies* 16 (1990), and Schliesser and Pack in *Journal of the History of Philosophy* 44 (2006).

3. bauble: "a gew-gaw; a trifling piece of finery" (Johnson).

4. Compare to Rousseau, *Discourse on Inequality*, penultimate paragraph of Part 2, and Smith's translation of this passage in his *Letter to the Edinburgh Review* (in *Essays on Philosophical Subjects*, p. 253); for commentary, see Force.

5. operose: "laborious; full of trouble and tediousness" (Johnson).

6. Here and below Smith responds to Rousseau; see esp. his translation of a key passage from the *Discourse on Inequality* in his 1756 "Letter to the Edinburgh Review" (*Essays*, pp. 251–52); for commentary, see Force and Rasmussen.

7. The relationship between self-interested behavior and the distribution of material goods is a principal theme of Smith's economics; in the present context see esp. *Wealth of Nations* 3.4.

8. Smith's famous "invisible hand" was invoked by many other

writers; Rothschild has noted it in Shakespeare, Voltaire, and Ovid; Force in Defoe, Rollin, and Charles Bonnet; and Hont in Rousseau. To these can be added (among many others), Swift ("To Lady Betty Berkeley"), Montesquieu (*Temple of Gnide*) and Fénelon (*Telemachus*). Smith himself only used the term on two other occasions (*History of Astronomy* 3.2 and *Wealth of Nations* 4.2.9).

PART IV, CHAPTER II

1. A précis of Hume's theory of the four sources of virtue—useful to self, useful to others, agreeable to self, and agreeable to others—summarized at *Treatise* 3.3.1.30 and *Enquiry Concerning Morals* 9.1–2, and developed at length in *Enquiry Concerning Morals* 5–8.
2. See Hume, *Treatise* 2.2.5.17 and *Enquiry Concerning Morals* 5.1 and n.
3. See 1.1.4 (p. 25).
4. Smith may have had several such defenses in mind, including d'Alembert's article on "Géométrie" for the *Encyclopédie*.
5. Compare to the discussion of the role of "a pleasing consciousness of the actual love, merited esteem or approbation of others" at Shaftesbury, *Inquiry Concerning Virtue* 2.2.1.
6. See 1.1.3 (p. 21).
7. Smith here intervenes in an eighteenth-century debate over the status of the modern virtue of humanity; compare his criticism here (and of the "the soft power of humanity" in 3.3, p. 156) to, e.g., Montesquieu, *Considerations on the Romans* 15; and Hume, *Enquiry Concerning Morals* 9.5–6.
8. "Women rarely make donations."
9. The Mediterranean island of Minorca, a key strategic outpost, was captured by the British in 1708, lost to the French at the outbreak of the Seven Years' War in 1756, returned to the British by the Treaty of Paris in 1763, and then recaptured by the French and given to the Spanish in 1783.
10. See Livy 2.5.

PART V, CHAPTER I

1. The question of whether the proportions of classical architecture were founded on nature or on custom was revived in the 1750s in the debates of the philosophical clubs of Edinburgh, as noted in Peter Jones's introduction to Kames's *Elements of Criticism*. Smith here follows the argument of Claude Perrault, the French architect

and translator of Vitruvius, who similarly argued that the proportions established by the ancients were arbitrary, but once established could not be altered (see Perrault, *A Treatise of the Five Orders in Architecture* 2.7).

2. Among "ancient rhetoricians," Aristotle examines such questions relative to both poetic meter (e.g., *Poetics* 24) and prose rhythm (*Rhetoric* 3.8). Smith's quotation is from a poem by Swift: "The Grand Question Debated . . . "

3. Quintilian's text reiterates and defends his earlier judgments on Seneca; see *Institutio Oratoria* 10.1.125–131.

4. Buffier, *Treatise on First Truths* 1.13.94.

5. On the complexion and face, see Buffier, *Treatise on First Truths* 1.13.101–103 (under the marginal note "beauty arbitrary").

PART V, CHAPTER II

1. Suetonius, Tacitus (*Annals* 11–14) and Cassius Dio (60–61) are the chief classical sources for the former's folly and the latter's wickedness.

2. Smith's invocations of various national stereotypes here and below reflect an interest typical of Enlightenment political thought, fueled by a boom in travel literature (including the works of Charlevoix and Lafitau cited below) that provided data on which philosophical inquiries into the ways in which institutions and cultural practices shape national character might draw (see, e.g., Montesquieu, *Spirit of the Laws* 19; and Hume, "Of National Characters").

3. The transition from savagery and barbarism to civilization was a preeminent theme of the historical and political inquiry of the Scottish Enlightenment and forms a crucial component of Smith's economic inquiry; see esp. the theory of the stages of social progress as developed in *Jurisprudence* A 1.27–35 and B 149–150. The Scottish Enlightenment also focused on the contrast of humane modern virtues with awful primitive virtues; see, e.g., Hume, *Enquiry Concerning Morals* 7.13–18; Kames, *Sketches of Man* 1.5.

4. In *Jurisprudence* A 4.5 Smith invokes Charlevoix and Lafitau as the best authorities on native North Americans. Their accounts are the principal sources for his comments here as well; "Spartan discipline" is a particularly prominent theme in particular in Lafitau's work; see, e.g., the comparison of the North Americans to the ancient Spartans at 1.6 (vol. 1, pp. 599–602). For commentary, see Maureen Harkin in *ELH* 72 (2005).

5. Lafitau discusses the deference of young men to their parents and the indifference of young men to their brides at *Manners of the*

American Savages 1.6 (vol. 1, pp. 561–564), and discusses the separation of newlyweds and compares it to ancient Spartan practice at p. 576.

6. Smith here draws on Charlevoix, *History of New France with Historical Journal* (Paris, 1744), Letter 14 (vol. 5, pp. 319ff.), Letter 16 (vol. 5, pp. 358–65), Letter 21 (vol. 6, pp. 8–10), and Letter 27 (vol. 6, p. 122ff.); and Lafitau, *Manners of the American Savages* 2.3. (vol. 2, pp. 275–281, 284–285).

7. From Dubos, *Critical Reflections* 1.42 ("Of our manner of reciting tragedy and comedy").

8. Cicero in his *Brutus* profiles the oratory of each of the figures here named, and occasionally signals the advent of the new eloquence (see, e.g., *Brutus* 82).

9. From Charlevoix, *History of New France with Historical Journal*, Letter 23 (vol. 6, p. 38).

10. See, e.g., Lafitau, *Manners of the American Savages*, 1.6 (vol. 1, pp. 592–593); Lafitau himself cites Plutarch on Lycurgus.

11. See Aristotle, *Politics* 7.16, 1335b20–21; Plato, *Republic* 5, 460c–461c.

PART VI, SECTION I

1. The whole of Part 6 was an addition to the sixth edition of 1790. In a letter to his publishers, Smith called it a "practical system of morality." It also contains his most complete answer to the first of the two questions posed in the introduction to Part 7 below, "wherein does virtue consist?" Smith's approach here is to answer this question in a manner akin to Aristotle and Cicero and much admired by Smith (see 7.4).

2. See 1.3.1 (p. 133).

3. Eighteenth-century histories of philosophy tended to classify ancient philosophers as Stoic, Epicurean, Academic (Platonic), or Peripatetic (Aristotelian).

4. Machiavelli was at Borgia's court as a Florentinian ambassador at the time (January 1503) of the events here described; he alludes to them in *Prince* 7 and describes them more fully in his "Description of the Method Used by Duke Valentino in Killing Vitellozzo Vitelli, Oliverotto da Fermo, and Others."

PART VI, SECTION II

1. This and the following two chapters describe three successive and ever-widening spheres of connections with others, a movement closely related to the classical conception of *oikeiosis* as described by Cicero among others (e.g., *De finibus* 3.62–64 and *De officiis*

1.50–57); for helpful commentary, see the books and articles by Brown, Vivenza, Montes, and Forman-Barzilai.

2. See 3.3 above.

3. Smith's argument for domestic education over boarding schools parallels Locke's argument in *Some Thoughts Concerning Education* 69–70. Smith's related critique of the Grand Tour at *Wealth of Nations* 5.1.f similarly parallels Locke's arguments here and in *Education* 212–213.

4. See, e.g., Aulus Gellius 13.3; Burke also discussed the Roman ties of necessitudo in his *Thoughts on the Present Discontents* (1770).

5. Among the classic distinctions between friendships of utility and friendships of virtue that Smith is likely to have in mind here are Aristotle, *Nicomachean Ethics* 8.3–4; and Cicero, *De amicitia* 5–6 and *De officiis* 1.55–56.

6. See also Smith's critique of casuistry in 7.4 below.

7. Smith refers to Voltaire, *L'Orphelin de la Chine*.

8. See Plutarch, *Lives*, "Marcus Cato" 27; Appian, *Punic Wars* 69.

9. The transcendence of national prejudice and the appreciation of the mutual benefits of free trade is a key component of Smith's argument against mercantilism in *Wealth of Nations* 4.

10. See Cardinal de Retz, *Mémoires* (p. 372 in the modern Pléiade edition).

11. See Plato, *Crito* 51b–c, as cited by Cicero in *Epistulae ad Familiares* 1.9.18; see also Cicero, *De officiis* 1.85.

12. See Plutarch, *Lives*, "Solon" 15; Montesquieu, *Spirit of the Laws* 19.21; Rousseau, *Letter to d'Alembert*.

13. For the context of Smith's discussion of universal benevolence, see, e.g., Hutcheson, *Essay with Illustrations* 1.2.2; Kames, *Essays on Morality and Religion* 1.2.

14. The *Meditations* were particularly admired by Smith's teacher Hutcheson, who had them translated and published in Glasgow.

15. The accusation is reported in the *Scriptores Historiae Augustae* ("Life of Avidius Cassius" 14.5). Smith's caveat that the accusation has been brought "perhaps unjustly" is crucial; the *Meditations* consistently emphasize the superiority of activity to passivity and our obligations to mutual benevolence (see esp. 5.1, 9.16, 9.42, 11.21). In general, Smith's critique of Stoicism seems to follow Cicero's critique; see, e.g., *De finibus* 4.68 and *De officiis* 1.19.

PART VI, SECTION III

1. Among such "ancient moralists," see, e.g., Plato, who distinguishes the control of anger from the control of pleasure (e.g., *Republic* 4, 429a–432a), and Aristotle, who in treating the virtues of the irra-

tional parts of the soul treats courage and temperance separately (*Nicomachean Ethics* 3.6–11; 1115a5–1119a21); see also Smith's accounts at 7.2 below.

2. On the nobility and dazzling splendor of Socrates' death, see, e.g., Xenophon, *Memorabilia* 4.8. Among commentators in "succeeding ages," see, e.g., Helvétius's identification of Socrates' magnanimity with "love of glory" (*De l'esprit* 3.16).

3. Smith refers to Birch, *The heads of illustrious persons of Great Britain* (1743). Birch's book contains entries for More, Raleigh, and Russell, all executed for treason or conspiracy. Birch's first edition has an entry for Sidney Godolphin and his later second volume includes one for Sir Philip Sidney, but not one for Algernon Sidney, presumably meant here.

4. Buccaneer: "a cant word for the privateers, or pirates of America" (Johnson).

5. Smith examines and compares Demosthenes' and Cicero's speeches at length in *Rhetoric* 25–26.

6. See, e.g., the concluding assessment of Catherine's character in Davila, *History of the Civil Wars in France* 9; Clarendon, *History of the Rebellion* 4.127–28; and Locke, "Memoirs relating to the life of Anthony, first Earl of Shaftesbury." All three of Smith's examples concern studies of principal figures in civil wars written by direct dependents.

7. See Cicero, *De officiis* 1.108–113. Contra Smith, these are less praises than reports; when Cicero speaks in his own name about these figures, his judgments are more critical (see 3.49, 3.73–75, 3.97–99).

8. The story here recounted received wide distribution in the eighteenth century through its inclusion in Abbé Raynal's *Anecdotes litteraires* (1750). But Smith likely knew it from the first volume of the 1729 edition of Despréaux's collected works, which he owned as part of his library. There it is to be found in a footnote glossing Satire II, "To Molière," lines 93–94 (which might be translated: "And always unhappy with what he had done, / He pleased the whole world, all except for one").

9. Alexander's belief in his divine lineage and his desire for divine recognition are prominent themes in the classic historical accounts; his attempt to secure his mother's apotheosis is mentioned only in Quintus Curtius Rufus 9.6.26 and 10.5.30.

10. On Socrates' *daimon*, see, e.g., Plato, *Apology* 31c–d; *Phaedrus* 242c; and Xenophon, *Memorabilia* 1.1.4; on the oracle's pronouncement and Socrates' response, see *Apology* 21a–23b.

11. See Suetonius 1.78.

12. With Cicero, Cato the Younger was a leading member of the *optimates*, who opposed the often unprincipled and demagogic *populares* with whom both Catiline and Caesar were aligned; Smith describes both parties in his rhetoric lectures (*Rhetoric* 2.155–161).

13. Parmenides' dates make it unlikely that he could have met Plato. A similar story is told in Cicero, *Brutus* 191, substituting Antimachus for Parmenides.

14. The original source for the first quote is Plutarch; for the second, Athenaeus. But both stories also appear in eighteenth-century sources on which Smith may have drawn; e.g., Thomas Leland, *The History of the Life and Reign of Philip King of Macedon* (London, 1758), vol. 2, p. 47. The story of Parmenio's execution is told in Quintus Curtius Rufus 7.2.11–33 (which also includes the account of Alexander's reliance on him); and Plutarch, *Lives*, "Alexander" 49.

15. See Clarendon, *History of the Rebellion in England* (1720–21), vol. 1, p. 55.

16. levee: "the concourse of those who crowd round a man of power in a morning" (Johnson).

17. See Aristotle, *Nicomachean Ethics* 4.3; 1124b6–9 and 1125a12–16.

18. Shakespeare, *Hamlet*, Act 1, Scene 5 (l. 76–79).

19. Smith again likely has Locke in mind, who likewise identifies as "the great secret of education" the utilization of the love of esteem to assist in the cultivation of virtue; see *Some Thoughts Concerning Education*, sec. 56–58, as well as Rousseau's discussion of "*le grand secret de l'education*" in *Emile* 4.

PART VII, SECTION I

1. On these conceptions of virtue, see 7.2.1–3 (p. 318).

2. Smith treats these conceptions of moral judgment in 7.3.1–3 (p. 318).

PART VII, SECTION II

1. Part 6, "Of the Character of Virtue," presumably provides Smith's own position on the question addressed in this paragraph.

2. Smith restricts his study of Plato's conception of virtue to *Republic*. For the analogy between the parts of the city and the parts of the soul, see esp. *Republic* 368c–369b, 434d–436b.

3. On reason as the governing principle of the city, see *Republic* 428a–429a; as governing principle of the individual, see *Republic* 442c.

4. On the objects and ends of the first class (spirit, or *thymos*) see, e.g., *Republic* 548c–550b; on those of the second (appetite, or *epithymia*) see, e.g., *Republic* 558c–561d; on the relationship between these, see *Republic* 439d–440e. On the Scholastic distinction

between the "irascible" and the "concupiscible," see, e.g., Aquinas, *Summa Theologiae*, First Part of the Second Part, Question 23.

5. See, e.g., *Republic* 442c, 579b–582e, which treat the cardinal virtue of wisdom (*sophia*), rather than prudence properly speaking (*phronesis*).

6. See, e.g., *Republic* 429a–430a, 442c, which treat the cardinal virtue of courage (*andreia*) rather than magnanimity properly speaking (*megalopsychia*), a term that does not seem to have been much used by Plato. Here and in his discussion of prudence Smith imports terms more associated with Aristotle. On the anger we feel toward ourselves upon succumbing to pleasure, see, e.g., *Republic* 439e.

7. See, e.g., *Republic* 430e–432b, which calls attention to the harmony afforded by the cardinal virtue of moderation (*sophrosyne*).

8. See, e.g., *Republic* 432b–434d, 442d–443e, which treat the virtue of justice (*dikaiosyne*). The view that Plato's conception of justice replicates Pythagorean views on justice as a form of harmony or proportion has been argued from Smith's day to our own; see, e.g., the history of ancient philosophy prefaced to the third volume of Monboddo's *Ancient Metaphysics* (London and Edinburgh, 1784), xxxii–xxxiii.

9. See 2.2.1 (p. 95).

10. For Grotius's distinction, see *Rights of War and Peace* 1.1.8. The distinction between Grotius and Aristotle is elaborated in a manner that anticipates Smith's note in Pufendorf, *Law of Nature and Nations* 1.7.9–12.

11. See esp. *Republic* 444d–e.

12. Smith's précis of Aristotle's definition of virtue emphasizes Aristotle's account of habituation (see *Nicomachean Ethics* 2.1–5, 1103a14–1106a13) and of the mean (see *Nicomachean Ethics* 2.6, 1106a14–1107a27), and perhaps underemphasizes the place of choice and deliberation.

13. On courage (*andreia*) as a mean, see *Nicomachean Ethics* 3.7 (1115b6–1116a15); on magnanimity (*megalopsychia*) as a mean, see *Nicomachean Ethics* 4.3 (1125a17–33). Smith's account of the "frugality" as the virtue pertaining to pursuit of objects of self-interest seems a combination of Aristotle's accounts of temperance (*sophrosyne*), the virtue concerning the pursuit of bodily pleasure (see *Nicomachean Ethics* 3.11, 1118b8–1119a20), and generosity (*eleutheria*), the virtue concerning proper use of wealth (see *Nicomachean Ethics* 4.2, 1120b28–1121a10).

14. See, e.g., *Nicomachean Ethics* 1.7, 1097b34–1098a20.

15. Smith here cites the *Magna Moralia*, whose attribution to Aristotle is now largely thought spurious. *Magna Moralia* 1.1, 1182a15–23

argues that Socrates overlooked the place of the irrational; 1183b9–18 argues more explicitly that the Socratic science of virtue overlooks activity. See also Aristotle's response to Socrates in *Nicomachean Ethics* 7.2, 1145b22–1146a8, as well as Smith's own insistence in 2.3 that "Man was made for action."

16. None of Zeno's writings have survived; Smith accordingly relies on the accounts of Zeno given in Cicero, *De finibus* 3 and Diogenes Laertius 7.

17. See, e.g., Cicero, *De finibus* 3.16, 3.59; Diogenes Laertius 7.85.

18. Cicero and Diogenes present Zeno and the Stoics as distinguishing the absolute good of moral worth—*to kalon* in Greek or *honestum* in Latin—from the lower class of objects (including health, wealth, and reputation) whose possession is preferable and whose opposites (including sickness, poverty, and ignominy) are undesirable, but which appear insignificant or indifferent when compared to virtue. See, e.g., Cicero, *De finibus* 3.10–11, 3.20–21, 3.43–46, 3.48–51, 3.56; and Diogenes Laertius 7.102, 7.106, 7.108.

19. For the Stoic understanding of propriety in choosing and rejecting and its relationship to living according to nature, see, e.g., Cicero, *De finibus* 2.34, 3.20, 3.26, 3.31, 4.15; Diogenes Laertius 7.87. The idea of "living according to nature" is esp. prominent in Marcus Aurelius (e.g., *Meditations* 1.17, 3.12, 5.3–4, 7.55–59, 10.15; see also Epictetus, *Discourses* 1.26.1–2) and central to the Scottish Enlightenment; see, e.g., Hutcheson, *Essay with Illustrations* 1.6.7; Kames, *Essays on Morality and Religion* 1.2.1.

20. The relationship of the doctrines of the Stoics to those of the Peripatetics is a principal concern of Cicero; see, e.g., *De finibus* 3.41.

21. On the "primary objects" recommended by nature, see Smith's note at 7.2.2 (p. 346) and the accompanying editor's note.

22. For the Stoic conception of providence and its direction of the universe, see, e.g., Epictetus, *Discourses* 1.6, 1.14, 1.16; Marcus Aurelius, *Meditations* 2.3, 6.36–39, 7.9.

23. See Epictetus, *Discourses* 2.5.24–26.

24. This and the three following paragraphs are a heavily revised version of Smith's treatment of Stoicism in Part 1 in editions prior to the sixth edition of 1790.

25. Smith here likely has in mind the line from the 1st c. AD Roman philosopher Demetrius the Cynic, as reported by his friend the Stoic philosopher Seneca, in *De providentia* 5.5.

26. See Epictetus, *Discourses* 2.5.10–14. On the individual's obligation to understand himself as part of the whole, see esp. Marcus Aurelius, *Meditations* 2.4, 2.9, 7.13, 8.34, 11.8.

27. In addition to the passage cited above, see also Epictetus, *Dis-

courses 1.25.1, 2.2.15–20, 2.5.1–5. For Smith's own very different view, see 2.3 (p. 111).

28. For the Stoic conception of gratitude for our enemies and our challenges, see, e.g., Seneca, *De providentia* 3.1–4, 4.4–8.

29. The remainder of this section was an addition to the sixth edition of 1790.

30. For the Stoic metaphor on life as a game, see, e.g., Epictetus, *Discourses* 2.5.15–17.

31. See Epictetus, *Discourses* 1.25.18–21.

32. The Stoics have long been understood as advocates of suicide. For more moderate views of the Stoic conception, see, e.g., Cicero, *De finibus* 3.60–61; Diogenes Laertius 7.130.

33. See Epictetus, *Discourses* 1.25.14–17.

34. See Cicero, *De finibus* 3.60.

35. For the Stoic views on bearing misfortune with constancy, see, e.g., Seneca, *De constantia sapientis* passim. On their indifference to death, see, e.g., Marcus Aurelius, *Meditations* 2.17, 9.3; Seneca, *De tranquillitate animi* 11. On the modern systems, see also 3.3 (p. 156).

36. Milton, *Paradise Lost* 2.568–569.

37. See Plutarch, *Lives*, "Cleomenes" 37 and Polybius 5.39.

38. Of the Messian hero Aristomenes, to whom Smith presumably refers, there is no story of suicide. Smith may have confused him with the Aristomenes who attempts suicide in Apuleius's *Metamorphoses* (1.16), or Aristodemus, a Messian hero of the previous century, who is reported to have committed suicide (Pausanias 4.13.4).

39. Ancient accounts of his suicide include Aristophanes, *Knights* 83–84; Plutarch, *Lives*, "Themistocles" 31; Diodorus Siculus 11.58; the story is rejected in Thucydides 1.138; Cornelius Nepos, "Themistocles" and Cicero, *Brutus* 42–43.

40. On Theramenes' death, see Diodorus Siculus 14.4–5; Cicero, *Tusculan Disputations* 1.40. On Phocion's death, see Plutarch, *Lives*, "Phocion" 34–37; Diodorus Siculus, 18.66–67. On Socrates', see note above.

41. The betrayal to which Smith refers happened after the battle of Gabiene (316 BC). On Eumenes' death, see Plutarch, *Lives*, "Eumenes" 17–19; Diodorus Siculus 19.43–44.

42. See Plutarch, *Lives*, "Philopoemen" 18–20; Livy 39.49–50; Pausanias 8.51.5–7.

43. Several stories of the suicides of various Greek philosophers are told or alluded to in Diogenes Laertius; see, e.g., 2.120, 2.144, 4.3, 6.76–77, 6.95, 6.100, 7.167, 8.40, 10.15–16.

44. All three accounts are in Diogenes Laertius 7.28–31; Diogenes himself accepts the first, as Smith notes below. The story of Niobe, whose children were killed by Apollo in retaliation for her pride in her fertility, was first told by Homer (*Iliad* 24) and then by Aeschylus and Sophocles (in lost works), but not Euripides.

45. Persaeus's ostensible slavery is reported in Aulus Gellius 2.18.

46. Augustus Caesar ruled 27 BC–AD 14; Zeno died c. 263 BC. On the Apollonius to whom Smith here refers, see Diogenes Laertius 7.6, 24, 28.

47. Zeno's death is noted in Lucian, *Long Lives* 19 (now thought spurious); and Lactantius, *Divine Institutes* 3.18.

48. See, e.g., Cicero, *De officiis* 3.99–111; Cicero, *De finibus* 2.65; Seneca, *De providentia* 3.9–11; Aulus Gellius 7.4; Augustine, *City of God* 1.15.

49. On the death of Cato, see also the note on Sallust above. Cicero's posthumous praises in his *Cato* in 46 BC were challenged in Caesar's much longer (though now largely lost) *Anticato*.

50. Smith's reference is untraced.

51. See Seneca, *De tranquillitate animi* 17.9.

52. Pliny frequently describes suicides and attempted suicides (see, e.g., 1.12, 3.7, 3.9, 3.16, 6.24), and himself sets down a rule for distinguishing noble from cowardly suicides (1.22).

53. The question of suicide's legitimacy was reopened in part by Hume's posthumous 1777 publication of his essay "Of Suicide" which sought to marshal "the sentiments of all the ancient philosophers" (though it only explicitly mentions Seneca, Tacitus, and Pliny) to defend a view of suicide as not blameworthy.

54. Smith's recognition of two distinct strains within Roman Stoicism— one emphasizing self-command, and the other benevolence— distinguishes his view from, e.g., Gataker ("Maxims of the Stoics") or Hume ("The Stoic"), who share Smith's emphases on providentialism and benevolence but emphasize self-command to a lesser degree. Some of the tensions in Smith's conception of Stoicism are traceable in part to his differentiation of these strains.

55. The slave is Epictetus. Domitian (AD 51–96), Roman Emperor from 81 to his death, banished the philosophers from Italy in 89, only eighteen years after Vespasian had banished philosophers from Rome (including Demetrius; see note above).

56. On the beauties of the ordinary, see esp. Marcus Aurelius, *Meditations* 3.2; on death and old age, see *Meditations* 9.3.

57. On the physician's prescriptions, see Marcus Aurelius, *Meditations* 5.8; on the loss of children, see *Meditations* 11.34, 12.26.

58. See Marcus Aurelius, *Meditations* 4.23.

59. Smith's critique of the Stoic paradoxes continues a line of critique dating back to antiquity; among others, see esp. Cicero's "Paradoxes of the Stoics" and *De finibus* 4.74–76.

60. Pope, *Essay on Man* 1.90.

61. Plutarch notes the utility of the wise man's stretching of his finger in his essay "Of Common Conceptions, Against the Stoics" 22; he also uses the example of finger-stretching to criticize Chrysippus in "Contradictions of the Stoics" 26; see also Cicero, *De finibus* 3.57.

62. The metaphor is frequently employed; see Cicero, *De finibus* 3.48, 4.64; cf. Diogenes Laertius 7.120, 7.127; Plutarch, "Of Common Conceptions, Against the Stoics" 10.

63. Smith's critical judgment is anticipated in Plutarch and Cicero and especially Diogenes Laertius 7.187–89.

64. Smith refers to Cicero's *De officiis*. Brutus is reported by Seneca (*Epistles* 95) to have written a lost work on propriety (*peri kathekontos*), but Smith may also have in mind the reference by Cicero (*De finibus* 1.8) to Brutus's now-lost work on virtue (*De virtute*). For Smith's own embrace of the distinction here drawn between "perfect virtue" and mere "proprieties" see 1.1.5 (p. 30).

65. Smith's account might be compared to Diogenes' account of the Stoic conception of the ends of life, which emphasizes the insufficiencies of both the life devoted strictly to contemplation and the life devoted strictly to practical activity, preferring instead a life that makes room for both contemplation and action in accord with our rational nature (7.130). See also Cicero's critique of Stoicism for focusing on the mind and ignoring the goods of the body pursued prudentially (*De finibus* 4.35–42). See also 6.2.3 (p. 276) and accompanying notes.

66. On the Stoic doctrine of *apatheia*, or freedom from passion, see, e.g., Cicero, *De finibus* 3.35; Diogenes Laertius 7.117.

67. See Clarke, *Discourse Concerning Natural Religion* Proposition 1; Wollaston, *Religion of Nature Delineated* 1.4, 4.7; and Shaftesbury, *Inquiry Concerning Virtue* 2.2.1 (under the marginal heading "Balance of the Affections"). Smith's précis here may be shaped by the more extensive précis of the same thinkers given by Hutcheson (see *Essay with Illustrations* 2.2–3, 5); Kames (*Essays on Morality and Religion* 1.2.9, which treated only Clarke and Wollaston in the editions prior to the first edition of *TMS*, adding Hutcheson, Hume, Rousseau and Smith himself in the third edition of 1779); and Hume (*Treatise* 3.1.1.4).

68. The allegation that Epicurus borrowed his metaphysics from Democritus and his ethics from Aristippus is reported in Diogenes Laertius 10.4; see also Cicero, *De finibus* 1.17, 1.23, 1.26.

69. None of Epicurus's works have survived aside from the three letters and the collection of maxims published by Diogenes; hence Smith's reliance again on Diogenes' and Cicero's accounts. For a glimpse into how Epicurus was regarded in the Scottish Enlightenment, see, e.g., the speech that Hume contrives for "Epicurus" in *Enquiry Concerning Understanding* 11.9–23; and his essay "The Epicurean."

70. On pleasure as the ultimate good and the occasional necessity of abstaining from present pleasures and withstanding present pains for greater future pleasures, see, e.g. Cicero, *De finibus* 1.23, 1.29, 1.32–33; Diogenes Laertius 10.34, 10.128–129.

71. Diogenes Laertius 10.124–125, 10.139.

72. On tranquility as absence of pain and the proper end of life, see Cicero, *De finibus* 1.37–41; Diogenes Laertius 10.128, 10.131. Epicurus in a related vein argues that natural philosophy is chiefly valuable for its alleviation of anxiety (Cicero, *De finibus* 1.63; Diogenes Laertius 10.79–85, 10.142); compare to Smith's account of the motives for scientific inquiry in *Astronomy*.

73. On the instrumentality of virtue, see Cicero, *De finibus* 2.73; Diogenes Laertius 10.150–151. On the instrumentality of the individual cardinal virtues, see Cicero, *De finibus* 1.48–53; Diogenes 10.144.

74. See Diogenes Laertius 10.132.

75. See, e.g., Cicero, *De finibus* 2.80; Diogenes Laertius 10.9–10.

76. In accusing Epicurus of accounting only for external goods and being indifferent to moral worth, Smith anticipates his critique of Mandeville (see note below), reiterates his own commitment to the supreme value of praiseworthiness (see notes above), and echoes Cicero's allegation that Epicurus fails to account for our commitment to genuine moral worthiness (*honestum*); see *De finibus* 2.44–50.

77. phasis: "appearance exhibited by any body; as the changes of the moon" (Johnson).

78. A free rendering of Xenophon, *Memorabilia* 1.7; Smith's quotation marks seem to indicate this as a speech of Socrates rather than a direct transcription of the source text. See also Cicero's similar discussion of "true glory" in *De officiis* 2.43.

79. On Epicurus's metaphysical doctrines and their debts to atomism, see, e.g., Diogenes Laertius 10.39f.

80. Hutcheson and Hume had both previously criticized self-love theorists on similar grounds; see, e.g., Hutcheson, *Essay with Illustrations* 1. Preface, and Hume, *Enquiry Concerning Morals* App. 2.6. Elsewhere Smith describes the utility of such an approach in natural philosophy; see, e.g., *History of Astronomy* 2.12.

81. Literally "the things primary by nature." In Stoicism these included the necessaries of the body essential to preservation and physical

well-being, but rigorously distinguished these from that which was in itself genuinely good or honorable (*honestum*); see, e.g., Cicero, *De finibus* 3.21.

82. See Smith's similarly worded account given in his own name in the closing paragraphs of 2.3.3 (p. 103).

83. Smith here refers to the school of Alexandrian thinkers from Potamon to Iamblichus who flourished between the reign of Augustus and the fall of Rome, were united in receptivity to Platonism and hostility to Epicureanism, and were often receptive to Christianity. Smith's likely sources include Diderot's essay "*Eclectisme*" in the *Encyclopédie* (which emphasizes efforts to imitate God through contemplation, and the wise man's duty to promote the well-being of others); Part II, Chapter 1 of the study of the 2nd c. AD in Mosheim, *Ecclesiastical History* (1726) (which especially emphasizes that the aim of Eclecticism is direct communication with God); and Hutcheson's comment on the Eclectics at the conclusion of his "Dissertation on the Origin of Philosophy" (1756).

84. Together the "Cambridge Platonists," collectively united by a suspicion of the materialist metaphysics of Descartes, Spinoza, and Hobbes, and a commitment to reconciling Platonic reason with Christian revelation. For their teachings on divine love, see, e.g., More, *An Essay on Disinterested Love* (Glasgow, 1756); and John Smith, *Select Discourses* 5.2–4.

85. On the double sympathy that recommends benevolence and its amiable weaknesses, see esp. 1.2.4 (p. 48).

86. Hutcheson's discussions of benevolence include *Inquiry into Beauty and Virtue* 2.2–3, on which several of Smith's discrete observations that follow depend.

87. Here and below Smith regards Hutcheson as a hard-line moral rigorist. As Smith notes, Hutcheson in various places suggests that self-interested motives can lessen moral merit; see, e.g., *Inquiry into Beauty and Virtue* 2.2.3; *Short Introduction* 2.3.6; and *System* 2.2.1. But elsewhere, Hutcheson's views are somewhat more moderate; see, e.g., *Inquiry into Beauty and Virtue* 2.3.5 (which presents the view of self-love as "indifferent" to which Smith refers) and *Essay with Illustrations* 2.4, as well as his discussions of the "sense of honor" (*Short Introduction* 1.1.13 and 1.2.8; and *System* 1.2.6 and 1.5).

88. On public good as a universal standard, see, e.g., *Inquiry into Beauty and Virtue* 2.3.3, in which Hutcheson references the "late debates about passive obedience, and the right of resistance" instigated by Berkeley's *Passive Obedience* (1712); see also Hume's intervention in "Of Passive Obedience."

89. For Hutcheson's equations of virtue with degrees of benevolence,

see *Inquiry into Beauty and Virtue* 2.3.8; *Short Introduction* 1.1.11, 1.3.1; *System* 1.4.10.

90. The similarity between this locution and Smith's use of the phrase "one of the multitude" on three occasions in *TMS* (2.2.2 and note above) suggests the influence of Hutcheson.

91. Smith's references are to *Inquiry into Beauty and Virtue* 2.2.4 and *Essay with Illustrations* 2.5. But Hutcheson's own claim seems rather to be that self-approbation presumes a natural regard for the happiness of others; see, e.g., *Essay with Illustrations* 1.1.3, 1.4.5, 2.1.

92. Hutcheson is not entirely silent on these (see, e.g., *Short Introduction* 1.3.3, 1.6.3, 1.7.2, 3.8.2–3), but Smith is right to suggest that Hutcheson's focus is on their utility or effects.

93. Smith here repeats his claim concerning Hume's four sources of virtue from 4.2 above. For Hume's "definition of virtue," see esp. *Enquiry Concerning Morals* 8n and 9.12; for the specific claim that moderation renders affections useful, see *Enquiry Concerning Morals* 6.2.

94. On the Epicurean view of the utility of virtue, see, e.g., Cicero, *De finibus* 1.42–54.

95. Earlier editions also mentioned La Rochefoucauld as another example of a "licentious system," but Smith withdrew his references after an objection from a descendent of La Rochefoucauld.

96. Smith's treatment here is anticipated in his 1756 letter to the *Edinburgh Review*, which described "the principles and ideas of the profligate Mandeville" as agents of "corruption and licentiousness" that were in turn "softened, improved, and embellished" by Rousseau.

97. For representative statements of Mandeville's views on the naturalness of self-preference, see "An Enquiry into the Origin of Moral Virtue," in Kaye's edition of the *Fable*, vol. 1, p. 41; and *Enquiry into the Origin of Honour* (London, 1732), 39. On vanity and the love of praise as motives of human action, see "Enquiry," 54–55; *Fable*, Remarks C, M, and R; and *Enquiry into the Origin of Honor*, 5–7.

98. A paraphrase of Mandeville's claim at "Enquiry," p. 51.

99. In emphasizing here against Mandeville "the honourable and noble," Smith likely has in mind not only the classical conceptions of *to kalon* and the *honestum* as described by Aristotle and Cicero (see note to 3.3 above), but also eighteenth-century attempts to recover these categories against champions of psychological egoism; see, e.g., Shaftesbury, *Characteristicks* Miscellany 3, Chapter 2, note; Berkeley, *Alciphron* 3; Hutcheson, *Short Introduction* 1.1.10 and his inaugural oration at the University of Glasgow, "On the Natural Sociability of Mankind"; cf. Mandeville "A Search into the Nature of Society," in *Fable*, vol. 1, pp. 323–326.

100. Smith's differentiation here of three distinct orientations to praise—
"vanity" (the indiscriminate love of praise), "the love of true glory"
(the desire to deserve and to claim praises), and "the love of virtue"
(the desire of becoming what is honorable and noble, whether rec-
ognized and praised or not) is a crucial element of his argument in
the sixth edition; see, e.g., Smith's restatement of these three levels
in his discussion of praiseworthiness in 3.2 (p. 136).

101. For Mandeville's rigorist views on luxury, see the opening of
Remark L of the *Fable*; on lust, see *Fable*, Remark N.

102. For representative statements of Mandeville's rigorist association
of virtue with self-denial, see, e.g., *Fable*, Remark O; and "Search
into the Nature of Society," p. 331; for his claim that "the generous Notions concerning the natural Goodness of Man are hurtful
as they tend to mis-lead, and are merely Chimerical," see, e.g.,
"Search into the Nature of Society," pp. 343, 365, 369; and *Fable*,
Remarks V, X, and Y.

103. See Descartes, *Principia philosophiae* 3. Smith elaborates on the
theory of vortices in *Astronomy* 4.61–66.

PART VII, CHAPTER III

1. Smith's account of the sources of approbation speaks to a key controversy in contemporary British moral philosophy; both Hutcheson
(see *Essay with Illustrations* 2. Preface) and Hume (see *Treatise*
3.1.1 and *Enquiry Concerning Morals* 1.3–10, App. 1) take the
grounds of approbation as their point of departure. Yet while this
remains the primary question for Hume, Smith calls it, in the paragraph above, "the next question of importance in Moral Philosophy." Hutcheson and Hume had an interchange over whether the
primary purpose of moral philosophy was the practical teaching of
virtue or the speculative inquiry into the origin of moral principles.
In a letter to Hutcheson (17 September 1739), Hume suggests that
Hutcheson identified with the former aim where Hume sides with
the latter—positions borne out in their published works (compare,
e.g., Hutcheson, *Short Introduction* Preface; and Hume, *Enquiry
Concerning Understanding* 1). Smith's identification of the question "wherein does virtue consist" as his primary question raises
the question of whether he sides with Hutcheson's rather than
Hume's understanding of the purpose of moral philosophy. Smith
treats Hutcheson and Hume below at 7.3.3 as representatives of the
sentiment view; the self-love view (Hobbes, et.al.) is treated at 7.3.1
and the reason view (esp. Cudworth) at 7.3.2.

2. To call Pufendorf a "follower" of Hobbes is misleading; more

accurate is Smith's claim at *Jurisprudence* B 3 that Pufendorf wrote partly to "confute Hobbes"; see also notes below.

3. For Hobbes's conception of the absence of natural sociability and the instrumental value of civil society, see, e.g., *De cive* 1.2; in a related vein, see Mandeville, "Search into the Nature of Society," pp. 344, 346. Other natural law theorists were considerably more optimistic about the possibility of natural sociability coexisting with self-love; see, e.g., Grotius, *Rights of War and Peace* Preliminary Discourse 6–8; Pufendorf, *Law of Nature and Nations* 2.3.14–16, 7.1.2–3; and esp. Hutcheson, *System* 1.2.11, 3.4 and "Natural Sociability of Mankind." Pufendorf particularly emphasizes how man's natural weakness renders him dependent upon the assistance of others and renders civil society necessary (see, e.g., *Duty of Man and Citizen* 1.3.3, 2.1.4, 2.1.9–10, 2.5; *Law of Nature and Nations* 7.1.7).

4. See 4.1 (p. 209).

5. In accord with the first line of the previous paragraph Smith here seems to delineate a second strain, distinct from Hobbes and his followers, of thinkers who account for approbation from self-love. His reference in the middle of the present paragraph to the discussion of beauty as utility in 4 may suggest that among the thinkers who celebrate the advantages of civilized over savage life that he has in mind is Hume (see esp. *Treatise* 3.2.1–2); see also Kames, *Essays on Morality and Religion* 1.2.1 and 1.2.8.

6. For the debate on the question of whether self-interest shapes our approbation of the characters of "distant ages," see, e.g., Hutcheson, *Inquiry into Beauty and Virtue* 2.1.2–4 and *Essay with Illustrations* 2. Preface; and Hume, *Enquiry Concerning Morals* 5.7–15.

7. On the state of nature as a state of war, see *De cive* 1.12, 5.2; *Leviathan* 13.8; and responses in Pufendorf, *Law of Nature and Nations* 2.2.6–9; Locke, *Essay Concerning Civil Government* 19; and Rousseau, *Discourse on Inequality* 1.

8. On the preeminence of self-preservation in our moral psychology, see, e.g., Hobbes, *De cive* 1.14; Pufendorf, *Duty of Man and Citizen* 1.3.2. On the necessity of obedience, see, e.g., *De cive* 5.7, 11, 6.13; *Leviathan* 17. For Hobbes's positivist conception that justice is the product of law, see, e.g., *De cive* 1.10, 15.17 and *Leviathan* 6.6, 13.12, 15.3; see also Locke, *Essay Concerning Human Understanding* 2.28.5, 2.28.10–11; and Hume, *Treatise* 3.2.8.4.

9. Smith describes Hobbes's aims similarly at *Jurisprudence* B 2, which explicitly mentions his argument that the origin of the Civil Wars lay in the conflict of ecclesiastical and civil powers. In both instances Smith likely has in mind the analysis of the dangers

posed by "two kingdoms in one and the same nation" and the claim that the "virtue of a subject is comprehended solely in obedience to the laws of the commonwealth" as developed in Part 1 of Hobbes's *Behemoth*. On the unification of these two kingdoms, see *De cive* 18.13; *Leviathan* 43.22.

10. Cudworth dedicated the first book of his *Treatise Concerning Eternal and Immutable Morality* to critique of ancient (esp. Epicurean) and modern (esp. Hobbesian) systems of positivism; see 1.1.3–4. For his critique of the materialist metaphysics underlying Hobbesian positivism, see 2.3–4, 4.3.15, 4.6.4–5.

11. For Cudworth's arguments that value exists antecedent to law and resides particularly in the nature of the internal operations of the mind, see, e.g., *Immutable Morality*, 1.2.3–4, 4.6.12.

12. See esp. Hutcheson, *Essay with Illustrations* 2.1.

13. Smith principally has Hutcheson in mind here, as the remainder of this chapter makes clear. Other authors well known to Smith also influential in the debates over moral sense include Shaftesbury, *Inquiry Concerning Virtue* 1.3.1–3; Hume, *Treatise* 3.1.2; and Kames, *Essays on Morality and Religion* 1.2.2.

14. Smith has Hume particularly in mind here, as the last paragraph of this chapter makes clear. For Hume's comparison of moral sense systems with those founded on sympathy, see esp. *Treatise* 3.3.6.3.

15. For Hutcheson's conception of approbation as not founded on self-love, see, e.g., *Inquiry into Beauty and Virtue* 2.1.4–5; for his conception of approbation as not founded on reason, see, e.g., *Essay with Illustrations* 2.1.

16. For Hutcheson's comparisons of the external and internal senses, see, e.g., *Inquiry into Beauty and Virtue* 1.10–11; and *Short Introduction* 1.1.3–4.

17. In referring here to the "Treatise of the Passions," Smith may have in mind Hutcheson's brief discussion of reflection in the Preface to the *Essay with Illustrations* (esp. in the 1742 edition, which names Locke explicitly). Hutcheson's distinction between the direct and the reflex senses is more fully drawn in his *Synopsis of Metaphysics* 2.1.3 and *Short Introduction* 1.1.3–4. Locke's distinction between sensation and reflection is drawn in his *Essay Concerning Human Understanding* 2.1.4 and 2.6.1–2.

18. For Hutcheson's conception of the moral sense as harmonious with the analogy of nature, see *System* 1.4.4; for an overview of the various senses, see *Essay with Illustrations* 1.1.

19. Smith's reference is to *Essay with Illustrations* 2.1, under the marginal heading "Objections from our judging even of our Affections and Senses themselves."

20. Johnson's definitions reiterate the wide scope emphasized by Smith; thus approbation is "the liking of any thing," and conscience, "the knowledge or faculty by which we judge of the goodness or wickedness of ourselves."

21. For Smith's account of Hume, see 4.1–2 above; on sympathy in this context, see *Treatise* 3.3.1–2; and Kames, *Essays on Morality and Religion* 1.1.

PART VII, SECTION IV

1. For their catalogues of the ethical virtues, see Aristotle, *Nicomachean Ethics* 3.6–5.11; Cicero, *De officiis* 1.18–151.

2. Casuistry is a form of moral reasoning that seeks to articulate comprehensive standards of judgment universally applicable to all discrete cases; see also Smith's critique at *Wealth of Nations* 5.1.f.

3. highwayman: "a robber that plunders on the public roads" (Johnson).

4. See note below.

5. On the debate over the promise owed to the highwayman, see esp. Pufendorf, *Law of Nature and Nations* 3.6.10–13, which cites in support of its position Cicero, *De officiis* 3.107–109 (itself part of the discussion of Regulus, cited above); and Hutcheson, *Short Introduction* 2.9.8–9.

6. Among the "eminent modern casuists" that Smith likely has in mind are two cited by Pufendorf: Grotius, *Rights of War and Peace* 2.11.7; and Hobbes, *De cive* 2.16 and *Leviathan* 14.19–20. Smith's footnote suggests he may also have in mind Augustine, *Letters* 125; and La Placette, *Traité de la conscience* (trans. 1705 as *The Christian Casuist: Or, a Treatise on Conscience*), 1.18.

7. punctilio: "a small nicety of behaviour; a nice point of exactness" (Johnson).

8. parole: "word given as an assurance" (Johnson).

9. rencounter: "loose or casual engagement" or "sudden combat without premeditation" (Johnson).

10. This and the following four paragraphs were additions to the sixth edition of 1790.

11. The first five sentences of this paragraph and the whole of the next three paragraphs were additions to the sixth edition of 1790.

12. piacular: "such as requires expiation" or "criminal; atrociously bad" (Johnson).

13. Smith's division of moral philosophy into ethics and natural jurisprudence does important work in his system though was itself common; see, e.g., Hutcheson, *Short Introduction* Preface.

14. Cicero's inquiry of the relationship of the right to the expedient

concludes with his pronouncements on a series of practical examples; see, e.g., *De officiis* 3.89–116, which also encompasses the discussion of promise-keeping referenced by Smith above.

15. Cicero describes justice in terms of obligation and benefit in *De officiis* 1.20–41 and 3.40–49; Aristotle describes justice as a mean in *Nicomachean Ethics* 5.

16. Smith further develops this distinction in *Jurisprudence* A 1.1–4 and 6.1–2 and B 5 and 203.

17. Smith has in mind *Rights of War and Peace*, whose point of departure is the insufficiency of the attempts of Aristotle to define justice in terms of a mean; see his Preliminary Discourse 43–45.

CONSIDERATIONS

1. The *Considerations* was first published in 1761 in *The Philological Miscellany*, a London periodical. Smith subsequently instructed his publisher to append it to *TMS*. Its first appearance in *TMS* came in the third edition of 1767, and it was included in all following editions of *TMS* published in Smith's lifetime, including the sixth edition of 1790, whose version is reprinted here. Despite Smith's solicitude for the piece, it has rarely been reprinted in modern editions of *TMS*, and has only recently begun to garner the scholarly attention it deserves; helpful treatments include Christopher Berry in *Journal of the History of Ideas* 35 (1974); James Otteson in *Smith's Marketplace of Life*, ch. 7; and Marcelo Dascal in *Cambridge Companion to Smith*, ch. 3.

2. Smith's essay is an intervention in an eighteenth-century debate over the origin of languages; central participants included Condillac (*Essay on the Origin of Human Knowledge*, 1746); Rousseau (*Discourse on Inequality*, 1755; and *Essay on the Origin of Languages*, published posthumously); and Monboddo (*Of the Origin and Progress of Languages*, 1773). Smith's own treatment focuses as much on the progress and development of language and its relationship to the progress of the mind as on language's origin, as has been noted (see esp. Dascal's comparison of Smith to Condillac in the *Cambridge Companion*, pp. 84–85). Smith's treatment here is also in keeping with his focus elsewhere on the stages and conditions of social development (see e.g. *Jurisprudence* A 1.27-35 and 5.2 above).

3. Smith's reference is presumably to vol. 1 of the two-volume 1760 "Amsterdam" edition of Rousseau's works; pp. 376–77 thus refer to what is in modern editions paragraph 29–30 of Part 1 of the *Discourse on Inequality*. Throughout the *Considerations* Smith engages several of the claims Rousseau sets forth in *Discourse on*

Inequality 1.25-32 and notes 13–14, and particularly Rousseau's claims regarding "abstraction" and "metaphysics."

4. In a contemporary letter (to George Baird, 7 February 1763), Smith volunteered that he was indebted to two works for his principal "instruction" in and "entertainment" on grammatical topics: Abbé Girard, *The True Principles of the French Language* (1747), and the grammatical articles of the *Encyclopédie* (of which vols. 1-7 had appeared between 1751 and 1757; the remaining vols. 8-17 were not published until 1765). Each work's prominently advertised aspirations to provide "systematic" treatments of its topics (see esp. Girard's "Preface") would likely have appealed to Smith, and their treatments of several topics, including the parts of speech, are likely to have been in his mind during the composition of this opening section of the *Considerations*. The tree example is likely drawn from Rousseau, *Discourse on Inequality* 1.30.

5. The elaboration of the specific qualities perceived by each of the senses is a key theme of Smith's essay on the "External Senses"; see e.g. 13–17.

6. Smith's discussion here of the derivation of general rules from generalized actual practices recalls his parallel discussion in *TMS* 7.3.2 above. It also parallels several treatments in *Wealth of Nations*, as has been noted; see esp. Otteson's discussion of "the invisible hand of rule formation" in *Smith's Marketplace of Life*, ch. 7.

7. Smith's reference is to a sixteenth-century work on Latin by Francisco Sanchez ("Sanctius"). More crucially, compare Smith's discussions above of how we "split and divide almost every event into a great number of metaphysical parts" and how we "divide words into their elements" to his famous discussions of the division of labor in *Wealth of Nations* 1.1

8. Smith's discussion of the progress of language in terms of simplicity and complexity parallels certain of his other treatments of the evolution and improvement of intellectual systems; see esp. *Astronomy* 4.

9. Key discussions of Smith's views on the simplification and perfection of machines include the conclusion of 4.1 above, *Wealth of Nations* 1.1.8–9 and *Jurisprudence* A 6.40-43.

10. Smith here quotes Milton's translation of Horace's ode "To Pyrrha" (1.5), l. 9–12.

11. Smith's decision to conclude his study of the progress of languages with a defense of the superiority of ancient to modern languages may be attributable in part to his engagement with Rousseau (see 4 and notes above) and his engagement with the Quarrel of the Ancients and the Moderns (see 3.2 and notes above).

Index

Addison, Joseph, 149, 231, 466n. 15
afterlife, 462–63n. 14
Ajax, 335
Alembert, Jean Le Rond d', 149–50, 466n. 14
Alexander the Great, 119, 253, 295, 298–99, 475n. 9
ambition, 62–73, 77, 201, 211, 397
amiability, 30–33, 50, 285, 361, 456–57n. 13
anger: and amiable virtues, 31; and self-command, 280–81, 283–85, 309–10; and sympathy, 15–16, 22; and temperance, 474n. 1; and unsocial passions, 44; variations of, 382
animals, 113–14, 463n. 2
Anne, of England, 272
Antigonus, 336
Antoninus (Marcus Antoninus), 279, 340, 467n. 6
Apollonius of Tyre, 336
approbation: and authority of conscience, 156–80; and beneficence, 310–11; and bodily pain, 39; and consequences of actions, 118–19; and duty, 204; and Epicureanism, 351; and modern philosophical systems, 345–46; and the nature of virtue, 370–71, 485–86n. 1; and praiseworthiness, 147; and propriety, 24, 94; and punishment, 110, 462n. 12; and reason, 370, 374–77; and self-love, 371–74; and sentiments, 378–85; and social status, 71–73; sources of, 485–86n. 1; and sympathy, 21–30, 86–88, 133–34, 382–83; and utility, 218–24; vs. self-love, 486n. 5
Aristides, 90
Aristippus, 346
Aristomenes, 335, 479n. 38

Aristotle: and character analysis, 473n. 1; and character of virtue, 318, 322–23; and Epicureanism, 352; and magnanimity, 303–4, 322; and Platonic system of virtue, 321; and prudence, 477n. 6; and rules of justice, 403; and rules of morality, 388; and social customs, 246; and temperance, 477n. 13; and vanity, 484–85n. 99
arrogance, 101, 275–76
Arundel, Thomas Howard, Earl of, 302
Attila, 298
Augustine, Saint, 488n. 6
Augustus Caesar, 353
Avaux, Claude de Mesmes, Comte d', 271–72
Avidius Cassius, 279

Barbeyrac, Jean, 390
beauty, 134–35, 209–17, 218–24, 227–33, 486n. 5
beneficence: and concern for others, 308; and friendships, 266; and justice, 95–99; and rules of morality, 197; and self-command, 309–10; and social order, 104–10; and social structure, 268–76
benevolence: and character of virtue, for others, 308; and friendships, 266; and human nature, 358, 455n. 1; and public spirit, 275; and Stoicism, 480n. 54; and systems of moral sentiments, 315–16
Birch, Thomas, 475n. 3
Biron, Charles de Gontaut, duc de, 62, 458–59n. 5
Boileau-Despréaux, Nicolas, 149, 293, 466n. 14, 475n. 8
Borgia, Cesare, 91, 255–56, 473n. 4
Bristol, George Digby, second Earl of, 284
Brutus (1) (Lucius Junius Brutus), 223–24
Brutus (2) (Marcus Junius Brutus), 343

Buccaneers, 282–83
Buffier, Claude, 231

Caesar (Gaius Julius Caesar), 78, 119,
    295–98, 337, 475n. 12
Calas, Jean, 465n. 7
Callisthenes, 299
Camillus, 90
capital punishment, 106
cardinal virtues, 477n. 6
casuistry, 389, 390, 393–95, 399–400,
    488nn. 2, 6
Catherine de Medici, 284, 469n. 5
Catiline, 297, 372, 475n. 12
Cato the Elder, 243, 270, 337, 458n. 3
Cato the Younger, 60, 297, 372, 475n. 12
Charles I, 65, 66, 459n. 8
Charles II, 235
Charlevoix, Pierre-François-Xavier de, 472n. 4
Christianity: and benevolence, 354; and
    compassion, 31; and duty, 198, 393; and
    the Eclectics, 483n. 83; and ethics, 469n. 1;
    and rules of morality, 388–89
Chrysippus, 164, 343
Cicero: and character analysis, 473n. 1;
    death, 337; and Epicureanism, 362,
    482nn. 69, 76; and honor, 484–85n.
    99; and imperfect virtues, 343; and
    interdependence, 462n. 9; and moral
    worth, 478n. 18; and the optimates,
    475n. 12; and praiseworthiness, 152; and
    propriety, 481n. 64; and public spirit,
    275; and rules of justice, 403; and rules
    of morality, 388, 390; and self-command,
    283, 284; and social customs, 243
Clarendon, Edward Hyde, first Earl of,
    284, 302
Clarke, Samuel, 316, 345–46
Claudius, 234
Cleanthes, 342–43
Cleomenes III, 335–36
compassion: and bodily passions, 38; and
    Christianity, 31; described, 13; and
    individual character, 255; limits of, 27–30;
    and rules of morality, 195, 205–6; and
    self-command, 286; and social custom,
    240–46; and social passions, 48; and social
    status, 66, 72, 266–67; and sympathy, 15,
    17, 61–62
Cowley, Abraham, 40
Crassus (1) (Marcus Licinius Crassus), 285
Crassus (2) (Lucius Licinius Crassus), 243
Cudworth, Ralph, 354, 375, 487n. 10

Davila, Arrigo Caterino, 284
Decalogue (Ten Commandments), 164
Demosthenes, 283
Descartes, René, 368
Diderot, Denis, 483n. 83
Diogenes Laertius, 337, 478n. 18, 480n. 44,
    481n. 65, 482n. 69
distributive justice, 321
divine law, 110, 154–56, 186–97, 204
Domitian, 340, 480n. 55
dryads, 113, 463n. 1
Dryden, John, 231
Dubos, Jean-Baptiste, Abbé, 243
duty, 196–97, 197–201, 201–6, 261–62,
    278

Eclectics, 353
Edward III, 428
English language, 415, 423–24, 425, 428,
    430–31
Enlightenment, 461–62n. 5, 472n. 2
envy, 51, 56–59, 118, 162, 294, 365
Epaphroditus, 340
Epictetus, 163, 164, 326, 331, 340,
    480n. 55
Epicurus/Epicureanism, 333, 346–53,
    361–62, 455n. 1, 482nn. 69, 72, 76, 483n.
    83
Eugene, Prince of Savoy, 296
Eumenes, 335–36
Euripides, 336, 457–58n. 3
evil, 93, 126–28, 329, 380
executions, 281–82, 458–59n. 5, 475n. 3

faction, 179–80, 273–75, 289, 333
fashion, 76–77, 227–33, 234–46
fear, 17, 46, 66, 99, 280–81, 282–85, 309
Fontenelle, Bernard Le Bovier, Sieur de, 149,
    465–66n. 13, 466n. 14
fortune. See also misfortune: and gratitude
    and resentment, 112–16; and individual
    character, 250–51; and intent of action,
    111–12, 116–21; and irregularity of
    sentiments, 125–29; and merit, 121–25;
    and social custom, 242; and Stoicism,
    326–28
Frederick II, 296, 460n. 16
Frederick Wilhelm I, 460n. 16
friendship, 48–49, 252, 259, 264–68, 387

Gaius Laelius the Elder, 243
Gaius Laelius the Younger, 243
Genghis Khan, 298

God: and benevolence, 277–79, 358; and duty, 197–98; and irregularity of sentiments, 126; and justice, 93, 105–6, 110; and laws of the Deity, 186–97; and rules of morality, 196

Godolphin, Sidney Godolphin, first Earl of, 475n. 3

Gracchus, Gaius Sempronius, 243

Gracchus, Tiberius Sempronius, 243

gratitude: and duty, 201–2; and fortune, 112–16; and intent of actions, 115; and justice, 92–94; objects of, 84–86; and propriety, 87, 89; and resentment, 84–86; and reward, 82–84; and sympathy, 86–88, 88–90, 90–92

Gray, Thomas, 148, 465n. 12

Greece: and factions, 333; Greek language, 415, 416, 419–21, 426–28; Greek tragedies, 38; and social customs, 245–46; and suicide, 335–36

grief: and approval/disapproval, 22–24; and propriety of passions, 34; and self-government, 31; and selfish passions, 51, 52–53; and sociability, 30; and social customs, 236–37; and sympathy, 16, 19, 20, 56–58, 85, 373; and unsocial passions, 46

Grotius, Hugo, 321, 403, 488n. 6

Gustavus Adolphus, 296

happiness: and the afterlife, 469n. 3; and choice, 332; and Epicureanism, 348, 361; and individual character, 250–56; and prudence, 308; and the public good, 357; and Stoicism, 171, 328, 334, 342; and universal benevolence, 279; and utility, 212–13; and virtue, 317

Hercules, 38

Hippolytus, 38, 457–58n. 3

Hobbes, Thomas, 371, 374–75, 486nn. 3, 5, 487nn. 9, 10, 488n. 6

Homer, 285

Horace, 40, 431

human nature: and authority of conscience, 158–59, 171; and benevolence, 358, 455n. 1; and bodily passions, 36; and inconsistency, 152; and rules of morality, 204; and self-interest, 455n. 1; and social order, 105–6; and Stoicism, 326, 455n. 1

Hume, David, 458n. 2, 459nn. 8, 10, 465–66n. 13, 480nn. 53, 54, 481n. 67, 485–86n. 1, 487n. 15

Hutcheson, Francis, 315–16, 354–56, 377–80, 390, 458n. 1, 467n. 4, 481n. 67, 483n. 87, 485–86n. 1, 487–88n. 17

imagination, 16, 18, 36–37, 39–42, 71, 213

intent of actions, 111–12, 112–16, 116–21, 123–29

James I, 216, 461n. 3

James II, 66, 87–88, 459n. 10

Joanna of Castile, 174–75, 468n. 21

Jocasta, 128

Jones, Peter, 471n. 1

judgment: and approbation, 24–27; and authority of conscience, 156–80; customs and fashion, 227–33; and factions, 179; and praiseworthiness, 136–56; and respectable virtues, 32, 33; and rules of morality, 186–97; and self-approbation, 133–36; and self-deceit, 180–86; and sense of duty, 197–206; and social status, 68; and Stoicism, 345

justice. *See also* law: and the afterlife, 462–63n. 14, 469n. 3; and approbation of punishment, 110, 462n. 12; and authority of conscience, 172, 178–79; and beneficence, 95–99; and casuistry, 395, 399–400; and character of virtue, 280; and concern for others, 308; and corruption of moral sentiments, 75; and duty, 201, 202–3; and happiness of others, 257; and individual character, 255; and intent of actions, 112, 123–24; and irregularity of sentiments, 125–29; and jurisprudence, 389–90, 401, 487n. 9; and morality, 386; and Platonic system of virtue, 320, 321, 477n. 8; and praiseworthiness, 141, 154–56; and prudence, 349–50; and resentment, 92, 96, 101–2; and rules of morality, 193, 196; and self-command, 309–10; and self-deceit, 181, 184; and self-interest, 100–103; and social order, 104–10; and unsocial passions, 44; and utility, 212, 221–22

Kames, Henry Home, Lord, 461n. 2, 471n. 1, 481n. 67

Lafitau, Joseph-François, 472nn. 4, 5

La Fontaine, Jean de, 149

La Motte, Antoine Houdar de, 149, 466n. 14

La Placette, Jean de, 488n. 6

Lares, 113, 463n. 1
La Rochefoucauld, François, Duc de, 70, 459n. 6
Lauzun, Antonin-Nompar de Caumont, Duc de, 172, 468n. 18
law. See also justice: and beneficence, 98–99; divine law, 110, 154–56, 186–97, 204; law of Scotland, 120, 123; laws of the Deity, 186–97; and moral distinctions, 375; natural law, 325, 486n. 3; positive law, 401–2; and property, 463–64m. 9; and rules of justice, 402–3; and self-command, 285; and social order, 106–7; and war, 109
licentiousness, 107–8, 235, 360–69
Locke, John, 284, 379, 476n. 19, 487–88n. 17
Louis II de Bourbon, Prince of Condé, 296
Louis XIII, 76
Louis XIV, 67–68, 76
love: and ambition, 70; and approbation, 24; and gratitude, 82; and mutual sympathy, 20, 21, 42; and passions of the imagination, 39–42; and social custom, 240; and social passions, 49; and social status, 65
Lucullus, 118
lying, 138, 252, 395–99
Lysander, 285

Machiavelli, Niccolò, 256, 473n. 4
magnanimity: and amiable virtues, 32; and Aristotelian system of virtue, 303–4, 322; Mandeville on, 366; Plato on, 477n. 6; and pride, 303–4, 307; and respectable virtues, 33; and rules of morality, 193; and self-command, 281–82, 287; and social custom, 240; and social status, 66; and Stoicism, 329; and sympathy, 60; and unsocial passions, 48
Malebranche, Nicolas, 181–82
Mandeville, Bernard, 362–69, 371, 459n. 6, 465n. 5, 482n. 76, 484n. 96, 484–85n. 99
Marcellus, 78
Marcus Antoninus, 279, 340, 467n. 6
Marivaux, Pierre Carlet de, 164
Marlborough, John Churchill, first Duke of, 296
Massillon, Jean-Baptiste, 155–56, 469n. 3
mercy, 107
Milton, John, 335, 431
Minorca, battle of, 223
misfortune. See also fortune: and approval/disapproval, 23; and authority of

conscience, 161, 165–80; and self-command, 288; and social status, 65; and Stoicism, 334–35, 479n. 35; and sympathy, 61–62
moral relativism, 464m. 1, 465n. 5
More, Henry, 354
More, Sir Thomas, 281, 475n. 3

Native Americans, 240–46, 334, 339
natural jurisprudence, 389, 401–2
natural law, 325, 486n. 3
natural philosophy, 148–49, 482n. 72
negligence, 123–24, 463nn. 2, 7, 463–64n. 9
Nero, 91, 234
Newton, Isaac, 148, 465–66n. 13
noun adjectives, 409–11, 412–13, 419
numbers, 418–19, 425

Oedipus, 128, 464m. 12
Olympia, 295
The Orphan of China (Voltaire), 268
Othello (Shakespeare), 43
Ovid, 40

paganism, 189
pain: and bodily passions, 36–39; and denial, 145–46; and Epicureanism, 346–48, 352–53; and praiseworthiness, 148; and sympathy, 14, 56, 165; and unsocial passions, 45; and virtue, 73
Parmenides, 298
Parmenion, 299
Pascal, Blaise, 467n. 7
passions: and approval/disapproval, 22, 23; and Aristotelian system of virtue, 323; and gratitude, 82; Mandeville on, 367; and modern philosophical systems, 345; and Platonic system of virtue, 318–19; and propriety, 34, 41–42; and rules of morality, 189; and self-command, 280–81, 285, 309; and self-deceit, 181–82, 185–86; and social custom, 240–46; and Stoicism, 329, 342
Paulus Aemilius, 69–70
Perrault, Charles, 149
Perrault, Claude, 471n. 1
Persaeus, 336
Peter the Great, 253
Petrarca, Francesco (Petrarch), 40, 458n. 6
Pharsalus, battle of, 78, 297
Philip of Castile (Philip I), 174–75
Philip of Macedon (Philip II), 253, 299
Philoctetes, 38, 457–58n. 3

Philopoemen, 336

Phocion, 335

Plato: and Aristotelian system of virtue, 323; and character analysis, 474n. 1; and character of virtue, 318; and courage, 477n. 6; and the Eclectics, 483n. 83; and Epicureanism, 352–53; and justice, 403, 477n. 8; and moral relativism, 465n. 5; and public spirit, 275–76; and social customs, 246; system of virtue, 318–22

pleasure. *See also* Epicurus/Epicureanism: and denial, 145–46; and Epicureanism, 346–49, 352–53; Mandeville on, 367; and mutual sympathy, 21; and Platonic system of virtue, 319; and self-command, 289–90; and temperance, 474n. 1

Pliny the Younger, 337–38, 480n. 53

Plutarch, 335, 481n. 61

Pompey, 118

Pope, Alexander, 148, 149, 231, 341, 466n. 15

positive law, 401–2. *See also* justice

positivism, 487n. 10

poverty: and authority of conscience, 161, 165–66; and corruption of moral sentiments, 73–78; and social status, 62–73; and Stoicism, 334–35; and virtue, 73

praiseworthiness, 136–56; and credulity, 396; and Epicureanism, 482n. 76; Mandeville on, 364; and moral relativism, 464m. 1; and vanity, 138, 141, 151, 485n. 100

propriety: and approval/disapproval, 24, 94; and authority of conscience, 160, 161, 164, 165; and customs and fashion, 227–30, 236–37; and gratitude, 87, 89; and justice, 97; and merit, 94; and modern philosophical systems, 345–46; and passions, 34, 41–42; and rules of morality, 188; and self-command, 285–86, 288–89, 309–11; and self-deceit, 186; and social status, 67, 68, 75; and Stoicism, 165, 324–25, 327–29, 344, 478n. 19; and sympathy, 21–25, 25–30, 34, 60; and utility, 210, 218–24; and virtue, 32–33, 318–46, 358, 360, 457n. 15

prosperity: and authority of conscience, 161; and envy, 58–59; and Epicureanism, 361–62; and resentment, 84–85; and rules of morality, 193; and self-admiration, 298; and selfish passions, 51–52; and

social status, 71–72; and Stoicism, 325–26

prudence: and character of virtue, 280, 318–19, 346–53, 358, 359, 361; and individual character, 250–56; and praiseworthiness, 152; and rules of morality, 201; and self-command, 309–10; Smith's use of term, 477n. 6; and Stoicism, 327; and utility of action, 220, 224

Pufendorf, Samuel, 371, 390, 486n. 3, 488n. 6

punishment: and animals, 113–14; approbation of, 110, 462n. 12; and authority of conscience, 160; and blame-worthiness, 142–44; capital punishment, 106, 281–82, 458–59n. 5, 475n. 3; and irregularity of sentiments, 127; and justice, 95–99, 102, 110, 462n. 12; and negligence, 463n. 2; and Platonic system of virtue, 320; and praiseworthiness, 155; and prudence, 350; and resentment, 82–84, 85–86, 89–90, 95, 109; and rules of morality, 196; and self-command, 281–82; and social order, 93–94, 104–10; and social status, 72–73; and Stoicism, 333; and treason, 119

Pyrrhus, 172–73

Pythagoras, 353, 477n. 8

Quinault, Phillipe, 149

Quintilian, 230–31

Racine, Jean, 148, 149, 164, 230, 465n. 9, 466n. 14

Raleigh, Sir Walter, 281, 475n. 3

ranks (social status): and ambition, 62–73; and compassion, 266–67; and custom, 235–39, 240, 244; and family structure, 262; and fashion, 228; and gratitude, 87–88; and individual character, 251, 253–55; and language, 414–17; and self-command, 287; and vanity, 303, 307

reason: and approbation, 370, 374–77; and character of virtue, 376; loss of, 16–17; and morality, 376–77; and Platonic system of virtue, 318–22

Reformation, 354

Regulus, 337

religion: and blame-worthiness, 144–45; and divine justice, 110; and duty, 197–206, 393–94; and happiness of others, 257; and rules of morality, 189–90, 196–97; and self-admiration, 296

resentment: and approval/disapproval, 22, 24; and fortune, 112–16; and justice, 92, 96, 101–2; objects of, 84–86; and propriety of passions, 34; and punishment, 82–84, 85–86, 89–90, 95, 109; and rules of morality, 195; and sociability, 30; and social status, 66, 69; and sympathy, 20–21, 85, 88, 92–94; and unsocial passions, 42–48

Retz, Paul de Gondi, Cardinal de, 73, 201, 271–72, 337

Riccoboni, Marie-Jeanne, 164

Richardson, Samuel, 164

Richelieu, Armand du Plessis, Cardinal de, 201

Roman Catholic Church, 205–6, 393–94

Roman culture: and the arts, 230–31; and friendships, 264; and patriotism, 270; and public spirit, 279; and rules of morality, 189; and self-command, 296; and social customs, 243; and social status, 69–70; and suicide, 337; and utility, 223–24

Rousseau, Jean-Jacques, 409, 462n. 9, 465n. 5, 466–67n. 2, 481n. 67, 484n. 96

Russell, William, Lord, 281, 475n. 3

Sallust, 231, 465n. 5

Santeuil, Jean, 293

savages, 240–46, 339, 407–8, 472n. 3

Scipio Aemilianus, 243

Scipio Africanus, 90, 243

Scipio Nascia, 270

Scottish Enlightenment, 456–57n. 13, 462n. 11, 472n. 3, 478n. 19

self-command. See also temperance: and authority of conscience, 166–69, 175–77, 180; and propriety, 285–86, 288–89, 309–11; and resentment of suffering, 93; and social custom, 240–46; and Stoicism, 180, 480n. 54; and utility of action, 220; and virtue, 30–33, 280–308

self-interest: and authority of conscience, 158–61; and beneficence, 105; and duty, 200–201; and human nature, 455n. 1; and Hutcheson, 483n. 87; and justice, 100–103; and perception of virtue, 316, 317; and prudence, 250–56; and the public good, 357; selfish passions, 50–54, 199–200, 308, 317–18, 362–63; self-love, 356, 363, 370, 371–74,

378; and Stoicism, 162–64, 258, 324, 461–62n. 5, 467–68n. 12; and survival instinct, 94; and vanity, 362–64

Seneca, 60, 180, 230–31, 337, 343, 362, 480n. 53

Shaftesbury, Anthony Ashley Cooper, first Earl of, 284

Shaftesbury, Anthony Ashley Cooper, third Earl of, 345

Sidney, Algernon, 281, 475n. 3

Sidney, Sir Philip, 475n. 3

Simson, Robert, 148

Smith, John, 354

sociability, 19, 30, 134–35, 177, 286–87, 290, 462n. 9, 486n. 3

social order: and ambition, 62–73; and beneficence, 104–10; and corruption of moral sentiments, 73–78; and fashion, 235–39; and natural jurisprudence, 401–2; and punishment, 93–94, 104–10; and selfish passions, 51–52; and virtue, 371; and wealth, 211–15

social status. See ranks (social status)

Socrates, 60–61, 281, 295–96, 335, 477–78n. 15

Solon, 275

Sophocles, 457–58n. 3

St. Bartholomew's Day Massacre, 205–6, 469n. 5

statesmanship, 461n. 3

Stewart, Matthew, 148

Stoicism, 324–45; and divine order, 45; and ends of life, 481n. 65; and Epicureanism, 362; and fortune, 326–28; and happiness, 171, 328, 334, 342; and human nature, 326, 455n. 1; and licentiousness, 360; maxims of, 467n. 6; and misfortune, 334–35, 479n. 35; and moral worth, 478n. 18; and natural desire, 352, 483n. 81; paradoxes of, 342–43; and propriety, 165, 324–25, 327–29, 344, 478n. 19; and self-command, 180, 480n. 54; and self-interest, 162–64, 258, 461–62n. 5, 467–68n. 12; and suicide, 333, 335–36, 336–38, 479n. 32

suffering, 14–15, 91–92, 92–94, 155–56

suicide: and Aristomenes, 479n. 38; and Cato, 458n. 3; Hume on, 480n. 53; and praiseworthiness, 139; and Stoicism, 333, 335–36, 336–38, 479n. 32

Sully, Maximilien de Béthune, Duc de, 76, 458–59n. 5

Sulpitius, 243

Swift, Jonathan, 231, 253

sympathy: and approbation, 21–30, 86–88, 133–34, 382–83; and authority of conscience, 161, 162–63, 168; and beneficence, 105; described, 13–18; and family structure, 259–62; and gratitude, 86–88, 88–90, 90–92; limits of, 27–30; and love, 20, 21, 42; and moral sense, 380–81; mutual sense of, 18–21; and physical passions, 35–36, 36–39; and propriety of passions, 21–25, 25–30, 34, 60; and resentment, 20–21, 85, 88, 92–94; and self-command, 286; and selfish passions, 50–54; and self-love, 373; Smith's use of, 456n. 6; and social customs, 240; and social passions, 48–50; and social status, 62–73; and sorrow and joy, 55–62; and universal benevolence, 277; and unsocial passions, 42–48; and utility, 385

Tacitus, 231, 480n. 53

Tamerlane, 298

taste, 24–27, 32, 134–35, 147, 224, 228

temperance. See also self-command: and amiable passions, 285; Aristotle on, 477n. 13; and Epicureanism, 349; Mandeville on, 366–67; and Platonic virtue, 320; and pleasure, 474n. 1; and prudence, 36; and social rank, 75; and Stoicism, 329; and utility, 224

Themistocles, 285, 335

Theramenes, 335

Tibullus, 40, 458n. 6

Tigranes II, 122

Timolean, 90

torture, 241–42, 340

Turenne, Henri de La Tour d'Auvergne, Vicomte de, 296

unsocial passions, 42–48, 199

utility, 209–17, 218–24, 359–60, 385, 486n. 5

vanity: and esteem, 459n. 7; and fashion, 76–77; Mandeville on, 366–68; and praiseworthiness, 138, 141, 151, 485n. 100; and self-command, 290, 298–308; and self-interest, 362–64; and social status, 63

vengeance: and atonement, 142–43; divine, 128; and justice, 114, 185; and pity, 102; and punishment, 92–94; and resentment, 86; and self-command, 283–84

Vertue, George, 281

Vespasian, 480n. 55

vices, 45, 74–76, 193–94, 218–19, 265, 371

virtue: amiable virtues, 30–33; and approbation, 370–71, 485–86n. 1; Aristotelian system of, 318, 322–23; and benevolence, 276–80, 317–18, 353–61; cardinal virtues, 477n. 6; and corruption of moral sentiments, 74–78; and customs, 239; and duty, 201, 206; and friendships, 265; imperfect virtues, 343; and individual character, 251; and kinship ties, 261–62; and licentiousness, 360–69; Mandeville on, 368; and modern philosophical systems, 345–46; Platonic system of, 318–22; and praiseworthiness, 140, 155, 485n. 100; and propriety, 32–33, 318–46, 358, 360, 457n. 15; and prudence, 280, 318–19, 346–53, 358, 359, 361; and reason, 376; and relativism, 465n. 5; and rules of morality, 193–94, 386–87; and self-command, 30–33, 280–308; and self-interest, 316, 317; and social order, 371; and social status, 69, 73; Socratic system of, 477–78n. 15; and Stoicism, 324–45; and systems of moral sentiments, 315–16; and unsocial passions, 45; and utility, 217, 219, 385

Voltaire, 148, 164, 230, 253, 268, 465n. 7, 466–67n. 2, 469n. 4

war: civil wars, 487n. 9; Grotius on, 403; and justice, 178–79; laws of, 109; and public spirit, 223, 273–74; and self-command, 282, 289; and state of nature, 374

wealth, 62–73, 73–78, 87–88, 101, 211–15, 297–98

William III, of England, 272

Wollaston, William, 345, 481n. 67

Zeno of Citium, 164, 318, 324, 336, 342–43, 352, 478n. 18